Macbeth

This volume offers a wealth of critical analysis, supported with ample historical and bibliographical information, about one of Shakespeare's most
enduringly popular and globally influential plays. Its eighteen new chapters
represent a broad spectrum of current scholarly and interpretive approaches,
from historicist criticism to performance theory to cultural studies. A substantial section addresses early modern themes, with attention to the protagonists and the discourses of politics, class, gender, the emotions, and the
economy, along with discussions of significant 'minor' characters and less
commonly examined textual passages. Further chapters scrutinize *Macbeth's*
performance, adaptation and transformation across several media—stage,
film, text, and hypertext—in cultural settings ranging from early nineteenth-
century England to late twentieth-century China. The editor's extensive
introduction surveys critical, theatrical, and cinematic interpretations from
the late seventeenth century to the beginning of the twenty-first, while
advancing a synthetic argument to explain the shifting relationship between
two conflicting strains in the tragedy's reception. Written to a level that will
be both accessible to advanced undergraduates and, at the same time, useful
to postgraduates and specialists in the field, this book will greatly enhance
any study of *Macbeth*.

Contributors: Rebecca Lemon, Jonathan Baldo, Rebecca Ann Bach, Julie
Barmazel, Abraham Stoll, Lois Feuer, Stephen Deng, Lisa A. Tomaszewski,
Lynne Dickson Bruckner, Michael David Fox, James Wells, Laura Engel,
Stephen M. Buhler, Bi-qi Beatrice Lei, Kim Fedderson and J. Michael
Richardson, Bruno Lessard, Pamela Mason.

Nick Moschovakis has published essays in academic and cultural journals
including *Shakespeare Quarterly*, *Milton Quarterly*, and *College Literature*.
He has taught courses on Shakespeare and early modern English literature at
The University of the South, George Washington University, Reed College,
and elsewhere.

Shakespeare Criticism

Philip C. Kolin, *General Editor*

Romeo and Juliet
Critical Essays
Edited by John F. Andrews

Coriolanus
Critical Essays
Edited by David Wheeler

Titus Andronicus
Critical Essays
Edited by Philip C. Kolin

Love's Labour's Lost
Critical Essays
Edited by Felicia Hardison Londré

The Winter's Tale
Critical Essays
Edited by Maurice Hunt

Two Gentlemen of Verona
Critical Essays
Edited by June Schlueter

Venus and Adonis
Critical Essays
Edited by Philip C. Kolin

As You Like it from 1600 to the Present
Critical Essays
Edited by Edward Tomarken

The Comedy of Errors
Critical Essays
Edited by Robert S. Miola

A Midsummer Night's Dream
Critical Essays
Edited by Dorothea Kehler

Shakespeare's Sonnets
Critical Essays
Edited by James Schiffer

Henry VI
Critical Essays
Edited by Thomas A. Pendleton

The Tempest
Critical Essays
Edited by Patrick M. Murphy

Pericles
Critical Essays
Edited by David Skeele

The Taming of the Shrew
Critical Essays
Edited by Dana E. Aspinall

The Merchant of Venice
New Critical Essays
Edited by John W. Mahon and Ellen Macleod Mahon

Hamlet
New Critical Essays
Edited by Arthur F. Kinney

Othello
New Critical Essays
Edited by Philip C. Kolin

Julius Caesar
New Critical Essays
Edited by Horst Zander

Antony and Cleopatra
New Critical Essays
Edited by Sara M. Deats

All's Well, That Ends Well
New Critical Essays
Edited by Gary Waller

Macbeth
New Critical Essays

Edited by Nick Moschovakis

Shakespeare Criticism Volume 32

Routledge
Taylor & Francis Group

NEW YORK AND LONDON

First published 2008
by Routledge
270 Madison Ave, New York, NY 10016

Simultaneously published in the UK
by Routledge
2 Park Square, Milton Park, Abingdon, Oxon OX14 4RN

*Routledge is an imprint of the Taylor & Francis Group,
an informa business*

Typeset in Times New Roman by
RefineCatch Limited, Bungay, Suffolk
Printed and bound in Great Britain by
Antony Rowe Ltd, Chippenham, Wiltshire

Library of Congress Cataloging in Publication Data
Macbeth : new critical essays / edited by Nick Moschovakis.
p. cm. —(Shakespeare criticism ; 32)
1. Shakespeare, William, 1564–1616. Macbeth.   I. Moschovakis,
Nicholas Rand, 1969–
PR2823.M235 2008
822.3'3—dc22
2007036627

British Library Cataloguing in Publication Data
A catalogue record for this book is available from the British Library

ISBN 10: 0–415–97404–6 (hbk)
ISBN 10: 0–203–93070–3 (ebk)

ISBN 13: 978–0–415–97404–2 (hbk)
ISBN 13: 978–0–203–93070–0 (ebk)

Contents

List of figures and acknowledgments

Every effort has been made to trace and contact copyright holders. The publishers would be pleased to hear from any copyright holders not acknowledged here, so that this acknowledgement page may be amended at the earliest opportunity.

Editor's acknowledgments

My first and most profuse thanks are due to the critics whose work appears in this volume. I admire their assiduity and perseverance as much as I appreciate the breadth and diversity of their expertise and the acuity of their insights. The editor of this series, Philip C. Kolin, has supplied welcome feedback and encouragement.

For much-needed assistance and helpful correspondence I am grateful to staff members at the Folger Shakespeare Library (especially Georgianna Ziegler), the Royal Collection (Karen Lawson), the Guildhall Art Gallery (Naomi Allen and Hannah Wardle), and the National Gallery (Vivien Adams). I am also thankful to Matt Byrnie at Routledge (NY) and to Polly Dodson, Huw Price, and Gabrielle Orcutt at Routledge (UK) for guiding me through the publication process. Polly claims a special debt of gratitude for her consideration and willingness to accommodate late changes. The last stages of production were actually pleasant, thanks to the admirable solicitude and professionalism of Rebecca Hastie, Tamsin Rogers, and Richard Willis (all of Swales & Willis), Emma Nugent (of Routledge UK), and our keen-eyed copy-editor, Liz Dawn.

I owe a more than ordinary debt to Bernice W. Kliman, my consulting expert on matters performative, textual, and orthographical, and an unfailingly supportive friend. Malcolm Smuts, Sarah Wall-Randell, William Proctor Williams, Iain Wright, and William C. Carroll were all kind enough to share their work with me when it was still unpublished or hard to procure. In several cases Al Braunmuller facilitated this favor. Al has also generously shown an interest in the progress of the volume as a whole, helpfully calling my attention to sundry errors and omissions in a late draft of my introduction.

For less formal advice, forbearance, good conversation, and good cheer on various occasions while I was putting the volume together with its introductory chapter, I have the following colleagues and friends to thank (in no particular order, and doubtless with some accidental elisions): Heather

James, Michael Mirabile, Jay Dickson, Lisa Steinman and Jim Shugrue, David Roessel, Pamela Beatrice, Joan and Yiannis Moschovakis, Anna Moschovakis and Matvei Yankelevich, Eddie Cushman, Andrew Majeske, and Jennifer Lewin.

Finally: I choose not to name my spouse here. No perfunctory public acknowledgment could do justice to her patience, which—however sorely tested by this project's demands on my time—has never slackened. I only hope she knows I'll never take it for granted.

General Editor's introduction

The continuing goal of the Shakespeare Criticism series is to provide the most significant and original contemporary interpretations of Shakespeare's works. Each volume in the series is devoted to a Shakespeare play or poem (e.g. the sonnets, *Venus and Adonis*, *Othello*) and contains eighteen to twenty-five new essays exploring the text from a variety of critical perspectives.

A major feature of each volume in the series is the editor's introduction. Each volume editor provides a substantial essay identifying the main critical issues and problems the play (or poem) has raised, charting the critical trends in looking at the work over the centuries, and assessing the critical discourse that has linked the play or poem to various ideological concerns. In addition to examining the critical commentary in light of important historical and theatrical events, each introduction functions as a discursive bibliographic essay, citing and evaluating significant critical works—books, journal articles, theater documents, reviews, and interviews—giving readers a guide to the vast amounts of research on a particular play or poem.

Each volume showcases the work of leading Shakespeare scholars who participate in and extend the critical discourse on the text. Reflecting the most recent approaches in Shakespeare studies, these essays approach the play from a host of critical positions, including but not limited to feminist, Marxist, new historical, semiotic, mythic, performance/staging, cultural, and/or a combination of these and other methodologies. Some volumes in the series include bibliographic analyses of a Shakespeare text to shed light on its critical history and interpretation. Interviews with directors and/or actors are also part of some volumes in the series.

At least one, sometimes as many as two or three, of the essays in each volume is devoted to a play in performance beginning with the earliest and most significant productions and proceeding to the most recent. These essays, which ultimately provide a theater history of the play, should not be regarded as different from or rigidly isolated from the critical work on the script. Over the last thirty years or so Shakespeare criticism has understandably been labeled the "Age of Performance." Readers will find information in these essays on non-English speaking production of Shakespeare's plays as well as landmark performances in English. Editors and contributors also include photographs from productions across the world to help readers see and further appreciate the ways a Shakespeare play has taken shape in the theater.

Ultimately, each volume in the Shakespeare Criticism series strives to give readers a balanced, representative collection of the most engaging and thoroughly researched criticism on the given Shakespeare text. In essence, each volume provides a careful survey of essential materials in the history of the criticism for a Shakespeare play or poem as well as cutting-edge essays that extend and enliven our understanding of the work in its critical context. In offering readers innovative and fulfilling new essays, volume editors have made invaluable contributions to the literary and theatrical criticism of Shakespeare's greatest legacy, his work.

Philip C. Kolin
University of Southern Mississippi

1 Introduction

Dualistic *Macbeth*?
Problematic *Macbeth*?

Nick Moschovakis

Shakespeare probably wrote his *Tragedy of Macbeth* just over four centuries ago. In the later seventeenth and eighteenth centuries, audiences and readers in the English-speaking world and Europe became well acquainted with the play. Since then, cultures around the globe have embraced it as a well-wrought drama of action and character—even as adapters and interpreters have presented radically different views of its overarching values and its larger outlook on human experience.

The play moves rapidly and suspensefully, climaxing in a battle. Its protagonists are alternately admired and abhorred; fortunate and miserable; self-assured and terrified; gratified and tormented. Its human plot speaks directly to any society where fears of treachery are felt; where blood is shed for advantage; and where crimes against unsuspecting allies, acquaintances, and friends are supposed to lead to remorse.

Macbeth joins these readily understood themes to a masque-like subplot involving conjurations, prophecies, and supernatural agency. It thus enlarges its scope beyond that of ordinary human relations. It invites speculation about the ultimate causes of pain and suffering, and may elicit our sympathy with reviled transgressors as we witness the betrayal of their extraordinary hopes.

The weïrd sisters have been variously understood by different individuals, times, and cultures. They embody humanity's perennial failure to impose its conscious will and its ideas of order upon the unruly energies of desire, the pride of the great, and the manifold horrors of war and tyranny. Last but not least, they conspire to bring us face to face with the ultimate disappointment of death.

The present introduction: purpose and terminology

Among the many questions *Macbeth* raises, one of the most encompassing is that of how to make choices in life—what the basis of our actions should be. Recent criticism has been energized by profound disagreements over whether or not *Macbeth* upholds a *dualistic* view of morality: one which measures human actions and objectives by their worth relative to polar opposites of 'good' and 'bad.' When Macbeth first hears the witches' prophecies, he sounds problematically unable to place their promises in either category: "This supernatural soliciting/ Cannot be ill, cannot be good" (1.3.129–30). His disinclination to differentiate between 'good' and 'ill' recalls his fondness for paradoxes elsewhere—"So foul and fair a day I have not seen" (1.3.36), "nothing is,/ But what is not" (140–41). Yet Shakespeare often explored such occasions for ambivalence elsewhere in his writing. We might suspect that he shared the view of the nineteenth-century American sage who proclaimed, "Good and bad are but names very readily transferable to that or this" (Emerson 290).

Is *Macbeth*, then, meant to throw doubt on our ability to distinguish 'good' from 'evil'? Or does it instead assure us, dualistically, that we *can* tell them apart (and that we must)? Does it, or does it not, illustrate the premise that men and women have an ability and an obligation to choose what is best—even when they fail to exercise this capacity? The very liveliness of recent controversies may attest to *Macbeth*'s ambivalent stance on the issue. Yet its characters often speak in ways that suggest a commitment to dualistic ideologies. Moreover, as we will see, a similar attachment to moral dualism consistently informed the work of both critics and performers from the later seventeenth century until the modern period. It was not until the twentieth century that Shakespeare's interpreters began explicitly arguing that *Macbeth* was designed to confound dualistic categories, problematizing our moral perceptions and judgments—and so substantiating the weïrd sisters' contention that "Fair is foul, and foul is fair" (1.1.12).

The present chapter will trace this modern shift from the dualistic *Macbeth* toward its opposite, which, for brevity's sake, I term the 'problematic' *Macbeth*. This approach, though narrowly focused, can afford many telling glimpses of representative moments in the play's history. By following the development of earlier, dualistic *Macbeth*s and, later, those that arose to rival them, I aim to present a continuous (if inevitably partial and abbreviated) guide to *Macbeth*'s evolution through time.

Part I begins with a summary of what scholars can and cannot claim to know, on the basis of textual and historical evidence, about *Macbeth* in its original context. By the 1660s—though not earlier—we can cite plentiful evidence for the reception of *Macbeth* as a morally polarized play about 'good' and 'evil.' After that, *Macbeth*s proliferated and diversified for three centuries or so, though almost always in keeping with a basically dualistic perspective; this rich, evolving strain in *Macbeth*'s reception remained dominant until the 1960s. Since then, problematic *Macbeth*s have become more culturally viable.

As I develop this narrative in Part I, my purpose is to highlight major features of critical, theatrical, and cinematic versions, while relating the most innovative to some of the cultural and social changes that informed them. Without trying to be comprehensive (an impossible aim), I have sought in Part I to illustrate both the breadth and the depth of *Macbeth*'s involvement with the historical and creative currents of four centuries.[1] Part I also briefly surveys a range of global *Macbeths*—though here, again, omissions have been inevitable (if regrettable)—and it concludes with a section contrasting two English productions from the past decade. My coverage of criticism in Part I ends with the 1960s; this is because I have chosen to address recent scholarship separately, in Part II.

Part II supplies numerous references to critical studies published from the 1980s through the early 2000s. Despite exigencies of space, I have tried to give some attention to a considerable proportion of this secondary literature, while identifying some of each critic's main concerns. In keeping with the Introduction's general argument, I have also arranged Part II into two sections, reflecting my rough dichotomy between dualistic and problematic views of the play. Of course I don't mean to reify these heuristic terms into a new and unhelpfully artificial binary of my own invention. As a recent essay on *Macbeth* has provocatively argued, professional and pedagogical habits of thought can lead us to overemphasize the dichotomous patterns a work explores, even as we aim to show how it complicates those patterns (Crane). The most effective critical readings of *Macbeth* often integrate insights from both dualistic and problematic traditions. If they veer toward one or the other pole—as most ultimately do—they may still attempt to take into account at least some of the considerations that have fueled opposing arguments in the past.

The organization of the volume

The same tension and interplay characterizes the critical voices convened between the covers of this book. Our contributors employ multiple critical approaches to *Macbeth*, and to the questions that proliferate around it: from new historicism and cultural studies, to the theory and history of performance. Their essays refer to a wealth of past work on the play, while also illustrating many trends that animate today's scholarship and creative practice.

Chapters 2 through 11 are arranged in a sequence roughly corresponding to the emergence of some of *Macbeth*'s major themes, as they arise in the tragedy and are taken up in turn by each contributor. Thus, the issues at play in *Macbeth*'s representations of monarchy and succession, Scottish history, and the male aristocratic community—all of which surface quickly in Act 1— are discussed in chapters 2, 3, and 4 (while some receive more scrutiny in chapter 8 and elsewhere). Chapters 4, 5, and 6 develop social and cultural, as well as psychological contexts for Macbeth and Lady Macbeth, who together dominate the play from the middle of Act 1 through the end of Act 3. Chapters 7, 8, and 9 address the interrelated discourses of socioeconomic instability and pathology, while spotlighting key passages in Acts 3, 4, and 5; two of these chapters illuminate the bit parts of the Murderers (3.1, 3.3) and both Doctors (4.3; 5.1). Chapter 10 is focused on depictions of emotion in two of the play's later scenes (4.3; 5.9). Finally, readers who may specifically seek a viewpoint on Macbeth's last soliloquy (5.5.16–27) may consult chapter 11.[2] In these thematic essays, each author's purpose has been to offer useful guidance to existing debates, while at times proposing to open new avenues of inquiry. Another aim has been to supply more, more deliberate, and, in some cases, more controversial examples of close reading—as well as fuller and rather more up-to-date bibliographical resources—than are ordinarily found in brief critical guides, handbooks, and the like.

Chapters 11 and 12 both concern topics in the theory of performance, which abut interpretive questions in *Macbeth*. Chapters 13 through 17 then consider some noteworthy moments in *Macbeth*'s peregrinations across several media—stage, film, text, and hypertext—from the late eighteenth century to the beginning of the twenty-first. Finally, chapter 18 offers perspectives on the First Folio text, its handling by modern editors, and the relationship between text and performance.

A collection of individually focused interpretive essays such as this cannot claim to 'cover' the vast ground under consideration, even on a casual or arbitrary understanding of this term. Still, the arguments set forth in these chapters—significant in themselves—may begin to suggest the much more extensive territory that lies open for readers to explore.

PART I: *MACBETH* OVER FOUR CENTURIES (1606–2005)

These sections will concern *Macbeth*'s fortunes in the creative media, in criticism, and in the context of wider cultural and historical changes since the seventeenth century. My account follows the play chronologically from the 1600s until a few years ago. After two brief initial sections discussing the play's date and possible early performances, Part I will go on to focus on the period since 1660. This is because our specific evidence concerning *Macbeth*'s early seventeenth-century composition, and its reception by its earliest audiences and readers, is sadly incomplete. Almost everything written about the 'original' *Macbeth*—i.e. the play as it was first performed and perhaps circulated in manuscript, or as it existed before Shakespeare's death in 1616—is based on indirect, circumstantial, and/or intertextual evidence. (To reflect the difficulties faced by scholars working in this largely hypothetical realm, I have deferred discussion of recent historicist debates over the 'original' *Macbeth* and its significance for Part II, "Recent criticism.")

From at least the 1660s until the twentieth century, theatrical and critical interpreters alike presented *Macbeth*'s design as a dualistic one, invoking stark moral oppositions—with a cautionary emphasis on the Macbeths' deviation from the good. This is not to say that dualistic *Macbeths* repeated themselves for three hundred years. Profound differences emerged as to just *how* the play defined 'evil.' Was it 'ambition' and regicide *Macbeth* chiefly warned against? Or was it the corruption of male honor by womanly temptation? Might it be, perhaps, the danger of tyranny under a monarchical system? Perceptions of 'evil' could embrace any and all possibilities that were greatly feared; and these changed with time.

Meanwhile, Romantic and later nineteenth-century readers began apprehending more ethically problematic possibilities. Some seemed to consider Macbeth less culpable than psychologically deviant. However, it was only in the modern era that interpreters first hinted at a radically problematic *Macbeth*. At first by fits and starts, but eventually in force, twentieth-century productions and readings came to see *Macbeth* as questioning the dualistic underpinnings of traditional morality, politics, and cosmology. *Macbeth* now became something potentially very different. At the same time, in many cultural contexts it continued to be understood according to older, dualistic conventions and assumptions.

My own opinions in Part I are often derivative, being based on secondary works that cite primary texts. Nevertheless, I shall occasionally infer and speculate where this seems appropriate as a way to advance a new angle on an old story.

Text and date: the 'original' *Macbeth*

The date 1606 is conventionally assigned to *Macbeth*. Though not proven, it is supported by statistical studies of Shakespeare's changing style (Wells and Taylor 128–29). *Macbeth* also contains apparent allusions to events that were topical around that time (see Braunmuller 5ff. and below, Part II).

The earliest surviving text appeared in 1623, in the First Folio of Shakespeare's plays, commonly known as "F" (online at Hinman, "*Macbeth*;" in print, see Hinman, *Norton;* de Somogyi). Modern editions base themselves on F as the only authoritative text (though Spencer thinks Davenant may preserve some early variants). For this reason, scholarly texts of *Macbeth* resemble F rather closely—at least by contrast with other plays, such as *Hamlet* or *King Lear*, for which early quartos offer alternative readings. Some theatrical practitioners prefer to use F as is, mistrusting later editors' interference. In fact, recent editors and scholars have questioned past editorial choices at length, though without rejecting the editor's role altogether (for discussion see e.g. Brooke 213–24; Braunmuller 245–63; Billings; Worster; Cordner; and Pamela Mason's essay, chapter 18 in this volume).

Other *Macbeth*s than F must have existed before Shakespeare's death in 1616, perhaps differing substantially from F. Unfortunately, none has survived—either in manuscript, or in a full and detailed report of a performance—so our arguments are conjectural. Still, the unusual brevity of the F *Macbeth* (and other features of the text) are often thought to indicate that it was shortened for the stage, either by Shakespeare or by another hand (see Brown, *Macbeth* 6, 8; Brooke 55–56; Braunmuller 247; Erne 189–91).

While we cannot be certain whether or not *Macbeth* is all Shakespeare's, it is an "almost inarguable" conclusion of textual scholars that the F *Macbeth* contains at least a small amount of material for which Shakespeare was not solely responsible (Braunmuller 259; cf. 259–65). The parts usually seen as 'non-Shakespearean' are the musical passages featuring the goddess Hecate (*Macbeth* 3.5; 4.1.38 SD–43 SD; see e.g. Wells and Taylor 128–29, 543; Braunmuller 255–59, 270–71; Carroll 155–59, with documents; cf. Ioppolo 121–24). The question of when and how these passages originated may affect the issue of *Macbeth*'s date (see Brooke 66; de Somogyi xxx–xxxi).

The 'original' *Macbeth* on stage: inference *vs.* evidence

Macbeth might have been performed for the first time in 1606 by Shakespeare's theatrical company—the King's Men—at the open-roofed Globe Theatre in Southwark. Somewhat later, between 1609 and Shakespeare's death in 1616, *Macbeth* might have been seen indoors on the Blackfriars stage, for a higher entrance fee and a more socially exclusive audience (see e.g. Kliman, *Shakespeare*, 1–4; Wilders 2–3; on stagings in early venues, see Thomson, *Shakespeare's* 142–66). The play could also have been presented at any time in a private hall, possibly for members and guests of the royal court (see now Farley-Hills). There is a theory that *Macbeth* was first performed during July and August of 1606 on the occasion of a visit to England by King Christian IV of Denmark (for the fullest, most influential statement see Paul 41 and *passim*). While this speculation is commonly entertained by academic critics and others, it has not been supported with direct evidence (see Braunmuller 8–9).

In fact, our only explicit "record of *any* pre-Restoration performance" of *Macbeth* is a single written report, made by Simon Forman after he saw the play at the Globe in 1611 (Orgel 165). Forman's account contains major discrepancies with F. Strikingly, it makes no reference to witches or witchcraft, assigning the initial prophecies instead to "3 women feiries or Nimphes" (quoted in Muir, *Macbeth* xv). These terms are "plucked directly" from Raphael Holinshed's *Chronicles of England, Scotlande, and Ireland* (1587)— the book which was *Macbeth*'s chief narrative source, and which Forman himself may have consulted in order to fill out his gappy memory of the play (Thomson, *Shakespeare's* 145). Forman's report also makes no mention of Hecate or the apparitions. Such intriguing differences raise tantalizing questions about the play's shape before 1623, though Forman's testimony has sometimes been regarded with extreme circumspection (e.g. Scragg, "Macbeth;" for a recent tendency to rehabilitate Forman, see Holderness; McLuskie, "*Macbeth*, the Present" 401–405; Brown, *Macbeth* 3–5; Whitney 147–53).

For a half-century after Forman wrote his account, little evidence survives of *Macbeth*'s theatrical existence. Allusions to *Macbeth* have been perceived in plays by Shakespeare's contemporaries, such as Francis Beaumont's *The Knight of the Burning Pestle* and the anonymous *The Puritan* (see Bartholomeusz 8; Kliman, *Shakespeare* 13; on other possibilities, see Braunmuller 59 n.

1, 58–60; Egan). In a surviving copy of the First Folio, *Macbeth* was marked—probably between 1625 and 1635—with cuts as if for the stage (see e.g. Orgel 23–25). Apart from such scattered signs, the tragedy fades from our modern performance histories until the English Restoration and the reopening of the public theaters.

The dualistic *Macbeth* in development: Davenant and Garrick

In the early 1660s, *Macbeth* was adapted and revived for the Restoration stage by Sir William Davenant, a Royalist who was England's Poet Laureate (see, e.g. Carroll 162–84, with excerpts; Brooke 36–40; S. Williams, "Taking" 56–59). The clear moral and ideological design of this adaptation inaugurated a three-hundred-year epoch of predominantly dualistic *Macbeth*s.

As printed in 1674, Davenant's *Macbeth* was a drastically rewritten version of Shakespeare's. Alterations included major cuts, added scenes, and heavily reworked dialogue. Macbeth himself became a more clear-cut moral example than the Folio had made him. He identified "ambition" as his overriding motive and flaw—and did so not just where F encourages this view (e.g. 1.7.27), but throughout the play. After fighting Macduff, Davenant's Macbeth is left to die alone on stage, where he confesses his folly and spends his final moments repudiating his "vain . . . *Ambition*" (Davenant 65; italics in original). Such closure gives Davenant's *Macbeth* an ideological "clarity" that the F text does not impose on the play, at least in the view of many modern interpreters (S. Williams, "Taking" 57; cf. e.g. Spencer 14–16; Rabkin 101–10).

Davenant's conclusive indictment of Macbeth's ambition registered the impact of historical events. It had been less than fifteen years since King Charles I was beheaded, and just a few since his son had resumed the throne as King Charles II. At such a time it was politically astute to trace tyranny strictly to the desires of overreaching *subjects*. 'Ambition' is a motive readily ascribed to private individuals like Macbeth (or, to name an example then still on English minds, Oliver Cromwell); it is less easily associated with a publicly proclaimed heir and successor, such as Malcolm—or the recently empowered Charles (cf. Kroll 844–61). By critiquing 'ambition,' Davenant linked social crisis to the effects of unmastered inward passions (cf. Rowe, "Humoral" 186ff.) while muting any suggestion that an established regime like Duncan's might provoke justified resistance.

Davenant's dualistic and pro-monarchical approach was emulated in key respects by *Macbeth*'s next memorable theatrical interpreter, the famous David Garrick, who played Macbeth on London stages beginning in the 1740s. Garrick replaced Davenant's moralizing death-speech with a longer one of his own, which, however, featured a similar denunciation of "Ambition" (Wilders 213 n.). Garrick undid, or redid, many of Davenant's other interpolations and revisions to F. Still, he kept Davenant's major cuts, and he made new cuts of his own (Wilders 13; see further Stone). One of them removed most of the pretended "detraction" Malcolm speaks against himself when testing Macduff's patriotism (4.3.124; see Wilders 184 n.). This helped to burnish the image of dynastic monarchy even more. Unlike Malcolm as portrayed in F, Garrick's Malcolm no longer recited a harrowing list of the violent abuses for which an absolute prince might claim impunity. With the scene purged of this worrisome material, Malcolm was not so obviously engaged (as the Folio's Malcolm was) in Machiavellian deception.

Garrick famously elicited audiences' pity for Macbeth, yet he accomplished this without blurring moral lines. His version implied that Macbeth might have remained faithful to Duncan, were it not for the promptings of his more manifestly 'evil' wife (discussed below). It was by allowing *her* ambition to tease forth his own that Garrick's Macbeth failed in his duty. Of course, he failed nevertheless, and Garrick's new dying speech conveyed Macbeth's deep contrition for this failure. One eyewitness wrote that "humanity triumphed" at this climactic moment (quoted in S. Williams, "Taking" 61).

Garrick's view of Macbeth as a hero who was fallible, yet humanly and pitiably so, arose in part from Enlightenment cultural imperatives. Audiences now idealized "the man of sensibility;" it was modish to show "masculine nobility through the expression of sensitive remorse" (Prescott 85; cf. S. Williams, "The Tragic Actor" 124). It also helped that Garrick was a singularly versatile, affecting performer (Kliman, *Shakespeare* 24–27; Wilders 11–12; cf. Bartholomeusz 69, 78, 80–81). Ultimately, though, Garrick perpetuated the dualistic ideology of Davenant's *Macbeth*—reproducing its conservative emphasis on 'ambition' as the root cause of public evils, while taking additional steps to clarify the virtuousness of Malcolm and his position as legitimate heir.

The witches and comic 'evil'

These early, dualistic reshapings of *Macbeth* by Davenant and by Garrick would exert a persistent influence on subsequent stage practice, even into modern times (Braunmuller, 62 n. 3). Of course, performance was not the only context for *Macbeth*'s reception. F had reappeared in several seventeenth-century editions, so Davenant's was never the only *Macbeth* in *literary* circulation. And by the early 1700s, readers could access new editions of Shakespeare—the first was Nicholas Rowe's (1709)—which reflected F far more faithfully than stagings did. Regardless, a large part of Shakespeare's eighteenth- and nineteenth-century audience knew *Macbeth* less from books than from theaters.

To playgoers *Macbeth* offered spectacular display and aural diversion. Davenant's version succeeded partly by enriching the element of 'musical theater' in the witch-scenes, making them nearly as lavish as Baroque opera (see Kliman, *Shakespeare* 16–19). This convention dominated *Macbeth*s through the late eighteenth century, and was often retained well into the nineteenth. Later, modern *Macbeth*s would reduce the musical element by cutting the Hecate passages (see Wilders 163, 171; for recent defenses of

Hecate and the singing, dancing witches, see Suhamy; Kliman, *Shakespeare* 15–16; on early stagings see Kiefer, *Shakespeare's* 101–27).

For a seventeenth-century audience, the comic witches need not have subverted the dualistic moral seriousness of *Macbeth* as a whole. Such figures could have been seen as strange demonic servitors, rather like those in Christopher Marlowe's play *Doctor Faustus*—itself a precursor of *Macbeth*, and often discussed in relation to it (see now Logan 201–11). For centuries, demonic and devilish beings on English stages had been grotesque and "antic" (4.1.129), yet "morally and spiritually serious" (Cox 82). Like Marlowe's mocking devils, Davenant's amusing weïrd sisters observed Macbeth's evil inclinations and answered his queries, while cuing the audience to hold him and his pride responsible.

Rather than letting the weïrd sisters appear as mysteriously powerful figures—an impression that might overshadow the evil of human choices—Davenant and his immediate successors instead stressed Macbeth's culpable embrace of 'ambition.' The witches, while entertaining the audience, supplied the deceptive occasion for this 'evil' choice.

Lady Macbeth and the dualists: Davenant, Pritchard, Siddons

Besides Macbeth's 'ambition' and the witches' predictions, there is of course another transgressive force to be reckoned with in the play. This is Lady Macbeth. As performers and critics have long recognized, a key question in *Macbeth* is the nature of her power over Macbeth, its extent and its manner of working. If one sees Macbeth as a man unlikely to plan a regicide without help, then a proportionate share of responsibility will accrue to his wife. Conversely, Lady Macbeth may seem less implicated in the plot if Macbeth seems bent on 'evil' from the start (either from his 'aside' at 1.3.127–41, or since before the action begins; see Braunmuller 69 and n. 2).

However, the mere fact that Lady Macbeth can sway her husband's will in the persuasion scene (1.7.28–82) inherently troubled generations of male interpreters. Early modern men were enjoined to 'rule' the women in their households. Macbeth lets himself be overruled instead. Davenant stressed the monstrous, 'unnatural' perversity of such negligence. In a new dialogue he added to Act 4, a briefly and repentantly lucid Lady Macbeth cast blame on Macbeth's "upsetting of the natural order . . . because he, as a man, failed to exercise his natural superiority over her" (S. Williams, "Taking" 59). Davenant also greatly expanded Lady Macduff's role, making her an example of virtuous womanhood and so clearly delineating the difference between a "good" wife and a wayward one like Lady Macbeth (Wilders 8).

Garrick's performances introduced a different interpretation of Lady Macbeth's role. It was now that she began to come into her own, not merely as a negative *exemplum* for wives—and their husbands—but as an independent and overbearingly 'evil' force. From 1748 through 1768, Garrick played opposite Hannah Vaughan Pritchard, whose Lady was a domineering villain

(Bartholomeusz 49, 69, 79; Kliman, *Shakespeare* 25; Wilders 14). With Pritchard taking the initiative in Duncan's murder, Garrick was freed to develop his version of Macbeth as "a noble man . . . urged to act by his wife" in ways that ran "counter to his essential nature" (Kliman, *Shakespeare* 24–25; cf. Bartholomeusz 46–47). Garrick proved so affecting in *Macbeth* that his fame would dwarf that of later rivals in the part (but cf. Rosenberg, "Culture" 286–87). Yet it was Pritchard's virago who absorbed the opprobrium that Garrick's ruined hero otherwise would have had to bear.

Pritchard's performance impressed and influenced critics of Shakespeare. Samuel Johnson—the essayist, lexicographer, poet, and Shakespearean editor—wrote in 1751 that "Lady Macbeth is merely detested" (62; cf. S. Williams, "Taking" 60). A few years later, Elizabeth Montagu denounced her "mind naturally prone to evil," contrasting it with Macbeth's "frail one warped by force of temptations" (though Montagu did add that the Lady showed "something feminine" in her inability to kill Duncan herself; 215).

Once Pritchard had shown that Lady Macbeth could drive the tragic plot, there were two dualistic *Macbeth*s in circulation: one about a man with unmastered 'evil' ambitions, and another about an honorable man yielding to an 'evil,' mannishly masterful wife. As already noted, F ambiguously supports both ways of apportioning agency and responsibility, especially in Acts 1 and 2 (see Rosenberg, *Masks* 67–72, 160–205). Yet by some point in Act 3, if Macbeth has not already had the initiative, he must inevitably assume it, as Lady Macbeth recedes into the background (until the sleepwalking scene). The question of when and how a performance will shift this balance toward Macbeth is a crucial one (Kliman xiv; cf. 62–79).

Another juxtaposition of an essentially 'good' Macbeth with an 'evil,' ambitious Lady occurred when John Philip Kemble was paired with his sister, Sarah Siddons, in the late eighteenth and early nineteenth centuries. Kemble made for a noble, yet "tortured" Macbeth (Bartholomeusz 145), who, despite differences, "tended to refine and highlight central features of Garrick's interpretation" (S. Williams, "The tragic actor" 125; cf. Wilders 23; see further Jenkin 90, citing eyewitness G.J. Bell).

Siddons's Lady Macbeth was, by contrast, a "powerful" and sublimely evil figure (Kliman, *Shakespeare* 28). It is surprising, therefore, that when Siddons described the Lady in writing, she envisioned a character with an underlying, if repressed, 'feminine' nature—one still somehow related to a recognizable "model of acceptable womanhood" (Ziegler 129; see also Laura Engel's essay, chapter 13 in this volume). Whether or not Siddons's acting bore out this conception, it is clear that her "Lady Macbeth overshadowed her brother's Macbeth" (Braunmuller 66). Her interpretation of the part remains more renowned than any other. It was emulated by later performers in the "Pritchard–Siddons tradition" of the Victorian age (Braunmuller 68, 74–76; Wilders 33–34; see further Rosenberg, *Masks* 160–65; Kliman, *Shakespeare* 28–39; McDonald, *Look* 36–49).

Conservative dualism in a revolutionary epoch: J.P. Kemble

The dualistic *Macbeth*s that held the stage between the Restoration and the 1800s might foreground either Macbeth's 'evil' agency or Lady Macbeth's. What was not in question was whether regicide could be anything *other* than 'evil.' From 1788 through 1816, J.P. Kemble kept Garrick's dying speech in his *Macbeth* (Wilders 214), repeating its dualistic indictment of "ambition."

Dualism also gained new political meanings at this time. With the American and French revolutions of 1776 and 1789, depictions of regicide and tyranny acquired an immediate relevance they had not enjoyed in England since shortly after the Restoration. Monarchs feared violent rebellion at the hands of radicalized subjects. Interpretations of *Macbeth* responded to these revolutionary developments. Kemble, in particular, has been characterized as "a natural Tory" (Thomson, *On Actors* 113; cf. Moody 43, 44, 48–49; Prescott 87–89). His decision to retain Garrick's speech against 'ambition' suggests conservatism, implicitly condemning all insurgencies.

In this light, it is significant that Kemble departed from earlier stagings of the weïrd sisters; one of his major contributions as an interpreter of *Macbeth* was to make them more sinister figures. In April 1794, he mounted a *Macbeth* that strove to "avoid all buffoonery" in the witch-scenes (Bartholomeusz 135, quoting W.C. Oulton, *History of the Theatres of London* [1796]). It was now common in England to invoke Shakespeare's witches as figures for political subversion—including that of the rebels in France, where King Louis XVI had been guillotined just over a year earlier (Bate, *Shakespearean* 88–91, plates 31, 32). To make witchcraft a solemnly nefarious business may have been to signal the gravity of a clear and present danger to the social order.

Along similar lines, Kemble's 1794 *Macbeth* was also the first staging to make Banquo's ghost an invisible and imagined presence in the banquet scene (3.4), rather than a gorily embodied one (Bartholomeusz 133–34; cf. Rosenberg, *Masks* 439ff.). Like Kemble's treatment of the witches, this innovation seems meant to make something deeply serious—as opposed to playfully theatrical—out of an encounter with the forces that tempt humanity to transgress imposed limits on its knowledge and power.

Revolutionary dualism?: the anti-tyrannical *Macbeth*s of Kean and Phelps

As the eighteenth century closed, conservative dualistic *Macbeth*s continued to portray treason and regicide as 'evil,' while tracing their origins to base 'ambition.' But this was a revolutionary age. New concepts of 'evil' were in circulation, equally dualistic yet politically dissimilar. To radicals, the misery of nations was caused by the arrogance of princes—whether they were "untitled," as Macduff calls Macbeth, or pedigreed royal "issue" like Malcolm (4.3.104, 106). Among *Macbeth*s at this time, some bore witness to this radical shift in the ground of ideological debate and the current meanings of 'evil.'

One sign that anti-tyrannical, pro-revolutionary readings were envisioned in this period is the suppression of *Macbeth* by European monarchies (for a Czech example, see Stříbrný, *Shakespeare* 60–61; on the fortunes of Giuseppe Verdi's *Macbeth* in Italian cities, see Bradshaw 51). *Macbeth* did not evoke such crude censorship in England, where Shakespeare was by now a 'national poet.' Still, anti-authoritarian readings were presumably available to English actors and audiences.

In the 1810s, Edmund Kean played Macbeth as an out-and-out villain, drawing comparisons with his own earlier appearances as Richard III (Bartholomeusz 145; cf. Prescott 88–89).[3] Kean's vigorous, generally 'vulgar' comportment (Wilders 26) gave his performances a stirring populist edge (Thomson, *On Actors* 114). Arguably he helped to displace the view of Macbeth as an honorable gentleman—born and bred to virtue, though since corrupted—with a more democratic vision of an enterprising opportunist. If this basely acquisitive Macbeth lacked the high scruples of more 'noble' Macbeths, perhaps it was because revolutionary discourse had spread the word that thanes, and even kings, were much like other men: some better, many worse. Indeed, to many in Kean's audience it might have been the bad Macbeth, not the 'good' Duncan, who seemed a more typical representative of his class.

Later, the Victorian Samuel Phelps disclosed further anti-monarchical resonances in *Macbeth*. Phelps is remembered for staging parts of the text that had been cut regularly since the Restoration. One passage restored in his 1847 *Macbeth* was the on-stage murder of Macduff's young son (4.2.76 SD–82). This gruesome act had been relegated off-stage in Garrick's version—and in all others prior to Phelps's (Wilders 36, 178, 180–81). To bring it back *on* served not only to alienate the audience utterly from Macbeth (cf. Honigmann, *Shakespeare* 137–38), but also to confront them with the full horror of royal power's potential for abuse.

The conclusion of Phelps's *Macbeth* may also have conveyed a sense of radical suspicion toward monarchy. By this time, actors had broken with the Davenant–Garrick tradition of letting Macbeth die 'nobly' with a sermon on his lips. Yet Phelps was the first to adhere to the letter of F—where Macduff, having butchered Macbeth, returns the severed head to public view (5.9.20 SD). The sight made it harder to remember the fallen "tyrant" (5.8.27) as an innately 'honorable' man, dying contritely. Rather than cultivating pity for a ruined nobleman, Phelps presented regicide as an act of rough justice executed against a king who had reigned brutally.

Shakespeare's canonical status in English culture allowed actors a certain license to explore bold, potentially subversive interpretations. Some may have used this freedom to turn *Macbeth*'s dualistic values against the established order, identifying evil with the monarchical system. Meanwhile, other writers of the Romantic period and afterward had begun feeling that all might not be well with moral dualism itself.

A nineteenth-century problematic: *Macbeth* and psychology

Though nineteenth-century writers did not deny that *Macbeth* depicted a conflict of 'good' and 'evil,' some began to find a more confusing human experience enacted in the play: one in which bafflement and delusion are as important as recognitions of moral truth. Literary critics, especially, began reading *Macbeth* as a study of the imagination's ascendancy over the reason. This notion would eventually help to erode the assumption that Shakespeare's tragedy evokes clear and objective intuitions about 'good' and 'evil.' The Romantics thus anticipated the later emergence of what I am calling a 'problematic' *Macbeth*.

Among the earlier nineteenth-century critics, it was William Hazlitt who perhaps came closest to formulating a problematic viewpoint. On the one hand, Hazlitt wrote in 1817 of *Macbeth*'s "systematic principle of contrast. . . . It is a huddling together of fierce extremes, a war of opposite natures" (23–24). On the other, Hazlitt argued that despite this dualism, *Macbeth* creates paradoxical conjunctions of opposite values: Lady Macbeth veers between feelings of "filial piety" and "thoughts [that] spare the blood neither of infants nor old age" (25; cf. *Macbeth* 2.2.12–13, 1.7.54–59). If people in *Macbeth* are both one thing and another, both good and bad, we may well begin wondering how to separate the two.

Europe also began to discover problematizing possibilities. In 1800, a German adaptation by Friedrich Schiller and J.W. von Goethe gave unprecedented importance to the weïrd sisters, making them statuesque embodiments of the delusive dreams that lead mortals to ruin (S. Williams, *Shakespeare* 94ff.). Schiller himself had said that behavior is motivated less by reason than by strong impressions on the imagination (see LeWinter 72); this was a general view at the time, though it had a prehistory in early modern accounts of emotion (for discussion in re. *Macbeth*, see Rowe, "Minds in Company," "Humoral"). In the Schiller–Goethe *Macbeth*, the weïrd sisters represented the power of a passionate imagination to obscure moral truths and distinctions that reason itself might have discerned. While Schiller and Goethe related the weïrd sisters to fantasy's delusive workings, they did not reject moral dualism. But they offered a glimpse of future readings that would deny the ability of Macbeth—or, eventually, his audience—to make confident dualistic judgments.

As we have seen, Hazlitt also hinted that *Macbeth* might perplex ethical analysis, undermining morality's rational structure. S.T. Coleridge posited another disconcerting separation between Macbeth's accusing conscience and his conscious mind; he saw the latter struggling to evade the former's clear perceptions of 'good' and 'evil,' seeking refuge in amoral "prudential reasonings" to avoid facing an "avenging conscience" (248, 250). Though Coleridge's explicit moral views were dualistic, he saw *Macbeth* as a dramatic illustration of the mind's ability to suppress—albeit only temporarily—the awareness of 'evil' and the claims of the 'good.' (On *Macbeth*'s relation to theories of the unconscious, see Abraham Stoll's essay, chapter 6 in this volume.)

Romantic readers developed new understandings of Shakespeare's psychological dimension, approaching *Macbeth* as a poetic representation of subjective experience (see e.g. Hazlitt 16, 18). Thomas De Quincey, in his famous commentary on the scene following Duncan's death (2.2.60 SD–2.3.17 SD), wrote that its purpose was to "throw the interest on the murderer" by making us "enter into his feelings" and "understand them" (91).[4] In accordance with this psychologizing impulse, nineteenth-century critics—however much they reiterated dualistic judgments against ambition, murder, etc.—also began discussing a subject harder to adjudicate morally: that of mental illness. George Fletcher in 1847 called "excessive morbid irritability" a "great moral characteristic of Macbeth" (quoted in Furness 404). The great French critic Hippolyte Taine, in his *Histoire de la Littérature Anglaise* (1863), regarded *Macbeth* as "the history of a monomania;" Macbeth suffers from a "hallucination" of "grand and terrible phantoms . . . the poetry of which indicates a generous heart, enslaved to an idea of fate" (212). Among these hallucinations was Banquo's ghost; yet in describing it as such, Taine all but asserted that moral dualism itself is a subjective mental construct (215). His viewpoint attested to a creeping doubt in later nineteenth-century culture about the essential existence of 'good' and 'evil' (while social conservatives, including Taine, continued to see the outward maintenance of moral dualisms as imperative).

Psychological approaches to Shakespearean interpretation were not new, even in the earlier nineteenth century; for example, in 1794, Walter Whiter had tried to explain *Macbeth*'s imagery in terms of Shakespeare's own associative process (see Wain 63–76). What was notable in Romantic and later nineteenth-century criticism was the perception that Shakespearean tragedy is fundamentally *about* mental experience and its caprices. *Macbeth* was a useful text for this thesis, with its unearthly apparitions. But the premise as such was motivated by a more general uncertainty about the relationship between consciousness and desire. If our deliberations are not under our rational control, but are subject to the vagaries of passion and imagination—making our judgments fickle and unaccountable to reason—what hope is there for a responsible pursuit of the 'good?'

As such questions became more and more urgent for the Victorians, the stage was set for modern and postmodern approaches to *Macbeth* as a revelation of subjectivity's paradoxical and unstable qualities, suggesting problematic perspectives on our ethical and ideological commitments.

Nineteenth-century *Macbeth*s on stage: dualism enhanced

While literary critics explored psychologistic avenues which would eventually threaten to erode dualism, theatrical interpreters were more tightly bound to dualistic assumptions. Moralistic melodramas now prevailed on European stages. Even "scenery . . . was required to signal a necessary quality of vice or virtue, peril or security, by the atmosphere of the set" (Styan, *Modern Drama* 3). In stage *Macbeth*s, dualistic premises remained broadly in evidence, and were enhanced by technical novelties.

Like other plays at this time, and perhaps more due to its supernatural subject-matter, *Macbeth* was a vehicle for elaborate visual designs. Large choruses of witches were common (Bradshaw 46). Sensational effects such as their disappearance (1.3.76 SD), Banquo's ghost, and the apparitions were achieved in diverse, ingenious ways (Wilders 40, 78 n., 152–53 n., 173 n.).

The importance of historical thinking at this time, as well as visual sensibilities, prompted increasing attention to scenic 'accuracy.' Clothing and topographical details evinced a fascination with national identity in an age of imperial rivalry and racialist ideology; thus, in 1877, F.J. Furnivall attributed Macbeth's "terrors" to his "Keltic imagination" (quoted in Furness 413). While eighteenth-century English audiences had not yet come to expect 'period' costumes and sets in Shakespearean performances, in 1773 Charles Macklin created the first Scottish-themed *Macbeth*. Later, in the 1790s, J.P. Kemble introduced 'medieval' scenery, heralding a trend that dominated large stages until the earlier twentieth century (Wilders 16–19, 24, 52ff.). Most Victorian stagings sought a Gothic effect, though one—presented in the mid-1800s by Charles Kean, the son of Edmund Kean—was ostensibly "Saxon" (see Wilders 39; cf. Bartholomeusz 180–86). Such conceptions incidentally attest to the period's unhappy notions about 'race' and its supposed role in a nation's historical and artistic achievements—including the more and more highly esteemed works of Shakespeare himself.

Shakespeare's growing international fame not only inspired literary translations, but also led to stagings, adaptations, and a more general assimilation of *Macbeth* into the European cultural consciousness. One mid-nineteenth-century German *Macbeth*, staged by Dingelstedt, matched its English counterparts in "operatic" stateliness, while weaving "realism" into its stark moral symbolism. For instance, "Macbeth's demand that the stars hide their fires [1.4.50] was accompanied by a sudden withdrawal of the back of Duncan's tent to reveal a panorama of the stars." Later in the century, another spectacle-laden German production (by the influential Meiningen company) had "Macbeth . . . slain by Macduff on the very steps which earlier he had ascended to murder Duncan" (S. Williams, *Shakespeare* 158, 170). In these examples, the grand visual conceptions of nineteenth-century *Macbeth*s became not just moralizing but overtly providentialist, forcefully reinscribing a dualistic pattern of crime and punishment.

Macready as Macbeth: a Romantic Satan?

Moral dualism, of one sort or another, prevailed in theatrical *Macbeth*s throughout the nineteenth century—even as literary critics were arguing that the play immerses its readers in a psychological and subjective experience of alienation from approved moral perceptions. It was not yet openly asserted that such experiences might encourage doubts about conventional morality's claim to objective truth. But a few critics came close to acknowledging this, clearing the way for later problematic readings.

If there was any actor during the earlier 1800s who may have helped audiences sense some of the troubling implications critics were finding in *Macbeth*, it was William Charles Macready (see Figure 1.1). For over thirty years, from 1820 to 1851, Macready played Macbeth opposite a number of actresses including Helen Faucit, Charlotte Cushman, and Fanny Kemble. Scholars agree that his studied approach, and constant attention to the play, yielded a subtle interpretation of Macbeth's character. He is said to have eluded existing paradigms, steering between the "hypersensitivity" of a Garrick or J.P. Kemble and the "ruthless determination" of an Edmund Kean (Wilders 31; see further Downer 318–38.)

Interestingly, certain moments in Macready's performances intimated a quality that contemporaries might identify as 'Satanic' sublimity (Bartholomeusz 155; Shattuck 1: 70). If Macready indeed evoked a Satan, it must have been Milton's Satan, whom some Romantics thought admirable in his rebelliousness—and who lurks within some Romantic accounts of Macbeth (see e.g. De Quincey 91, echoing "The hell within him" [*Paradise Lost*, IV, 20]). By embodying such Satanic transgression appealingly, Macready might have hinted at a rethinking of dualistic pieties.

Macready's career is also remembered for an episode that shows how ideological differences within nineteenth-century Shakespearean culture could manifest themselves in more materially disruptive ways. In the 1830s–1840s Macready fell into a transatlantic rivalry with the American actor Edwin Forrest, whose broad and energetic style recalled Edmund Kean's. In 1849, on a stage in Manhattan, Macready appeared as Macbeth while Forrest played the same role nearby. Class tensions flamed up, as a domestic exponent of Kean's populist idiom came up against an actor associated with un-American aristocracy and social stratification. Demonstrations for the "Freemen" and against the "English" met with official violence, concluding in over a score of deaths and many more injuries and arrests (see Shattuck 1: 82–85; cf. Braunmuller, *Macbeth* 74 and n. 5).

A few nights before this episode—known as the Astor Place Riot—another U.S. audience had cheered Forrest for his rousing delivery of Macbeth's plea to "scour these English hence" (5.3.57; Shattuck 1: 82). The later incident suggests how a tragedy's evocations of bloody conflict might conduce to an outbreak of actual bloodshed. It is surely significant that a combatively anti-aristocratic crowd felt able to identify with a regicidal protagonist—albeit one who was also, paradoxically, a tyrannical king.

Terry as Lady Macbeth: a problematically 'good' woman

As noted earlier, a division had emerged within nineteenth-century views of Lady Macbeth. As critics tried to comprehend her in relation to "the parameters of Victorian womanhood," they simultaneously elaborated "two images of the Lady—as barbaric and passionate or domesticated and caring" (Ziegler 122, 137; cf. Desmet 49–51; see Figure 1.1). Actresses who favored the more "domesticated" reading included Helen Faucit in 1843 (Braunmuller 69–71; Wilders 32–33; cf. Rosenberg, *Masks* 174ff.) and, in 1888, the famed Ellen Terry (Braunmuller 77–78; McDonald, *Look* 94–100; cf. Shattuck 2: 180),

Figure 1.1 Detail of Henry Maclise, *The Banquet Scene in Macbeth* (1840). By permission of the Guildhall Art Gallery, Corporation of London. The actor William Charles Macready was reportedly Maclise's model for Macbeth (Clary). The painting was a success on its first exhibition. However, one Victorian critic would object to its physically formidable Lady Macbeth, advocating instead for a more visibly 'soft' and feminine Lady. "What was Lady Macbeth's form and temperament? In Maclise's great painting of the banquet scene, she is represented as a woman of large and coarse development; a Scandinavian amazon, the muscles of whose brawny arms could only have been developed to their great size by hard and frequent use; a woman of whose fists her husband might well be afraid ... Was Lady Macbeth such a being? Did the fierce fire of her soul animate the epicene bulk of a virago? Never! Lady Macbeth was a lady beautiful and delicate ... Could the Lady Macbeth of Mr. Maclise, and of others who have painted this lady, have been capable of the fire and force of her character in the commission of her crimes, the remembrance of them would scarcely have disturbed the quiet of her after years" (Bucknill 44–46).

followed by Lillie Langtry in 1889 (Shattuck 2: 119–20). Others, who adhered more closely to the Pritchard–Siddons line, nevertheless began to suggest 'feminine' sensitivity in the Lady's later scenes (Rosenberg, *Masks* 168–70).

The portrayal of Lady Macbeth as "a tender, companionate wife" (Braunmuller 68) proved congenial to dualistic versions where Macbeth was obviously 'evil.' For a malicious Macbeth, a 'feminine' Lady made a useful foil. In 1888 such a Lady was required to complement the ignoble Macbeth of Henry Irving (see next section). Ellen Terry developed an unprecedentedly "soft" characterization (Rosenberg, "Macbeth" 84). Reviewers were ambivalently "awed by her beauty, intrigued by her fragility," yet "disappointed by her lack of wicked grandeur" (McDonald, *Look* 99; cf. 98; Bartholomeusz 206–207). Perhaps, though, the Victorian critics simply did not want to see how a servile wife who obeyed her husband—for good or for ill—might thereby exemplify 'evil' at its most chilling. Perhaps Terry's Lady disturbingly revealed deference to corrupt authorities as a form of complicity.

For a Victorian woman to serve her husband unquestioningly was, if not perfectly 'good,' yet 'good' enough. Terry may have subverted this stereotype by incorporating it into her Lady Macbeth, insinuating that women could be *too* 'good': that to love, cherish, and obey a Macbeth was in fact 'bad.' This in turn implied a problematic recognition that 'good' and 'evil' might not always be neatly distinguishable, even in the most exemplary Victorian housewife.

Irving as Macbeth: the dualistic tradition diminished

The later nineteenth century was the period of realistic and naturalistic revolts in European drama and literature. Zola's *Thérèse Raquin*, a novel dispassionately following the fortunes of an adulterous, murderous couple, was published in 1867 and adapted for the stage in 1873. It was followed by more plays, such as Ibsen's and Strindberg's, that challenged melodrama's clear dualistic values and insistence on the natural predominance of the 'good.' Such works were encouraged by a larger, Darwinian movement toward the view that life was to be explained physically, not metaphysically; they were also in step with Nietzsche's attack on the use of the terms 'good' and 'evil' to dignify prevailing cultural imperatives and institutions (Styan, *Modern Drama* 6–11, 17–30, 37–44).

Neither English nor American productions of Shakespeare would quickly absorb these changes. However, in Henry Irving's *Macbeth*s of the 1870s and 1880s, we may glimpse a tendency to problematize dualistic views of the conflict between virtue and vice. Until now this conflict had been presented as an inner struggle or a clash of opposed wills. Irving's Macbeth, however, was no agonist but a corrupt self-seeker, lacking either a conscience or a 'noble' sense of shame. In the second half he was not so much sensible to his guilt as simply afraid. In the banquet scene, during an 1875 performance, he hid from the ghost under his own cloak (Hughes 108; cf. 113; cf. Shattuck 2: 176–78; Braunmuller 77 n. 4; Wilders 44; see also S. Williams, "The tragic actor" 129–30). Irving described Macbeth in writing as an "intellectual voluptuary," though one who had cultivated "a true villain's nerve and callousness" (quoted in Furness 470–71).

To the reviewers, Irving's dastardly Macbeth seemed implausibly "neurasthenic" (Odell 2: 384). One scholar has tried to explain this "largely negative critical response" as an expression of gendered anxieties: male reviewers identified enough with Macbeth, if only because of his sex, to feel queasy at the sight of his spinelessness (Prescott 94). This must be at least partly right; in 1888, it was left to Ellen Terry's Lady Macbeth to sustain her craven husband through his humiliating collapse. Still, considering that Irving himself regarded Macbeth as an 'immoralist,' it may be that the critics' hostility involved more than gender. Whereas nineteenth-century thinkers often debated morality's relationship to human nature, many still assumed that normal people in civilized societies had some respect for morality. To be greatly 'evil,' one would need to have an audacious and determined spirit, not a shrinking one; the works of Darwin, Nietzsche, and Freud (or their popularizers) had not yet persuaded many to believe that despite laws and customs, people were intrinsically driven by their most selfish appetites. So we may suspect that Irving's 1888 *Macbeth* dismayed late Victorian reviewers because it seemed to belittle morality's perceived impact in human life. To imagine a small-souled man murdering and tyrannizing, without either an indomitable will of his own or a shrewishly 'evil' wife to pressure him into unethical acts, was to minimize the influence of the moral law itself.

Chafing against Victorian sensibilities, Irving's *Macbeth* thus resonated with emergent modern anxieties. In some ways it was comparable to Zola's *Thérèse Raquin*, with its shabby picture of lustful murderers who behave as "human animals, nothing more" (Zola 22). Along similar lines, when Sarah Bernhardt played Lady Macbeth in London in 1884, reviewers attacked the eroticism of her performance; the persuasion scene—where she flaunted her physical, sexual power over Macbeth—was especially disparaged (Wilders 49). To identify Shakespearean 'evil' with such basic human desires was at once morally unacceptable and—at the same time—all too close to the conflicted heart of Victorian selfhood. Whereas Macready's Macbeth evoked Romantic visions of Milton's fallen Lucifer, Irving's and Bernhardt's performances seem to have anticipated later, naturalistic depictions of murder such as Dreiser's *American Tragedy* (1925), or even the sordid killers who populate 1950s film noir.

Into the twentieth century: the new Shakespearean stage

The turn of the century saw both continuity and change on Shakespearean stages. On the one hand, the grand illusionism of nineteenth-century sets survived in some early twentieth-century *Macbeth*s (for examples see Shattuck 2: 283–85; Braunmuller 78–79; Wilders 50–52; Bartholomeusz 226–30). On the other hand, a rethinking of Shakespearean performance was stirring, as

William Poel attempted to research and reconstruct the spatial and technical elements employed in Renaissance theaters. In an important sense, Poel's Elizabethan revival represented a consummation of the Victorian search for 'authenticity' through historical accuracy. But Poel's path toward this end was a new one. Key innovations included platform stages and protruding apron stages (*vs.* the recessed proscenium), permanent and often minimal sets, and accelerated speech, as well as scripts that were faithful to the early texts (see e.g. Styan, *Shakespeare* 45ff.).

In 1909 Poel applied these principles to a production of *Macbeth* in "Elizabethan costume" (Bartholomeusz 221). In his quest for the authentic Shakespeare, Poel presented the F text far more completely than anyone since Phelps (Wilders 53; cf. Styan, *Shakespeare* 49). Such experiments enriched and diversified the repertory of performance strategies available to larger productions, contributing to a wider theatrical ferment in which prominent English Shakespeareans—such as Edward Gordon Craig (Ellen Terry's son) and Harley Granville-Barker—were taking part (see e.g. Styan, *Shakespeare* 79–81, 82ff.).

This wider artistic movement would never simply adopt Poel's vision of an 'Elizabethan' Shakespeare in all its antiquarian specificity. Instead, it assimilated Poel's technical insights and fused them with other modern artistic and intellectual currents. By the 1920s these converging tendencies had created new resources for the Shakespearean stage. Some directors of the interwar period even started challenging the dualism of traditional *Macbeth*s—though it was not until the 1960s that a concerted or fully articulate movement would arise to reject dualistic conventions altogether.

Modernity and the problematic *Macbeth*: Bradley to Freud

Early twentieth-century thought was preoccupied with depth psychology and the mysterious recesses of the self. Western culture at this time was undergoing a wrenching encounter with "the post-Nietzschean notion of nature as an immense amoral force;" modern thinkers and artists responded with a psychological "turn inward, to experience or subjectivity" (Taylor 462). Yet the self's own claim to a deeper moral integrity had been irreparably damaged by Darwinian, Nietzschean, and—soon—Freudian theses about human nature. The inner life offered no clear model of the 'good' to compete with Judeo-Christian and Enlightenment traditions (which modernism was critiquing, and in many ways, rejecting).

Modernity's morally problematic subjectivism helped to impose an increasingly blurred lens upon the ethical perceptions of *Macbeth*'s early twentieth-century readers and audiences. This trend appeared first in criticism, where it had been in preparation since the nineteenth century; on stage, it would emerge during the 1920s and 1930s. As noted earlier, Romantic and mid-nineteenth-century literary critics had already focused attention on Macbeth's mental experience, suggesting how a man's conscious grasp on moral distinctions might weaken, to the point of exposing an underlying inconstancy in our moral intuitions themselves. One expression of this problematic insight is found in the work of A.C. Bradley, whose book *Shakespearean Tragedy* (1904) made him the foremost modern exponent of a psychologizing approach to Shakespeare.

Like his nineteenth-century precursors, Bradley used terms that made him *sound* like a moral dualist; he cited and endorsed Coleridge's view of Macbeth as a man trying to repress his inward "imagination," where his moral conscience—"the best of him"—resided (Bradley 106–107). Yet Bradley was much less clear than Coleridge about *our* ability to discern good from bad within Macbeth. To him, the play's "atmosphere" of "darkness" and "storm," with its "violent and gigantic images," suggested "the presence of evil . . . all through and around our mysterious nature" (Bradley 101–103). And in concluding his discussion, Bradley revealed an even more problematic strain in his thought by hinting at the existence of a "tragic point of view"—far from that of morality—in which a character such as Lady Macbeth seems "too great to repent" (129). To call an 'evil' character "great" is to imply that tragic protagonists are best evaluated aesthetically, not ethically. The idea resonates with an older Romantic Satanism, but also with the "tragic poeticism of Nietzsche," which was attracting interest in these decades (Safranski 332).

Before Bradley, most critics had judged Shakespeare's protagonists dualistically even when analyzing them psychologically (see e.g. Furness 412–13). By the early 1900s this censorious note would not be so predictably sounded. Some modernist writers saw *Macbeth* as reflecting an alienation from common values and/or rational perceptions (see e.g. Hofmannsthal 337–38; Maeterlinck xiv). Theories of unconscious motivation could also work against dualism in the new intellectual climate. Sigmund Freud himself, in 1916, suggested that Macbeth and his wife resembled "two disunited parts of a single psychical individuality," so that "what he feared in his pangs of conscience is fulfilled in her" (137). As novel as Freud's psychology, here, was his view of dramaturgy, according to which different characters might represent dispersed pieces of a self. To take this idea seriously would be to suppose that a tragedy can represent something wholly beyond the characters' individual powers of apprehension: if so, then the very notion of judging their choices *morally* is quite beside the point. Freud's essay might well have suggested to some modern Shakespeareans how "the turn inward may take us beyond the self as usually understood, to a fragmentation of experience which calls our ordinary notions of identity into question" (Taylor 462).

The modern *Macbeth* on stage: Jackson and Komisarjevsky

Theatrical *Macbeth*s would eventually begin expressing a modernist subjectivism. Already, earlier stagings may sometimes have intimated the mind's submerged workings through their theatrical design. Irving's *Macbeth* had used lighting and music to make the weïrd sisters appear awful and inscrutable (Bartholomeusz 199; Rosenberg, *Masks* 13; Braunmuller 78; Wilders 84 n.). Witches who seem truly strange and remote from conscious experience may imply that the Macbeths' crimes are not done out of malice so much as impelled by occult intentions; the supernatural can signify our own secret will, radiating from the unknowable depths of the worlds our minds project.

In the new century, theatrical artists began psychologizing *Macbeth* much more deliberately. Two new styles, expressionism and primitivism, evoked the modern descent into the psyche. In 1922 and 1923, two German expressionist directors created *Macbeth*s aimed at "heightening emotional states to the point where the subjective turns into the archetypal" (Innes 48; see Hortmann, *Shakespeare* 66ff.). Expressionist and primitivist influences are also noted in several American and English *Macbeth*s mounted between 1921 and 1932 (Kennedy, *Looking* 141–42; Bartholomeusz 231, 237). Later, Orson Welles's 1936 *Macbeth* would combine both styles to memorable effect (discussed below).

However, the first modernist *Macbeth* to have a resounding impact on English audiences was that of a Russian stage designer and director, Theodore Komisarjevsky. In 1933, his *Macbeth* was performed at Stratford, England. Certain visual details, such as military uniforms and prop guns, alluded to World War I (Wilders 57–58). Yet as a whole, Komisarjevsky's design depicted a world outside history, objectivity, and reason. The action was bathed in changing lights (often red) and set among curved metallic shapes with constructivist and surrealist affinities. (On an earlier 1921 Russian modernist *Macbeth*, with designs by Sergei Eisenstein, see Baer 192.)

According to one reviewer, Komisarjevsky aimed to "relate Shakespeare to an age dominated by psychological conceptions, rationalizing . . . magic and witchcraft" (quoted in Mullin, "Augures" 21; cf. 25 and Kennedy, *Looking* 129). That is, the supernatural was not allowed to exist objectively within the play-world, but only to exist within the mind and *its* world. The point was not to discredit Macbeth's perceptions, but rather to make the audience share them while conveying their radical subjectivity—their particularity to his personal experience. Komisarjevsky suggested this by making Banquo's ghost (3.4) into, literally, "a shadow cast by Macbeth" upon an opposing wall. The apparitions (in 4.1) likewise visited Macbeth in his bedroom, not as physical presences, but as figments of shadow and light (Mullin, "Augures" 29; cf. Wilders 173 n.). This *Macbeth* offered a theatrical counterpart to subjectivist criticism; it implied that world views are produced by individual minds, that they lack the guarantee of an objective or transcendent reality.

Komisarjevsky's work at Stratford in the 1930s was seminal, "preparing the ground for the revolution in British theatre in the second half of the twentieth century" (Střibrný, *Shakespeare* 78). His 1933 *Macbeth* substituted dreamlike presentation for naturalistic representation, subjective for objective statement. Since it did make allusions to the Great War, it may be that Komisarjevsky's conception—like the "archetypal" vision of the German expressionists—did not simply disclaim any relationship to a possible shared morality. Regardless, it distanced the play from earlier ideological frames of reference, in part through its physical setting.[5]

However, another innovator—a few years earlier—had already done something to prepare English audiences for the shock of Komisarjevsky's *Macbeth*. Barry Jackson is remembered for having introduced modern dress to the Shakespearean stage in the mid-1920s. In 1928 he produced a *Macbeth* in London, directed by H.J. Ayliff, which featured machine guns at the beginning (Farjeon 136) and updated the rest of the play accordingly. "Lady Macduff . . . was murdered over a cup of afternoon tea . . . Macduff . . . received the news of their deaths wearing a felt hat and a lounge suit," and "Macbeth emptied his revolver into the charmed Macduff at point-blank range" (Styan, *Shakespeare* 149–50). Reviewers found these effects jarring, and judged Jackson's *Macbeth* less successful than his earlier contemporizing experiments. Yet the production probably did more to disturb dualistic presuppositions than any other English *Macbeth* prior to Komisarjevsky's. It revealed contradictions between the dualistic values that audiences associated with *Macbeth*, and the modern pressures that in real life seemed to be eroding those values.

In one scholar's view, Jackson defamiliarized *Macbeth*, "blurring the struggle between essential good and evil" (Bartholomeusz 232) and dislodging received dualisms. Another suggests that "Lady Macbeth's part . . . [was] to stand for the amoral modern world outside Macbeth's consciousness . . . until in the end she herself follows into his world of shadow and terror" (Mullin, " 'Macbeth' in Modern" 182; cf. Kennedy, *Looking* 112). Some aspects of that terrible world, such as Macduff's invulnerability to gunfire, had a dreamlike unreality suggesting the subjective distortion of experience by the 'primitive' mind. A dualistic world view was now part of the archaic baggage borne by a *pre*-modern Macbeth; it no longer reflected modern reality.

Dualism and historicism: earlier twentieth-century scholarship

Jackson's anachronistic *Macbeth* challenged audiences to confront the ideological chasm now separating modernity, with its psychologistic outlook, from earlier dualistic mentalities. Meanwhile, Shakespearean scholars also began to see this historical distance as a problem. Academics during the 1910s, 1920s, and 1930s became concerned that modern views of human nature obscured a historical view of Shakespeare. They began emphasizing differences between 'Elizabethan' and modern discourses of ethics, character, and politics. Against modern psychologistic critics such as Bradley, these early twentieth-century historicists found moral lessons in *Macbeth* that were even more stringently dualistic than those adduced by Victorian critics. Their insistence that Shakespeare was *more* dualistic than modernity appears in the most influential scholarly work on *Macbeth* from this period (e.g. Knight; Spurgeon; Campbell).[6]

The same historicist dualism informed an important early effort to distinguish modern, 'realistic' dramaturgy from Shakespeare's nonnaturalistic theater. E.E. Stoll was an American professor who, from the 1910s, maintained that Shakespeare's characters were made not to resemble 'real' people but to serve dramatic effects, including that of moral contrast—even at the cost of 'realistic' continuity. In a 1933 study Stoll wrote that Macbeth's despair is caused, not by a doomed "inner struggle" against his "righteous nature" (as Coleridge and Bradley thought), but by a more "theological" and "traditional conception of conscience," as "the voice of his creator" cries out to torment him (*Art* 79).

Dualist historicism offered somewhat contradictory possibilities for modern stage interpretations. On the one hand, it implied that *Macbeth* was misinterpreted by directors and performers who projected problematizing, subjectivist psychologies into the tragedy. If so, then the best way for moderns to appreciate *Macbeth* 'authentically' might be to frame it with suggestions of its Renaissance context, perhaps by implementing Poel's 'Elizabethan' staging practices. On the other hand, modern historicist scholarship could also imply that modern audiences necessarily stood at a distance from *Macbeth*'s moral dualism, simply because twentieth-century values *were* more problematic than those of 1606. Scholars like E.E. Stoll may be termed 'historicists' precisely because they saw ethical perceptions as historically and culturally relative. Perhaps, then, the 'original' *Macbeth* was lost to moderns beyond recovery, and the only viable option for artists was to pursue a self-consciously 'modern *Macbeth*.'

It is telling that the tide of dualistic scholarship began flowing in force during the first half of the 1930s—shortly after Jackson had irritated his London audiences with the first modern-dress *Macbeth*, and around the time of Komisarjevsky's production. Hand in hand, academic historicism and cultural modernism precipitated a crisis in Shakespearean interpretation in the study and on the stage. Yet from the 1930s until the 1960s, this crisis would only drive most critics and directors to underscore, ever more clearly, the dualistic presuppositions they read into *Macbeth*.

The causes of this dualistic turn were largely political and ideological, as we shall see. First, though, it will be necessary to turn back to the early 1920s. At that time, in Eastern Europe, a stunningly different and problematic approach to *Macbeth* had briefly appeared. Then, just as abruptly, it disappeared from the annals of the twentieth-century theater—not to be recovered for Western scholarship until very recently.

Les Kurbas in 1924: the first thoroughly problematic *Macbeth*

I have been tracing the emergence of several interpretive possibilities that would furnish mid-twentieth-century Shakespeareans with the ingredients for a problematic *Macbeth*. As it happens, though, another set of possibilities had already been deployed to sensational effect in 1924—but in a place geographically far away from the English-speaking world, and politically even farther. This was Kharkiv, Ukraine, where the Berezil theater staged an avant-garde *Macbeth* under the direction of Les Kurbas.

Kurbas had directed three previous *Macbeth*s in 1919 and 1920, all made possible by the lifting of tsarist censorship immediately after the Russian revolution. In 1924 he undertook "a reexamination of representation itself." Kurbas devised techniques of alienation—anticipating Brecht's—whereby "every theatrical convention was questioned, including the idea of the tragic hero" (Makaryk 78, 94; cf. 42, 65, 92). These aims were quite different from those of the Romantic and modernist interpreters who had begun to problematize *Macbeth* so far, filtering it through Macbeth's psychology and replacing objective values with subjective perceptions. In a revolutionary socialist context, such psychologism surely would have seemed unacceptably 'bourgeois' and individualistic. Kurbas did not follow the cult of interiority that led Western modernists to conflate the world with the self, or selves with their unconscious motives. Rather than psychologize the play-world, he did the opposite: he reduced Macbeth, with every other character, to a superficial stock type. Macbeth became "a common, unimaginative soldier" and his wife "a caricature of the new stereotype of the heroic Soviet woman." Even more disorientingly, Kurbas chose to make "Duncan . . . a drunken fool, whose death at first seemed, if not deserved, then at least not completely reprehensible" (Makaryk 94–95).

Kurbas also used farce to mock the solemnity of bourgeois tragedy and criticize contemporary politics. Above all, he greatly expanded the Porter's role, costuming him in "traditional fool's clothing" and giving him "a bulbous nose which occasionally lit up" (associating the Porter with the witches, who were also "wired" with "electric lights"). The Porter/Fool acquired a series of functions throughout the performance, for example making jokes that changed with the daily headlines (Makaryk 99; cf. 101, 96).

Most importantly, Kurbas sought to expose human materialism and demystify the causes of 'tragic' conflict. This was clearest at the conclusion, when the Porter/Fool made his reappearance as a bishop to place the crown on Malcolm's head, but "a new pretender approached, killed the kneeling Malcolm, and seized the crown. Without pause, the clownish bishop unperturbedly once again intoned the same words, 'There is no power, but from God.' As the new king began to rise, yet another pretender murdered him and the ritual was repeated" (Makaryk 101).

This treatment of monarchical rituals and claims to legitimacy shocked one Ukrainian aristocrat, who felt that by "making idiots of Duncan and his son," Kurbas had "destroy[ed] the whole play" (Makaryk 103). Indeed, nothing could have been further from earlier, dualistic *Macbeth*s with their vision of 'evil' challenging 'good,' or their message that only anointed kings can guarantee stability in the face of 'ambitious' subjects. Yet Kurbas was not just mocking the repressive institutions of the past; he also critiqued those of the present and future. While satirizing monarchies, his *Macbeth* also "gave the lie to early Soviet narratives which attempted to mythologize the Revolution"

(103). "The audience's difficulty and confusion lay in its inability to choose sides. Rather than presenting simple oppositions . . . this production stressed the universal complicity of society in acts of evil" (110).

Macbeth can seem inimical to Marxist interpretation, thanks to its supernatural elements and its suggestions of the sanctity of kingship. Indeed, the play is said to have frustrated Bertolt Brecht's best efforts to interpret it in terms that might "make sense to a modern (socialist) audience" (Hortmann, *Shakespeare* 67 n. 50; cf. Stříbrný, *Shakespeare* 123–24).[7] Kurbas had cut this Gordian knot by turning *Macbeth* virtually inside out, exposing the moral dualism of its rhetoric as a mask for the uniform selfishness of its characters; but this required him to forgo any clearly positive political message. To distribute 'evil' motivations among all the characters is to prevent us from endorsing any one character's cause as 'good.' Moreover, when characters lack interiority we cannot endorse the 'good' *within* any individual on stage— or within any larger vision of humanity. The Berezil *Macbeth* was, then, radically problematic. Its subject was not a conclusive struggle between good and bad, but an endlessly repetitive cycle of victory and defeat, perpetuated by an infinite succession of ridiculous, mediocre rivals.

Despite all this, Kurbas's *Macbeth* has been called "optimistic" in its suggestion "that new modes of art, new modes of thinking, new politics could indeed be created" (Makaryk 109). If so, then perhaps the production stirred its audiences to replace the old dualisms with a more realistic dualism grounded in a truer vision of community. Be that as it may, the director's hopes were not to be realized; in 1937 he would die in Stalin's bloody mass purge of Ukraine. His memory was then effaced by a Soviet establishment committed to "socialist realism" and to a more Stanislavskian theater (Makaryk 198–99).

Les Kurbas was unknown to Westerners until after the fall of Communism. His *Macbeth* stood alone in its time. Perhaps its nearest early twentieth-century analogue was Barry Jackson's 1928 production, which sometimes created "an uncomfortable effect of farce" (Styan, *Shakespeare* 150). Yet this "effect" was perhaps unintentional, and the Jackson–Ayliff *Macbeth* shared nothing with Kurbas technically or theoretically. If there was a precedent for Kurbas in any earlier *Macbeth*-related work it was probably Alfred Jarry's absurdist play of 1896, *Ubu Roi*, long regarded as a travesty of *Macbeth* (though the resemblances are very general, and *Macbeth* probably was not a model; see Morse 117–19; cf. Innes 24ff.).

Welles's "Voodoo" *Macbeth*: psychologism, primitivism, dualism?

In the West, no *Macbeth*s were as radically new as that of Kurbas, either in the 1920s, the 1930s, or indeed until the 1960s. However, the interwar period saw at least one American *Macbeth* that paralleled Kurbas's banishment of 'good' from the play-world. In 1936, in Harlem, New York, Orson Welles directed what came to be known as his "Voodoo" *Macbeth*. Welles directed *Macbeth* for the Negro People's Theatre, a unit within the U.S. Federal Theatre Project that employed African Americans. The tragedy was adapted to a Caribbean setting, where witchcraft could seem an accepted cultural fact. Welles used ritualistic spectacles to evoke 'primitive' religion and superstition.

The modernist aesthetic of primitivism had strongly psychologistic connotations. Many modernists romanticized the forms of 'primitive' culture, thinking they revealed the unconscious mind. African cultures were especially said to express the subjectivity of a primordial, 'savage' self that civilization had concealed. Some modern artists tried to do the same, self-consciously appropriating the cultural forms that they saw through an exoticized and racialized lens.

The 1936 *Macbeth* was Welles's virtual primitivist exhibition. While the rulers' costumes suggested a colonial-style palace life (Kliman, *Shakespeare* 115–16), this only made the "Voodoo" elements all the more vivid. The playwright Eugene O'Neill had employed a similar contrast in his 1921 drama, *The Emperor Jones*. Much like O'Neill's play, Welles's *Macbeth* suggested a primitivist revelation of repressed human nature at its most violent and irrational. This was clearest in his treatment of the supernatural; he made the witches "dominant and powerful through repetition and through their constant presence" on stage. Hecate now became "a huge man . . . with a twelve-foot bullwhip," and appeared in numerous scenes throughout the production (Kliman, *Shakespeare* 118, 113–14). Here and elsewhere Welles made free with F, cutting liberally and remixing the text to create unfamiliar combinations of word and image (117).

Welles's changes tended to accent the hostility of the play-world. They eliminated most expressions of goodness, while occluding the larger prospects for social redemption (Kliman, *Shakespeare* 120–21). To confirm this "pessimistic" view of humanity, Welles resolved the play on an ominous note: Hecate concluded with the words "Peace! The charm's wound up" (Kennedy, *Looking* 147; cf. Kliman, *Shakespeare* 119).

The "Voodoo" *Macbeth* was a significant milestone for American interpretations of Shakespeare, as well as for Welles's own directorial career, and (by some measures at least) for the African-American theater. Jack Carter was admired as Macbeth, despite the heavily conceptual and in some respects demeaning nature of the production around him. Scholars have discussed the play from all these angles (see e.g. Hill 103–107; Kennedy, *Looking* 143–48; Kliman, *Shakespeare* 112–22; for surviving film footage from a touring version—with a different actor replacing Carter—see *We Work Again*, online at Scarborough). Performances in Harlem were well received by audiences and local reviewers, but more critical notices appeared elsewhere. The latter resulted in some cases from conservative discomfort with Welles's textual manipulations, and in others from disappointment with the performances of amateur cast members; also, unfortunately but predictably, racism played a part (Hill 103–107).

Welles had thrown a partly problematic light on the moral landscape of *Macbeth*. His primitivist conventions suggested a correspondence between the 'savage' mentalities on display and the deepest instincts of the human psyche. Humanity's grasp on the 'good' was weakened. But from another standpoint the "Voodoo" *Macbeth* conveyed a qualified dualism. While the ostensibly Caribbean milieu seemed inimical to goodness, it kept its distance from its audience's world (unlike the settings of Jackson's or Kurbas's *Macbeth*s). The culture of witchcraft could be seen as a cautionary example of what *might* happen if 'civilized' societies lapsed into barbarism.

Itself a product of socioeconomic crisis, Welles's "Voodoo" *Macbeth* might thus have warned audiences to be vigilant against 'evil.' It can be seen as a mirror for fears of the "Voodoo"-like politics then in the ascendant in Germany and elsewhere (cf. Kennedy, *Looking* 148). To many audience members, either fascism or Communism—or both—would have seemed a grave and imminent threat to Western culture and values. Dualistic values increasingly seemed to require affirmation, not qualification.

Finally, despite its pessimistic portrayal of 'primitive' humanity, the "Voodoo" *Macbeth* was optimistic in another respect. Though Welles reinforced racist stereotypes by enlisting African Americans in a primitivist performance (see comments in Buhler's essay, chapter 14 in this volume), it is also said that the Negro People's Theatre helped to overcome those stereotypes in the long run, merely by entrusting Shakespeare to the talents and skills of African-American artists. Producing *Macbeth* in Harlem affirmed the possibility of canonical 'high' culture flourishing among a people whose bodies marked them, in all too many minds, as socially and culturally inferior; the "Voodoo" *Macbeth* presented its creators—if not without ambiguity—as producers of 'civilized' work (cf. Innes 194). While the terms of the assertion are (and were) objectionable, we might note that in the United States, even now, some Shakespearean productions with minority casts and/or non-Western settings are advertised as affirmations of ethnic and cultural worth.

Whether or not the more problematic side of Welles's *Macbeth* was generally seen as such in the 1930s, it is clear that during the upcoming global conflict of the 1940s and the Cold War of the 1950s, fewer Shakespeareans would be inclined to problematize *Macbeth*. The 'evil' that had long been perceived in the play-world was now understood to be all too real; what was needed was a firmer commitment to the 'good.'

Dualism reaffirmed: *Macbeth* scholarship in the 1940s and 1950s

By the early 1930s, as noted earlier, scholars began favoring strongly dualist accounts of *Macbeth*'s moral significance. This tendency was furthered by World War II and the Cold War. Some postwar readings attest to the revival of Christian humanism that was then occurring in literary culture (see e.g.

Auden). Many others share a stalwartly moralizing rhetoric that helped to keep dualistic *Macbeth*s in the majority until the 1960s.

Macbeth especially invited dualistic interpretation in the 1940s and 1950s, first, because reality seemed to reflect its subject-matter—murder, tyranny, war, unhallowed rites—and second, because its characters make such clear moral distinctions. Scholars echoed their claims that good and evil are locked in mutual conflict, that we must choose one or the other. "Evil" was being spelled with a capital "E" (G. Hunter, " 'Macbeth' " 10; see further Tredell 54–63, 68–89; cf. Coursen, *Macbeth* 84–91). Some dualists produced 'New Critical' close readings of *Macbeth*'s language and imagery (see esp. Brooks; cf. Traversi 150–66; Wain 202–54; G. Hunter, " 'Macbeth' " 6–7). Meanwhile, historicists directed ever more attention to *Macbeth*'s religious, cultural, and ideological 'backgrounds.' W.C. Curry, in 1937, thus gave intellectual–historical reasons for thinking the witches "demons or devils" (quoted in G. Hunter, " 'Macbeth' " 4; cf. Farnham 99–104). Others argued that *Macbeth* had been written specifically to please King James I, since he had been both a vigorous prosecutor of witchcraft and a promoter of true religion (see esp. Paul).

One hallmark of dualist readings was—and is—to take Malcolm's final speech at face value (5.9.27–42), accepting his triumph as an act of providential deliverance (see e.g. Tillyard 317). Such readings often reflected wartime patriotism; tellingly, Winston Churchill "said *Macbeth* was the only Shakespeare play he knew completely by heart" (Hortmann, "Berlin" 97). Similarly, Macbeth's tyrannical reign also had a contemporary application; as one critic put it in 1951, "Shakespeare's monarchs do usually color the spiritual life of their realms. . . . We, who remember Hitlerite Germany, can understand that" (Fergusson 38–39). In the same year, another dualist defended Macduff against the charge that his flight from Macbeth makes him a traitor to his family (4.2.5, 4.3.26–31): "In 1942 I had the honour to meet in London one of the highest officers of the French Navy, who had escaped from France after the German occupation to fight from this country. He too left his wife and child exposed to the retaliation of the enemy. In those days no one asked him why" (Bradbrook 36).

This urgent postwar dualism influenced the Shakespearean 'scholarship industry' at a time when it was expanding. The resultant outpouring of dualistic work must have had an impact on directors and actors; it may have done much to retard the emergence of more problematic *Macbeth*s on the Western stage until the later upheavals of the 1960s.

Mostly dualistic: wartime, postwar, and Cold War *Macbeth*s

By the 1940s, modern dress and sets had lost their ability to shock. Period settings varied, as often as not; abstract scenery was not unusual. Commentary on stagings at this time tends to concentrate on star performances, which—however accomplished—did little in themselves to challenge familiar dualisms (for representative 1930s and 1940s productions see e.g. Bartholomeusz 235; Wilders 55–56, 61; Wheeler 767–68, 770–72). A 1941 Broadway version, directed by Margaret Webster, gave Macduff the rabble-rousing gesture of "throwing Macbeth over the battlements at the end;" this version was in fact adapted for U.S. military audiences during the war (Kliman, *Shakespeare* 81).

One exception to this wartime dualism hailed from a nation that had at least officially maintained wartime neutrality. Ingmar Bergman directed three theatrical *Macbeth*s in Sweden during the 1940s (Fridén 173–74). The third, in 1948, aimed to signify "that evil is always with us" (Kennedy, *Looking* 197). Bergman's problematic production responded to the unhappy implications— especially in hindsight—of his and his country's disinclination to take sides against the Nazis.

The year 1948 also saw the release of Orson Welles's cinematic *Macbeth*, which differed from his earlier staging, lacking both its Caribbean locale and its African-American cast. Once again, though, Welles problematized the tragedy by withholding any vision of a sustainably 'good' society; at the end, humanity remains noticeably subject to 'evil' influence (Holland, " 'Stands' " 379–80; cf. Kliman, *Shakespeare* 123–24). The film's expressionist style (Rothwell 73) can be seen as "an externalization of Macbeth's . . . mind" (Jorgens 151–52), as moral distinctions dissolve into swirls of fog. Yet—as in the "Voodoo" *Macbeth*'s primitivist setting—this problematizing view of the protagonist's experience can also be seen as a cautionary gesture, reflecting the *danger* associated with moral dissolution in postwar minds. Welles's heavy use of Christian symbolism may support this dualistic analysis of the play's overarching values (see Holland, " 'Stands' " 379; on the film, see further, e.g. Mason 188–93).

A conjunction of conventional dualism with ambivalence about the prospects for the 'good' was characteristic of the most memorable *Macbeth*s staged during the 1950s. In 1954, Michael Benthall directed a thrilling version (see David) that, however, omitted Malcolm's closing speech; one critic protested the cut's problematizing effect (Wheeler 626; cf. 773). Presumably the demoralized reviewer would have preferred the *Macbeth* performed at London's Royal Exchange in 1953, when a mock-Renaissance stage was erected and the supposed 'royal play' staged to celebrate the Queen's coronation (Styan, *Shakespeare* 193).

In 1955, Glen Byam Shaw directed a *Macbeth* in Stratford, England, starring Laurence Olivier, that became one of the most celebrated of its century. Shaw took a basically dualistic view, calling the tragedy a "play . . . against evil & sin" (quoted in Mullin, *Macbeth* 16–17; cf. 249, 252). Moral contrasts were vividly expressed through staging; after the murder of Macduff's family (4.2), the set quickly changed to present an idyll of "humane, civilized England" in the next scene (David 131; for online images, see Royal Shakespeare Company).

Shaw put the principals, especially Olivier, at the center of his production—and this was the decisive factor in its success. It was Olivier's second

Macbeth, but his first triumph in the role; his performance elicited empathy (Kliman, *Shakespeare* 69, 72; cf. David 125). Vivien Leigh, as Lady Macbeth, at first projected confident temerity and then declined; meanwhile, Olivier rose from an initially reserved mood to a high pitch of "hysteria" and "fury" (David 128; Kliman, *Shakespeare* 75; cf. 62–79, *passim*). Byam Shaw's dualistic reading seems to have made an effective foil for Olivier's rather more problematic characterization, with its implicitly psychologistic and modern understanding of inner conflict. While the play-world created clear oppositions between 'good' and 'evil,' audiences experienced that world through Olivier's charismatic *persona*.

At least one technical detail of the production helped audiences appreciate Macbeth's vantage point; this was the mysterious evanescence of the weïrd sisters—a visual trick inviting spectators to identify with Macbeth's perspective from the outset (Kliman, *Shakespeare* 67–68; David 128). In fact, it seems possible that Byam Shaw meant to problematize his *Macbeth* in other ways, but failed to do so. For instance, he tried striking a pessimistic note in the character of Malcolm, whom he imagined as a "rather effete young man . . . rather decadent," according to the actor who played the part (quoted in Mullin, *Macbeth* 252). The actor, though, resisted Byam Shaw's interpretation; on stage, Malcolm became "a mere boy" inspiring "pity and sympathy" (David 125). Byam Shaw also made cuts suggesting a wish to limit the audience's sympathy for Macduff (Brown, *Macbeth* 126–27).

However, such efforts to detract favor from supporting characters may simply reflect Byam Shaw's plan to make audiences identify first and foremost with the protagonists. Another attempted injection of pessimism only tends to confirm the essential dualism of Byam Shaw's assumptions. On the one hand, his direction "hinted at Banquo's tacit acceptance" of the regicide; on the other hand, Byam Shaw justified this choice by claiming that Banquo "is a guilty man & to some extent gets what he deserves" (Kliman, *Shakespeare* 77, quoting Shaw from Mullin, *Macbeth*).

A most problematic *Macbeth:* Kott and the 1960s

A Polish ex-Communist, Jan Kott, is credited with spurring Western reevaluations of Shakespeare during the 1960s. In his radically problematizing book *Shakespeare Our Contemporary*, Kott pronounced: "there are no bad kings, or good kings . . . there is only the king's situation, and the system" (17). In *Macbeth*, "history" is a "murder-cycle" (87); Macbeth kills "to put himself on a level with the world in which murder . . . exists" (91). By the tragedy's end, he "can accept himself at last, because he has realized that every choice is absurd, or rather, that there is no choice" (96). Kott's existentialist ideas were not entirely new to Western Shakespeareans (cf. Collmer); what was new was his hearty endorsement of Macbeth's final, nihilistic outlook.

Kott's work did not swiftly prompt theatrical reinterpretations of *Macbeth* that would influence all subsequent productions, as it did with respect to some other plays (e.g. *King Lear*; Styan, *Shakespeare* 217–23). A Kottian *Macbeth* was staged in 1966 with Alec Guinness and Simone Signoret; but it did not succeed (260 n. 34; cf. Wheeler 661, 785). Still, many future directors would gravitate toward Kott's view that Macbeth's opponents were less 'good' than dualist readings assumed. In a 1967 *Macbeth* at Stratford, England, director Peter Hall "meant to show a vision of evil;" for instance, the production suggested that "megalomania . . . underlies Malcolm's virginal purity." Ironically, the production may have fallen short because Paul Scofield preferred to play Macbeth as a "man of conscience," thus upsetting Hall's vision (Wheeler 787, 668). On the other hand, perhaps Hall himself was not consistently committed to a problematic *Macbeth*; he followed earlier directors (including Shaw) in making England a "green world" to contrast with spiritually barren Scotland (Rosenberg, *Masks* 543).

Certainly the problematizing shift of the 1960s did not occur all at once. Scholars of the mid-1960s, for their part, were not quick to abandon dualism (see e.g. Muir, *Shakespeare Survey*). But as U.S. bombers rained napalm on Vietnam, it became harder for Shakespeareans in the West to identify complacently with self-proclaimed political saviors such as Malcolm. One liberal critic of *Macbeth* ambivalently described "all acts of violence" as "grotesque and sickening," even if they were sometimes "necessary" (Sanders 274; cf. Tredell 89–93). Over the next few decades, Shakespearean scholars would move *en masse* to develop new critical lenses through which a more problematic view of *Macbeth* would appear (see below, Part II; for discussion cf. Kranz 380–82; Tredell 94–149, *passim*.).

Polanski's problematic *Macbeth*

Kott's impact is most prominently seen in a *Macbeth* that was filmed by another Pole, Roman Polanski, and released in 1971 (Coursen, *Macbeth* 184, citing Crowl; D. Williams 149; see further Pearlman; Kliman, *Shakespeare* 190–216; Rothwell 146–53; Hatchuel). Polanski's screenwriting collaborator, Kenneth Tynan, described *Macbeth* explicitly as containing "evil but no organized good" (quoted in Holland, " 'Stands' " 375). Indeed, the film denies its characters any clear view of 'good' as a viable choice. Its world obeys harsh, Hobbesian laws of human nature; "Duncan's reign is . . . callous and bloody" (Buhler 85). Slaughter, whether of pigs or of men, is constantly in view. Lady Macduff is implicitly raped before dying (Kliman, *Shakespeare* 192–93). Although the Macbeths share some disarming moments, even the marital bed harbors violent designs; it is here that Macbeth tells Lady Macbeth, "We are yet but young in deed" (4.3.144).

One critic argues that Polanski may evoke a potentially 'good' alternative to this abattoir-like world in the society of the weïrd sisters, women who "have stepped outside" their warring culture and give "evidence of human feeling within a community" (Kliman, *Shakespeare* 215). Another critic contends, however, that these characters "seem less-than-human," and calls

Polanski as hostile to "feminists" of this sort as to other figures of "sixties communalism"—such as the Mansonite cult members who had murdered his wife (D. Williams 156; cf. 145). Either way, one doubts whether any idea of 'good' could gain wide currency in Polanski's film-world. Moreover, we may feel that this world is all too much like our own, its violent characters merely less fortunate versions of ourselves; Polanski thus "makes his audience sympathise" with the hired assassins by accentuating their poverty (Kliman, *Shakespeare* 197; on these characters, cf. Lois Feuer's essay, chapter 7 in this volume).

Polanski makes Macbeth himself "not [a] tragic figure," but a typical product of a brutalized and brutalizing society (Kliman, *Shakespeare* 206). More problematically still, Polanski uses his medium to cast doubt on the validity of human perceptions and judgments. The apparitions resemble subjective hallucinations—complete with 1960s psychedelic iconography—and the witches themselves seem too human to inspire dread; nevertheless, the question of their epistemological authority is confused by the uncanny accuracy of their prophecies (Kliman, *Shakespeare* 204, 201). All appearances threaten to deceive, as Polanski relativizes our view through the lens. This subjectivizing tendency culminates when Polanski's camera briefly sees as if through the eyes of Macbeth's severed head, leaving us uncertain about the reality of what it displays (for different views see Rothwell 151; Buhler 89). All we can feel sure of, finally, is that things *seem* to change very little in Scotland; "Donalbain's return to the witches' cave suggests . . . usurper will replace usurper in an infinite regression" (Rothwell 151).

Marowitz, Schechner, Ionesco: the witches in the 1968 era

During an earlier revolutionary age, William Hazlitt had called *Macbeth* "an unruly chaos of strange and forbidden things, where the ground rocks under our feet" (24). For a few years around and after 1968, Western society and culture were shaken—or so it seemed—"to their foundations" (4.1.57). To juxtapose Polanski's *Macbeth* with another movie filmed a decade earlier, starring stage actors Maurice Evans and Judith Anderson (see Kliman, *Shakespeare* 81–89), is to apprehend the vast cultural distance between 1960 and 1971.

In the midst of sociocultural crisis, *Macbeth* spawned multiple 'rewritings' into new idioms (see generally Cohn, *Modern* 60–105). Indeed, *Macbeth* became "almost . . . an avant garde trademark" (Innes 194). Whatever their intentions, "almost all offshoots" during this period involved an expansion of "the roles of Lady Macbeth and the witches" (Cohn, *Modern* 101). Two examples from 1969 were *A Macbeth* by Charles Marowitz and *Makbeth* by Richard Schechner. In different ways, both works made "the witches . . . omnipresent and omnipotent," identifying them with psychic and/or social forces repressed by society but affirmed through performance (Innes 194–95). Such adaptations could evince dualistic impulses even while affronting traditional sensibilities. If the old values were false, it might seem 'good'—if only in a relative, problematic sense—to embrace the way of witchcraft. This more or less optimistic, countercultural inversion of postwar values would take time to find favor with scholars; yet by 1986, a prominent academic proclaimed the witches "heroines" (Eagleton 2; for discussion cf. Braunmuller 28; Tredell 123–25).

The Romanian-French dramatist Eugène Ionesco wrote an absurdist *Macbett*, staged in Paris in 1972, "to show . . . that all politicians are paranoids and all politics leads to crime" (quoted in Morse 121 n. 30). Ionesco cited both Jarry's influence and Kott's. His "Lady Macbett" was effectively merged with the witches—either to "represent . . . subconscious urges" (Innes 196) or, on another view, to indicate Ionesco's "conservative" suspicion toward feminism and other rhetorics of liberation (Morse 120). Thus, both partisans and opponents of the counterculture arrived at problematized views of *Macbeth*, even as some offered to redefine the 'good' for an ideologically polarized era. (On a U.S. topical spin-off that also reflects this period's eventfulness, see Stephen M. Buhler's essay, chapter 14 in this volume.)

Nunn's *Macbeth*: a mostly dualistic standard

Trevor Nunn directed *Macbeth* at Stratford, England, in 1976, in a production that was later adapted for television (Kliman, *Shakespeare* 127–47; cf. Wilders 68–70). A compromise between more and less dualistic *Macbeth*s, Nunn's version drew clear lines between 'good' and 'evil' while questioning the former's efficacy. Duncan was an aged and "feeble" man at prayer, Malcolm a conscientious but insecure "college boy" (Kliman, *Shakespeare* 131, 138). The brilliant principals, Ian McKellen and Judi Dench, performed in an intimate space delineated by a chalk circle and movable crates, on which the actors might sit and observe even when not 'on stage' (127–28; see Kennedy, *Looking* fig. 16; for online images, see Royal Shakespeare Company).

Nunn left the play-world's governing order ambiguous. His witches behaved as if posessed; yet it was unclear whether this was literally or only metaphorically the case, or if they possessed actual powers (for contrasting views see Kliman, *Shakespeare* 131–33; Braunmuller 82). While the visions were drug-induced (Mullin, "Stage" 358), their conjuration was ritualistic—rather than trippy, as in Polanski—and this gave them starkly 'evil' connotations. Yet whatever the real nature and force of the play's 'evil,' McKellen's Macbeth seemed quite unable to resist its appeal. In this way the production made its own dualistic conventions feel problematically at odds with human capacities. (On Nunn, see further Fedderson and Richardson, chapter 16 in this volume.)

Since the success of Nunn's version, the English stage has seen a number of weak Macbeths who—like Irving in the previous century—evinced neither a conscience nor a heroic spirit. Examples include Jonathan Pryce, co-starring with Sinead Cusack in a 1986 RSC production (see Wilders 71; cf. Rutter), and Derek Jacobi at London's Barbican in 1994 (see esp. Jacobi 342; cf. Wilders 71; Prescott 81; Holland, *English Shakespeares* 213). These productions—both directed by Adrian Noble—illustrate the pitfalls of the modern "tendency . . . to mitigate Macbeth's tragic stature" (Bevington et al. 809). The consequences of this approach for *Macbeth* as a whole are, perhaps, *too* problematic to be managed easily—Polanski's and Nunn's versions being the exceptions to prove the rule. Perhaps a diminished Macbeth is most readily accepted in contemporary adaptations, where action and context are familiarized (e.g. *Men of Respect*; cf. Greenhalgh; see Fedderson and Richardson, chapter 16, for other instances).

*Macbeth*s around the world

Outside England, Europe, and the United States, versions of *Macbeth* have multiplied over the past century or so; they continue to do so at an ever-accelerating pace. The present survey can only hope to touch on a few of the play's intercultural transformations.

British colonialism was the earliest engine of *Macbeth*'s global expansion. An 1835 law mandated the teaching of *Macbeth* in India (Viswanathan 54). Between the 1890s and the 1950s, at least nine translations or adaptations into Marathi, Hindi, and Bengali appeared (Loomba 119f., figs. 4–5; Das 66–68; cf. Sengupta 252; Trivedi, " 'Folk' " 174, 178–80). In 1979, B.V. Karanth's Hindi play *Barnam Vana* successfully adapted *Macbeth* into a "folk" mode informed by Vedantic philosophy, rather than Western dualistic categories (Trivedi, " 'Folk' " 184–85; cf. Hapgood, "*Macbeth*;" Gillies et al. 276–78, with images; Trivedi, "Interculturalism"). In 1988, Ekbal Ahmed directed a *Gombe* ("toy," or puppet) *Macbeth* written in Kannada by children's author Vaidehi, in which "only the witches" are "human beings," while "the rest of the characters [are] puppets" (Chandrashekar 196; cf. 196–200; on other recent Indian *Macbeth*s, cf. Lanier, "Hours" 31).

In Japan, during the early years of the twentieth century, *Macbeth* was adapted into the localized Shimpa ("new school") style (Brandon 39). However, it was Akira Kurosawa's 1957 film *Throne of Blood*—more literally translated *The Castle of the Spider's Web*—that would become the signal Japanese *Macbeth*. The film's feudal Japanese setting is also the domain of spiritual powers—though these may exist objectively, or may be understood as cinematic equivalents to the characters' subjective perceptions. Violence is endemic to the film-world; yet there are limits to the harm one can do to one's friends before one begins to *see* one's deeds as 'evil,' and to suffer accordingly (Kliman, *Shakespeare* 187–88; cf. Braunmuller 85–86; Holland, " 'Stands' " 367–71). Thus, *Throne of Blood* envisions a dualistic universe, but its vantage-point is problematized in that the forces of 'good' may emanate from a collective imaginary.

In the 1980s, director Yukio Ninagawa again set *Macbeth* in early modern

Japan (Nouryeh 261). The production toured abroad, beguiling Western audiences with its sensual beauty (see esp. Harvey and Kliman 159–82; cf. Kishi 115–16). Yet its initial inspiration had come from an incident of self-consuming political violence that derailed the Japanese radical left in 1972 (162–63; cf. Senda 24–25; on a later Ninagawa *Macbeth*, cf. Kliman, "Another"). In the early 1990s Tadashi Suzuki directed two "distantly related" theatrical works (Mulryne 87) that incorporated material from *Macbeth: Greetings from the Edge of the Earth, Part One* and *The Chronicle of Macbeth*. Suzuki's work is described as deconstructively "postmodern," mixing Shakespearean and non-Shakespearean "texts and allusions," yet sustained by a rigorous "discipline of physical stage-movement" (Mulryne 90, 88; cf. Carruthers).

Recent scholarship tantalizes with its hints of the complex elaborations that directors and adapters of *Macbeth* have created around the world. For instance, in León Felipe's adaptation or *paráfrasis* ("paraphrase") of *Macbeth*—performed in Mexico City in 1955—the loss of "peace, a remembrance of a better, but lost world," is imagined in terms of an *asesino del sueño* or "murderer of sleep" (cf. *Macbeth* 2.2.39; Zaro 95, 102, 104). Echoes of *Macbeth* are also apparent to casual readers of colonial and postcolonial anglophone works. In 1968, for example, Ghanaian dramatist Kwesi Kay echoed aspects of *Macbeth* in his play *Maama*, about witchcraft, barrenness, birth, and nature. (On other *Macbeth*s since 1968 in Ghana, Nigeria, and Mauritius, see Banham et al. 289–97.)

Eastern Europeans have interpreted *Macbeth* as a political play, adding to its already substantial legacy of anti-tyrannical readings. A Russian *Macbeth* produced in 1955—shortly after Stalin's death—"dealt with the responsibility of a leader to his people and . . . the role of a people when the leader has been compromised" (Carmeli). Two later stagings in Bulgaria (1977) and Prague (1981) made Malcolm a villain, implicitly critiquing official histories (Shurbanov and Sokolova 110; Stříbrný, "Shakespeare" 276, 277). In 1978, another Czech *Macbeth* was recorded on audiotape "by three dissident artists who were forbidden to perform publicly" (called the "Living-Room Theatre"). In the words of adapter Pavel Kohout, their goal was to achieve "a catharsis uplifting their downcast souls" (quoted in Stříbrný, "Shakespeare" 277; the performance inspired part of Tom Stoppard's work *Dogg's Hamlet, Cahoot's Macbeth*, published 1979).

In 1971, East German playwright Heiner Müller rewrote *Macbeth* in a ruthlessly pessimistic mode, with "corpses stacked to serve as Duncan's throne." Some asked whether a work this "negative" had anything to offer politically (Hortmann, *Shakespeare* 238, 240). But, since the production was set in "the courtyard of a run-down East German tenement" (Guntner, "Brecht" 130), others interpreted Müller's Macbeth as a Stalin figure and his Banquo as a version of Trotsky. Müller denies that this was his intention, yet affirms the pertinence of such readings in context (Müller 184; cf. 185, 188).

The effect of political circumstances on theatrical interpretation was also seen in post-Communist Ukraine, where two *Macbeths* were staged in 1991. One dualistically opposed tyranny to justice; the other, by contrast, reduced "high tragedy" to "quotidian violence" (Makaryk 203). In Bulgaria in 1995, a *Macbeth* appeared, full of historical allusions, which did not merely acknowledge the triumph of capitalism but participated in it materially. It was dominated by a "red label of Johnnie Walker, looming large over the entire production and reminding everybody of its sponsors" (Shurbanov and Sokolova 110).

Macbeth has often been made to speak for politically oppressed and dissatisfied communities around the world. In 1992, Michael Bogdanov's staging for the English Shakespeare Company registered global concerns with U.S. imperialism and militarism, particularly in its dystopian set design (Hodgdon; cf. Parsons and Mason 125–29; the production should not be confused with the same director's video adaptation). Québec's independence movement inspired Michel Garneau's 1978 "tradaptation" of *Macbeth* into Québécois (see Lieblein), which in 1993 became part of director Robert Lepage's celebrated *Shakespeare Cycle* (Salter; Hodgdon). A Nigerian pro-democracy adaptation, *Makbutu*, was staged in 2000 (Banham et al. 297).

Such examples show how dualistic *Macbeths* remain relevant today. In other contexts dualism can signify compliance, complacency, or an uncritical celebration of 'Shakespeare' as a non-controversial source of cultural affirmation. Welcome Msomi's South African adaptation *uMabatha*, written in the early 1970s under apartheid, was revived in the 1990s and toured for appreciative international audiences. Yet it has been argued that despite the play's Zulu language and setting, its positive reception—at home and abroad—has always been contingent on the adapter's "uncontentious and antiquarian way" with the classic text (Orkin 274; cf. McLuskie, "*Macbeth/ Umabatha;*" cf. Braunmuller 54 n. 1).

Several English-language studies have been published on *Macbeth* in China. A new one, included in this book, discusses the variety seen in Chinese adaptations from 1986 to 1999, revealing their common tendency to problematize the play's values in response to social disruptions and cultural change (see Lei's essay, chapter 15; cf. Li and Gillies; Huang). A much larger study, however, would be needed to offer anything like an adequate survey of the diverse *Macbeths* that have flourished around the world. (For notes on Swedish and Hungarian productions, see Leiter; on more recent *Macbeths* worldwide, cf. Lanier, "Hours;" online, see "Shakespeare Around the Globe").

Two recent English *Macbeths*: problematizing the mainstage

In England, two notable *Macbeths* have recently presented distinctly problematic visions. One was directed by Gregory Doran at Stratford in 1999, starring Antony Sher and Harriet Walter (later remade for DVD). Doran's Scottish warriors were a gang of testosterone-soaked partisans, echoing "images . . . familiar on the television screen" during the Balkan conflict and other 1990s wars (Sher 108; cf. Brown, *Macbeth* 131). The contemporaneity of this setting was underscored by the Porter, "an impersonation of Tony Blair" (Doran 17.) By bringing the action closer to his audiences, Doran implicitly challenged them to account for their own relationship to a world in which warrior values were horribly realized.

In the DVD version of Doran's production, Sher's Macbeth begins as a proverbial 'good soldier.' His reluctance to kill Duncan proceeds not from humane principles, or a sense of the victim's transcendent goodness, but from his loyalty to his male cadre. In light of this homosocial setting, it seems appropriate that Macbeth's manhood is again at issue during a heavily eroticized persuasion scene. When he tells his wife—played with consummate intensity by Walter[8]—to "[b]ring forth men-children only" (1.7.72), his arousal underscores his already implicit need to feel secure in his masculinity. Sher's Macbeth is choosing not so much between ideals of 'good' and 'evil,' as between two divergent avenues toward male self-assurance.

In the event, the course chosen by Sher's Macbeth leads him only to dread his tainted self. He adopts a nervously ironic mask, as if to avoid recognizing himself. His "Tomorrow" soliloquy (5.5.18–27) becomes a "sardonic" dismissal of the part he is now playing; in the stage production Sher actually walked away from the set, breaking the 'fourth wall' (Wilders 73; cf. Shuttleworth; S. Williams, "The tragic actor" 134). This gesture enacted Macbeth's wishful fantasy of escape from a version of manhood that has betrayed him.

Doran's *Macbeth* is basically psychologistic; it presents Macbeth's inner struggle not in terms of 'good' and 'evil,' but rather as his quest for a self that he can admire. Even more problematically, the courses of action that seem to promise Macbeth the security he seeks are all more or less equally violent. Doran's allusions to modern war remind us that this warring reality is part of our own world, however distant it may seem to the more fortunate among us. (On the DVD version, see further Greenhalgh.)

Another *Macbeth* was staged at London's Almeida Theatre in 2005, directed by John Caird, with Simon Russell Beale and Emma Fielding (see Figure 1.2). Russell Beale writes that he was concerned with "Macbeth as a poet, as the creator of a new vision, rather than a soldier or a king" (108). Caird's direction supported this view of the play-world as an internal one, informed not by sociopolitical realities—as in Doran's and Sher's version—but rather by Macbeth's closed-off consciousness and his progressive alienation from the world around him (107, 114; cf. Wolf; Billington; Swanston). Russell Beale understood Macbeth's violent motives in relation to his childless marriage (114); Caird developed this theme by adding children to several scenes (Billington).

At the end, Russell Beale's Macbeth opened himself to Macduff's knife-thrust in "a sort of assisted suicide" (Russell Beale 118). This final gesture bleakly epitomized the centrality of Macbeth's despairing mind to the performance, which is said to have evoked a kind of "void," drawing compar-

Figure 1.2 Almeida Theatre production of *Macbeth* (2005). Photograph by permission
of Hugo Glendinning.

isons to the drama of Samuel Beckett (Billington; cf. Wolf). Unlike Sher's
futile self-evasions, Russell Beale's embrace of annihilation seems most problematic in its projection of a world where personal suffering can make
notions of objective 'good' and 'evil' fade into meaninglessness. Nevertheless,
dualistic values survived in at least one aspect of the Caird production,
which—according to Russell Beale—represented Macbeth's "murder of
children" as finally "unforgivable" (117).[9]

Drawing the line in *Scotland, PA*: the limits of the problematic

The question of what is 'forgivable' and what is not—of where we must,
finally, recognize 'evil' in human conduct—is one that *Macbeth* still poses. To
recognize life's problematic complexities is intellectually responsible, but it
makes our every decision difficult to defend. Even if we approve no choice
as 'good,' we make choices. In practice, most of us constantly reassert our
position in an unjust, often violent world. We embrace our comforts and
pleasures while knowing the toll that many of them exact on others. Do we
excuse such complicity as inevitable? Are we deferring judgment indefinitely?
How many of our moments are spent in the cynical expectation that, unlike
Macbeth, *we* will never be compelled by dualistic judges (or avengers) to "try
the last" (5.8.32)?

   Near the end of the 2001 film *Scotland, PA*—a comic travesty of *Macbeth*,
set in the 1970s United States—the cornered protagonist "Mac" says of
Duncan's murder: "That's kinda hard to explain, you sorta had to be there."

This movie parodies the dualistic conventions of crime thrillers, and it employs other problematizing strategies (e.g., Duncan is a jerk). Yet at times it transmutes the deadpan indifference of irony into a more acutely affecting ambivalence. For instance, the film makes Macduff a vegetarian, establishing a sustained parallel between meat-eating and murder (cf. Shohet 188–89). This is ostensibly funny, but, in fact, many would now find this equation far from absurd. Do our disparate views mean that the morality of meat is insolubly problematic today? Or do those who ridicule such parallels thereby disclose themselves—to 'good' vegetarians—as 'evil'?

The difficulty of justifying human actions increases with the scope of ethical debate, and with the variety of subjective viewpoints from which we make—or avoid making—dualistic judgments. Reflecting this diversity, contemporary critical accounts of how Shakespeare's contemporaries might have understood *Macbeth* are rich in both dualistic and problematizing perspectives. It is to these studies that I now turn.

PART II: RECENT CRITICISM

Since the 1980s, much of the most influential scholarly work on *Macbeth* has involved historicist inquiry into the play's 'original' meanings. These 'new' historicist readings are often far more problematic than those of the earlier twentieth century—a change reflecting cultural developments since the 1960s. Still, the dualistic *Macbeth* continues to claim many adherents. I will address dualistic and problematic currents separately in the first and second sections below. Of course they are not really isolated from each other; exponents of each sometimes try to account for the meanings revealed by the other, and to reconcile those impressions to their own vision. For example, many critics would now argue that even as *Macbeth* seems to endorse binary moral distinctions, it simultaneously deconstructs those antinomies by exposing the rhetorical and ideological artifice behind them (Kastan, *Shakespeare* 166; cf. Kastan, " 'A rarity' " 16–19). Conversely, a recent scholar has ably argued that in *Macbeth* "one can forego moral absolutes and still differentiate between good and bad characters." He thus reasserts the case for a *Macbeth* that is *relatively* dualistic, but leaves some room for ethical and ideological "ambiguity" (McCoy 28, 27).

There are also exceptions to the hegemony of historicism in recent criticism. Not all critics took part in the 'new historicist' turn of the 1980s and 1990s to the same extent, or with similar aims; some have actively dissented. I try to acknowledge these outliers in a third section below. Finally, the study of Shakespeare in performance—a large field in itself—has been dealt with sufficiently in Part I. Nevertheless, a fourth section here will reflect briefly on distinctions between textual *Macbeth*s and those in other media.

The 'original' *Macbeth*: dualistic versions

Many critics still endorse a dualistic understanding of the 1606 *Macbeth*. Dualistic readings draw substantial support from the way *Macbeth*'s characters make strong moral judgments. Shakespeare's dialogue is frequently informed by the language of a cosmic struggle between heaven and hell. God's confessed enemy, Macbeth, pits himself against the proclaimed defenders of virtue and the common good. Dualists take this moral language seriously—some would say uncritically.

Numerous scholars have linked the play's dualistic language to religious beliefs. Some see *Macbeth* as an exploration of Christian teachings on damnation (see e.g. Nosworthy; Wilks 125–43; for a thoughtful dualistic account, see R. Hunter 159–82; cf. Braunmuller 42–43; see also Lake 387–88). Dualists also point to a more specifically apocalyptic tendency in the play's language. Macbeth envisions Duncan's "virtues" preserving the king from hell at the Last Judgment (1.7.18); Lady Macbeth calls the alarm sounded after the murder's discovery a "trumpet," using eschatological imagery despite herself (2.3.75; cf. 5.6.9; see also Kinney, *Lies* 200–205, for a discussion not committed to dualism). Such allusions conjure up a traditional, Christian cosmic vision often compared with that of medieval mystery plays (Wickham; Creeth 4–7, 40–72; Jones 80–83; Lancashire; Hassel; Miola, *Shakespeare* 109–10).

Whole shelves of studies have explicated *Macbeth*'s dualistic symbols, many of them Christian. Some are scriptural, such as Lady Macbeth's advice to Macbeth to be a "serpent" (1.5.64). If the word alludes to the Bible (Genesis 3: 1ff.), then by implication, Macbeth recapitulates the Christian "myth of the fall from a state of grace" (Coursen, "In Deepest" 377; cf. Kolin, "Macbeth" 159–60). A high density of scriptural echoes is found in Macbeth's "Tomorrow" soliloquy (5.5.18–27; see Shaheen 640–41). More Christian emblems include Macbeth's image of "Vaulting ambition," recalling "medieval and later depictions of Pride" (Braunmuller 1.7.27 n., citing Belsey, "Shakespeare's"); Duncan's gift to Lady Macbeth of a diamond (2.1.15–17), signifying "purity and constancy;" and the apparitional dagger (2.1.33–47), symbolizing "the Deadly Sins of Wrath and Envy" (Doebler 115, 128). Lady Macbeth's habit of writing and reading in her sleep (5.1.3–7) has been related to the "writing that occurs within the conscience," a trope of Christian psychology (Kiefer, *Writing* 125).

Some images, though confusingly hard to picture, still seem Christian: for example "pity, like a naked newborn babe/ Striding the blast," or "heaven's cherubin horsed/ Upon the sightless couriers of the air" (1.7.21–23; see Braunmuller's notes on these lines; on cherubs, cf. Gardner). Two scholars suggest the indebtedness of Macbeth's "newborn babe" to Catholic meditations on the infant Jesus (Edgecombe; Baynham; cf. Milward 57–58). Finally, a rich vein of symbolism is found in the "castle that both symbolizes the law and also shelters foul customs," though such settings can of course be interpreted ambivalently and problematically as well as dualistically (Ross 127; cf. 1.6.1; 5.7.25, 30).

Devout Christians studied human history, and temporal events generally, for signs of God's will. Ross reports convulsions in the natural order after the regicide: Duncan's horses have "Turned wild" and eaten each other (2.4.16; cf. 18–20). Dualists interpret such passages as portents of God's displeasure, and see the play's resolution as a return to the divine—or, at least, the natural—order. Thus Macbeth's reign is ended by a "green wood of . . . liberating armies," evoking springtime seasonal rituals of rebirth and renewal (Laroque, "Magic" 77; cf. Brooks 199; Holloway 57–74; Long 117–20; such restorative readings are usefully reexamined in Woodbridge, *Scythe* 132–35).

Dualist critics see the Macbeths as overreachers, would-be exceptions from God's temporal dispensation (see esp. Kermode 83–89). When Lady Macbeth feels "the future in the instant" (1.5.56), she illicitly aspires to transcend the 'natural' order of time (see e.g. Mahood, *Shakespeare's* 131–36; Snyder 64–66; Honigmann, *Myriad-Minded* 93–102). Christians expect such rebels to suffer at the end of time and in the afterlife, but also from "judgement here" (1.7.8)—i.e., in their temporal lives. Thus in most early modern accounts of murder, the murderers are providentially exposed and punished (Jorgensen 14–40).

Dualists cite Renaissance texts that linked Christian morality to conservative ideology, sanctifying the monarch and anathematizing resistance. One widely quoted source is the *Homily against disobedience and willful rebellion* (1570), a sermon which was officially disseminated during the sixteenth and earlier seventeenth centuries. The *Homily* warned against the spiritual as well as temporal repercussions of insubordination (for documents see e.g. Carroll 231–32, 238–41). It related all disobedience to the first sin of rebellion against God, much as murders were then said to recapitulate Cain's crime (cf. Jorgensen 79–80).

Many dualists argue or assume that *Macbeth* in its time was a 'royal play.' Soon after his accession in 1603, King James I (earlier King James VI of Scotland) had granted his patronage to Shakespeare's theatrical company (see e.g. Kernan 75–88).[10] *Macbeth*'s subject was singularly pertinent to the new regime because the chronicles identified Banquo as an ancestor of the Stuart dynasty, to which the king belonged (see e.g. Paul 212; Braunmuller 2–3; Carroll 189–90). Accordingly, the "two-fold balls and treble sceptres" in the apparition scene (4.1.120) allude to James's possession of multiple kingdoms (Braunmuller 243–44). The play's alliance between a Scottish royal claimant, Malcolm, and the English Edward I may seem to celebrate the realms' unification under King James—an early promoter of the notion of an "Empire of Great Britain."

When James became England's king, some writers had recounted flattering predictions of the glorious role that history had supposedly reserved for the Stuarts. In 1605, James was welcomed on a visit to Oxford with a Latin performance by three boys dressed as "nymphs" or "sibyls," who related the old prophecy of the "fatal sisters" concerning Banquo's line—the tale that Holinshed had retold in his *Chronicles* and that Shakespeare adapted for *Macbeth* (Gwinne, sigs. H3r-v; cf. Braunmuller 5–6; Carroll 333–34; and see now I. Wright, "Perspectives"). *Macbeth* recalls such panegyrics, most obviously in its "show of . . . kings" descending from Banquo (4.1.110 SD). At the same time, the prophecies that falsely encourage Macbeth (4.1.78–80, 91–93) can be related to official denunciations of popular political prophecies, a genre often seen as subversive (Jaech; Carroll 330–43, with documents).

Macbeth is often thought to fit with a general outpouring of praise for James, and righteous indictments of his enemies, following the abortive 'Powder Plot' (Gunpowder Plot) of late 1605. This was a failed plan to kill many of England's leading men and spark a revolt by its Roman Catholic minority. Allusions to Catholics connected with the plot are found in the Porter's speech (2.3.1–17; for background, see Braunmuller 5–6; Carroll 249–63, with documents; Kinney, *Lies* 116ff.). These allusions have prompted dualistic readings of *Macbeth* as a tribute to James, the plot's most prominent intended victim (see esp. Paul 237–47; Wills; for a problematizing view see Lemon's essay, chapter 2 in this volume).[11]

Accounts of *Macbeth* as a dualistic "Gunpowder play" (Wills 9) often note that the Porter's allusions to the would-be regicides are associated with images of the Last Judgment and hell; some critics infer that *Macbeth* exploited, or stoked, anti-Catholic feelings. (King James presented himself as a devout Protestant.) Also cited is the early modern controversy over "equivocation," a practice to which *Macbeth* alludes (5.5.42; cf. 2.3.7–9). This was, in effect, a verbal stratagem enabling subjects to mislead Church and state authorities—even when placed under oath—without feeling dishonest about the deception. The aim was to avoid religious persecution without seeing oneself as perjured. In Protestant England, Catholics were at risk of finding themselves in situations where they might be compelled to choose or reject such casuistic methods. Following the exposure of the Powder Plot, an English Catholic priest who was tried and executed for treason was especially vilified as an exponent of equivocation theory (Braunmuller 5 and n. 2; Carroll 263–70, with documents). Allusions to equivocators would have called forth images of Catholics deluding Protestants, much as Macbeth is deceived by—or deceives himself with respect to—the prophetic words of the weïrd sisters and the apparitions. (For the point that Shakespeare may have wished to dissociate himself from equivocation even if he himself were Catholic, see Milward 64–65; cf. Wilson 186–205.)

Macbeth's depiction of witchcraft can seem to add to its pro-monarchical tenor. The figure of the witch was a paradigmatic construct of early modern dualistic thinking. On one influential reading, Shakespeare used witchcraft precisely to create "ideological closure" (Stallybrass 205). While the weïrd sisters also recall such figures as the classical Fates or Furies, dualists argue that Christians considered these figures devilish (McGee). Lady Macbeth, by invoking "spirits" (1.5.38), may seem to practice "black" magic or "necromancy" (Laroque, "Magic" 67; this impression is enhanced if one imagines the speech as a ritual conjuration, as in many modern productions).

Some historians suggest that the actual witch-hunting craze in early modern England expressed fears of "a suddenly and drastically disrupted moral realm," due to socioeconomic change and upheaval, and we may see the same fears reflected in Scotland under Macbeth's tyrannical rule (Sokol 265). If persecutions of witches resolved social tensions symbolically, then *Macbeth* itself may exhibit an identical pattern: its curse on Scotland is traceable to malefic individuals, who must therefore be hunted down and slain. One historicist even thinks that *Macbeth* "may have influenced the contemporary criminalisation of witchcraft as . . . conspiracy;" for, if there was a 'royal' performance in 1606, "the courtiers and lawyer" present would have been the first English playgoers ever to behold "the full repertoire of the black mass . . . complete with the pact, infanticide, cannibalism and necromancy" that would later be alleged against the infamous 'witches of Lancashire' (Wilson 187–88).

Whatever the play's possible impact on audiences' attitudes toward witchcraft, dualists agree that *Macbeth* appealed to their existing notions about the causes of social evil. Besides witchcraft and murder, these included less lurid factors. One scholar sees Macbeth's reign as a vision of social breakdown; the "dependent relations" which, in early modern belief, ought to underpin public order—and even "political freedom"—are corrupted into relations dominated by force and terror (Weil 107; on the social fabric, see further the essays in this volume by Bach [chapter 4] and by Feuer [chapter 7]).

Macbeth draws on a whole complex of early modern social attitudes and beliefs linking "sexuality, witchcraft, and violence," as areas where human sin was seen at its most shameless (Biggins 268). Gendered codes of behavior are especially regarded as fundamental; of all the dualistic claims typically advanced about *Macbeth*, probably the most widely accepted is that it portrays the Macbeths as deviants from 'good' male and female ideals. (In this area, the 'new' historicism often benefits from—and reciprocally informs—feminist and psychoanalytic criticism. Many of the studies cited below have integrated one or both of these approaches with historicist arguments.)

In one well-established dualistic view, *Macbeth* warns against the cultural and rhetorical conflation of masculinity with aggression—a conflation Lady Macbeth relies on when persuading Macbeth to kill Duncan (1.7.45–51; cf. e.g. Montagu 214; Waith; Asp).[12] Similarly, most historicists share a generally dualistic view of the play's attitude toward female roles. Some see *Macbeth* as a radically misogynistic text, even by early modern standards. It demonizes non-male 'others,' the witches and Lady Macbeth, and erects against them a fantasy of exclusively masculine authority (see esp. Adelman 130–47). The Lady, called "fiend-like" (5.9.36; see e.g. Merchant; Ewbank), embodies the male assumption that "the kingdom of darkness is unequivocally female" (Callaghan, "Wicked" 358–59; cf. Belsey, *Subject* 184ff.). Her manipulation of Macbeth reflects legal constructions of female recalcitrance in the patriarchal household as "petty treason" (Dolan 227; cf. 225–30).

Shakespeare thus displaces the onus of Macbeth's sin onto his 'evil' wife (cf. Braunmuller 33–38). Furthermore, by enlisting the Lady along with the three "sisters" as *agents provocateurs* in the regicide, Shakespeare protected patriarchal institutions from any suspicion that *they* might be at fault. *Macbeth* implied that it was women, not men, who were to blame for nurturing men's transgressive ambitions. Historicists thus relate Lady Macbeth's conduct to early modern writings on women's biological nature (Klein; La Belle) and/or 'female' medical disorders (Levin), as well as to the maternal functions prescribed for early modern women (Chamberlain; on all these topics cf. Carroll 344–68). It is also suggested that *Macbeth*'s depiction of witchcraft is complicit in a larger early modern (male) project to demystify witch-lore, thus eroding belief in a hitherto credible form of female agency (Purkiss 207; for a response cf. McLuskie, "Humane" 1–3).

Some dualists prefer the related but different view that Shakespeare located evil and disorder in a zone of sexual *ambiguity*, represented by the witches (see esp. 1.3.43–45), against which a definitively and exclusively male order ultimately establishes itself (Garber; cf. Purkiss 213). Still others claim that *Macbeth*'s representation of gender does the opposite, constructing androgyny as a 'good' synthesis of 'feminine' and 'masculine' elements superior to either sex. Perhaps *Macbeth* envisions this ideal negatively, through the contrast between Macbeth and a better ruler who "integrates his conscience and his feelings with his valor" (Kahn 179; cf. Freud 137; for a reading that combines Freudian with early modern psychology, cf. Kirsch, esp. 273, 290ff.). Alternatively, early modern audiences may have sensed their need for more 'feminine' kings through their revulsion from Macbeth's "terrifying 'masculinity' " after his accession, when his dissociation from Lady Macbeth is accompanied by an escalation of his tyrannical crimes (Bushnell 131). Of course, if *Macbeth*'s warning against excessive or misconstrued 'manliness' ends by suggesting that *men* should combine 'male' and 'female' good qualities to rule more virtuously, then it may finally seem to recuperate patriarchy by making its failings seem contingent and remediable through a reclamation of women's powers on its own behalf. Thus, one historicist reads *Macbeth*'s series of 'good' father-figures as an appropriation of the force of fertility for the male; the play's endowment of "fathers with life-bestowing power" was related in 1606 to an "emerging Jamesian model" of benign patriarchy, a model "stressing love, peace, and nurturance" (Tiffany 154–55; cf. Trubowitz 311–12).

Possibly *Macbeth* suggested in 1606 that male rulers could, and should, absorb the virtues of the 'feminine.' On the other hand, perhaps it advocated a total purgation of the female from the political domain (see e.g. Tennenhouse 128–32; cf. esp. Trubowitz 314–19). Either way, it may have pleased those English subjects who had looked askance at several decades of 'womanly' rule under Queen Elizabeth I, and who, after 1603, could feel relieved to see

England again governed by a man. Like the Scots at *Macbeth*'s finale, they might now hope for an "emergent establishment of patrilineal inheritance as the most legitimate source of royal authority" (McLuskie, "Humane" 9; see further Smuts).

The 'original' *Macbeth*: problematic versions

Many critics have argued, especially in recent decades, that the 1606 *Macbeth* was a morally and/or ideologically problematic play. While recognizing how its characters appeal to concepts of 'good' and 'bad,' problematizing critics suggest that *Macbeth* ironizes these appeals. It makes them seem confused, contingent, mutually contradictory, disingenuously partial and self-serving, or simply in conflict with other values and intuitions available to an early modern audience.

A first line often taken against dualistic readings is based on the perception that *Macbeth*'s putatively 'good' characters are not necessarily so. No matter how much the characters seem to insist on the viciousness of Duncan's murder (for instance), one need not believe everything that a given individual says—even one whom others valorize, or who attains power at the play's conclusion. This point was made by William Empson, a New Critic who resisted his generation's prevalent moral and political dualisms. Empson eloquently stresses *Macbeth*'s ambiguity, noting its evocation of "immense confusion" in a society in the throes of civil unrest, and its "general atmosphere of fog and suspicion" (146). It is worth quoting his brisk, skeptical retort to dualistic arguments about equine cannibalism (2.4.18–20): "Ross is telling lies" (144).[13]

The characters whom dualists have labeled 'good' are now frequently criticized. Disquietingly, the play's most fulsome flattery of Malcolm is uttered by Malcolm himself (4.3.120–31). Such false modesty may sound like self-mystification. Also, Duncan can seem culpable so far as practical kingship is concerned. He appears to have a weak hold on his throne at the play's outset, since military action is required to keep him there. (Scholars have noted for centuries that if Shakespeare meant to make Duncan's rule look ineffective, he was merely following his source in Holinshed; see e.g. Furness 436, 441.) Finally, considering what Duncan now owes Macbeth, we may think that he shows less than due gratitude in nominating Malcolm—not Macbeth—as his successor (1.5.35–42; cf. Berger 70–97). Many new historicists note that to audience members in 1606 who knew something about medieval Scottish history, Malcolm's nomination could have appeared as a tendentious move to alter the customary principles of royal succession in his son's favor; Duncan thus could have seemed a self-serving, dynastically 'ambitious' overreacher, much like Macbeth (cf. Nielsen; Norbrook; Braunmuller 15–16; Valbuena 79–96; on Duncan and Macbeth, see the essays in this volume by Lemon [chapter 2] and by Deng [chapter 8]).

At times the absence of a presumably well-known historical detail from

Macbeth may suggest that Shakespeare was inviting his audience to see the play's view of events as a self-consciously distorted and partial one, casting an ironic light on its pro-Jamesian gestures. Thus the vision of Banquo's descendants, which traces the Stuart lineage up to (and beyond) King James, contains *"eight kings"* (4.1.110 SD) but no queens. Omitted is James's late mother, Mary Stuart—Scotland's most famous queen, and Queen Elizabeth I's most notorious enemy and victim. Audiences in 1606 would perceive Mary's fate as a deeply problematic chapter in recent English history, not least since she was a key link in the genealogy that had put James on England's throne (Goldberg 259; Coddon 497). Such suggestive absences might have made *Macbeth* a reminder of still reverberating conflicts, rather than a paean to the shared values now undergirding a triumphant Jacobean order.

Along similar lines, audience members who read Holinshed or other historical authorities could have been troublingly aware that in their narratives Macbeth's reign does not look so consistently 'evil' as it does in Shakespeare's tragedy (see e.g. Carroll 115–50, with documents). Conversely, Shakespeare's 'good' English king—Edward I—was not admired in all quarters as he is in *Macbeth* (Hadfield, *"Macbeth;"* cf. 3.6.24–29; 4.3.139–61). Certain audience members may have known, too, that the Stuarts' supposed derivation from Banquo did not survive unscathed by the critical turn in Renaissance historiography (see e.g. Carroll 121, 190). If *Macbeth* was performed—or read—at court, it would likely have found such a well-informed audience in King James himself, along with some of the other Scots who had come to join him in England (see Baldo's essay, chapter 3 in this volume; cf. Carroll 274–75).

Still, the historicist critique of dualism may run into an objection at this point: just how much can we legitimately assume about the knowledge available to *Macbeth*'s early audiences? Some problematizing readings ask us to believe that *Macbeth* was understood in 1606 as a sophisticated commentary on rather specialized legal and historical debates: for example those concerning the source of the monarch's authority, and whether it is a subject's duty to obey a tyrant (see Lemon, chapter 2 in this volume; cf. Carroll 185–299, with documents; Kinney, *Lies* 86–124). A comparable question was whether King James was justified in claiming to rule with "imperial" authority (cf. 1.3.128) because of his multiple royal titles (see Baldo, chapter 3; Kinney, *Lies* 88–93).[14] Perhaps some early audience members reflected expertly on such matters. Surely, though, many did not (Norbrook 96; cf. Hawkins 175). Both dualists and problematizers who adduce intertextual evidence must admit that the play does not *include* most of what is found in these intertexts. And it can seem perverse to find problematic resonances in the fact that *Macbeth*'s language is *more* dualistic than that of, for example, Holinshed (a point noted in Kastan, *Shakespeare* 173; cf. Stoll, "Source").

Such checks on historicists' contextualizing efforts should be taken seriously, yet they need not invalidate the insights of the problematizing critics. Even if some intertexts were not generally available in 1606, they may still have been important for a few, well-informed and possibly powerful individuals. And we must remember that every text (or performance) prompts individual, highly variable responses, emerging from contingent acts of reception and cognition, and potentially differing widely between people. A play is not a treatise with just one, authoritative sense for all who read it 'correctly' (see esp. Kinney, *Lies*, where the study of contexts is guided by this important principle). For this reason one may plausibly claim that a given early modern English context is "inscribed within [*Macbeth*] as a stubborn subtext," even if it is largely or wholly absent from the text itself (Norbrook 80; see also Sinfield 104). We need never exclude the possibility that *someone* in 1606 interpreted *Macbeth* in relation to a given piece of information, so long as it was available in some form at that time. Of course, there are ways of pressing this hermeneutic freedom to a point where some might consider it unhistorical license.

The new historicism has not just yielded problematic views of *Macbeth*'s attitude toward historiography and dynastic politics. Over the past two decades, problematizing critics have addressed many English events and circumstances in 1606. Some dispute dualistic readings of the Powder Plot and equivocation allusions; to them, the play's ostensible compliments to James seem no less equivocal than the prophecies that delude Macbeth (see esp. Mullaney; Coddon). Others argue that "the King's Men did not treat their royal patronage over-deferentially," pointing out that tragedies concerning regicidal plots were not always or necessarily flattering (Dutton 138; cf. Kinney, *Lies* 68ff.).[15]

Some recent historicists problematize *Macbeth*'s position on religious politics (see esp. Wilson 186–205; cf. Hunt). Others observe that the union of "Great Britain," though dear to King James, was not to be formalized until 1707, and in the early 1600s was highly contentious—not least because of intercultural tensions (see Baldo's essay, chapter 3; on union, cf. Marshall 35; Kinney, *Lies* 90; on images of Scotland in *Macbeth*, cf. Carroll 271–99, with documents; Riach 32–52). With respect to English hopes for dynastic stability, one historicist argues that *Macbeth* displaces the "lineal, sequential order" of succession with a "cyclical progress of speech, action, and, in [the show of kings], history itself;" the "Tomorrow" soliloquy suggests "that all forms of successive order are specious appearances" (Baldo, "Politics" 533, 556).

I have remarked that where sex, gender, and sexuality are concerned, *Macbeth* is usually read as a dualistic play—often extremely so. Not many critics would demur from the view that *Macbeth* overtly sanctions an androcentric social order. Yet some claim that the destruction wrought by male rivalries in *Macbeth* must be seen as a critique of male power, not just—as dualists assert—a warning against the misconstrual of 'manliness.' For one critic, *Macbeth* undercuts a key principle in male pretensions to natural social entitlement through its "erasure of the . . . distinction between positive and negative violence," which patriarchies claim to uphold (Cohen, *Shakespeare's* 128). Another critic draws fruitful intertextual links to Vergil's *Aeneid*, a poem tracing the problematic nexus between male violence and 'virtue' (Headlam-Wells 117–43).

Macbeth's views on heterosexual marriage and male sexuality have also been problematized, if not yet thoroughly. Dualistic interpreters have long worried over how Macduff—apparently a 'good' patriot—seemingly becomes a 'bad' husband by deserting his family (see e.g. Furness 269). The only obvious way to clear him from his wife's imprecations, and Malcolm's insinuations (4.2.1–14; 4.3.25–27), is to devalue marital and paternal obligations themselves by contrast with national service. But if we admit that the 'good' of the household must thus be sacrificed to Scotland's 'greater good,' we are faced with a problematic conflict of values.

A recent critic has suggested that *Macbeth* questions heterosexual norms. Noting incisively that "Macduff's desertion of his family is Shakespeare's addition to the story," resulting from a reordering of the events in Holinshed, he goes on to emphasize the play's strong homosocial subtext (its "astonishingly male-oriented and misogynistic" tone). In view of all this, is it possible that Shakespeare envisioned Macduff fleeing to Malcolm's side for personal reasons—not just public ones? The same critic sees the Macbeths' union as problematic for the heterosexual ideology of marriage, simply because they lack the sort of specifically marital conflict that shows up elsewhere in Shakespeare (Orgel 169). Of all the marriages Shakespeare depicted, why is it *this* one that he chose to imagine as relatively 'good?' (For Macbeth and Lady Macbeth's bond, see e.g. Braunmuller 243, 3.2.45 n.; *contra*, see Leinwand.)

Along different lines, a feminist critic sees *Macbeth*'s purgation of females from the commonwealth as disturbing to early modern audiences; in a society still attuned to agricultural cycles and fertility symbols, the triumph of an all-male cohort could only have foreboded "an illusory order emerging out of paradox and contradiction." Moreover, details such as Macduff's "unusual birth" and Malcolm's "virginity suggest no potential for procreative renewal" (Liebler 222; on impotence, see Barmazel's essay, chapter 5 in this volume). Another study claims that despite the play's attraction to bountiful, nurturing kings—an image James cultivated (Tiffany, as discussed previously)— *Macbeth* ultimately demystifies this ideal by deconstructing the gender codes that inform it (Perry 137–47).

The subject of bodies in *Macbeth* has also been problematized in ways not chiefly concerned with sex and gender. One critic relates the play to early modern funereal, anatomical, and religious practices and discourses (Zimmerman). Another discusses geohumoral contexts, citing English views of the Scots as a people susceptible to corrupting environmental influences. The witches are seen as figures for the power of the elements, which they manipulate, and Macbeth as their largely passive victim (Floyd-Wilson). Critics focusing on early modern medical and physiological discourses also suggest that Lady Macbeth's somnambulism is not just a dualistic sign of bad conscience, but a more problematic signifier, since the early modern boundaries between spiritual and physical illness were contested (Neely 57ff.;

cf. Floyd-Wilson 154–56; cf. the essays in this volume by Stoll [chapter 6] and by Tomaszewski [chapter 9], respectively offering more problematic and more dualistic views).

Recent studies find problematic implications in *Macbeth*'s handling of many other early modern issues and customs. Some address the unstable cultural dynamics of post-Reformation religious conversion (Cartwright), the shady world of state surveillance networks (Kinney, "Macbeth's"), England's wars in Ireland (Hadfield, " 'Hitherto' " 61–63), and the 'scaffold speeches' made by convicted traitors on the point of death (Coddon 494; Lemon, "Scaffolds;" cf. 1.4.1–14). A biographical study notes that the practice of grain-hoarding—with which editors gloss the suicide of the "farmer" in the Porter's speech (2.3.3–4; see e.g. Brooke 130, at 2.3.4–5 n.)—was one that Shakespeare, like other early modern businessmen, had engaged in (Duncan-Jones 121–22).

Problematizing insights are also sought in representations of the supernatural. On one account, Banquo's ghost exemplifies the play-world's uncertain location "on the border between fantasy and reality;" far from assuring us that murder will be revealed and punished providentially, *Macbeth* instead registers a crisis of belief, "a bleeding of the spectral into the secular" and vice versa (Greenblatt, *Hamlet* 192–94; cf. Calderwood 127–31). *Macbeth*'s witches may suggest similar doubts, especially in light of some post-Reformation writers' growing skepticism about the reality of witchcraft—a movement connected with the Protestant rejection of exorcism among other Catholic rites. James I himself may have leaned in this direction by 1606 (see Greenblatt, "Shakespeare;" cf. Carroll 302–12, with documents).

An insightful article has compared the function of prophecies in *Macbeth* to that of riddles in early modern popular culture, finding the play's riddling witches ultimately problematic (Gorfain). Literary intertexts have yielded some problematizing readings. An example is the corpus of Senecan tragedy, which *Macbeth* seems to echo frequently, recasting it into forms more ambivalent than the original (Miola, *Shakespeare* 92–121; Peyré; cf. Boyle 154–66, 173–75). *Macbeth* may also glance at ambivalence in biblical prophecy narratives (Snyder 175–79). Most studies of mythological symbolism take a dualistic approach; one rare exception addresses Renaissance lore concerning Hecate (DiMatteo).

Finally, many critics seek to problematize *Macbeth*'s larger conception of the universe and humanity's place in it. Whereas 'old' historicists saw Macbeth and Lady Macbeth as transgressors of God's temporal order (as already discussed), there may be other ways to understand the strangeness of their situation in time. Their "dislocation" from past experience is puzzling (Cohen, *Searching* 135; cf. 123–38). *Macbeth* may seem "a curious temporal palimpsest, in which a variety of different times coexist" (Berry 119). A materialist critic enlarges on this theme when examining the explosive effects that made "thunder, lightning" possible on the early modern stage (1.1.2); the ensuing smoke and stink may have conveyed a volatile mix of mnemonic and historical associations (Harris). *Macbeth*'s plot and form, on the other hand, seem to problematize linear temporality in so far as the action does not have "a beginning, a middle, and an end," but instead seems to be "all middle," the last battle being uncannily reminiscent of the first (Booth, *King Lear* 90–91). Whereas dualists often assert that such effects conduce to a sense of cyclicity and regeneration—like those nourished by myth and religion—it has been argued that even if *Macbeth*'s end does suggest rejuvenation, Shakespeare undercuts this suggestion with trenchantly historicist insights into the "processes of civilization-under-construction and the difficult and problematic birth of structure and hierarchy" (Liebler 223; on time and temporality, cf. Hapgood, *Shakespeare* 41–48; cf. Wells's essay, chapter 12 in this volume).

Several topics that many critics have dealt with dualistically—e.g. the discourses of conscience, the image of Duncan's "golden blood" (2.3.105), and the hired Murderers—are understood in somewhat more problematic terms by contributors to this volume (see respectively the essays by Stoll [chapter 6], Deng [8], and Feuer [7]).

Beyond the historical: problematics of representation

Apart from these historicist lines of interpretation, but often running in parallel with them, are studies of *Macbeth*'s verbal and dramaturgical art. The play can appear problematic simply in virtue of its metatheatrical concern with deception, delusion, and mystification. Its language and stagecraft are self-consciously artificial and manipulative. By employing such a style to represent ostensibly historical and political subject-matter, *Macbeth* can seem to make ideology and facticity interchangeable.

Various critics have noted how *Macbeth* foregrounds the poet's art through its prosody (G. Wright 66–67), its grammar (Poole; Woodbridge, "Shakespeare"), its prose style (Vickers, *Artistry* 386), and its prominent verbal repetitions (see e.g. Dean; Poole; Kranz; cf. Braunmuller 51–53; on all these and more, cf. McDonald, *Shakespeare's* 44–52). The same might be said about *Macbeth*'s intricately recurring poetic imagery, its puns (Willson)—some of them obscured by the 'standardized' orthography of modern editions, but evident in F (De Grazia and Stallybrass 263–66)—and its deployment of numerical patterns (see e.g. Kranz 369–79; cf. Baldo, "Politics" 548–57; Braunmuller 25–27).

Words and speech-patterns circulate among the voices of different characters in *Macbeth*, even those who have not conversed together. A.C. Bradley noted Macbeth's unwitting echo of the weïrd sisters, "So foul and fair a day I have not seen" (1.3.36; cf. 1.1.12), and made it an example of Shakespeare's ironic technique, whereby our "dread of the presence of evil" is "enhanced" throughout the play (Bradley 103). A recent critic extends this dualistic insight by following traces of witch-talk in Banquo's lines, arguing that these progressively chart a "deterioration" in his moral stance (G. Williams 246).

Such reverberations become most problematic when they cross the boundaries separating individual *human* consciousnesses. It is not only the witches whose words infiltrate the discourse of other characters. Macbeth's "language . . . recurs in other speakers, most conspicuously Lady Macbeth," while the form of Lady Macbeth's soliloquy (1.5.36–52) returns uncannily in Macbeth's "Come, seeling night" speech (3.2.46–53; Brooke 10, 16). Verbal slippages of this sort insinuate how the ordinary limits of human identity and agency may be suspended in the play-world. Linguistically, it seems, *Macbeth* might inhabit the company of Shakespeare's 'late plays,' with their "supra-characterological energy, located in the sleepless metaphorical patterns into which . . . characters dip and out of whose processes they emerge" (Palfrey 265; cf. Young 114ff.; on *Macbeth* and the romances, cf. Leggatt). Characters so constituted are quite unlike the bounded, autonomous ethical agents posited by traditional law and ethics; we may well suppose that dualistic concepts of personal, moral accountability would fail to apply to such fluid entities, or projections.

Macbeth also makes us aware of the dramatist's art, for example in its repetition of things seen (Brown, *Shakespeare*: The Tragedy 104). Visual "illusion" is "a central preoccupation" (Brooke 1; cf. 1–34). Among other things, *Macbeth* allows considerable room for "special optical effects" (Laroque, "*Macbeth*" 163). One scholar thinks the dagger might have been a stage trick in 1606, achieved—literally—with smoke and mirrors (I. Wright, "All Done" cf. 2.1.33ff.). The same writer speculates that the show of kings might have been projected by a machine like the later seventeenth-century 'magic lantern' (I. Wright, " 'Come' "); other suggestions include "a shadow show," emphasizing "unreality and . . . ambiguity" (Laroque, "*Macbeth*" 165). Perhaps these illusive aspects invited early audience members to doubt their own perceptions; certainly they may do so in our postmodern context. To insist that human minds are highly fallible is perforce to question our competence as interpreters and moral judges.

Deconstructively inclined critics—including historicists with a deconstructive bent[16]—have sometimes raised such points, making *Macbeth* an occasion for problematic reflections on the nature and functions of representation. One historicist finds *Macbeth* insinuating "how far superior the poet is to the king" (Foster 341). Another understands equivocation, not just as a topically charged theme in its time, but as one with pervasively unsettling epistemological implications (Scott). The ubiquity of death in the tragedy hints at a preoccupation with problems of mimesis, too, since death is "unrepresentable" on stage in ways that other human actions are not; in a deconstructive (and psychoanalytic) account, "Duncan's absent corpse signifies as the play's most powerful presence" (Zimmerman 334–35). Finally, one deconstructive historicist figures *Macbeth* itself as a site of endlessly ironic historicities, infinitely reflecting the "heterogeneous dispersal" of agency that haunts and bedevils inquiries into its production (Goldberg 242).

Such theoretical readings, even while departing from strictly historicist premises, may remind us of the limits of a prescriptive (or proscriptive) historicist criticism. The issue of how *we* ought to judge a given character, or action, cannot be settled by reducing a play's significance to the responses available to 'original' audiences. We are sure to respond in our own ways, for our own reasons (see e.g. Sprengnether). Nor is historical objectivity about *Macbeth* a possibility anyway, given our lack of a complete record of its textual history. Thus, the Folio text may seem to offer one reason for disputing a dualistic view of witchcraft in *Macbeth:* "At the end . . . the weïrd sisters are left unmentioned, their role unresolved" (Greenblatt, *Will* 354); but is this because the witches were meant to disappear from "the play," in accordance with an 'original' intention that hinged on their doing so? Or is it that the F *Macbeth* has been trimmed for performance—carelessly perhaps, or with regret for certain passages that were sacrificed to purely practical and theatrical (or political and prudential) needs? What is *Macbeth* after all? Is it simply *The Tragedie of Macbeth* as printed in F? Or is the 'original' *Macbeth* finally a false creation of the historicist brain?

Mediated *Macbeth*s: a plea for complexity

A final brief for subtle and variegated, rather than uncompromisingly dualistic or problematic, views of *Macbeth* might be made on the basis of differences between media. *Macbeth*'s meanings are found not only in the text, nor in its various stagings, nor in its reception and critical legacy, but in *all* these diffusely refracted phenomena. In each medium different considerations create various advantages—or disadvantages—for a given approach to a line or scene.

For instance, readers have long found implausibilities and inconsistencies in the plot, most notoriously in matters of character development.[17] A problematizing critic may infer from these "gaps" that *Macbeth*'s representations of character and motive are intentionally deficient or incoherent (Bell, *Shakespeare's* 238; cf. Empson; Bell, "*Macbeth*;" Rabkin 101–10). Yet much that a literary reader deems improbable will pass unnoticed on stage (cf. Braunmuller 262).

Again, critics may interpret a character partly through tracing connections with language used by other characters. Thus the Captain compares Macbeth and Banquo to "cannons over-charged with double cracks" that "doubly redoubled strokes upon the foe" (1.2.37–38), and—much later—the witches chant their refrain, "Double, double" (4.1.10, 20, 35). For a close reader, this links "Macbeth and the dark sisters" (Norbrook 100). But in the theater, who will notice such a belated echo? Such questions are only resolved in practice. Here, the putative 'link' may illuminate not only Macbeth's character, but also Banquo's, which F leaves ambiguous. Performers characterize Banquo diversely, often making him a 'good' victim in dualistic versions and an ambivalent figure in problematic ones (Kliman, *Shakespeare* 7–8; Rosenberg, *Masks* 108–10; cf. Muir, *Macbeth* lvi). If the lines adumbrate a larger pattern binding Macbeth *and* Banquo to the witches, this pattern may emerge in different ways and different degrees, subject to the medium's constraints. Many theatrical *Macbeth*s will *not* consistently support the perception of such patterns.

Countless interpretive perceptions thus presuppose *Macbeth*'s reception in a given medium. Another example bearing on Banquo's character is Duncan's wordplay on his name: "worthy *Banquo* . . . in his commendations I am fed;/ It is a *banquet* to me" (1.4.54–56). If we see—or hear—this as an echo, it may ironically foreshadow the banquet scene; on one dualistic view, the paronomasia is "psalmic" and "sacramental," pointing toward Banquo's future inclusion in the saints' "eternal banquet" with God (Fendt 205, 206). Such readings are only as far-fetched as we individually think them. Surely this echo is more easily *heard* in performance than that of "double," which stretches over three acts. Still, an actor may or may not emphasize the pun. Further, any attempt to relate it to the *upcoming* "banquet" must presume either that audiences are *re*reading the play and seeking such patterns, or that they already know *Macbeth* and have prior knowledge about Banquo's fate. Finally, the Christian reading presupposes a familiarity with scripture that not everyone could be presumed to have, even in 1606. (For other recent close readings that make much of verbal and syllabic echoes, see e.g. McDonald, *Shakespeare and the Arts* 158–60; G. Williams 244, 248–49 n. 21.)

Another instance of meaning's contingency on the medium appears in battles, which loom much larger on the stage than in the text. Reading inclines us to attend to utterances rather than actions; characters say less while they are fighting, and moreover, readers must construe such scenes for themselves without swashbuckling action to help them. To evaluate Macbeth's defeat, Macduff's revenge, and Malcolm's triumph—either dualistically or problematically—is a task inseparable from the medium of reception. (On the staging of the final battle, see Pamela Mason's discussion, chapter 18 in this volume.)

In short, reading and performance involve fundamentally different interpretive acts, each with its own contingent dynamics. While the Folio text of *Macbeth* is one of the shortest in the Shakespearean canon—and hence more feasibly performed in full than other 'major' tragedies, such as *Hamlet*—it arguably contains intellectual perplexities that exceed the scope of any staging, and that emerge only through reading and reflection (Berger 98–125). A close reader may thus approach Lady Macbeth's "Come, you spirits" soliloquy (1.5.36–52) as an "insistently discontinuous speech," dazzlingly affirming the importance of even "contextually impossible potential meanings" (Booth, "Close" 50, 51; cf. 50–55ff.). Could any actor communicate this?

Meanwhile, stage-centered criticism can reveal meanings that even the closest readers cannot appreciate without the benefit of its insights. In the sleepwalking scene, for example, it is helpful to realize that this "presentation of an isolated figure, in a way that . . . will puzzle an audience and is beyond the understanding of informed onlookers," is unique in Shakespeare (Brown,

Shakespeare Dancing 47). Again, historicist critics may find *Macbeth*'s use of the early modern theatrical space significant (Weimann).

Some theorists might argue that a play performed is more complex than a solitary reading, since embodied actions and interactions are richer in semantic density than any individual mind's response to a text. Still other critics might characterize reading, itself, as a sort of performance. The cinema and, more recently, interactive digital media (see Lessard's contribution to this volume [chapter 17]) have further augmented the mediated diversity of contemporary *Macbeth*s.

Conclusion: from *Macbeth* to *Macbeth*s

While the abundance of scholarly commentary on *Macbeth* can seem daunting, it is also the case that technology has made it easy for us to access a wide range of creative *Macbeth*s. The whole catalog of contemporary 'offshoots' and 'appropriations' is much too vast to document here. A web search may turn up anything from Kurosawa's *Throne of Blood*, to fringe-theater productions such as *Tiny Ninja Theater Presents Macbeth* (with its 'cast' of small cheap plastic toys). One of the most striking features of recent Shakespearean scholarship is the extent to which it brings such various phenomena into its purview.

Paradoxically, this quantitative increase also makes us less and less able to assign *Macbeth* the status of a cultural touchstone, resonating in a few predictable ways for the members of a given population. Instead, the text has become a site of fascination where countless, globally dispersed vectors of interest converge occasionally, incidentally, and in part accidentally. However we now interpret *Macbeth* individually—or as members of a particular subculture—the play itself continues to exist as an object of multiple forms of attention and varied, divergent concerns.

Dualistic *Macbeth*s and problematic *Macbeth*s will both continue to proliferate, of course. Yet the tug-of-war between them, being nearly half a century old, seems unlikely to hold the interest of Shakespeareans much longer. We can only trust that whatever their values, future *Macbeth*s will at least keep answering in some way to our understandings of choice and consequence, and to our sense of how it feels—and what it might mean—to desire, to wonder, to fear, to kill, to grieve, and to die.

Notes

1 Some areas that I have not been able to explore in Part I—or barely touched on— include silent films, *Macbeth*s made for television, and spin-offs. For references in these categories see Braunmuller (84–85 n. 2); Bulman and Coursen; Wheeler (e.g. 821–22); McKernan and Terris (90–101); Lanier, *Shakespeare*, Lehmann; Rothwell (346–48); Lanier, "Hours;" Tredell (167–70). Another subject I have avoided here, merely for lack of space, is that of allusions to *Macbeth* in post-Shakespearean literature and culture; for some significant discussions, see e.g. Bate (*Shakespeare,*

228ff.); Rowe ("Politics"); Novy; Finnerty; Harries (133–50); Kolin ("*All God's;*" "Shakespeare Knocks"); cf. O'Connor (177–86).

2 Throughout this chapter, citations and quotations of *Macbeth* are from Braunmuller.

3 For other comparisons and contrasts between Macbeth and Richard III, see Vickers (*Shakespeare* 6: 407–29, cited in Miola, *Macbeth* 226 n. 3); Braunmuller (71 and n. 3); Scragg (*Discovering* 185–93).

4 De Quincey added a dualistic caveat, distinguishing this "sympathy of comprehension" from "a sympathy of . . . approbation," which he did *not* wish to allow (91).

5 For a contrary view, arguing that abstract modernist sets reified moral binaries, cf. McLuskie (*Macbeth/Umabatha* 162).

6 Of course, twentieth-century historicist readings had a long prehistory (dating back to Johnson, if not earlier). For some nineteenth-century examples, see Furness.

7 In 1946, a Soviet critic would produce a historicist analysis of *Macbeth* (Smirnov). While interesting—and notably problematic, by contrast with 'old historicism' in the West at this time—its tortuous and ultimately self-contradictory rhetoric does nothing so much as remind us of the author's Orwellian predicament while writing under Stalin. Outside Communist countries, there would seem to have been few socialist *Macbeth*s. Joan Littlewood directed one in London in 1957 (Callaghan, "Shakespeare" 119); a later version was Howard Brenton's spin-off, *Thirteenth Night* (Cohn, "Shakespeare" 53–54).

8 Walter's subtlety may be noted in her interpretation of a signal crux: Lady Macbeth's words "We fail." This phrase "can represent either interrogation . . . or exclamation" (Braunmuller 1.7.59 n.; cf. Kliman, *Shakespeare* 35). In the Doran DVD, Walter manages the feat of conveying both (cf. Coursen, *Macbeth* 114).

9 For remarks on some other recent U.K. *Macbeth*s, see Wilders (62–75). Less critically successful recent versions include a Pidgin translation, *Makbed blong Willum Sekspia*, directed by Ken Campbell in 1998; and two 2004 stagings, directed by Andrew Hilton and by Dominic Cooke (on the latter cf. Thomas). Some positive notices were garnered by Sean Bean and Samantha Bond in a vigorous *Macbeth* directed by Edward Hall in 2002; Max Stafford-Clark reportedly made Macbeth resemble Idi Amin in a 2005 production. Most recently—and to far greater initial acclaim than any of the others listed here—Patrick Stewart appeared in director Rupert Goold's *Macbeth*, which evoked Stalinist Russia; it opened at Chichester's Minerva Theatre in 2007, and was transferred to London later that same year.

10 Possibly a 1606 audience might have seen Shakespeare's "bleeding Captain" (1.2.0 SD) as an allusion to the knight who, in 1603, travelled to Scotland to apprise King James VI of his succession to England's throne—bloodying himself in a mishap along the way (Loomis).

11 Dualists seeking pro-Jacobean meanings in *Macbeth* also interpret the dagger vision (2.1.33–49) as a reminiscence of the 'Gowrie Plot,' which had targeted James in 1600, before his accession to the English throne; during the botched attempt, James was menaced with a dagger (Kinney, *Lies* 113; cf. Kozikowski; Clark; Carroll 255–56).

12 A nineteenth-century critic, Gervinus, observed that "for the murder of Banquo Macbeth employs the very incitements which had wrought most effectually upon himself; he appeals to the manhood of the murderers" (quoted in Furness 441; cf. 3.1.101–103).

13 This suspicion that Ross, in particular, is dishonest was raised in the nineteenth century by M.F. Libby (see Furness). Polanski's film memorably made Ross "a kind of evil genius" (Kliman, *Shakespeare* 198).

14 For another historicist essay invoking specialized legal contexts, cf. Fowler.

15 In 1604, when the King's Men—in a play now lost—dramatized the Gowrie Plot

(see n. 11 above), they were said to have evoked displeasure from "great counsellors" (quoted in Carroll 256 n. 5).

16 I use this term loosely here; strictly deconstructionist projects are rare in Shakespeare studies. Both Calderwood (27–31) and Cohen (*Searching* 123–38) gesture toward deconstructive readings of Macbeth's experience, yet both—especially Calderwood—qualify this gesture by insisting that form and value are reimposed on that experience. For an outlook that seems more thoroughly indebted to deconstruction, see Evans (113–22, 133–37).

17 See e.g. Tredell (19, citing William Richardson's discussion from 1774); Furness (5.1.7 n., quoting the eighteenth-century editor George Steevens); Furness (406, quoting the Victorian Joseph Hunter); Freud (133–36). In 1947, the editor J. Dover Wilson tried to explain perceived implausibilities by hypothesizing that F reproduced a heavily cut *Macbeth;* Muir responded in his edition (*Macbeth* xxiv–xxv). Empson's position, that *Macbeth*'s details were "*meant* to seem puzzling" (146), is championed in a recent essay (Lewin).

Works cited

Adelman, Janet. *Suffocating Mothers: Fantasies of Maternal Origin in Shakespeare's Plays*, Hamlet *to* The Tempest. London: Routledge, 1992.

Asp, Carolyn. " 'Be bloody, bold, and resolute:' Tragic Action and Sexual Stereotyping in *Macbeth*." *Studies in Philology* 78.2 (1981): 153–69. Rpt. *Macbeth: Critical Essays*. Ed. S. Schoenbaum. New York: Garland, 1991. 377–95.

Auden, W.H. "*Macbeth*." *Lectures on Shakespeare*. Reconstructed and edited by Arthur Kirsch. Princeton: Princeton UP, 2000. 208–18.

Baer, Nancy Van Norman. *Theatre in Revolution: Russian Avant-Garde Stage Design, 1913–1935*. London: Thames & Hudson, 1991.

Baldo, Jonathan. "The Politics of Aloofness in *Macbeth*." *English Literary Renaissance* 26.3 (1996): 531–60.

Banham, Martin, Roshni Mooneeram, and Jane Plastow. "Shakespeare and Africa." *The Cambridge Companion to Shakespeare on Stage*. Ed. Stanley Wells and Sarah Stanton. Cambridge: Cambridge UP, 2002. 284–99.

Bartholomeusz, Dennis. Macbeth *and the Players*. Cambridge: Cambridge UP, 1969.

Bate, Jonathan. *Shakespeare and the English Romantic Imagination*. Oxford: Clarendon, 1986.

—— *Shakespearean Constitutions: Politics, Theatre, Criticism 1730–1830*. Oxford: Clarendon, 1989.

Baynham, Matthew. "The Naked Babe and Robert Southwell." *Notes and Queries* 50.1 (2003): 55–56.

Bell, Millicent. "*Macbeth* and Dismemberment." *Raritan* 25.3 (2006): 13–29.

—— *Shakespeare's Tragic Skepticism*. New Haven: Yale UP, 2002.

Belsey, Catherine. "Shakespeare's 'vaulting ambition.' " *ELN* 10 (1972): 198–201.

—— *The Subject of Tragedy: Identity and Difference in Renaissance Drama*. Methuen: London, 1985.

Berger, Harry, Jr. *Making Trifles of Terrors: Redistributing Complicities in Shakespeare*. Stanford: Stanford UP, 1997.

Berry, Philippa. *Shakespeare's Feminine Endings: Disfiguring Death in the Tragedies*. London: Routledge, 1999.

Bevington, David, Anne Marie Welsh, and Michael L. Greenwald. *Shakespeare: Script, Stage, Screen*. New York: Pearson-Longman, 2006.

Biggins, Dennis. "Sexuality, Witchcraft, and Violence in *Macbeth.*" *Shakespeare Studies* 8 (1975): 255–77.

Billings, Timothy. "Squashing the 'Shard-borne Beetle' Crux: A Hard Case with a Few Pat Readings." *Shakespeare Quarterly* 56.4 (2005): 434–47.

Billington, Michael. "*Macbeth.*" Rev. of *Macbeth*, dir. John Caird. *The Guardian* 21 Jan. 2005. Rpt. 18 Jan. 2006 <http://www.guardian.co.uk>.

Booth, Stephen. "Close Reading without Readings." *Shakespeare Reread: The Texts in New Contexts*. Ed. Russ McDonald. Ithaca: Cornell UP, 1994. 42–55.

—— King Lear, Macbeth, *Indefinition, and Tragedy*. New Haven: Yale UP, 1983.

Boyle, A.J. *Tragic Seneca: An Essay in the Theatrical Tradition*. London: Routledge, 1997.

Bradbrook, M.C. "The Sources of *Macbeth.*" *Shakespeare Survey* 4 (1951): 35–48.

Bradley, A.C. "*Macbeth* (1904)." *Shakespeare:* Macbeth. Ed. John Wain. Casebook series. 1969. Rpt. Nashville: Aurora, 1970. 97–130.

Bradshaw, Graham. "Operatic Macbeths: What We Could Still Learn from Verdi." Kliman, Bernice W. *Shakespeare in Performance:* Macbeth. 2nd ed. Manchester: Manchester UP, 2004. 44–61.

Brandon, James. "Shakespeare in Kabuki." *Performing Shakespeare in Japan*. Ed. Minami Ryuta, Ian Carruthers, and John Gillies. Cambridge: Cambridge UP, 2001. 33–53.

Braunmuller, A.R., ed. *Macbeth*. The New Cambridge Shakespeare. Cambridge: Cambridge UP, 1997.

Brooke, Nicholas, ed. *The Tragedy of Macbeth*. The Oxford Shakespeare. Oxford: Oxford UP, 1990.

Brooks, Cleanth. "The Naked Babe and the Cloak of Manliness (1947)." *Shakespeare:* Macbeth. Ed. John Wain. Casebook series. 1969. Rpt. Nashville: Aurora, 1970. 183–201.

Brown, John Russell. *Macbeth*. The Shakespeare Handbooks series. Houndmills: Palgrave, 2005.

—— *Shakespeare:* The Tragedy of Macbeth. London: Arnold, 1963.

—— *Shakespeare Dancing: A Theatrical Study of the Plays*. Houndmills: Palgrave Macmillan, 2005.

Buhler, Stephen M. *Shakespeare in the Cinema: Ocular Proof*. Albany: State U of New York P, 2002.

Bulman, J.C., and H.R. Coursen, eds. *Shakespeare on Television: An Anthology of Essays and Reviews*. Hanover: UP of New England, 1988.

Bushnell, Rebecca W. *Tragedies of Tyrants: Political Thought and Theater in the English Renaissance*. Ithaca: Cornell UP, 1990.

Calderwood, James L. *If It Were Done:* Macbeth *and Tragic Action*. Amherst: U of Massachusetts P, 1986.

Callaghan, Dympna. "Shakespeare at the Fun Palace: Joan Littlewood." *Cross-Cultural Performances: Differences in Women's Re-Visions of Shakespeare*. Ed. Marianne Novy. Urbana: U of Illinois P, 1993. 108–26.

—— "Wicked Women in *Macbeth:* A Study of Power, Ideology, and the Production of Motherhood." *Reconsidering the Renaissance: Papers from the Twenty-First Annual Conference*. Ed. Mario A. Di Cesare. Binghamton: Medieval & Renaissance Texts & Studies, 1992. 355–69.

Campbell, Lily B. *Shakespeare's Tragic Heroes: Slaves of Passion*. Cambridge: Cambridge UP, 1930.

Carmeli, Audrey Ellen. "Allegory and metaphor: Soviet productions of Shakespeare in the post-Stalin era." Diss. U of Illinois at Urbana-Champaign, 2002. *DAI* 63 (2002): 423.

Carroll, William C., ed. Macbeth: *Texts and Contexts*. Boston: Bedford/St. Martin's, 1999.

Carruthers, Ian. "The *Chronicle of Macbeth*: Suzuki Tadashi's Transformation of Shakespeare's *Macbeth*." *Shakespeare: World Views*. Ed. Heather Kerr, Robin Eaden, and Madge Mitton. Newark: U of Delaware P, 1996. 214–36.

Cartwright, Kent. "Scepticism and Theatre in *Macbeth*." *Shakespeare Survey* 55 (2002): 219–36.

Chamberlain, Stephanie. "Fantasizing Infanticide: Lady Macbeth and the Murdering Mother in Early Modern England." *College Literature* 32.3 (2005): 72–91.

Chandrashekar, Laxmi. " 'A sea change into something rich and strange': Ekbal Ahmed's *Macbeth* and *Hamlet*." *India's Shakespeare: Translation, Interpretation, and Performance*. Ed. Poonam Trivedi and Dennis Bartholomeusz. Newark: U of Delaware P, 2005. 193–203.

Clark, Arthur Melville. *Murder Under Trust: or The Topical* Macbeth *and other Jacobean Matters*. Edinburgh: Scottish Academic, 1981.

Clary, Frank Nicholas. "Maclise and Macready: Collaborating Illustrators of *Hamlet*." *Shakespeare Bulletin* 25.1 (2007): 33–59.

Coddon, Karin S. " 'Unreal Mockery': Unreason and the Problem of Spectacle in *Macbeth*." *ELH* 56.3 (1989): 485–501.

Cohen, Derek. *Searching Shakespeare: Studies in Culture and Authority*. Toronto: U of Toronto P, 2003.

—— *Shakespeare's Culture of Violence*. Houndmills: St. Martin's, 1993.

Cohn, Ruby. *Modern Shakespeare Offshoots*. Princeton: Princeton UP, 1976.

—— "Shakespeare Left." *Theatre Journal* 40.1 (1988): 48–60.

Coleridge, Samuel Taylor. *Notes and Lectures Upon Shakespeare and Some of the Old Poets and Dramatists, With Other Literary Remains of S.T. Coleridge*. Ed. H.N. Coleridge. Vol. 1. London: William Pickering, 1849.

Collmer, Robert G. "An Existentialist Approach to *Macbeth*." *The Personalist* 41 (1960): 484–91.

Cordner, Michael. " 'Wrought with things forgotten': Memory and Performance in Editing *Macbeth*." *Shakespeare, Memory, and Performance*. Ed. Peter Holland. Cambridge: Cambridge UP, 2006. 87–116.

Coursen, H.R. "In Deepest Consequence: *Macbeth*." *Shakespeare Quarterly* 18.4 (1967): 375–88.

—— Macbeth: *A Guide to the Play*. Greenwood Guides to Shakespeare. Westport: Greenwood, 1997.

Cox, John D. *The Devil and the Sacred in English Drama, 1350–1642*. Cambridge: Cambridge UP, 2000.

Crane, Mary Thomas. " 'Fair is Foul': *Macbeth* and Binary Logic." *The Work of Fiction: Cognition, Culture, and Complexity*. Ed. Alan Richardson and Ellen Spolsky. Aldershot: Ashgate, 2004. 107–25.

Creeth, Edmund. *Mankynde in Shakespeare*. Athens: U of Georgia P, 1976.

Crowl, Samuel. *Shakespeare Observed*. Athens: Ohio UP, 1992.

Das, Sisir Kumar. "Shakespeare in Indian Languages." *India's Shakespeare: Translation, Interpretation, and Performance*. Ed. Poonam Trivedi and Dennis Bartholomeusz. Newark: U of Delaware P, 2005. 47–73.

Davenant, William. *Macbeth, a Tragaedy* [sic]. *With all the Alterations, Amendments, Additions, and New Songs. As it's now Acted at the Duke's Theatre.* London: P. Chetwin, 1674.

David, Richard. "The Tragic Curve." *Shakespeare Survey* 9 (1956): 122–31.

De Grazia, Margreta, and Peter Stallybrass. "The Materiality of the Shakespearean Text." *Shakespeare Quarterly* 44.3 (1993): 255–83.

De Quincey, Thomas. "On the Knocking at the Gate in *Macbeth.*" 1823. *Shakespeare: Macbeth.* Ed. John Wain. Casebook series. 1969. Rpt. Nashville: Aurora, 1970. 90–93.

De Somogyi, Nick, ed. *The Shakespeare Folios:* Macbeth / The Tragedie of Macbeth. London: Nick Hern, 2003.

Dean, Paul. "Murderous Repetition: *Macbeth* as Echo Chamber." *English Studies* 80.3 (1999): 216–23.

Desmet, Christy. " 'Intercepting the Dew-Drop': Female Readers and Readings in Anna Jameson's Shakespearean Criticism." *Women's Re-Visions of Shakespeare: On the Responses of Dickinson, Woolf, Rich, H.D., George Eliot, and Others.* Ed. Marianne Novy. Urbana: U of Illinois P, 1990. 41–57.

DiMatteo, Anthony. " 'Antiqui Dicunt': Classical Aspects of the Witches in *Macbeth.*" *Notes and Queries* 41.1 (1994): 44–47.

Doebler, John. *Shakespeare's Speaking Pictures: Studies in Iconic Imagery.* Albuquerque: U of New Mexico P, 1974.

Dolan, Frances E. *Dangerous Familiars: Representations of Domestic Crime in England, 1550–1700.* Ithaca: Cornell UP, 1994.

Doran, Gregory. "As Performed By the Royal Shakespeare Company at the Swan Theatre in Stratford-upon-Avon in 1999." *Macbeth.* Ed. William Proctor Williams. The Sourcebooks Shakespeare. Naperville: Sourcebooks mediaFusion, 2006. 11–19.

Dover Wilson, John, ed. *Macbeth.* The New Shakespeare. Rev. ed. Cambridge: Cambridge UP, 1950.

Downer, Alan S. *The Eminent Tragedian: William Charles Macready.* Cambridge: Harvard UP, 1966.

Duncan-Jones, Katherine. *Ungentle Shakespeare: Scenes From His Life.* London: Thomson Learning, 2001.

Dutton, Richard. *William Shakespeare: A Literary Life.* Houndmills: Macmillan, 1989.

Edgecombe, Rodney Stenning. "Southwell's 'Burning Babe' and the 'Naked New-Born Babe' in *Macbeth.*" *Notes and Queries* 48.3 (2001): 295–96.

Egan, Gabriel. "The Early Seventeenth-Century Origin of the *Macbeth* Superstition." *Notes and Queries* 49.2 (2002): 236–37.

Emerson, Ralph Waldo. "Self-Reliance." 1841. *The American Intellectual Tradition: A Sourcebook.* 2nd ed. Vol. I. Ed. David A. Hollinger and Charles Capper. Oxford: Oxford UP, 1993. 288–302.

Empson, William. *Essays on Shakespeare.* Ed. David B. Pirie. Cambridge: Cambridge UP, 1986.

Erne, Lukas. *Shakespeare as Literary Dramatist.* Cambridge: Cambridge UP, 2003.

Evans, Malcolm. *Signifying Nothing: Truth's True Contents in Shakespeare's Text.* Athens: U of Georgia P, 1986.

Ewbank, Inga-Stina. "The Fiend-Like Queen: A Note on 'Macbeth' and Seneca's 'Medea'." *Shakespeare Survey* 19 (1966): 82–94.

Farjeon, Herbert. *The Shakespearean Scene: Dramatic Criticisms.* London: Hutchinson, n.d.

Farley-Hills, David. "The Entrances and Exits of *Macbeth.*" *Notes and Queries* 50.1 (2003): 50–55.

Farnham, Willard. *Shakespeare's Tragic Frontier.* Berkeley: U of California P, 1950.

Fendt, Gene. "Banquo: A False *Faux Ami?*" *Notes and Queries* 52.2 (2005): 204–206.

Fergusson, Francis. "Macbeth as the Imitation of an Action." *English Institute Essays, 1951.* Ed. Alan S. Downer. New York: Columbia UP, 1952. 31–43.

Finnerty, Páraic. *Emily Dickinson's Shakespeare.* Amherst: U of Massachusetts P, 2006.

Floyd-Wilson, Mary. "English Epicures and Scottish Witches." *Shakespeare Quarterly* 57.2 (2006): 131–61.

Foster, Donald W. "*Macbeth*'s War on Time." *English Literary Renaissance* 16.2 (1986): 319–42.

Fowler, Elizabeth, "The Rhetoric of Political Forms: Social Persons and the Criterion of Fit in Colonial Law, *Macbeth*, and *The Irish Masqve at Covrt.*" *Form and Reform in Renaissance England: Essays in Honor of Barbara Kiefer Lewalski.* Ed. Amy Boesky and Mary Thomas Crane. Newark: U of Delaware P, 2000. 70–103.

Freud, Sigmund. "From 'Some Character-Types Met With in Psycho-Analytical Work' (1916)." *Shakespeare:* Macbeth. Ed. John Wain. Casebook series. 1969. Rpt. Nashville: Aurora, 1970. 131–38.

Fridén, Ann. Macbeth *in the Swedish Theatre 1838–1986.* Malmö: Liber Förlag, 1986.

Furness, Horace Howard, Jr., ed. *A New Variorum Edition of Shakespeare:* Macbeth. Rev. ed. New York: Dover, 1963 [1903].

Garber, Marjorie. "Macbeth: the Male Medusa." *Shakespeare's Late Tragedies: A Collection of Critical Essays.* Ed. Susanne L. Wofford. Upper Saddle River: Prentice Hall, 1996. 74–103.

Gardner, Helen. "From *The Business of Criticism.*" *Shakespeare:* Macbeth. Ed. John Wain. Casebook series. 1969. Rpt. Nashville: Aurora, 1970. 246–54.

Gillies, John, Ryuta Minami, Ruru Li, and Poonam Trivedi. "Shakespeare on the Stages of Asia." *The Cambridge Companion to Shakespeare on Stage.* Ed. Stanley Wells and Sarah Stanton. Cambridge: Cambridge UP, 2002. 259–83.

Goldberg, Jonathan. "Speculations: *Macbeth* and Source." *Shakespeare Reproduced: The Text in History and Ideology.* Ed. Jean E. Howard and Marion F. O'Connor. New York: Routledge, 1987. 242–64.

Gorfain, Phyllis. "Riddles and Tragic Structure in *Macbeth.*" *Shakespeare and Folklore.* Ed. Philip C. Kolin. *Mississippi Folklore Register* 10.2 (1976): 187–209.

Greenblatt, Stephen. "Shakespeare Bewitched." *New Historical Literary Study: Essays on Reproducing Texts, Representing History.* Ed. Jeffrey N. Cox and Larry J. Reynolds. Princeton: Princeton UP, 1993. 108–35.

—— *Will in the World: How Shakespeare Became Shakespeare.* New York: Norton, 2004.

Greenhalgh, Susanne. " 'Alas poor country!': Documenting the Politics of Performance in Two British Television *Macbeth*s since the 1980s." *Remaking Shakespeare: Performance across Media, Genres and Cultures.* Ed. Pascale Aebischer, Nigel Wheale, and Ed Esche. Houndmills: Palgrave Macmillan, 2003. 93–114.

Guntner, Lawrence. "Brecht and Beyond: Shakespeare on the East German Stage." *Foreign Shakespeare: Contemporary Performance.* Ed. Dennis Kennedy. Cambridge: Cambridge UP, 1993. 109–39.

Gwinne, Matthew. *Vertumnus, sive Annus Recurrens.* London, 1607.

Hadfield, Andrew. " 'Hitherto she ne're could fancy him': Shakespeare's 'British'

Plays and the Exclusion of Ireland." *Shakespeare and Ireland: History, Politics, Culture.* Ed. Mark Thornton Burnett and Ramona Wray. Houndmills: Macmillan, 1997. 47–67.

—— "*Macbeth,* IV.iii.140–58, Edward the Confessor, and Holinshed's *Chronicles.*" *Notes and Queries* 49.2 (2002): 234–36.

Halio, Jay L., ed. *Approaches to* Macbeth. Belmont: Wadsworth, 1966.

Hapgood, Robert. "*Macbeth* Distilled: A Yakshagan Production in Delhi." *Shakespeare Quarterly* 31.3 (1980): 439–40.

—— *Shakespeare the Theatre-Poet.* Oxford: Clarendon, 1988.

Harries, Martin. *Scare Quotes from Shakespeare: Marx, Keynes, and the Language of Reenchantment.* Stanford: Stanford UP, 2000.

Harris, Jonathan Gil. "The Smell of *Macbeth.*" *Shakespeare Quarterly* 58.4 (2007): 465–86.

Harvey, Paul A.S., and Kliman, Bernice W. "*Ninagawa Macbeth:* Fusion of Japanese and Western Theatrical Styles." Kliman, Bernice W. *Shakespeare in Performance:* Macbeth. 2nd ed. Manchester: Manchester UP, 2004. 159–82.

Hassel, R. Chris, Jr. " 'No Boasting Like a Fool'? Macbeth and Herod." *Studies in Philology* 98.2 (2001): 205–24.

Hatchuel, Sarah. " 'Prithee, see there! Behold! Look! (3.4.69): The Gift or the Denial of Sight in Screen Adaptations of Shakespeare's *Macbeth.*" *Borrowers and Lenders: The Journal of Shakespeare and Appropriation* 1.2 (2005). 20 Jan. 2007 http://atropos.english.uga.edu/cocoon/borrowers/archive>.

Hawkins, Michael. "History, Politics, and *Macbeth.*" *Focus on* Macbeth. Ed. John Russell Brown. London: Routledge and Kegan Paul, 1982. 155–88.

Hazlitt, William. *Characters of Shakespear's Plays.* London: R. Hunter and C. and J. Ollier, 1817.

Headlam-Wells, Robin. *Shakespeare on Masculinity.* Cambridge: Cambridge UP, 2000.

Hill, Errol. *Shakespeare in Sable: A History of Black Shakespearean Actors.* Amherst: U of Massachusetts P, 1984.

Hinman, Charlton, ed. *The First Folio of Shakespeare: The Norton Facsimile.* 2nd ed. New York: W.W. Norton, 1996.

——, ed. "*Macbeth* (1623 First Folio Edition)." U of Virginia Library Electronic Text Center. 17 March 2006 <http://etext.virginia.edu/shakespeare/folio/>.

Hodgdon, Barbara. "*Macbeth* at the Turn of the Millenium." *Shakespearean Illuminations: Essays in Honor of Marvin Rosenberg.* Ed. Jay L. Halio and Hugh Richmond. Newark: U of Delaware P, 1998. 147–63.

Hofmannsthal, Hugo von. "Shakespeare's Kings and Noblemen." Trans. James Stern and Tania Stern. *Shakespeare in Europe.* Ed. Oswald LeWinter. Cleveland: Meridian-World, 1963. 321–39.

Holderness, Graham. *Textual Shakespeare: Writing and the Word.* Hatfield: U of Hertfordshire P, 2003.

Holland, Peter. *English Shakespeares: Shakespeare on the English stage in the 1990s.* Cambridge: Cambridge UP, 1997.

—— " 'Stands Scotland Where It Did?': The Location of *Macbeth* on Film." Macbeth: *Authoritative Text, Sources and Contexts, Criticism.* Ed. Robert S. Miola. New York: W.W. Norton, 2004. 357–80.

Holloway, John. *The Story of the Night: Studies in Shakespeare's Major Tragedies.* Lincoln: U of Nebraska P, 1961.

Honigmann, E.A.J. *Myriad-Minded Shakespeare: Essays on the Tragedies, Problem Comedies and Shakespeare the Man*. 2nd ed. Manchester: Manchester UP, 1998.
—— *Shakespeare: Seven Tragedies Revisited: The Dramatist's Manipulation of Response*. New ed. Houndmills: Palgrave, 2002.
Hortmann, Wilhelm. "Berlin—Zürich—Düsseldorf: Aspects of German Theatre During the Nazi Period and After." *Shakespeare and His Contemporaries in Performance*. Ed. Edward J. Esche. Aldershot: Ashgate, 2000. 89–108.
——, with Maik Hamburger. *Shakespeare on the German Stage: The Twentieth Century, with a Section on Shakespeare on Stage in the German Democratic Republic by Maik Hamburger*. Cambridge: Cambridge UP, 1998.
Huang, Alexander C.Y. "The Politics of an 'Apolitical' Shakespeare: A Soviet–Chinese Joint Venture, 1950–1979." *Borrowers and Lenders: The Journal of Shakespeare and Appropriation* 1.2 (2005). 20 Jan. 2007 <http://atropos.english.uga.edu/cocoon/borrowers/archive>.
Hughes, Alan. *Henry Irving, Shakespearean*. Cambridge: Cambridge UP, 1981.
Hunt, Maurice. "Reformation/counter-reformation *Macbeth*." *English Studies* 86.5 (2005): 379–98.
Hunter, G.K. " 'Macbeth' in the Twentieth Century." *Shakespeare Survey* 19 (1966): 1–11.
Hunter, Robert G. *Shakespeare and the Mystery of God's Judgments*. Athens: U of Georgia P, 1976.
Innes, Christopher. *Avant Garde Theatre 1892–1992*. London: Routledge, 1993.
Ioppolo, Grace. *Revising Shakespeare*. Cambridge: Harvard UP, 1991.
Jacobi, Derek. "Macbeth." Macbeth: *Authoritative Text, Sources and Contexts, Criticism*. Ed. Robert S. Miola. New York: W.W. Norton, 2004. 328–42.
Jaech, Sharon L. Jansen. "Political Prophecy and Macbeth's 'Sweet Bodements.' " *Shakespeare Quarterly* 34.3 (1983): 290–97.
Jenkin, H.C. Fleeming. "Mrs. Siddons as Lady Macbeth and Queen Katherine." *Papers on Acting*. Ed. Brander Matthews. New York: Hill and Wang, 1958. 75–114.
Johnson, Samuel. "From Johnson's *Shakespeare* (1765)." *Shakespeare:* Macbeth. Ed. John Wain. Casebook series. 1969. Rpt. Nashville: Aurora, 1970. 51–62.
Jones, Emrys. *The Origins of Shakespeare*. Oxford: Clarendon, 1977.
Jorgens, Jack J. *Shakespeare on Film*. Bloomington: Indiana UP, 1977.
Jorgensen, Paul A. *Our Naked Frailties: Sensational Art and Meaning in* Macbeth. Berkeley: U of California P, 1971.
Kahn, Coppélia. *Man's Estate: Masculine Identity in Shakespeare*. Berkeley: U of California P, 1981.
Kastan, David Scott. " 'A rarity most beloved': Shakespeare and the Idea of Tragedy." *A Companion to Shakespeare's Works: Volume 1, The Tragedies*. Ed. Richard Dutton and Jean E. Howard. Malden: Blackwell, 2003. 4–22.
—— *Shakespeare After Theory*. New York: Routledge, 1999.
Kay, Kwesi. *Maama. Ten One-Act Plays*. Ed. Cosmo Pieterse. London: Heinemann, 1968. 231–53.
Kennedy, Dennis. *Looking at Shakespeare: A Visual History of Twentieth-Century Performance*. Cambridge: Cambridge UP, 1993.
Kermode, Frank. *The Sense of an Ending: Studies in the Theory of Fiction*. Oxford: Oxford UP, 1967.
Kernan, Alvin. *Shakespeare, the King's Playwright: Theater in the Stuart Court, 1603–1613*. New Haven: Yale UP, 1995.

Kiefer, Frederick. *Shakespeare's Visual Theatre: Staging the Personified Characters.* Cambridge: Cambridge UP, 2003.

—— *Writing on the Renaissance Stage: Written Words, Printed Pages, Metaphoric Books.* Newark: U of Delaware P, 1996.

Kinney, Arthur F. *Lies Like Truth: Shakespeare, Macbeth, and the Cultural Moment.* Detroit: Wayne State UP, 2001.

—— "Macbeth's Knowledge." *Shakespeare Survey* 57 (2004): 11–26.

Kirsch, Arthur. "Macbeth's Suicide." *ELH* 51.2 (1984): 269–96.

Kishi, Tetsuo. "Japanese Shakespeare and English Reviewers." *Shakespeare and the Japanese Stage.* Ed. Takashi Sasayama, J.R. Mulryne, and Margaret Shewring. Cambridge: Cambridge UP, 1998. 110–23.

Klein, Joan Larsen. "Lady Macbeth: 'Infirm of purpose.' " *The Woman's Part: Feminist Criticism of Shakespeare.* Ed. Carolyn R.S. Lenz, Gayle Greene, and Carol Thomas Neely. Urbana: U of Illinois P, 1980. 240–55.

Kliman, Bernice W. "Another Ninagawa *Macbeth.*" *The Shakespeare Newsletter* 52.4 (2002/3): 93, 106.

—— *Shakespeare in Performance:* Macbeth. 2nd ed. Manchester: Manchester UP, 2004.

Knight, G. Wilson. "The Milk of Concord: An Essay on Life-Themes in *Macbeth.*" 1931. *Shakespeare:* Macbeth. Ed. John Wain. Casebook series. 1969. Rpt. Nashville: Aurora, 1970. 139–67.

Kolin, Philip C. "*All God's Chillun Got Wings* and *Macbeth.*" *Eugene O'Neill Newsletter* 12.1 (1988): 55–61.

—— "Macbeth, Malcolm, and the Curse of the Serpent." *The South Central Bulletin* 34.4 (1974): 159–60.

—— "Shakespeare Knocks: *Macbeth* in Adrienne Kennedy's *Funnyhouse of a Negro.*" *Contemporary Literature* 34.4 (2004): 8–10.

Kott, Jan. *Shakespeare Our Contemporary.* 1962. Trans. Boleslaw Taborski. Garden City: Anchor-Doubleday, 1966.

Kozikowski, Stanley J. "The Gowrie Conspiracy Against James VI: A New Source for Shakespeare's *Macbeth.*" *Shakespeare Studies* 13 (1980): 197–212.

Kranz, David L. "The Sounds of Supernatural Soliciting in *Macbeth.*" *Studies in Philology* 100 (2003): 346–83.

Kroll, Richard. "Emblem and Empiricism in Davenant's *Macbeth.*" *ELH* 57.4 (1990): 835–64.

La Belle, Jenijoy. " 'A strange infirmity': Lady Macbeth's Amenorrhea." *Shakespeare Quarterly* 31 (1980): 381–86.

Lake, Peter, with Michael Questier. *The Antichrist's Lewd Hat: Protestants, Papists, & Players in Post-Reformation England.* New Haven: Yale UP, 2002.

Lancashire, Anne. "The Dualistic Castle in Shakespeare and Middleton." *Mirror up to Shakespeare: Essays in Honour of G.R. Hibbard.* Ed. J.C. Gray. Toronto: U of Toronto P, 1984. 223–41.

Lanier, Douglas. " 'Hours Dreadful and Things Strange': *Macbeth* in Popular Culture." *Macbeth.* Ed. William Proctor Williams. The Sourcebooks Shakespeare. Naperville: Sourcebooks mediaFusion, 2006. 21–33.

—— *Shakespeare and Modern Popular Culture.* Oxford: Oxford UP, 2002.

Laroque, François. "Magic in *Macbeth.*" *Cahiers Élisabéthains* 35 (1989): 59–84.

—— "*Macbeth:* Theatre of Image to Shadow Theatre." *Spectacle & Image in Renaissance Europe: Selected Papers of the XXXIInd Conference at the Centre d'Études*

Supérieures de la Renaissance de Tours, 29 June–8 July 1989. Ed. André Lascombes. Leiden: E.J. Brill, 1993. 147–75.

Leggatt, Alexander. "*Macbeth* and the Last Plays." *Mirror up to Shakespeare: Essays in Honour of G.R. Hibbard*. Ed. J.C. Gray. Toronto: U of Toronto P, 1984. 189–207.

Lehmann, Courtney. "Out Damned Scot: Dislocating *Macbeth* in Transnational Film and Media Culture." *Shakespeare, The Movie II: Popularizing the Plays on Film, TV, Video, and DVD*. Ed. Richard Burt and Lynda E. Boose. New York: Routledge, 2003. 231–51.

Leinwand, Theodore B. "*Coniugium Interruptum* in Shakespeare and Webster." *ELH* 72.1 (2005): 239–57.

Leiter, Samuel L., ed. "Macbeth." *Shakespeare Around the Globe: A Guide to Notable Postwar Revivals*. Ed. Samuel L. Leiter. New York: Greenwood, 1986. 355–93.

Lemon, Rebecca. "Scaffolds of Treason in *Macbeth*." *Theatre Journal* 54 (2002): 25–43.

Levin, Joanna. "Lady Macbeth and the Daemonologie of Hysteria." *ELH* 69 (2002): 21–55.

Lewin, Jennifer. "Murdering Sleep in *Macbeth:* The Mental World of the Protagonist." *The Shakespearean International Yearbook* 5 (2005): 181–88.

LeWinter, Oswald, ed. *Shakespeare in Europe*. Cleveland: Meridian-World, 1963.

Li, Ruru, and John Gillies. *Shakespeare in China*. Stanford University. 19 Jan. 2007 <http://sia.stanford.edu/china/FILES/HOMEPAGE.HTM>.

Lieblein, Leanore. " 'Cette belle langue': The 'Tradaptation' of Shakespeare in Québec." *Shakespeare and the Language of Translation*. Ed. Ton Hoenselaars. London: Thomson Learning, 2004. 255–69.

Liebler, Naomi Conn. *Shakespeare's Festive Tragedy: The Ritual Foundations of Genre*. London: Routledge, 1995.

Logan, Robert A. *Shakespeare's Marlowe: The Influence of Christopher Marlowe on Shakespeare*. Aldershot: Ashgate, 2007.

Long, Michael. *Macbeth*. Twayne's New Critical Introductions to Shakespeare. Boston: Twayne, 1989.

Loomba, Ania. "Shakespearian Transformations." *Shakespeare and National Culture*. Ed. John J. Joughin. Manchester: Manchester UP, 1997. 109–41.

Loomis, Catherine. " 'What Bloody Man is That?' Sir Robert Carey and Shakespeare's Bloody Sergeant." *Notes and Queries* 48 (2001): 296–98.

Macbeth. Dir. Gregory Doran. Perf. Antony Sher and Harriet Walter. Royal Shakespeare Company/Channel 4, 2001. DVD. Illuminations, 2003.

Macbeth. Dir. Trevor Nunn. Perf. Ian McKellen and Judi Dench. Thames Television, 1978. DVD. Fremantle Home Entertainment, 2004.

Macbeth. Dir. Roman Polanski. Perf. Jon Finch, Francesca Annis, and Martin Shaw. Columbia Pictures, 1971. DVD. Tristar Home Entertainment, 2002.

McCoy, Richard C. " 'The Grace of Grace' and Double-Talk in *Macbeth*." *Shakespeare Survey* 57 (2004): 27–37.

McDonald, Russ. *Look to the Lady: Sarah Siddons, Ellen Terry, and Judi Dench on the Shakespearean Stage*. Athens: U of Georgia P, 2005.

—— *Shakespeare and the Arts of Language*. Oxford: Oxford UP, 2001.

—— *Shakespeare's Late Style*. Cambridge: Cambridge UP, 2006.

McGee, Arthur R. "*Macbeth* and the Furies." *Shakespeare Survey* 19 (1966): 55–67.

McKernan, Luke and Olwen Terris. *Walking Shadows: Shakespeare in the National Film and Television Archive*. London: British Film Institute, 1994.

McLuskie, Kathleen. "Humane Statues and the Gentle Weal: Historical Reading and Historical Allegory." *Shakespeare Survey* 57 (2004): 1–10.

—— "*Macbeth*, the Present, and the Past." *A Companion to Shakespeare's Works: Volume 1, The Tragedies.* Ed. Richard Dutton and Jean E. Howard. Malden: Blackwell, 2003. 393–410.

—— "*Macbeth/Umabatha:* Global Shakespeare in a Post-Colonial Market." *Shakespeare Survey* 52 (1999): 154–65.

Maeterlinck, Maurice, trans. *La Tragédie de Macbeth.* Paris: Librairie Charpentier et Fasquelle, 1910.

Mahood, M.M. *Shakespeare's Wordplay.* London: Methuen, 1957.

Makaryk, Irena R. *Shakespeare in the Undiscovered Bourn: Les Kurbas, Ukrainian Modernism, and Early Soviet Cultural Politics.* Toronto: U of Toronto P, 2004.

Marshall, Tristan. *Theatre and Empire: Great Britain on the London Stages under James VI and I.* Manchester: Manchester UP, 2000.

Mason, Pamela. "Orson Welles and Filmed Shakespeare." *The Cambridge Companion to Shakespeare on Film.* Ed. Russell Jackson. 2nd ed. Cambridge: Cambridge UP, 2007. 187–202.

Men of Respect. Dir. William Riley. Perf. John Turturro, Katherine Borowitz, and Dennis Farina. Arthur Goldblatt Productions/Central City Films/Grandview Avenue Pictures, 1990. DVD. Sony Pictures, 2003.

"The Mercury Theatre on the Air." Kim Scarborough. 14 January 2007 <http://www.mercurytheatre.info/>.

Merchant, W. Moelwyn. " 'His Fiend-Like Queen.' " *Shakespeare Survey* 19 (1966): 75–81.

Milward, Peter. *Shakespeare's Religious Background.* Bloomington: Indiana UP, 1973.

Miola, Robert S., ed. Macbeth: *Authoritative Text, Sources and Contexts, Criticism.* Norton Critical Editions. New York: W.W. Norton, 2004.

—— *Shakespeare and Classical Tragedy: The Influence of Seneca.* Oxford: Clarendon, 1992.

Montagu, Elizabeth. "The Genius of Shakespeare." Macbeth: *Authoritative Text, Sources and Contexts, Criticism.* Ed. Robert S. Miola. Norton Critical Editions. New York: W.W. Norton, 2004. 211–15.

Moody, Jane. "Romantic Shakespeare." *The Cambridge Companion to Shakespeare on Stage.* Ed. Stanley Wells and Sarah Stanton. Cambridge: Cambridge UP, 2002. 37–57.

Morse, Ruth. "Monsieur Macbeth: From Jarry to Ionesco." *Shakespeare Survey* 57 (2004): 112–25.

Muir, Kenneth, ed. *Macbeth.* The Arden Shakespeare. Rev. ed. with new introduction. 1984. Rpt. London: Routledge, 1988.

——, ed. *Shakespeare Survey: An Annual Survey of Shakespearian Study and Production.* Vol. 19. Cambridge: Cambridge UP, 1966.

Mullaney, Steven. "Lying Like Truth: Riddle, Representation, and Treason in Renaissance England." *ELH* 47 (1980): 32–47.

Müller, Heiner. " 'Like Sleeping with Shakespeare.' A Conversation with Heiner Müller and Christa and B.K. Tragelehn." *Redefining Shakespeare: Literary Theory and Theater Practice in the German Democratic Republic.* Ed. J. Lawrence Guntner and Andrew M. McLean. Newark: U of Delaware P, 1998. 183–95.

Mullin, Michael. "Augures and Understood Relations: Theodore Komisarjevsky's 'Macbeth.' " *Educational Theatre Journal* 26.1 (1974): 20–30.

—— " 'Macbeth' in Modern Dress: Royal Court Theatre, 1928." *Educational Theatre Journal* 30.2 (1978): 176–85.

—— Macbeth *Onstage: An Annotated Facsimile of Glen Byam Shaw's 1955 Prompt-book*. Columbia: U of Missouri P, 1976.

—— "Stage and Screen: The Trevor Nunn 'Macbeth.' " *Shakespeare Quarterly* 38.3 (1983): 350–59.

Mulryne, J.R. "The Perils and Profits of Interculturalism and the Theatre Art of Tadashi Suzuki." *Shakespeare and the Japanese Stage*. Ed. Takashi Sasayama, J.R. Mulryne, and Margaret Shewring. Cambridge: Cambridge UP, 1998. 71–93.

Neely, Carol Thomas. *Distracted Subjects: Madness and Gender in Shakespeare and Early Modern Culture*. Ithaca: Cornell UP, 2004.

The New Deal Stage: Selections From the Federal Theatre Project, 1935–1939. 1999. Library of Congress. 25 January 2007 <http://memory.loc.gov/ammem/fedtp/fthome.html>.

Nielsen, Elizabeth. "Macbeth: The Nemesis of the Post-Shakespearian Actor." *Shakespeare Quarterly* 16.2 (1965): 193–99.

Norbrook, David. "*Macbeth* and the Politics of Historiography." *Politics of Discourse: The Literature and History of Seventeenth-Century England*. Ed. Kevin Sharpe and Steven N. Zwicker. Berkeley: U of California P, 1987. 78–116.

Nosworthy, J.M. "*Macbeth, Doctor Faustus*, and the Juggling Fiends." *Mirror up to Shakespeare: Essays in Honour of G.R. Hibbard*. Ed. J.C. Gray. Toronto: U of Toronto P, 1984. 208–22.

Nouryeh, Andrea J. "Shakespeare and the Japanese Stage." *Foreign Shakespeare: Contemporary Performance*. Ed. Dennis Kennedy. Cambridge: Cambridge UP, 1993. 254–69.

Novy, Marianne L. *Engaging With Shakespeare: Responses of George Eliot and Other Women Novelists*. Iowa City: U of Iowa P, 1998.

O'Connor, John. *Shakespearean Afterlives: Ten Characters with a Life of Their Own*. Thriplow: Icon, 2005.

Odell, George C.D. *Shakespeare from Betterton to Irving*. 2 vols. 1920. Rpt. New York: Dover, 1966.

Orgel, Stephen. *The Authentic Shakespeare and Other Problems of the Early Modern Stage*. New York: Routledge, 2002.

Orkin, Martin. " 'I am the Tusk of an Elephant'—*Macbeth, Titus* and *Caesar* in Johannesburg." *Shakespeare and the Language of Translation*. Ed. Ton Hoenselaars. London: Thomson Learning, 2004. 270–86.

Palfrey, Simon. *Late Shakespeare: A New World of Words*. Oxford: Clarendon, 1997.

Parsons, Keith and Pamela Mason, eds. *Shakespeare in Performance*. London: Salamander, 1995.

Paul, Henry N. *The Royal Play of* Macbeth. New York: Macmillan, 1950.

Pearlman, E. "*Macbeth* on Film: Politics." *Shakespeare Survey* 39 (1987): 67–74.

Perry, Curtis. *The Making of Jacobean Culture*. Cambridge: Cambridge UP, 1997.

Peyré, Yves. " 'Confusion now hath made his masterpiece': Senecan Resonances in *Macbeth*." *Shakespeare and the Classics*. Ed. Charles Martindale and A.B. Taylor. Cambridge: Cambridge UP, 2004. 141–55.

Poole, Adrian. "*Macbeth* and the Third Person." *Proceedings of the British Academy* 105 (2000): 73–92.

Prescott, Paul. "Doing All That Becomes a Man: The Reception and Afterlife of the Macbeth Actor, 1744–1889." *Shakespeare Survey* 57 (2004): 81–95.

Purkiss, Diane. *The Witch in History: Early Modern and Twentieth-century Representations*. London: Routledge, 1996.

Rabkin, Norman. *Shakespeare and the Problem of Meaning*. Chicago: U of Chicago P, 1981.

Riach, Alan. *Representing Scotland in Literature, Popular Culture, and Iconography: The Masks of the Modern Nation*. Houndmills: Palgrave Macmillan, 2005.

Rosenberg, Marvin. "Culture, Character, and Conscience in Shakespeare." Macbeth: *Authoritative Text, Sources and Contexts, Criticism*. Ed. Robert S. Miola. New York: W.W. Norton, 2004. 282–93.

—— "Macbeth and Lady Macbeth." *Focus on* Macbeth. Ed. John Russell Brown. London: Routledge and Kegan Paul, 1982. 73–86.

—— *The Masks of* Macbeth. Berkeley: U of California P, 1978.

Ross, Charles. *The Custom of the Castle: From Malory to Macbeth*. Berkeley: U of California P, 1997.

Rothwell, Kenneth S. *A History of Shakespeare on Screen: A Century of Film and Television*. 2nd ed. Cambridge: Cambridge UP, 2004.

Rowe, Katherine. "Humoral Knowledge and Liberal Cognition in Davenant's *Macbeth*." *Reading the Early Modern Passions: Essays in the Cultural History of Emotion*. Ed. Gail Kern Paster, Katherine Rowe, and Mary Floyd Wilson. Philadelphia: U of Pennsylvania P, 2004. 169–91.

—— "Minds in Company: Shakespearean Tragic Emotions." *A Companion to Shakespeare's Works: Volume 1, The Tragedies*. Ed. Richard Dutton and Jean E. Howard. Malden: Blackwell, 2003. 47–72.

—— "The Politics of Sleepwalking: American Lady Macbeths." *Shakespeare Survey* 57 (2004): 126–36.

Royal Shakespeare Company. "Plays in Focus: *Macbeth*." 19 Jan. 2007 <http://www.rsc.org.uk/picturesandexhibitions/action/showAllExhibitions>.

Russell Beale, Simon. "Macbeth." *Performing Shakespeare's Tragedies Today: The Actor's Perspective*. Ed. Michael Dobson. Cambridge: Cambridge UP, 2006. 107–18.

Rutter, Carol, with Sinead Cusack, Paola Dionisotti, Fiona Shaw, Juliet Stevenson, and Harriet Walter. *Clamorous Voices: Shakespeare's Women Today*. London: Routledge, 1989.

Safranski, Rüdiger. *Nietzsche: A Philosophical Biography*. 2000. Trans. Shelley Frisch. New York: W.W. Norton, 2002.

Salter, Denis. "Between Wor(l)ds: Lepage's Shakespeare Cycle." *Theater* 24.3. Rpt. *Alternative Theater*. 15 August 2005 <http://www.alternativetheater.com>.

Sanders, Wilbur. "The 'Strong Pessimism' of *Macbeth*." 1966. Rpt. in *Shakespeare*: Macbeth. Ed. John Wain. Casebook series. 1969. Rpt. Nashville: Aurora, 1970. 255–75.

Scotland, PA. Dir. Billy Morrissette. Perf. James LeGros, Maura Tierney, and Christopher Walken. Lot 47, 2001. DVD. Sundance Channel Home Entertainment, 2005.

Scott, William O. "Macbeth's—And Our—Self-Equivocations." *Shakespeare Quarterly* 37.2 (1986): 160–74.

Scragg, Leah. *Discovering Shakespeare's Meaning: An Introduction to the Study of Shakespeare's Dramatic Structures*. London: Longman, 1994.

—— "Macbeth on Horseback." *Shakespeare Survey* 26 (1973): 81–88.

Senda, Akihiko. "The Rebirth of Shakespeare in Japan: From the 1960s to the 1990s." *Shakespeare and the Japanese Stage*. Ed. Takashi Sasayama, J.R. Mulryne, and Margaret Shewring. Cambridge: Cambridge UP, 1998. 15–37.

Sengupta, Debjani. "Playing the Canon: Shakespeare and the Bengali Actress in Nineteenth-Century Calcutta." *India's Shakespeare: Translation, Interpretation, and Performance*. Ed. Poonam Trivedi and Dennis Bartholomeusz. Newark: U of Delaware P, 2005. 242–59.

Shaheen, Naseeb. *Biblical References in Shakespeare's Plays*. Newark: U of Delaware P, 1999.

"Shakespeare Around the Globe." *Internet Shakespeare Editions*. University of Victoria. 18 Jan. 2007 <http://ise.uvic.ca/Library/Criticism/shakespearein/index.html>.

Shattuck, Charles H. *Shakespeare on the American Stage*. 2 vols. Washington: Folger Shakespeare Library, 1976, 1987.

Sher, Antony. "Leontes in *The Winter's Tale*, and Macbeth." *Players of Shakespeare* 5. Ed. Robert Smallwood. Cambridge: Cambridge UP, 2003. 91–112.

Shohet, Lauren. "The Banquet of Scotland (PA)." *Shakespeare Survey* 57 (2004): 186–95.

Shurbanov, Alexander and Sokolova, Boika. "*Macbeth* in the Context of Twentieth-Century Totalitarianism." *International Shakespeare: The Tragedies*. Ed. Patricia Kennan and Mariangela Tempera. Bologna: CLUEB, 1996. 105–11.

Shuttleworth, Ian. "*Macbeth*." Rev. of *Macbeth*, dir. Gregory Doran. *Financial Times*. Rpt. *Ian Shuttleworth*. 19 Jan. 2007 <http://www.compulink.co.uk/~shutters>.

Sinfield, Alan. *Faultlines: Cultural Materialism and the Politics of Dissident Reading*. Berkeley: U of California P, 1992.

Smirnov, A. "Shakespeare, Renaissance and the Age of Barroco." *Shakespeare in the Soviet Union: A Collection of Articles*. Ed. Roman Samarin and Alexander Nikolyukin. Trans. Avril Pyman. Moscow: Progress, 1966. 58–83.

Smuts, Malcolm. "Banquo's Progeny: Hereditary Monarchy, the Stuart Lineage and *Macbeth*." *Renaissance Historicisms: Essays in Honor of Arthur F. Kinney*. Ed. James M. Dutcher and Anne Lake Prescott. Newark: U of Delaware P (forthcoming).

Snyder, Susan. *Shakespeare: A Wayward Journey*. Newark: U of Delaware P, 2002.

Sokol, B.J. "*Macbeth* and the Social History of Witchcraft." *Shakespeare and History*. Ed. Holger Klein and Rowland Wymer. Shakespeare Yearbook. Vol. 6. Lewiston: Edwin Mellen, 1996. 245–74.

Spencer, Christopher. *Davenant's* Macbeth *from the Yale Manuscript: An Edition, with a Discussion of the Relation of Davenant's Text to Shakespeare's*. New Haven: Yale UP, 1961.

Sprengnether, Madelon. "Reading as Lady Macbeth." *Women's Re-Visions of Shakespeare: On the Responses of Dickinson, Woolf, Rich, H.D., George Eliot, and Others*. Ed. Marianne Novy. Urbana: U of Illinois P, 1990. 227–41.

Spurgeon, Caroline. "From *Shakespeare's Imagery and What it Tells Us* (1935)." *Shakespeare*: Macbeth. Ed. John Wain. Casebook series. 1969. Rpt. Nashville: Aurora, 1970. 168–77.

Stallybrass, Peter. "*Macbeth* and Witchcraft." *Focus on* Macbeth. Ed. John Russell Brown. London: Routledge and Kegan Paul, 1982. 189–209. Rpt. *Shakespeare's*

Late Tragedies: A Collection of Critical Essays. Ed. Susanne L. Wofford. Upper Saddle River: Prentice Hall, 1996. 104–18.

Stoll, E.E. *Art and Artifice in Shakespeare*. Cambridge: Cambridge UP, 1933.

—— "Source and Motive in *Macbeth* and *Othello*." *Review of English Studies* 19 (1943): 25–32.

Stone, George Winchester, Jr. "Garrick's Handling of *Macbeth*." *Studies in Philology* 38 (1941): 609–28.

Stříbrný, Zdeněk. *Shakespeare and Eastern Europe*. Oxford: Oxford UP, 2000.

—— "Shakespeare as Liberator: *Macbeth* in Czechoslovakia." *Shakespeare and Cultural Traditions: The Selected Proceedings of the International Shakespeare Association World Congress, Tokyo, 1991*. Ed. Tetsuo Kishi, Roger Pringle, and Stanley Wells. Newark: U of Delaware P, 1994. 274–79.

Styan, J.L. *Modern Drama in Theory and Practice*. Vol. 1: *Realism and Naturalism*. Cambridge: Cambridge UP, 1981.

—— *The Shakespeare Revolution*. Cambridge: Cambridge UP, 1977.

Suhamy, Henri. "The Authenticity of the Hecate Scenes in *Macbeth*: Arguments and Counter-Arguments." *French Essays on Shakespeare and His Contemporaries: "What would France with us?"* Ed. Jean-Marie Maguin and Michèle Willems. Newark: U of Delaware P, 1995. 271–88.

Swanston, Roderick. "*Macbeth*, by William Shakespeare, Almeida Theatre." Rev. of *Macbeth*, dir. John Caird. *Times Literary Supplement* 21 Jan. 2005. Rpt. *Online Review London*. 18 Jan. 2006 <http://www.onlinereviewlondon.com>.

Taine, Hippolyte. "From *A History of English Literature*." Trans. H. Van Laun. *Shakespeare in Europe*. Ed. Oswald LeWinter. Cleveland: Meridian-World, 1963. 191–222.

Taylor, Charles. *Sources of the Self: The Making of the Modern Identity*. Cambridge: Harvard UP, 1989.

Tennenhouse, Leonard. *Power on Display: The Politics of Shakespeare's Genres*. London: Routledge, Chapman and Hall, 1986.

Thomas, Sian. "Lady Macbeth." *Performing Shakespeare's Tragedies Today: The Actor's Perspective*. Ed. Michael Dobson. Cambridge: Cambridge UP, 2006. 95–105.

Thomson, Peter. *On Actors and Acting*. Exeter: U of Exeter P, 2000.

—— *Shakespeare's Theatre*. 2nd ed. London: Routledge, 1992.

Tiffany, Grace. "*Macbeth*, Paternity, and the Anglicization of James I." *Studies in the Humanities* 23.2 (1996): 148–62.

Tillyard, E.M.W. *Shakespeare's History Plays*. London: Chatto & Windus, 1944.

Tiny Ninja Theater Presents Macbeth. 2001. Tiny Ninja Theater. 12 Dec. 2006 <http://www.tinyninjatheater.com/macbeth/>.

Traversi, Derek A. *An Approach to Shakespeare*. 2nd ed. Garden City: Doubleday Anchor, 1956.

Tredell, Nicolas. *Shakespeare, Macbeth: A Reader's Guide to Essential Criticism*. Houndmills: Palgrave Macmillan, 2006.

Trivedi, Poonam. "Interculturalism of Indigenization: Modes of Exchange, Shakespeare East and West." *Shakespeare and His Contemporaries in Performance*. Ed. Edward J. Esche. Aldershot: Ashgate, 2000. 73–88.

—— " 'Folk Shakespeare': The Performance of Shakespeare in Traditional Indian Forms." *India's Shakespeare: Translation, Interpretation, and Performance*. Ed. Poonam Trivedi and Dennis Bartholomeusz. Newark: U of Delaware P, 2005. 171–92.

Trubowitz, Rachel. " 'The single state of man': Androgyny in *Macbeth* and *Paradise Lost*." *Papers on Language & Literature* 26.3 (1990): 305–33.

Valbuena, Olga L. *Subjects to the King's Divorce: Equivocation, Infidelity, and Resistance in Early Modern England*. Bloomington: Indiana UP, 2003.

Vickers, Brian. *The Artistry of Shakespeare's Prose*. London: Methuen, 1968.

——, ed. *Shakespeare: The Critical Heritage*. 6 vols. London: Routledge & Kegan Paul, 1974–81.

Viswanathan, Gauri. *Masks of Conquest: Literary Study and British Rule in India*. New York: Columbia UP, 1989.

Wain, John, ed. *Shakespeare:* Macbeth. Casebook series. 1969. Rpt. Nashville: Aurora, 1970.

Waith, Eugene M. "Manhood and Valor in Two Shakespearean Tragedies." *ELH* 17.4 (1950): 265–68.

We Work Again. U.S. Works Progress Administration, 1937.

Weil, Judith. *Service and Dependency in Shakespeare's Plays*. Cambridge: Cambridge UP, 2005.

Weimann, Robert. "Theatrical Space in Shakespeare's Playhouse: Revisiting *Locus* and *Platea* in *Timon* and *Macbeth*." *The Shakespearean International Yearbook* 2 (2002): 203–17.

Wells, Stanley, and Gary Taylor, with John Jowett and William Montgomery. *William Shakespeare: A Textual Companion*. Oxford: Clarendon, 1987.

Wheeler, Thomas. Macbeth: *An Annotated Bibliography*. New York: Garland, 1990.

Whitney, Charles. *Early Responses to Renaissance Drama*. Cambridge: Cambridge UP, 2006.

Wickham, Glynne. "Hell-Castle and Its Door-Keeper." *Shakespeare Survey* 19 (1966): 68–74.

Wilders, John. *Macbeth*. Shakespeare in Production series. Cambridge: Cambridge UP, 2004.

Wilks, John S. *The Idea of Conscience in Renaissance Tragedy*. London: Routledge, 1990.

Williams, Deanne. "Mick Jagger Macbeth." *Shakespeare Survey* 57 (2004): 145–58.

Williams, George Walton. " 'Time for such a word': Verbal Echoing in *Macbeth*." *Shakespeare Survey* 47 (1995): 153–59. Rpt. *Shakespeare and Language*. Ed. Catherine M.S. Alexander. Cambridge: Cambridge UP, 2004. 240–50.

Williams, Simon. *Shakespeare on the German Stage, Volume I: 1586–1914*. Cambridge: Cambridge UP, 1990.

—— "Taking Macbeth Out of Himself: Davenant, Garrick, Schiller and Verdi." *Shakespeare Survey* 57 (2004): 54–68.

—— "The Tragic Actor and Shakespeare." *The Cambridge Companion to Shakespeare on Stage*. Ed. Stanley Wells and Sarah Stanton. Cambridge: Cambridge UP, 2002. 118–36.

Wills, Garry. *Witches & Jesuits: Shakespeare's* Macbeth. New York: Oxford UP, 1995.

Willson, Robert F., Jr. "Fearful Punning: The Name Game in *Macbeth*." *Cahiers Élisabéthains* 15 (1979): 29–34.

Wilson, Richard. *Secret Shakespeare: Studies in Theatre, Religion and Resistance*. Manchester: Manchester UP, 2004.

Wolf, Matt. "*Macbeth*." Rev. of *Macbeth*, dir. John Caird. *Variety* 31 Jan. 2005. Rpt.

Variety. 18 Jan. 2006 <http://www.variety.com/review/VE1117926013?categoryid=33&cs=1&s=h&p=0>.

Woodbridge, Linda. *The Scythe of Saturn: Shakespeare and Magical Thinking.* Urbana: U of Illinois P, 1994.

—— "Shakespeare and Magical Grammar." *Style: Essays on Renaissance and Restoration Literature and Culture in Memory of Harriet Hawkins.* Newark: U of Delaware P, 2005. 84–98.

Worster, David. "Performance Options and Pedagogy: *Macbeth*." *Shakespeare Quarterly* 53.3 (2002): 362–78.

Wright, George T. "Shakespeare's Metre Scanned." *Reading Shakespeare's Dramatic Language: A Guide.* Ed. Sylvia Adamson, Lynette Hunter, Lynne Magnusson, Ann Thompson, and Katie Wales. London: Thomson Learning, 2001. 51–70.

Wright, Iain. "All Done with Mirrors: Macbeth's Dagger Discovered." *Heat* 10 (2005).

—— " 'Come like shadowes, so depart': The Ghostly Kings in *Macbeth*." *The Shakespearean International Yearbook* 6 (2006): 215–29.

—— "Perspectives, Prospectives, Sibyls and Witches: King James Progresses to Oxford." *Renaissance Perspectives.* Ed. Jan Lloyd Jones and Graham Cullum. Melbourne: Australian Academic, 2006 (forthcoming).

Young, David. *The Action to the Word: Structure and Style in Shakespearean Tragedy.* New Haven: Yale UP, 1990.

Zaro, Juan J. "Translating from Exile: León Felipe's Shakespeare *Paraphrases*." *Latin American Shakespeares.* Ed. Bernice W. Kliman and Rick J. Santos. Madison: Fairleigh Dickinson UP, 2005. 92–111.

Ziegler, Georgianna. "Accommodating the Virago: Nineteenth-century Representations of Lady Macbeth." *Shakespeare and Appropriation.* Ed. Christy Desmet and Robert Sawyer. London: Routledge, 1999. 119–41.

Zimmerman, Susan. "Duncan's Corpse." *A Feminist Companion to Shakespeare.* Ed. Dympna Callaghan. Oxford: Blackwell, 2000. 320–38.

Zola, Émile. "Preface to the Second Edition." 1868. *Thérèse Raquin.* Trans. Leonard Tancock. Harmondsworth: Penguin, 1962. 21–27.

2 Sovereignty and treason in *Macbeth*

Rebecca Lemon

However much treason and sovereignty, Macbeth's supernatural dagger and Duncan's "golden blood" (2.3.110) might appear distinct in *Macbeth*, a generation of Shakespeare scholars have helped highlight the unsettling connections between these two categories of political philosophy. Challenging the emphasis on *Macbeth* as a royalist celebration of King James VI and I's absolute sovereignty against the threat of treason—a reading carefully articulated by Alvin Kernan and Henry Paul—critics have drawn attention to the play's "radically ambigious effects" or, as Stephen Mullaney writes, its "amphibology" (Coddon 485; Mullaney).[1] This ambiguity appears most pointedly in the play's political representations: even as it depicts the horrors of treason, the play offers a critique of sovereign power, at least as such power relies on treason and tyranny to establish and maintain its rule (Coddon; Mullaney). Indeed, rather than supporting sovereign power at any cost, the play legitimates tyrannicide as Malcolm and his allies unseat Macbeth. The play thus purports, as Alan Sinfield cogently argues, "to discriminate Macbeth's violence from that legitimately deployed by the state" (101), but this distinction serves merely to justify tyrannicide in the name of the state. David Scott Kastan also illuminates the persistent connection of traitors to sovereigns in the play, evident in the doubling of Malcolm and Macbeth as monarchomachs: "the play both begins and ends with an attack upon established rule, with a loyal nobility rewarded with new titles, and with the execution of a rebellious thane of Cawdor" (174).

Contributing to these studies of political philosophy in *Macbeth*, this chapter filters the categories of treason and sovereignty through the titular hero. Specifically, I analyze the tensions defining Macbeth: what are the political and dramatic effects of combining the categories of sovereignty and treason in this character? Why might Shakespeare, particularly in 1606, create a play about sovereigns who are usurpers, and rebels who are legitimate rulers? In order to answer these questions, this essay begins by assessing the portraits of treason and sovereignty represented by Duncan, Macbeth, Malcolm, and Edward. I then turn to debates about legitimate kingship, tyranny, and rebellion, contemporary to Shakespeare's audience, in order to deepen our understanding of the play's nuanced depiction of treason. Although *Macbeth*, on one level, offers a highly sensational depiction of the crime, its subtlety appears in Shakespeare's attempt to split tyrannicide from king-killing. As a result, he differentiates between two types of treason, one committed in the name of the state and the common good, and the other out of personal interest. Treason, the play suggests, like sovereignty, takes multiple forms. Since the law of treason in Shakespeare's time does not make such a distinction, and since royal polemicists condemned tyrannicide, Shakespeare's portrait paradoxically challenges contemporary theories of absolute sovereignty and definitions of treason while at the same time celebrating the role of legitimate and even mystical kingship in stabilizing the state.

Four sovereigns

Duncan's virtues are so evident that even the Macbeths, as they prepare to murder him, praise him as well. Macbeth hesitates, telling his wife of Duncan, "We will proceed no further in this business:/ He hath honour'd me of late" (1.7.31–32). Lady Macbeth too, famously, pauses before the murder: "Had he not resembled/ My father as he slept, I had done't" (2.2.12–33). Duncan makes treason a challenge—he is a grateful leader and a father figure. Shakespeare helps establish the legitimacy of Duncan's rule through a strain of natural imagery running throughout the play, as Derek Traversi and G. Wilson Knight have convincingly shown. Traversi writes, for example, how Duncan's function in the play lies in "the images of beauty and fertility which surround his person and confer substance and consistency upon the 'symbolic' value of his rule" (151). As the sun, Duncan shines gratitude and warmth on all his noblemen who as a result appear "like stars" (1.4.41). Further, he claims "to plant" Macbeth and "will labour/ To make [him] full of growing" (1.4.28–29). As Banquo puts it, he can serve as Duncan's "harvest" (1.4.33), the fruits of his careful rulership.

Such natural imagery, reinforcing Duncan's sovereignty, contrasts starkly with the images surrounding Macbeth. Even as Duncan celebrates his noblemen as stars, Macbeth finds the light of stars threatening: "Stars, hide your fires!/ Let not light see my black and deep desires" (1.4.50–51). Lady Macbeth also celebrates such darkness, summoning "thick Night" filled with the "dunnest smoke of Hell" (1.5.50–51). This strain of imagery climaxes with Macbeth's "Come, seeling Night" speech as he prepares to murder Banquo and Fleance (3.2.46–55). Here, the heavy-handed imagery of night and day, associated with Macbeth and Duncan respectively, continues: "Good things of Day begin to droop and drowse,/ Whiles Night's black agents to their preys do rouse" (52–53). Macbeth's language is riddled with visual oppositions that recall the brightness of Duncan's "silver skin lac'd with his golden blood" (2.3.110). Other natural images reinforce the opposition of Duncan to Macbeth, helping to idealize the murdered king even before his death. The cheerful "martlet" (1.6.4) noted by Banquo and Duncan contrasts with the "raven" (1.5.38), the "owl" (2.2.3), and the "crow" (3.2.50), the carnivorous birds invoked by the Macbeths.

Macbeth's highly sensational portrait of treason resonates with contemporaneous texts by crown-sponsored authors. King James's speech to Parliament after the discovery of the 1605 Gunpowder Plot, the Catholic attempt to blow up the Parliament building on its opening day of November 5, rehearses the "fearfull Chaos" of the treason which would have "sent forth of the bottome of the Stygian lake such sulphured smoke, furious flames, and fearefull thunder, as should have by their diabolicall Domesday destroyed and defaced" the country (*The King's Book* sig. E3r).[2] William Barlow's sermon after the plot also employs such language: the "false-hearted rebels" dwell in "the lowest pit," while the king's "resplendent brightness" shines so that "all the kingdomes of Christendome may receive their light" (sigs. E2r–E3r). With the attempted treason, "these lights thus gloriouslie shining in this golden candlesticke . . . would have at once blowne out" (sig. E3r).

The portraits of treason and sovereignty in *Macbeth* are more subtle, however, than the above, schematic analysis admits. While opposing Duncan to Macbeth, sovereign to traitor, gardener to sorcerer, Shakespeare also exposes, appropriately in this play, how "fair is foul, and foul is fair" (1.1.11). Not only is Macbeth a paradoxical combination of traitor and sovereign, a point I develop below, but also Duncan, despite his evident virtues, demonstrates a host of often-noted weaknesses—Shakespeare thus compromises what we might initially view as an idealized portrait of sovereignty. Duncan is, after all, a baffled king. His first line is a question: "What bloody man is that?" (1.2.1), and his interrogative mood, to adopt Maynard Mack's famous characterization of *Hamlet*, continues over the next scenes: "Who comes here?" (46), "Whence cam'st thou?" (49), "Is the execution done on Cawdor? Or [*sic*] not/ Those in commission yet return'd?" (1.4.1–2), "Where's the Thane of Cawdor?" (1.6.20). He seems, as Harry Berger, Jr. aptly writes, "almost as unclear about the rapidly changing state of war as he is about his thanes of Cawdor" ("The Early Scenes" 17; see also Berger, "Text against Performance").

When not questioning his subjects for crucial information on the war, Duncan plays the perfect audience member, offering brief affirmations of the speeches delivered by his subjects: "O valiant cousin! Worthy gentleman!" (1.2.24), "Great happiness!" (59), "My worthy Cawdor!" (1.4.47). Duncan's demeanor, that is to say, is hardly sovereign, in the sense of a ruler governing over his subjects and nation. Instead, he seems more dependent upon them, relying on their narratives in order to rule effectively. Of course, one might ask what king is not dependent on his subjects, and Duncan's questioning manner could be a sign of a good rather than a tyrannous ruler. He depends on his captains and foot soldiers, and does not pretend otherwise.

In addition to his questioning stance, however, Duncan seems, more worryingly, out of touch with his environment. In some of the play's funniest lines, Duncan famously describes his soon-to-be coffin, namely Macbeth's castle, as a "pleasant seat" whose "air/ Nimbly and sweetly recommends itself/ Unto our gentle senses" (1.6.1–3). If we hesitate to fault Duncan for trusting the hospitality of his recently-decorated subject, the king's timing in electing his son as his successor makes him more culpable. As David Norbrook has most clearly articulated, *Macbeth*'s immediate narrative sources record that the Scottish practice of succession, tanistry, would place Macbeth as Duncan's successor, not Malcolm: through elective kingship or tanistry, succession was determined by alternating between royal lines, rather than simply through primogeniture (86).[3] Yet Duncan elects his own son in 1.4, of which Norbrook writes, "if Duncan has to nominate his son, presumably the implication is that he could have nominated someone else, that the system is not one of pure primogeniture" (94). Electing to follow the newer system of primogeniture rather than tanistry, which would favor Macbeth, Duncan nominates his own son as king as part of the postwar spoils, an action that is ill-timed and impolitic given Macbeth's own recent triumph in the war in contrast to Malcolm's captivity.

Not only does Duncan fail to read his environment correctly but he also seems to lack the interpretive skills necessary to understand his enemies. This is particularly true, as I have argued elsewhere, in the episodes concerning the first Thane of Cawdor (Lemon). Duncan can hardly be faulted for passing the traitor's title onto Macbeth, although the dramatic irony of this decision only reinforces the king's unfortunate choices. But when he claims of Cawdor, "he was a gentleman on whom I built/ An absolute trust" (1.4.14–15), he highlights the instability of his own sovereignty. He builds his kingdom with trust for traitors, not only with the first Thane of Cawdor, as he admits here, but with the second Cawdor as well. As Duncan claims, Macbeth is "so valiant" that "in his commendations I am fed;/ It is a banquet to me" (1.4.54–56). Betrayed in his absolute trust for one traitor, Duncan now finds temporary nourishment in the poison of another. Beginning the play with a series of questions, relying on his subjects for answers, and trusting two sets of traitors while his country is at war, Duncan erodes monarchical sovereignty through his seemingly benign misrule. As Michael Hawkins writes, "many of the attributes ascribed to Duncan have a questionable double edge in a king" (173).

What, then, do these two readings of Duncan—as idealized and culpable—tell us about Shakespeare's portrait of sovereignty in the play? Duncan, it seems, for all his virtues cannot rule effectively during a time of traumatic crisis. Too trusting, he fails to battle effectively those mutinous traitors that fill Scotland's landscape: Cawdor, Macdonwald, Macbeth, and the "Kerns" and "Gallowglasses" of the "western isles" (1.2.12–13). If the vulnerability of Duncan's rule, given his evident virtues, seems perplexing, the sovereignty theory of Niccolò Machiavelli helps illuminate precisely the difficulties facing such generous rulers. In *The Prince* Machiavelli writes, "There is nothing so self-consuming as generosity: the more you practise it, the less you will be able to continue to practise it" (57). In the case of Duncan, this self-consuming generosity appears first with his announcement of Macbeth's promotion to Cawdor, and second with his election of Malcolm as successor.

Since each honor is inimitable, once it has been rewarded, Duncan has ceded power away from himself onto the traitor who will kill him and the son who will succeed him.[4]

Duncan's vulnerability comes, as Machiavelli might diagnose it, in being loved rather than feared. "It is," Machiavelli famously writes, "much safer to be feared than loved" (59). This is because, he elaborates, "love is sustained by a bond of gratitude which, because men are excessively self-interested, is broken whenever they see a chance to benefit themselves" (59). The direct influence of Machiavelli on Shakespeare has been the subject of much speculation, with Quentin Skinner and Richard Tuck helping to establish the influence of Machiavelli throughout continental Europe in the sixteenth century and in England primarily in the later seventeenth century.[5] If a direct relation between Machiavelli's theories of statecraft and Shakespeare's representation of rulership in *Macbeth* is unlikely, nevertheless Machiavelli's emphasis on self-interest helps bring forward the apparently contradictory elements of Macbeth's relation to Duncan: he at once celebrates the king's rule, acknowledging his generosity, and destroys such rule as a means of benefiting himself.

While Shakespeare offers a model of love-based sovereignty in Duncan, he also offers its opposite through Macbeth: rule based in fear. Under Macbeth's rule, as his opponents claim, "each new morn/ new widows howl, new orphans cry" (4.3.4–5), a description by Macduff that reinforces the opposition of Macbeth and daylight. The country is, as Rosse claims, "almost afraid to know itself" (4.3.165). Yet the fear and horror in Scotland does not aid Macbeth's sovereignty, primarily because he inspires, as Machiavelli warns, not only fear but hatred: "a ruler must make himself feared in such a way that, even if he does not become loved, he does not become hated" (59). Through excessive cruelty, attempting to murder Banquo and Fleance, as well as Macduff and his family, the Macbeths appear as a "butcher and his fiend-like Queen" (5.9.35). As a result, Macbeth cannot govern effectively, being an illegitimate and murderous ruler: "those he commands move only in command,/ Nothing in love" (5.2.19–20)—his troops desert him or fail to fight with conviction.

Furthermore, in ruling Scotland the Macbeths inspire not only fear and hatred in others, but also experience fearful anxiety themselves. After the murder, Lady Macbeth's first line, "I am afraid" (2.2.9), anticipates Macbeth's: "I am afraid to think what I have done" (50). Macbeth later confesses "fears in Banquo" (3.1.48), he and Lady Macbeth "eat [their] meal in fear" (3.2.17), and he suffers, as he claims, the "initiate fear" (3.5.142) of the novice to murder. Only the witches can set his "fear aright" (4.1.74). The fear Macbeth inspires in others offers him little repose, instead infecting his experience of his own rule from the moment he plots it.

Machiavelli's political theory helps draw attention to the play's starkly contrasting portraits of sovereignty, one practiced by Duncan, the other by Macbeth, one vulnerable and legitimate, and the other treasonous. Yet the play's representation of sovereignty extends beyond this opposition. In its second half, Shakespeare introduces, in Edward and Malcolm, two ruler-figures who complicate the contrast evident in Duncan and Macbeth between legitimate and treasonous sovereignty. This complication occurs because, even as the English king Edward represents a model of godly rule, the companion portrait of Malcolm is more tangled: he practices both sovereignty (he is the legitimate heir seeking to protect the state) and treason (he rebels against the ruling king). Through his combination of treason and sovereignty, Malcolm ironically combines, as we shall see, the rulership of his father and his opponent.

Two traitors

While Malcolm represents himself as one who "never was forsworn" (4.3.126), who has barely "coveted what was mine own," and who never falsely speaks, in gaining the Scottish throne he must nevertheless overthrow the fearful, usurping, but still-reigning king. The play appears to legitimate this rebellion on a number of levels. In condensing his source material in Holinshed, Shakespeare makes the reign of Macbeth appear short-lived and bloody. The historical Macbeth, by contrast, ruled successfully for ten years, a point that Norbrook effectively explores in detail. In revising his sources, Shakespeare signals his primary interest in depicting Macbeth as a usurper and tyrant, rather than as a legitimate ruler.

The argument for disobedience and even tyrannicide gains further credit through Malcolm's position as legitimate, but not eager, successor. Nominated by Duncan, Malcolm exhibits a notable lack of ambition for the throne, and thus his attacks on Macbeth seem the product of his interest in the common good, not his own welfare. The play insists that he is cajoled into rebellion, living in comfort in England and only agreeing to counter Macbeth when approached by his desperate countrymen. He repeatedly positions himself as a follower of a rebellion organized by others, telling Macduff "I put myself to thy direction" (4.3.122), and "What I am truly,/ Is thing, and my poor country's, to command" (131–32).[6] Here, the future king is careful to place the agency of rebellion elsewhere, thereby protecting himself from accusations of self-interest.

With Malcolm as legitimate successor, Macbeth's enemies call the usurping king "untitled" (4.3.104), and therefore not sovereign. Since Macbeth never held office of king at all, despite his coronation ceremony at Scone, he can be lawfully deposed. Furthermore, characters repeatedly emphasize that Macbeth is a "tyrant," "usurper," and "traitor," terms that help reinforce the illegitimacy of his kingship and the righteousness of rebellion.[7] Starting in 3.6 in a brief scene with Lennox, characters including Macduff, Malcolm, Rosse, Menteth, Siward, and an unnamed Lord repeatedly level the charge of tyrant against the reigning king.[8] Indeed, as Mary Ann McGrail most recently argues, Macbeth "presents us with a tyrant distilled to his essentials" (32).

He embodies the contemporary definition of a tyrant: he is usurping and self-interested, fulfilling George Buchanan's claims that "it is of the nature of tyrants that they seize office without being legally chosen, and rule autocratically." Further, he writes, tyrants have "power neither circumscribed by any bonds of the laws nor subject to any judicial investigation" (Buchanan 89).[9] Similarly, as the author of *Vindiciae Contra Tyrannos*, likely the Huguenot resister Philippe Duplessis-Mornay, defines it, "rulers are called 'kings' when they promote the people's interest and are called 'tyrants,' as Aristotle says, when they seek only to promote their own" (*Vindiciae* 172).[10]

Macbeth's opponents also offer a religious justification for their rebellion. Macbeth is, as they claim, "devilish" (4.3.117), he is "damn'd" (56), while his opponents represent the "holy king" (3.6.30), or "holy angel" (45). The groundwork has already been laid for such religious rhetoric, in the depiction of Duncan's "golden blood" and the Macbeths' "smoke of hell." But now this rhetoric does more powerful work, given that it justifies tyrannicide. The portrait of Edward bolsters such a religious call to arms since the model of sanctified kingship helps support a fantasy of anointed rule destroyed by Macbeth but potentially achievable under Malcolm and Banquo's descendants. With God's aid, Scotland could then receive the curative powers exhibited by the divinely anointed Edward, who heals "a crew of wretched souls" (141), "strangely-visited people,/ All swol'n and ulcerous, pitiful to the eye" (151). "This good King" touches "the Evil" (4.3.146–47) in his sick subjects by hanging "a golden stamp about their necks" (4.3.154). While the king's healing touch refers to his cure for scrofula, not treason, terms such as "evil," "strangely-visited" and "wretched souls" recall the witches and the Macbeths, characters who appear to be, as Edward's visitors are, "the despair of surgery" (152). In addition to curing his country's ill, Edward boasts a form of self-protection lacking in Scotland. While Macbeth's utter faith in the witches creates the blindspot that precipitates his downfall, Edward, by contrast, does not need to trust in his subjects. Instead, he "hath a heavenly gift of prophecy" (157), precisely what Macbeth disastrously seeks in the form of the witches.

The play's portrait of Edward—a brief fantasy of legitimate, godly kingship—is delivered by Malcolm, as if to suggest that the future Scottish king, by proxy, enjoys such favor as well. Unlike his two Scottish predecessors, Malcolm also "touches" his subjects, attempting to cure or at least expose their illnesses. That is to say, he directly engages with the possible corruption of his countrymen: through the elaborate and forced ritual with Macduff in 4.3, Shakespeare depicts a future king who tests loyalties in order to protect himself and his country. Malcolm pretends, in his exchange with Macduff, to be voluptuous and avaricious, claiming that, were he king, he would "pour the sweet milk of concord into Hell/ Uproar the universal peace, confound/ All unity on earth" (4.3.97–99). These lines, exaggerating the characteristics of tyrannous rule, resonate with the sensational depictions of Macbeth earlier in the play. Malcolm, however, unlike Macbeth, controls this portrait.

Indeed, Andrew Hadfield describes this scene as one in which Malcolm puts "his scholarly book-learning into practice, testing out what he has learned from authorities in the real political world" (56). He willingly depicts himself in such hyperbolic terms as a means of testing his subjects—he has not capitulated to witches nor lost command of his own desires. He can "touch" evil, representing himself as a cistern of vice, only to "abjure/ The taints and blames" (4.3.123–24).

Malcolm's self-sufficiency appears, more specifically, in his virginity. As Janet Adelman most powerfully argues, the future king, being "yet/ Unknown to woman" (125–26), avoids the frightening specter of female sexuality evident in both Lady Macbeth and the witches (Adelman 146). Malcolm thus represents a form of patriarchal power untainted by femininity. In relation to questions of sovereignty, his virginity proves his self-dependence, verifying his almost inhuman lack of need for his countrymen or women. Barely speaking after the murder of his father, he flees to England alone. Then, planning his return to battle Macbeth, he nevertheless practices "modest wisdom" rather than "over-credulous haste" (4.3.119–20) in deceiving Macduff. Only when Macduff deems his father "a most sainted King" and his mother to have been "oft'ner upon her knees than on her feet" (109–10) does Malcolm relent, suggesting how the future king participates in an idealization of his own origins: with his saintly parents acknowledged, Malcolm is able to reassert himself as equally virtuous and untainted.

Associated with the kingship of Edward, Malcolm offers a model of self-sovereignty through his restrained speech and virginal body. Unlike Duncan and Macbeth, Malcolm refuses to trust his countrymen or women in any form. This model of kingship is discomforting because his use of deception resonates with the equivocation of traitors and witches: his tactics of misrepresentation recall the Macbeths greeting Duncan into their deadly castle. Macduff acknowledges such discomfort in his initially silent response to Malcolm's trickery, excusing himself by claiming "such welcome and unwelcome things at once/ 'Tis hard to reconcile" (4.3.138–39). Macduff's word "reconcile" is particularly apt here: how can he simultaneously celebrate Malcolm's virtues and recover from the future king's hazing ritual? Apparent reconciliation becomes possible only in the name of necessity, when Macduff turns his attention away from his discomfort with Malcolm to a much more immediate tragedy: the murder of his family by Macbeth. Now Malcolm's suspicion, isolation, and trickery seems a "welcome" and justified form of protectionism given Macbeth's butchery. Temporarily displaced is consideration of Malcolm's more "unwelcome" practice of absolutist self-sovereignty.

One tyrant

However strong the play's argument in favor of unseating Macbeth may be, it nonetheless challenges both legal statute and royal polemics among Shakespeare's contemporaries, which condemn king-killing even in the case

of tyranny. English treason law, in the form of the 1534 Treason Act, regu-
lated not only murder attempts against the king, but also slanderous name
calling, known as "treason by words." This 1534 Act condemned as traitors
those subjects who

> do maliciously wish, will or desire by words or writing, or by craft imagine,
> invent, practice or attempt any bodily harm to be done or committed to
> the King's most loyal person, the Queen's or their heir's apparent, or
> to deprive them or any of them of the dignity, title or name of their
> royal estates, or slanderously and maliciously publish and pronounce, by
> express writing or words, that the King our sovereign lord should be
> heretic, schismatic, tyrant, infidel or usurper of the crown.
>
> (Record Commission 508)[11]

This legislation regulates, then, precisely the type of language on tyranny and
usurpation employed by Malcolm and his allies against Macbeth.

Of course, a strong body of resistance theory, including the often-reprinted
Vindiciae Contra Tyrannos, counsels subjects to resist tyranny by arguing that
government exists by popular consent rather than divine right. The author of
Vindiciae argues that subjects have a pressing duty to rebel against the illegal
rule of usurping tyrants. As he writes,

> The obligation between prince and people is ever reciprocal and mutual.
> He promises to be a just prince; they, to obey him if he is one. The people,
> therefore, is obligated to the prince conditionally, he to the people abso-
> lutely. If the condition is not fulfilled, the people are released, the com-
> pact voided, and the obligation nullified. . . . The officers of the kingdom,
> therefore, when all or a good number have agreed, are permitted to use
> force against a tyrant. And they are not only permitted but obliged, as
> part of the duty of their office, and they have no excuse if they should fail
> to act.
>
> (*Vindiciae* 191)[12]

According to this theory of government by contract, subjects owe no duty to
an illegal tyrant. Indeed, in the name of the law and the state, subjects must
rebel in order to restore order. To do otherwise would be, as Duplessis-
Mornay argues, base.[13]

An equally vigorous counter-argument, mounted by those theorists of
absolute sovereignty, condemned rebellion as ungodly and illegal. In his 1576
Six livres de la république, French political theorist Jean Bodin writes that it is
illegal for "any subject individually, or all of them in general, to make an
attempt on the honor or the life of the monarch, either by way of force or by
way of law, even if he has committed all the misdeeds, impieties, and cruelties
that one could mention" (115).[14] Here, obedience does not hinge on the ruler's
merit, but instead on the subject's duty. King James and his supporters

offered similar arguments against tyrannicide. As James writes in *A Remonstrance for the Right of Kings* (1615), a text produced in the political controversy surrounding post-Gunpowder Plot legislation, "I will not deny that an heretical Prince is a plague . . . but a breach made by one mischief must not be filled up with greater inconvenience: an error must not be shocked and shouldered with disloyalty, not heresie with perjurie, not impietie with sedition and armed rebellion against God and King" (235). James develops a familiar line of argument: bad kings, however tyrannical, are a form of godly "plague" that people must endure before God offers deliverance. Subjects cannot take matters into their own hands, because this action would simply heap disease on disease, rather than offering a true remedy for the plague itself.

A sermon delivered after the Gunpowder Plot spells out this logic in greater detail, elaborating on St. Paul's statement in Romans 13 that "he that resisteth receiveth unto himself damnation." The preacher, John Buckeridge, writes:

> If hee be a good Prince, causa est, hee is the cause of thy good, temporall and eternall; if any evill prince, occasio est, He is an occasion of thy eternall good, by thy temporall evill. Si bonus, nutritor est tuus; si malus, tentator tuus est; if he be a good King, he is thy nourse, receive thy nourishment with obedience; If he be an evill Prince, hee is thy tempter, receive thy trial with patience; so there's no resistance, either thou must obey good Princes willingly, or endure evill tyrants patiently.
>
> (Buckeridge 3)

Like Bodin and James, this minister acknowledges the difficulties of tyranny. However evil and heretical such a ruler may be (and here we can view Macbeth as the limit case), nevertheless the proper solution lies in passive obedience to authority.

The stakes in the tyrannicide debate were particularly high after the 1605 plot. As David Wootton writes, "in James's reign, particularly after the Gunpowder Plot of 1605, tyrannicide was a doctrine that only Catholics dared defend: to deny the absolute authority of the king appeared to open the way to the legitimation of Catholic plotting" (Wootton 30).[15] Positioning *Macbeth* in relation to such debates on tyrannicide complicates the long-held association of the play with royalist celebrations after the Gunpowder Plot. Certainly, the play has historical associations with the plot, which Garry Wills's book-length study of *Macbeth* carefully illustrates (Wills). First, in the comic relief of the Porter's speech, the play refers directly to a figure involved in the plot, Father Henry Garnet—the famous "farmer" who is "hanged on expectation of plenty." Furthermore, on August 7, 1606, the play was allegedly performed before Queen Anne and her brother, King Christian of Denmark, in a celebration of the plot's failure.[16] Henry Paul, in *The Royal Play of Macbeth*, and Alvin Kernan, in *Shakespeare, the King's Playwright*, offer the most detailed explorations of the play's alleged role in royal celebrations.

Kernan notes that *Macbeth* was "probably written especially for this import-ant occasion" of royal performance before Anne and Christian, pointing to the play's references to equivocation, Father Garnet, and, most significantly, to James's own royal lineage stretching back to Banquo (Kernan 76–77).[17] Kernan describes the play, especially in relation to its source in Holinshed, as "the synthesizing work of the propagandist" by which Shakespeare "trans-formed, to fit his patron's political myth, a petty power struggle in a primitive society . . . into a sacred event in the history of divine-right legitimacy" (78). The ascension of Malcolm, followed by that of Banquo's descendants, initiates this godly monarchy in Scotland.

Given that James wrote directly against tyrannicide in his political tracts and that English law deemed king-killing to be treason, however, Malcolm's triumph over the usurping Macbeth is not simply cause for celebration. Since Macbeth is the reigning sovereign, his deposition, while arguably necessary, is nevertheless treasonous. Indeed, Macbeth and Malcolm both practice a form of treasonous sovereignty, coming to the throne through violent murder rather than through simple succession. Malcolm's violence is underscored even before his attack on Macbeth, when he attempts to capitalize on Macduff's losses. He counsels the grieving widower to make "med'cines of our great revenge" (4.3.214), using the loss of his wife and children as a spur in the fight against Scotland's king: "let grief/ Convert to anger" (228–29). Having begun this scene feigning reluctance to take up the crown, Malcolm now betrays such eagerness that he hardly pauses to comfort Macduff, and instead seeks "manly" (235) action from personal loss. This response to grief reminds the audience that, while a grieving son himself, Malcolm never appears sorrowful onstage. Instead, in 2.3 he converts, as he counsels Malcolm to do, loss into action when he immediately flees the murder scene as a means of self-protection.

Between Malcolm's awkward trickery in 4.3 and his willing participation in revolt, the play demonstrates the new king's familiarity with deception, recall-ing the tactics of Macbeth more than his father Duncan. Indeed, Malcolm's battle strategy fulfills the witches' equivocating warning about Birnam wood: he orders that every soldier chop a branch and "bear't before him" in order to "shadow/ The numbers of our host, and make discovery/ Err in report of us" (5.4.5–6). Dwelling in "shadow" and error as a means of deceiving his enemies, Malcolm relates to the natural landscape, which supplied the images of fertility characteristic of Duncan, through a destructive impulse: he hews down the wood to fuel his cause. Furthermore, he evinces a comfortable familiarity with precisely the types of deceitful practices that neither Duncan nor Macbeth could anticipate or understand.

Despite his deceptive and violent bid for the throne, in his final speech Malcolm attempts to restore precisely the oppositional vocabulary that opens the play, as he divides sovereign and traitor, natural ruler and fiend. He first returns to his father's images of natural fertility, tending to tasks that "would be newly planted with the time" (5.9.31). Having chopped down Birnam wood, he now strives to become the fruitful gardener in keeping with his new role as king.[18] He also reiterates the play's structuring opposition between traitor and sovereign. Not naming Macbeth, Malcolm labels him a "dead butcher" who, with "his fiend-like Queen" ruled through "snares of watchful tyranny" (33–35). He will, he claims, by contrast, rule by "the grace of Grace" (38). He takes up his task with gratitude and generosity, evident in the creation of earls from thanes. This political shift from Scottish nobility towards the English model constitutes, as several scholars have noted, a fresh start for the country. No longer will the Thane of Cawdor's tainted title belong to any subject of Scotland. At the same time, this reordering helps align Malcolm's state with that of Edward's even more closely, reinforcing the political education he received in exile. He effects this revolution in government and cleanses his country of its traitorous thanes, however, by attempting to restore the rhetorical opposition of sovereign and traitor—an opposition perhaps appropriate in Edward's England, but belied in Scotland by his own treasonous sovereignty.

Macbeth constructs, then, a pardoxical case on the relationship of treason and sovereignty. Written in a context that would suggest a royalist argument, the play certainly celebrates legitimate sovereignty in the form of Edward. Yet this character never appears, as if to suggest that such divine rule in the context of troubled Scotland remains distant, foreign, and unachievable. Furthermore, the supposedly idealized figure of Duncan practices a baffled and ineffectual form of rule, inadequate to Scotland's crisis. Finally, Malcolm, despite evident merits and the right of succession, is a type of absolutist, who usurps the throne from the reigning, albeit illegitimate, king. The portraits of sovereignty and treason in *Macbeth* are thus richly various: on the one hand, the play condemns treason in language that could not be clearer. Indeed, the sensationalism of its portrait resonates with contemporary propaganda to such a degree that its inset scaffold speech and images of day and night could derive directly from pamphlets produced after the 1605 Gunpowder Plot. Yet this sensationalism only helps feed an argument in favor of tyrannicide, an argument that King James challenges in his own political writings. The play thus makes the radical move of supporting rebellion, but it does so in the name of Malcolm's absolutist, patriarchal, Christian orthodoxy. Whatever stability this second usurpation might offer Scotland, its terms are such that, for many audience members, it produces uneasiness just like the first.

Notes

1   Mullaney traces the term "amphibology" through George Puttenham's *The Arte of English Poesie*: it is the Greek term for ambiguity, and signifies the dangers of false prophecy.

2   *The King's Book* was printed only a month after the plot, and presents the official version of events. It is a composite publication containing "His Majesties Speech in this Parliament, together with a discourse of the manner of the discovery of this late intended treason," quoted here, and the "Discourse of the maner of the

discovery of this late intended Treason joyned with an Examination of some of the prisoners" (London, 1605).

3 Norbrook analyzes the representation of elective succession in Buchanan's *Rerum Scoticarum Historia* (Edinburgh, 1582).

4 We might contrast Duncan's nomination of his successor with Queen Elizabeth I's refusal to do so. As a result of her much-criticized reluctance, she continued to exercise royal power late into her reign rather than contending with a rival courtly circle surrounding England's future monarch.

5 On Tacitus, Bodin, and Machiavelli in England, see Skinner (1: 152–89; 2: 284–301); and Tuck (104–19).

6 However much Malcolm might claim to be in another's "direction," events of the play have repeatedly shown him to be someone in control of his destiny, rather than overwhelmed by it.

7 On tyranny in *Macbeth*, see McGrail; see also Bushnell.

8 The charge begins with the unnamed Lord in 3.6.22, 25, moves through Macduff, Malcolm, and Rosse's conversations in 4.3.12, 36, 45, 178, and then appears on the battlefield with 5.2.11 and 5.4.8.

9 Buchanan's text, published in 1579, was dedicated to young King James VI. The connection between Buchanan's resistance theory and Shakespeare's play has attracted significant critical attention. See especially Hadfield (43–58) and Norbrook.

10 The *Vindiciae* appeared in partial English translation in 1588, and a full translation in 1648.

11 On Thomas Cromwell and Thomas Audley's process of drafting the treason legislation between 1531 and 1534, see Elton; see also Bellamy (31).

12 In addition to *Vindiciae* and Buchanan's *De Jure Regni Apud Scotos* (1579) (see n. 9 above), see Ponet; see also Kingdon.

13 This contract theory reappears in the writings of Catholic resistance theorists, who defended rebellion in England on the grounds of the civil and religious tyranny of its monarchs (Holmes 150). For Catholic resistance theory, see [Persons]; Allen. See also Clancy; Milward (114–15); Salmon.

14 For the source of Carlisle's speech in Bodin, see Benjamin.

15 Wootton's use of the term "Catholics" elides seditious recusants with loyal Catholics, many of whom experienced increased persecution after the plot despite their allegiance to the Jacobean crown. He nevertheless helps illuminate the post-1605 atmosphere, when regicide, even against tyrants, became less defensible. See also Figgis (135). Since James's succession to the English throne challenged English law (namely the will of Henry VIII and the Act of 1584), the king would undermine his claim to the throne if he upheld English law over royal sovereignty, a point made by both Wootton and Figgis.

16 For debates about this first performance see Muir (xv–xxv); Paul (15–24). On the Gunpowder Plot, see Durst; Fraser; Haynes; Nicholls.

17 On this royal performance, in addition to Muir, Paul, and Wills listed above, see also Barroll (147) who discusses, in association with the question of Macbeth's topicality, the closing of the public theaters due to plague in June 1606, only one month after Garnet's execution.

18 On the links between kingship and gardening, see especially Shakespeare's *Richard II*, Act 3, scene 4.

Works cited

Adelman, Janet. *Suffocating Mothers: Fantasies of Maternal Origin in Shakespeare's Plays*, Hamlet *to* The Tempest. New York: Routledge, 1992.

Allen, Cardinal William. *A True, sincere and modest defence of English Catholics* (1584). Ed. R.M. Kingdon. Ithaca: Cornell UP, 1965.

Anonymous [attributed to Philippe Duplessis Mornay]. *Vindiciae Contra Tyrannos: or, concerning the legitimate power of a prince over the people, and of the people over a prince* (1579). In *Constitutionalism and Resistance in the Sixteenth Century: Three Treatises by Hotman, Beza, and Mornay*. Trans. Julian H. Franklin. New York: Pegasus, 1969.

Barlow, William. "The Sermon preached at Paules Cross, the tenth day of November, being the next Sunday after the discovery of this late horrible treason." London: Mathew Law, 1606.

Barroll, Leeds. *Politics, Plague, and Shakespeare's Theatre*. Ithaca: Cornell UP, 1991.

Bellamy, John. *The Tudor Law of Treason*. London: Routledge and Kegan Paul, 1979.

Benjamin, Edwin B. "Sir John Hayward and Tacitus." *Review of English Studies*, n.s. 8 (1957): 275–76.

Berger, Harry Jr. "The Early Scenes of *Macbeth*: Preface to a New Interpretation." *ELH* 47 (1980): 1–31.

—— "Text against Performance in Shakespeare: The Example of *Macbeth*." *Genre* 15: *The Power of Forms and the Form of Power in the English Renaissance*. Ed. Stephen Greenblatt. Norman: Pilgrim, 1982. 49–79.

Bodin, Jean. *On Sovereignty: Four Chapters from the Six Books of the Commonwealth*. Ed. and trans. Julian H. Franklin. Cambridge: Cambridge UP, 1992.

Buchanan, George. *The Powers of the Crown in Scotland [De Jure Regni Apud Scotos]*. Trans. Charles Flynn Arrowood. Austin: U of Texas P, 1949.

Buckeridge, John. "A sermon preached at Hampton Court before the Kings Majestie, on Tuesday the 23 of September, 1606 by John Buckeridge." London: Robert Barker, 1606.

Bushnell, Rebecca W. *Tragedies of Tyrants: Political Thought and Theater in the English Renaissance*. Ithaca: Cornell UP, 1990.

Clancy, T.H. *Papist Pamphleteers: The Allen–Persons Party and the Political Thought of the Counter-Reformation, 1572–1615*. Chicago: Loyola UP, 1964.

Coddon, Karin S. " 'Unreal Mockery:' Unreason and the Problem of Spectacle in *Macbeth*." *ELH* 56.3 (1989): 485–501.

Durst, Paul. *Intended Treason: What Really Happened in the Gunpowder Plot*. London: W.H. Allen, 1970.

Elton, G.R. *Policy and Police: The Enforcement of the Reformation in the Age of Thomas Cromwell*. Cambridge: Cambridge UP, 1972. 265–92.

Figgis, J. Neville. *The Theory of the Divine Right of Kings*. Cambridge: Cambridge UP, 1896.

Fraser, Antonia. *Faith and Treason: The Story of the Gunpowder Plot*. New York: Doubleday, 1996.

Hadfield, Andrew. *Shakespeare, Spenser, and the Matter of Britain*. Basingstoke: Palgrave Macmillan, 2004.

Hawkins, Michael. "History, Politics and *Macbeth*." *Focus on Macbeth*. Ed. John Russell Brown. London: Routledge, 1982. 155–87.

Haynes, Alan. *The Gunpowder Plot: Faith in Rebellion*. Dover: Alan Sutton, 1994.

Holmes, Peter. *Resistance and Compromise: The Political Thought of the Elizabethan Catholics*. Cambridge: Cambridge UP, 1982.

James VI and I. *The King's Book*. London: Robert Barker, 1605.

—— *A Remonstrance for the Right of Kings, and the independence of their crowns. The*

Political Works of James I. Ed. Charles Howard McIlwain. New York: Russell and Russell, 1965. 169–268.

Kastan, David Scott. *Shakespeare after Theory*. New York: Routledge, 1999.

Kernan, Alvin. *Shakespeare, the King's Playwright: Theatre in the Stuart Court, 1603–13*. New Haven: Yale UP, 1995.

Kingdon, Robert M. "Calvinism and Resistance Theory, 1550–1580." *Cambridge History of Political Thought 1450–1700*. Ed. J.H. Burns with the assistance of Mark Goldie. Cambridge: Cambridge UP, 1991. 193–218.

Knight, G. Wilson. *The Imperial Theme*. London: Methuen, 1957.

Lemon, Rebecca. "Scaffolds of Treason in Macbeth." *Theatre Journal* 54 (2002): 25–43.

McGrail, Mary Ann. *Tyranny in Shakespeare*. Lanham: Lexington, 2001.

Machiavelli, Niccolò dei. *The Prince*. Ed. Quentin Skinner and Russell Price. Cambridge: Cambridge UP, 1988. Rpt. 2001.

Milward, Peter. *Religious Controversies of the Elizabethan Age: A Survey of Printed Sources*. London: U of Nebraska P, 1977.

Muir, Kenneth. "Introduction." *Macbeth*. The Arden Shakespeare. London: Methuen, 1984. xiii–lxv.

Mullaney, Stephen. *The Place of the Stage: License, Play and Power in Renaissance England*. Ann Arbor: U of Michigan P, 1995.

Nicholls, Mark. *Investigating Gunpowder Plot*. Manchester: Manchester UP, 1991.

Norbrook, David. "*Macbeth* and the Politics of Historiography." *Politics of Discourse: The Literature and History of Seventeenth-Century England*. Ed. Kevin Sharpe and Steven N. Zwicker. Berkeley: U of California P, 1987. 78–116.

Paul, Henry. *The Royal Play of Macbeth*. New York: Macmillan, 1950.

[Persons, Robert.] *A Conference about the next succession to the crown of England*. n.p., 1594.

Ponet, John. "A Short Treatise of Politic Power." n.p., 1556.

Record Commission. *Statutes of the Realm*. Vol. 3. London: G. Eyre and A. Strahan, 1817.

Salmon, J.H.M. "Catholic Resistance Theory, Ultramonanism and the Royalist Response, 1580–1620." *Cambridge History of Political Thought 1450–1700*. Ed. J.H. Burns with the assistance of Mark Goldie. Cambridge: Cambridge UP, 1991. 219–53.

Sinfield, Alan. *Faultlines: Cultural Materialism and the Politics of Dissident Reading*. Berkeley: U of California P, 1992.

Skinner, Quentin. *The Foundations of Modern Political Thought*. 2 vols. Cambridge: Cambridge UP, 1978.

Traversi, D.A. *Approach to Shakespeare*. 2nd ed. New York: Doubleday Anchor, 1956.

Tuck, Richard. *Philosophy and Government, 1572–1651*. Cambridge: Cambridge UP, 1993.

Wills, Garry. *Witches and Jesuits: Shakespeare's* Macbeth. Oxford: Oxford UP, 1995.

Wootton, David. *Divine Right and Democracy: An Anthology of Political Writing in Stuart England*. London: Penguin, 1986.

3 "A rooted sorrow"

Scotland's unusable past[1]

Jonathan Baldo

Revisionist historians have recently disputed the assumption that a radical break separated Tudor and Stuart England, producing an overwhelming nostalgia for Elizabethan England upon the old queen's death. Challenging entrenched notions of an "idyllic national consensus" in the waning years of Elizabeth's reign and of the "Stuarts' universal unpopularity," John Watkins begins his study of Stuart representations of Elizabeth by questioning the widely held assumption "that the Stuarts departed so dramatically from Elizabeth's example that the differences were apparent to everyone" (Watkins 4–5). Still, the accession of James arguably produced at least one sudden and startling change: the inheritance by the more prosperous of the two nations of what many Elizabethans regarded as a troubling and violent past. If a nation is defined as a people who share a common history, invented or imagined through extensive, tacit agreements about what to remember and what to suppress, then what happens when a nation—already having substantially shaped and been shaped by an invented past—suddenly inherits a new one? That strikes me as the larger question posed by *Macbeth* to its first English audiences, who, armored with xenophobia and longstanding stereotypes about Scotland,[2] were likely to have interpreted the play very differently from Shakespeare's patron, King James.

Macbeth, a play that is often discussed for its value as Stuart propaganda, bears strong and troubling implications for the timely union question. After it was established in 1604, the Anglo-Scots Union Commission drew up proposals for the formal legal and political union of the two countries that were recently linked dynastically. From about 1603 to 1607, the union question was debated vigorously throughout England. A union of two kingdoms, however, requires at least a partial union of their pasts. *Macbeth* might be seen as Shakespeare's attempt to pose, if not to answer, the questions of how well these two histories might be united, and what use this newly acquired history might be to the English nation.[3]

*

When King James VI of Scotland assumed the English throne in 1603 to become James I of England, he immediately strove to unite the two kingdoms over which he ruled. The English Lower House refused to grant him his desired title of King of Great Britain by statute, whereupon he seized it by royal proclamation in November, 1604: the same means by which he required his British flag, the Union Jack, to be flown on both English and Scottish ships. He met with less success in trying to bring Scots onto the Privy Council and into the Court (Wormald 147). Though the same ruler occupied two thrones, it may be said that James even failed to unite the two crowns, which were governed by different rules of dynastic descent, let alone two Parliaments, judiciary systems, churches, cultures, and nations.[4] In 1606, the year in which *Macbeth* was most likely written, the union of the kingdoms was still the foremost theme of James's reign, though the play has rarely been discussed from the vantage point of the union issue.[5] Most topical readings of *Macbeth* have focused (quite successfully, I should add) on the Gunpowder Plot. An excellent recent essay by Neil Rhodes on Shakespeare and the union question makes no mention of *Macbeth*, noting instead the way in which James's political texts "can be seen to interact in significant ways with Shakespeare's own representation of union and kingship, most obviously in the second tetralogy of history plays and *King Lear*" (Rhodes 38). *King Lear*, with its potent image of a map of Britain divided into three regions, has for some time now been interpreted powerfully and persuasively in terms of the union question (Marcus 148–59). It is with the less obvious ways in which *Macbeth* comments on union, in however dubious, uncertain, and equivocating a manner, that I am concerned in this essay.

When Shakespeare's Scottish play was first staged, James's most strenuous and impassioned argument for union before the English Parliament was yet to take place, in 1607. Before he could deliver that speech, however, the idea had all but run aground in both kingdoms. As Jenny Wormald writes, "What the Union of the Crowns produced . . . was not the joy and peace of new Anglo-Scottish friendship. It meant loss of face on both sides. The English saw their court and government threatened by the influx of the Scots. The Scots were all too aware that they were unwelcome in London" (147). The hostility of the English was met with passionate arguments on the Scottish side "against being relegated to the status of a province," even though James desired the union largely in order "to protect Scottish interests and prevent his ancient kingdom simply becoming, as he himself said, 'as the northern shires, seldom seen and saluted by their king' " (Wormald 148, 147).

James projected a vision of "one king, one faith, one language; one law, one Parliament, one people alike in manners and allegiance" (Willson 250–51), in which the old names of England and Scotland would be submerged in the old/new name of Britain. Adopting the title King of Great Britain, he traced his ancestry back to one Brutus, King of all Britons, rewarding antiquarians like Thomas Lyte who supported the historical myth. He spoke of the union of the kingdoms as a reunion: "the blessed Union, or rather reuniting, of these two mighty, famous, and ancient kingdoms of England and Scotland under one Imperial Crown" (*Constitutional Documents* 32).

In laying before a recalcitrant English Parliament on March 19, 1604, the "great benefits that by that Vnion [of England and Scotland] do redound to the whole Island," James recalled a time when not only England but other great monarchies as well were "diuided, and euery particular Towne or little Countie, as Tyrants or Vsurpers could obtaine the possession, a Segniorie apart." England in particular was divided into seven Saxon kingdoms: "Do we not yet remember, that this Kingdome was diuided into seuen little Kingdomes, besides Wales? And is it not the stronger by their vnion? And hath not the vnion of Wales to England added a greater strength thereto?" As Jean Howard has written, "Scotland to the English was very much a foreign country" (299). James, however, greatly exaggerated the cultural uniformity of England and Scotland, as well as that of each separate kingdom.[6] As if seeking to mask the degree to which he seemed a foreigner to his new subjects, he asked Parliament, "Hath not God first vnited these two Kingdomes both in Language, Religion, and similitude of manners?" Now they were to be united further in his royal person, "alike lineally descended of both the Crownes" (King James VI/I 135).

In his next sentence James naturalized the process of nation-building, transforming it from a contingent historical result of uncertain wars and conquest to an inevitable, natural process:

> For euen as little brookes lose their names by their running and fall into great Riuers, and the very name and memorie of the great Riuers swallowed vp in the Ocean: so by the coniunction of diuers little Kingdomes in one, are all these priuate differences and questions swallowed vp.
>
> (King James VI/I 137)

Union, like a court of law, settles disputes among principalities, which are denigrated as "priuate differences and questions." The impermanence of the identities of "little Kingdomes" is suggested by the simile of the river, commonly associated with the passage of time as well as territorial boundaries. The sea, by contrast, is permanent and also primordial, like Britain itself, according to the myth subscribed to by James and supported by Jacobean antiquarians. In a startling anticipation of Ernest Renan's analysis late in the age of European nationalism, James implied, toward the very beginning of that age, that it is not so much the strengthening of collective memories as their attenuation that leads to unification and produces nations.[7]

James's argument that union would require—or achieve with the inevitability of natural processes—an erosion of regional memories may have owed something to an unease or embarrassment over the violent history he brought with him from the north. Alvin Kernan notes how "the severed heads of the Stuarts seemed to end up in London with fatal regularity" (43), a pattern consistent with what Keith Brown characterizes as "the stereotyped image that English men had of the Scots, as violent, uncivilized, poor, and rapacious": a view that was "very much alive when James VI ascended the throne of England" (140). *Macbeth*, I want to argue, is a masterful piece of doublespeak. While seeming to support James's case for union, it simultaneously telegraphs to English anti-unionists the hazards of joining their nation to one whose history, a monotonous tale of violence and regicide in the least charitable estimation, might have seemed to the most virulently xenophobic among them "a tale/ Told by an idiot, full of sound and fury,/ Signifying nothing" (5.5.27–28): the epitome of an unusable past.

*

Malcolm leads an English army against Macbeth in Act 5, suggesting a united purpose that the new monarch of a nominally united Great Britain no doubt applauded. For the most part, however, England remains modestly and diffidently on the margins of Shakespeare's Scottish play.[8] The only English ruler referred to in the play, Edward the Confessor, remains invisible and offstage. As befits a character that is represented as spiritual to the point of saintliness, he is denied a bodied, theatrical presence. Historically, Edward received Malcolm at his court during the first year of his reign (1042–43). In Shakespeare's play, Malcolm makes a false confession at the English court in order to root out Macduff's true loyalties. England is the place of confession, the antithetical counterpart to the nation where "There's no art/ To find the mind's construction in the face" (1.4.11–12).[9] In Scotland, deception accompanies treason, rebellion, bloodshed, and brutal retaliation, whereas in England, it leads to the discovery of authentic feeling and the forging of alliances: between the exiled Scot Malcolm and the English, and between Malcolm and Macduff.

The pervasive link between Scotland, secretive plotting, and deception would not have seemed unfamiliar to a predominantly English audience in 1606. Plots involving Mary Stuart, including the Ridolfi Plot of 1571 and the Babington Plot of 1586, had the aim of assassinating Queen Elizabeth and replacing her with Mary. In addition, memory of the Gowrie Conspiracy of 1600 was kept alive in annual sermons and commemorative bell-ringing in most English parishes (Cressy 57). This complicated and still unresolved episode, in which John Ruthven, 3rd Earl of Gowrie and his brother Alexander were dispatched by attendants of King James in Gowrie House apparently to prevent them from murdering the king, was represented on stage by the King's Men in 1604, though as David Norbrook notes, it "displeased the authorities, presumably because direct representation on the stage was felt to demean the king's dignity. The utmost tact and circumspection were needed even when paying the king the highest compliments" (83). With the example of the Gowrie play fresh in his mind, Shakespeare achieved circumspection in spades in *Macbeth*, a play that might actually allude to the Gowrie conspiracy.[10] James's attendants successfully protected him from his murderous host; Duncan's attendants, heavy with wine, did not.

The beginning of *Henry V* brings up the "auld alliance" between Scotland and France, an agreement dating from 1295 that specified that if England attacked one of their countries, the other would retaliate.[11] Debating the wisdom of leaving the kingdom undefended from "the weasel Scot" (1.2.170), the court is reminded by the Bishop of Ely of the "auld alliance" between France and Scotland: "But there's a saying very old and true:/ *'If that you will France win,/ Then with Scotland first begin'* " (1.2.166–68).[12] Canterbury reminds Henry of England's having captured and sent to France the Scottish monarch David II when Edward III was preoccupied with the French wars: a historical error, because David II was not sent to France, though the scenario remains apt for the historical Henry, who would take the young Scottish king, James I, prisoner and transport him "to the French wars in an effort to stop the Scots from helping the French king" (Ferguson 37).[13] Although the Treaty of Edinburgh (1560) had formally put an end to the "auld alliance," certain provisions remained in effect long after. The opinions voiced by the Bishop about "the weasel Scot" were far from obsolete in Elizabethan England. Keith Brown notes, "At the height of the crisis caused by the Spanish Armada in 1588 Gilbert Gifford warned Walsingham that 'England will find Scotland, old Scotland still, and traitorous in the greatest need.' Even as late as 1600 an Englishman could still write of 'an old beggarly enemy, the Scot' " (Brown 140).

Although the Protestants achieved ascendancy in Scotland in 1560, there were strong Counter-Reformation pressures within that nation (Ferguson 92).[14] Long after the Scottish Reformation, doubts among English Protestants lingered, akin to those voiced by Duncan toward the former Thane of Cawdor: "There's no art/ To find the mind's construction in the face;/ He was a gentleman on whom I built/ An absolute trust" (1.4.11–14).[15] English attitudes toward Scotland, to be sure, stopped well short of absolute trust. Early in James's reign, some English Catholics hoped that James, son of the Catholic heroine Mary Queen of Scots and husband to a Catholic wife, Anne of Denmark, would declare himself a Catholic, and return England once again to the traditional faith. At any rate, he was more tolerant of recusant Catholics in England than Elizabeth had been,[16] and he had even elevated the crypto-Catholic Earl of Northumberland[17] and Henry Howard to important posts. There must have been some in Shakespeare's audience in 1606 who felt that James's loyalty to his new nation and to Protestantism, like Macduff's loyalty to Scotland in the play, stood in need of a test. He was, after all, the son of a traitor who had plotted against the life of the English queen.

Furthermore, English mistrust of James's motives for pushing the union issue was the order of the day. In the Parliamentary debates on union from 1606, the probable date of *Macbeth*, the Scots were "eclectically damned as beggars, thieves and murderers" (Ferguson 102–103). Allegations were common that "the benefits of incorporation would lie with the Scots at the expense of the mere English" (101). James himself referred to the atmosphere of suspicion early in his reign. In his closing speech to his first English Parliament late in 1604, he contrasts the trust granted him by his Scottish subjects with the suspicion of the English: "There [in Scotland] all things warranted that came from me. Here all things suspected" (quoted in Notestein 84).[18] James associates transparency and suspicion with Scotland and England, respectively, an association that Shakespeare would also have come across in Holinshed's *Chronicle of Scotland*: after Malcolm's three-part "confession" of the vices he harbors within, Macduff imputes these to his time at the English court. Malcolm "is so replete with the inconstant behavior and manifest vices of Englishmen that he is nothing worthy to enjoy it; for by his own confession he is not only avaricious and given to insatiable lust but so false a traitor withal that no trust is to be had unto any word he speaketh" (Holinshed 2: 75). Shakespeare's play inverts these associations, in keeping with England's longstanding distrust of the perennial ally of its perennial enemy France.

I would argue that English subjects' mistrust of their new monarch over the union issue stemmed, in part, from the threat the union posed to a sense of nationhood forged during Elizabeth's reign. When James ascended the throne in 1603, some English must have sensed their nation, in its new configuration with Scotland, reverting to a dynastic state, whose unity was derived only from the person of the hereditary ruler and not by the unity of language, customs, or laws. By contrast with the relatively new idea of the nation, writes Benedict Anderson in his celebrated study of the origins of nationalism, "in the older imagining" of the "dynastic realm," "states were defined by centers, borders were porous and indistinct, and sovereigns faded imperceptibly into one another" (19). In her comparative study *Nationalism: Five Roads to Modernity*, Liah Greenfeld argues that the modern western construct of the nation first took shape in sixteenth-century England: "by 1600, the existence in England of a national consciousness and identity, and as a result, of a new geo-political entity, a nation, was a fact" (30).[19] John Guy makes a similar point when discussing "the shift from 'realm' to 'state' " in the Tudor period. The concept of a "state," a "defined territory" with "a sovereign government which recognized no superior in political, ecclesiastical, and legal matters," was well established by the 1590s (Guy 352). The newer concept was supported by "three underlying beliefs," according to Guy: "(1) that humanity was divided into races or nations; (2) that the purity of the English nation would be sullied by foreign admixtures; and (3) that English language, law, and customs (including dress) were the badges of nationality" (352). Both Greenfeld and Guy point toward terminological shifts—largely from "realm" and "kingdom" to "state" and "nation"—that register the conceptual shift from dynastic realm to unitary nation whose identity and stability do not depend entirely on a principle of legitimate succession (Guy 352; Greenfeld 31f.). A similar terminological shift is discernible over the course of Shakespeare's chronicle histories. "Nation" and "state" appear with increasing frequency in the later histories, gradually supplanting "realm," which predominates in the early *Henry VI* plays.[20] *Macbeth* registers a convulsion within the idea of nationhood as England confronted a monarch and a history that seemed marginal, at best, to its own.

*

The cultural differences between the two newly conjoined nations, as they are represented in *Macbeth*, are perhaps most economically revealed through the two doctors, sounding boards for two radically different attitudes toward history. Hoping that his wife is not beyond medicinal cure, Macbeth tries to efface a personal history in these incantatory lines addressed to the Scottish Doctor:

> Canst thou not minister to a mind diseased,
> Pluck from the memory a rooted sorrow,
> Raze out the written troubles of the brain,
> And with some sweet oblivious antidote
> Cleanse the stuffed bosom of that perilous stuff
> Which weighs upon the heart?
>
> (5.3.39–44)

Although Macbeth's lines refer to a personal history, they might serve as well for a national one: especially given the extent to which the play connects crimes against the family (notably Macduff's) with crimes against the state. Specifically, they might have spoken to an English desire to efface this new and burdensome history that England so recently inherited. Macbeth's desperate hope for oblivion for his wife reflects the meaning of history for the English nation in this strange play that, aside from assuring its monarch that his dynasty would rule Scotland "to the crack of doom," bore no trace of a usable past for the English people. Shakespeare's predominantly English audience would certainly have felt the full force of Macbeth's desire for "some sweet oblivious antidote." A history play that must have struck English audiences as a rooted sorrow, one that they would just as soon pluck from their collective memory, as much as royal propaganda, *Macbeth* bore the potential to support anti-union pamphleteers and propagandists at least as much as it would have flattered James. Macbeth's desire for the Scottish Doctor to provide a medicinal antidote to a poisonous memory seems oddly consonant with James's prescription for the English people in his first speech to Parliament, cited earlier in this chapter. The rhetoric of that speech, which underscored the importance of forgetting for producing national unity, could only have confirmed anti-unionist fears of "England" disappearing into the ocean of "Great Britain." As if recalling James's argument, *Macbeth* casts Scotland as the place of harrowing memories that cannot be expunged and one where some antidote to memory is devoutly to be wished.

In England, by contrast, the king's power of healing is linked not to forgetting but to foreknowledge. After the English Doctor describes Edward in saintly terms, Malcolm picks up the theme of Edward's miraculous healing powers. In response to Macduff's question, "What's the disease he [the Doctor] means," Malcolm explains,

> 'Tis called the Evil.
> A most miraculous work in this good King,
> Which often since my here remain in England
> I have seen him do. How he solicits Heaven
> Himself best knows; but strangely visited people,
> All swoll'n and ulcerous, pitiful to the eye,
> The mere despair of surgery, he cures,
> Hanging a golden stamp about their necks
> Put on with holy prayers; and 'tis spoken,
> To the succeeding royalty he leaves
> The healing benediction. With this strange virtue,
> He hath a heavenly gift of prophecy;
> And sundry blessings hang about his throne,
> That speak him full of grace.
>
> (4.3.146–59)

Whereas Macbeth's conversation with the Scottish Doctor expresses a wish for oblivion, Malcolm's exchange with his English counterpart reveals a commanding view of history akin to that of the witches. Such command issues from the gift of prophecy, which in *2 Henry IV* the Earl of Warwick associates with the careful study of history. In a speech that is a near kinsman to Macbeth's "Tomorrow, and tomorrow, and tomorrow," King Henry laments,

> O God, that one might read the book of fate
> And see the revolution of the times
> Make mountains level, and the continent,
> Weary of solid firmness, melt itself
> Into the sea.
>
> (3.1.44–8)

To Henry's despairing lines Warwick responds,

> There is a history in all men's lives
> Figuring the natures of the times deceased,
> The which observed, a man may prophesy,
> With a near aim, of the main chance of things
> As yet not come to life, which in their seeds
> And weak beginning lie intreasurèd.
>
> (3.1.79–84)

In Warwick's speech, the ability to "prophesy," attributed to Edward in *Macbeth*, is tied to a view of history as eminently practical, usable by the present to predict future trends and patterns of events and thereby avoid calamity. England, then, as constructed by the Scottish play, is partnered with a view of the usefulness of history, tied to a power to heal, prophesy, and command. Scotland, by contrast, is a place of new beginnings (under Malcolm Canmore) and wished-for oblivion: in both cases a place where the past bears little utility for the present.

Malcolm's speech about Edward the Confessor's healing powers is frequently cited as evidence of how well Shakespeare had learned to modify any historical detail that might embarrass his patron.[21] Shakespeare undoubtedly made many other revisions to Holinshed's account in order to flatter or at least not offend the king and his purported ancestor Banquo, and most of these are well known. In Holinshed it is clear that Macbeth was Duncan's cousin and bore a strong claim to the throne. Banquo was complicit in the murder of Duncan, whereas Shakespeare makes him guiltless. Shakespeare's Duncan is at once more saintly than Holinshed's and less ineffectual. Shakespeare omits any reference to Macbeth's ten years of peaceful and effective rule, when he was "accounted the sure defense and buckler of innocent people" (Holinshed 2: 171). Less widely remarked is Holinshed's tendency to assign more credit to Earl Siward of Northumberland, Malcolm's uncle, than does Shakespeare. In the section referring to "the battle in which Earl Siward vanquished the Scots," Holinshed comes close to making Malcolm seem a puppet king of Siward.[22] Like the medieval chroniclers before him, Holinshed grants,

> Siward the noble Earl of Northumberland, with a great power of horsemen, went into Scotland and, in battle, put to flight Macbeth, that had usurped the crown of Scotland; and, that done, placed Malcolm surnamed Canmore, the son of Duncan sometime King of Scotland, in the government of that realm.
>
> (Holinshed 2: 192)

Shakespeare's Siward, by contrast, extends credit to his client: "The day almost itself professes yours," and not "ours," he tells Malcolm (5.7.28). The underlying scenario, however—of Scottish dependency on England's military might and prowess—bore very timely implications for the union question, especially from the Scottish side, where many of James's subjects feared that union would mean that Scotland would be treated like Ireland: "a conquered and slavish province to be governed by a Viceroy or Deputy" (Ferguson 103, citing *Register of the Privy Council of Scotland* 7: 536).

Like the whirling military riddle of the play's beginning, where Scotland seems nearly simultaneously under assault from without and within, by the rebel Macdonwald and by Sweno of Norway,[23] Siward's assault has equivocal implications. Is it a war of liberation or of conquest? There was certainly a historical tradition, represented in the *Chronicle of Huntingdon* (late thirteenth century), for instance, that saw it as the latter: "Whereupon Siward led an army into Scotland, and having defeated the King and ravaged the whole kingdom, he reduced it to subjection himself" (quoted in Robinson 90). Medieval English chroniclers tended to give credit for the victory to Siward, a circumstance about which the fourteenth-century Scottish chronicler John of Fordun complained in his *Scottichronicon* (or Chronicle of the Scots). The prevailing English view led Edward I in 1301 to write to Pope Boniface to claim overlordship of Scotland partly on the grounds that "St. Edward, the King of England, gave the kingdom of Scotland to Malcolm, to be held of him" (A.O. Anderson 1: 593). That Malcolm had payed homage to Edward must have been well known to Shakespeare's audiences. As David Norbrook writes, "English supporters of a Stuart succession had tried to combat hostility toward rule by a foreigner by arguing that many Scottish kings had paid homage to English monarchs, that in this sense Scotland was already united with England. One of the examples often cited was Malcolm's paying homage to Edward the Confessor. Several plays in Elizabeth's last years— including a lost play about King Malcolm—treated this theme of homage, drawing on Holinshed" (95).[24] The precise nuance given to Siward's action has wide ramifications. For instance, it could confirm or confute the proud Scottish boast, widely known in Shakespeare's England, that the Scots, unlike the English, had never been conquered.

Certainly the prominence Shakespeare gives to Siward's declaration of the number of Scots who have defected to Malcolm's side would have appealed to James. The sight of Scotsmen and Englishmen fighting side by side in united purpose and a righteous cause looks like good propaganda for the cause of union. Finally, Malcolm's anglicizing gesture of creating Scotland's first earls in his final speech, also remarked in Holinshed, would tend to support the case for union insofar as it hints at a long history of convergence of the two cultures, though even this innovation was variously interpretable, as Shakespeare could have known solely from Holinshed. Thus, the sixteenth-century Scottish historian Hector Boece, in the introductory "Description of Scotland" included in Holinshed, characterizes these new titles as "vain puffes" and links Malcolm's reign in particular to a decline from the old staunch Scottish virtues into a decadent and diminished present (quoted in Norbrook 86).

Some of Shakespeare's alterations that are cited as evidence of the play's service in the cause of royal propaganda, however, bear double implications that allowed the playwright to equivocate with his pro-union monarch and largely anti-union audience. The elimination of all reference to Macbeth's ten years of even-handed, peaceful, and judicious rule, for example, is arguably necessary both to telescope a long reign into a five-act play and to make Macbeth that much darker by contrast with his rivals Banquo and Duncan. But this excision also accentuates prevailing stereotypes of Scotland as a brutally violent land with scarcely breathing space in its history between coup and counter-coup.[25] A single alteration, in other words, could make concessions towards prejudices on both sides, so that, like the Jesuit Father Garnet and the equivocating fiends who lie like truth, Shakespeare could telegraph opposing messages to his Scottish monarch and the nobles he had brought with him from the north, on the one hand, and his largely English audience, on the other. Even the union of Scots and English ranged against Macbeth on the battlefield, rather than being represented as a sentimental bi-national band of brotherhood, bears more than the hint of a dark paradox akin to those of the riddling witches. Siward remarks, "The tyrant's people on both sides do fight" (5.7.26). Malcolm echoes, "We have met with foes/ That strike beside us" (5.7.29–30). It is as if both characters are describing the play that contains them: Shakespeare's play itself "do[es] fight," it seems, "on both sides" of the union issue.

Leah Marcus notes that early in James's reign even a modified plan for union which respected the distinct legal systems of the two countries was foundering on English prejudice and mutual suspicion: "In England the Scots were scorned as aliens, mercilessly pilloried in plays and satires. Numerous duels were fought between Englishmen and Scotsmen. . . . On ceremonial occasions, English parvenus would elbow out Scots of the old nobility" (124). With a widely publicized court case decided in 1608 on the Post Nati or those Scots born after James ascended the English throne, Marcus notes, James sought to remove "the mark of the stranger" from his fellow countrymen and thereby pave the way for union. The case "hinged on whether a Scotsman born since the proclamation of union had the right to defend his ownership of property held in England in a court of English law." The judges found nearly unanimously that the Post Nati were indeed citizens "entitled to recourse at English law despite their continuing ties to the alien Roman system" (Marcus 124). When he wrote *Macbeth*, Shakespeare had already specialized in writing plays in which a character—a Shylock, for example, or an Othello—bore "the mark of the stranger." In *Macbeth*, I would suggest, nearly the entire cast functions that way. *Macbeth* is a topsy-turvy play not only in terms of gender relations—Lady Macbeth is, among other things, a study in the unnatural phenomenon of "the female dominance which had haunted James throughout his early life" (Marcus 105)—but also in terms of larger cultural norms. The play's center, Scotland, bears "the mark of the stranger,"[26] whereas the margins—in this case, England—represent the norm, all the more powerfully because they are nearly invisible, with the exceptions of the English Doctor, Siward, and his son. The precise relation between margin and center remains ambiguous largely because of Edward's invisibility, but the play certainly speaks to anxieties on both sides, Scottish as well as English, of becoming marginalized under James's project for union.

Shakespeare's histories frequently pose the question of the uses the past holds for the present. The historical figures in his plays often plot to use the past—or, as often, occlude it—for private as well as public ends, teaching Elizabethan audiences by example or counter-example the uses and disadvantages of history for a sense of nationhood. *Macbeth*, like its predecessor *Hamlet*, moves away from the relative optimism of the histories regarding the utility of the past for the present. Like Macbeth's wish for "some oblivious antidote" for his wife, Hamlet's memory is a debilitating burden rather than an enabling call to action. Hamlet is stymied by his father's ghost's injunction, "Remember me," in part because the martial, heroic past he represents is, from the prince's perspective, an unusable one. In both tragedies memory bears a purgatorial aspect for the protagonists: "Heaven and earth,/ Must I remember?" (*Hamlet*, 1.2.142–43).[27] In *Macbeth*, Shakespeare, not unlike the infamous Father Garnet, equivocated with his monarch and patron. Under the guise of complimenting James and projecting his line to rule Scotland, as an appalled Macbeth guesses during the Show of Kings, "to th' crack of doom" (4.1.132), Shakespeare's riddling play hints to his English audiences how futile it will be to unite this new past, suddenly bequeathed to them with the accession of the Scottish monarch, with their own. A dubious experiment in uniting Scotland's history with England's, reflecting James's failed attempt to unite the administrations of the two nations, *Macbeth* shows English and Scottish history to be tragically divided. Like James's Project for Union, all but defunct at the time of the Scottish play's premiere, the potential union of the two histories seems to have run aground.

Notes

1   An earlier version of this chapter was presented at the 2006 meeting of the Shakespeare Association of America in Philadelphia. I would like to thank all the members of "The Scottish Play" seminar, particularly leader Al Braunmuller and respondents Linda Levy Peck and F.J. Levy, for a lively and productive discussion. Linda Peck especially deserves thanks for detailed suggestions that helped improve the final draft. I would also like to thank the editor of the current volume, Nick Moschovakis, for his excellent bibliographic and editorial suggestions.
2   For an account of the range of English attitudes toward Scotland at the time of *Macbeth*, see William C. Carroll's excellent edition of the play.
3   Any essay referring to the past as "usable" or "unusable" automatically incurs a debt to Friedrich Nietzsche's essay, "On the Uses and Disadvantages of History for Life."
4   As William Ferguson summarizes James's progress on the issue, "Strenuous efforts by James to unite the realms of England and Scotland failed, and their general laws and administration remained separate and distinct, as did their crowns and the rules of succession thereto" (97). Other useful investigations of the union issue in James's reign include Galloway; Levack. For a useful set of early Jacobean pamphlets on both sides of the union issue, see Galloway and Levack.
5   Two exceptions are Kinney (88) and David Norbrook. Although Norbrook grants some attention to the implications of the play for the union issue (see esp. 95–96), that is certainly not the primary focus of his essay.
6   See Highley (53–66) for a discussion of the linguistic diversity in James's Scotland and a more thorough examination of ways in which contemporary "claims about a community of language between England and Scotland ring hollow" (54). Highley suggests that *Macbeth*, with its relative linguistic uniformity (using very few "linguistic markers of Scottish identity"), stages the unionist fantasy of cultural

uniformity, though adding the caveat that "we do not know how a production of *Macbeth* would have actually sounded. We can only speculate as to whether individual actors disguised their native accents in favour of a company standard of pronunciation" (57–58). On the other hand, it is possible that early productions of the play stressed linguistic diversity and strangeness: "although there is no evidence that actors adopted Scottish accents, we cannot rule out the possibility that they took unscripted and impromptu liberties in this regard" (57). Citing evidence that the company used regional accents in other productions, Andrew Gurr has suggested that "we might give some thought to the awesome possibility that for *Macbeth* in 1606 the company all adopted Scottish accents. . . . Some of the Blackfriars company boys certainly used northern voices in the same year as *Macbeth* for *The Isle of Gulls*, a sharp satire on the Scottish presence at the English court, of which Thomas Edmondes reported, 'all men's parts were acted of two diverse nations.' London was full of Scottish accents in 1606. If boys could copy it, the professionals, well-travelled through most of the country, and always alert to local accents, surely could too" (44–45).

7 See Renan. For an application of Renan's idea to Shakespeare's *Henry V*, see my "Wars of memory in *Henry V*."

8 Jean Howard notes the "borderland settings" favored by Jacobean tragedies, arguing that they "furnish Shakespeare with a temporal or geographic analogue for a period of crisis in the ruling order" (315).

9 All citations from *Macbeth* refer to the Oxford Shakespeare edition, ed. Nicholas Brooke. Citations from *King Henry V* and *The Second Part of King Henry IV* refer to the New Cambridge Shakespeare editions, ed. Andrew Gurr (1992) and Giorgio Melchiori (1989), respectively.

10 Arthur Melville Clark attempts to establish this connection in *Murder Under Trust*.

11 The alliance was renewed under Elizabeth's father, when King James IV of Scotland, armed by the French, invaded England in order to divert Henry VIII from his invasion of France under Louis XII. (Henry himself was emulating his famous ancestor Henry V.) The Scots were defeated at the Battle of Flodden Field on September 9, 1513.

12 The Quarto assigns this speech to an anonymous "Lord," the Folio to Ely. Gurr thinks the latter allocation unlikely and attributes it to Westmorland, who speaks it in Holinshed.

13 Of course, Shakespeare's *Henry V* does not allude to this.

14 These fears persisted in James's reign, as Ferguson notes: "Many in England feared the spread of absolutism on the continent, which was equated with the Counter-Reformation, and James' reliance on favourites and rough dealing with an admittedly ill-defined constitution raised alarms for the preservation of constitutional government" (105).

15 As Garry Wills has argued, Shakespeare's contemporaries would have recognized James as in many ways the antithesis of Duncan. Sermons and speeches by Launcelot Andrewes and Sir Edward Coke lauded him as one who could see through lies and deceptive appearances. About Duncan's speech, Wills writes, "Nothing could be more at odds with the way James faced plots against him (not only the Powder Plot, but the Gowrie Plot, also commemorated in annual sermons that claimed he kept his head and baffled his assailants shrewdly). James *did* have an art to find the construction (construing) of deceptive appearances" (30). I am suggesting, however, that James, the unraveler of conundrums, was himself a "questionable shape," as Hamlet says of his father's Ghost, to his new subjects.

16 For instance, he ended recusancy fines, at least until after the Hampton Court Conference, when he reinstated them. In a speech before Parliament on November 9, 1605, he conceded, "Many honest men, seduced with some errors of Popery, may yet remaine good and faithfull subjects" (King James VI/I 152).

17 The earldom of Northumberland, the title held by Siward in *Macbeth*, had been a troublesome one throughout Elizabeth's reign, from the Northern Rising of 1569 in which Thomas Percy, seventh Earl of Northumberland took part, to the activities of the Catholic sympathizer and intriguer, Henry Percy, ninth Earl of Northumberland, including the Somerville Plot discussed by Richard Wilson in his *Secret Shakespeare* (105–108). The alliance between Siward and Malcolm might very well have suggested to the most suspicious Protestants in Shakespeare's audience, or at least those most prone to conspiratorial thinking, the link between this northern earldom held by a largely Catholic family and the country that many English Protestants still suspected for its "auld alliance" with France.

18 James also struck a conciliatory note at the end of his final speech to his first English Parliament, claiming to understand English suspicions: "So on the other part I confesse, if I had bene in your places at the beginning of this Parliament, (which was so soone after mine entry into this Kingdome, wherein ye could not possibly haue so perfect a knowledge of mine inclination, as experience since hath taught you,) I could not but haue suspected, and mis-interpreted diuers things" (King James VI/I 158).

19 Many literary critics have recently supported the contention that the modern nation predates the Enlightenment. See, for example, McEachern.

20 For example, in the first tetralogy "realm(s)" appears a total of thirty-eight times by comparison with five mentions of "nation(s)." In the second tetralogy, the frequencies of the two words are nearly even: eleven for "realm(s)" and ten for "nation(s)." The dying John of Gaunt's reference to "this earth, this realm, this England," like other feudal rhetoric (e.g, his opening line, "I have, my liege"), makes him seem a superannuated figure. For a reading of this speech as a proto-nationalist performance, see McEachern, (5–6).

21 Alvin Kernan, following the precedent set by Henry Paul, regards *Macbeth* as the work of a royal "propagandist" who "transformed, to fit his patron's political myth, a petty power struggle in a primitive society between a weak and a strong warrior into a sacred event in the history of divine-right legitimacy." Thus, Shakespeare circumspectly converts the historical Edward's practice of touching the bodies of those afflicted with the King's Evil (tuberculosis of the skin, or scrofula), into James's practice of "hanging a golden stamp [coin] about their necks," in order not to embarrass the present king who, with his intense dislike for crowds and for illness, refused to touch the bodies of the diseased (Kernan 76–78; cf. Paul).

22 Some medieval chroniclers even represented Siward as bent on subjugating Scotland.

23 Macdonwald's assault alone is equivocal in this respect. Jean Howard notes that the Western Isles from which Macdonwald's invasionary force heralds may be the Hebrides or, "just as likely, . . . Ireland" (319).

24 See Axton (21–22, 79–80, 101–15). Norbrook also notes that in 1605 Sir George Buc wrote a panegyric, *Daphnis Polystephanos*, which "presented the alliance between Malcolm and Edward as prefiguring the Union and traced James's ancestry on the English side back to Edward" (96).

25 Kernan remarks, "Nine of the ten kings who preceded Macbeth were murdered, and earlier times had been equally bloody" (78).

26 As Highley points out, we simply do not know whether actors in performance used English and Scottish accents to differentiate characters and to give the Scottish the "mark of the stranger" (see note 6 above).

27 Andrew Hadfield draws out numerous connections to Scotland and Scottish history in *Hamlet*. In his reading, *Hamlet* seems almost a second "Scottish play." Perhaps this helps explain the way in which memory produces a purgatorial suffering in both plays.

Works cited

Anderson, A.O., ed. *Early Sources of Scottish History*. 1922. Rpt. Stamford: Paul Watkins, 1990.

Anderson, Benedict. *Imagined Communities: Reflections on the Origin and Spread of Nationalism*. Rev. ed. London: Verso, 1991.

Axton, Marie. *The Queen's Two Bodies: Drama and the Elizabethan Succession*. London: Royal Historical Society, 1977.

Baldo, Jonathan. "Wars of Memory in *Henry V.*" *Shakespeare Quarterly* 47 (1996): 132–59.

Brown, Keith M. "The Price of Friendship: The 'Well Affected' and English Economic Clientage in Scotland before 1603." *Scotland and England 1286–1815*. Ed. Roger A. Mason. Edinburgh: John Donald, 1987.

Carroll, William C., ed. *Macbeth: Texts and Contexts*. Boston: Bedford/St. Martin's, 1999.

Clark, Arthur M. *Murder Under Trust: The Topical "Macbeth" and Other Jacobean Matters*. Edinburgh: Scottish Academic, 1981.

Constitutional Documents of the Reign of James I. Ed. J.R. Tanner. Cambridge: Cambridge UP, 1930.

Cressy, David. *Bonfires and Bells: National Memory and the Protestant Calendar in Elizabethan and Stuart England*. Berkeley: U of California P, 1989.

Ferguson, William. *Scotland's Relations with England: A Survey to 1707*. Edinburgh: Donald, 1977.

Galloway, Bruce. *The Union of England and Scotland, 1603–1608*. Edinburgh: John Donald, 1986.

Galloway, Bruce, and Brian Levack, eds. *The Jacobean Union: Six Tracts of 1604*. Scottish History Society, Fourth Series, vol. 21. Edinburgh: Clark Constable, 1985.

Greenfeld, Liah. *Nationalism: Five Roads to Modernity*. Cambridge: Harvard UP, 1992.

Gurr, Andrew. *The Shakespeare Company, 1594–1642*. Cambridge: Cambridge UP, 2004.

Guy, John. *Tudor England*. Oxford: Oxford UP, 1988.

Hadfield, Andrew. "*Hamlet*'s Country Matters: The 'Scottish Play' within the Play." *Shakespeare and Scotland*. Ed. Willy Maley and Andrew Murphy. Manchester: Manchester UP, 2004. 87–103.

Highley, Christopher. "The Place of Scots in the Scottish Play: *Macbeth* and the Politics of Language." *Shakespeare and Scotland*. Ed. Willy Maley and Andrew Murphy. Manchester: Manchester UP, 2004. 53–66.

Holinshed, Raphael. *Chronicles of England, Scotland and Ireland*. 2nd ed. London, 1587.

Howard, Jean. "Shakespeare, Geography, and the Work of Genre on the Early Modern Stage." *Modern Language Quarterly* 64 (2003): 299–322.

Kernan, Alvin. *Shakespeare, The King's Playwright: Theater in the Stuart Court, 1603–1613*. New Haven: Yale UP, 1995.

King James VI and I. *Political Writing*. Ed. Johann P. Sommerville. Cambridge: Cambridge UP, 1994.

Kinney, Arthur. *Lies Like Truth: Shakespeare, Macbeth, and the Cultural Moment*. Detroit: Wayne State UP, 2001.

Levack, Brian. *The Formation of the British State: England, Scotland, and the Union 1603–1707*. Oxford: Clarendon Press, 1987.

McEachern, Claire. *The Poetics of English Nationhood, 1590–1612*. Cambridge: Cambridge UP, 1996.

Marcus, Leah S. *Puzzling Shakespeare: Local Reading and Its Discontents*. Berkeley: U of California P, 1988.

Nietzsche, Friedrich. "On the Uses and Disadvantages of History for Life." *Untimely Meditations*. Trans. R.J. Hollingdale. Cambridge: Cambridge UP, 1983. 59–123.

Norbrook, David. "*Macbeth* and the Politics of Historiography." *Politics of Discourse: The Literature and History of Seventeenth-Century England*. Ed. Kevin Sharpe and Steven N. Zwicker. London: U of California P, 1987. 78–116.

Notestein, Wallace. *The House of Commons, 1604–10*. New Haven: Yale UP, 1971.

Paul, Henry. *The Royal Play of* Macbeth. New York: Macmillan, 1950.

Renan, Ernst. "What Is a Nation?" *Nation and Narration*. Ed. Homi K. Bhabha. London: Routledge, 1990. 8–22.

Rhodes, Neil. "Wrapped in the Strong Arms of the Union: Shakespeare and King James." *Shakespeare and Scotland*. Ed. Willy Maley and Andrew Murphy. Manchester: Manchester UP, 2004. 37–52.

Robinson, Tony. *Macbeth: Man and Myth*. Phoenix Mill: Sutton Publishing, 1999.

Shakespeare, William. *King Henry V*. Ed. Andrew Gurr. Cambridge: Cambridge UP, 1992.

—— *Macbeth*. Ed. Nicholas Brooke. Oxford: Oxford UP, 1990.

—— *The Second Part of King Henry IV*. Ed. Giorgio Melchiori. Cambridge: Cambridge UP, 1989.

Watkins, John. *Representing Elizabeth in Stuart England: Literature, History, Sovereignty*. Cambridge: Cambridge UP, 2002.

Wills, Garry. *Witches and Jesuits: Shakespeare's* Macbeth. New York: Oxford UP, 1995.

Willson, David Harris. *James VI and I*. New York: Oxford UP, 1956.

Wilson, Richard. *Secret Shakespeare: Studies in Theatre, Religion and Resistance*. Manchester: University of Manchester Press, 2004.

Wormald, Jenny, ed. *Scotland: A History*. Oxford: Oxford UP, 2005.

4 The "peerless" Macbeth

Friendship and family in *Macbeth*

Rebecca Ann Bach

Resolving to take his rest at Macbeth's castle in Inverness, Duncan says of his new Thane of Cawdor, "[i]t is a peerelesse Kinsman" (TLN 346; 1.4.58).[1] Duncan's compliment could not be more prophetic, although it does not prophesy as Duncan would have wished. Duncan means to call Macbeth "matchless," "unequalled" (*OED* "peerless" a.). Even this meaning for "peerless" may signify danger for Duncan since it could foreshadow Macbeth's ascent to the kingship. As we shall see, however, Duncan's word may also prophesy Macbeth's rejection of "peers," his rejection of family and friends in their premodern senses. Macbeth proves himself "peerless" in his inability to keep or make peers, if "peers" means noblemen, the only meaning that Shakespeare acknowledges. Shakespeare consistently uses "peer" to mean "[a] member of one of the degrees of nobility in the United Kingdom" or "[i]n generalized sense . . . a noble" (*OED* "peer" 4a., 5). *The Oxford English Dictionary* documents a broadening of meaning for "peer" beginning at the end of the seventeenth century, one that seemingly culminates in the sociological sense of "An equal; a contemporary; a member of the same age-group or social set" (2b), the sense often intended in late-modern usage of the word. As the dictionary's categorization of usages documents, this usage evolved from an earlier sense that coexisted with the meaning "noble": "an equal in any respect" (2a). But, as the usages the dictionary collects under each category suggest, these senses are not identical. Prior to the end of the seventeenth century, when "peer" is used about people to mean "an equal in any respect," the people in question are generally nobility. Macbeth will be a king without nobles, a king without peers.

Like the word "peerless," the word "peer" occurs only once in the play, in Lady Macbeth's plea to the men at Macbeth's dinner table to disregard his wild ravings at the ghost that they cannot see. Lady Macbeth calls the men at table "good Peeres," and she is hardly claiming an equal relation to them (TLN 1373; 3.4.95). Her epithet is a piece of what Lynne Magnusson calls "negative politeness," speech that establishes respect from the speaker to the addressee and recognizes the social distance between them (21). Lady Macbeth could also be desperately attempting to establish Macbeth as among his peers in Shakespeare's sense of the word: that is, among the men who should owe him their allegiance and their love. The play will show this attempt as entirely fruitless for, as Lisa Hopkins suggests, "from the time of the disrupted banquet, [Macbeth] converses only with those conspicuously beneath him" (104).

Shakespeare's usages of "peer" and "peerless" in *Macbeth* point to the play's devotion to a network of kinship and friendship between noblemen, and they offer us a window into a premodern *Macbeth* that has been seldom seen by modern critics of the play. Put another way, modern critics of the play, from the eighteenth century forward, have seen Macbeth as their "peer" in the modern sense of the word, while the play is clearly a product of a world that did not recognize that sense. Robert Heilman, in his 1966 assessment of Shakespeare's dramatic technique, declares that "we become Macbeth, or at least assent to complicity with him" (14). And more than thirty years later, in his introduction to the play in *The Norton Shakespeare*, Stephen Greenblatt asserts that "the caldron is in every one of us" (2562).[2] However, Macbeth belongs to a world in which most people could not be peers. Macbeth is "peerless" in the play, and Duncan is destroyed, precisely because Macbeth is without a "peer" in Shakespeare's sense of the word.

Although ostensibly entirely unconcerned with Shakespeare's plays, Alan Bray's last book, *The Friend*, which focused on friendship and family relations between noblemen, offers us a new way to read *Macbeth*.[3] Bray's book exposes the absolute centrality of friendship and other bonds between men, what he calls "voluntary kinship" bonds, to the culture that Shakespeare inherited and in which he lived, a culture that Bray calls "traditional society." In such a culture, Bray claims, "the friendship that kinship could create was in itself only one part of a larger whole. . . . Within this larger frame, a multi-plicity in the forms of kinship readily overlapped and created that web of obligations and friendship that held the society of England together" (105). Ann Rosalind Jones and Peter Stallybrass describe this society as subscribing to what they call "the long regime of livery," whose "aim . . . is to mark the body with its debts—debts of love, of solidarity, of servitude, of obedience" (275, 273).

The language of "obligations" and "debts of love" appears forcefully in *Macbeth* at its start when Duncan makes Macbeth a greater peer, the Thane of Cawdor, saying, "More is thy due, then more than all can pay" (TLN 304; 1.4.21). That language surfaces again at the play's close when Malcolm ele-vates his thanes to be Scotland's first earls: "We shall not spend a large expence of time/ Before we reckon with your seuerall loues/ And make vs euen with you" (TLN 2513–15; 5.11.26–28). This language, far from intimat-ing crass economic interests, is the love language that binds men to one another in "traditional society." While in the modern world love is ideally separated from economic interests, in the English Renaissance the economic language of debt and obligation was love language. This was the language of ideal relations between men, the language of premodern kinship and friendship. Both Bray's book and Jones and Stallybrass's suggest that it is "the concept of the individual" that replaces "traditional society" with its "regime of livery" (Jones and Stallybrass 275).[4]

The historical stories Jones and Stallybrass and Bray tell should help us to understand *Macbeth*'s critical history, which emerged at the same time as the novel, a history of what might be called, broadly, individualistic readings of the play. For most of its critical history, *Macbeth* has been read as the story of either of two men, Macbeth or, more recently, King James; critics have also focused on the witches and on Lady Macbeth, but most of those studies read the play's women for their effects on its protagonist. That critical history is, from one perspective, entirely proper in that it attends to what is seductive for modernity about Macbeth, what A.C. Bradley calls Macbeth's "instinct of self-assertion" (244). However, the play's criticism effectively ignores the play's own construction of propriety, the propriety of "traditional society." Macbeth as a man may be devoted to "self-assertion," but *Macbeth* is devoted to a society that rejects self-assertion apart from friendship and kinship relations. It is Macbeth's failure to perform as a peer, a creator of peers, a kinsman, and a friend that destroys him. His devotion to his wife rather than to his friends is a major feature of that failure. Paradoxically, however, because his radically misplaced devotion (misplaced in the eyes of the play) appeals to modernity, critics have focused on the man and his wife rather than on the network of men that the play suggests Macbeth should have better loved.

Macbeth, himself, recognizes that his loss of men's love is crucial: "Were not they forc'd with those that should be ours" he says, "We might haue met them darefull, beard to beard,/ And beate them backward home" (TLN 2325–27; 5.5.5–7). Indeed, the Scottish thanes whom we see at Macbeth's dinner table should be his. He has every opportunity to create the loving family of men who should form a king's household, the men whose love would have let him beat off the English army and some Scottish thanes. But he chooses away from his peers, and his choices indicate his inability to create the love between men that signifies in "traditional society." As Hopkins notes, Macbeth never bestows a title: "There are no nobles of his creation" (104). However he does cherish his ties with women. Bray asks whether "women figure" in "the stories of sworn friendship" that he reads. And he answers, "emphatically yes, not as friends, but as the enemies of friendship" (175). *Macbeth* functions like those stories of sworn friendship, as its women, the witches and Lady Macbeth, are the ultimate enemies of friendship between men. Macbeth chooses them as his counselors and friends rather than choosing the noble men upon whom he should rely, and Shakespeare signals Macbeth's mistaken choice explicitly in his language. Banquo calls Macbeth "My Noble Partner" when they are talking with the witches (TLN 154; 1.3.52), and when Banquo describes Macbeth's subsequent reverie to Ross and Angus, he says "Looke how our Partner's rapt" (TLN 254; 1.3.141). Macbeth, however, uses the word "partner" only to describe his wife: "*my dearest Partner of Greatnesse*" (TLN 357–58; 1.5.9–10). His selection of his wife as his "partner" indicates his deep inability to construct a family around him except in the modern sense. As Stephen Orgel suggests, "The notion that your wife is your friend and your comfort is not a Shakespearean one" (353). Unlike so many of his Shakespearean cohorts, Macbeth can love his wife, but he cannot love his friends.

Just as *Macbeth*'s love language between men violates modernity's distinction between love and economic interest, *Macbeth* speaks in a language of friendship and kinship foreign to modernity's systems of distinctions between immediate family, extended family, and friends. Bray's work shows us the significance of this language. While modernity separates friends from kin and kin from immediate family, "traditional society" recognizes friends as family and, in the case of kings, peers as friends/family. Reading literary and religious discourses from the sixteenth century, Bray argues that "different kinds of kinship terminology overlap and shade into each other and are not clearly distinguished from friendship" (83). We can see this lack of distinction in Malcolm's final speech; he calls the men around him "Thanes and Kinsmen" and promises to call "home [his] exil'd Friends abroad" (TLN 2515, 2519; 5.11.28, 32). The play implies that these friends may also be thanes and/or kinsmen. Malcolm promises to recreate in Scotland a network of men, a network of loving friends. This is also the family a king should have, a family of fighting men, and it is also by no means a model of family restricted to medieval Scotland. One of Bray's primary examples of this model of family is King James's relation to his peer, Buckingham, the peer whom James loved deeply and used familial terms to address.[5]

Macbeth applauds this model of male family, a family of friends who will die for one another. As Orgel suggests, that male family is seen by the play as considerably more significant than the immediate family so embraced by modernity: "Those claims on Macduff that tie him to his wife and children, that would keep him at home, that purport to be higher than the claims of masculine solidarity, are in fact rejected quite decisively by the play" (Orgel 353).[6] And that male family with its "claims of masculine solidarity" was a family by every definition based in blood. Although, as Harry Berger, Jr. points out, Duncan's Scotland is fraught with treachery and rebellion and attacked from without, its male–male love relations are not entirely illusory even though they are enacted in violence. After the men whom Duncan believes are his loyal defenders defeat his internal and external enemies, Duncan is surrounded immediately by "Sonnes, Kinsmen, [and] *Thanes*" (TLN 322; 1.4.35), none treacherous except Macbeth; and the Scottish Lord whom Lennox approaches at the end of Act 3 longs for a life where the peers "may againe . . . Do faithfull Homage, and receiue free Honors,/ All which [they] pine for now" (TLN 1506, 1509–10; 3.6.33, 36–37). His "againe" signifies that the men in the play see Duncan's kingship as a relative paradise of male–male relations. Lennox, Ross, and Macduff were Duncan's faithful kin, and nothing indicates that they will not be Malcolm's friends. This is hardly what Terry Eagleton calls "the routine state of cut-throat rivalry between noblemen" (6). Indeed, Eagleton's assessment narrows the play's focus to noblemen as represented by the former Thane of Cawdor, Duncan, and the new Thane of Cawdor, Macbeth; although it is a brilliant deconstructive reading of the play, Eagleton's reading is another manifestation of Macbeth as the critic's peer. The play, however, creates a world of many loving noblemen revenging themselves against a renegade cut-throat.

Critics such as Berger and Eagleton, dissatisfied with, or leery of, male family-making based in bloodshed, are responding more to a modern world view—one that chooses life in the world over death in battle—than they are to the energy of *Macbeth* or, indeed, any of Shakespeare's history plays or tragedies. A play that applauds the loss of Siward's son in battle does not anticipate the modern world devoted to the immediate family. In fact, it is Shakespeare's villains, such as Iago, who value life above male friendship.[7] Michel Foucault suggests that "For a society in which the systems of alliance, the political form of the sovereign, the differentiation into orders and castes, and the value of descent lines were predominant; for a society in which famine, epidemics, and violence made death imminent, blood constituted one of the fundamental values" (147). Foucault is describing a premodern society like that depicted in *Macbeth*, but Shakespeare's society shared all of these attributes.[8] And Bray teaches us to add male friendship to Foucault's list of characteristics of a society with blood as a fundamental value. The strain of *Macbeth* criticism that sees the play as somehow critical of violence and that, therefore, dismisses the play's friendship bonds between men as always incipiently treacherous may be epitomized in William Carroll's fine topical introduction to the Bedford *Texts and Contexts* edition of the play which ends thus:

> Finally, the presence of the witches exposes the violence inherent in the dominant cultural system of the play, the savage customs of the Scots whereby honors and titles derive directly (and, in the play, entirely) from murderous violence. How does one become thane of Cawdor? By his death. How does one become king? By killing him. How does one become an earl, as at the end of the play? By killing. After each killing, the victim is described as a traitor or a tyrant or a "dead butcher" (5.8.70), and the victor is described as thane, earl, or king. Such is the basis of kingship in the play. The witches lead us, as they lead Macbeth, to the heart of kingship's darkness.
>
> (Carroll 19–20)

As appealing as Carroll's condemnation of violence might be, Carroll rejects a model of family and friendship that the play itself loves. His rhetoric reveals his critical investment in Macbeth as his peer in the word's dominant modern sense. Carroll's repetition of the word "one" asserts an essential equality between the characters in question and a sense of identity between those equal men and the reader. But the play does not identify all of the "one[s]" in question as identical. It says, instead, that Macbeth becomes the Thane of Cawdor by his king's gift for his loyal battle service, and that he becomes king by repaying that gift with treachery. Similarly, it says that Malcolm's loyal friends become earls by his gift. The play never suggests that killing in battle is the same as murder. Indeed, it would be very difficult to make that argument even today—although Terry Eagleton tried to in 1986.[9] *Macbeth* also never suggests that just any "one" could become a thane or earl or king by killing; the people in question are all noblemen. Likewise, Carroll's words "victim" and "victor" and the passive voice "is described" imply that the descriptions of Macbeth as "tyrant" and "butcher" may be wrong, and that Macbeth might be accurately described as a "victim." Only a critic's deep investment in Macbeth as his peer could enable such a description. Carroll's rhetoric might seem an easy target, but it exemplifies a critical tradition that collectively sees Macbeth as our peer, not as a man among family and friends defined in a way entirely foreign to modernity. Put another way, this assessment of the play subscribes to a logic only available to modernity rather than to the premodern logic of the play. The play knows well the difference between its "bloody man" who is a "braue friend" and its "man of Blood" who murders a friend (TLN 18, 23; 1408; 1.2.1, 5; 3.4.125).

Macbeth, himself, as his laments toward the end of the play indicate, understands that premodern logic well. He says,

> My way of life
> Is falne into the Seare, the yellow Leaf,
> And that which should accompany Old-Age,
> As Honor, Loue, Obedience, Troopes of Friends,
> I must not looke to haue: but in their steed,
> Curses, not lowd but deepe, Mouth-honor, breath
> Which the poore heart would faine deny, and dare not.
>   (TLN 2239–45; 5.3.23–29)

Macbeth's list of things that will not come to him with age is a list of male relations: he will not have the titles given by men, men's love and willing duty paid to him, a group of loving men around him. And it is significant that he calls this world of male family and friendship "My way of life." At this late moment in the play, he sees his identity in relational terms, in the terms Duncan understands when he invests his son as the Prince of Cumberland and invokes the "signes of Noblenesse" that "like Starres, shall shine/ On all deseruers" (TLN 328–29; 1.4.41–42). These are the same relational terms that this son will invoke, in turn, when he makes his thanes and kinsmen earls. Macbeth's assessment of his own lack of relation with men is quite accurate, and the play stresses its significance. Angus, discussing the battle situation with three other thanes loyal to Malcolm, says of Macbeth, "Those he commands, moue onely in command,/ Nothing in loue" (TLN 2197–98; 5.2.49–50). And Malcolm reiterates the sentiment, telling Siward and Macduff, "none serue with him but constrained things,/ Whose hearts are absent too" (TLN 2307–308; 5.4.13–14). Bray's book teaches us that we should not read so quickly past the language of love in lines like these: "such language," he suggests, "always and necessarily signified in the public context of power and place that to modern eyes it seems to belie" (67). Angus and Malcolm are asserting more than that Macbeth is an autocratic ruler. Angus is affirming the love he and the thanes he fights with have for the man they serve, and Malcolm is promising to keep the hearts of the men who serve him.

Because that love between men is enmeshed in violence, it may look unreal to modern readers. We may read a male world in which love and violence coexist easily as somehow confused, but, as Bray suggests about the terms of premodern friendship and family, "the confusion lies not in these terms from the past but with us" (104). The violence that is a part of these love relations does not falsify them; rather, men who will kill and die for one another are the family a king should have. They, not his wife, are the family Macbeth misses at the end of his life.

Although Lady Macbeth seems well versed in the language of friendship, her fantasies are of Macbeth's singular rule. These are fantasies antithetical to "traditional society," which celebrated reciprocal, not "singular," relations of inequality: relations such as the ones between Malcolm and his peers and between Malcolm's peers. Thus Lady Macbeth welcomes Duncan with the elaborate "negative politeness" and the language of obligation that suits a peer's wife addressing her husband's benefactor king:

> All our seruice,
> In every point twice done, and then done double,
> Were poore, and single Businesse, to contend
> Against those Honors deepe, and broad,
> Wherewith your Maiestie loades our House.
> (TLN 450–54; 1.6.14–18)

And later she asks Macbeth to "Pronounce" her "welcome" to "all our Friends" (TLN 1262–63; 3.4.6–7). Nonetheless, she and the witches have set Macbeth's singular course. Introducing her plan to kill Duncan, Lady Macbeth asks her husband to let her manage the "Businesse" "Which shall to all [their] Nights, and Dayes to come,/ Giue solely soueraign sway, and Masterdom" (TLN 423–25; 1.5.66–68). Lady Macbeth calls the Macbeths' service to the king "poore, and single Businesse" after she has called the murder their "Businesse" in her conversation with her husband. This repetition should alert us to the resonance between the "solely soueraign sway" she offers Macbeth and the "single Businesse" that would so poorly "contend" against the honor Duncan has given Macbeth. For it is precisely that "single Businesse" that she conducts and that she offers Macbeth. She is offering Macbeth "single" status, a life "unaccompanied or unsupported" by his peers (*OED* "single" a. 1.). Her gift to him is his "solely soueraign sway," a "sway" that does not grant other men "free Honors," that does not create premodern peer relations. Obeying Lady Macbeth rather than responding to his peers' needs has given Macbeth a "sole name" that "blisters" the Scottish peers' "tongues" (TLN 1827; 4.3.12). These are Malcolm's words, describing the "Tyrant" Macbeth to Malcolm's own peers (men whose hearts should have belonged to Macbeth). Editors, almost universally, gloss "sole" in this line as "mere," certainly a reasonable gloss in the context of Malcolm's line alone.[10] But in the context of Lady Macbeth's earlier lines, we can hear Macbeth's "name" as "sole," as in "[w]ithout companions; apart from or unaccompanied by another or others" (*OED* "sole" a. 2a.). Such is Macbeth's condition since his response to his wife.

Likewise, Macbeth's response to the first witch's "All haile, *Macbeth*, haile to thee *Thane* of Glamis" and the second witch's "haile to thee *Thane* of Cawdor" signals his disregard of men and peer relations (TLN 148–49; 1.3.46–47). We can see the witches' naming Macbeth both Thane of Cawdor and "King hereafter" as the preemptive parody of Duncan's naming Macbeth his own Thane of Cawdor (TLN 150; 1.3.48). The witches hail him as the Thane of Cawdor and as king before Duncan can hail him as his thane. Macbeth never makes a peer himself, but he accepts the witches' grants of honor. And unlike the witches and Duncan, he cannot hail his own men, or the men who should be his own. Duncan and the witches call him Thane of Cawdor, but when his lords hover around his table waiting for his command, he says, "You know your owne degrees, sit downe" (TLN 1256; 3.4.1). His language fundamentally refuses premodern peer relations. The lords' "degrees" are indeed their "owne," but they are only their own by virtue of the king's gift, and their degrees measure and reflect their relations with the king and with each other. In Shakespeare's plays, kings address their peers by the names that indicate their social statuses and the relations between them. Compare, for example, Richard II's address to his Duke of Lancaster, "Old *Iohn of Gaunt*, time-honoured Lancaster" (*Richard II* TLN 1; 1.1.1), or Henry V's address to his nobles, "My lord of *Cambridge*, and my kinde lord of *Masham*,/ And you, my gentle Knight" (*Henry V* TLN 642–43; 2.2.13–14), to Macbeth's "You know your owne degrees." Henry is addressing traitors to his throne, and so the invocation of relation in his case is double-edged and even poignant, depending on one's perspective on Henry. But even when Henry speaks with men who genuinely love him, he calls them "my Princes and my Noble Peeres" (TLN 713; 2.2.81). Macbeth has no peers to call his own, and he refuses to make Scotland's peers his own by naming them, even when they present themselves to him. In that same scene, Lady Macbeth reminds him, "Your Noble Friends do lacke you," and he composes himself enough to say, "I do forget:/ Do not muse at me my most worthy Friends" (TLN 1358–59; 3.4.83–84). Yet he cannot name them himself; he follows his wife's lead, and he has forgotten his relations with his peers.

Perhaps then, Duncan's "peerelesse" is prophetic in another sense detrimental to his interests in that it hints at Macbeth's links to women instead of to men. The *OED*'s entries under the definition "Without peer; unequalled, matchless" reveal that the word was customarily used to describe women or feminine or effeminate qualities. From the fourteenth century, the *OED* cites Gower in *Confessio Amantis* describing Apollonius of Tyre's daughter as "piereles of beaute" (8.286–87); and from the fifteenth century, the dictionary cites Robert Fabyon who, in his chronicle history of England and France, characterizes Henry II as "peereles in chyualry, in warre, and in lechery" (*OED* "peerless" a.). Spenser, in the June ecologue of *The Shepheardes Calender*, has Hobbinoll offer Collin the "pierlesse pleasures" to be found when the nine sister muses make music under *Pheobe*'s light, and Milton may be picking up Spenser's reference to the feminine moon in *Paradise Lost* when he calls the moon an "Apparent queen" who unveils "her peerless light" (4.608). Except in the case of *Macbeth*, Shakespeare also uses the word to describe female or effeminate characters. "Peerless" appears only once in any early Shakespeare play, in *1 Henry VI*, when Suffolk tempts Henry to marry Margaret because of her "peerelesse feature" (TLN 2890; 5.7.68). Then we find a small spate of usages: two in *The Winter's Tale*, one in a servant's description of Perdita and one by Paulina describing Hermione's life (TLN 2843; TLN 3202; 5.1.94; 5.3.14); one in *The Tempest*, where Ferdinand uses the word to court Miranda, calling her "So perfect, and so pee[r]lesse" (TLN 1291; 3.1.47); and one use of the word by Antony to describe his lovemaking with Cleopatra (TLN 51; 1.1.42). In Antony's case, what he describes as "peerless" is the stance of the two lovers embracing while the world melts around them; this, like Henry II's alleged lechery signifies effeminacy in the English Renaissance. Shakespeare's other usage of "peerless" occurs in *Pericles*, where Gower uses the word in a description of Cleon's wife's murder plans: she plans to murder Marina so that the wife's daughter, Philoten, "Might stand peerless by this slaughter" (15.40). Again, it is a woman who may "stand peerless" in the world. Thus, in the context of Shakespeare's customary usage of the word, Duncan's word marks Macbeth as feminine or effeminate even while the occasion for the praise is Macbeth's battle triumph. Macbeth is a man among women rather than a man among his peers.

The only attempts Macbeth makes to initiate what might be a king–peer relation come under the witches' auspices. After they have seen the witches together, Macbeth says to Banquo, "let vs speake/ Our free Hearts each to other" (TLN 273; 1.3.153–54). And when Banquo recounts his dream of the witches, Macbeth seems to offer him a title dependent on the outcome of their "Businesse": "it shall make Honor for you," he says to Banquo (TLN 600, 604; 2.1.22, 25). Yet if this is a conditional offer of a title, this is Macbeth's only acknowledgment of a peer relation. When he meets Banquo as his king, Macbeth calls him "our chiefe Guest" and "sir," never his thane or his peer (TLN 994, 998; 3.1.11, 14).

Just as Macbeth's response to the witches' call rather than to Duncan's shows us his deficiencies as a peer of his king, his relations with the murderers and with much lesser men, generally, indicate his failure as a peer-maker.

Once again Shakespeare invokes the language customary between noble men to mark Macbeth's debased male relations. If the second witch's "haile to thee *Thane* of Cawdor" parodies Duncan's "my worthy *Cawdor*" proleptically (TLN 335; 1.4.47), Macbeth's conversations with the murderers parody the acts of peer-making by Duncan and his son. Macbeth congratulates the murderer to whose "assistance" he has made "loue" (TLN 1127; 3.1.125), saying, "Thou art the best o' th'Cut-throats,/ Yet hee's good that did the like for *Fleans*./ If thou did'st it, thou art the Non-pareill" (TLN 1274–76; 3.4.16–18). Though Macbeth uses the language of love between men when he enlists the murderers for their jobs, even to them he acknowledges his expediency and their debased nature in contrast to the "certaine friends" before whom he must save face. He must not "drop" those friends' "loues," yet he "make[s] loue" to a murderer of his "certaine friends"'s friend (TLN 1124–25; 3.1.122–23). Once the murderer has done the deed, Macbeth rewards him, offering him one title—"Cut-throat"—and the prospect of another—"the Non-pareill." This second title, "Non-pareill," recalls Duncan's naming of Macbeth as "peerelesse" in that Shakespeare almost always uses the word to describe a woman.[11] Where Duncan, sadly for him, believes that Macbeth is both "peerelesse" and his peer, even as his adjective, "peerelesse," betrays him, Macbeth seems to know that the title he offers his murderer is illegitimate. He does not call him a thane; he almost calls him "the Non-pareill," a word with feminized connotations like "peerelesse." But "the Non-pareill" and "Cut-throat" are the only titles he gives or almost gives out. He only makes male relations with men who could never be his peers. So, in addition to the murderers, he connects himself with his thanes' traitorous servants: "There's not a one of them but in his house/ I keepe a Seruant Feed" (TLN 1414–15; 3.4.131). This king should be paying his debts to his thanes; instead he is paying their servants to spy on their masters.

Arguably, the closest male–male relationship that Shakespeare allows Macbeth is the one between him and his officer or armor-bearer Seyton.[12] This relationship seems tender, perhaps because Seyton employs the "negative-politeness" language of love and respect that should surround a king but that Macbeth no longer gets from his peers; and Seyton seems to be a man in intimate relation to Macbeth's body, either arming him himself or calling in the armorers.[13] Jones and Stallybrass argue that "[i]n an aristocratic society the most privileged markings of identity are those of the knight. . . . The surface (the armored body) is elaborately identified . . . not as an 'individual' but as a genealogical body, a body marked, on the shields that surround it, by its kinship connections" (250). The gentry wills in which armor is left to men's heirs "make clear that the identity of the gentry is not the same as individuality. It is shaped from the outside by the value and the honors it can absorb into itself" (251). This deep link between a nobleman's most significant clothing, his armor, and his kinship relations shows us the significance of the pattern of clothing imagery that Caroline Spurgeon, seventy years ago, first noted in *Macbeth*. As Spurgeon suggests, "[t]he idea constantly recurs that Macbeth's new honours sit upon him, like a loose and badly fitting garment, belonging to someone else" (325). Macbeth should wear the livery of his king, and, once king, he should robe other men. But he does neither. Under his reign, Macduff fears that the peers' "old Robes" may "sit better than [their] new" (TLN 975; 2.4.39). And they will, because Macbeth's efforts to dress himself (TLN 513; 1.7.36) will leave him unable to properly wear the robes that should signify his kinship ties.

In Macbeth's figurative acceptance of the robes stripped from Cawdor, and in his subsequent theft of Duncan's robes, critics have seen a pervasive cynicism about kinship ties in the play. But Macbeth's exploitation of Duncan's love may instead be a sign of Shakespeare's deep awareness of "the resentment and dangers" the "obligations of friendship" and kinship "carried with them" (Bray 174). The word "cousin," which appears six times in *Macbeth*, shows us the breadth of friendship and kinship in the English Renaissance, and it is also a microcosm of the double-edged sword of friendship in both the play and Shakespeare's England. "Cousin" is a word that seems confusing to modern readers, so much so that Shakespeare editions gloss this seemingly familiar word. It could mean "a kinsman," or it could be used "[a]s a term of intimacy, friendship, or familiarity," or it could be "[u]sed by a sovereign in addressing or formally naming another sovereign, or a nobleman of the same country" (*OED* 1., 5., 5a.). Bray comments about terms like this that this "apparent confusion, in which different kinds of kinship terminology overlapped and shaded into each other, corresponded with precision to the actual social context in which they figured" (105). In *Macbeth*, Duncan calls Macbeth his "valiant Cousin" (TLN 43; 1.2.24) and addresses him as "worthyest Cousin" (TLN 297; 1.4.14). Banquo addresses Ross and Angus as "Cousins" (TLN 237; 1.3.125). Macbeth denounces Malcolm and Donalbain as "Our bloody Cozens" after their father's murder (TLN 1016; 3.1.31). Macduff welcomes Ross to the English court, saying "My euer gentle Cozen, welcome hither" (TLN 1995; 4.3.162). And Malcolm uses the word two times, first to address his thanes generally before the battle (TLN 2291; 5.4.1), and then, in what looks like a more specific reference, to talk about young Siward: "You (worthy Vnkle)/ Shall with my Cosin your right Noble Sonne,/ Leade our first Battell" (TLN 2383–85; 5.6.2–3).

For many of these usages it would be useless to try to discriminate between meanings. Duncan is surely calling Macbeth his friend, as well as his kinsman, as well as his nobleman, for example. But just as the pun queen/quean signified the sexual suspicion attached to woman as a category in the Renaissance, the pun cousin/cozen, which was equally and always available to the ear and the eye, signified the suspicion attached to the figure of the friend. In the folio text of *Macbeth*, the word is spelled sometimes "Cousin," sometimes "Cosin," and twice "Cozen." To cozen, of course, was a verb that meant "to cheat" and to "impose upon" (*OED* 1., 2.). And the noun and verb bled into one another, a great example of the "semantic slipping and sliding" available before standardized spelling (de Grazia and Stallybrass 265).[14] Duncan wants

Macbeth to be his cousin, but Macbeth is ready to cozen only in the negative sense. This, however, does not mean that Ross and Angus will cozen Malcolm. As Bray suggests,

> [t]he friendship of traditional society did indeed depend on an exchange of signs that could never wholly be assured . . . [its] rhetoric was Utopian. . . . But that emphatically does not mean that the rhetoric was false. It was precisely in being Utopian that it protected an endangered honor, when the obligations of friendship were created or called upon, or when the heart grew cold. Traditional society had need of such Utopias, and knew well how to make use of them.
>
> (Bray 204)

Macbeth's cold heart manifests itself in his rejection of his friends, but *Macbeth* may be a plea for the efficacy and primacy of friendship in Shakespeare's world.

Notes

1 I will quote all Shakespeare plays from the Hinman facsimile folio. They will be cited by through line numbers (TLN). After the TLN, I provide act, scene, and line numbers from *The Norton Shakespeare*.

2 See also Kenneth Muir's comment, "Shakespeare can make us feel our kinship with his client, can make us recognize that if we had been so tempted, we too might have fallen" (xliv).

3 Bray does discuss Shakespeare's sonnets, where we see male–male friendship and love most distinctly rendered, but his account of friendship should enable a conceptual leap for critics of the plays as well.

4 Although I will be invoking Jones and Stallybrass's work in this reading of *Macbeth*, Bray's lens is most useful, I think, because Bray explores in detail the male–male kin, peer, and friend relations that matter most to the play.

5 See Bray (96–104). See also David Bergeron.

6 See also Kathleen McLuskie's comment, "It is tempting to sentimentalize Macduff's relations with his family in a modern world that has privatized familial relations. However, the play provides a different set of relationships that link kin and kingship" (6).

7 Eagleton makes a version of this same point when he calls Shakespeare's villains "bourgeois individualist[s]" (4).

8 A number of *Macbeth* critics see the play as depicting a "feudal" world quite different than Shakespeare's own. Although Duncan's Scottish kingdom with its thanes is certainly not Shakespeare's own, I am arguing that the value of blood is shared between the two worlds.

9 See his comment, "it is hard to see why [Lady Macbeth's] bloodthirsty talk of dashing out babies' brains is any more 'unnatural' than skewering an enemy soldier's guts" (6).

10 See, for examples, *The Norton Shakespeare* (2063), David Bevington's Pearson/Longman *The Complete Works* (1283), *The Riverside Shakespeare* (1380), Robert Miola's Norton Critical Edition (61), Carroll's Bedford edition (87). Kenneth Muir's Arden edition attributes its gloss "the mere mention of whose name" to E.K. Chambers (123); The Everyman Shakespeare glosses "sole name" as "name

alone" (132); the Signet Classic edition edited by Sylvan Barnet glosses "sole" as "very" (105).

11　Caliban says that Prospero describes Miranda this way; Viola uses the term to talk about Olivia; and Posthumus sarcastically categorizes Imogen as "the nonpareil" in his appallingly misogynistic rant. The only exception besides Macbeth's usage is, again, in *Antony and Cleopatra*. This usage is complicated: Enobarbus uses the word in an imitation of Lepidus's fawning praise of Caesar. In the scene, Agrippa and Enobarbus mercilessly mock Lepidus as effeminate.

12　See the note in Kenneth Muir's Arden edition of *Macbeth* on the Setons as "hereditary armour-bearers to the Kings of Scotland" (5.3.29 n.).

13　Seyton asks Macbeth, "What's your gracious pleasure," and calls him "my good lord" and "my lord." The Doctor and the messenger use the same language, but both incur Macbeth's wrath.

14　There may well be another example of this "slipping and sliding" in Duncan's "it is a peerelesse kinsman." Were the middle "e" sounded, the word could slip into the word "perilous."

Works cited

Berger, Harry Jr. "The Early Scenes of *Macbeth*: Preface to a New Interpretation." *ELH* 47 (1980): 1–31.

Bergeron, David M. *King James and Letters of Homoerotic Desire*. Iowa City: U of Iowa P, 1999.

Bradley, A.C. "The Tragedy of *Macbeth*." *Macbeth: A Norton Critical Edition*. Ed. Robert S. Miola. New York: Norton, 2004. 237–53.

Bray, Alan. *The Friend*. Chicago: U of Chicago P, 2003.

Carroll, William C. "Introduction." William Shakespeare. *Macbeth: Texts and Contexts*. Boston: Bedford, 1999. 1–20.

De Grazia, Margreta and Peter Stallybrass. "The Materiality of the Shakespearean Text." *Shakespeare Quarterly* 44.3 (1993): 255–83.

Eagleton, Terry. *William Shakespeare*. Oxford: Basil Blackwell, 1986.

Foucault, Michel. *The History of Sexuality: Volume 1: An Introduction*. New York: Vintage Books, 1980.

Gower, John. *Confessio Amantis*. Toronto: U of Toronto P, 1980.

Greenblatt, Stephen. "Introduction." *Macbeth*. William Shakespeare. *The Norton Shakespeare*. New York: Norton, 1997. 2555–63.

Heilman, Robert. "The Criminal as Tragic Hero: Dramatic Methods." *Shakespeare Survey* 19 (1966): 12–24.

Hopkins, Lisa. "Household Words: *Macbeth* and the Failure of Spectacle." *Shakespeare Survey* 50 (1997): 101–10.

Jones, Ann Rosalind and Peter Stallybrass. *Renaissance Clothing and the Materials of Memory*. Cambridge: Cambridge UP, 2000.

McLuskie, Kathleen. "Humane Statute and the Gentle Weal: Historical Reading and Historical Allegory." *Shakespeare Survey* 57 (2004): 1–10.

Magnusson, Lynne. *Shakespeare and Social Dialogue: Dramatic Language and Elizabethan Letters*. Cambridge: Cambridge UP, 1999.

Milton, John. *Paradise Lost*. New York: Norton, 1993.

Muir, Kenneth. "Introduction." *Macbeth*. William Shakespeare. London: Routledge, 1984.

Orgel, Stephen. "*Macbeth* and the Antic Round." *Macbeth: A Norton Critical Edition*. Ed. Robert S. Miola. New York: Norton, 2004. 237–53.

Shakespeare, William. *Macbeth. The Norton Facsimile. The First Folio of Shakespeare*. Prep. Charlton Hinman. New York: Norton, 1968.

—— *The Norton Shakespeare*. Gen. Ed. Stephen Greenblatt. New York: Norton, 1997. 2555–618.

—— *Macbeth. The Arden Shakespeare*. Ed. Kenneth Muir. London: Routledge, 1984.

—— *Macbeth. The Complete Works of Shakespeare*. Ed. David Bevington. 5th ed. New York: Pearson, 2004.

—— *Macbeth. The Everyman Shakespeare*. Ed. John F. Andrews. London: J.M. Dent, 1993.

—— *Macbeth: A Norton Critical Edition*. Ed. Robert S. Miola. New York: Norton, 2004.

—— *Macbeth: Texts and Contexts*. Ed. William C. Carroll. Boston: Bedford/St. Martin's, 1999.

—— *The Tragedy of Macbeth. The Riverside Shakespeare*. Ed. Gen. ed. G. Blakemore Evans. 2nd ed. Boston: Houghton Mifflin, 1997. 1355–90.

—— *The Tragedy of Macbeth. The Signet Classic Shakespeare*. Ed. Sylvan Barnet. New York: New American Library, 1963.

Spenser, Edmund. *The Shepheardes Calender. The Yale Edition of the Shorter Poems of Edmund Spenser*. Ed. William A. Oram, Einar Bjorvand, Ronald Bond, Thomas Cain, Alexander Dunlop, and Richard Schell. New Haven: Yale UP, 1989.

Spurgeon, Caroline F.E. *Shakespeare's Imagery and What it Tells Us*. Cambridge: Cambridge UP, 1935.

5 "The servant to defect"

Macbeth, impotence, and the body politic

Julie Barmazel

> Th' attempt and not the deed/ Confounds us.
> Lady Macbeth (2.2.10–11)[1]

The question of the Macbeths' children—or lack thereof—has given a number of recent critics cause to contemplate Lady Macbeth's potentially vexed relationship with menstruation and childbirth, her role as a madwoman or hysteric moved to murderousness by the vagaries of her womb as well as those of her mind.[2] Alice Fox, in particular, has noted that "a major function of the imagery of obstetrics and gynecology in *Macbeth*" is to make us "aware of the protagonists as human beings who want to have children ... as human beings whose desire for living children has been frustrated" ("Obstetrics" 138). Indeed, the play returns relentlessly to images of bodily frustration and inadequacy, especially with regard to reproduction, evidencing what Gail Paster has characterized as a typically early modern preoccupation with "bodily refinement and exquisite self-mastery" (14)—both of which the Macbeths apparently lack. Such frustration with the body, evoking fears of the inability to master one's sexual and/or reproductive functions, speaks to a profound anxiety about physiology characteristic of the Renaissance imaginary: Shakespeare's was an age, Paster reminds us, "newly preoccupied with corporeal self-discipline" (10) and deeply influenced by the notion of the humoral body, the idea that the body operated fundamentally as a storehouse of unwieldy fluids that determined one's temperament.[3]

This body was thought to have very much a mind of its own: "Humoral physiology ascribes to the workings of the internal organs an aspect of agency, purposiveness, and plenitude to which the subject's own will is often decidedly irrelevant" (Paster 10). For early moderns, that is, the body was viewed increasingly as a site of shameful unruliness, in which corporeal imbalance would likely determine one's state of mind and course of action (or inaction). Through the metaphor of the body politic, the workings of the body could also be used to understand the state of the state. As Gil Harris has argued,

[t]o an extent that has not been fully acknowledged, early modern English versions of organic political analogy are similarly fixated with illness: extensively informed by the emergent discourses of Renaissance physiology, nosology, and pathology, elaborate accounts of the body politic's sundry diseases and their remedies make their first appearance in the literature of the period. Political writers, playwrights, and pamphleteers attempted to explain . . . the nature of the *corpus politicum*'s ills.

(Harris 3)

Macbeth can be viewed productively as one such text, as a play in which the frailties and imbalances of the body are made to speak to state ills, and vice versa. And while it has become a commonplace to view theater as "one of the Renaissance's most powerful and most ubiquitous mechanisms for explaining and enforcing political structure" (Raber 299), I would redirect our attention to the ways Shakespeare's play also does the reverse: to the playwright's tendency to characterize political structures as both inheriting and reflecting the body's infirmities—weaknesses over which the subject may have disturbingly little control. If, as Frank Whigham has suggested, "[d]uring the early seventeenth century Renaissance drama increasingly presented the body politic in *privacy* [and] Elizabethan political and social sins once portrayed with armies and rebels and maps were often recast in terms of sexual deviation and bodily excess" (Whigham 333), then *Macbeth* illustrates the extent to which its playwright is also concerned with the body's role in public politics; with the primacy of the private(s), as it were. And while the play opens with references to scenes of bloody battle, it reads for the most part as a tragedy of a highly personal, bodily, and domestic nature, in which the intrapersonal stakes are raised to the status of state business and state business is understood primarily in terms of the body—and the marital bed.

Although a good deal of critical attention has been paid to the potentially physiologically inflected language of Lady Macbeth's speeches, the play's numerous allusions to her husband's physiology have remained largely underexplored.[4] In this chapter, I would like to (re)turn our gaze to Macbeth's problematic body by looking at the play's elaborate network of puns about and allusions to Macbeth's sexual dysfunction. These work to connect the fruitlessness of Macbeth's political aspirations with those of his body, ironically making both images more potent. Macbeth's political sterility—his pointless destructiveness, his lack of political heirs—reenacts and confirms the sterility of his bed chamber; his power-lust is depicted in terms of poorly managed bodily lust and a related imbalance of bodily fluids. In short (and I use this term pointedly), Macbeth is impuissance embodied, and I shall devote the rest of this chapter to underscoring the many ways in which the play suggests a link among his physical, political, and moral disequilibria. Such connections resonate with those made by James I and other writers of the period, who saw kingship as bound up fundamentally with fatherhood, and fatherhood with bodily mastery: for James, "a king is truly *Parens patriae*, the politic father of his people," and is "rightly compared to a father of children, and to a head of a body composed of divers members" ("A Speech to the Lords and Commons of the Parliament at Whitehall [1610] and "The True Law of Free Monarchies [1598], cited in Carroll 216–17).[5] As Alexandra Shepard has noted, "[a]lthough domestic advice dwelt extensively on men's mastery of others, it also emphasized that this was predicated on their mastery of themselves" (77–78). Masculine self-governance, in turn, was intimately linked with the management of bodily fluids: as Mark Breitenberg has suggested, early moderns possessed a

> model of normative humoural masculinity in which the body's fluids are carefully (and anxiously) regulated according to what is allowed to enter and what must be expelled and in which all members of the body act properly in accordance with their assigned places and designated functions—an idealized vision of the masculine body as well as utopian political state.
>
> (Breitenberg 38–39)

If, as Shepard has said of the early modern period, "[t]he self-government expected of manhood was the basis of men's claims to authority" and "[m]en could not govern others if they were unable to govern themselves" (70), then Macbeth's inability to master his sexuality and/or impregnate his wife implies that he is also incapable of legitimately fathering a nation. (In the words of Sir Robert Filmer [*c.*1630], "there is no monarchy, but paternal" [cited in Stallybrass 131].) This would have been particularly pleasing to James I, who traced his lineage to Malcolm and Fleance:[6] the more "unnatural" Macbeth's sexuality appears, that is, the more "natural" the lines of descent from Malcolm and Fleance to James I come to seem.

Among a cast of principals who appear either as parents or children or both, it has often been noted, the Macbeths stand alone as childless and un(re)productive: Duncan is at once the father of a nation and of Malcolm and Donalbain; Banquo is aligned throughout the drama with his son Fleance; Macduff with his wife and precocious son; and the elder Siward with Young Siward. While the drama revolves around what Shakespeare calls in his tenth sonnet the making of "another self," or procreation, only the Macbeths, the Weird Sisters, and the Three Murderers lie outside the circle of generation, in the "unnatural" realm of explicit self-interest and unapologetic self-promotion, where a lack of offspring hints at a concomitant lack of concern for the well-being of society at large.[7]

The marked contrast between the fruitfulness of the play's major—and law-abiding—figures and the barrenness of the Macbeths encourages questions: Why are the Macbeths alone without heirs? "Or who is he so fond will be the tomb/ Of his self-love to stop posterity?" (Sonnet 3). Has the pair's lack of children generated their present self-absorption, or vice versa? Have they in fact chosen not to reproduce, or has their fate been determined by their physiology? By the end of the first act it is clear that Lady Macbeth's current state of childlessness is not likely due to any incapacity to bear children on *her* part. She has, after all, "given suck, and know[s]/ How tender 'tis to love the babe that milks me" (1.7.54–55). We are made to understand from this speech that Lady Macbeth *has* mothered a child.[8] Had she, then, a previous husband? Did her babe, or possibly babes, die during infancy? Such speculation, encouraged by both the structure and language of the play, leads to further questions still:[9] What of Macbeth's role in the marriage's current state of childlessness? Is Macbeth incapable of reproducing, or has he become so estranged from his wife that they no longer expect intimacy? The couple's closeness at the start of the play would indicate the contrary: before the Macbeths' bloodlust changes them so much as to make their personalities almost unrecognizable, the two clearly function in concert, something made obvious both by the content of Macbeth's letter to his wife in Act 1 and by the fact of his having written to her immediately after having heard the "perfectest report" of the Weird Sisters (1.5.2). She is his "dearest partner of greatness" (1.5.9–10), his "dearest chuck" (3.2.45), and theirs appears to be a far from loveless marriage.

Given such intimacy, and in light of Lady Macbeth's comments about having nursed an infant in the past, the play seems to suggest that the responsibility for any reproductive problems the couple might have lies squarely with Macbeth—and this despite the dominant early modern belief that "[b]arrenness was . . . the fault of the woman" (Pollock 41).[10] Lady Macbeth's explicit preoccupation with her body, and the suggestive language through which she expresses this concern, help to underscore the notion that she is (or at least believes herself to be) all too fertile, too womanly; so much so that she must call upon the gods to "unsex" her if she is to commit murder (1.5.39)—an act that, to the early moderns, was decidedly masculine.[11] The play's implicit references to menstruation reinforce the notion that Lady Macbeth is entirely too much dominated by her fertility, her female physiology, her "nature," to commit the "unnatural" act of murder:[12] in a drama blood-soaked from the start, Lady Macbeth is—to her frustration—steeped not only in the innocent blood of her victims, but in her own menstrual blood, the bodily issue that indicates both the possibility of giving birth and the (temporary) death of this opportunity, the very condition that defines the Macbeths and their "unlineal" rule. Lady Macbeth is still susceptible to the "compunctious visitings of nature" (1.5.43), to use the colloquial Renaissance term for menstruation, and would have the spirits "make thick my blood" and "Stop up th'access and passage to remorse" (1.5.41–42), which is to say that her blood has *not* been "stopped-up" and that the reproductive capacity she spurns is still very much extant within her.[13] So, too, is the quality of mercy that was thought to have attended it, and that will—by way of remorse—eventually lead to her madness.[14] Thus, while Macbeth refers to his wife's (masculine-inflected) "undaunted mettle" (1.7.73), we also sense that he protests too much. The "masculine" vigor and violence with which Lady

Macbeth attempts to renounce her body indicate that it possesses an equally strong "femininity," a femininity that is, ironically, the worthy opponent of her malevolence—in large part because of its reproductive capacity and fluids. Macbeth's fearful, half-critical, half awe-filled urging that his wife "[b]ring forth men-children only" (1.7.72) further underscores Lady Macbeth's reproductive potential, while simultaneously distancing Macbeth from the process of generating heirs himself. His comment almost suggests a fantasy of willful parthenogenesis on the part of his wife: it implies that Lady Macbeth alone might assume responsibility for creating (and possess the power to produce) her own issue—and to decide its sex, no less—while Macbeth's language clearly places him on the periphery of the process, passive and inconsequential.

Such irrelevance will characterize Macbeth's reign, as well. And throughout the play, the king's ultimate political inconsequentiality—his inability to produce heirs who might legitimate and extend his reign—is made to resonate with the language of bodily insufficiency, with the suggestion that Macbeth is unable to extend himself physically, at least when it comes to pleasing his wife. He appears in the play surrounded, variously, by the language of sexual insufficiency and inadequacy (or "unmanned" manhood [3.4.73]) and masturbatory excess—both of which would have arguably connoted humoral imbalance to a Renaissance audience.[15] If Lady Macbeth is too wet to commit murder, in other words, her husband is depicted as too dry to act the part of the proper man—in large part, we suspect, because he has already drained himself "dry as hay" (to paraphrase the curse of the First Witch in 1.3.17). In Act 3, for example, Macbeth claims that his "strange and self-abuse/ Is the initiate fear that wants hard use" (3.4.142–43). While these lines are usually taken to mean that Macbeth sees himself as an insufficiently hardened criminal, as one who has allowed his fears about immoral acts to lead him to hallucinate, the phrases "hard use" and "strange and self-abuse" may have possessed masturbatory overtones.[16] Like the subject of Shakespeare's first sonnet, Macbeth, too, apparently "[f]eeds't [his] light's flame with self-substantial fuel,/ Making a famine where abundance lies." Or, as Hecate says directly on the heels of Macbeth's comment, Macbeth "[l]oves for his own ends" (3.5.13)—a pronouncement that resonates with Macbeth's own description of "a barren scepter in my gripe/ Thence to be wrenched with an unlineal hand,/ No son of mine succeeding" (3.1.63–65), and his assertion: "[s]trange things I have in head, that will to hand" (3.4.139). Lady Macbeth's "compunctious visitings" would have served as a monthly reminder of her husband's shortcomings in this regard: because his "will" is in his hand, rather than her body, she will continue to bleed instead of becoming pregnant. "Yet here's a spot . . . Out, damned spot! Out, I say! One, two. Why, then, 'tis time to do't," she famously says (5.1.27–31). Might not Lady Macbeth's horror at these imagined bloodstains reenact the monthly reminder that she is not yet with child—a reminder still audible in her insistence that it is, once again, "time to do't"?[17] Finally, if some of Macbeth's own lines may be supposed to have had masturbatory implications, then so too might Angus's suspicion that Macbeth "does . . . feel/ his secret murders sticking on his hands" (5.2.16–17).

Terms denoting sterility, and possibly connoting masturbation, abound in this play—and why not? The Macbeths' is, after all, a masturbatory reign, insofar as its end is only to satisfy the couple's (political) desires, without a concern for the future of the nation. Macbeth's "will"—signifying both his political ambitions and his member—is, of course, mishandled; is insufficient to the task at hand. Macbeth speaks of having "no spur/ To prick the sides of my intent" (1.7.25–26), but the implication is that this "rat without a tail"— to paraphrase the First Witch again—actually has no "prick" to use with his wife.[18] His member is his first disobedient subject. The Porter's innuendo-riddled speech about drunken impotence, given just after Macbeth murders the king and just before he returns to the scene to face Duncan's sons, thus serves as more than a brief comic interlude in the midst of profound horrors; it strikes directly at the heart of the matter of the play. Drink, the porter says, gives one the desire for sex while removing the means, making one unable to "stand to." In Macbeth's words, "Our will became the servant to defect,/ Which else should free have wrought" (2.1.18–19). Shakespeare indicates that Macbeth has been singularly unable to master his body, and by implication will fail to master the body politic. Again, political and bodily terms are conflated—so much so that Shakespeare even has his would-be king envision his ascent to the throne in terms of penile sufficiency: on the heels of the Weird Sisters' prophesy, Macbeth muses over what he describes as "the swelling act/ Of the imperial theme" (1.3.127–28), suggesting a link between the act of becoming king and the ability to maintain an erection. This line also speaks to the Captain's earlier description of Macbeth's adventures in battle: "So from that spring whence comfort seemed to come/ Discomfort swells," he says (1.2.27–28). We are, in other words, encouraged to associate Macbeth with a dysfunctional member—a defunct spring—from the start of the play, and to view his rise to kingship as an unnatural attempt to shore up the masculinity that he himself has weakened. Lady Macbeth will eventually reinforce this image by accusing her husband of "unbend[ing]" his "noble strength" (2.2.48), implying that both Macbeth's political aspirations and his sex have been mishandled.[19] Macbeth, in turn, associates his ultimate commitment to murderous deeds with a working penis: "I am settled," he says in response to his wife's demands, "and bend up/ Each corporal agent to this terrible feat" (1.7.79–80). The line implies that Macbeth sees murder as a means of "bend-ing up" his "corporal agent," as a way to have in marriage what he has only recently had in battle: "cannons over-charged with double cracks,/ So they doubly redoubled strokes upon the foe" (1.2.37–38). Lady Macbeth has cer-tainly implied that her husband's "cannon" has not been "overcharged" of late, nor "stroking" at all, let alone "doubly." Bearing in mind that "courage" had indicated "lustiness" and "vital force" since at least the fifteenth century and "sexual vigour and inclination" since at least the mid-sixteenth (*Oxford*

English Dictionary 3), Lady Macbeth's insistence that her husband "screw [his] courage to the sticking-place" (1.7.60) also serves as a less-than-subtle reminder of his usual failure in this regard.[20]

Lady Macbeth's oft-cited aspersions against her husband's manliness[21] thus have a distinct materiality. The would-be queen's rhetoric suggests that Macbeth's physical, emotional, and political weaknesses are unthinkable in isolation—and that each must be corrected if the couple's desires are to be satisfied. Lady Macbeth's promptings seem designed as a spur to a man who has none, as a means to seeing her husband finally endowed by virtue of being enthroned, and vice versa. All of this is necessary, she suggests, because her husband's "nature . . . is too full o'th'milk of human kindness/ To catch the nearest way" (1.5.14–16), too full of womanly humor to carry out its requisite functions. Again, bodies and wills collide in Shakespeare's language. "Nature" connotes menstrual blood, as well as the female genitalia;[22] the "milk of human kindness" that supposedly fills Macbeth's "nature" betokens a range of female bodily fluids (menstrual blood, mother's milk), but at the same time also suggests semen (*OED* 2b). Macbeth is thus both too much a woman and too little a man. He is saturated with the bodily fluids associated with childbearing, but without the children that should, to a Renaissance mind, accompany them.[23]

Lady Macbeth's charges do not refer merely to Macbeth's metaphorical "womanliness" or slack effeminacy, then, but to what she characterizes as a distinctly physical/sexual inadequacy, as well. "Are you a man?" she taunts. "What, quite unmanned in folly?" (3.4.58 and 73).[24] Lady Macbeth makes clear that her opinion of her husband depends very much on Macbeth's proving that he is *not*, ultimately, to be "unmanned":

> . . . From this time
> Such I account thy love. Art thou afeard
> To be the same in thine own act and valour,
> As thou art in desire? . . .
> When you durst do it, then you were a man.
> And to be more than what you were, you would
> Be so much more the man.
>
> (1.7.38–51)

Again, political ambitions are allied with sexual desire and ability. Bearing in mind the bawdy implications of the First Witch's "I'll do, I'll do, and I'll do" (1.3.9), Lady Macbeth's "When you durst do it, then you were a man" reinforces her already strong case against Macbeth's potency (i.e. he hasn't yet "done it" with her) while simultaneously highlighting the couple's working assumption that Macbeth's identity is dependent on his sexual proficiency, on his ability to manage his member properly.[25] Thus, while commentators sometimes encourage us to think of Macbeth's murderousness as "in part an act of love done to please his wife" (Wintle and Weis 143), his actions are perhaps better viewed as the desperate behavior of an "unmanned" man than they are those of a simply doting, even uxorious, husband. The marriage that first appears to us as supportive and collaborative turns out to be based on—or perhaps to have devolved into—an "unnatural" alliance in which the "masculine" female is forced to compensate for her husband's physical insufficiency: "Infirm of purpose!" she accuses him, "Give me the daggers" (2.2.55–56). It is because Macbeth's dagger is infirm, in other words, and because he has kept hold of it, that his wife must make such a demand. By this point in the play, it is clear that the Macbeths equate the king's ability to rule with his ability to master his sex. Not surprising, then, that Macbeth should describe his murder of Duncan in terms of sexual conquest, equating his approach to the king with that of Tarquin to Lucrece (2.1.55), and proclaiming after the murder that he has finally "done the deed" (2.2.14).[26] Perhaps more importantly, he has attempted to prove to himself that he can truly make good use of his dagger. The tragedy of Macbeth, of course, is that his daggers (his knife, his member) are misused, and thus lead only to destruction without increase, to a (not so) *petit mort* that fails to provide what should "naturally" follow: the planting and growth of Macbeth's seed.

Given the logic of sex and death—or climax without result—that guides *Macbeth*, it is fitting that the drama should repeatedly invoke the specter of orgasm, as well. The term "come"—which the *OED* notes appeared in print with its present connotation of reaching orgasm in 1650 (17), and which, I suggest, would have held that meaning for Shakespeare at the start of the century[27]—appears in Macbeth's speeches and in speeches relating to him with a noticeable regularity: "Macbeth doth come" (1.3.29); "Come what come may" (1.3.145); "our thane is coming" (1.5.32); "Come, let me clutch thee," he says to the vision of the dagger (2.1.34); and "To bed, to bed; . . . Come, come, come, come, give me your hand . . . to bed, to bed, to bed" (5.1.56–58) his wife says to him in her reverie. The witches sing "Come away, come away" (3.5) after discussing the fact that Macbeth, perhaps a man whom they have already decided to "drain . . . as dry as hay" (1.3.17) and who "loves for his own ends" (3.5.13), will "come to know his destiny" (3.5.17). A common enough word, but it appears almost too often in *Macbeth*. Perhaps this is because the doomed king has already "come" too much—but to no good end—or because he will never come into his own, as it were. Perhaps the witches are implying that Macbeth must "come" *in order* to fulfill his destiny, while Lady Macbeth urges him to do what she knows all too well he cannot. "The cry is still 'They come!' " (5.5.2), Macbeth says of his enemies as the play ends, in a comment that at once announces the presence of Malcolm, Siward, and Macduff and reminds us of the fundamental difference between Macbeth and the rightful heirs to their titles. Malcolm has already hinted at this discrepancy, in the account of his own character that he gives Macduff:

> *Malcolm.*   I grant [Macbeth] bloody,
>   Luxurious, avaricious, false, deceitful,

> Sudden, malicious, smacking of every sin
> That has a name. But there's no bottom, none,
> In my voluptuousness: your wives, your daughters,
> Your matrons, and your maids could not fill up
> The cistern of my lust, and my desire
> All continent impediments would o'erbear,
> That did oppose my will. Better Macbeth
> Than such an one to reign.
>
> (4.3.57–66)

The suggestion is that Macbeth represents the antithesis of Malcolm's putative sexual prowess. If "Better that your wives, your daughters,/ Your matrons, and your maids" should be unsafe in Malcolm's presence than that they should be ruled by one who poses no sexual threat whatever—whether he be "luxurious" (i.e. lustful) or no. Taken as a whole, the play illustrates precisely the dangers of having such a one as king.

Together, Shakespeare's myriad allusions to Macbeth's sexual dysfunction promote the idea that his marriage has been as sterile as will be his reign, and as terminal. The material and the marital thus speak to the martial and the monarchical. In her longest speech about Macbeth, Hecate says "There hangs a vap'rous drop profound;/ I'll catch it ere it come to ground" (3.5.24–25), indicating that Macbeth's seed will never germinate, that, in contradistinction to Banquo, Macbeth will not be "planted," will not be "full of growing," as Duncan says Banquo will be (1.4.28–29). For all of Macbeth's coming, then, he never arrives, his self-love remaining always his goal and obstacle, and leading, finally, to his *un*doing. In the end, Macbeth loses the scepter he had never learned to hold on to properly (despite, or because of, his many attempts to do so), and, in a final emasculating blow that lends itself to these sorts of readings, loses his head as well, making explicit the condition that we have already been led to imagine throughout the body of the play.

Notes

1 This and all other quotations from *Macbeth* are taken from A.R. Braunmuller's New Cambridge Shakespeare edition of the play.

2 I am referring to L.C. Knights's famous question, "How Many Children Had Lady Macbeth?" (See his essay of the same title, reprinted in *Explorations* [London: Chatto and Windus, 1946]). For treatments of the theme of childlessness in *Macbeth* generally, see especially Calderwood; Davis; and Omberg. For discussions of Lady Macbeth's physiology in relation to this issue, see Fox ("Obstetrics") and Fox (" 'How Many Pregnancies' "); Adelman; Bristol; Levin.

3 "Every subject grew up with a common understanding of his or her body as a semipermeable, irrigated container in which humors moved sluggishly. People imagined that health consisted of a state of internal solubility to be perilously maintained" (Paster 8).

4 For more on Lady Macbeth's body and the critics, see note 2, above. A notable exception to the general critical neglect of Macbeth's body is Biggins, who pays

significant attention to the metaphorical language surrounding Macbeth's vexed sexuality.

5 For more on the perception that patriarchy and monarchy were linked, see Jean E. Graham, "The Performing Heir in Jonson's Jacobean Masques"; Peter Stallybrass, "Patriarchal Territories: The Body Enclosed"; and Jonathan Goldberg, "Fatherly Authority: The Politics of Stuart Family Images."

6 Wintle and Weis write: "James I and his children could claim descent from two of the characters in *Macbeth*, Malcolm and Fleance, both sons of fathers murdered in the play by the childless hero. . . . Banquo and his son Fleance were invented to extend and dignify the somewhat obscure genealogy of the Stuarts when they came to power in Scotland" (128).

7 Cf. Shakespeare's Sonnet 9:

> The world will be thy widow and still weep,
> That thou no form of thee hast left behind . . .
> No love toward others in that bosom sits
> That on himself such murd'rous shame commits.

8 For a contrary view, see especially Stallybrass.

9 The play begins *in medias res*, a device that encourages an audience's questions. As James Calderwood has rightly noted: "We come in on the play . . . not at the beginning, but in mid-hurly-burly . . . of course, under the classical heading of *in medias res*, this is a perfectly respectable way to (not)-begin a play" (79).

10 Pollock goes on to suggest that "[i]f a male was capable of erection, he was presumed potent; if he achieved penetration and ejaculation and yet conception did not occur, then it was assumed that the woman was infertile" (41). I am arguing that the play gives us every reason to imagine that Macbeth has not achieved penetration.

11 For more on this subject, see especially Sandra Clark's "*Hic Mulier, Haec Vir*, and the Controversy over Masculine Women." As Clark notes: "Many references to masculine women mention their weapons and aggressive behavior" (170). Karen L. Raber sums the situation up nicely:

> Lady Macbeth's apparent lack of children and her capacity to over-write her mothering instinct with political ambition have been the subject of any amount of critical speculation. It is fair to say at a bare minimum that Shakespeare uses her present childlessness and her murderous speech to emphasize the unnatural role she adopts when she seeks to move out of the position of wife and mother and into the position of political advisor and schemer. (313)

12 Cf. Bristol on the normative nature of such a view:

> Knights expounds Lady Macbeth's lines about murdering her own child as the elaboration of the general theme of "unnatural" feelings. But why is it unnatural to feel like dashing out the brains of your own baby? The interpretation here obviously depends on a judgement about Lady Macbeth as a mother. Her intended behaviour is "unnatural" only in relation to a normative inference that says mothers are supposed to love and protect their babies. (24–25)

13 I owe this discussion of Lady Macbeth and menstruation to Fox and La Belle (see especially Fox, "Obstetrics" 129 and La Belle 381–82). La Belle suggests that "[w]hen [Lady Macbeth] pleads to 'make thick my blood,/ Stop up th'access and

passage to remorse,' she is asking for the periodic flow to cease, the genital tract to be blocked. Renaissance medical texts generally refer to the tract through which the blood from the uterus is discharged as a 'passage' " (382). Regarding Lady Macbeth's speech, I would also stress the strangeness of her describing her monthly "visitings" as "compunctious" (i.e. conscience-stinging) rather than simply unwelcome, or perhaps bothersome. What is it about menstruation that would produce in Lady Macbeth a conviction of sin or suggest the need for remorse, rather than mere sadness? It seems more likely that the compunction she speaks of belongs to her husband—it is he, she suggests, who should feel responsible for the couple's childlessness. This reading is strengthened when one considers that "*spirit* is used to mean 'semen' in the opening line of Sonnet 129" (Biggins 265). In this case, Lady Macbeth's request in 1.5.38–46 might be paraphrased as, "Come, semen . . . Make me pregnant."

14 Note Gail Paster's suggestion that "among. . . the several idioms of the Elizabethan-Jacobean stage, [blood] is most often metonymy for important and laudable qualities such as mercy, sacrifice, or passion" (65). Again, the play implies a concordance between the body and the larger social order: in order to violate the latter, Lady Macbeth insists that she must first experience bodily disorder (by way of de-feminization).

15 Paster writes:

> [S]exual intercourse was understood in the humoral economy as the bodily expenditure of seminal fluid, to be regulated in both men and women for the maintenance of health. Doctors had the support of humoral theory in prescribing therapeutic sexual intercourse for sexually mature men and women since the unnatural retention or expenditure of seed could produce humoral imbalance or disease. (168–69)

For more on the complicated history of the cultural career of masturbation, specifically, see especially Stolberg, and cf. Laqueur. Also note that masturbation and impotence had been linked long before *Macbeth* (Stolberg 703).

16 The term "use" would have signified sexual pleasure to a Renaissance audience. (See especially Shakespeare's twentieth sonnet.) As for "self-abuse," in 1728, Chambers notes that "Self-Abuse is a Phrase used by some late Writers for the Crime of Self-Pollution" (cited in the *OED*). Whether or not Shakespeare was one such late writer is debatable, but while Thomas W. Laqueur suggests in *Solitary Sex* that masturbation was not viewed, specifically, as disease-inducing "self-abuse" until 1712, the word "abuse" does figure in Shakespeare's fourth sonnet, in which masturbation (and its pitfalls) is the implied topic. (Sonnet 6 is similarly focused.)

17 For more on Shakespeare's use of "do" to connote the sex act, see especially Biggins 262.

18 The *OED* notes examples of "prick" meaning penis as early as 1592, and suggests that "tail" was used colloquially to mean penis as early as 1483. As Dennis Biggins writes in "Sexuality, Witchcraft, and Violence in *Macbeth*," the Witch "undoubtedly refers to her intention of draining the unfortunate man of his semen" (Biggins 257).

19 As Biggins suggests, "Lady Macbeth scornfully equates Macbeth's quailing from regicide with sexual nonperformance" (267).

20 The *OED* notes that "screw" first appeared in print with its sexual connotation in 1725 (which suggests that it would have been in common currency long before this), and that a "sticking-place" refers to "the screwing-up of the peg of a musical instrument until it becomes tightly fixed in the hole" (*OED* 2). As for the term "courage," Michael Davis treats the subject at length in "Courage and Impotence

in Shakespeare's *Macbeth*," but without highlighting the sexual charge latent in the word. "Courage is a martial virtue," he writes (223), but I would take Lady Macbeth's speech to mean that she also values it as a marital virtue.

21 Patrick Colm Hogan, for example, writes of Lady Macbeth "chiding Macbeth for his femininity" (388). Wintle and Weis note "her jibes at his lack of manliness" (142). Stephanie Chamberlain complicates the question. She writes:

> Scholars have traditionally read . . . her . . . "unsex me here" invocation as evidence of Lady Macbeth's attempt to seize a masculine power to further Macbeth's political goals. To overcome her husband's feminized reticence, Lady Macbeth assumes a masculinity she will prove unable to support. While she clearly seeks power, such power is, I would argue, conditioned on maternity, an ambiguous, conflicted status in early modern England. (72–73)

22 The *OED* gives examples of these uses in texts dated 1481, 1569, and 1607.

23 Cf. Biggins 262.

24 Here, "folly" can refer to sexual as well as irrational behavior. The term definitely connotes the former in *Othello* ("She turned to folly; and she was a whore" [5.2.131]) and *Measure for Measure*, where Isabella describes the licentious Angelo as an "outward-sainted deputy,/ Whose settled visage and deliberate word/ Nips youth i'th head, and follies doth enmew" (3.1.89–91). Lady Macbeth's suggestion seems to be both that Macbeth is unreasoning in thinking he has seen a ghost, and emasculated—unable to act the part of a man during sex. Paster's discussion of early modern conceptions of the womb's "thirst" for semen and its role in female melancholy is also apt here (see especially Paster 58–62).

25 Cf. Carolyn Asp:

> Only if he dares to do the deed will he be a man, and so much more the man, in her esteem. The whole argument to murder is couched in sexual terms: she accuses him of arousing her expectations and then failing to follow through with action . . . When Macbeth appears after the murder she calls him "my husband," the only time in the play she addresses him by that familiar title that emphasizes the sexual bond between them. (160–61)

Joanna Levin notes similarly: "As Lady Macbeth goads Macbeth on to murder, their interaction can be read as a sexualized relation in which murderous intent emerges as the final product" (42).

26 James L. Calderwood notes that "one way to interpret the Macbeth–Tarquin equation would be to regard the murder as a metaphoric substitute for the sexual act" (70).

27 For a compelling discussion of Shakespeare's use of "come" to imply orgasm in *Julius Caesar*, see Parker. Shakespeare implies a familiarity with the sexual implications of the term "come" in *Measure for Measure*, as well. In a particularly innuendo-ridden conversation between Pompey and Escalus—in which the clown alludes to pregnancy, prostitutes, and pudenda—the two exchange the following dialogue:

> *Escalus.* Come, you are a tedious fool, to the purpose: what was done to Elbow's wife, that he hath cause to complain of?
> *Come me to what was done to her.*
> *Pompey.* Sir, your honour cannot come to that yet.
> *Escalus.* No, sir, nor I mean it not. (2.1.103–107)

My suggestion is that Lady Macbeth, unlike Escalus, does mean it.

Works cited

Adelman, Janet. *Suffocating Mothers: Fantasies of Maternal Origin in Shakespeare's Plays*, Hamlet *to* The Tempest. New York: Routledge, 1992.

Asp, Carolyn. " 'Be bloody, bold and resolute': Tragic Action and Sexual Stereotyping in *Macbeth*." *Studies in Philology* 78.2 (1981): 153–69.

Biggins, Dennis. "Sexuality, Witchcraft, and Violence in *Macbeth*." *Shakespeare Studies* 8 (1975): 255–77.

Breitenberg, Mark. *Anxious Masculinity in Early Modern England*. Cambridge: Cambridge UP, 1996.

Bristol, Michael D. "How Many Children Did She Have?" *Philosophical Shakespeares*. Ed. John Joughin. London: Routledge, 2000. 18–33.

Calderwood, James L. " 'More Than What You Were': Augmentation and Increase in *Macbeth*." *ELR* 14.1 (1984): 70–82.

Carroll, William C., ed. Macbeth: *Texts and Contexts*. Boston: Bedford/St. Martin's, 1999.

Chamberlain, Stephanie. "Fantasizing Infanticide: Lady Macbeth and the Murdering Mother in Early Modern England." *College Literature* 32.3 (2005): 72–91.

Clark, Sandra. "*Hic Mulier, Haec Vir*, and the Controversy over Masculine Women." *Studies in Philology* 82 (1985): 157–83.

Davis, Michael. "Courage and Impotence in Shakespeare's *Macbeth*." *Shakespeare's Political Pageant: Essays in Literature and Politics*. Ed. Joseph Alulis and Vickie Sullivan. Lanham: Rowman and Littlefield, 1996. 219–36.

Fox, Alice. "How Many Pregnancies Had Lady Macbeth?" *University of Dayton Review* 14 (1979–80): 33–37.

——— "Obstetrics and Gynecology in *Macbeth*." *Shakespeare Studies* 12 (1979): 127–41.

Goldberg, Jonathan. "Fatherly Authority: The Politics of Stuart Family Images." *Rewriting the Renaissance: The Discourse of Sexual Difference in Early Modern Europe*. Ed. Margaret W. Ferguson, Maureen Quilligan, and Nancy J. Vickers. Chicago: U of Chicago P, 1986. 3–32.

Graham, Jean E. "The Performing Heir in Jonson's Jacobean Masques." *Studies in English Literature 1500–1900* 41.2 (2001): 381–98.

Harris, Jonathan Gil. *Foreign Bodies and the Body Politic: Discourses of Social Pathology in Early Modern England*. Cambridge: Cambridge UP, 1998.

Hogan, Patrick Colm. "*Macbeth*: Authority and Progenitorship." *American Imago* 40.4 (1983): 385–95.

Knights, L.C. "How Many Children Had Lady Macbeth?" *Explorations: Essays in Criticism*. London: Chatto and Windus, 1946. 1–39.

La Belle, Jenijoy. " 'A Strange Infirmity': Lady Macbeth's Amenorrhea." *Shakespeare Quarterly* 31 (1980): 381–86.

Laqueur, Thomas W. *Solitary Sex: A Cultural History of Masturbation*. New York: Zone Books, 2003.

Levin, Joanna. "Lady Macbeth and the Daemonologie of Hysteria." *ELH* 69.1 (2002): 21–55.

Omberg, Margaret. "Macbeth's Barren Sceptre." *Studia Neophilologica* 68 (1996): 39–47.

Parker, Barbara L. "The Whore of Babylon and Shakespeare's *Julius Caesar*." *Studies in English Literature, 1500–1900* 35.2 (1995): 251–70.

Paster, Gail Kern. *The Body Embarrassed: Drama and the Disciplines of Shame in Early Modern England*. Ithaca: Cornell UP, 1993.

Pollock, Linda A. "Embarking on a Rough Passage: The Experience of Pregnancy in Early-Modern Society." *Women as Mothers in Pre-Industrial England*. Ed. Valerie Fildes. London: Routledge, Chapman and Hall, 1990. 39–67.

Raber, Karen L. "Murderous Mothers and the Family/State Analogy in Classical and Renaissance Drama." *Comparative Literature Studies* 37.3 (2000): 298–320.

Shakespeare, William. *Macbeth*. Ed. A.R. Braunmuller. Cambridge: Cambridge UP, 1997.

—— *Julius Caesar*. Ed. Marvin Spevack. Cambridge: Cambridge UP, 2004.

Shepard, Alexandra. *Meanings of Manhood in Early Modern England*. Oxford: Oxford UP, 2006.

Stallybrass, Peter. "Patriarchal Territories: The Body Enclosed." *Rewriting the Renaissance: The Discourse of Sexual Difference in Early Modern Europe*. Ed. Margaret W. Ferguson, Maureen Quilligan, and Nancy J. Vickers. Chicago: U of Chicago P, 1986. 123–42.

Stolberg, Michael. "The Crime of Onan and the Laws of Nature: Religious and Medical Discourses on Masturbation in the Late Seventeenth and Early Eighteenth Centuries." *Paedagogica Historica* 39.6 (2003): 701–17.

Whigham, Frank. "Reading Social Conflict in the Alimentary Tract: More on the Body in Renaissance Drama." *ELH* 55.2 (1988): 333–50.

Wintle, Sarah and René Weis. "Macbeth and the Barren Sceptre." *Essays in Criticism* 41.2 (1991): 128–46.

6 *Macbeth*'s equivocal conscience

Abraham Stoll

Macbeth dramatizes the functioning of conscience in the sinful mind. Macbeth and Lady Macbeth take the path of willfully ignoring conscience as they kill their sworn king, and in the aftermath of that action they experience conscience redounding upon them. Lady Macbeth's unfolds slowly, finally communicating to her in Act 5. But Macbeth's conscience works immediately and expansively in the moments after the murder, dominating his thoughts and the drama of Act 2. These two parts of the play furnish a portrait of how conscience communicates—how it sounds and looks, and how it feels to find oneself within the workings of conscience.[1]

Far more than ours, Shakespeare's period put considerable energy into anatomizing and understanding the conscience. *Macbeth* is written soon after two important theorizations of conscience, Alexander Hume's *Ane Treatise of Conscience* (1594) and William Perkins's more expansive *A Discourse of Conscience* (1596). These are but the beginnings of England's extensive entanglement with conscience in the seventeenth century, which Keith Thomas has called "the Age of Conscience" (29).[2] With conscience emerging as a central object of inquiry, theorists such as Hume and Perkins take up the challenge of explaining how this inward faculty functions. The array of metaphors which emerges in such discourse shows just how hard it is to describe: conscience is to be found pricking, gnawing, biting, stinging, murmuring, accusing, and witnessing; it is figured as fiery darts, a worm, a notary with a pen, a prison keeper, a little god within the heart, a cutthroat, and a continual feast. One of the most commonly discussed conceptions is the idea that the conscience functions through a sharing of knowledge with an other.

This sharing of knowledge is related to the metaphor of a witness, one of longest-standing and most common ways of describing conscience.[3] But the notion that conscience is a *knowing with* some other agent is based upon the eytmology of the word, and the explanatory force of etymology substantiates it to the point that it is no longer metaphor but a literal description. Hume explains that: "the significatioun and pith of the word it self doth import: For the latine word, *Conscientia*, (from the which the worde, *Conscience* comes) is composed of the Preposition, *cum*, which signifies in our language, *with*, &

Scientia, which signifies *Science*, or *Knawledge*" (13, with some modernization of spelling). Or, as Perkins puts it: "*Scire*, to know, is of one man alone by himselfe: and *conscire* is, when two at the least know some one secret thing; either of them knowing it togither with the other" (*Discourse* 5). This way of understanding the early modern conscience C.S. Lewis calls the "together branch," distinguishing it from the "weakened branch" which functions through knowledge but not through a knowledge shared with an other (181–82).[4] This chapter uses the phrase *knowing with* to describe how this stronger and widespread conception of conscience causes extreme difficulty for the Macbeths.

Shakespeare picks up this sense of *knowing with* in *Richard III* when Richard cries out, "My conscience hath a thousand several tongues,/ And every tongue brings in a several tale,/ And every tale condemns me for a villain" (5.3.193–96).[5] Shakespeare is hyperbolical, seizing upon *knowing with* to turn Richard's bad conscience into a scene of overwhelming communication. Such troping marks Shakespeare's imaginative interest in the dynamics of *knowing with*, an interest which reappears in *Macbeth*. For Richard, conscience communicates with terrifying clarity and in overwhelming unison, just as the play itself moves inexorably toward divine justice. But in *Macbeth*, *knowing with* brings to conscience a crisis of signification. When Shakespeare returns in *Macbeth* to the conception of conscience as an overcrowded, over-loud space, the signifiers are not so easily interpretable, and the communication is not so neatly effective.

Shakespeare gets from Holinshed's *Chronicles* the kernel of his investigation, as Kenneth, who furnishes part of the character of Macbeth, murders Malcolm, and is then stricken by conscience. Kenneth

> could not but still live in continuall feare, least his wicked practise concerning the death of Malcome Duffe should come to light and knowledge of the world. For so commeth it to passe, that such as are pricked in conscience for anie secret offense committed, have ever an unquiet mind. And (as the fame goeth) it chanced that a voice was heard as he was in bed in the night time to take his rest, uttering unto him these or the like woords in effect: "Thinke not Kenneth that the wicked slaughter of Malcolme Duffe by thee contrived is kept secret from the knowledge of the eternall God."
>
> (Holinshed 5: 247)

The voice clearly conveys his guilt, and goes on to lay out his sure punishment. The next morning Kenneth confesses. In reworking Holinshed, Shakespeare turns up the volume on Kenneth's unquiet mind and fractures the communicating voice until Macbeth's mind reverberates with an overcrowded, overwhelming conscience. If conscience is a *knowing with*, Shakespeare undermines the Macbeths' ability to interpret the object of that preposition—to understand *with what* or *with whom* they know. And in this unstable experience, conscience communicates in such a chaotic way that it fails to bring about repentance.

Beginning with a reading of the aftermath of Duncan's murder, this chapter reveals how the cacophony of sounds and the chaos of sights which greet Macbeth fail to convey the judgments of conscience with clarity. This failure to communicate not only challenges the viability of the early modern conscience, but even its existence, as *Macbeth* draws repeatedly near to the conclusion that conscience is a *knowing with* no other agent but oneself. This solipsism is legible in the play in three ways. First, conscience is undermined by the possibility that it is indistinguishable from the symptoms of melancholy, suggesting that it is merely a physical, and not a supernatural, experience. Second, the play raises the suspicion that, in the vocabulary of Freud's essay "The 'Uncanny,' " it is a projection of the unconscious, and so has no origin outside of the self. And third, *Macbeth* entertains the skeptical possibility that conscience, as Hobbes later argues, is merely a metaphor. This essay handles these as three separate but overlapping approaches to conscience in the play. But it refrains from giving theoretical precedence to any of the three epistemes. Cumulatively, they reveal how *Macbeth* counters the period's generally sanguine theorists by developing a vision of conscience as a tragically equivocal moral guide.

Act 2, Scene 2

Immediately after the murder, Macbeth experiences conscience as a chamber of sights and sounds, with each signifier potentially, but incompletely, representing that witness who will communicate his guilt. Macbeth kills his liege in the second act, between the first and second scenes, and his entrance in Scene 2 shows us Macbeth in the first throes of conscience. In his first words he is startled, and worries that someone is out there: "Who's there? What ho?" (2.2.8). And then, "I have done the deed. Didst thou not hear a noise?" (2.2.14). Macbeth goes from the deed right to the sense that there is a person or a noise within a communicable distance. In the immediate aftermath of the murder, and throughout the course of Scene 2, we can see the implications of *knowing with*: Macbeth expects to experience his conscience and conceives of it as an exchange of information with some other being.

Not knowing how to interpret the noise, Macbeth first guesses that it issues from a person, and then more generically identifies it as a noise. In the following lines Macbeth and Lady Macbeth desperately try to understand the noise:

Macb.	I have done the deed. Didst thou not hear a noise?
Lady M.	I heard the owl scream and the crickets cry.
	Did not you speak?
Macb.	When?
Lady M.	Now.
Macb.	As I descended?

Lady M.   Ay.
Macb.   Hark! who lies i' th' second chamber?
Lady M.   Donalbain.
Macb.   This is a sorry sight.
Lady M.   A foolish thought to say a sorry sight.

(2.2.14–19)

To answer Macbeth's confusion, Lady Macbeth provides an interpretation of the sound which views it as a natural phenomenon. The possibility that it is an owl or crickets would quiet the fear that it is a supernatural noise connected to the conscience. But Lady Macbeth immediately undermines her rational explanation by betraying that she too thinks the sound is a person. "Did not you speak?" suggests that the owl and crickets have not set to rest in her own mind the possibility that a voice made the noise. They continue inquiring into the sound, but the exchange takes on a dizzying sense of anxiety and doubt: "When?/ Now./ As I descended?/ Ay./ Hark!" Here the switching of the stichomythia creates a sense of searching in audience and reader alike, as we ask suddenly, Who is speaking? Where on stage or in the line of pentameter is that sound? The question of where he was when the previous sound echoed remains unresolved, however, as Macbeth jumps to another line of inquiry. "Hark," implies that a new sound is at that very moment audible. And then he makes another jump to a different topic, the tenant of the second chamber. This seems to be motivated by the fear of a witness to his deed, and now the sense of some other being has developed from the uninterpretable sound to the possibility of his sin becoming known by that other. Lady Macbeth's answer, that it was the king's son Donalbain, sinks Macbeth into the despair of "This is a sorry sight," which may refer to himself, or to the tableau he imagines in which he murders the king in the chamber next to the king's son, or to the possibility that Donalbain has seen the deed and is a witness.[6]

As ambiguity in expression plagues Macbeth, so does ambiguity in sense perception. In his disorienting shift from sound to sight, Macbeth seems unable to organize the sounds and sights around him, seems to be focusing now on one, now on the other. But the organizing principle is his apparent feeling that, somewhere within this chamber of echoing sounds and difficult to perceive sights, there is a witness. In the moments after the murder, Macbeth is both wary of and searching for that other who, in the logic of *knowing with*, is privy to his secret and is communicating that shared knowledge.

In these opening moments of their experience with conscience, Lady Macbeth reaches for explanations which would set aside the logic of *knowing with*. First she claims the sound is an owl or crickets, implying that it is merely an accidental noise from the natural world, and not therefore loaded with moral value. She then turns to an argument from fancy, when she calls his "sorry sight" a "foolish thought." Again, she is denigrating the possibility of conscience *knowing with* by urging that the sight is a product of Macbeth's unreliable mind rather than some actual other. Lady Macbeth must work hard to set aside conscience in herself and her husband—as has been seen, she immediately slips out of her feigned innocence of the supernatural with "Did not you speak?" She struggles in the attempt to shove their thoughts away from the portentous world of communicating sights and sounds, but nevertheless continues to reassert her Machiavellian denial of conscience. Macbeth, however, is still caught in the the play's echo chamber. After "A foolish thought to say a sorry sight," Macbeth then says "There's one did laugh in 's sleep, and one cried, 'Murther!' " (2.2.20). Lady Macbeth again tries to push aside Macbeth's sense of a supernatural voice with a rational, if partial, explanation: "There are two lodg'd together" (2.2.23). But Macbeth carries the voice far into the world of supernatural communication with "Methought I heard a voice cry, 'Sleep no more!/ Macbeth does murther sleep' " (2.2.32–33). The voice, he fears, cries out "to all the house" (2.2.38)—sharing in the knowledge of the sin and, as a witness, crying out its tale. Exasperated, Lady Macbeth cuts in: "Who was it that thus cried? Why, worthy thane,/ You do unbend your noble strength, to think/ So brain-sickly of things" (2.2.41–43). She pushes beyond "foolish thought" to the outright assertion that Macbeth is sick in the head and therefore is hearing things which are not true.

Macbeth has already thought of this possibility. Before the murder is committed but after the decision to kill is made, as Macbeth prepares himself, he is haunted by a conscience which is experienced in even more equivocal terms. Conscience here does not communicate with voices and sounds, but as a vision—the "dagger of the mind" which confronts Macbeth in his solitude. Macbeth's preoccupation is whether the dagger he sees is really there, or if it is a product of his mind:

> Is this a dagger which I see before me,
> The handle toward my hand? Come, let me clutch thee:
> I have thee not, and yet I see thee still.
> Art thou not, fatal vision, sensible
> To feeling as to sight? or art thou but
> A dagger of the mind, a false creation,
> Proceeding from the heat-oppressed brain?
>
> (2.1.33–39)

When he cannot touch what he sees, Macbeth assumes that the dagger is "of the mind," and this leads immediately to it being false and a product of a diseased brain. In turning to his own brain as the source of the dagger, Macbeth cuts off the possibility that it issues from an other—rejecting the interpretation of the dagger as a part of the supernatural *knowing with* of conscience. The most common metaphor for conscience's action, that it pricks, is implicit in the image of the dagger.

Macbeth explains away a vision that clearly feels like a warning from his conscience—but then conscience sneaks back into his thoughts in an indirect

manner by means of the figure of Tarquin. Contemplating his own intentions, Macbeth personifies "withered murder" who "with his stealthy pace,/
With Tarquin's ravishing strides, towards his design/ Moves like a ghost"
(2.1.54–56). In Shakespeare's earlier imagining of the scene in "The Rape of
Lucrece," the rapist Tarquin takes his ravishing strides—he "stalks" towards
Lucrece (354)—only after a long period of indecision which is resolved when
he corrupts conscience to such a point that vileness looks like virtue:

> Thus graceless hold he disputation
> 'Tween frozen conscience and hot burning will,
> And with good thoughts makes dispensation,
> Urging the worser sense for vantage still;
> Which in a moment doth confound and kill
> All pure effects, and doth so far proceed
> That what is vile shows like a virtuous deed.
>
> (246–52)

Macbeth imagines murder on the other side of Tarquin's encounter with
conscience—that is, his language reveals how his own murderous action
will proceed only in the wake of failed conscience. If Macbeth has begun to
undermine conscience, as Lady Macbeth will do extensively (in 2.2), his mind
shows itself to be, on some level, very aware of what he is doing.

The complexity of the allusion to Tarquin, and the fact that murder is also
ghostly, however, registers just how equivocal Macbeth's experience of conscience is at this moment. Unlike the unanimous chorus of voices judging
Richard III a villain, Macbeth's conscience flickers with the impossibility of
deciding whether the dagger is real or not, and hints at its knowledge through
the trails of literary allusion. In fact, Macbeth's preoccupation with what is
real and what is not covers over the alternative possibility that the dagger is
ghostly precisely because it is legitimately a thing of the conscience. With this
in mind, Macbeth's conclusion concerning the dagger appears as perfectly
contradictory: "There's no such thing:/ It is the bloody business which
informs/ Thus to mine eyes" (2.1.47–49). He decides that the dagger is unreal,
and at the same time names it as a piece of information issuing from the
bloody business—as a signifier of conscience.

The play itself, mischievously taking on the role of Lady Macbeth, further
attenuates Macbeth's conscience by suggesting that the dagger is real, a
material weapon. For in the next scene surfaces a pair of real daggers whose
materiality is all too obvious. Just after she charges Macbeth with thinking
"so brainsickly of things," she discovers the incriminating daggers in his
hand: "Why did you bring these daggers from the place?" (2.2.45). The audience is left wondering whether there wasn't an actual dagger on stage in the
previous scene—a prop that went unnoticed. Such an effect depends largely
on staging, but by making both Macbeth's vision and the murder weapon
daggers, Shakespeare leaves the audience as uncertain as Macbeth. The entire

echo chamber of (2.2) ends, moreoever, with a similar materializing of the sound of knocking. When Lady Macbeth leaves and Macbeth again finds himself alone, he hears a knock within and declares, "Whence is that knocking?/ How is 't with me, when every noise appalls me?/ What hands are here?" Once again in the realm of overheard sounds, everything is feeling portentous and barely understood to Macbeth. For all we know the hands are hands of the mind. But then Lady Macbeth returns to insist that the knocking is an ordinary sound, part of the material world, which she says is coming from the south entry (2.2.63). And in the Porter scene which follows, the knocking is parodied in its utterly mundane materiality, both as sounds now clearly emanating from a door, and in the Porter's mimicking of the noise: "Knock, knock, knock!" (3.1.3). We emerge from the experience of Macbeth's conscience caught by the suspicion that, as Lady Macbeth insists, none of the sounds and sights were anything but the physical and material phenomena found in the everyday world.

Melancholy and conscience

By persistently questioning whether Macbeth is experiencing conscience as *knowing with*, or whether the sights and sounds are merely physical, Shakespeare is engaging with a problem which frequently captured the attention of the theorists of conscience, the problem of distinguishing between conscience and that physical and psychological condition called melancholy. So Perkins asks in *The Whole Treatise of the Cases of Conscience* (1606): "it may be demanded, whether there be any difference betweene the trouble of Conscience and Melancholy? for many hold that they are all one" (194). Perkins answers that they differ much, and, in fact, every theorist in the period says that they are different—an insistence which itself clearly shows, as Perkins admits, that many people cannot distinguish conscience from melancholy. The symptoms are similar, but much is at stake in the distinction, for melancholy is a physical condition explained as an imbalance of the bodily humours. To explain a patient's symptoms as melancholy rather than afflicted conscience is, as Lady Macbeth does, to allow a physical explanation to elide conscience.

It is a measure of how intertwined conscience and melancholy were in the period that Timothy Bright's *A Treatise of Melancholy* (1586), offers a cure, as it says on the title page, "for such as have thereto adjoyned an afflicted conscience"; and that in a neat converse, Perkins's *The Whole Treatise of the Cases of Conscience* (1606) includes a discussion of melancholy. Bright devotes several chapters to conscience, and is particularly interested in distinguishing it from melancholy. For Bright, melancholy manifests itself in vain fancy, while conscience is theologically and ontologically more real: "Whatsoever molestation riseth directly as a proper object of the mind, that in that respect is not melancholicke, but hath a farther ground then fancie, and riseth from conscience" (193). Perkins, too, carefully distinguishes between the afflictions of conscience, which have "a true and certain cause," and melancholy, in which "the imagination conceiveth a thing to be so, which is not so" (*Treatise*, 195).

Despite attempts to distinguish conscience and melancholy—the one aligned with truth the other with false imaginings—they produce undeniably similar experiences. Melancholy cannot cause the pricks of conscience, but, Bright argues, a bad conscience can lead a person into melancholy, as "infinite feares and distrust" wastes the spirit and "congealeth the lively bloud" (195). This results in, among other things, "vaine feares, and false conceits of apparitions, imagination of a voyce sounding in your eares, frightfull dreames, distrust of consumption, and putrifying of one part or other of your bodie" (195). And such melancholic symptoms in turn contribute to the difficulty of clearing the conscience because it "increaseth the terrour of the afflicted minde, doubling the feare and discouragement, and shutteth up the meanes of consolation" (196). Perkins also focuses on the way melancholy leads to an overactive and deceptive imagination:

> For this humour being corrupted, it sends up noysome fumes as cloudes or mists which doe corrupt the imagination, and makes the instrument of reason unfit for understanding and sense. Hence followes the first effect, strange imaginations, conceits and opinions, framed in the minde.
>
> (Perkins, *Treatise* 192)

This condition could well be indistinguishable from the experience of a conscience which is structured by the logic of *knowing with*. If conscience unfolds as communication with an other, the sounds and visions which form that communication may appear to be nothing more than products of melancholy. So Alexander Hume hints: for someone with a bad conscience, "it wil appeare to himselfe, that al the creatures of God are animate, as it were, and conspired against him" (43).

Perkins and Bright both insist on the primacy of conscience, viewing melancholy as a mere physical condition which might exacerbate the difficulties of conscience. However, the later theorist of melancholy, Robert Burton, disagrees on this crucial distinction: "much melancholy is without affliction of conscience, as Bright and Perkins illustrate by four reasons; and yet melancholy alone again may be sometimes a sufficient cause of this terror of conscience" (3.4.2.3). The radicalness of Burton's position can be felt: if conscience may result from the physical condition of melancholy, then potentially it can be removed from genuine consideration, for the workings of conscience are interpreted not as a divine witness, but rather as mere symptoms of the humours in the mind. What Lady Macbeth calls thinking "brain-sickly of things" is a position anticipating Burton's subversion of conscience.

As much as Bright and Perkins want to distinguish conscience and melancholy, the two bleed back into each other—and Lady Macbeth encourages their confusion. *Macbeth* itself neither sides with nor rejects Lady Macbeth's physical explanations in (2.2), but instead can be seen as dramatizing the difficulty of making this crucial distinction. The standard diagnosis that melancholy leads to a corrupt imagination itself sounds very like the chaos of sight and sounds in the aftermath of Duncan's murder.

When the Macbeths hear an owl, a voice, then a knocking, they and the audience cannot know if they are experiencing melancholy or conscience—a position captured by the problem of the dagger: "Is this a dagger which I see before me,/ The handle toward my hand?"; or "A dagger of the mind, a false creation,/ Proceeding from the heat-oppressed brain?"

If confusion with melancholy serves the Macbeths' desire to ignore con-science, it is a fitting reversal that in Act 5 the physical perspective comes back to haunt them in the figure of the Doctor. As Lady Macbeth sleepwalks and guiltily recounts her role in the murder of Duncan, her earlier rejection of conscience is proven disastrous—we learn that her conscience is alive and well. And at this very moment Shakespeare reminds us of the argument for melancholy that served as a means of explaining away conscience. Observing Lady Macbeth in the throes of conscience, the physician represents the linger-ing hope that her symptoms are merely physical, and so curable. The Doctor's diagnosis, however, is succinct: "This disease is beyond my practice" (5.1.59). The Doctor here voices what the theorists of conscience insist upon. Perkins says of the symptoms of conscience, "melancholy may be cured by phisicke; this sorrow cannot be cured by any thing but by the blood of Christ" (*Dis-course*, 87). And Hume succinctly develops an absolute division between the material world of physical disease, which he calls "natural," and the divine, "supernatural" realm of conscience: "the diseases before rehearsed are natu-rall; the disease of the *Conscience*, supernaturall . . . The melancholious humors may be purged, and the body brought to a gude temperature and constitution: But all the Phisitians, and all the natural medecine under heaven, can na mair remeid the woundit *conscience*" (Hume 37).

The "natural" world is what Lady Macbeth has worked so hard to privilege—interpreting the sights and sounds of (2.2) as either the sounds of nature or the products of Macbeth's physically diseased brain. In the figure of the Doctor, however, the natural explanation is thoroughly parodied. In Macbeth's desperation, it becomes apparent just how impossible it would be for a physician to cure conscience:

> Canst thou not minister to a mind diseas'd,
> Pluck from the memory a rooted sorrow,
> Raze out the written troubles of the brain,
> And with some sweet oblivious antidote
> Cleanse the stuff'd bosom of that perilous stuff
> Which weighs upon the heart?
>
> (5.3.40–45)

Macbeth's repetition of the vague and untheological "stuff" marks his willful distance from the real workings of conscience. And when he then asks the Doctor to "cast/ The water of my land" (5.3.50–51), the remedies of the physician are laid bare as utterly beside the point. Macbeth's questions, though, are poignant. In seeking a medical cure, he is again wishing away conscience, but only weakly this last time. Supernatural conscience has fully reasserted itself in the tragic order of the play.

The uncanny conscience

In early modern conceptions of conscience, as Lewis points out, "A person cannot help thinking and speaking of himself as, and even feeling himself to be (for certain purposes), two people" (187).[7] For Perkins, conscience actually forms a doppelganger:

> For there must be two actions of the understanding, the one is simple, which barely conceiveth or thinketh this or that: the other is *a reflecting* or doubling of the former, whereby a man conceives and thinkes with himselfe what he thinks. And this action properly pertaines to the conscience. The minde thinks a thought, now conscience goes beyond the minde, and knowes what the minde thinks; so as if a man would go about to hide his sinnefull thoughts from God, his conscience as an other person within him, shall discover all. By meanes of this second action conscience may beare witnes even of thoughts, and from hence also it seemes to borrow his name, because conscience is a science or knowledge joyned with an other knowledge: for by it I conceive and know what I know.
>
> (Perkins, *Discourse* 7)

More than a figure of speech, this process of "doubling" and of creating "an other person," confers on *knowing with* a significant degree of psychological reality—and complexity, for it must be a strange moment when the individual suddenly becomes multiple.[8] Perkins does not register such a psychological shock, but the presence of a double as conscience draws very near to Freud's skeptical analysis in his essay on the uncanny. There Freud uses the figure of the double to explain the basic conception of the conscience as a witness:

> The idea of the "double" does not necessarily disappear with the passing of primary narcissism, for it can receive fresh meaning from the later stages of the ego's development. A special agency is slowly formed there, which is able to stand over against the rest of the ego, which has the function of observing and criticizing the self and of exercising censorship within the mind, and which we become aware of as our "conscience."
>
> (Freud 17: 235)

Freud's "special agency" picks up the sense of *knowing with* which preoccupied seventeenth-century theorists of conscience. But in Freud's hands the conscience as a double is markedly different than in Perkins's. For Freud locates the witness not within a divine economy ultimately linked to God, but within the ego. Making conscience into a formation of the mind implies, as melancholy does, a human explanation for the experience, and so eclipses the supernatural authority of conscience. But what Freud's insertion of the unconscious most of all does is insert a far less stable epistemology, disrupting the knowledge which is the foundation of *knowing with*.

Perkins assumes a seemingly unimpeded self-knowledge: "science or knowledge joyned with an other knowledge: for by it I conceive and know what I know." Contrary to our modern assumptions, self-consciousness does not muddy the waters, but rather seems to increase clarity. Perkins, moreover, locates the double within the understanding, which is the seat of reason. He begins *A Discourse of Conscience* by insisting that conscience resides in the faculty of "Understanding" rather than in the "Will," the seat of passions and desires (1). The understanding functions through the multiplication of voices, but these doubles speak crystalline logic. In describing the "manner of judgement" of the conscience, Perkins says that it operates with the precision of the syllogism—"by a kind of reasoning or disputing, called a *practical syllogism*" (*Discourse* 83). So conscience functions, he says, as a logical argument:

> Every murderer is accursed, saith the minde.
> Thou art a murderer, saith conscience assisted by memory.
> Ergo, Thou art accursed, saith conscience, and so giveth her sentence.
> (Perkins, *Discourse* 84)

There are several speaking parts in Perkins's conscience, and every voice conveys another layer of unequivocal knowledge. Doubling forms the basis of Perkins's optimistic notion of the logical and clear functioning of conscience.

The double in Freud, on the other hand, is a deeply ambiguous figure which locates the conscience not in the rational clarity of syllogism, but in the murky epistemology of the uncanny. As Freud describes it, the uncanny is a strange feeling of both otherness and familiarity which is often associated with perceived appearances of the supernatural. It is especially pronounced, he says, when we find ourselves unable to distinguish the natural from the supernatural: "an uncanny effect is often and easily produced when the distinction between imagination and reality is effaced" (17: 244). The necessary condition is doubt—so while the supernatural has no uncanny effect in fairy tales, because the reader expects magic, the uncanny emerges when "there is a conflict of judgement as to whether things which have been 'surmounted' and are regarded as incredible may not, after all be possible" (17: 250). The double serves as one of Freud's primary examples of the uncanny, and when

Freud describes conscience as a double, he thrusts it into that space of doubt in which imagination and reality cannot be distinguished.

It is toward just such a conscience that Shakespeare draws us in (2.2), as the competing possibilities of conscience and melancholy confront Macbeth with a perfect pattern of the uncanny. The owl and crickets which immediately follow Macbeth's deed, the voices which seem to accuse him, and the knocking which so startles him, all seem to be supernaturally portentous. But, at the same time, a skeptical interpretation is always present, as Lady Macbeth insists that the sounds are merely physical. As unsure as Macbeth how to interpret the sights and sounds, the reader is led by the play into the uncanny conflict of judgment in which things regarded as incredible "may not, after all be possible." This conflict between the natural and the supernatural confronts Macbeth most explicitly in the shape of the dagger, which he sees but cannot grasp, and which may be real or may be merely "A dagger of the mind, a false creation,/ Proceeding from the heat-oppressed brain." Macbeth finds himself unable to distinguish between a supernatural vision and a real dagger, and this doubt immediately leads him to the possibility of an unhealthy mind. To use Freud's terms, which in some important respects replace the early modern vocabulary of melancholy, Macbeth wonders whether he is experiencing the projections of his unconscious mind.[9]

Uncanny visions such as the dagger or a double are explained by Freud as a return of the repressed. We have repressed what Freud calls the "omnipotence of thoughts," which is "the old animistic conception of the universe" in which spirits populate the world and magic works upon us (17: 240). This primitive understanding of the world is a thing of the past: the modern mindset disbelieves in the omnipotence of thoughts, and carries around the memory of it only in the unconscious. From within a present skepticism, the uncanny is felt as a return of repressed animism and belief in magic. The supernatural breaks through our conscious, skeptical position:

> We—our primitive forefathers—once believed that these possibilities were realities, and were convinced that they actually happened. Nowadays we no longer believe in them, we have *surmounted* these modes of thought; but we do not feel quite sure of our new beliefs, and the old ones still exist within us ready to seize upon any confirmation. As soon as something *actually happens* in our lives which seems to confirm the old, discarded beliefs we get a feeling of the uncanny.
>
> (Freud 17: 247–48)

The uncanny, then, arises when we are skeptical of the supernatural, but are momentarily challenged to reconsider that skepticism. It names the condition felt by an unbeliever when he or she suddenly doubts that unbelief. By insisting upon a natural interpretation of the sounds of (2.2), Lady Macbeth becomes a figure for the repression of the omnipotence of thoughts. Within the context of *knowing with*, this skeptical repression functions as a rejection of conscience itself: conscience appears superstitious and ineffective. But when these sounds simultaneously strike the Macbeths as portentous, the uncanny conscience breaks through into consciousness. They experience the uncanny and terrible possibility—after the sin has been committed—that conscience is not a superstition but is real, and will really operate upon them.

Identifying conscience as a return of an explicitly disbelieved perspective casts conscience into a heap with old wives' tales. Moreover, it taints the experience of conscience with psychological fearfulness. For conscience only fully enters the play with the sense of an involuntary reemergence, a return of the repressed.[10] The Macbeths try hard to interpret the signifiers of (2.2) as purely material, but then that skepticism fails and the supernatural conscience returns with all the force of a repressed memory. This uncanny conscience produces knowledge through the fleeting and fractured images which, as in dreams, are symptoms of repressed memory.[11] Quite unlike the syllogisms in Perkins's understanding, such a conscience communicates outside of the order of the conscious mind. This is what happens to Macbeth as he sinks into the panicked and desperately uncertain state in which "every noise appalls me."

And so the "manner of judgement" of conscience, to use Perkins's phrase, is severely compromised: rendered uncanny, *knowing with* fails to produce a coherent other as a witness, and conscience collapses into solipsism. The object of the preposition in *knowing with* becomes the self—one knows with oneself. Here can be felt the expansion of the modern subject, as conscience becomes congruent with the vagaries of self-consciousness. Such solipsism brings *Macbeth* near to Freud, and nearer to the vexed self-consciousness of *Hamlet* where "conscience," as was common in the seventeenth century, means both the moral witness and consciousness.[12] Macbeth enters (2.2) with "I have done the deed. Didst thou not hear a noise?" And by his departing speech, *knowing with* has descended into the despairing language of self-consciousness which we associate with *Hamlet*: "To know my deed, 'twere best not know myself" (2.2.70).

Metaphoric conscience

Perkins's syllogism assumes that the *knowing with* of conscience functions by means of fully transparent and knowable language—like the tales told by the tongues of Richard's conscience, each speaker in Perkins's syllogism "saith" unequivocally. Perkins, like Alexander Hume, gives scant attention to language itself, essentially assuming that it signifies unproblematically. However Perkins's student, William Ames, rethinks this assumption in *Conscience and the Cases Thereof* (1639). Ames maintains most of Perkins's ideas, including the notion that conscience functions according to the structure of the syllogism. But just before describing conscience's syllogistic judgment, Ames specifically departs from "the most grave Divine, William Perkins" in his insistence on the presence in conscience of "discourse" (2). Ames argues against Perkins's claim that conscience resides in the faculty of understanding, insisting on a less reified and more active conception of "practical judgement." Rather than the conscience's judgment proceding by means of immediate apprehension, conscience "belongs to judgement discoursing" (3). Conscience still functions with the logic of the syllogism, but the significant awareness Ames arouses is that even a syllogism is part of discourse. And once discourse is given a place in the functioning of conscience, judgment becomes subject to the ambiguities of rhetoric and language. Ames remains quite orthodox, but the interjection of a rhetorical component into conscience has far-reaching and subversive consequences.

The radical endpoint of the admission of discourse into conscience is reached by the middle of the seventeenth century, in Hobbes's *Leviathan* (1651). Hobbes voices a deep skepticism towards discourse, which, he argues, cannot lead to certain judgment but only personal opinion: "But if the ground of such Discourse, be not Definitions; or if the Definitions be not rightly joyned together into Syllogismes, then the End or Conclusion, is again OPINION" (1.7). Hobbes has little expectation that discourse can be grounded in definition or can proceed with the precision of syllogism, and this leads him immediately into a discussion of conscience which is astounding in its subversiveness:

> When two, or more men, know of one and the same fact, they are said to be Conscious of it one to another; which is as much as to know it together. And because such are fittest witnesses of the facts of one another, or of a third; it was, and ever will be reputed a very Evill act, for any man to speak against his *Conscience*; or to corrupt, or force another so to do: Insomuch that the plea of Conscience has been always hearkened unto very diligently in all times. Afterwards, men made use of the same word metaphorically, for the knowledge of their own secret facts, and secret thoughts; and therefore it is Rhetorically said, that the Conscience is a thousand witnesses. And last of all, men, vehemently in love with their own new opinons (though never so absurd,) and obstinately bent to maintain them, gave those their opinions also that reverenced name of Conscience, as if they would have it seem unlawfull, to change or speak against them; and so pretend to know they are true, when they know at most, but that they think so.
>
> (Hobbes 1.7)

Conscience is Hobbes's illustration of the human tendency to elevate personal opinion to the exalted level of truth, even divine law: men with mere opinions invoke the "reverenced name" of conscience to make those opinions inviolable.[13] This is not just an abuse of conscience, but an indication of the abusiveness of the notion of conscience itself. For the conception of conscience as a witness is mere rhetoric—not a true description of the actual functioning of conscience, but a dangerous figure of speech. The inward faculty of conscience is merely a metaphor for the more mundane and entirely un-supernatural act of *knowing with* another person. For Hobbes, metaphor is a name for discourse which is false: it is one of the "abuses of speech" when people "use words metaphorically; that is, in other sense than that they are ordained for; and thereby deceive others" (1.4). By calling conscience a metaphor, he categorizes it as a deceiving and unreliable form of discourse. It is, moreover, removed from its divine authority, and made into a human creation.

If by mid-century conscience can be conceived of as mere metaphor, in 1606 we can find Shakespeare contemplating the same Hobbesian possibility. The functioning of conscience in *Macbeth* is rendered equivocal by the possibility that it is only figural language. As the Macbeths experience conscience in (2.2) and beyond, the legibility of conscience's signifiers, and so the efficacy of the faculty, is compromised by the difficulty of sorting metaphor from literal language.

At key moments in the play, metaphor does seem to be an adequate signifier for conscience. Before the murder, for example, Lady Macbeth prays to "Stop up th' access and passage to remorse,/ That no compunctious visitings of nature/ Shake my fell purpose" (1.5.44–46). Here the word compunction, which in modern usage is only a synonym for regret, actually carries within it the metaphor of the prick of conscience: reflecting its etymology, the first definition of "compunction" in the *Oxford English Dictionary* is "Pricking or stinging of the conscience or heart" ("Compunction," 1). In this case Lady Macbeth seems to have succesfully named conscience, for she does banish it. The action of pricking or stinging later returns in Macbeth's lament, "O, full of scorpions is my mind, dear wife!" (3.2.36). Again, the metaphor surfaces as a signifier for a functional conscience—by Act 3 Macbeth knows very clearly what is bothering him, and figural language seems to name it adequately.

But if the pricking conscience signifies unequivocally, the conscience that is a *knowing with* leads to deeply equivocal language. Macbeth is thrown into the chaos of *knowing with*—"I have done the deed. Didst thou not hear a noise?"—by the sound of an owl. Lady Macbeth's explanation that it is merely an owl materializes the sound, implying that it has no connection to the conscience. Yet just before Macbeth's entrance, Lady Macbeth herself had read this same owl's shriek as deeply metaphorical, for he is "the fatal bellman,/ Which gives the stern'st good-night" (2.2.3–4). Lady Macbeth's materializing of the sound is also a literalizing: what she had instinctively read as a metaphoric "fatal bellman" she now insists is a mere owl. She forces herself to adhere to the skeptical and literal interpretation, for, like the argument for materiality, it elides the functioning of conscience. Similarly, Macbeth first interprets the knocking as deeply figural, part of the echo chamber in which "every noise appalls me." In response, Lady Macbeth again insists that it is a physical—and so literal—knocking at the gate of the castle. In both cases, conscience depends upon metaphor, as the literal interpretation implies that it is a natural sound and not conscience communicating. And in both cases Lady Macbeth's skeptical interpretation serves her desire to ignore conscience.

But Lady Macbeth's instinctive metaphorical reading of the owl suggests a figural signification which is prior to her skepticism. Just as Freud's omnipotence of thoughts breaks in upon the conscious mind, so metaphor emerges from Lady Macbeth's unconscious, and must be repressed. In the case of the knocking, Lady Macbeth suppresses metaphor—and so conscience—in her husband. But in the following scene the play itself stages the return of the repressed in the form of the Porter. Lady Macbeth's literal reading of the knocking is reinforced by the Porter laboriously answering the door in the following scene. But his ironic mutterings as he makes his way to the door reinsert the knocking sound into a figural mode: "I'll devil-porter it no further," the Porter declares, "I had thought to have let in some of all professions that go the primrose way to th' everlasting bonfire" (2.3.17–19). The gate of Enverness is appropriately called the gate of hell—the metaphor signifies very accurately that in the supernatural economy of Christian morality, Macbeth and Lady Macbeth have indeed entered Hell (O'Connell 159; cf. Wickham). Lady Macbeth's literalizing efforts cannot stand up to the Porter's ironic language, as metaphoric signification uncannily returns.

Like the omnipotence of thoughts, the metaphoric conscience returns to haunt the skeptical mind. This return to the figural interpretation of the sights and sounds of (2.2) brings *Macbeth* near to Hobbes. And, as in *Leviathan*, it threatens to demolish conscience by viewing it as merely metaphor—an abuse of language and a purely human creation. Indeed, Lady Macbeth's entire strategy of closing off "compunctious visitings" depends upon such a Hobbesian dismissal of the reality of conscience. But dismissively saying *merely* a metaphor would be deceptive. In the redemptive economy of *Macbeth*, metaphor proves uncannily effective. This becomes clear in the most famous metaphor for conscience, Lady Macbeth's spotted hands.

Lady Macbeth begins by insisting that the blood on Macbeth's hands is merely physical blood, and not a metaphor for his guilt: "Go get some water,/ And wash this filthy witness from your hand" (2.2.43–44). Even while advancing the material signification, however, she cannot prevent the momentary return of the metaphoric interpretation: "witness" recalls the conscience she is at pains to repress. Macbeth is disinclined to ignore the metaphoric dimensions, crying out, "Will all great Neptune's ocean wash this blood/ Clean from my hand?" (2.2.57–58). But Lady Macbeth persists: "A little water clears us of this deed;/ How easy is it then!" (2.2.64–65). Insisting that the blood functions only as blood, Lady Macbeth makes the remarkable assertion that water alone clears them of the murder.

But of course by Act 5 it has become not at all easy. Lady Macbeth's great emblematic struggle with her conscience takes the form of the return of the metaphor she had denied: "Out, damn'd spot! out, I say!"; "What, will these hands ne'er be clean?"; "Here's the smell of the blood still. All the perfumes of Arabia will not sweeten this little hand. O,O,O!" (5.1.35, 43, 50–52). The spot is another metaphor for conscience, and, in returning to figural language conscience at last is functioning with the clarity experienced by Richard and assumed by Perkins. There is, in a special and strict sense, poetic justice here: not only in the appropriateness of Lady Macbeth being tormented by the thing she has denied; but because the just functioning of conscience is shown to be dependent on metaphor—that is, on poetic language.[14]

When Lady Macbeth's conscience reproduces the very metaphor she had used in (2.2), it becomes possible to read the spot not as an assertion of any supernatural witnessing, but as her dreams siezing upon her mind's own conceptions. Conscience, this fact suggests, may originate in the human mind, and it may be merely a metaphor—as in Hobbes. Moreover, when conscience finally functions it does so in a dream, making this moment of justice available only within her unconscious mind. It communicates only there, where she cannot fully know of the *knowing with*—and so conscience remains uncanny, as in Freud. For some readers, such insights may be enough to undermine the divine authority of conscience altogether. In the world of *Macbeth*, however, conscience does still operate. Lady Macbeth does feel conscience at work, in fact for the first time in the play she feels it witness her guilt with clarity. But this last moment of a succesfully communicating conscience is deeply tragic nerverthelesss. Our tragic understanding is that even if conscience is merely a metaphor and merely a product of the unconscious mind, it still works upon us. Our pity for Lady Macbeth, such as it is, becomes a pity for the skeptical project of willfully ignoring conscience. We pity her, and in tragic fashion we fear—for ourselves if, like Lady Macbeth we doubt the efficacy of conscience; and for humanity, because of the deeply equivocal ways in which conscience must communicate with it.

Notes

1 A number of studies have read *Macbeth* in light of conscience, including A.L. and M.K. Kistner, Garber (108–17), Wilks (125–43), Lukacher (162–93), and Kinney (226–42). Critics have particularly focused on Shakespeare's allusions to Henry Garnet and the public crisis of conscience which his involvement in the Gunpowder Plot touched off, e.g. Wills (93–105) and Mullaney (116–34).

2 Other seventeenth-century theorists include Immanuel Bourne, *The Anatomie of Conscience* (1623), Ephraim Huit, *The Anatomy of Conscience* (1626), William Ames, *Of Conscience and the Cases Thereof* (1639), and Jeremy Taylor, *Ductor Dubitantium* (1660). For modern critical accounts see: Wood, Slights, Leites, and Gallagher.

3 Conscience as a witness goes back to Romans 2: 15: "Which shewe the effect of the Lawe written in their heartes, their conscience also bearing witnesse, and their thoughts accusing one another, or excusing." The conscience as witness also appears in Aquinas, as Elizabethan proverb, and as a commonplace of the seventeenth century. Thomas Aquinas, *Summa Theologica*, 1.79.13, *Quaestiones disputatae de veritate*, 17.1. See Potts (131), Tilley (116). Later in the century, Joseph Hall declares, "I can do nothing without a million witnesses: the conscience is as a thousand witnesses; and God is as a thousand consciences" (7: 514).

4 Lewis calls this sense of conscience "consciring" (184).

5 All citations of Shakespeare are from *The Riverside Shakespeare* (second edition).

6 The Riverside and many other modern editions include the stage direction

"[*Looking on his hands.*]" after "This is a sorry sight." I have followed the Folio in omitting the stage direction, which closes off the wide variety of possible referents for this line.

7 *Richard III* examines this dynamic in Richard's soliloquy, "What do I fear? Myself? There's none else by./ Richard loves Richard, that is, I am I" (5.3.182–83).

8 The functioning of conscience by means of a double is familiar to modern readers in the image of the good angel on one shoulder and the bad angel on the other. As a way to dramatize conscience, it was also a construct in Elizabethan theater, for example in Christopher Marlowe's *Doctor Faustus* as well as morality play precedents, such as William Wager's *The Conflict of Conscience*.

9 Freud in fact names *Macbeth* as like the fairy tale, in that we simply give ourselves to the fiction of witchcraft (17: 230). Several studies, especially by Wills, support Freud's reading by emphasizing that the play is entirely credulous of magic and not aimed at eliciting skepticism. But the literal truth of magic, like the actual functioning of conscience, does not change the fact that it can be disbelieved. The reality of the witches only emphasizes that Lady Macbeth is willfully repressing the supernatural. Her repression of the supernatural signification of conscience is rendered obtuse and tragic by the reality of the supernatural elsewhere in the play. For Freud's many other readings of *Macbeth*, see Lukacher (168–83).

10 As Lukacher argues, "Conscience clings the way the blood clings to the hands of the Macbeths, not as a physical stain but as an irrepressible and incontrovertible compulsion to repeat" (185).

11 Freud is inconsistent in "The Uncanny" as to the relationship between the uncanny and the unconscious. He places the double within the ego rather than within "what is unconscious and repressed" (235 n. 2). But he regularly discusses the uncanny in terms of a return of the repressed, and as an experience closely allied to the dynamics of dreams and memory traces. In particular, he allies it with the unconscious compulsion to repeat explicated in *Beyond the Pleasure Principle* (238).

12 "Thus conscience does make cowards of us all" (3.1.82). On this line see Lewis (207) and Belsey. Also see Butler.

13 This becomes known as enthusiasm—see, for example, Locke's chapter "Of Enthusiasm," in the *Essay*, 4.19.

14 This resembles Pater's adjustment of poetic justice in his essay on *Measure for Measure*: "It is not always that poetry can be the exponent of morality; but it is this aspect of morals which it represents most naturally, for this true justice is dependent on just those finer appreciations which poetry cultivates in us the power of making, those peculiar valuations of action and its effect which poetry actually requires" (184). For an account of traditional concepts of poetic justice, see Dollimore (72–82).

Works cited

Ames, William. *Of Conscience and the Cases Thereof*. London, 1639.

Belsey, Catherine. "The Case of Hamlet's Conscience." *Studies in Philology* 76 (1979): 127–48.

Bright, Timothy. *A Treatise of Melancholy*. London, 1586.

Burton, Robert. *The Anatomy of Melancholy*. New York: New York Review of Books, 2001.

Butler, Judith. "Conscience Doth Make Subjects of Us All." *Yale French Studies* 88 (1995): 6–26.

Dollimore, Jonathan. *Radical Tragedy: Religion, Ideology and Power in the Drama of Shakespeare and his Contemporaries*. 3rd ed. Durham: Duke UP, 2004.

Freud, Sigmund. *The Standard Edition of the Complete Psychological Works of Sigmund Freud*. Trans. James Strachey. 24 vols. London: The Hogarth Press, 1955.

Gallagher, Lowell. *Medusa's Gaze: Casuistry and Conscience in the Renaissance*. Stanford: Stanford UP, 1991.

Garber, Marjorie. *Dream in Shakespeare: From Metaphor to Metamorphosis*. New Haven: Yale UP, 1974.

Hall, Joseph. *Meditations and Vows, Divine and Moral. The Works of Bishop Hall*. 10 vols. Oxford: Oxford UP, 1863.

Hobbes, Thomas. *Leviathan*. Ed. Richard Tuck. Cambridge: Cambridge UP, 1997.

Holinshed, Raphael. *Holinshed's Chronicles of England, Scotland, and Ireland*. 6 vols. 1808. New York: AMS, 1965.

Hume, Alexander. *Ane Treatise of Conscience*. Edinburgh, 1594.

Kinney, Arthur. *Lies Like Truth: Shakespeare*, Macbeth *and the Cultural Moment*. Detroit: Wayne State UP, 2001.

Kistner, A.L and M.K. "Macbeth: A Treatise of Conscience." *Thoth* 13 (1973): 27–43.

Leites, Edmund, ed. *Conscience and Casuistry in Early Modern Europe*. Cambridge: Cambridge UP, 1988.

Lewis, C.S. *Studies in Words*. Cambridge: Cambridge UP, 1996.

Locke, John. *An Essay Concerning Human Understanding*. Ed. Peter H. Nidditch. Oxford: Clarendon, 1979.

Lukacher, Ned. *Daemonic Figures: Shakespeare and the Question of Conscience*. Ithaca: Cornell UP, 1994.

Mullaney, Steven. *The Place of the Stage: License, Play, and Power in Renaissance England*. Chicago: U of Chicago P, 1988.

O'Connell, Michael. "Vital Cultural Practices: Shakespeare and the Mysteries." *Journal of Medieval and Early Modern Studies* 29.1 (1999): 149–68.

Pater, Walter. "Measure for Measure." *Appreciations: With an Essay on Style*. New York: Macmillan, 1910, 170–84.

Perkins, William. *A Discourse of Conscience*. London, 1596.

—— *The Whole Treatise of the Cases of Conscience*. London, 1606.

Potts, Timothy C. *Conscience in Medieval Philosophy*. Cambridge: Cambridge UP, 1980.

Shakespeare, William. *The Riverside Shakespeare*. Gen. ed. G. Blakemore Evans, with the assistance of J.J.M. Tobin. 2nd ed. Boston: Houghton Mifflin, 1997.

Slights, Camille Wells. *The Casuistical Tradition in Shakespeare, Donne, Herbert, and Milton*. Princeton: Princeton UP, 1981.

Thomas, Keith. "Cases of Conscience in Seventeenth-Century England." *Public Duty and Private Conscience in Seventeenth-Century England*. Ed. John Morrill, Paul Slack, and Daniel Woolf. Oxford: Clarendon Press, 1997. 29–56.

Tilley, Morris Palmer. *A Dictionary of the Proverbs in England in the Sixteenth and Seventeenth Centuries*. Ann Arbor: University of Michigan Press, 1950.

Wickham, Glynne. "Hell Castle and Its Door-keeper." *Shakespeare Survey* 19 (1966): 68–74.

Wilks, John S. *The Idea of Conscience in Renaissance Tragedy*. London: Routledge, 1990.

Wills, Garry. *Witches and Jesuits: Shakespeare's* Macbeth. Oxford: Oxford UP, 1995.

Wood, Thomas. *English Casuistical Divinity During the Seventeenth Century, With Special Reference to Jeremy Taylor*. London: S.P.C.K., 1952.

7 Hired for mischief

The masterless man in *Macbeth*[1]

Lois Feuer

Readers long have paused over the catalogue of dogs in 3.1 of *Macbeth*, intrigued by the apparently unnecessary specificity of its listing:

> *1st Murderer:* We are men, my liege.
> *Macbeth:*   Ay, in the catalogue ye go for men,
>   As hounds and greyhounds, mungrels, spaniels, curs,
>   Shoughs, water-rugs, and demi-wolves are clept
>   All by the name of dog; the valued file
>   Distinguishes the swift, the slow, the subtle,
>   The house-keeper, the hunter, every one,
>   According to the gift which bounteous nature
>   Hath in him clos'd; whereby he does receive
>   Particular addition, from the bill
>   That writes them all alike: and so of men.
>   (3.1.91–100)[2]

Macbeth recites this list to the two murderers he hires to kill Banquo. In this otherwise brief exchange, the detailedness of the catalogue puzzles us, for its details are seemingly unneeded. But, as I shall argue, this episode links Macbeth to his hirelings; the passage places them all within a dual social context, first of the feudal society represented in the play, and then of a rapidly changing society at the time of its composition. Though *Macbeth* is far less commonly studied for a glimpse of Shakespeare serving as social historian than, say, *Lear*, taking a closer look at the hired killers reveals this play's insight into the socioeconomic realities of Shakespeare's time.

The killers resemble their new master, Macbeth, in their rootlessness and their amoral readiness to do whatever will advance them. In their focus on the mechanics of murder rather than its morality, they resemble the play's early version of Lady Macbeth, attending to creating circumstantial evidence such as the blood-smeared grooms. The hired killers resemble also the later Macbeth, whose original recognition of the evil of murdering Duncan ("Whose horrid image doth unfix my hair/ And make my seated heart knock at my ribs/Against the use of nature," 1.3.135–37) gives way to the mechanistic elimination of even those who pose no threat, such as Lady Macduff and her children. By using the catalogue of dogs to draw our attention to the desperate alienation of the hired killers, Shakespeare focuses for us Macbeth's own growing, self-imposed, and ravenously destructive alienation.

But the passage also foregrounds conditions in Shakespeare's society. Shakespeare's time was one of significant and rapid social change, what A.L. Beier calls "profound social dislocations." Increasing and increasingly visible poverty, "disastrous economic and demographic shifts and massive migration" mark this period (Beier 3). Poverty increased in part because of a major population increase—historians estimate that the population of England rose as much as 35 percent during the forty-five years (1558–1603) of Elizabeth's reign. This growth in population, especially urban population, drove up the price of land and drove down the price of labor, so much so that historians refer to the "price revolution" brought about by inflation (Jones 34). Though all ranks of society underwent great change, the poor suffered most, being displaced from their homes by changes in the pattern of landownership such as the enclosure for private use of land formerly shared by villagers, and the disappearance of the monasteries which had dispensed charity (Carroll 21–23). They received less in wages while food prices rose (as much as 600 percent in the sixteenth century; see Jones 34), and were often displaced from the aristocratic households which kept far fewer servants as the century wore on (Beier 23–24). A bad harvest—and there were several in the 1590s—spelled disaster for those already living on the margins: "hunger and privation never disappeared in the Tudor–Stuart period, even when harvests and other economic conditions were good; and when such conditions were bad, the poor died in the streets, and the beggars and vagabonds of the kingdom multiplied—like vermin, it was said, 'in swarms' " (Carroll 23).

The comparison to vermin should indicate the sometimes surprisingly harsh attitudes toward the poor that arose at this time, resulting in a series of laws that represent the "criminalization of poverty" over the course of the Tudor century (Woodbridge 232). Beginning in 1531 and renewed at frequent intervals, Parliamentary acts establish what seems to us savage treatment of the poor, the mentally ill, and vagabonds. Their wandering in search of work or food is familiarly described in More's *Utopia*, where More's analysis of the problem in Book I establishes the need for the remedies he proposes in Book II. This wandering is seen as a threat to order—people, it was thought, should stay in their places, both social and geographic—and was punished by whipping, branding, the amputation of ears, imprisonment, and forced transportation to servitude or slavery in the New World (Carroll 21–69).

I am most concerned here with those called "masterless men" in the early modern period; this term, like "beggar," "rogue," and "vagabond" (terms used almost interchangeably in that era; Carroll 17) assumes that the natural, normal state for a man is as part of the complex social hierarchy, a holdover from feudalism's social order. As Neill notes, "it was almost impossible [for them] to conceive of a properly human existence outside the hierarchy of masters and servants" (21). Masterless men, "belonging" to no one, were seen as *outside* the social order, and were feared as a vivid reminder of great social inequity and of the vulnerability of the ruling class. (Women, "belonging" to fathers and husbands, were seen as firmly fixed within the order; though many of them were homeless, it is the men who were perceived as the greater threat.) Without a master to govern and supervise him, it was thought, such a man would lack the restraint necessary for order (Brown 210). Further, those in power feared the undermining of the shared values which, it was believed, held together the traditional social fabric of hierarchy and deference. A new kind of economy was emerging in which "the old commonwealth ideal began to break down" (Jones 37). The governors of Elizabethan England showed their awareness of a link between shifts in social values and in economic contingencies, producing statements such as that of Elizabeth's principal adviser, Lord Burghley: "There is nothing will sooner lead men into sedition than dearth of victual."[3]

A series of measures was thus taken in the sixteenth century lest the very poor have no stake in the status quo and, desperate, rise to rend the social fabric which served the interests of their superiors. The Privy Council's order to provide work for unemployed clothworkers, issued in 1586, nicely blends charity and fear: this is "a matter not onlie full of pittie in respect of the people but of dangerous consequence to the state if speedie order be not taken theirin."[4] Like these governors of the realm, Shakespeare marked the link between social values and economic contingencies, and he described the issues with his usual precision and his uncanny feel for the particularity of human beings enmeshed in the fabric of history. We would consider most representations of the poor on the Renaissance stage and in other contemporary literature to be woefully unrealistic: they are actually noblemen in disguise, they're jolly and not really suffering at all, or they're witty thieves like the brilliant con-artists of Jonson's *Alchemist*.[5] In this regard as in so many others, Shakespeare stands out; he interrogates these representations of the poor and marginalized in a fashion that seems radical even today.

Shakespeare's plays give us individuals rather than types, but when we examine these individuals in the aggregate of the canon, we can distinguish at least four groups which tie social value to economic status. There are the masterless men, such as the hired killers of *Macbeth* and *Lear*; there is also the more specific category of the vagabond, including both the peddler Autolycus in *Winter's Tale*—though his masterlessness is incidental to his role—and the disguised Edgar in *Lear*, whose poverty is the core of his disguised identity. We see also the figure of the social rebel, as in Jack Cade or the hungry peasants of *Coriolanus*, and, finally, that of the ambitious striver, as in *Lear*'s Oswald, *Henry VIII*'s Wolsey, or (more lightheartedly, but with his own sinister edge) *Twelfth Night*'s Malvolio. Each of these groupings, extending beyond the boundaries of the individual play, enables us to connect one play to another in order to illuminate both the individual plays and the body of Shakespeare's work.

To glance briefly at the groups that I have distinguished from the subject of our special interest, the masterless man: the vagabond is a specific sub-type of masterless man, one forced out of his community by upheaval, and this figure receives its fullest Shakespearean expression in *Lear*, with Edgar's disguise as a Bedlam beggar.[6] In the figure of "Poor Tom," Shakespeare links poverty with the skepticism it raises about the possibility of justice and the integrity of society. Taking up "the basest and most poorest shape/ That ever penury, in contempt of man,/ Brought near to beast" (2.3.7–9), Edgar both personifies "houseless poverty" himself and evokes in Lear and Gloucester not mere sympathy for their inferiors, but a critique of the very structure of their society, which their former complacent greatness had left unquestioned. When Lear realizes that he has "ta'en/ Too little care of this" (3.4.32–33) and acknowledges that wealth corrupts justice, "Through tatter'd clothes [small] vices do appear;/ Robes and furr'd gowns hide all" (4.6.164–65), he goes beyond pity to indictment of the whole social order.

Cade of *2 Henry VI* and the desperate rebels described by Queen Katherine in *Henry VIII*, whose plight has "flaw'd the heart of all their loyalties," exemplify my third category: the rebellious subject. As Burghley's words imply, rebellion is the most overt manifestation of the relationship between economic crisis and dissent from the traditional values of the hierarchical society: rebels demand change. Shakespeare's aristocrats are depicted as varied in their responses to rebellion, ranging from the sympathetic Queen Katherine to the contemptuous Coriolanus, but Shakespeare is impressively specific about the depicted reality of the peasant plight and about the causes of rebellion, whether the latter be the exorbitant one-sixth tax of the "Amicable Grant" and its disastrous effects on clothworkers in *Henry VIII*, or the dearth of corn in *Coriolanus*, topically timely in the England of 1607–1608.[7]

Who profits by the displacement and consequent suffering of the masterless man, the vagabond, and the peasant rebel? It is my fourth figure, the ambitious seeker, who benefits by the dissolution of the social fabric and of the moral and economic order. Such men form a category notable for its conjunction of strange bedfellows—Tyrell of *Richard III*, Oswald of *Lear*, Malvolio of *Twelfth Night*, and Wolsey of *Henry VIII*, for example. The category also bears an affinity to the upwardly mobile "civil servant" who was, says Fernand Braudel, "invariably of humble origin" everywhere in the sixteenth century and whose arrival as agent of state power "marks a political revolution coupled with a social revolution" (Braudel 2: 681).[8] The opportunity of these ambitious men comes with the decay of old families and old values both, and thus provides a fourth example of Shakespeare's linking economic and value shifts in the "new man" who, rootless and amoral, seeks his fortune by filling the vacuum left by the departure of the traditional order.[9] Many see a "sharp historical divide" in social attitudes:

> On one side of it lies the "society of orders" described by social historians —a society that still imagines itself as an organically connected hierarchy

bound by reciprocal duties and obligations, insisting that to be a man
at all is to be another's "man"; on the other lies a world of competitive individuals, organized by the ruthless and alienating power
of money into something that is beginning to resemble a society of
classes.

(Neill 45)

The masterless men in *Macbeth* provide an interesting intermediate case,
sharing aspects of all the others: they are marginalized like vagabonds, and
disenfranchised like rebels, but they profit, like the ambitious climber, by
increased opportunity in a time of rapid change.

We are accustomed to saying that the gradual shift to a market economy
produced a loosening of the ties of the "highly integrated and mutually interdependent village society;" at the extreme end of this road lies the highly
mobile and individualistic society of our own time (McFarlane 197). But what
happens to that historical abstraction, the masterless man, when enclosure,
the relative lowering of wages, the rise of prices and rents, the growth of
commerce, and the growth of population combine to create the social mobility of the Elizabethans? From one angle, this mobility looks like freedom and
opportunity. But social mobility, of course, works in both directions. Though
the crash of old aristocratic families makes a more resounding echo, the
"lesser" person, having less far to fall because of his already tenuous footing
on the social ladder, may suffer the slippage more keenly. I take this to be the
case of the hired killers in *Macbeth*. The play has as one of its subjects social
disintegration; on the level of the action this disintegration has Macbeth
rather than the commercial revolution as its agent. On another level, though,
the plight of the hired killers is an economic and social one: they are driven to
this employment by desperation. The masterless men in *Macbeth* need to be
doubly contextualized, first within the play itself, as outcasts from community, and then in the context of their fellows in Shakespeare's canon, as
examples of a social group characterized by its desperate willingness to do
anything to survive.

The desperate poor are brought near to the condition of animals in their
struggle to survive, and Macbeth's comparison of the masterless men to dogs
has the initial effect of degrading their human status. Discussing the implications of the early modern habit of analogizing humans to animals, Gail Kern
Paster reminds us that such comparisons are "grounded in the premodern
doctrine of sympathies and correspondences" by which all of creation is
drawn together (145). Yet in the hierarchy of creation, humans ranked above
all other animals in the Renaissance mind.[10] The comparison to dogs seems
also to erase the men's individuality, already faint, as they are defined by their
social status and their function as hired killers. The Arden editor may well be
right in citing, as the ultimate source of the catalogue of dogs, a then-well-
known comparison of men and dogs by Erasmus; but surely the many cata-
logues of types of beggars, vagabonds, and rogues in the pamphlets of the

time had made such listings familiar and also provide a telling analogy (Muir 81).[11] Thus the particularization of *kinds of dogs* marks the passage in our memories, while perhaps also anticipating our question: and what *kind of animal* is a hired killer?[12]

Here, in one of the play's many familiar inversions (beginning with the witches' "fair is foul"), Macbeth inscribes a sort of sub-humanity as true manliness: "to qualify as an authentic man you must raise your head above the pack and kill, as [Macbeth] himself rises above Glamis to be Cawdor and above Cawdor to be King of Scotland" (Calderwood 124). Dogs, emblematized in the Renaissance for their loyalty, are ironically appropriate animals for Macbeth, whose loyalty to his king has failed but who wants to evoke that emotion in the desperate men before him. Such motivation in fact seems unnecessary, since they are men whose situations are so desolate that they no longer care what they do:

> *2nd Murderer:*   I am one, my liege,
> Whom the vile blows and buffets of the world
> Hath so incens'd that I am reckless what
> I do to spite the world.
> *1st Murderer:*   And I another,
> So weary with disasters, tugg'd with fortune,
> That I would set my life on any chance,
> To mend it, or be rid on't.
>   (3.1.107–13)

Though we have no objective means of verifying the cause of their plight, Macbeth tells them that Banquo is to blame, and they don't—or can't— disagree; how much are we to believe of Macbeth's accusations?[13] What is more to our purpose is that, even though the origin of the murderers' masterless condition is not specified, they are linked by it to characters like Poor Tom whose marginalization is more fully detailed.

Shakespeare doesn't pause on the question of Banquo's responsibility, because he wants the emphasis to be on the power of Macbeth's appeal here.[14] Macbeth's words suggest that the hired killers' misfortune is financial as well as (perhaps) political. He says,

>   Know
> That it was he in the times past which held you
> So under fortune, which you thought had been
> Our innocent self? This I made good to you
> Our last conference, pass'd in probation with you:
> How you were borne in hand, how cross'd, the instruments,
> Who wrought with them, and all things else . . .
>   Are you so gospell'd
> To pray for this good man, and for his issue,

Whose heavy hand hath bow'd you to the grave
And beggar'd yours for ever?

(3.1.75–90)

As a further incentive, Macbeth offers not only revenge on their supposed wronger, but "a station in the file," a distinctive position in the society from which they feel themselves set apart. To their "we are men, my liege," Macbeth replies with the catalogue of dogs and suggests that if the murderers distinguish themselves from the general crew, as a particular kind of dog may be distinguished from others of the species, they will find him a master who will "grapple you to the heart and love of us." They respond with obedience—"We shall, my lord, perform what you command us"—and thus, in another of the play's inversions of fair and foul, the desperate man alienated by want from his society is perversely reintegrated into that society, regaining a master by performing his murders for him; rejoining the community by violating its most fundamental prohibition.[15] In so doing, the hired killers threaten the hierarchy on which the play's society is built, and thus resemble their new master, Macbeth, whose own subversion of this hierarchy is one of the play's most frequently iterated themes.[16] Carroll puts this subversiveness in a broader context for us: "The lean beggar serves not just as an antithesis to the fat king, but as an opposing principle to all authority that derives from the sociopolitical hierarchy that maintains and justifies the monarchy, the court, and the social gradations ramifying from it" (175). Macbeth's marginality is self-created, unlike that of his hirelings, but all subvert the moral order through what Carroll calls their "antihierarchical status" (36). Macbeth himself, having killed his king, is a masterless man as well as—deserted by his followers at the end—a manless master.

Macbeth's hired killers thus take their place alongside other hired killers in Shakespeare's plays. We recall Cordelia's hangman in *Lear*, who offers to perform any task required without regard to ethical considerations: "If it be man's work, I'll do't" (5.3.39). These words, spoken by the Captain in response to Edmund's promise of advancement to "noble fortunes," leave us to wonder what "man's work" is. Likewise, Tyrell in *Richard III* is instantly ready to kill Richard's princely nephews, who stand in the way of Richard's rise to the throne. "I will dispatch it straight" (4.2.82), Tyrell responds to Richard's whispered command, accompanied by a promise of preferment. Tyrell and the Captain may look at first glance quite like the murderers of *Macbeth*: all, in fact, are promised advancement for their deeds. But Tyrell and the Captain are not shown as driven by desperation as the masterless men are; murder is merely their means to rise, a ready path for the ambitious man.

The willingness to serve any purpose, seen in Tyrell and the Captain, is the hallmark of Shakespeare's "new men." They are distinguished from the more prominent villains of the plays such as Macbeth or Claudius by their subordinate positions as well as by their roles as opportunistic factotums. Oswald in *Lear*, happy to raise his fortunes above his station as steward by apprehending the blinded Gloucester; Wolsey in *Henry VIII*, manipulating Henry's vanity while drawing all threads into his own hands; even the pretentious steward Malvolio of *Twelfth Night*, whose ridiculous willingness to believe his mistress in love with him lightens his hypocrisy and masks his resemblance to his more dangerous counterparts in other plays, are "new men" in the sense of being "self-made," seeking their fortunes as their historical counterparts did in the opportunity provided by a time of major social dislocation. *Macbeth*'s hired killers, driven by desperation, should be categorized as "masterless men" rather than "new men." The men in *Macbeth* are needy and rootless, these facts explaining if not justifying their actions, whereas the ambitious strivers such as Tyrell or the Captain are given no such rationale beyond their own desire for advancement.[17]

Macbeth presents us with many areas of moral indeterminacy, such as Malcolm's ambiguous testing of Macduff at the English court, Macduff's desertion of his family, Banquo's silence about his suspicions of Macbeth, and the question of the relative responsibility of Lady, Witches, and Thane.[18] A larger ambiguity, as Alan Sinfield has shown, characterizes the play's stance on the tyranny of the state and its accumulating violence. Should we prefer the Macbeth of the play's opening battle, whose efficient butchery on behalf of Duncan "unseam'd" his opponent "from the nave to th' chops" to the Macbeth who turns that skill upon Duncan himself (1.2.22)?[19] By suggesting that this question may have no certain answer, *Macbeth* glances tellingly at the contemporary problem of the "newly unemployed soldier" (Carroll 175), a trained killer who must turn his training to peacetime use—but how? (The point was noted as early as 1516, in More's *Utopia*.)

For all the seeming intractability of such questions, Shakespeare does represent Macbeth and his hired killers as violators of certain values, which others in the play hold, or at least profess to hold. What are these values, then, and how are they depicted? In the feudal world of *Macbeth's* thanes, the loyalty of the clan is a signal value, and Macbeth's obligation of loyalty to Duncan is the bond that he most obviously violates.[20] In such a world, a place in the social order, a station in the file, is essential. By providing the seemingly extraneous details of the motivation of the masterless men who kill Banquo and the lengthy list of dogs, Shakespeare gives us a chilling sense of the emptiness of a world without these communal bonds: the world of Macbeth's final soliloquies on the meaninglessness of the Scotland without "honor, love, obedience, troops of friends" (5.3.25). Making himself into a masterless man like the killers he hires, Macbeth is a self-created outcast whose growing isolation in the play, even from his "dearest partner of greatness," Lady Macbeth, culminates in his being labeled a "monster" and "butcher," outside the circle of human communion. The extremity of the labels indicates the extent of his fall from the most admired to the most hated of men.

At the end, Macbeth's followers desert him, and he becomes a king without subjects: a manless master. The remedy, the play suggests on one level, is the "med'cine of the sickly weal" (5.1.27) represented by Malcolm and Macduff;

Macbeth is a disease to be purged. Yet, one of the play's many puzzling echoes points to still another indeterminacy: Macbeth, seeking legitimacy after his murder of Duncan, goes to be crowned at Scone, the traditional site for this ceremony. Malcolm's last words in the play are his invitation to his followers "to see us crown'd at Scone." Are we to wonder if a pattern is about to repeat as Malcolm echoes Macbeth's action? The play refuses to yield that certainty which we'd prefer, though surely most of the indicators are that Malcolm has liberated his country from the destruction of its human fabric created by Macbeth. Malcolm's follower, the anonymous lord of 3.6, gives us the description of that human, natural, social fabric, hoping that the end of Macbeth will enable the people of Scotland to

> again
> Give to our tables meat, sleep to our nights;
> Free from our feasts and banquets bloody knives,
> Do faithful homage and receive free honors,
> All which we pine for now.
>
> (33–37)

Such hopes for restoration contrast strongly with the sleepless nights of Lady Macbeth, or the banquet disrupted by Macbeth's hallucination of the murdered Banquo, emblematizing Scotland in disarray under the murderous Macbeth. The passage on types of dogs with which we began this inquiry has led us to understand the hired killers, outlaws beyond the pale of society, as representatives not only of the social upheaval of Shakespeare's time, but as figures standing in for Macbeth, royal outlaw, self-hired for mischief.

Notes

1 The Geneva Bible's marginal comment on the passage in Acts 17: 5 about "vaga-bonds and wicked fellowes" glosses these as "Certaine companions which doe nothing but walk the streetes, wicked men, to be hired for every mans money to doe any mischiefe, such as we commonly call the rascals and very sinks and dung-hill knaves of all townes and cities" (Sheppard 65). Though Shakespeare's famil-iarity with this popular translation and its marginal commentaries is not pertinent to my use of this gloss, Burnet and Black provide the evidence for that familiarity. My attention was drawn to this passage by Christopher Hill, who uses the Geneva gloss as an epigraph to his chapter on Masterless Men (32).

   It is a pleasure to record here my indebtedness to Professor Lamar Hill, Uni-versity of California, Irvine, for first drawing my attention to the puzzle of Macbeth's catalogue of dogs, and for his counsel and encouragement of my work on a much earlier essay on this topic. Versions of this paper have been presented to a workshop on Poverty and Vagrancy at the Shakespeare Association of America's 1997 meeting, and to the Shakespeare Symposium of the California State Uni-versity. I am grateful to my Symposium colleagues, especially Michael Flachmann and Renèe Pigeon, for their suggestions, and to Bryan Feuer for his support and encouragement.

2 *The Riverside Shakespeare* is the source of all quotations from Shakespeare.

3 As cited in Fletcher (112). For further discussion of early modern English representations of rogues and vagabonds, see now Dionne and Mentz.

4 Cited in Buchanan Sharp (66–67).

5 See extensive discussions of these representations in Carroll, Woodbridge, and Howard.

6 "Bedlam" was the era's shortening of the name of the hospital for the mentally ill, Bethlehem.

7 See Fletcher (19). Sharp (3, 7) surveys food riots occurring in the period 1586 to 1631.

8 For a more recent discussion of the professionalization of government service and the origin of these servants, see Williams (144); Elton earlier made this case in regard to England (423).

9 Like most writers on this topic, I am happily in the debt of Colie. I trust it is clear that by "new man" I intend no narrow reference to a particular social group, even given the contemporary references to the advancement of the humbly born; we are looking at a broader phenomenon than the phrase "rise of the gentry" can describe, I think. The locus classicus for the controversy over rising gentry and falling aristocracy is Hexter. Wrightson (13) gives a more recent discussion of this point.

10 See Boehrer's nuanced discussion of early modern attitudes as a useful amplification of my generalization.

11 For such lists in pamphlets, see Carroll (71, 80, 82), and Woodbridge. Many such pamphlets are reprinted in Kinney.

12 Paster notes the opposite case: "denying individual difference among animals within the same species in order to fix it exclusively in human beings is fundamental to humanist praises of the dignity of man" (163).

13 Rosenberg debates the credibility of these accusations of Banquo in his discussion of this scene (401).

14 See Rosenberg (402–403): "the performance is dazzling: he holds out promise of friendship, but no specific bribes (though in the theatre coins have changed hands); subjects them—as he was subjected—to an appeal to a masculinity they must hold dear. He allows them to be partners with him in crime, while challenging them to find a place for themselves not too far below."

15 Macbeth's taint corrupts even this perverse revival of lordship, however; when the two murderers gather to strike down Banquo, they are joined by a mysterious third, sent by Macbeth, the second murderer suggests (3.3.2), out of mistrust of the bloody service of his new followers. How, after all, could Macbeth, destroyer of the bonds to king, guest, and kinsman in his murder of Duncan, expect deference and loyalty even from the outcasts whom need drove to his service?

16 Calderwood (124–25) and Rosenberg (402) both assert that *degree*—the English Renaissance's term for the ordered hierarchy of society—is part of the point of this passage and of the ranks of dogs therein.

17 In his humorlessness and pretense of having greatness thrust upon him, Malvolio is strangely allied to the "vile politician" Bolingbroke. Grandson of Edward III, Shakespeare's Henry is hardly a "new man" in his social status. Yet, he too is an equivocating seeker, finding the ultimate preferment by overthrowing Richard (with, admittedly, a good deal of help from Richard himself), professing loyalty while, as he later boasts to Hal in *1 Henry IV*, he devises policy to pluck allegiance from men's hearts. What greater rise than to the throne?

18 Berger sees a fundamental complicity in all the major characters; he concludes "that there is something rotten in Scotland—that something intrinsic to the situation of Scottish society, something deeper than the melodramatic wickedness of one or two individuals, generates these tendencies toward instability, conflict, sedition, and murder" (5). Norbrook, too, has a fine essay from this perspective.

19 Sinfield argues that the play is about the distinction "between the violence which the play considers legitimate and that which it does not," between, for example, Macbeth's bloody killing of Macdonwald in battle and the murder of Duncan. "Violence is good, in this view, when it is in the service of the prevailing dispositions of power; when it disrupts them it is evil." The play interrogates this received view of state violence, Sinfield asserts (93).
20 See Berry (especially 117).

Works cited

Beier, A.L. *Masterless Men: The Vagrancy Problem in England 1560–1640*. London: Methuen, 1985.

Berger, Harry Jr. "The Early Scenes of *Macbeth*: Preface to a New Interpretation." *ELH* 47 (1980): 1–31.

Berry, Ralph. *Shakespeare and Social Class*. Atlantic Highlands: Humanities, 1988.

Black, James. *Edified by the Margent: Shakespeare and the Bible*. Calgary: U of Calgary, 1979.

Boehrer, Bruce. *Shakespeare among the Animals: Nature and Society in the Drama of Early Modern England*. New York: Palgrave, 2002.

Braudel, Fernand. *The Mediterranean and the Mediterranean World in the Age of Philip II*. 2 vols. 1949. Trans. Siân Reynolds. New York: Harper & Row, 1972–73.

Brown, Paul. " 'This Thing of Darkness I Acknowledge Mine': *The Tempest* and the Discourse of Colonialism." *The Tempest: A Case Study in Critical Controversy*. Ed. Gerald Graff and James Phelan. Boston: Bedford, 2000. 205–29.

Burnet, R.A.L. "Shakespeare and the Marginalia of the Geneva Bible." *Notes and Queries* 26 (1979): 113–14.

Calderwood, James L. *If It Were Done: Macbeth and Tragic Action*. Amherst: U of Massachusetts P, 1986.

Carroll, William C. *Fat King, Lean Beggar: Representations of Poverty in the Age of Shakespeare*. Ithaca: Cornell UP, 1996.

Colie, Rosalie L. "King Lear and the Crisis of the Aristocracy." *Some Facets of King Lear*. Ed. Rosalie Colie and F.T. Flahiff. Toronto: U of Toronto P, 1974. 185–219.

Dionne, Craig and Steve Mentz, eds. *Rogues and Early Modern English Culture*. Ann Arbor: U of Michigan P, 2004.

Elton, G.R. *The Tudor Revolution in Government*. Cambridge: Cambridge UP, 1953.

Fletcher, Anthony. *Tudor Rebellions*. London: Longman, 1968.

Hexter, J.H. "Storm over the Gentry." *Reappraisals in History*. 1961. New York: Harper, 1963. 117–62.

Hill, Christopher. *The World Turned Upside Down*. New York: Viking Press, 1972.

Howard, Jean. *The Stage and Social Struggle in Early Modern England*. London: Routledge, 1994.

Jones, Norman. "Shakespeare's England." *A Companion to Shakespeare*. Ed. David Scott Kastan. Oxford: Blackwell, 1999. 25–42.

Kinney, Arthur, ed. *Rogues, Vagabonds, and Sturdy Beggars*. Amherst: U of Massachusetts P, 1990.

McFarlane, A.D.J. *Witchcraft in Tudor and Stuart England*. New York: Harper, 1970.

More, Thomas. *Utopia*. Ed. and trans. David Wootton. Indianapolis: Hackett, 1999.

Muir, Kenneth, ed. *Macbeth*. The Arden Shakespeare. Cambridge: Harvard UP, 1951.

Neill, Michael. *Putting History to the Question: Power, Politics and Society in English Renaissance Drama.* New York: Columbia UP, 2000.

Norbrook, David. "*Macbeth* and the Politics of Historiography." *Politics of Discourse: The Literature and History of Seventeenth-Century England.* Ed. Kevin Sharpe and Steven N. Zwicker. Berkeley: U of California P, 1987. 78–116.

Paster, Gail Kern. *Humanizing the Body: Emotions and the Shakespearean Stage.* Chicago: U of Chicago P, 2004.

Rosenberg, Marvin. *The Masks of* Macbeth. Berkeley: U of California P, 1978.

Shakespeare, William. *The Riverside Shakespeare.* Ed. G. Blakemore Evans and J.J.M. Tobin. 2nd ed. Boston: Houghton Mifflin, 1997.

Sharp, Buchanan. *In Contempt of All Authority.* Berkeley: U of California P, 1980.

Sheppard, Gerald T., ed. *The Geneva Bible: The Annotated New Testament, 1602 Edition.* New York: Pilgrim, 1989.

Sinfield, Alan. "*Macbeth:* History, Ideology, and Intellectuals." *Critical Quarterly* 28 (1986): 63–77. Rpt. *Materialist Shakespeare: A History.* Ed. Ivo Kamps. London: Verso, 1995. 93–107.

Williams, Penry. *The Later Tudors: England, 1547–1603.* Oxford: Clarendon, 1995.

Woodbridge, Linda. *Vagrancy, Homelessness, and English Renaissance Literature.* Urbana: U of Illinois P, 2001.

Wrightson, Keith. *English Society 1580–1680.* 1982. New Brunswick, NJ: Rutgers UP, 1984.

8 Healing angels and "golden blood"

Money and mystical kingship in *Macbeth*

Stephen Deng

Following Malcolm's testing of Macduff's loyalty in Act 4, Scene 3 of *Macbeth*, an English doctor informs the two that there is a "crew of wretched souls" suffering from some disease and awaiting the English king Edward the Confessor, at whose "touch,/ Such sanctity hath heaven given his hand,/ They presently amend" (4.3.143–45).[1] Macduff inquires about this disease, and Malcolm responds with a description of a peculiar ceremony whereby Edward cures patients suffering from scrofula or "the king's evil":

> 'Tis call'd the evil:
> A most miraculous work in this good king,
> Which often, since my here-remain in England,
> I have seen him do. How he solicits heaven,
> Himself best knows; but strangely-visited people,
> All swoll'n and ulcerous, pitiful to the eye,
> The mere despair of surgery, he cures,
> Hanging a golden stamp about their necks,
> Put on with holy prayers, and 'tis spoken,
> To the succeeding royalty he leaves
> The healing benediction. With this strange virtue,
> He hath a heavenly gift of prophecy,
> And sundry blessings hang about his throne
> That speak him full of grace.
>
> (4.3.146–59)

Critics have generally concluded that the passage served as a royal compliment to King James, who saw an early production of the play, and who continued this ceremony of "touching" for the king's evil.[2] For example, in *Bell's Edition of Shakespeare's Plays* (1773–74), the actor Francis Gentleman accuses Shakespeare of having "lugged in, by neck and heels, a doctor for the strange purpose of paying a gross compliment to that royal line, which ridiculously arrogated a power of curing the evil, by a touch," adding that the "scene is properly left out" in performance, which it has often been (1: 55).

I argue, however, that the passage, and especially the detail of the king "hanging a golden stamp"—a gold coin called an *angel*—around the necks of patients, resonates with a general economy of monetary representation in the play. In this chapter I situate *Macbeth* within the socio-cultural context of early modern money, which circulated in both material and representational economies. The use of this gold coin in the healing ceremony began only with Henry VII, which explains why there is no mention of its employment by Edward the Confessor in Shakespeare's main source, Holinshed's *Chronicles*. With the Tudors, however, the coin came to be considered essential to the healing ceremony, and subjects who removed the coin were reported to have suffered relapses. This putative power was based on a tradition that saw mystical powers in coins, whose combination of precious metal, royal effigy, and "magical" inscription made them suitable for healing purposes. As a result, the coin served to promote royalty by helping to produce the ideology of mystical kingship. Although both Elizabeth and James considered terminating the ceremony because of its idolatrous implications, they realized its importance for the promotion of the English monarchy, and continued to hang angels around patients' necks as part of the ritual.

The dissemination of healing coins, then, circulated money within mystical as well as financial economies. Historically, however, the strategies and motivations of the two were often at odds. In *Macbeth*, the financial economy is represented by a system of tribute and reward between Duncan and Macbeth as well as the material "sinews of war" Macbeth attempts to use to maintain power, especially by hiring mercenaries and establishing a system of paid spies. The mystical economy is emblematized by Macbeth's vision of Duncan's "silver skin lac'd with his golden blood" (2.3.112), the trope of money as blood flowing through the immortal body politic. I argue that the usurper Macbeth gets caught in between these two economies. Whereas he feels an initial tension between the financial and mystical economies of monetary representation, he temporarily suppresses the mystical in his decision to murder Duncan. However, immediately after the murder, the mystical reemerges in Macbeth's conscience, especially in Macbeth's description of Duncan's body. Despite his financial investment in surveillance and security as king, he believes that the "true" blood of the social body "is stopp'd" as long as his own, illegitimate reign continues (2.3.99). Macbeth's insecurities reveal that money is not a *sufficient* mechanism for legitimacy despite its effective deployment in what Max Weber calls the "routinization of charisma." Although he acquires the resources of state, Macbeth cannot recreate the aura surrounding Duncan's gold. While royal investment in the two economies promoted the belief that money guaranteed the health of the country in addition to being a measure of material resources, Macbeth's perception of a diseased Scotland evidences the belief that all money is not equivalent—only the money produced by the legitimate king has the power to preserve the state.

The money fetish and the routinization of charisma

The practice of "touching" most likely began in France under Robert the Pious (996–1031), but soon after it is reported that Edward the Confessor performed a similar healing in England.[3] From its inception, the ceremony included economic in addition to therapeutic aid from the king,[4] yet it was not until around the time of Henry VII that the angel—a gold coin initially worth six shillings, eight pence—became a central component of the ceremony.[5] According to a late seventeenth-century pamphlet entitled *The Ceremonies for the Healing of Them that be Diseased with the King's Evil used in the Time of King Henry VII* (1686), the king's chaplain would repeat a verse from the first chapter of John, "That light was the true light which lighteth every man that cometh into the world," while "the King shall be crossing the Sore of the Sick Person with an Angel of Gold Noble." After the king crossed the sores, the patient would "have the same Angel hanged about his Neck, and . . . wear it until he be full whole" (12–13).[6] Henry's liturgy attached a mystery to the coin that clearly transcended economic charity. After all, why would he ceremoniously hang the coin around patients' necks rather than just hand it to them like alms?

The significance of the angel can be understood from the earliest known contemporary account of the practice, during the reign of Queen Mary. A letter describes how Mary

> made the sick people come up to her . . . and taking a gold coin—viz. an angel—she touched the place where the evil showed itself, signed it with the Cross and passed a ribbon through the hole which had been pierced in it, placing one of them round the neck of each of the patients, and making them promise never to part with that coin, save in case of extreme need.[7]

According to this contemporary account, Mary placed special emphasis on the coin as a memento of the wondrous event, but the qualification "save in case of extreme need" acknowledges that the memento bore economic value. While Mary's initial request encourages an interpretation of the coin as a personally meaningful object outside of commodity-exchange cycles, her modification concedes the coin's economic origin—the monetary alms that supplemented the healing touch. By the time of James, however, the monarchy upheld the view that the coin was an essential component of healing, and *not just* economic aid, so that the cure would be ineffective if subjects parted with the angel. In 1625 James issued a proclamation warning against patients who "were formerly cured, but then disposed of the gold coins in unlawful ways," presumably selling them or even using them as common currency, "and consequently experienced a relapse" (quoted in Bloch 183). This concern about subjects employing the king's healing coins as common currency may explain why later monarchs replaced the angel with a non-current, though still gold, "touchpiece."

With monarchs hanging this gold coin around the necks of patients and telling them not to part with it, it was only a small step to the perception that the coin was an amulet bearing protective power. In fact, one unintended consequence was that subjects began to believe the coin itself was enough to effect a cure. The angels or touchpieces used in the ceremonies were thought to maintain the healing power of the king, and they were often given to other scrofula sufferers who had not gone through the ceremony. In *Adenochoirade-logia* (1684), John Browne tells an amusing anecdote about a father and son both suffering from the evil. Only the father had been "touched," but he would let his son borrow the gold whenever the son had an outbreak:

> The Father being distempered and ill, keeps the Gold about his neck, which kept him in health, and gave him speedy ease and relief: The Son falling ill, he borrows his Fathers Gold from his neck, and puts it about his own, which likewise gave him ease and relief. The Father after this by leaving his Gold, had his Destemper seized him afresh, and then took the Gold again, and this made it as readily vanish. And thus by the inter-course or change of Gold from Father to Son, and from Son to Father, whoever of them kept the Gold, was defended against any new approach or appearance of his Distemper; and this was kept and maintained by them for many years together.
>
> (Browne 138)

The story suggests that the curative power had been transferred from the king's touch to the gold itself, which even began to circulate as a "sacred commodity" separated from its point of origin in the touching ceremony.[8] According to Browne (93), touchpieces used in the ceremony could be found for sale in goldsmiths' shops; Bloch discovers that coins of Charles I had been passed down from generation to generation for healing scrofula in the Shetland Islands well into the nineteenth century (223). Even after the healing ceremonies had ceased, coins or touchpieces that had been used in them continued to circulate as remnants or relics of the mystical event.

Such relics circulating as healing agents could of course be considered idolatrous in Protestant England. James was concerned about endorsing a ritual that was ingrained in England's Catholic past, and particularly one associated with the iconic Edward the Confessor.[9] Among three requests he made when first coming to England, he asked specifically that he not be required to touch for scrofula, "not wishing to arrogate vainly to himself such virtue and divinity, as to be able to cure diseases by touch alone."[10] In a letter dated June 4, 1603, a Venetian representative reports to the Doge and Senate, "King James says that neither he nor any other King can have any power to heal scrofula, for the age of miracles is past, and God alone can work them."[11] But James's English Council, headed by Cecil, eventually made James understand that discontinuing the ritual would detract from the dignity of the crown. So "inasmuch as it was an ancient usage and for the good of his subjects," as it was recorded in an October 9, 1603 letter, he finally "resolved to give it a trial, but only by way of prayer, in which he begged all present to join him." Considering his initial aversion to the ceremony, it is surprising that James eventually made a significant contribution to the conviction that the coins had assumed the healing power of the king.

Nevertheless, in order to allay his concerns, James altered the ritual to exclude papist and idolatrous elements, all of which involved the coin. He excluded the practice of crossing patients' sores with the angel. In addition, James removed from the reverse side of his angel a small cross on a ship's mast, and he excluded "*et EST MIRABILE*" from Mary and Elizabeth's motto on their coins: "*A DOMINO FACTUM EST ISTVD et EST MIRA-BILE in oculis nostris*" ("This was the Lord's doing, and it is marvelous in our eyes"). He wanted to eliminate any suggestion that the "touching" ceremony involved a miracle performed by the monarch. Still, James continued to use the coin in his healing ceremony. His service calls for the verse from John to be repeated "as often as the King putteth the Angel about their neckes."[12] Considering all the anxiety that induced James to change the coin and its use, why did he continue to use the coin at all? Why was the coin so important to the healing ritual?

A key reason seems to be that it made the ceremony more convincing.[13] Elizabeth's physician William Clowes describes a seemingly incurable scrofu-lous individual who, having been wondrously transformed by the queen's touch, shows his angel as proof: "And that I should credit him the more he showed me the Angell of golde, which her Majesty did put about his neck" (50). Moreover, there was a long tradition of employing coins as amulets, a tradition on which Henry VII likely drew when he incorporated the angel into his healing ceremony. For example, during the late Middle Ages, soldiers sometimes used coins for protection on the battlefield, worn either around their necks—as English soldiers wore Edward III nobles—or attached to their helmets.[14]

Gold coins like the angel were particularly suitable as amulets. First, gold was thought to have inherent natural properties that could effect a cure for certain ailments. The most common medicinal use of gold was the *aurum potabile*, drinkable gold, which was believed to cure a number of diseases and even to be an elixir of long life.[15] Gold could cure by being worn *on* the body as well, especially in the form of a ring. For example, the "cramp rings" produced by monarchs were thought to cure epilepsy. As with the angels, there was an elaborate ceremony involved in turning cramp rings into healing agents. From the time of Edward II through Henry V, the king would place freshly minted gold and silver coins on an altar. The king would then "redeem" the coins by exchanging for them an equivalent sum in ordinary coin. Finally, he would have these new coins melted down and produce rings from the metal. In the Tudor version, the rings were made ahead of time, and the ordinary coin redeemed the rings themselves from the altar.[16]

In addition to being comprised of curative gold, coins typically bore the images of rulers, which from the classical to the Byzantine periods were considered protective agents.[17] Some early modern rulers, especially Elizabeth I, exploited this tradition. Roy Strong links the English cult of Elizabeth to the Byzantine icon, arguing that the royal portrait filled "the vacuum left by the pre-Reformation image cult." Strong finds that subjects would wear Elizabeth's image as a kind of talisman, making her cult "draw to itself mysterious traditions" (39). But rather than the portrait of the monarch, the angel depicted the Archangel Michael, whose image might constitute a remnant of the "pre-Reformation image cult." The figure of Michael slaying the dragon, which has been read as a type for the healer Apollo trampling the serpent of pestilence, is an appropriate representation for mystical healing.[18] Moreover, the circulation of this sacred image on coins could signify the monarch's divine favor. For example, Shakespeare's Richard II employs a common pun on "angels" to affirm his royal prerogative:

> For every man that Bullingbrook hath press'd
> To lift shrewd steel against our golden crown,
> God for his Richard hath in heavenly pay
> A glorious angel; then if angels fight,
> Weak men must fall, for heaven still guards the right.
>
>   (3.2.58–62)

Richard compares the men that Bullingbrook has "press'd" to worthless, steel currency contesting his pure, golden angels. His control over coinage allows Richard to "press" both coins, as in the stamping process, as well as soldiers, who are impressed into his army.[19] He implicitly transforms the coins he produces into an army of angels sent by God to defend "his Richard." The angels therefore embodied the protective power of God's agents, both for those suffering from scrofula and for the monarch bearing the divine gift.[20]

A source of divinity could also be found in the coins' imprinted mottoes, typically borrowed from Scripture. We saw that in Henry VII's ceremony the passage from John accompanied the crossing of patients with the angel, and that James initially wanted to cure "only by way of prayer."[21] Although reformists would deny such a connection, prayers might be compared to charms and incantations, which were believed to materially affect the air in order to influence the sufferer, resembling transubstantiation, in which the mere ritualistic pronunciation of words changed material objects.[22] Prayers could be so physically powerful that even writing them down on a piece of paper and wearing them around one's neck could allegedly effect a cure. There is an interesting version of this phenomenon in the Gowrie Plot to murder James, recorded in *The Earl of Gowries Conspiracie Against the Kings Majestie of Scotland* (1600), which many critics have related to *Macbeth*.[23] Although Gowrie was cut down in the attempt, his body refused to bleed until James removed from his pocket a "little close parchment bag." Once the bag was displaced, "blood gushed out in great abundance" from the corpse.

Gowrie's bag was found to be "full of Magicall characters, and words of inchantment, wherin it seemed that hee had put his confidence, thinking himselfe never safe without them," which suggests Gowrie's belief in the protective power of these characters (sig. C2^r). The words on coins were thought to bear similar powers. The motto on James's angels, "*A DOMINO FACTUM EST ISTVD*" ("This was the Lord's doing"), attested to God's presence in the original healing ceremony. It is easy to see why the continued wearing of this remnant could be considered constant protection from the king's evil.

Since angels combined the power of gold, the figure of Michael and royal images, and a prayer or "charm" in the form of the coin's legend, they were potent devices for promoting allegiance to the monarch; it was therefore politically expedient for James to adopt their use. Although the touch of the king was the primary agent in the ceremony, the gold coin, which for James became the mediator between the king's touch and the body of the ill subject, also factored significantly in the ritual's perceived efficacy. To guarantee his position, James would employ the energy of what Thomas calls a "primitive piece of magic" while surrounding it with a religious ceremony to serve as "a protective framework" against charges of idolatry (197). Henry VII, whose records first indicate the adoption of the angel into the ceremony, drew from a long tradition of monetary amulets; a tradition based on the belief that there was something magical about coins, whose material and inscription contributed to the mystery of kingship, primarily because of their association with the monarch. Although money, in Shakespearean terminology, served as a "common drudge/ 'Tween man and man," it also constituted a "visible god" circulating among the populace.[24]

Indeed, the visible power of money was not limited to perceptions of its numeric value. In addition to facilitating economic transactions, coins represented a critical point of contact between state and subject. As with the earlier passage from Clowes, in which the patient shows the angel he had received from the king, the coin provided not only a source of pride for patients, but also material evidence of the monarch's gift. Many in Shakespeare's audience would likely have seen one of these "golden stamps" and been reminded of the present king. Although the amuletic quality of the coins might border on idolatry, the wearing of the coins conspicuously displayed allegiance to a powerful monarch. They became an essential component in the circulation of state authority, and distribution of the coins helped to produce what Max Weber calls the "routinization of charisma." Weber asserts that the legitimacy of a ruler is based on *charisma*, which he defines as "a certain quality of an individual personality by virtue of which he is considered extraordinary and treated as endowed with supernatural, superhuman, or at least specifically exceptional powers or qualities" (241). But beyond the "individual personality," charisma may exist as an "objective, transferable entity" transmitted from one individual to another, constituting what Weber terms the "*charisma of office*" (248). It was indeed the "charisma of office" that James's advisors appealed to when they encouraged him to keep the royal healing ceremony alive. The public's perception of James's powers, regardless of whether he himself believed he actually possessed them, offered proof of his legitimacy. The "routinization of charisma" embodied in the touching ceremony therefore provided a constant, everyday reminder of the king's legitimacy.

Moreover, the healing ceremony exploited another form of routinized charisma: minted money. The use of money signaled the public's acceptance of the king's stamp as a guarantor of value; acceptance of the legitimacy of the king's office as the producer of money. M.T. Clanchy describes how Henry II's dispersion of writs, especially with their royal seals depicting Henry crowned and seated on his throne, represented an early instance of the "routinization of charisma" for the English state because the laws of the realm were accompanied by a visual representation of the monarch's majesty (156). I would argue the king's coins served a similar function. Weber himself writes that "the process of routinization of charisma is in very important respects identical with adaptation to the conditions of the economy, since this is the principal continually operating force in everyday life" (254). The everyday use of money and the state's monopoly on money production represented an early version of this routinization of charisma ingrained in economic activity. The pinnacle of monetary charisma was reached when the state could produce valuable paper money independent of the state's supply of gold—in fact, dependent only on the public's faith in the state. What better sign of the modern state's charisma, its supernatural or superhuman powers, than its ability to turn an ordinary piece of paper into a valuable commodity? But it would take years for the state to develop such a capability. All legitimate money in early modern England contained precious metals, either gold or silver, and, as we shall see, perceptions of the state's own legitimacy depended on the routinized charisma produced by a healthy flow of metallic money.[25]

Macbeth, money and mystical kingship

The state's charismatic power embodied in money sheds light on the issue of royal legitimacy in *Macbeth*. Before Duncan's murder, Macbeth experiences fierce tension between the idealistic view of a loyal subject's unequivocal duties to the king and the realization of an unequal relation of material tribute and reward with Duncan. In murdering Duncan, he temporarily suppresses the former and foregrounds the latter. Initially, with the "golden round" staring him in the face, Macbeth becomes intent on claiming what he feels he deserves according to the logic of the balance sheet. Moreover, once he gains the throne, he attempts to depend entirely on the material economy to defend his position. But after the king's murder he recognizes how Duncan's money—the money produced by the legitimate king—bears the mystical power of maintaining a healthy state. He sees Duncan's "silver skin lac'd with his golden blood" as an emblem of blood-like money coursing through the king's second body, the immortal body politic. Despite the fact that he acquires the "sinews of war" by buying an army and even a system of surveillance for information gathering, he nonetheless intuits some lack in his money's power due to the perceived illegitimacy of his kingship. The lack ultimately attributes to the "gild" that Macbeth and Lady Macbeth have acquired through Duncan's death; the "guilt" that destroys the psyche of Lady Macbeth and extends to the general diseased state of Scotland, which needs to be "purged" by the rightful heir. Futilely trying to attribute the disease to an external source—Malcolm's army—Macbeth eventually locates the source within, his gold that lacks the aura of Duncan's blood flowing through the body politic. This internalization of Macbeth's crime, I contend, is symptomatic of an early modern perception that all money is not equivalent, not alone a sufficient mechanism for legitimacy. Charisma, even in its routinized form, requires a general perception of legitimacy that itself determines the preservative power of the money flowing throughout the body politic.

As the play begins, we find a conspicuous exchange of courtesies between Macbeth and Duncan, but with an implicit system of accounting for the unequal relation of tribute and reward. Harry Berger notes that the "tone is courtly and effusive, but the language is that of competition, debt and payment" (20). Such coding of courtesy using accounting terms gradually produces tension in the relationship between Macbeth and Duncan. Early on, there is a suggestion of even exchange when the loyal Macbeth receives the title Thane of Cawdor from the rebel initially holding the same: "What [Cawdor] hath lost, noble Macbeth hath won" (1.2.67). Although Angus claims that Rosse and he come not to "pay" Macbeth for his service (1.3.103), Macbeth's prior description of Cawdor as a "prosperous gentleman" (73) suggests the "addition" (106) he receives from that title is substantial. Along with the material rewards, Macbeth has "bought . . . from all sorts of people . . . golden opinions," which he wears "now in their newest gloss" and would "not cast aside so soon" by going against Duncan (1.7.32–35). Such honors come heaping in at the start, as Rosse tells how the posts came to Duncan "as thick as tale" bearing Macbeth's "praises in his kingdom's great defense,/ And pour'd them down before him" (1.3.97–100). The editors of the *Riverside Shakespeare* explain the phrase "as thick as tale" to mean "as fast as they could be 'told' or counted," as if there is an implicit attempt to enumerate Macbeth's praises within a financial reckoning.[26] Nevertheless, the financial reckoning initially connotes a measure of social or communal value of individuals based on the "golden opinions" of others rather than a purely self-interested metric of personal worth to be cashed in for material benefits.

But the dialogue gradually intimates that Macbeth's tribute and service to the king far outweigh the rewards and honors Duncan has bestowed on him. Macbeth's generosity extends from the courtesies of food and shelter to the provision of military service the king needs to maintain his position. Duncan even uses the metaphor of feeding off of the "commendations" of "so valiant" Macbeth, whose glories provide a veritable "banquet" for him, conflating the luxuries he enjoys from Macbeth's military service and hospitality (1.4.54–56). Moreover, when Rosse describes how "as thick as tale" messengers poured down Macbeth's "praises in his kingdom's great defense," the image connotes tribute given to Duncan rather than to the loyal soldier. The honors that Macbeth receives are immediately bestowed on his king, and Rosse states that when Duncan reads about Macbeth's "personal ventures in the rebels' fight,/ His wonders and his praises do contend/ Which be" Macbeth's and which Duncan's (1.3.90–93). Duncan is in fact profiting from Macbeth's exploits, and we get the sense of conflict even within this outpouring of courtesy. The king explicitly acknowledges, albeit in courteous terms, the imbalance in exchange between Macbeth and himself:

> O worthiest cousin!
> The sin of my ingratitude even now
> Was heavy on me. Thou art so far before,
> That swiftest wing of recompense is slow
> To overtake thee. Would thou hadst less deserv'd,
> That the proportion both of thanks and payment
> Might have been mine! Only I have left to say,
> More is thy due than more than all can pay.
>
> (1.4.14–21)

Despite the gracious tone, we sense Duncan's resentment about having to repay Macbeth for all he has done. He later confesses that "The love that follows us sometime is our trouble,/ Which still we thank as love" (1.6.11–12). Duncan feels uncomfortable for all the courtesies and service Macbeth has shown since he can imagine it would only lead to resentment.

Outwardly, Macbeth and Lady Macbeth deny any imbalance in the system of reward and tribute. They profess that the honor Duncan has bestowed on them outweighs all that they have provided. For example, Lady Macbeth states that their service even "in every point twice done, and then done double/ Were poor and single business" when compared with the "honors deep and broad wherewith" Duncan "loads [their] house" (1.6.15–18). They identify themselves as Duncan's mere "servants," who "have theirs, themselves, and what is theirs, in compt,/ To make their audit at [Duncan's] pleasure,/ Still to return [his] own" (1.6.25–28). Rather than a *quid pro quo* economy amongst strangers, Macbeth describes a hierarchical family unit based on loyalty:

> The service and loyalty I owe,
> In doing it, pays itself. Your Highness' part
> Is to receive our duties; and our duties
> Are to your throne and state children and servants;
> Which do but what they should, by doing every thing
> Safe toward your love and honor.
>
> (1.4.22–27)

Macbeth revises accounting practices so that his glories as well as his debts become Duncan's assets. But although the Macbeths object that their obligation to Duncan transcends the accounting metaphors they employ, nevertheless the very employment of a financial calculus to convey these sentiments suggests the scarcity and unequal distribution underlying the courtesy. From this perspective, Duncan has unfairly profited from the generosity of the Macbeths, and he has not come close to redeeming their service.

The discourse surrounding the murder of Duncan, and especially the assumed motive of the alleged murderers, maintains the early financial language of the play, but it also incorporates Macbeth's recognition of money's mystical implications. In Macbeth's description of Duncan's body, the golden blood of Duncan atop the faces of the grooms intimates a motive of avarice:

> Here lay Duncan,
> His silver skin lac'd with his golden blood,
> And his gash'd stabs look'd like a breach in nature
> For ruin's wasteful entrance; there, the murtherers,
> Steep'd in the colors of their trade, their daggers
> Unmannerly breech'd with gore.
>
> (2.3.111–16)

When Macbeth describes the murderers "Steep'd in the colors of their trade," we are reminded of Lady Macbeth's earlier plan to "gild the faces of the grooms" with Duncan's blood, which "must seem their guilt" (2.2.53–54). The Folio's spelling of "guild," which is even closer to the latter "guilt," makes the pun transparent.[27] The references to Duncan's "golden blood" and Lady Macbeth's "gilding" of the suspects' faces indicate a material purpose for the murder—the desire for gold.[28] Donalbain later expresses a similar concern that he and Malcolm might be implicated based on a material motive when he quotes to Malcolm what seems like a proverb appropriate for their situation: "the near in blood/ The nearer bloody" (2.3.140–41). The lines suggest that Donalbain fears the person who killed Duncan would want to kill them as well since they are those closest in blood to him. However, the lines also imply that the two might seem to have a motive for killing Duncan because they are in line to inherit from the king. They might be considered "nearer bloody" not from being murdered but from gilding themselves with the material rewards of the act, the golden blood of Duncan, thereby falsely presenting their "guilt." But by fleeing the scene, they merely raise more suspicion, and Macbeth uses this suspicion for his own ascent. Macbeth therefore "lies like truth" by assigning to the false agents the true motive of the crime, the "golden round" and all its ancillary material benefits. The "breach" in Duncan's body lets the Macbeths—and according to Lady Macbeth's theatrical scheme, the murderers—"breech" themselves in luxury, following the oft-recognized motif of clothing as a sign of position and status throughout the play.[29]

A consummate materialist, Macbeth attempts to use his acquired resources to maintain his position, subscribing to Cicero's popular epithet for money: the "sinews of war."[30] He gathers information from paid spies to discover Macduff's intentions: "There's not a one of them but in his house/ I keep a servant fee'd" (3.4.130–31). And when Macduff finally returns to Scotland with an army, he complains that he "cannot strike at wretched kerns, whose arms/ Are hir'd to bear their staves" (5.7.17–18), implying that Macbeth has purchased mercenaries for his defense. These material resources used to bolster Macbeth's position echo earlier financial tropes, but unlike Duncan, Macbeth will keep his books balanced by paying those who support him according to the value of their service.

Nevertheless, although Macbeth has acquired the "sinews of war" to buy an army and even a system of surveillance for information gathering, his money lacks the mystical aura of the golden blood flowing from Duncan's body. Macbeth's own description of the murdered Duncan, a "breach in nature/ For ruin's wasteful entrance" depicts an image of violated nature. Moreover, this "breach" in Duncan's body resonates with classical and contemporary images of the avaricious plundering of nature. In *The Metamorphoses* Ovid explains how during the Iron Age, people "eft . . . gan to digge,/ And in the bowels of the ground unsaciably to rigge,/ For Riches couch and hidden deepe, in places nere to Hell" (I: 154–57). While gold naturally inheres in the veins of the earth, greed drives people to breach the earth in search of riches, which in Ovid are "the spurres and stirrers unto vice, and foes to doing well" (158). And in Book 2 of *The Faerie Queene*, Spenser's knight Guyon describes to Mammon, the figure of avarice, the fall from the "antique world" into the "pride" of "later ages" (2.7.16):

> Then gan a cursed hand the quiet wombe
>   Of his great Grandmother with steele to wound,
>   And the hid treasures in her sacred tombe,
>   With Sacriledge to dig. Therein he found
>   Fountaines of gold and siluer to abound,
>   Of which the matter of his huge desire
>   And pompous pride eftsoones he did compound;
>   Then auarice gan through his veines inspire
> His greedy flames, and kindled life-deuouring fire.
>
> (2.7.17)

Spenser adds to Ovid's vivid violation of nature the sense of "Sacriledge" in looting the "sacred tombe" of the earth. The search for riches therefore becomes an affront both to nature and God. The resonance between such images and Duncan's "golden blood" flowing from a "breach in nature" suggests not only the excessive greed motivating Duncan's murderers, but the very sacrilege and violence against nature inherent in the act of stabbing the king's body.

But the "golden blood" flowing from Duncan's body points to another common early modern trope similarly implying sacrilege and the violation of nature: *money as the blood of the body politic.*[31] For example, the author of *Usurie Arraigned and Condemned* (1625) compares the coins generously flowing from the monarch's mint to the blood that maintains and defends "politike bodies":

> Is not money minted by politicke Princes, out of their owne Bullion to bee imployed to the publike good of their publike Common-wealths, both in trading for the whole bodies maintenance, as also in Warres for the whole bodies defence. How graciously doe they disperse it in favours and rewards, that it may runne as charitably from member to member . . . throughout those politike bodies, like bloud in the naturall, in the veines of trading, for all and euery ones maintenance, and retire to those royall centres againe, by many iust rights for all and euery ones defence. (1–2)

The image of Duncan's "golden blood" should be interpreted in light of the monetary system and the political theology of the king's two bodies. In a healthy commonwealth, the golden blood is disbursed by the mint in order to course through the king's second body, the immortal body politic. In addition to the "sinews of war" whose strength defends the borders of the commonwealth, money provides daily nourishment to the body's interior through trade and commerce.

A healthy flow of money keeps the body sound, but if for some reason there is a disturbance in the flow, the health of the commonwealth may suffer. Thomas Hobbes calls such a disruption in the flow of money one of the "Diseases of a Common-wealth," and he specifically compares it to

> an Ague; wherein, the fleshy parts being congealed, or by venomous matter obstructed; the Veins which by their naturall course empty themselves into the Heart, are not (as they ought to be) supplyed from the Arteries, whereby there succeedeth at first a cold contraction, and trembling of the limbes; and afterwards a hot, and strong endeavour of the Heart, to force a passage for the Bloud; and before it can do that, contenteth it selfe with the small refreshments of such things as coole for a time, till (if Nature be strong enough) it break at last the contumacy of the parts obstructed, and dissipatheth the venome into sweat; or (if Nature be too weak) the Patient dyeth.
>
> (Hobbes 373–74)

Following his depiction of Duncan's body, Macbeth describes a similar obstruction of blood flow when he tells Malcolm and Donalbain, "The spring, the head, the fountain of your blood/ Is stopp'd, the very source of it is stopp'd" (2.3.98–99). Duncan's internal blood flow, however, is disrupted by the *external* wound from Macbeth rather than from some internal ague.

Although this fountain of blood does not allude explicitly to a monetary flow, it does prefigure the developing sickness in Scotland due to an external obstruction in legitimate inheritance. Therefore, Macbeth's violation of nature also represents a disturbance in the health of the commonwealth, which depends for its maintenance on normal blood flow. And the fact that Duncan's blood is "golden" suggests the salutary benefits of money, which keeps the commonwealth vigorous. The spilled golden blood signals renewed awareness in Macbeth that the health of the body politic is inextricably bound with legitimacy, and that only the *legitimate* king has the capacity to produce the *kind* of money necessary to maintain the country's health.

The introduction of Edward the Confessor and the touching ceremony, which points to the contemporary dissemination of healing coins, dramatizes the stakes of Macbeth's temporary suppression of money's mystical dimension prior to Duncan's murder. The healing power of the legitimate king's money serves as a counterpoint to the various images of disease that proliferate after the murder of Duncan, first in reference to the mental condition of Lady Macbeth, but later in reference to Scotland itself. In her mad ramblings, Lady Macbeth expresses surprise at the excessive blood flowing from Duncan: "Yet who would have thought the old man to have had so much blood in him?" (5.1.39–40). Her madness provides Shakespeare with an occasion to introduce a second doctor, whose commentary amplifies the motif of disease. The doctor knows that Lady Macbeth's disease goes beyond her mental state; he realizes that these "unnatural troubles" are merely signs of "unnatural deeds" (5.1.71–72); Scotland in fact suffers from the "king's evil." Moreover, Malcolm and his troops abroad see themselves as the cure, inverting Macbeth's assertion that they are its disease. Cathness describes Malcolm as "the med- 'cine of the sickly weal,/ And with him pour we, in our country's purge,/ Each drop of us" (5.2.27–29). Only by resuming the blood flow from the legitimate line, only by restoring the "due of birth" (3.6.25) to the rightful heir, can Scotland be "purged" of its "king's evil." It is therefore significant that Malcolm "is receiv'd/ Of the most pious Edward" (26–27). Like Edward curing the king's evil from scrofula sufferers in England and thereby maintaining a healthy state, Malcolm hopes to rid Scotland of its own evil.

We find in this connection a site for the production of the ideology of legitimate kingship, the belief that Scotland will be made healthy with the purgation of Macbeth and that the blood of the body politic will flow again. Jonathan Goldberg argues that the ideology of kingship is at first an obstacle for Macbeth, but it also becomes a source of legitimacy for him. By sanctifying Duncan, Macbeth is able to produce a mystical aura around his own reign: "Macbeth succeeds as the king of the image repertoire" (250). While it is true that Macbeth employs an "image repertoire" surrounding kingship, his perceptions of the golden blood flowing from Duncan, the "stopp'd" blood of Duncan's line, and the diseased state of Scotland suggest that he buys into a substantial part of this repertoire. The "blood of the body politic" signifying a healthy state will refuse to flow again until the rightful heir, whom Macbeth *knows* to be Malcolm, is restored to the throne. The difference is that Macbeth's gold is not blessed, not the sacred "blood of the body politic" that sprang from the "now stopp'd" fountain of Duncan. His inability to appropriate the monetary mysticism means his "gild" cannot be separated from his guilt. The only way to restart the fountain in Macbeth's eyes is to restore the rightful ruler to the throne. Although externally he can separate the "golden round" from Duncan's head, internally Macbeth cannot generate the "golden blood" of a legitimate king to keep his country healthy. He thereby learns that all money is not equivalent. Although producing the blood of the social body had become routinized, it still depended on the ability to recreate the charisma of legitimacy.

However, while Macbeth perceives his ultimate failure to generate monetary charisma for the maintenance of his state, this does not necessarily imply a "conservative" reading of the play, a providential distinction between the illegitimate Macbeth and the legitimate monarch—Duncan and especially James. James himself showed that he did not believe in this mystical economy per se. When he took the throne, he knew that he needed to continue distributing angels in the ceremony of "touching," despite his belief that "the age of miracles is past," because he recognized an intimate connection between the gold coin and the health of his state. He could eschew concerns about idolatry because the healing coin connected more strongly to the *symbolic* economy of state—riding on top of a magical or religious economy—than to the *mystical* prerogative of kingship. Macbeth, unlike James, is ultimately unable to differentiate between the mystical economy of kingship and the symbolic economy of state because he perceives a critical difference between his own "sinews of war" and Duncan's "golden blood." Therefore, Macbeth remains unable to recreate the charisma of legitimacy, despite his apparent efficiency in adopting routinized state structures, because he believes in the mystical prerogative, whereas James discovered a potent form of charisma in the healing ceremony *despite his disbelief*. If James did not believe that the ceremony actually cured individual patients, he at least believed that it contributed to the political strength of his state. The outflow of coins for the ceremony of the "king's evil" circulated signs of a healthy state just like the golden blood flowing through the mystical body politic.

Notes

I would like to thank several people for their helpful suggestions on this paper, especially Nick Moschovakis, Richard Helgerson, Patricia Fumerton, Alan Liu, Mark Rose, and Elizabeth Williamson.

1 All Shakespeare quotations are from *The Riverside Shakespeare*.
2 See for example Clark (23) and Wills (122). See also Paul (379–86) for an elaborate theory that James's plotting council influenced the passage's inclusion.
3 The monk Helgald provided the first record of the healing ceremony, translated in Crawfurd (12). See Bloch (21) for a summary of the likely chain of events initiating the healing ceremony in France. Edward the Confessor's healing is recorded in the

anonymous *Vita Aeduardi qui apud Westmonasterium requiescit*; the relevant part is translated in Crawfurd (19).

4 According to Helgald, Robert the Pious would visit the houses of the sick and "give them with his own hand a sum of pence" to supplement the healing. The *Vita Aeduardi* records that Edward the Confessor "maintained [the patient] from day to day at his own cost, until she should be restored to full health." The "Computus Hospitii" of Edward I (trans. in Crawfurd 34) records a number of instances of "pence given to sick persons blessed by the King." Similar records survive for Edward II and Edward III.

5 The angel, whose obverse depicted the Archangel Michael, was not introduced until the period of the War of the Roses, during Edward IV's reign.

6 This part of the office seems to have remained mostly the same through Elizabeth, whose office is recorded in William Tooker's treatise *Charisma: Sive Donum Sanationis* (1597); the relevant part is translated in Crawfurd (73).

7 M.A. Faitta to Ippolito Chezzuola, London, 3 May 1556, Archives of Venice, trans. in Crawfurd (67).

8 I take the term "sacred commodity" from Geary.

9 Healing coins also strikingly resemble the fetishes and emergent fetishism described by Pietz.

10 Roman transcripts, General Series, 88.8.11, trans. in Crawfurd (84). Henry Stubbe reports that Elizabeth had similarly considered terminating the ceremony because of its idolatrous implications (9).

11 *Calendar of State Papers—Venetian* (44). James's reluctance may also be due to his repulsion to disease. See Crawfurd (70–71, 87).

12 The service is found in a broadside of 1618, "Hum. Dyson. tempore Jacobi Regis," and was included in the Book of Common Prayer of 1634.

13 Some even believed that the ceremony would not be effective without it (see for example Bloch 56). See also Bloch (65–67) on the significance of the angel being first used by competing claimants to the throne during the War of the Roses.

14 See also Maguire on the use of coins as amulets in the late Roman period and early Middle Ages (1039–45).

15 See *2 Henry IV* 4.5.161–63 for a reference to the practice.

16 See Bloch (92–107). Thomas locates the practice's source in the belief that offertory coins and communion silver, along with nearly everything else in the Catholic Church, were thought to have magical curative powers and to protect one from various dangers (33).

17 See Maguire (1039–40).

18 See Farquhar (69–70) and Woolf (101).

19 In *1 Henry IV*, Falstaff employs a similar conflation of the two meanings of "pressing" when he has "misused the King's press damnably" by turning "a hundred and fifty soldiers" into "three hundred and odd pounds" (4.2.12–14).

20 The reverse side of the angel depicted the royal coat of arms, which could stand in for the monarch. Bilson writes that respect for the coats of arms or other royal images "is accepted as rendred to their owne persons, when they can not otherwise be present in the place to receive it" (561). According to Strong, this is consistent with Renaissance Platonism, in which the ruler was portrayed "not as an individual, but as the embodiment of the 'Idea' of kingship" (35).

21 The multiplicity of the ritual allowed for numerous identifications of the cure's source. Reginald Scot states that in identifying the source of the cure, "some refer to the propriety of [the monarchs'] persons, some to the peculiar gift of God, and some to the efficacy of words" (171). *Macbeth* represents this uncertainty about the cure's source. The first mention of it by an English doctor attributes the cure to the king's touch: "at his touch,/ Such sanctity hath Heaven given his hand,/ They presently amend" (4.3.144–46). But Malcolm's subsequent description, which

adds the detail of the coin, leaves the curative process more ambiguous. Recounting how "strangely-visited people . . . he cures,/ Hanging a golden stamp [a gold coin] about their necks,/Put on with holy prayers" (4.3.151–55), Malcolm allows either the "golden stamp" or the spoken prayers accompanying its placement to be interpreted as the source.

22 See Thomas (33, 227).

23 See Mullaney (116) and Clark (109–26). There is also an interesting connection between the healing ceremony and the Gunpowder Plot of 1605: in 1611 James performed the ritual on the plot's anniversary (see Rye 144–45). For other examples of written prayers worn on the body see Thomas (179, 183).

24 *Merchant of Venice* 3.2.103–104; *Timon of Athens* 4.3.386.

25 James I did experiment with copper farthings in 1613, but widespread counterfeiting of the tokens ultimately led to their withdrawal in 1644 (see Gaskill 126, 163).

26 See definitions 2.8 and 2.9 of "Tale" in the *Oxford English Dictionary*.

27 For a discussion of Shakespeare's various puns on "gild," "gilt," and "gelt," see Egan (166–72).

28 The image of "golden blood" partially relies on an early modern perception of gold as "red" in color. In *Econolingua* Sandra Fischer lists "ruddock" or "ridduck" was a slang term for a gold coin because of its reddish color (117). Fischer also cites the phrase, "Kissing the ruddie lips of angels," in *Old Fortunatus* (41).

29 See Spurgeon (324–27) and Brooks (38–39) for interpretations of clothing imagery in *Macbeth*.

30 Cicero's term in the *Phillipics* is "*nervos belli, pecuniam infinitam*" (5.2.5). The translated term "sinews of war" came to be a common epithet for money in early modern England. For example, in *A Discourse of the Common Weal of this Realm of England*, from around 1550, the anonymous author writes, "these coines and treasures be not with out cause called of wise men [nervi] bellorum, that is to saie, The senowes of warre" (86–87).

31 On the significance of the body politic in political theology, see Kantorowicz (7–23). The "golden blood" flowing from Duncan has traditionally been read as a sign of the king's sanctity. See for example Jorgensen (87–88) and Murray (42). For an earlier (fourteenth-century) example of the flow of humors in the body compared to the flow of riches, see Nicholas Oresme's influential text on coinage *De Moneta* (43–44).

Works cited

Berger, Harry. "The Early Scenes of *Macbeth*: Preface to a New Interpretation." *English Literary History* 47 (1980): 1–31.

Bilson, Thomas. *The True Difference between Christian Subiection and Vnchristian Rebellion*. Oxford, 1585.

Bloch, Marc. *The Royal Touch*. Trans. J.E. Anderson. New York: Dorset, 1989.

Brooks, Cleanth. "The Naked Babe and the Cloak of Manliness." 1947. Rpt. *Twentieth-Century Interpretations of Macbeth*. Ed. Terence Hawkes. Englewood Cliffs: Prentice-Hall, 1977. 34–53.

Browne, John. *Adenochoiradelogia*. London, 1684.

Calendar of State Papers—Venetian. Vol. 10. London: HM Stationery Office, 1900.

The Ceremonies for the Healing of Them that be Diseased with the King's Evil used in the Time of King Henry VII. London, 1686.

Cicero, Marcus Tullius. *Philippics*. Trans. Walter C.A. Ker. Cambridge, MA: Harvard UP, 1926.

Clanchy, M.T. *England and its Rulers 1066–1272*. Totowa, NJ: Barnes and Noble, 1983.

Clark, Arthur Melville. *Murder Under Trust or The Topical* Macbeth. Edinburgh: Scottish Academic, 1981.

Clowes, William. *Treatise for the Artificial Cure of Struma*. London, 1602.

Crawfurd, Raymond. *The King's Evil*. Oxford: Clarendon, 1911.

A Discourse of the Common Weal of this Realm of England. Ed. Elizabeth Lamond. Cambridge: Cambridge UP, 1954.

The Earl of Gowries Conspiracie Against the Kings Majestie of Scotland. London, 1600.

Egan, Gabriel. "Gilding Loam and Painting Lilies: Shakespeare's Scruple of Gold." *Connotations* 11.2–3 (2001/02): 165–79.

Farquhar, Helen. "Royal Charities, Part I—Angels as Healing-pieces for the King's Evil." *British Numismatic Journal* 12 (1916): 39–135.

Fischer, Sandra K. *Econolingua: A Glossary of Coins and Economic Language in Renaissance Drama*. Newark: U of Delaware P, 1985.

Gaskill, Malcolm. *Crime and Mentalities in Early Modern England*. Cambridge: Cambridge UP, 2000.

Geary, Patrick. "Sacred Commodities: The Circulation of Medieval Relics." *The Social Life of Things*. Ed. Arjun Appadurai. Cambridge: Cambridge UP, 1986. 169–91.

Goldberg, Jonathan. "Speculations: *Macbeth* and Source." *Shakespeare Reproduced*. Ed. Jean E. Howard and Marion F. O'Connor. New York: Methuen, 1987. 242–64.

Hobbes, Thomas. *Leviathan*. Ed. C.B. Macpherson. London: Penguin, 1985.

Jorgensen, Paul A. *Our Naked Frailties: Sensational Art and Meaning in* Macbeth. Berkeley: U of California P, 1971.

Kantorowicz, Ernst H. *The King's Two Bodies: A Study in Mediaeval Political Theology*. 1957. Princeton: Princeton UP, 1997.

Maguire, Henry. "Money and Magic in the Early Middle Ages." *Speculum* 72 (1997): 1037–54.

Mullaney, Steven. *The Place of the Stage*. Ann Arbor: U of Michigan P, 1995.

Murray, W.A. "Why Was Duncan's Blood Golden?" *Shakespeare Survey* 19 (1966): 34–44.

Oresme, Nicholas. *The De Moneta of Nicholas Oresme and English Mint Documents*. Trans. Charles Johnson. London: Thomas Nelson and Sons, 1956.

Ovid's Metamorphoses. Trans. Arthur Golding. Ed. John Frederick Nims. Philadelphia: Paul Dry, 2000.

Paul, Henry. *The Royal Play of* Macbeth. New York: The Macmillan Company, 1950.

Pietz, William. "The Problem of the Fetish I." *Res* 9 (1985): 5–17.

Rye, William Brenchley. *England as Seen by Foreigners*. London, 1865.

Scot, Reginald. *The Discovery of Witchcraft*. London, 1665.

Shakespeare, William. *Bell's Edition of Shakespeare's Plays as They are Now Performed at the Theatres Royal in London*. London, 1773–74.

—— *The Riverside Shakespeare*. 2nd ed. Ed. G. Blakemore Evans and J.J.M. Tobin. Boston: Houghton Mifflin, 1997.

Spenser, Edmund. *The Faerie Queene*. Ed. Thomas P. Roche, Jr. London: Penguin, 1978.

Spurgeon, Caroline F.E. *Shakespeare's Imagery and What It Tells Us*. Cambridge: Cambridge UP, 1935.

Strong, Roy. *Portraits of Queen Elizabeth I*. Oxford: Clarendon, 1963.

Stubbe, Henry. *The Miraculous Conformist*. Oxford, 1666.

"Tale." *Oxford English Dictionary*. 2nd ed. Oxford: Oxford UP, 2005. 26 July 2005 <http://dictionary.oed.com>.

Thomas, Keith. *Religion and the Decline of Magic*. New York: Charles Scribner's Sons, 1971.

Usurie Arraigned and Condemned. London, 1625.

Weber, Max. *Economy and Society: An Outline of Interpretive Sociology*. Ed. Guenther Roth and Claus Wittich. New York: Bedminster, 1968.

Wills, Gary. *Witches and Jesuits: Shakespeare's* Macbeth. Oxford: Oxford UP, 1995.

Woolf, Noël. "The Sovereign Remedy: Touch Pieces and the King's Evil." *British Numismatic Journal* 49 (1979): 99–115.

9 "Throw physic to the dogs!"

Moral physicians and medical malpractice in *Macbeth*

Lisa A. Tomaszewski

Only seven physician-characters appear in all of Shakespeare's plays,[1] and two of them are found in his most compact tragedy, *Macbeth*. Although neither of these characters have names, they are both present at key moments of the play and provide spiritual and moral commentary that appears to exceed their professional boundaries. In a play charged with supernatural themes, why would two "men of science" be burdened with such responsibilities?

The symbolic weight of the doctors in *Macbeth* has received some scrutiny, primarily surrounding the concepts of physical, spiritual, and symbolic "healing." A Shakespearean physician-character often inhabits a position of authority that offers credibility to his diagnosis of ills—physical as well as metaphysical. The Scottish Doctor serves in this capacity when he alerts Macbeth that his wife's illness is beyond physical treatment and she is instead suffering from a moral affliction. Furthermore, the presence of a doctor on the stage complements the use of medical metaphors that occur so often in Shakespeare's plays (e.g. a kingdom is sick).[2]

Philip C. Kolin devotes an entire chapter to the physicians in *Macbeth* and sums up his view of their purpose: "The English physician is important for his symbolic endorsement of a more powerful medicine than his own, and the Scottish doctor serves as a chronic reflector of retribution" (107). This analysis certainly works within the framework of the play; however, the figures gain a further significance when set against the backdrop of Renaissance medical history. The Shakespearean physician is a powerful symbol on stage, in part because of his historical meaning. The history of the Renaissance physician, in particular, should not be neglected when examining this play.[3]

Macbeth's plot teeters on medical revelations, culminating in a misinterpreted caesarian. Thematically, the play moves on two continually intersecting planes: the supernatural/deceitful and the scientific/moral. Juxtaposing *Macbeth*'s physicians with medical history, I shall argue that Shakespeare crafts the role of medical doctor as a foil for Macbeth and the immorally supernatural world that drives him to impassioned acts of violence. This is not to say that the physicians do not participate in the supernatural dialogue of the play; they do participate, but their interaction with the supernatural is always curative, spiritual, and focused on the moral good.

If one were to generalize regarding Shakespeare's opinion of physicians based on the evidence of his complete works, one would find the result to be less than complimentary.[4] Nor was Shakespeare alone among his contemporaries in his assessment of the medical profession. The doctors of his time were highly educated and highly compensated professionals who could quote Greek medical scholars but who were very limited in their treatment options. Health care in the Renaissance gained little advancement (i.e. in terms of curing patients) from the classical texts that were reclaimed and employed during this period. These classical doctrines were vital to a Renaissance doctor's education and were readily available in translation either from Greek or Arabic sources. For example, Thomas Linacre, founder of the Royal College of Physicians contributed a translation of Galen's works into English in 1517 and the complete works of Galen in Greek were available in 1525 (Davies 26). Medical scholars clung to Galen and the like, for the "first priority for medical humanists lay in sound new translations of original Greek texts" (Porter 170). In other words, the Renaissance physician advanced as a scholar, but made only slight gains in clinical insights. Of course, it would be wrong to assert that no medical progress was made during the Renaissance. There were leaders in the field like Andreas Vesalius (1514–1564), who made great strides in anatomy, advancing the knowledge of the physicians of Shakespeare's generation. But even Vesalius "never moved out of the penumbra of Galenic physiology and believed as firmly as any in the central tenets of the system" (Lindemann 72).

Licensing or guilding the practice of medicine was nothing new in Europe, but it was not until 1518 that London enforced its own set of rules on doctoring. In this year, the College of Physicians was chartered by Henry VIII to govern the medical profession: "[T]he College of Physicians grew in power and in prestige, taking control of medical licensing away from religious authorities and using strict regulations to enhance the status of approved physicians" (Magner 155). Lawful doctoring, however, didn't always imply morality, and the Renaissance stage was quick to voice its criticisms. A very common Renaissance theatrical convention was the "quack" physician, who

> provided a score of convenient and conventional jokes about his profession. In most plays his cameo appearance supplies no more than a comic vignette. . . . If their noses were not fastened to urinals and their eyes were not scanning the heavens, then their hands were in a patron's pocket.
>
> (Kolin 35)

Shakespeare certainly exploits this convention in *The Merry Wives of Windsor* with the character of Doctor Caius.[5]

Apart from their shared professional title, the doctors in *Macbeth* bear no resemblance to their comic counterpart in *Merry Wives*. However, all of Shakespeare's physician-characters seem to suggest his acute awareness that physicians are mortal men, bound by mortal laws. Marjorie Garber emphasizes the recurrence of the theme throughout Shakespeare's plays that "physicians, however gifted, are mortal and therefore, limited in their powers" (Garber 107). If doctors promised otherwise, they deserve ridicule and suspicion. But when a physician-character is aware of his professional shortcomings and respectful of his own limitations, Shakespeare often holds him up as a moral guardian. As we shall see, these are the doctors we meet in *Macbeth*. They are not money-hungry, self-centered quacks.

Practically speaking, the Renaissance physician had very little to guide him through the science of human health. Testing and diagnosing were painfully limited. Aside from superficial urine and fecal analysis and treatments involving bloodletting, the doctors had little in their medical arsenal to diagnose and cure patients. Renaissance doctors, despite their scholarship and professional title, were ill-equipped to combat the mysteries of illness. The ability to cope with and accept these obstacles is what separated the "good" doctors from the "bad" doctors in Shakespeare's plays. In many ways Shakespeare was illustrating the status quo of Renaissance medicine: doctors are very limited in their ability to cure, so if they boast otherwise they are overstepping their bounds and are lying for the sake of profit.

A Renaissance doctor's spirituality was also the subject of criticism. As the cliché goes, medicine and atheism go hand in hand. According to Paul H. Kocher in an article written in 1954 that is still crucial to understanding the significance of the physicians in *Macbeth*:

> The evil reputation of Elizabethan doctors for atheism may be summed up in the proverb quoted by La Primaudaye, 'Of three Physitions one Atheist.' This ill fame rested in part on the tendency of Elizabethan medicine, Galenic or Paracelsan, to minimize the agency of God as the sender of health and disease, and to concentrate instead on such physicial causes as diet, corrupt air, evacuation, exercise, and sleep. Similiarly, medical science of Shakespeare's day paid scant heed to the human soul as an independent factor whose spiritual state of good and evil might effect the body's health.
>
> (Kocher 341–42)

The doctors in *Macbeth* buck this trend; spirituality is one of their common drives. And while the Scottish Doctor makes this stand in a clearly religious way, the English Doctor acknowledges the spiritual in a morally supernatural way.

After Malcolm and Macduff lament the sad state of their country, and just before Macduff learns of the cruel fate of his family, the English Doctor enters the scene and describes the supernatural healing abilities of the English king:

> Ay, sir. There are a crew of wretched souls
> That stay his cure. Their malady convinces
> The great essay of art; but at his touch—

Such sanctity hath heaven given his hand—
They presently amend.

(4.3.142–45)

The English Doctor whisks in and out of the scene. He simply bestows his knowledge of the King's healing power and then leaves. Shakespeare could have easily had Malcolm describe the situation—Malcolm is apparently very familiar with this phenomenon, as he explains it in detail to Macduff after the English Doctor leaves. This moment, when a doctor bestows medical credibility on a supernaturalistic legend, is in some ways a contradiction. Weren't Renaissance doctors supposed to be atheists and slaves to their Greek scholarship? Granted, we know very little about the English Doctor; he has only a handful of lines. All that we know about him is his profession, and that profession seems the least likely to endorse a king's magical healing powers.

On the one hand, the physician in this scene serves as a medical authority: the King is able to cure patients with ailments that would stump even a trained and licensed physician, and the English Doctor can verify that the sick are cured. On the other hand, the English Doctor's presence is even more significant: he separates the supernatural event of the healing touch of the king from the prophetic specter of the Weird Sisters. Up to this point in the play, anything performed beyond the boundaries of human limitations has trod on unholy ground. For Garber, this is a case of medical metaphor:

> This firm dividing line between the professional healer and the miracle worker or god is bridged by one medical figure in the plays: the English king, Edward the Confessor, who is described in act 4 scene 3 of *Macbeth*. Edward's touch was said to be able to cure scrofula, a disease therefore known as "the king's evil" . . . Edward is a holy king who cures, as opposed to the unholy Macbeth who infects his land and his subjects. And Edward's holy medicine of prayer also balances and contrasts with the unholy medicine of the witches.
>
> (Garber 107)

Macbeth is a bad king who brings death, and Edward is a good king who restores life. We might say, therefore, that Macbeth is metaphorically a bad doctor because his actions are self-indulgent and steeped in malpractice, whereas Edward is a good doctor because he focuses on the welfare of his patients and seeks no reward but the good of his kingdom. The English Doctor's presence emphasizes this implied analogy; he does not appear until the fourth act of the play, just as Macbeth is beginning to crumble under the weight of his stolen crown.

Notably, it is no doctor but the Weird Sisters who until now have tended to the condition of Macbeth and his wife. Given that Shakespeare makes a point of including legitimate doctors within the play, it may be useful to consider the Weird Sisters as their antithesis. After all, witchcraft, as it was conceptualized during Shakespeare's time, did have its connections with medicine. Furthermore, the women who continued to practice medicine—midwifery, herbology, etc.—in London after the establishment of the College of Physicians were not only outcasts, but outlaws.[6] The possible analogies between the Weird Sisters and unlicensed practitioners may suggest the danger that Macbeth encounters when he associates with them. When commenting on the surreal experience of meeting the Witches, Banquo describes it in terms of taking a drug: "Were such things here as we do speak about?/ Or have we eaten on the insane root/ That takes the reason prisoner?" (1.3.83–85). When Macbeth seeks out the witches in Act 4, Scene 1, he is completely overcome by the images of the cauldron; he sees what is before him, but is unable to process it rationally. It is appropriate, then, to have Macbeth actually drink of the brew before he sees the visions—as in Roman Polanski's 1971 film, in which "Macbeth drinks the witches' brew from the goblet used by his wife to drug the grooms" (Harris 128).

It is not until Act 5 that Macbeth goes outside of the services of the Weird Sisters, finding the well-being of his wife threatened to the point where he finds it necessary to bring in a licensed medical professional. The Scottish Doctor acts in a way that appears to represent his profession admirably. He specifically follows Galenic principles of medical observation as he begins his examination, observing and interacting with the patient to find a diagnosis: "Galen set a high value on evidence derived from personal observation and experience" (Siraisi 5; cf. Maclean 93). Thus the Scottish Doctor first questions at length those who have witnessed Lady Macbeth's condition, refusing to confirm their observations until he, too, has witnessed them in Act 5, Scene 1. After a preliminary formulation of the situation, gathered from the disturbing testimony of the Gentlewoman, the Doctor decides to record his own observations of his patient: "Hark, she speaks. I will set down what comes/ from her, to satisfy my remembrance the more strongly" (5.1.31–32).

The Scottish Doctor is interactive, trying to pull conclusions from the information he has been given. He continually questions, points out, and remarks upon what he is witnessing, struggling to understand the cause of Lady Macbeth's behavior. His dedication to finding a cause is sincere, but there is nothing extraordinary in his actions; he proceeds in a manner that would be routine according to the classical texts from which he has procured his knowledge of medicine. What is extraordinary is his conclusion—that the ailment is beyond medicine:

> Foul whisperings are abroad. Unnatural deeds
> Do breed unnatural troubles. Infected minds
> To their deaf pillows will discharge their secrets.
> More needs she the divine than the physician.
> God, God forgive us all! Look after her . . .
>
> (5.1.71–75)

Would a Renaissance doctor turn to religion so quickly? Not if he strictly adhered to the teachings of Hippocrates, Galen, and other Greco-Roman authors, whose major contribution to the practice of medicine was the separation of the divine from the physical in terms of diagnosis and treatment: "Galen, like all Greco-Roman physicians, was interested in medical practice and believed in natural causes of disease and nonsupernatural cures. Galenic medicine was in addition rational and learned" (Lindemann 68). The radical notion garnered by Renaissance physicians from these sources was that when a person is ill, a doctor should not look to the heavens for the cause and subsequently for the cure, but instead look to the physical imbalances of the patients. But the Scottish Doctor honestly and, from what we know of Lady Macbeth's crimes, truthfully diagnoses her condition as beyond the scope of his practice, despite the fact that this course of action is contrary to his training.

If Shakespeare's conception of a good doctor is that of one who recognizes and respects his human limitations, then the Scottish Doctor fits the profile through his refusal to diagnose a physical cause where none is present. Another Renaissance doctor might have diagnosed Lady Macbeth with melancholy and ordered a course of treatments aimed at balancing the humors. This method of care might have been more warmly received by the Doctor's employer, Macbeth, who in the scene that follows has a very difficult time accepting the Scottish Doctor's diagnosis that Lady Macbeth is suffering from a moral affliction.

Kocher's discussion of the Scottish Doctor's diagnosis as "conscience and nothing but conscience" (344) underlines the unorthodox nature of the Doctor's conclusion:

> The intense interest of Elizabethans in pathological melancholy, their predominantly physical approach to it, the resemblance between the self-blame of melancholia and that of a troubled conscience—all these factors made it easy for many people to confuse or identify the two conditions.
>
> (Kocher 343)

As Kocher explains, these two diagnoses were kept separate, one under the jurisdiction of medicine and the other under the jurisdiction of religion. The Scottish Doctor consciously takes himself out of the equation; he recognizes that he has no skill in this arena: "More needs she the divine than the physician" (5.1.74).

Interestingly, the Scottish Doctor never actually suggests that another healer, religious or otherwise, be brought to "minister" to Lady Macbeth. Instead he leaves Macbeth with somewhat of a paradox—"Therein the patient/ Must minister to himself" (5.2.48). In other words, Lady Macbeth, the cause of her own disease, must serve as her own healer. The same can be said of Macbeth, who cannot even begin to fathom the Doctor's advice.

It seems as though Macbeth would have been more satisfied with the tricks of a charlatan than the honest diagnosis of a good physician:

> Cure her of that.
> Canst thou not minister to a mind diseased,
> Pluck from the memory a rooted sorrow,
> Raze out the written troubles of the brain,
> And with some sweet oblivious antidote
> Cleanse the stuffed bosom of that perilous stuff
> Which weighs upon the heart?
>
> (5.3.41–47)

Macbeth longs for an easy solution, one that the Scottish Doctor is unwilling (and unable) to provide. This moment is pivotal to understanding the character of Macbeth—he is always seeking the answers and solutions he wants to hear. From the Doctor he wants a course of treatment that avoids scrutinizing moral accountability; he wants a doctor who will administer some medications to his wife so that the difficulties of her plight will be resolved quickly and easily. Specifically, Macbeth uses the word "antidote," implying that there is a treatment available that will counter the poison from which Lady Macbeth is suffering. Macbeth refuses to accept that the poison is, in fact, their own treachery and that no medical treatment can cure it.

For a less scrupulous physician this would have posed a very financially advantageous opportunity. The Scottish Doctor could have profited heavily from Macbeth's desperation. But the Doctor refuses to contribute to Macbeth's delusions and denial of wrongdoing; instead he chooses to be true to his own integrity, and does not profit from Macbeth's fiendishness. "Were I from Dunsinane away and clear,/ Profit again should hardly draw me here" (5.3.62–63).

Although the Scottish Doctor attempts to focus his attention on physical facts—"You see her eyes are open" (5.1.23); "Look how she rubs/ her hands" (5.1.25–26); and "What a sigh is there! The heart is sorely/ charged" (5.1.52–53)—he cannot ignore Lady Macbeth's murderous confession. For the Scottish Doctor, personal gain is not as important as his professional integrity.

How the doctor interacts with Macbeth after he has formulated his medical and moral diagnosis is what sets him apart from the typical Renaissance doctor, raising him to a level of morality and selflessness that begins to establish him as a foil to Macbeth. When the Scottish Doctor honestly refuses to treat Lady Macbeth because he knows her illness lies beyond his skills, Macbeth viciously dismisses him: "Throw physic to the dogs! I'll none of it" (5.3.49). If the Scottish Doctor refuses to conform to what Macbeth wants to hear, he will be cast aside, just as morality and loyalty are cast aside as Macbeth seizes and then protects his corrupt crown. Significantly, Macbeth puts on his armor during this exchange with the Doctor. He wants to be shielded from the Doctor's honesty. Macbeth is clearly preoccupied with his own interests, and even if the health of his once beloved partner hangs in the balance, Macbeth refuses to turn his thoughts to anything but his own success.

In a way, medicine dominates the later part of *Macbeth*.[7] The first doctor is not introduced until 4.3, and this is immediately followed by the Scottish Doctor's examination of Lady Macbeth. With such a weighty medical presence on the stage, it is apparent that Shakespeare is preparing his audience for the answer to the riddle left by the Witches' second apparition in Act 4, Scene 1: "Be bloody, bold, and resolute; laugh to scorn/ The power of man, for none of woman born/ shall harm Macbeth" (4.1.79–81).

In most cases, from antiquity through the Renaissance, a caesarian was only performed on a woman who was already dead or who was dying (Duffin 245–46). In addition, "a surgeon would occasionally slit open a woman dying in labour to deliver a baby, but caesarians were desperate measures and there is no record of a mother surviving one in Britain until the close of the eighteenth century" (Porter 277). Therefore, if Macduff's mother were dead or dying when he was "untimely ripped" from her womb, she, a woman, truly had no part in his birth. Furthermore, caesarians were usually performed by surgeons, who were men. Although on occasion a midwife would perform the procedure out of desperation, for the most part, a child of a caesarian birth would be born quite literally by the hands of a man.[8]

In fact, Shakespeare plants the seed of surgery in the audience's mind at the very start of the play when a brave and patriotic soldier is praised for the wounds he sustained in battle defending the king against a traitor. King Duncan sends him to surgeons for medical attention: "So well thy words become thee as thy wounds;/ They smack of honor both.—Go get him surgeons" (1.2.43–44). Significantly, though subtly, this opening scene raises the station of surgeon to servant of the king. Normally, surgeons were thought of as far beneath the doctor in status: "Judged a manual skill rather than a liberal science, the cutter's art had traditionally carried scant prestige" (Porter 277). Shakespeare in this minor reference may have been laying the groundwork for the medical revelations to come. Instead of Macduff being born through the handiwork of a crude "barber" or "cutter," because of this precedent in the play, he is born by the same hands that tend to wounded soldiers.

In *Macbeth*, Shakespeare effectively uses the medical professionals of his time to craft a foil for his title character and the seers that point him toward the path of destruction. The doctors in this play are a credit to their profession and Shakespeare emphasizes this by linking them with forces of moral good (e.g. the piety of the English King, with his healing touch, and the repercussions of conscience). Macbeth's unrealized salvation would lie in respecting his own boundaries, something that Shakespeare highlights in his doctor-characters.

Notes

1 This number is subject to debate. Kail claims that Shakespeare introduces eight physicians into seven of his plays. He counts the following characters as doctors: Doctor Caius in *The Merry Wives of Windsor*, a doctor in King Lear, an English doctor in *Macbeth*, a Scottish doctor in *Macbeth*, Cornelius in *Cymbeline*, Cerimon in *Pericles*, Dr. Butts in *Henry VIII*, and Gerard de Narbon in *All's Well That Ends Well* (represented posthumously through his daughter Helena). It is this final doctor which I do not include in my tally because he is physically not present in the play. His daughter Helena was under his tutelage and is skilled enough to cure the king's illness. Despite this accomplishment, Helena cannot historically be recognized as a physician because, for the most part, women were not permitted to study medicine at that time.

2 According to Spurgeon, "Various medical facts and theories are made use of for images, such as the well-known one that mental trouble drives out physical pain" (135). Throughout the plays illness is also used by Shakespeare to convey evil and corruption. Spurgeon offers the example of Lear calling Goneril "a boil, a plaguesore, an embossed carbuncle" as an illustration of her evil (161). Placing the figure of the doctor among these metaphors gives them a greater sense of urgency, because the doctor is often agent of health and healing.

3 Although the setting of *Macbeth* is in a period prior to the Renaissance, the concept of a physician within this play is based upon Renaissance notions of the profession. Each doctor is identified by his professional title. Their appearance on stage was based on Renaissance perception of medical practice.

4 In fact, an entire novelty book has been dedicated to Shakespeare's insults for doctors: *Shakespeare's Insults to Doctors*, by Wayne F. Hill and Cynthia J. Ottchen. This is not to say that Shakespeare was anti-doctor. He simply relayed in his plays some of the frustration that his contemporaries experienced with the medical profession. Shakespeare does create some very benevolent doctor-characters in his plays.

5 According to Shakespeare's caricature, Doctor Caius is an immoral character as well as a bad doctor because his preoccupations are self-serving, his intelligence is highly questionable, and he is more concerned with his own interests than the welfare of his patients. Doctor Caius is a handy example of what a Renaissance audience abhorred about the medical profession. His name refers historically to John Caius (1510–1573), the English medical humanist and a primary figure in the leadership of the College of Physicians. Although several critics, including Kail, suggest that Shakespeare's character and the historical figure are not meant to be seen as one and the same, it may be interesting to reexamine this character as Shakespeare's attempt to criticize organized medicine as crafted, in part, by Dr. John Caius.

6 "Because women were not admitted to the universities, female practitioners were easy targets for licensing reforms" (Magner 155).

7 Fox makes a strong argument for the importance of medical language in the earlier acts of the play. Specifically, she asserts that the use of language regarding childbearing, miscarriage, and abortion by Macbeth and Lady Macbeth shapes these "protagonists as human beings who want to have children" (138) but are somehow unable to do so. Fox does not, however, pursue the caesarian birth of Macduff as it relates to the ongoing use of obstetrical language and Lady Macbeth's barrenness. Macduff was born because his mother made the ultimate sacrifice for him; she died in order to give him life. Perhaps, if one were to press Fox's line of inquiry, one could conclude that Lady Macbeth is unable to produce a living heir because she is incapable of this level of selflessness. Driving this point home, Lady Macduff, another mother we meet in this play, also dies protecting her child.

8 Bicks suggests that Macduff's caesarian birth excuses him from having a debt to "the female" for his existence: "Macduff, then, is the product of a double patriarchal fantasy: birth without a mother and without her midwife" (156).

Works cited

Bicks, Caroline. *Midwiving Subjects in Shakespeare's England.* Burlington: Ashgate, 2003.

Davies, Gill, ed. *Timetables of Medicine: An Illustrated Chronology of the History of Medicine from Prehistory to the Present Time.* New York: Black Dog & Leventhal, 2000.

Duffin, Jacalyn. *History of Medicine: A Scandalously Short Introduction.* Toronto: U of Toronto P, 1999.

Fox, Alice. "Obstetrics and Gynecology in *Macbeth*." *Shakespeare Studies* 12 (1979): 127–41.

Garber, Marjorie. "The Healer in Shakespeare." Ed. Enid Rhodes Peschel. *Medicine and Literature.* New York: Neale Watson Academic, 1980.

Harris, Suzanne. "The Plays: Macbeth." *Shakespeare in Performance.* Ed. Keith Parsons and Pamela Mason. London: Salamander, 1995. 125–29.

Kail, Aubrey C. *The Medical Mind of Shakespeare.* Balgowlah, NSW: Williams & Wilkins, 1986.

Kocher, Paul H. "Lady Macbeth and the Doctor." *Shakespeare Quarterly* 5.4 (1954): 341–49.

Kolin, Philip C. *The Elizabethan Stage Doctor as a Dramatic Convention.* Salzburg: Institut für Englische Sprache und Literatur, Universität Salzburg, 1975.

Lindemann, Mary. *Medicine and Society in Early Modern Europe.* Cambridge: Cambridge UP, 1999.

Maclean, Ian. *Logic, Signs and Nature in the Renaissance: The Case of Learned Medicine.* New York: Cambridge UP, 2002.

Magner, Lois N. *A History of Medicine.* New York: Marcel Dekker, 1992.

Porter, Roy. *The Greatest Benefit to Mankind: A Medical History of Humanity.* New York: W.W. Norton, 1997.

Shakespeare, William. "Macbeth." *The Complete Works of Shakespeare.* 4th ed. Ed David Bevington. New York: Longman, 1997.

Siraisi, Nancy G. *Medieval and Early Renaissance Medicine: An Introduction to Knowledge and Practice.* Chicago: U of Chicago P, 1990.

Spurgeon, Caroline F.E. *Shakespeare's Imagery and What It Tells Us.* Cambridge: Cambridge UP, 1935.

10 "Let grief convert to anger"
Authority and affect in *Macbeth*

Lynne Dickson Bruckner

In recent years Act 4, Scene 3 of *Macbeth* has garnered the attention of scholars interested in the historicity of emotion. These scholars have focused on Macduff's immense sorrow in this scene and Malcolm's advice to "dispute it like a man" (4.3.259), though none have analyzed this textual moment in relation to the play's larger treatment of grief.[1]

This chapter reads 4.3 with grief and the expressivity of affect foremost in mind. Most of the scene can be accounted for in terms of how masculine grief is incited, expressed, and managed in *Macbeth*. My opening section reviews how masculine grief was understood in the period.[2] Under certain conditions—the loss of a son, the love of country—male tears were expected.[3] It is excessive sorrow that gets labeled as feminine or adolescent. Next I look at the patterning of grief in the play. In *Macbeth*'s Scotland, grief—even the most extreme anguish—is continually and damagingly deferred. Transmuted into anger and revenge, the absence of mourning only generates further bloodshed. In the final section, I conclude that in *Macbeth* the dynamics of power intrude on and even organize affective experience, exploiting the way grief can readily be reconfigured as revenge. Throughout, I argue that *Macbeth* highlights the tension between internal affective mandates and the demands of the power structure—between Macduff's grief and Malcolm's authority.

Masculine grief in Shakespeare's era

A number of Shakespeare's plays focus on sorrow and grief. Despite being accused of "unmanly grief" (1.2.94), Hamlet insists on the authenticity of his anguished response to the death of his father. While Lear initially rejects his own tears as womanly, he comes to a full articulation of his sorrow in the "Howl, howl, howl, howl" (5.3.256) with which he meets Cordelia's death. Shakespeare seems to have had a strong interest in expressions of grief, especially those which resulted from the loss of a child or parent. Significantly, Shakespeare's only son, Hamnet, died in 1596 at the age of 11, and Shakespeare's father died in 1601, several years before he writes *Macbeth*.[4] One of the most permissible early modern occasions for mourning—the process of giving grief its time—is when a parent loses a child, and particularly a son. It is not surprising that this is the case: any break in patrilineal ordering—the generational continuity between father and son—is a threatening disruption of patriarchal culture. *Macbeth* is deeply concerned with lineage. Macbeth who "has no children" (4.3.255) is driven to kill the sons of other men, and particularly "the seeds of Banquo" (3.1.75).[5] And the play ends with a debate about whether or not the death of Siward's son—young Siward—should be mourned. While Siward Senior refuses to grieve, Malcolm—the new leader of Scotland—insists, "he's worth more sorrow, and that I'll spend for him" (5.8.59). Overall, the tragedy of *Macbeth* is the tragedy of a world so violent that grief is not given its time. For when there is no time taken to grieve, blood supplants tears. As Donald Foster has written, "Revenge cannot, in fact, cure deadly grief, for it is revenge itself which makes grief deadly" (334).

The maxim that "boys don't cry" did not hold in Jacobean England. A more appropriate Renaissance phrasing might be that boys and men do cry, but for the right reason, and in the right way. Recent scholarship has found that the seventeenth century ushered in a greater acceptance of expressions of grief—though not without anxiety. George W. Pigman has argued that in the early seventeenth century, there is a shift away from the counsel to be stoic when confronted with loss. Margo Swiss and David Kent also locate the evolution of a "greater freedom to express grief in early seventeenth century culture" (8). Written *c.*1606, *Macbeth* rests on the cusp of this rise in the permissibility of grieving.

Thomas Wright's *The Passions of the Minde in Generall* (1604) analyzed and structured the working of emotions for early modern readers. The passions, when appropriately engaged, serve as proof of masculine subjectivity and inspired individuals to virtuous, even Christ-like, action. As Wright avers, "Christ our Saviour, in whom neither sinne, nor inordinate affection could fall, no doubt, was subject to these passions" (15).[6] Provided that men's expressions of mourning were neither excessive nor prolonged, they were seen as an appropriate emotional and physiological response to loss. Wright notes, moreover, that the melancholy humors could congeal, imprisoning the heart and trapping the mind. Some purging or release was necessary to keep the body from developing an excess of black bile or melancholy humor. As Bridget Lyons explains, Malcolm's advice to "give sorrow words" (4.3.246) "is based on the belief that the heart of a bereaved sufferer who could not unburden himself by speech was literally oppressed and suffocated by griefs which cut the heartstrings" (14). In essence, expressing grief was a matter of health, a necessary purging.

In *The Anatomy of Melancholy*, Robert Burton resists censuring either grief or its attendant tears.[7] Burton "does not 'forbid men to grieve, but to grieve overmuch' " (Shiesari 254). The adolescent or womanish griever is one who weeps immoderately, or without any cause, which Burton notes is "familiar with many gentlewomen" (393). Letter-writing handbooks also show that masculine grief in measure is acceptable. While such manuals were guides to epistolary decorum, they simultaneously modeled early modern emotions. William Fulwood's *The Enemie of Idlenesse* offers sample letters of consolation that affirm masculine grief and tears. Consider "The Example wherein one friend comforteth another, for the death of his son:"

> I had one litle sonne, so sweete, pleasant, and amiable, in whome I tooke all my comfort and recreation. For his onely presence, or his only speech, did often resolve me from my great fantasies, taking from me all melancholy . . . but now I power out teares of sadnes so much the more, for that I know death hath beene cruel unto mee, hee hath killed my onely hope, my consolation, my life . . . and therefore do I now sustaine great griefe and melancholy, I know not where to seeke comfort, nor what I should doe, or say. (71–72)

"Comforting him for his losse," the friend's response is driven by matching expressions of affect:

> I Bitterly bewailed (my most singular and perfect friend,) & could not keepe in my teares, when I reade the Letters which you sent me, making mention of the death of your sonne. And I doe advertise you, that I was constrained so to doe, for the good love that of so long time hath beene, and is betwixt us two, the which causeth me to feele the like dolor & griefe that you have in loosing the presence of a childe so well taught, and of so good a wit & entrance in good manners. (73–74)

Expressing feelings of "like dolor & griefe," the respondent affirms the emotions of the grieving father. Only after such validation does he urge moderation, depicting grief "beyond the limits of reason" in terms of behaviors that "better beseeme the female kind." Thus, while it may have been thought that "obstinate condolement" (to quote *Hamlet*'s Claudius) did not suit men, early modern culture denied men neither feelings of grief, nor expressive tears.

Shakespeare's primary historical source, Holinshed's *Chronicles* (1587), offers powerful images of masculine grief. Holinshed notes that Macduff visits Malcolm in England, to seek redress for "the detestable cruelties exercised by the tyrant Makbeth" (37).[8] Consonant with the topos of patriotic tears, Macduff begins his plea by "bewailing the miserable state of his countrie" (38), and Malcolm utters a matching "deepe sigh" and becomes "verie sorrowfull for the oppression of his countriemen the Scots" (38).[9] Holinshed goes on to show Macduff's highly emotional response to Malcolm's tripartite "proof" that he would be an even worse tyrant than Macbeth: " 'Adieu, Scotland, for now I account my selfe a banished man for ever, without comfort or consolation': and with those woords the brackish teares tricked downe his cheekes verie abundantlie" (40). Macduff's sorrow culminates in an indelible image of abundant tears, and nowhere does the text suggest that these are less than manly. Shakespeare—perhaps because he sought in *Macbeth* to show that the violent and disordered world the play depicts does not allow time to grieve—nowhere provides such a vivid image of masculine weeping.

Macbeth's representation of affect participates in the discourse of interiority. Early modern critics have debated the degree to which early modern subjects experienced an inner life—that "within which passes show" (1.2.85), as Hamlet insists.[10] Certainly, there were discursive registers for an inner life (see, e.g. Ferry). *Macbeth* gestures toward interiority, showing how it is inflected by and in dialogue with the structures of power. One way the play summons the notion of this internal reality is through its characters' claims to sorrow. Another way—a way ineluctably tied to affective claims—is through its depiction of the permeable body. *Macbeth* is a play steeped in blood—a play that opens with a "bloody man" (1.2.1) whose "gashes call for help" (1.2.46). Blood and tears share the mysterious capacity to reveal the inner man. As they can move from inside the body out to the visible world, both mark the subject as dangerously penetrable, revealing that the boundary between interior and exterior lives is, in fact, liquid—continually redefined and renegotiated.[11] It is at this nexus of interior and exterior that I locate my discussion. *Macbeth* shows that the very claim to sorrow makes it vulnerable to public appropriation; simultaneously, it registers the necessity of expressing emotion. Macbeth sought to become "perfect,/ Whole as the marble, founded as the rock" (3.4.23–24). Perhaps the point in this play is not to be whole and impenetrable. Perhaps the point is to be open, and willing to feel. Perhaps in a world of tears, we could have fewer men *and women* with bleeding wounds.

Reading grief in *Macbeth*

Macbeth is rife with anxiety about gender, and Macbeth, as oft noted, buys into a particularly narrow (read violent) definition of manhood.[12] Closely related to notions of manhood and patriarchy are issues of lineage and progeny. Macbeth's is a "barren scepter" (3.1.68), a fact that can not be separated from his veritable war against children (Brooks 50). He plots Fleance's death; commands that young Macduff and his siblings be murdered with their mother; and, in his final act, kills young Siward. Drawing our attention to these deaths, the play, as famously noted by Cleanth Brooks, includes recurrent images of babes and children (46). Such imagery, taken in conjunction with the deaths of sons in this play, amplifies the importance of their loss.

Harry Berger has written that "Warriors are trained to be suspicious of gentleness in themselves as a threat to their manhood" (27). Macbeth is readily mobilized by Lady Macbeth's insistence that a "man" acts quickly and with violence. Lady Macbeth's ability to play on Macbeth's gendered anxiety is underwritten by the larger social order in the play, an order that rewards Macbeth for warlike brutality. While Macbeth is labeled a "butcher" by the final scene, in the opening scenes he is hailed as "Bellona's bridegroom" and applauded for his skill in killing:

> For brave Macbeth (well he deserves that name)
> Disdaining Fortune, with his brandished steel
> Which smoked with bloody execution,
> Like valor's minion, carved out his passage
> Till he faced the slave;
> Which ne'er shook hands, nor bade farewell to him,
> Till he unseamed him from the nave to th' chops
> And fixed his head upon our battlements.
>
> (1.2.18–25)

Macbeth's bloody actions win him the title of Thane of Cawdor, and he is celebrated for "unseaming" MacDonald "from the nave to th' chops" or, as Adelman notes, performing a symbolic C-section on his opponent, further suggesting the obliteration of heirs (106). In prodding her husband with taunts like "Are you a Man?" (3.4.70), Lady Macbeth reiterates the message he has received from a nation-state that relies on violent action.

Even so, Macbeth initially recognizes that there is another mode of masculine being, a mode more complicated than vengeful physical power. This mode entails honor, poetry, courage, and the capacity to mourn. In the final scene of Act 1, deciding not to kill Duncan, Macbeth states, "I dare do all that may become a man;/ Who dares do more is none" (1.7.51–52). One wonders, therefore, at Lady Macbeth's ability to drive him beyond his resolution not to commit regicide. Critics have identified her leverage as sexual, and connected it to the larger specter of feminine power manifested by the witches. Yet, the dynamic between Macbeth and Lady Macbeth may also be driven by the shared loss of a child. Lady Macbeth has either had a child or fantasized one (1.7.62–67). And Macbeth's resounding "Bring forth men children only" (1.7.83) rings not only with his horror at his wife's brutality, but also his enduring desire for an heir. The possibility of a dead child makes all the more intelligible Macbeth's bloody attacks on other men's sons; he is not just childless, he has suffered the loss of a child. Rather than tears, Macbeth sheds blood.

The concern for sons in *Macbeth* is more than political. Although fleetingly, the play reminds the audience that sons are wonderful, and that fathers and sons can be close. Consider the late evening ride when Banquo in fatherly tones asks Fleance, "How goes the night, boy?" (2.1.1). A simple exchange of gear ensues as father and son debate the hour. On the night they are attacked, and just before they are ambushed, Banquo comments to Fleance on the weather: "It will be rain tonight" (3.3.23). The play, in the very pedestrian quality of their interaction, conveys the habitual tenderness between father and son—tenderness that makes all the more gruesome Macbeth's decision to kill Banquo and all his "seeds."

Macbeth also draws attention to the importance of children when Lady Macduff converses with her son after Macduff has fled to England. Lady Macduff worries—with good reason—over Macduff's "unnatural" abandonment of his family.[13] Yet, the precocious boy knows his "father is not dead" (4.2.42) for all of Lady Macduff's saying he is: "If he were dead you'd weepe for him" (4.2.63). This moment works rather differently from the one between Banquo and Fleance; rather than an image of the tenderness evinced by daily familiarity, it is the precocity of the boy that makes him important. Precocious children were a cultural ideal in the early modern period. When this child, in the moment before he is slain, is reduced to an "egg"—to the "young fry of treachery" (4.2.94–95)—the audience shudders at the loss.[14] His final words—"He has killed me mother. Run away, I pray you" (4.2.96–98)—construct him as an ideal child, one not unlike the "childe so well taught, and of so good a wit" mourned by Fulwood's letter writer. Young Macduff's concern for his mother and his effort to stand up for his father's honor in his last moments underscore his value as a boy, and shadow forth the honorable and caring man he would have become. The play emphasizes the immensity of this loss and the depth of filial love. Lady Macbeth—despite her claim willingly to dash the brains of her suckling child—asserts that she could have killed Duncan "had he not resembled/ My father as he slept" (2.2.16–17). Even she cannot deny the deep emotional pull between parent and child.

The prefix of "Mac" alone means "son of," and is shared by Macbeth, Macduff, and MacDonald (Garber 89). Moreover, while critics including Susanne Wofford have noticed the play's frequent rumination over dismemberment, it is equally littered with references to conception, birthing, and babies, for birth and destruction (at least for Macbeth) are competing sides of the same emotional coin. Duncan welcomes Macbeth with the lines "I have begun to plant thee, and will *labor*/ To make thee full of growing" (1.4.32–33, emphasis mine); Banquo ironically describes the Macbeths' castle as a "procreant cradle" (1.6.9); and the witches include "a finger of [a] birth strangled babe" (4.1.30) in the mix that moments later generates a "bloody child" (4.1.87). It can hardly be by chance that Macbeth's final act of violence is to kill Siward's son.

Macbeth includes multiple examples of male sorrow and tears. Male characters primarily grieve over filial losses, though patriotic tears are also depicted. The earliest tears in the play are Duncan's patriotic tears of joy. With the news of stability (however provisional) in Scotland, Duncan addresses "Sons, kinsmen, thanes," and notes that his "plenteous joys,/ Wanton in fullness, seek to hide themselves/ In drops of sorrow" (1.4.39–41).[15] These tears locate a measure of affect in the king, and hint at the authority over emotion that the crown claims in the play. Duncan is entitled not only to shed his tears, but also to gloss them: his tears look like sorrow, but signal joy. This textual moment reminds us of Duncan's status as good father and good king, affirming how family and state are ineluctably linked.[16] Interpreted by

Freud and others as parricide, Duncan's death connects to notions of familial bonds and their attendant affect. Contemplating the murder, Macbeth anticipates that "pity, like a naked newborn babe . . . shall blow the horrid deed in every eye,/ That tears shall drown the wind" (1.7.21–25).[17] Even Macbeth knows that the appropriate response to the death of such a good, tearful king is more tears—tears so forceful that they will "drown the wind." Yet, in the world that Macbeth ushers in with Duncan's death, there is no time for tears; there is only time to say there is no time.

Indeed, when Malcolm and Donalbain hear the news of their father's murder, their response is markedly contained. Malcolm's initial response is "O, by whom?" (2.3.118). Donald Foster has commented that Malcolm's terse question "displays nothing but an empty bosom, a cunning mind, and a ready tongue" (2.3.320). There are other possibilities. Malcolm might be wary and sorrowful at the same time. The flatness of his question suggests a state of shock, and the silence of both brothers indicates their recognition that they can ill afford to become impassioned with grief. When Duncan's sons speak together (in an aside), they already understand that Dunsinane is not safe for them:

Malcolm: Why do we hold our tongues,
    That most may claim this argument for ours?
Donalbain: What should be spoke here, where our fate,
    Hid in an auger hole, may rush and seize us?
    Let's away. Our tears are not yet brewed.
Malcolm: Nor our strong sorrow upon the foot of motion.
                                            (2.3.140–46)

Duncan's sons see the affective disjunction between themselves and the others who are visibly mourning the King's death. Containing their grief, the brothers have already begun the process of turning their tears into violence. Donalbain states, "Our tears are not yet brewed"—associating their tears immediately with fermentation, boiling, and the violence of storms (*OED* defs. 1a, 3). Malcolm's reply, "Nor our strong sorrow upon the foot of motion," indicates that their sorrow will be the foundation for their actions, which we sense will be violent ones. Truncated, their sorrow is already manifesting itself in terms of revenge—tears reconstituted as blood. Before taking leave of his brother, Malcolm pointedly observes, "To show an unfelt sorrow is an office/ Which the false man does easy" (2.3.161–62). Sorrow can be performed for calculated reasons. Yet sometimes, when there are the greatest of reasons, there is no time for grief.

Arguably, Macbeth experiences just this reality later in the play. His famous "Tomorrow, and tomorrow, and tomorrow" speech (5.5.20–31) is elicited by the news of the Queen's death. It opens with the ambiguous statement, "She should have died hereafter" which embeds both the callous thought that she would have died eventually, and the more grief-stricken recognition that she should have died at a different time, a time perhaps when Macbeth could have mourned. Of this passage, Harold Bloom has written, "grief, in any sense we could apprehend, is not expressed by [Macbeth]. Instead of an elegy for Queen Macbeth, we hear a nihilistic death march, or rather a creeping of fools, of universal victims" (541). Despite this, Bloom is drawn to concede the immense poetry of the passage. It is nihilistic, but its very poetry disturbs its claim that life is pointless. Furthermore, while not elegiac, the lines do convey Macbeth's pain, and offer an appreciably verbal response to loss—a response far more feeling than butchery. The problem Macbeth suffers from is the one that he, in fact, has created. There is no time to mourn.

Affect and authority

While grieving was well within the parameters of early modern masculine behavior, characters in *Macbeth* must continually truncate their grief. The chaos and violence endemic to Scotland prohibit sufficient time for sorrow. Act 4, Scene 3 makes the correlation between authority and affect explicit, showing that emotional expressivity is a privilege arrogated to and controlled by those in positions of power. In essence, Malcolm works to incite, control, and curtail Macduff's sorrow in this scene. Malcolm's efforts to produce and govern Macduff's affective responses suggest a Machiavellian quality to his character.[18] This quality complicates the traditional reading of the future king as purely benevolent, yet it is a quality that may—if we compare him to Duncan—be necessary in a realm that seeks to maintain control over its subjects. From the perspective of realpolitik, Malcolm may have the affective attributes essential in a king; he can feel, yet he is not controlled by his passions. Of equal importance, he can orchestrate the emotions of those who serve him.[19]

When Macduff first encounters Malcolm, the future king calls for sorrow: "Let us seek out some desolate shade and there/ Weep our sad bosoms empty" (4.3.1–2). Like his father, he sees a time for tears, and elects to take that time. While Malcolm potentially sounds like Shakespeare's Richard II who wants "with rainy eyes" to "write sorrow on the bosom of the earth" (*Richard II*, 3.2.142–43), he is less paralyzed by sorrow than Richard and far more willing to take action. Indeed, later in the scene we, along with Macduff, learn that Malcolm already has forces lined up and plans shortly to invade Scotland with Old Siward (4.3.152–54).[20] Such immediate military plans raise the possibility that Malcolm's initial call for weeping is merely a stance assumed to draw Macduff into his plan, and/or part of the test to which he will subject the thane. While expressions of genuine sorrow and Machiavellian displays of grief are not mutually exclusive categories, Malcolm's call for sorrow seems calculated when read in the larger context of the scene.

Macduff has no knowledge of Malcolm's military plans; consequently, he attempts to reconfigure Malcolm's sorrow as revenge. Grief between men, it seems, acts as a kind of currency that can be exchanged for action:

> Let us rather
> Hold fast the mortal sword and, like good men,
> Bestride our downfall'n birthdom. Each new morn
> New widows howl, new orphans cry, new sorrows
> Strike heaven on the face, that it resounds
> As if it felt with Scotland, and yelled out
> Like syllable of dolor.

(4.3.3–9)

Macduff displays the sorrow endemic to Scotland to urge Malcolm to take action. The dramatic irony of Macduff's speech is painful to witness; he describes how new widows and orphans cry daily, yet he does not yet know he is already a widower and father who has outlived his children. Macduff calls on Malcolm to fight, to stand over their fallen "birthdom," as one would protect a fallen comrade on the battlefield.[21] Scotland, like Duncan, is "the spring, the head, the fountain" (2.3.115) of Malcolm's blood, and he must protect it now. The sorrow evoked in these lines does not alter Malcolm's behavior, as the future king has already decided his course of action. The real issue is whether Macduff will be included.

Rather than replying to Macduff or mirroring his sorrow, Malcolm shifts his (real or performed) emotional gears, and expresses his suspicion: "What I believe, I'll wail;/ What know, believe; and what I can redress,/ As I shall find the time to friend, I will" (4.3.10–12). Malcolm sets conditions on his willingness to exchange his sorrow for the action Macduff desires. In the protracted dialogue that ensues, Malcolm puts Macduff through an extended test of his loyalty. *Macbeth* is a play in which no one has time to grieve, yet Malcolm has time to administer a lengthy and probing exam to Macduff. Malcolm begins by comparing himself to a "weak, poor innocent lamb" to be offered up by Macduff to "appease an angry god" (4.3.19–20). When Macduff retorts that "[he is] not treacherous" (4.3.21), Malcolm asks why he left his wife and children unprotected in Scotland. Macduff has no response to this other than near despair: "Bleed, bleed, poor country!" (4.3.39). We, however, know that the thane's wife and children have already become Macbeth's sacrificial lambs. Here the audience may become impatient with Malcolm's suspicions, particularly as his testing lies maneuver Macduff through a series of emotional upheavals. As the dialogue progresses, Malcolm makes it abundantly clear that he is opposed to every kingly virtue (4.3.108–10); rather than initiating just rule, he will "uproar the universal peace, confound/ All unity on earth" (4.3.115–16). Subjected to Malcolm's self-proclaimed litany of sins, Macduff becomes overcharged with sorrow: "O my breast,/ Thy hope ends here!" (4.3.131–32). And it is this exclamation of extreme passion that makes Macduff trustworthy in Malcolm's eye: "Macduff, this noble passion,/ Child of integrity, hath . . . reconciled my thoughts/ To thy good truth and honor" (4.3.133–36). Unlike his father, Malcolm is well aware of the possible disjunctions between face and mind. For Malcolm, the passions are the barometer of integrity. He has seen what he needed to, but Macduff, not surprisingly, now has trouble assimilating the news that Malcolm is not the tyrant he has painted himself to be. Malcolm has the authority to "Unspeak mine own detraction," to "here abjure/ the taints and blames I laid upon myself" (4.3.142–43), yet his claims to supreme innocence rest uneasily with his skillful discursive machinations.[22]

With a heightened sense of Malcolm's skills at emotional manipulation, we watch his response to Macduff's unfathomable loss. Macduff's grief is powerfully depicted in the scene, though Malcolm works to cut it short. When Malcolm is urging him to "give sorrow words," Macduff is still trying to grasp that his wife and children are dead.[23]

Macduff: My children too?
Ross: Wife, children, servants, all that could be found.
Macduff: And I must be from thence? My wife killed too?
Ross: I have said.
Malcolm: Be comforted.
            Let's make us med'cines of our great revenge
            To cure this deadly grief.
Macduff: He has no children.

                                        (4.3.248–55)

The play dramatizes with exquisite care the horror of Macduff's reality. His disbelief—"My wife killed too?"—stands as a formidable articulation of sorrow; it also points up how very hasty Malcolm is to turn this grief into action. After the extended time frame during which he tested Macduff's loyalty, Malcolm now expects the Thane of Fife in the space of ten lines to speak his grief, be comforted, and join him in "great revenge." Macduff's line "he has no children" can be read as referencing Macbeth, averring that revenge is impossible because the tyrant is childless. The meaning that doubles with this one, however, is that Malcolm must have no children, for he is incapable of hearing his own callousness. Invoking the narrow definition of manhood that led to his father's murder, Malcolm tenaciously urges Macduff toward revenge.

Malcolm: Dispute it like a man.
Macduff: I shall do so,
          But I must also feel it as a man.
          I cannot but remember such things were
          That were most precious to me. Did heaven look on
          And would not take their part? Sinful Macduff,
          They were all struck for thee! Naught that I am,
          Not for their own demerits, but for mine,
          Fell slaughter on their souls. Heaven rest them now.
Malcolm: Be this the whetstone of your sword. Let grief
          Convert to anger. Blunt not the heart; enrage it.

Macduff: O, I could play the woman with mine eyes
      And braggart with my tongue! But, gentle heavens,
      Cut short all intermissions! Front to front
      Bring thou this fiend of Scotland and myself.
      Within my sword's length set him. If he scape,
      Heaven forgive him too.
Malcolm: This tune goes manly.

(4.3.259–76)

Macduff claims a capacious masculinity, one that can "feel" things "as a man." Moreover, he takes a level of personal responsibility for the deaths of his wife and children; he should never have left them. In his love for Scotland, Macduff left his wife and children. Now Malcolm asks him to leave off mourning to answer state demands with a more "manly" tune. As James Calderwood succinctly puts it, Malcolm "makes revolutionary grist of Macduff's grief" (104). Malcolm's authority trumps affect.

Given that 4.3 demonstrates Malcolm's gift for exploiting emotion, his insistent emotional response to young Siward's death in 5.8 may seem surprising. Certainly the play struggles over masculine expressions of loss, and the final scene's competing responses to the death of young Siward demonstrate that the struggle is far from resolved:

Ross [to Siward]: Your son, my lord, has paid a soldier's debt.
      He only lived but till he was a man,
      The which no sooner had his prowess confirmed
      In the unshrinking station where he fought,
      But like a man he died.
Siward: Then he is dead?
Ross: Ay, and brought off the field. Your cause of sorrow
      Must not be measured by his worth, for then
      It hath no end.
Siward: Had he his hurts before?
Ross: Ay, on the front.
Siward: Why then, God's soldier be he!
      Had I as many sons as I have hairs,
      I would not wish them to a fairer death;
      And so his knell is knolled.
Malcolm: He's worth more sorrow, and that I'll spend for him.
Siward: He's worth no more.
      They say he parted well and paid his score,
      And so, God be with him. Here comes newer comfort.
      Enter Macduff with Macbeth's head

(5.8.44–64)

Laced with the language of quantification, the passage queries the value of a boy's life, and the economic troping serves to remind us of Macduff's "fee-grief" (4.3.229). Siward's response is almost startlingly a-poetic; his son's manly death requires no tears, as he has become God's soldier. Siward's resistance to mourning exemplifies "one ideal—the soldier's, or as Plutarch says, the Roman's ideal—of what it is to be a man" (Waith 265). We can readily draw a comparison to Titus Andronicus, with his 25 buried sons—a literalized precursor to Siward's pun on hairs and heirs. Critics have taken various positions both on Siward's refusal to grieve and Malcolm's contrasting insistence that young Siward is "worth more sorrow." Jonathan Goldberg, for example, finds that the battle concludes with Siward's "celebration of the ritual slaughter of his son" (104). Maynard Mack explains Siward's decision barely to lament his son as a matter of loyalty to the king—a refusal to privilege his son over the needs of the state (182). Like Mack, I am inclined to read Siward's response to his son's death at face value, particularly as it adheres to a passage in the Holinshed source text. If anything, Shakespeare tempers what we read there—that Siward, hearing that his son "died of a wound which he had received in fighting stoutly . . . and that his face towards the enemy, he greatlie rejoiced thereat, to heare that he died so manfullie" (44). In both texts, Siward recognizes that some must die for the public good and accepts the death of his son as an honorable and patriotic one.[24]

The play, however, disturbs Siward's patriotic response to his son's death with Malcolm's insistent: "He's worth more sorrow, and that I'll spend for him" (5.8.60). This line, a significant addition to Holinshed, invites the audience to query Siward's response, to think back through the play's depiction of death and grief, and to find perhaps that now that the "time is free," we should grieve—not just for Siward's son, but for all deaths that have gone unmourned in *Macbeth*. Such a response may lead us to applaud Malcolm's insistence on spending sorrow on Siward's son. Along these lines, Marilyn French finds that Malcolm speaks here to the more compassionate mode of manhood:

> The implication of this remark, plus the different tone of the dialogue at the close of this battle—saddened, heavy—compared to that of the triumphant dialogue at the close of the battle scene that opens the play, suggests that feeling will be at least an item in the new governance of Scotland.
>
> (French 22)

I am attracted to French's optimism, and in the past I have read the final act in just this way. I would like to think that Malcolm ushers in a world in which individual claims to affect are sanctioned and valued. Yet the present chapter's line of inquiry has led me to a less charitable interpretation of Malcolm's insistent sorrow. We have seen that Malcolm values, perhaps even requires, visible emotion in his subjects. The test of Macduff's fealty was his impassioned response to the sorrowful state of Scotland. Moreover, Malcolm readily transformed Macduff's agonized grief into state-sanctioned (and incited) violence. The more realistic reading of Malcolm's insistent grief is that he is modeling a state in which emotion is felt and expressed—not to usher in a time of feeling, but rather to usher in a time in which emotion becomes a commodity that the state can exploit to great effect. While some, perhaps Malcolm most of all, may perform their emotions for strategic reasons, others will live to feel fear, joy, despair, love, desire, hope, anger, and, of course, sorrow. A ruler driven by the mandates of realpolitik will know how strategically to reveal his own emotions, more readily to make use of those of others. Malcolm is one such ruler.

Notes

I would like to thank Nick Moschovakis, whose fine perceptions and gentle editorial prodding greatly enhanced this chapter.

1 Swiss and Kent find that Malcolm's call for anger and violent revenge marks a departure from "the stoical counsel to suppress grief" (2). Conversely, Kurtz describes it as "the normative relation of grief and anger" (182) in which "men transmute grief to rage and rage to vengeance" (183).
2 For recent scholarship on early modern grief, see Schiesari, Pigman, and essays in Paster et al., Swiss and Kent, and Vaught with Bruckner.
3 As Vaught writes, men's tears "were sometimes represented as a necessary sign of their humanity" (5). See Strier on how humanist and Reformation traditions defended "ordinary human emotions and passions" (32).
4 Thompson and Taylor connect the death of Hamnet to *Hamlet*.
5 All quotations from *Macbeth* come from the *New Folger Library* edition, ed. Mowat and Werstine. All other Shakespeare quotations are from *The Norton Shakespeare*, ed. Stephen Greenblatt et al.
6 With the exception of updating specific letters (e.g. "u" to "v") and writing out abbreviations, I preserve early modern spellings and punctuation in Wright, Burton, Fulwood, and Holinshed.
7 While written in 1621, the *Anatomy* is relevant to *Macbeth* as Burton culls from earlier sources. For Burton's understanding of the grief associated with filial loss, see "Causes of Melancholy" (subsection VII.1: 357–59).
8 Quotations from Holinshed come from Boswell-Stone.
9 According to Lutz, in "Western warrior tales, men cry most often about issues of war, peace, and ideals" (64).
10 Maus deftly outlines these debates; see 157–59.
11 See Marshall and Paster ("In the Spirit of Men") on how blood and wounds speak to interiority, gender, and the dynamics of power. Floyd-Wilson writes of the porous body in *Macbeth*.
12 Adelman summarizes major studies on *Macbeth* and manhood (113). See Garber and Wofford on gender anxiety in *Macbeth*.
13 She insists Macduff "wants the natural touch" (4.2.11). As state and family ideally complement each other, Macduff's decision to leave his family more accurately signals the "unnatural" (2.4.13) state of Scotland.
14 See Miller and Reeder on precocity.
15 While some critics see Shakespeare's Duncan as weak and feminized, he is a far more successful ruler than Holinshed's Duncan.

16 Duncan's "benevolent" power relies on rewarding and promoting bloodiness, as in 1.2.

17 See Brooks's discussion of the power of pity.

18 Critics have diverse views on Malcolm's motivations in this scene. While Goddard gives a positive view (544). Mack sees Malcolm as both flexible and expert in 4.3 (155). For Riebling Malcolm is a pure Machiavel (277).

19 As Rowe writes: "The monarch's challenge is . . . to reliably govern his own emotions and those of others, and to control how widely privy knowledge of his mind circulates. . . . Malcolm's handling of Macduff in 4.3 shows skillful governance of his own emotions and those of others" (185).

20 In Holinshed Malcolm is less of a Machiavel; there, Siward is appointed to go into Scotland with him only *after* Macduff visits England (48).

21 Here I follow Mowat and Werstine's annotation of this image (138 n. 5).

22 In Holinshed, after Malcolm explains he was only testing Macduff, the two embrace and fall "in consultation" (40).

23 Fred Tromly's argument that in Shakespeare's works the consoler occupies a position of authority in relation to the grieving subject could be extended to Malcolm here.

24 James Calderwood interprets Siward's refusal to grieve as a productive decision to break the cycle of revenge that has continually resulted in bloodshed (113).

Works cited

Adelman, Janet. " 'Born of Woman': Fantasies of Maternal Power in *Macbeth.*" *Cannibals, Witches, and Divorce: Estranging the Renaissance*. Ed. Marjorie Garber. Baltimore: Johns Hopkins UP, 1987. 90–121.

Berger, Harry. "The Early Scenes of *Macbeth:* Preface to a New Interpretation." *ELH* 47 (1980): 1–31.

Bloom, Harold. *Shakespeare: The Invention of the Human*. New York: Riverhead Books, 1998.

Boswell-Stone, W.G. *Shakespeare's Holinshed: The Chronicle And The Historical Plays Compared*. (1896). New York: Benjamin Blom, 1966.

Brooks, Cleanth. "The Naked Babe and the Cloak of Manliness." 1947. Rpt. *Twentieth-Century Interpretations of Macbeth*. Ed. Terence Hawkes. Englewood Cliffs: Prentice-Hall, 1977. 34–53.

Burton, Robert. *The Anatomy of Melancholy*. London: J.M. Dent & Sons, 1978.

Calderwood, James, L. *If It Were Done: Macbeth and Tragic Action*. Amherst: U of Massachusetts P, 1986.

Ferry, Ann. *The "Inward" Language: Sonnets of Wyatt, Sidney, Shakespeare, Donne*. Chicago: U of Chicago P, 1983.

Floyd-Wilson, Mary. "English Epicures and Scottish Witches." *Shakespeare Quarterly* 57.2 (2006): 131–61.

Foster, Donald, W. "Macbeth's War on Time." *English Literary Renaissance* 16.2 (1986): 319–42.

French, Marilyn. "Macbeth and Masculine Values." *Macbeth: New Casebooks*. Ed. Alan Sinfield. New York: St. Martin's, 1992. 14–24.

Fulwood, William. *The Enemie of Idlenesse*. 1598. *Early English Books On-Line*. Proquest Information and Learning Company. STC (2nd ed.) 11482.

Garber, Marjorie. "Macbeth: The Male Medusa." *Shakespeare's Late Tragedies*. Ed. Susanne L. Wofford. New Jersey: Prentice Hall, 1996. 74–103.

Goddard, Harold C. "From the *Meaning of Shakespeare.*" *Macbeth: Critical Essays.* Ed. S. Schoenbaum. New York: Garland, 1991. 239–74.

Goldberg, Jonathan. "Speculations: *Macbeth* and Source." *Macbeth: New Casebooks.* Ed. Alan Sinfield. New York: St. Martin's, 1992. 92–107.

Kurtz, Martha. "Tears and Masculinity in the History Play: Shakespeare's *Henry VI.*" *Grief and Gender: 700–1700.* Ed. Jennifer Vaught with Lynne Dickson Bruckner. New York: Palgrave, 2003.

Lutz, Tom. *Crying: The Natural and Cultural History of Tears.* New York: Norton, 1999.

Lyons, Bridget. *Voices of Melancholy: Studies in Literary Treatments of Melancholy in Renaissance England.* New York: Norton, 1975.

Mack, Maynard. *Killing the King: Three Studies in Shakespeare's Tragic Structure.* New Haven: Yale UP, 1973.

Marshall, Cynthia. "Wound-Man: Coriolanus, Gender, and the Theatrical Construction of Interiority." *Feminist Readings of Early Modern Culture: Emerging Subjects.* Ed. Valerie Traub, Lindsay Kaplan, and Dympna Callaghan. Cambridge: Cambridge UP, 1996. 98–118.

Maus, Katherine. "Proof and Consequences: Inwardness and Its Exposure in the English Renaissance." *Representations* 34 (1991): 29–52.

Miller, David Lee. *Dream of the Burning Child: Sacrificial Sons and the Father's Witness.* Ithaca: Cornell UP, 2003.

Mowat, Barbara and Paul Werstine, eds. *The Tragedy of Macbeth.* The New Folger Library. New York: Washington Square, 1992.

Oxford English Dictionary. OED Online. Oxford UP, 2005. <http://dictionary.oed.com/>

Paster, Gail Kern. " 'In the Spirit of Men there is no Blood': Blood as Trope of Gender in *Julius Caesar.*" *Shakespeare Quarterly* 40.3 (1989): 284–98.

Paster, Gail Kern, Katherine Rowe, and Mary Floyd Wilson, eds. *Reading the Early Modern Passions: Essays in the Cultural History of Emotion.* Philadelphia: U of Pennsylvania P, 2004.

Pigman, G.W. *Grief and English Renaissance Elegy.* Cambridge: Cambridge UP, 1985.

Reeder, Robert. " 'You are now out of your text': The Performance of Precocity on the Early Modern Stage." *Renaissance Papers* (2001): 35–44.

Riebling, Barbara. "Virtue's Sacrifice: A Machiavellian Reading of *Macbeth.*" *Studies in English Literature, 1500–1900* 32.2 (1991): 273–86.

Rowe, Katherine. "Humoral Knowledge and Liberal Cognition in Davenant's *Macbeth.*" *Reading the Early Modern Passions: Essays in the Cultural History of Emotion.* Ed. Gail Kern Paster, Katherine Rowe, and Mary Floyd Wilson. Philadelphia: U of Pennsylvania P, 2004. 169–91.

Schiesari, Juliana. *The Gendering of Melancholia: Feminism, Psychoanalysis, and the Symbolics of Loss in Renaissance Literature,* Ithaca: Cornell UP, 1992.

Shakespeare, William. *The Norton Shakespeare.* Ed. Stephen Greenblatt, Walter Cohen, Jean E. Howard, and Katharine Eisaman Maus. New York: W.W. Norton, 1997.

Strier, Richard. "Against the Rule of Reason: Praise of Passion from Petrarch to Luther to Shakespeare to Herbert." *Reading the Early Modern Passions: Essays in the Cultural History of Emotion.* Ed. Gail Kern Paster, Katherine Rowe, and Mary Floyd Wilson. Philadelphia: U of Pennsylvania P, 2004. 23–42.

Swiss, Margo, and Kent, David A. "Introduction." *Speaking Grief in English Literary*

Culture: Shakespeare to Milton. Ed. Margo Swiss and David A. Kent. Pittsburgh: Duquesne UP, 2002. 1–19.

Thompson, Ann, and Neil Taylor. " 'Father and Mother Is One Flesh': Hamlet and the Problems of Paternity." *Paternity and Fatherhood: Myths and Realities.* Ed. Lieve Spaas. New York: St. Martin's, 1998. 246–58.

Tromly, Fred B. "Grief, Authority and the Resistance to Consolation in Shakespeare." *Speaking Grief in English Literary Culture: Shakespeare to Milton.* Ed. Margo Swiss and David A. Kent. Pittsburgh: Duquesne UP, 2002. 20–41.

Vaught, Jennifer C. "Introduction." *Grief and Gender: 700–1700.* Ed. Jennifer C. Vaught with Lynne Dickson Bruckner. New York: Palgrave. 2003. 1–14.

Waith, Eugene M. "Manhood and Valor in Two Shakespearean Tragedies." *ELH* 17.4 (1950): 262–73.

Wofford, Susanne L. "The Body Unseamed: Shakespeare's Late Tragedies." *Shakespeare's Late Tragedies: A Collection of Critical Essays.* Ed. Susanne L. Wofford. New Jersey: Prentice Hall, 1996. 46–60.

Wright, Thomas. *The Passions of the Minde in Generall.* 1604. Facsimile rpt. Urbana: U of Illinois P, 1971.

11 Like a poor player

Audience emotional response, nonrepresentational performance, and the staging of suffering in *Macbeth*

Michael David Fox

Macbeth and audience complicity with "crimes that murder sleep"

Western performance theory, at least since Denis Diderot's insistence in the eighteenth century on the erection of an imaginary "fourth wall" as an invisible yet impenetrable barrier separating the performers from the audience, has assumed that there is a reciprocal relationship between the closure of representational illusion and the emotional involvement of the audience (Roach 155.) Similarly, modern acting theory, whether from the pro-emotionalist perspective of Stanislavski or the anti-emotionalist perspective of Brecht, has axiomatically presumed that the extent of the audience's emotional response in the theatre is dependent on the completeness of referential illusion and the de-realization of the actor. This assumption has become so ingrained in our thinking about the relationship between representational illusion and audience emotional response that even the most anti-representational contemporary performance theory "has not questioned the dogma that representational illusion is necessary for empathetic response" (Fox 361).

But in sharp contradiction to this assumption regarding a reciprocal relationship between representational illusion and audience emotional response, Shakespeare in *Macbeth* repeatedly breaches the fourth wall and reminds the audience of the presence of the performing actor *at precisely those points in the drama when audience response to the fictional character's fate must be at its height*. Exploring these moments and their emotional context in *Macbeth*, this chapter demonstrates that, in contradiction to the assumption of a reciprocal relationship between representational illusion and an audience's emotional response, a primary source of the deep affective response that Shakespeare elicits for Macbeth and his Lady is, in large part, the ways that Shakespeare uses nonrepresentational modes of performance to create a remarkable transparency of actor and role, simultaneously staging the fictional character and the existentially present performer, and undermining illusion in order to heighten the affective response of the audience.

An unlikely hero of a tragedy, Macbeth is a usurper and murderer, not only of men, but of defenseless women and children. Malcolm properly calls him "bloody, luxurious, avaricious, false, deceitful, sudden, malicious, smacking of every sin that has a name" (4.3.56–61).[1] He is vicious, ambitious, disloyal, indecisive, reckless, bullied by his wife, a nihilist, and a tyrant. And yet Macbeth still usually wins the audience, at least emotionally, to his side, seducing the spectators, as Lady Macbeth seduces her husband, into complicity with "crimes that murder sleep." As A.C. Bradley long ago noted, Macbeth and his Lady, although drenched in the blood of innocents, "remain to the end tragic, even grand" (321–22). How does Shakespeare conjure such a profound emotional response for such monsters, guilty "of every sin that has a name"? This chapter argues that the answer to the seeming paradox of the audience's empathetic response to Macbeth and his Lady lies not in the narrative of their bloody lives and deaths, nor primarily in the poetic force of their language, but above all in the ways in which Shakespeare in *Macbeth* uses modes of nonrepresentational performance to reveal the actors' faces behind the mask of their monstrous character. The great myth of the theatre is that we go to see fictions disguised as reality. The truth is that we go to the theatre to see reality disguised as fictions.

Bringing forth the bodies

Nonrepresentational performance heightens audience emotion because it foregrounds, and therefore heightens the audience's somatic experience of, the reality of the actor's physical and emotional presence. Bodied presence heightens emotional connectedness. Such heightening of emotional connectedness through bodied or somatic processes is a crucial aspect of cultural bonding. As anthropologist Thomas J. Csordas has written, "embodied experience is the starting point for analyzing human participation in a cultural world" ("Somatic" 135; cf. *Body/Meaning/Healing* 156). Without rejecting the usefulness of semiological and textual approaches to questions of the body, Csordas advocates an understanding of the body that "makes a place for a complementary appreciation of embodiment and being in the world alongside of textuality and representation" (*Body/Meaning/Healing* 243). More specifically, drawing from his field work in anthropology and the work of the philosopher Maurice Merleau-Ponty, Csordas proposes that we become aware of the critical importance in culture of what he terms "somatic modes of attention," which he defines as "culturally elaborated ways of attending to and with one's body in surroundings that include the embodied presence of others" (244). Csordas emphasizes that a somatic mode of attention "refers to both attending 'with' and attending 'to' the body. . . . To attend to a bodily sensation is not to attend to the body as an isolated object, but to attend to the body's situation in the world" and that "a somatic mode of attention means not only attention to and with one's own body, but includes attention to the bodies of others" (244–45).

Among the embodied cultural practices that Csordas sees as forms of somatic modes of attention are dancing, making love, sports, various psychological obsessions with the body such as anorexia and bulimia, the phenomenon of *couvade*, the practice of meditation, and ritual healing (Csordas, "Somatic" 139–46; Csordas, *Body/Meaning/Healing* 216–52). To this list of embodied cultural practices and somatic modes of attention, we must add the theatre, which is certainly a "culturally elaborated way[s] of attending to and with one's body in surroundings that include the embodied presence of others." The advantage of seeing the theatre from this perspective is that it allows us to step back from an often too exclusive concern with textuality and the theatre's signifying functions and, instead, foreground the ways in which the theatre directs and focuses the attention of the audience on the performer as more, and other than, a textual or rhetorical instrument.

Seeing the theatre as a somatic mode of attention also allows us to see the spectator's engagement with performance as being as much through the tactile and sensory receptors of the body as the cognitive and imaginative faculties of the mind. It therefore draws our attention to the ways in which the theatre directs the spectators to implicate their own bodies in the act of spectatorship. Adopting Csordas's emphasis on the delineation of somatic modes of attention to an analysis of Shakespeare and other early modern playwrights allows us to see the ways that the early theatre focused and directed the audience's experience of embodiment through early modern theatre conventions such as the soliloquy, the aside, extemporization, and the uses of metadramatic and anachronistic references. More particularly, seeing the theatre as a somatic mode of attention allows us to see how various nonrepresentational performance modalities of the early modern theatre affect the emotional response of spectators. Because affective response is a bodied response, it is heightened by the somatic mode of attention of the theatre, where physical co-presence "is a powerful factor in both communicating and generating emotion" (Planalp 63–64). Accordingly, when these nonrepresentational modes of performance are employed with great skill, as in *Macbeth*, the audience feels a profound emotional connection even with villains whose crimes murder sleep.

Shakespeare and the staging of the real

Scholars have now recognized the great extent to which the dramaturgy of Shakespeare and other early modern playwrights incorporates the theatrical traditions, techniques, and conventions of earlier popular drama. The staging conventions of medieval drama that early modern theatre incorporated into performance practices, such as the scaffold and inn-yard stages, allowed for an extremely high degree of contact and complicity between actors and the audience. This direct contact and complicity between actor and spectator often came at the expense of representational illusion. As Stephen Greenblatt has observed, the early modern stage was primarily a place of audience "complicity rather than belief" (Greenblatt 176–77). While early modern dramaturgy could certainly create and sustain representational illusion, it also frequently included breaks, disruptions, and subversions of illusion, through the use of nonrepresentational staging conventions inherited from both the medieval drama and the players' own performance traditions, which allowed the performers to "narrow the psychic distance between the tiring house and the yard-and-galleries" (Mack 281).

Robert Weimann has shown that an essential aspect of Shakespeare's dramaturgy was to retain and revitalize certain spatial elements and self-expressive, nonrepresentational performance practices of the medieval popular theatrical tradition (*Shakespeare* 139–46). In particular, Weimann has shown that certain spatial constellations of the early modern platform stage, which he calls the *locus* and *platea*, derived from popular medieval pageants and mystery plays, were utilized by Shakespeare to bring the audience closer to, or distance the audience from, the representing actor whose own energy and passion fueled the imaginary pathos of the represented role (224). In Weimann's schema, the *locus* is the particularized site of the represented action—a throne, a tent, a bed—that is both physically and psychically distant from the audience. The theatrical space of the *locus* is associated with imitative mimesis, the illusion of verisimilitude, dialogic speech, and the "specifying capacities of an enacted role." The *locus* is the theatrical space of fiction, imaginative transformation, and the closure of representational illusion, in which the wooden boards of the daylight stage become the dark halls of Macbeth's castle and the actor is transformed into the fiction of the enacted role. The *locus*, therefore, "provided an authorized specification of discursive space . . . a fairly verisimilar topos removed from direct audience address" (Weimann, "Representation" 499).

But while the early modern theatre was characterized by a hitherto unprecedented degree of imaginary diegesis and the projection of representational illusion, it also, at the same time, retained and revitalized the players' traditional practices of body-oriented, self-expressive, extemporaneous, and non-representational performance. Closer to the audience than the *locus*—often literally closer, as downstage theatrical space suited for direct audience address—is what Weimann has called the *platea*, the unspecified theatrical space associated with the earlier medieval conventions of non-illusionistic acting, extemporization, non-dialogic speech, direct address, anachronism, and identification with the audience (Weimann, *Shakespeare* 121–24). In contrast to the *locus* as the site of illusionary locales and characters, the *platea* is the theatrical space "not of what was represented . . . but what was representing and who was performing" (Weimann, "Representation" 503). Rather than projecting the "imaginary puissance" of a fictional role in a fictional world, the actor in *platea* performance plays in and brings to the audience's consciousness the here and now of the theatre itself, projecting the power of the actor's own body and passion in the theatre's shared, bodied space. Crucially, therefore, the *platea* is the non-illusionistic theatrical space of the player's *self*-representation; by staging the actor outside the represented role, the *platea* mode of performance is the staging "not of fiction but existence" (499).

This division between representational and nonrepresentational modes of performance was, of course, never absolute, or often not clearly delineated, in practice. Indeed, the particular theatrical energy of the plays of Shakespeare and his contemporaries is in large measure the result of the ease, as well as the complexity, which these plays shift between, and even overlap, representational and nonrepresentational modes of performance. The early modern theatre, and above all the plays of Shakespeare, is characterized by constant and often subtle shifts between representational and nonrepresentational performance practices, as well as by performance that consciously plays on the often indistinct margins between representation and self-presentation. These shifts in the plays' performance modalities take place not only throughout the course of the plays, but within individual scenes, and even within individual speeches. As a result of this constant, subtle, and complex interplay between representation and the actors' self-presentation, the audience in Shakespeare's plays was led to perceive, at a more or less conscious level, simultaneously both the representation of illusory locales and roles, and actors' concrete existence in their own identities in the here and now of the theatre.

The best known nonrepresentational performance convention of the early modern theatre is the soliloquy spoken as direct address to the audience. As Michael Mooney has noted, a distinguishing feature of early modern drama is "the frequency with which actors . . . appear to step out of their role to address—or otherwise break the illusion to communicate with—the spectators" (2). The roots of the early modern soliloquy are in the medieval popular theatre, in which "the actors speak to the audience repeatedly during the play and take them into their confidence, making them privy to the entanglements which are to follow" (Clemen 4). By being spoken directly to the audience, the early modern soliloquy created and employed an intimate and reciprocal relationship between the actor and the audience within the present time and space of the theatre. As Wolfgang Clemen has explained, "This direct address of the audience is important for the understanding of Shakespeare's soliloquies. The open stage protruding right into the pit, with the audience on three sides, favored close contact, even intimacy, and a secret understanding between the audience and the soliloquizing actor who was able to project his emotions by means of gestures, physiognomy and stage business" (4–5). In contrast to their adaptation to later practices of fourth wall illusionism, where Shakespearean soliloquies have been performed as private thoughts "overheard" by spectators cast as unacknowledged eavesdroppers (as, for example, in Olivier's 1948 *Hamlet* and Polanski's 1972 *Macbeth*, in which the crucial soliloquies are presented through voice-overs as the internal and unspoken thoughts of the protagonists), in the early modern theatre "the actors did not address the audience as if it were in another world . . . the audience could participate in the drama as easily as the actors could share a joke or enlist sympathy" (Clemen 5). By breaking the illusion of dialogic speech, the early modern soliloquy asserts itself against the fiction of the speaking character's existence and reveals the representing actor within the fiction of the representation. The soliloquy thus simultaneously creates a privileged and intimate relationship between the audience and the character and between audience and actor.

A similarly privileged and intimate, although less sustained, relationship between both audience and character, and audience and actor, was created by the nearly ubiquitous early modern theatrical convention of the aside. In the aside, a character speaks to the audience while other characters are on stage, but is imagined to be unheard by them. As Jeremy Lopez has noted, "The aside is one of the most pervasive conventions of English Renaissance drama, and one of the most potentially disruptive [of representational illusionism]." The pervasiveness of the aside in early modern drama cannot be appreciated simply by reference to the editorial constructions of stage directions marked in the texts of the plays. Rather, as Lopez has observed, "while there are many examples of stage directions specifically ordering characters to 'turn aside and speak' or to 'speak to the people', their number is disproportionately small compared to the vast number of unmarked but evident asides" (56).

Like the soliloquy, the aside fuses "a conspiratorial bond" between the speaker and the audience. Moreover, the aside "calls attention to the power of the stage to represent a multiplicity of actions, dialogues, points of view— that is, it helps create a convincing theatrical space; but as a consequence it opens up a variety of problems. . . . Even as playwrights ask their audience to focus on the intricacies of poetic dialogue, they also break up that focus by giving characters moments of (frequently intricate) direct address that comment on, misinterpret, break into, or sound over that dialogue" (Howard 346). Thus, the aside, like the soliloquy, breaks the cohesiveness and closure of representational space, creating moments that stand outside from, and sometimes in direct conflict with, the illusions of the represented action, as well as the represented time and place, of the play.

The early modern theatre is also characterized by the extensive use of anachronistic and metatheatrical references that served to undermine the represented time and place of the dramatic action. Like the soliloquy and the aside, the uses of anachronistic references in the early modern theatre are rooted in the players' performance traditions and the practices of medieval drama, where figures in biblical fabula often made reference to contemporary people, places, and events. As in the medieval drama, in the early modern theatre such anachronistic references were fully accepted, and even demanded, by audiences even though they broke the illusion of the play's fictional world and returned the audience to the time and place of performance.

Similarly, the early modern theatre often utilized metatheatrical references, such as Macbeth's analogizing himself to a "poor player," that also undermined the illusion of the represented action and called attention to the concrete presence of the performers. While the pervasiveness of metatheatrical references in Shakespeare's plays have often been noted in regard to the plays' articulation of thematic material, its theatrical import, and in particular its effect on audience consciousness and emotional response, has not been fully recognized. Richard Hornby defined metadrama as "drama about drama," in which "the subject of a play, turns out to be, in some sense, drama itself" (31). James L. Calderwood similarly points to Shakespeare's extensive use of theatrical metaphors to argue that "Shakespeare's plays are not only about the various moral, social, political, and other thematic issues with which critics have so long and quite properly been busy but also about Shakespeare's plays. Not just 'the idea of the play' ... but dramatic art itself—its materials, its media of language and theater, its generic forms and conventions, its relationship to truth and the social order—is a dominant Shakespearean theme, perhaps his most abiding subject" (*Shakespearean* 5). As Hornby properly notes, Shakespeare, like other playwrights, "is constantly drawing on his knowledge of drama as a whole (and, ultimately, culture as a whole) as his 'vocabulary' or his 'subject matter' " (31), and, as Calderwood observes, "It is hardly surprising that a playwright like Shakespeare would project his concerns about drama not only into his life but even into the fictional life of his play" (*Metadrama* 5).

But while the analysis of critics like Calderwood and Hornby may help us to see that metadramatic references support and underscore the themes of the plays (for example, that the metadramatic references in Macbeth's "poor player" speech links the transitoriness of Macbeth's kingship to the ephemeral performance of an actor in the theatre), their analysis does not help us understand why the breach in representational illusion caused by Macbeth's reference to himself as a "poor player" speech would be so emotionally powerful, or why Shakespeare *at this precise moment in the play* chooses to have the murderous Macbeth compare himself to an actor. Nor does the thematic analysis of metadrama explain the fact that instead of emotionally distancing the audience, as we would expect based on the traditional assumption of a reciprocal link between illusion and audience emotional response, Shakespeare's uses of metadrama often occur when the audience's emotional engagement with the play must be, and is, at its height. Our approach, on the other hand, which sees the early modern theatre's convention of metadramatic references as a way of focusing the spectators' somatic attention toward the concrete presence of the performing actors, allows us to see that metadramatic allusions increase the audience's emotional response by enabling the actors to distance themselves momentarily from the fiction of the role and stand before the spectators in their own concrete bodily and psychic presence.

The best known early modern comment on the players' practice of extemporizing is that of Hamlet. Hamlet's speech to the players condemns clowns who "speak more than is set down for them" (3.2.38–39). Such "villainous" behavior by "fools" possessed of "a most pitiful ambition" not only usurped the authority of the playwright, who "set down for them" both the words to be spoken and—since the actor must also "suit the action to the word"—the actions to be played on the stage. Moreover, such disruptions of representation by the players through modes of performance that called attention to their own concrete existence, apart and distinct from any referential figure within the play's fictional world, threaten to destroy the process of dramatic illusionism itself. As Howard Felperin has noted, "Hamlet's speech [to the players] is predominantly a plea for the new doctrine of dramatic illusionism and falls into line with the special pleading of such Elizabethan classicists as Sidney and Jonson" (376). This issue was of critical concern to early modern humanists, and especially to playwrights, who had to contend in the theatre with the countervailing anti-illusionistic traditions and impulses of the players. A century and a half before Diderot's dramaturgical revolution fundamentally changed the relationship between Western theatre and its audience, the nature and function of theatrical performance—"the purpose of playing"—and its relationship to the audience was being vigorously contested in early modern England by humanist writers such as Sir Philip Sidney, William Webbe, and George Puttenham, and playwrights such as Christopher Marlowe, Robert Greene, John Marston, Thomas Dekker, Ben Jonson, George Chapman, John Fletcher, Francis Beaumont, and John Webster.

It would be a mistake, however, to conclude that hostility toward the players' own performance traditions on the part of early modern playwrights— especially Shakespeare—was thoroughgoing or clear-cut. Even as the writers railed against what they perceived to be the vulgarity and disruptiveness of the players' self-expressive, extemporaneous, and nonrepresentational performance practices, they also consistently employed these very same practices in their plays and inscribed them into their texts. Playwriting was, after all, an emerging and extremely competitive commercial enterprise in early modern England, and achievement was measured by ticket sales. As Suzanne R. Westfall has observed, in the England of the late sixteenth and early seventeenth centuries "the theatre was rapidly becoming commodified and patronage shifted from the upper strata of society to include the general public" (41). Walter Cohen similarly notes that "The monarchy, the nobility, the clergy, the bourgeoisie all crucially shaped the cultural, political, social, and economic functioning of the theatre industry. Yet on matters of immediate production and consumption—actors and companies, stages and playhouses, playwrights and audiences—popular influences were paramount" (86). It did not pay, therefore, for the playwrights to ignore the tastes and expectations of the general public—that is, customers who would determine whether their enterprise was a success. Thus, despite the invective that the early modern playwrights often delighted to direct toward the spectators, the playwrights of the period had what David Bevington and Milla Riggio called a "push–pull relationship" with the audience, signified powerfully in "Prospero's proud and yet needful begging for applause in the Epilogue, where 'Prospero' and the actor playing his part and the dramatist are all meaningfully indistinguishable one from the other" (131–32). Even the notoriously cantankerous Ben Jonson, whose publicly stated contempt for the judgments and demands of theatre audiences was perhaps more severe than that of any other

early modern playwright, in *Bartholomew Fair* (1614) sarcastically acknowledges the right of every member of the audience, in strict proportion to ticket
price, to "haue his or her free-will of censure, to like or dislike at their owne
charge, the *Author* hauing now departed with his right: it shall be lawfull for
any man to iudge his six pen'orth, his twelue pen'orth, so as to his eithteen
pense, 2. shillings, halfe a crowne, to the value of his place," albeit with this
caveat: "Prouided alwaies his place get not aboue his wit" (Jonson 491).

Thus, in this highly contested, evolving, and interdependent theatrical
landscape—in which the authors of textually inscribed meaning often confronted the practice of performers in the no-man's-land of the public theatre,
and each side in the dispute was acutely aware of their mutual need to
cooperate in order to please a paying audience—Hamlet's insistence on a
singular "purpose of playing," requiring the complete and unconditional
surrender of the players to an orderly regime of closed representation under
the authority of the playwright, cannot be taken as expressing Shakespeare's
beliefs or his dramaturgical practice. Indeed, as Roy Battenhouse and others
have shown, Hamlet's discourse on the purpose and practice of playing
should probably be understood not as prescriptive, but ironic, since Hamlet
himself (and, of course, Shakespeare) repeatedly violates the neoclassical
rules of theatrical representation that he presumes to establish for the players
(Battenhouse 7–16). Moreover, not only does Hamlet himself violate these
rules, but he "makes us realize what intolerable drama we would have if he
did not" (Weimann, "Mimesis" 280).

Hamlet's humanistically informed and aristocratically assured advice to
the players is not, therefore, a reliable guide to an authentically "Shakespearean" performance, but instead an articulation of the energizing tension
between neoclassical theory and theatrical practice that characterizes the
early modern theatre. We need also keep in mind that Shakespeare, unlike the
majority of his playwrighting contemporaries, was a player and theatre company shareholder as well as a playwright, and that his apprenticeship took
place on the scaffolds of the practical theatre rather than in the classrooms
and libraries of the university. The early modern players' performance traditions and their impulses to fuse deep ties of complicity and mutual recognition with audiences, including the uses of various forms of self-expressive,
extemporaneous, and nonrepresentational performance, were at least as
important a part of Shakespeare's cultural inheritance as the early modern
playwrights' commitment to the new doctrine of dramatic illusionism.

In addition to various forms of self-expressive, extemporaneous, and nonrepresentational performance that the early modern theatre inherited from
the players' medieval traditions, another medieval theatre practice relevant
to the relationship between illusion and audience emotional response is
what Jody Enders has called "the hyperreality that characterizes so many
early performances," particularly in regard to the staging of scenes of violence and the infliction of pain (167). Early modern audiences were well
acquainted with reality presented as spectacle, and with spectacle that slipped

indeterminately between reality and illusion, particularly in the public staging of violence and suffering. In modern performance theory, the supposed paradox of pleasurable audience response to staged representations of violence and pain has often led to the supposition that the audience must be "at least marginally aware, on the critical level of consciousness, that the violence is not really happening" (Wilshire 250–51). Freud, among others, claimed that the pleasure of empathetic suffering on the part of the spectator is made possible by awareness that the suffering presented as spectacle is an illusion (Freud 306). But, as Enders has shown, in the medieval and early Renaissance theatre "it is clear that, sometimes, the violence really *was* happening or . . . that it had, that it could, or that it would" (197). Enders points to "the well-documented possibilities of real violence on [the medieval and early Renaissance] stage along with the widespread staging of public chastisement as a form of spectacle." In the numerous medieval dramas in which extreme violence was inflicted and endured, "there could be no such [audience] awareness of artistic limits if there were no limits. If anything, the language of many scourging scenes compounds the problem by raising the question whether the torturers are 'really' beating Christ or 'just pretending' " (166). As Enders notes, "Assuming a role in a mystery play was dangerous" (196). Similarly, Gustave Cohen observes that the medieval stage direction "*il faut sang*" ("there must be blood") should be extended to all medieval and early Renaissance mystery plays (152).

When characters bled in the early modern theatre, audiences knew that, at least in some cases, the blood was real. Moreover, well into the early modern period, real pain and suffering could be seen—and presented explicitly as spectacle—in stocks and whipping posts, public hangings, burnings, and dismemberments, lazar houses, and insane asylums. As John Spalding Gatton notes, "the sight of cruelty, suffering, and blood attracted rather than repelled" the audiences of medieval and early modern Europe (80). The early modern theatre not only competed with these spectacles of real violence and pain, but shared with them the existential reality of suffering put on display. Early modern audiences were accustomed both to the public staging of the existential reality of pain as spectacle, and to slippage and indeterminancy between the existentially real and the theatrically imagined in regard to the performative staging of violence and suffering.

Like a poor player

There are moments in narrative drama that Carl Plantinga has called "scenes of empathy." These are scenes "in which the pace of the narrative momentarily slows and the interior emotional experience of a favored character becomes the focus of attention" (239). Such scenes must succeed in engaging the spectators' emotional investment in the fictive suffering of the characters. According to the traditional assumption of a reciprocal relationship between the audience's emotional engagement and the completeness of representational illusion, one would expect that in scenes of empathy the representational illusion would be complete and assured.

But in the scenes of empathy in Shakespeare's tragic plays, the performers playing the leading tragic figures are made to engage in self-expressive, extemporaneous, and nonrepresentational modes of performance that move them into a theatrical space that reveals the existential presence of the representing actor within the represented role. At these crucial moments, the leading characters undermine the representational mode and enter a theatrical space revealing the theatre itself and the existential presence of the representing actor. Shakespeare's tragic works therefore reveal that the audience's emotional response is increased and deepened by the participation of the audience in a theatrical movement away from awareness of represented events, and toward awareness of the existential presence of the actor. It is through the actor's self-expressive and nonrepresentational modes of performance in these scenes that Shakespeare's tragic characters achieve their deepest emotional connection to the audience.

This inversion of the traditionally assumed relationship between the audience's emotional engagement and representational performance is nowhere clearer than in *Macbeth*. Macbeth and Lady Macbeth live, kill, and die in a theatrical space dominated by nonrepresentational modes of performance. Both speak directly to the audience in their first scenes. As Macbeth realizes that the first of the witches' prophecies has been fulfilled, he breaks the mode of dialogic speech and shares his thoughts with the audience: "Glamis, and Thane of Cawdor./ The greatest is behind" (1.3.114–15) and then quickly returns to dialogue with other characters: "Thanks for your pains" (1.3.115). A few lines later, this same devise of moving in and out of dialogic speech is repeated, and as Banquo talks apart with Ross and Angus, Macbeth enters into a secret confidence with the audience, sharing with them the temptation drawing him toward the "horrid image" of regicide (1.3.129–40). Macbeth is so bonded to this secret confidence with the audience that not even Banquo's dialogic interruptions can break it:

Banquo: Look how our partner's rapt.
Macbeth: If chance will have me king, why, chance may crown me
               Without my stir.

(1.3.143–46)

Macbeth repeatedly uses theatrical imagery—such as "happy prologues to the swelling act" (1.3.127)—to present his hopes and fears to the audience, and plays upon the thin line between reality and illusion: "and nothing is/ But what is not" (1.3.140–41). Here, in what is representationally a battle-scarred heath in ancient Scotland, and from the mouth of a character who is representationally a feudal warrior unlikely ever to have seen or read a play, Shakespeare's limitless resources of metaphor and images produce the image of a theatre. Macbeth also uses couplets extensively when speaking to the audience—"The eye wink at the hand; yet let that be,/ Which the eye fears, when it is done, to see" (1.5.51–52)—which further calls attention to the theatrical event and therefore foregrounds the existentially present actor performing the imaginary role (Weimann, *Shakespeare* 134). As we have noted, metatheatrical speech in general foregrounds for the audience the actor through whose real body and passion the imaginary character lives; where the represented character foregrounds its own theatricality, the figure on stage both "is and is not a character, because this same individual simultaneously is and is not the voice and body of the actor impersonating an artificial person through his own embodiment" (Weimann, "Representation" 507). The dual representation performed in these scenes—the actor performing both the character and himself—subtly forces the audience to a heightened awareness of themselves as theatrical spectators and of the representing actor submerged within the represented role. Thus, the audience hears and sees both the represented king and the representing actor. The duality performed in this scene—the actor simultaneously *representing* the character and *presenting* himself—creates in the audience an awareness of the representing actor within the represented role, simultaneously perceiving both the actor and the represented character.

This transparency of actor and character achieves a remarkable culmination in Macbeth's famous fifth act speech after learning of the death of Lady Macbeth. Macbeth, Seyton, and Macbeth's soldiers are on stage as the scene begins in a fully representational mode as Macbeth battles Macduff's siege. An off-stage cry is heard and Macbeth sends Seyton to discover its cause. When Seyton returns, Macbeth asks:

Macbeth: Wherefore was that cry?
Seyton: The Queen, my lord, is dead.
                        (5.5.15–16)

In Macbeth's response, only the first two lines are conceivably addressed to Seyton:

   She should have died hereafter.
   There would have been a time for such a word.
                        (5.5.17–18)

The remainder of the speech has no dialogic content:

   Tomorrow, and tomorrow, and tomorrow
   Creeps at this petty pace from day to day
   To the last syllable of recorded time,
   And all our yesterdays have lighted fools
   The way to dusty death. Out, out, brief candle.
   Life's but a walking shadow, a poor player

That struts and frets his hour upon the stage,
And then is heard no more. It is a tale
Told by an idiot, full of sound and fury,
Signifying nothing.

(5.5.19–27)

Narrative time has been suspended. Although Macbeth is not alone on stage, his words and actions neither call for nor receive a response from any of the other characters on stage. In this scene of empathy, the focus of the play is drawn in as tightly as in a cinematic close-up, but with the additional *theatrical* force of the audience being aware of the existential presence of the actor performing the characters, and the character-actor being able to see, feel, and acknowledge the presence of the spectators.

To say that Macbeth is talking to himself here is to miss the theatrical purpose and effect of the speech. Macbeth's speech dissolves both the other characters and the represented action. As the focus is pulled in, what the audience hears and sees is both the represented Macbeth and the concrete presence of the "poor player" who "struts and frets his hour upon the stage/ And then is heard no more." The effect of Macbeth's most famous speech is to stop the forward movement of the plot and connect the audience to the representing actor within the represented role, in contrast to dialogic speech that, however long, remains contained within the illusion of "the events portrayed" and adds to the momentum of the represented action. The audience thus perceives the body before them as being both the suffering character within the fictional world of the play, and, at the very same time, the actor *as an actor* immediately present before them, and offering his own pain and passion in the concrete here and now of the theatre. In this transparent staging of actor and role, *Macbeth* reaches its tragic apogee.

Even more than Macbeth, the audience's response to Lady Macbeth is a function of Shakespeare's uses of nonrepresentational performance. Indeed, from the perspective of close contact with the audience, Lady Macbeth is perhaps the most intimate character that Shakespeare ever created. Lady Macbeth enters and exits the play in a theatrical twilight that hovers between representational illusion and the actor's concrete self-presentation. Strikingly, nearly one-third of Lady Macbeth's part is non-dialogic. She has 129 lines alone with Macbeth, and a mere 47 lines are in dialogue with other characters. The vast majority of her lines are spoken either while alone on stage, or, as in the famous candle scene, while in the sway of madness that obliterates the other characters from her consciousness. In her scenes with Macbeth, Lady Macbeth and her husband appear to meet in an unlocalized secret passageway between *locus* and *platea* that is known only to them and the audience. When they speak to each other it is often between their individual turns speaking directly with the audience. For example, in 1.5 where Lady Macbeth first speaks alone on stage, and then she and Macbeth speak together; 1.7 where Macbeth first speaks alone on stage, then he and Lady

Macbeth speak together; 2.2 where Lady Macbeth first speaks alone, then she and Macbeth speak together, then Macbeth speaks alone, and then at the close of the scene they speak together again. This close contact between the character and audience produces not merely an intimacy with the character, but also with the actor, and, as we have seen, allows for audience perception, at a more or less conscious level, of the "relations between the representation of fictional roles and the actors' existence in their own identities" (Weimann, "Representation" 498).

The candle scene in the fifth act begins with a waiting-gentlewoman and a doctor discussing Lady Macbeth's sleepwalking. The doctor has watched for two nights and has failed to see Lady Macbeth leave her bed. The woman insists that she has seen her mistress "rise from her bed, throw her nightgown upon her, unlock her closet, take forth paper, fold it, write upon't, read it, afterwards seal it, and again return to bed, yet all this while in a most fast sleep" (5.1.3–7). The doctor asks:

> In this slumbery agitation besides her walking and other actual *performances*, what at any time have you heard her say?
>
> (5.1.9–11)

Now Lady Macbeth enters, not as herself, but, as the waiting-gentlewoman says, in "her very guise" (5.1.16). When she speaks, the elevated language and the represented royal dignity of her character are gone. As Bradley remarked, "Lady Macbeth is the only one of Shakespeare's great tragic characters who on a last appearance is denied the dignity of verse" (365). Lady Macbeth's loss of verse is also a loss of the trappings of represented dignity; it therefore frees the character from the constraints of representational performance, and creates an opening in theatrical space for the audience's awareness of the performing actor.

Bradley observed that the emotional response that Lady Macbeth inspires in this scene is inexplicable, since it is incompatible with the inhumanity of her character. In attempting to solve this riddle, Bradley postulated that there must be humanity in her character, even if it is not apparent, not only to reconcile her steely murderousness in the earlier scenes with her fragility in the candle scene, but also to explain the profound emotional effect of her suffering on the spectator. Yet Bradley admitted that he could find "nothing in the play to show this, and several passages subsequent to the murder-scene supply proof to the contrary" (338). What Bradley failed to see, because for him the character was a construction of reading rather than live performance, is that Lady Macbeth's humanity is provided not so much by the character, whose heart and actions are indeed those of a monster, as by the actor, whose energy and passions in producing the role are made perceptible to the audience though the modality of *platea* performance at precisely the moment in the play when the audience's emotional response to the suffering of Lady Macbeth is most required.

Note

1 All citations from Shakespeare are taken from *The Norton Shakespeare*, ed. Stephen Greenblatt (New York: W.W. Norton, 1997).

Works cited

Battenhouse, Roy. "The Significance of Hamlet's Advice to the Players." *The Drama of the Renaissance: Essays for Leicester Bradner*. Ed. Elmer Blistein. Providence: Brown UP, 1970. 3–26.

Bevington, David, and Milla Riggio. " 'What revels are in hand?' Marriage Celebrations and Patronage of the Arts in Renaissance England," in *Shakespeare and Theatrical Patronage in Early Modern England*. Ed. Paul Whitfield White and Suzanne R. Westfall. Cambridge: Cambridge UP, 2002. 125–49.

Bradley, A.C. *Shakespearean Tragedy: Lectures on* Hamlet, Othello, King Lear *and* Macbeth. 1904. Rpt. London: Penguin, 1991.

Calderwood, James L. *Shakespearean Metadrama: The Argument of the Play in* Titus Andronicus, Love's Labor's Lost, Romeo and Juliet, A Midsummer Night's Dream, *and* Richard II. Minneapolis: U of Minnesota P, 1971.

—— *Metadrama in Shakespeare's Henriad:* Richard I *to* Henry V. Berkeley: U of California P, 1979.

Clemen, Wolfgang. *Shakespeare's Soliloquies*, London: Methuen, 1987.

Cohen, Gustave. *Histoire de la mise en scène dans la thèâtre religieux français du Moyen Age*. 2nd ed. Paris: Champion, 1951.

Cohen, Walter. "The Merchant of Venice and the Possibilities of Historical Criticism." *Materialist Shakespeare: A History*. Ed. Ivo Kamps. London: Verso, 1995. 71–92.

Csordas, Thomas J. *Body/Meaning/Healing*. New York: Palgrave, 2002.

—— "Somatic Modes of Attention." *Cultural Anthropology* 8 (1993): 135–56.

Enders, Jody. *The Medieval Theater of Cruelty: Rhetoric, Memory, Violence*. Ithaca: Cornell UP, 1999.

Felperin, Howard. "O'erdoing Termagant: An Approach to Shakespearean Mimesis." *Yale Review* 63 (1974): 372–91.

Fox, Michael David. " 'There's Our Catastrophe': Empathy, Sacrifice, and the Staging of Suffering in Beckett's Theatre." *New Theatre Quarterly* 68 (2002): 357–72.

Freud, Sigmund. "Psychopathetic Characters on Stage," in *The Standard Edition of the Complete Psychological Works of Sigmund Freud*, ed. James Strachey. London: Hogarth, 1953.

Gatton, John Spalding. " 'There Must Be Blood': Mutilation and Martyrdom on the Medieval Stage." *Violence in Drama*. Ed. James Redmond. *Themes in Drama* 13. Cambridge: Cambridge UP, 1991. 79–91.

Greenblatt, Stephen. "Shakespeare and the Exorcists." *Shakespeare and the Question of Theory*. Ed. Patricia Parker and Geoffrey Hartman. New York: Methuen, 1985. 163–87.

Hornby, Richard. *Drama, Metadrama, and Perception*. New York: Associated UP, 1986.

Howard, Jean E. "Shakespearean Counterpoint: Stage Technique and the Interaction Between Play and Audience." *Shakespeare Quarterly* 30.3 (1979): 343–57.

Jonson, Ben. *Five Plays*. Ed. G.A. Wiles. Oxford: Oxford UP, 1999.

Lopez, Jeremy. *Theatrical Convention and Audience Response in Early Modern Drama.* Cambridge: Cambridge UP, 2003.

Mack, Maynard. "Engagement and Detachment in Shakespeare's Plays." *Essays on Shakespeare and Elizabethan Drama in Honor of Hardin Craig.* Ed. Richard Hosley. Columbia: U of Missouri P, 1962. 275–96.

Mooney, Michael. *Shakespeare's Dramatic Transactions.* Durham: Duke UP, 1990.

Planalp, Sally. *Communicating Emotion: Social, Moral, and Cultural Process.* Cambridge: Cambridge UP, 1999.

Plantinga, Carl. "The Scene of Empathy and the Human Face." *Passionate Views: Film, Cognition, and Emotion.* Ed. Carl Plantinga and Greg M. Smith. Baltimore: Johns Hopkins UP, 1999. 239–55.

Roach, Joseph R. *The Player's Passion: Studies in the Science of Acting.* Ann Arbor: U of Michigan P, 1993.

Weimann, Robert K. "Mimesis in *Hamlet*." *Shakespeare and the Question of Theory.* Ed. Patricia Parker and Geoffrey Hartman. New York: Methuen, 1985. 275–91.

—— "Representation and Performance: The Uses of Authority in Shakespeare's Theater." *PMLA* 101.3 (1992): 497–510.

—— *Shakespeare and the Popular Tradition: Studies in the Social Dimension of Dramatic Form and Function.* Ed. Robert Schwartz. Baltimore: Johns Hopkins UP, 1978.

Westfall, Suzanne R. "The Useless Dearness of the Diamond: Theories of Patronage Theatre." *Shakespeare and Theatrical Patronage in Early Modern England.* Ed. Paul Whitfield White and Suzanne R. Westfall. Cambridge: Cambridge UP, 2002. 13–42.

Wilshire, Bruce. *Role Playing and Identity: The Limits of Theatre as Metaphor.* Bloomington: Indiana UP, 1991.

12 "To be thus is nothing"

Macbeth and the trials of dramatic identity

James Wells

The epigraphic title of this chapter comes from Macbeth's soliloquy in 3.1. It represents the first uncompromised thought we hear from the new king after he becomes—to borrow from a usurping king at a critical moment in another play—possessed of the effects for which he did the murder: "To be thus is nothing, but to be safely thus" (47).[1] Macbeth's first words sound the vacuity of his predicament as an illegitimate king without issue, and underscore the surprising and ironic letdown he encounters after having obtained exactly what the Weird sisters promised him and for which he played "most foully." The audience must derive the agony of Macbeth's existence from a statement that is an apparent paradox. Only the proform "thus," fulfilled subsequently by Macbeth's deep-sticking fears of Banquo's royal nature and his own childlessness, gives meaning to his otherwise nonsensical statement. Yet, such knowledge does not erase the sentiment's essential paradox. To *be* in any way by definition is the opposite of *nothing*. Moreover, even with the benefit of explanation, Macbeth's sentiment remains paradoxical at its core. We make sense of the apparent paradox only when we replace it with a real one whereby Macbeth experiences two temporally distinct, and therefore mutually exclusive, selves at once—the present self of kingship and the future self obliterated by the failure to produce a tender heir who might bear his memory—and lives, like Lady Macbeth, in the heady intoxication of royal hope, in a perpetual state of feeling "the future in the instant" (1.5.58).

Surprisingly, Macbeth's paradoxical enunciation of his quandary does not really mark a change in him at all but merely rearticulates a self-alienation that he has been experiencing since he first heard the witches' prophecies. This alienation or dispossession is the result of a similar coincidence of temporally distinct selves. Banquo first describes this temporal self-dislocation immediately after the witches give Macbeth and him precocious awareness of Macbeth's fate: "My noble partner/ You greet with *present* grace and great *prediction*/ Of noble having and of royal hope,/ That he seems rapt withal" (1.3.54–57).[2] When Ross confirms the second article of the witches' forecast by conferring the title Thane of Cawdor upon him, Macbeth himself articulates the same experience of temporal self-displacement that results this time from the imaginary invasion of his future self as regicide: "My thought, whose murder yet is but fantastical,/ Shakes so my single state of man/ that function is smothered in surmise/ And nothing is but what is not" (1.3.139–42). Macbeth speaks of the thought of his own imaginary future as if it were a material presence, an intruder that dislodges and incapacitates his present self and leaves him trapped in the experience of a world governed by what is not there. Therefore, Macbeth's complaint in 3.1 shows that far from resolving the incapacitating paradoxical condition, the realization of the witches' prophecy has merely deferred it to another time and recreated it in another form.

In all three cases, the simultaneity of present and future selves in Macbeth results in an enraptured state, an aporia, in which the self is transported and identity recedes. Furthermore, Macbeth's aporias occur at critical moments of self-definition where identity is predicted, announced, and realized, respectively. Thus, the play presents Macbeth's identity as a problem; the moment that identity is asserted is the moment that identity dissolves. The play's iterations of Macbeth as a paradox of being and non-being not only form an important part of the play's environment, they are themselves environmental, the result of Macbeth's engagement with the particular atmosphere of the play's world. This environment, where supernatural creatures impart prescience, where the events of nature recoil in sympathy to the unnatural event of Duncan's murder, where characters make their entrances on stage seemingly upon the conjuration of their names, has long struck readers as uncanny. In applying the term "uncanny" to Macbeth's environment, I follow Lisa Hopkins who uses its technically specific, Freudian sense of a weirdness born out of distorting the familiar (106).[3] *Macbeth*'s environment is uncanny because it distorts experiences already common to the audience. They are the experiences of drama itself. These experiences take the form of paradoxes, and they are the essential and irreducible conditions of being a member of any play's viewing or reading audience.

The paradoxes of dramatic experience are the genre-specific forms of paradoxes intrinsic to all fiction and include paradoxes of character, time, and agency. The world that Macbeth inhabits, in which present and future exist at once and the self repeatedly collapses into a state of being-as-otherness, is one where the paradoxes that normally distinguish the way audiences experience characters from the way those characters experience their own world prevail, a world where these paradoxes have come alive and taken on a frightening character of their own. In this world governed by drama's paradoxes Macbeth undergoes his primary struggle, which is to acquire, fix, and maintain not just an identity ("to be safely thus"), but the one he is fated to become. The larger paradox of Macbeth's identity emerges from the collision between his struggles for fixity and the paradoxes of drama, which contravene such fixity. In a rehearsal of his own paradoxical nature, the more Macbeth strives to establish the singular identity promised to him, the more he works against not only the very identity he tries to create but also against identity itself. Inasmuch as Macbeth's struggles render his existence paradoxical, they merely point up the particular manner in which the play rehearses and redoubles the paradoxes of drama that the audience by necessity is already experiencing. Thus, the particular tragic thrust of *Macbeth* dramatizes the problems of maintaining identity in a medium where identity is always volatile, where neither the world nor the self can ever fully coalesce.

*

The growing sense of the suspended self as a normal state of affairs for Macbeth is avouched by his wife in the banquet scene when she tries to account for her husband's sudden outburst by explaining it as a chronic medical disorder: "My Lord is often thus, And hath been from his youth. . . . The fit is momentary" (3.4.52–54). Although we know that Lady Macbeth is merely trying to cover for her husband's evident lunacy, her medical pretext still takes on an accidental veracity because it accords so squarely with repeated experiences the audience has had with Macbeth since first encountering him. Banquo, were he there—and he is (in spirit)—could confirm her diagnosis having twice himself observed his fit (his thus-ness) on the heath. Critics too have also noticed Macbeth's recurrent problems with identity similar to the ones Lady Macbeth and Banquo propose. The humanist critic Richard Horwich, for one, argues that for Macbeth the lack of psychological integrity is "one of the central pre-occupations" (366).[4] According to Horwich, "the mere fantasies of murder induce in Macbeth a psychic dissociation," one which he spends the remainder of the play trying to mend (366). Horwich's choice of the term "integrity" to describe Macbeth's problems of identity is fitting because it encompasses simultaneously the moral and ontological deterioration that occurs with the conferral of his new titles. Horwich's argument takes a counterintuitive turn when he insists that it is not so much the mere presence of Macbeth's moral and psychic contradictions in his own nature that causes him to choose evil over good but his inability to endure such contradictions. By contrast, Macduff, who shares the same contraries with Macbeth (e.g. he abandons his family but kills Macbeth), is able to maintain his integrity because he embraces the contraries in his own nature, contraries that Horwich claims are natural to the human condition: "He [Macduff] retains 'the single state of man' because he is in every real sense a man, and demands no more of himself than that he should be one" (372).

Horwich was writing in 1978, and the seismic shifts in our profession engineered by materialist and feminist critics of the 1980s and 1990s, by virtue of which human beings were re-categorized as "subjects," induce autonomic jerks in readers when they encounter arguments grounded in phrases such as "in every real sense a man." Materialists would be more likely to use Macbeth's shaken single state and Macduff's bearing and feeling grief like a man to speculate upon the real state of men and women outside of the play, or, in the words of one of cultural materialism's founders, Jonathan Dollimore, on "the real historical conditions in which the actual identity of people is rooted"

(153). It was with this play that L.C. Knights expostulated against treating characters in plays as if they were real, urging instead that "the only profitable approach to Shakespeare is a consideration of his plays as dramatic poems" (20). Although Knights could not possibly have envisioned materialists' pursuit of the ideological reality that sustains theatrical illusions as the point of reading Shakespeare, his remonstrance against confusing fiction and reality is especially applicable in the case of the problem of identity in *Macbeth*. Neither the humanism of Horwich nor the now mainstream historicisms of the past twenty-five years allow for an understanding of how the critical moments in the play lead audiences away from the real world by engaging experiences that they are already having with the fictional one. For neither Macbeth nor his vanquisher Macduff is in any *real* sense a man. They are characters in a play, who, as such, have a dual, paradoxical relationship to the real human beings upon which they depend for animation. The "single state of man," if it exists at all, must lie outside of the fictional world of drama where being is by necessity disintegrated, even when it least appears to be so. Therefore, Macbeth's onstage experiences of the disintegrated self intensify experiences that the audience is already having with him because they are experiences of paradoxes that audiences have with character *qua* character.

To understand *Macbeth*'s systematic intensification requires us to understand how drama's paradoxes are themselves rooted in the broader duality of all fiction, of which drama is a specialized form. The recent work of Amittai Aviram on the distinction between fiction and non-fiction helps illuminate how such intensification works. Aviram's analysis of this distinction is rooted in a refreshing and original reconsideration of the role of mimesis in fiction in Aristotle's *Poetics*. Aviram first clarifies that by "poetry" Aristotle intended all fiction as part of the larger category of mimesis or imitation. The originality of Aviram's reading lies in his reconsideration of how the general concept of *recognition*, traditionally considered an exclusive attribute of tragedy, is germane to the experience of mimesis, and therefore fiction, itself:

> The broader concept of matching what one encounters with what one already knows [i.e. recognition] from a previous encounter comes into play early [in the *Poetics*] and is directly linked to the play of imitation. "For it is for this reason," Aristotle explains, "that people enjoy viewing images: that, observing them, they get the chance to find out and to figure out what each thing is, such as that this [figure] is that [person]; since, if one does not happen to have seen [the original] beforehand, [the image] would give pleasure not *qua* imitation (*mímêma*), but because of its construction or its color or some other such cause."
>
> (Aviram 64–65)[5]

This "play of imitation" refers to a paradox of recognition and its pleasures that are the phenomenological conditions separating the experience of imitation from that of its objects. Mimesis is a paradoxical experience because it requires the mind of the observer to carry out two opposing mental operations at once: the recognition of the object being imitated and the recognition of the object as an imitation. One recognition requires the observer to treat the imitation as real, while the other requires that observer to recognize its artifice. Imitation, therefore, presents itself a game of recognition in which the mind constantly avers two irreconcilable perceptions, that the imitated object is and is not the object imitated. Such a game is what Aviram has in mind when he reconnects fiction to its mimetic origins and defines the aesthetic experience of it as "a kind of *divided attention*, a pull in opposing directions with regard to the same object of perception or apprehension" (67).

Drama, because it is a type of fiction, not only carries the paradox of recognition that is a necessary quality of mimesis, it also intensifies and exaggerates the tensions involved in this paradox. It does so because it establishes mimesis through the same objects that it imitates (i.e. human bodies) and thus makes object and medium empirically indistinguishable from one another, unlike other forms of imitation such as poetic and narrative fiction, painting, as well as sculpture. Hence, drama amplifies imitation's game of recognition, requiring audiences to play it at a higher level and a more intense pace. Accordingly, drama entails its own set of paradoxes, each of which is a redoubling, an intensification of the general paradoxes of fiction and mimesis. The first of these is the paradox of dramatic character. This paradox arises from the dual nature of dramatic character, which combines a fictional self, with its own will and identity, with a real actor, whose animating presence both supplies and contravenes that fictional identity. The experience of dramatic character is a redoubled experience of the mimetic paradox of recognition in which the audience must register the real human bodies on stage (or their imaginary counterparts on the page) as both being and not being real people.

In a similar way, drama intensifies what Aviram calls the paradox of "dual temporality" intrinsic to fiction:

> On the one hand, the work of fiction, as a sequence of words and of events, has a beginning, a middle to which it leads, and, issuing in turn from the middle, an end. And yet, as a complete unity, the work of fiction 'already' contains the end even when we are only reading or hearing the beginning. We know this without even knowing precisely what the end will be—or already is.
>
> (Aviram 70)

While the experience of dual temporality is part of the experience of all fiction, the performed and finite nature of the dramatic event activates the dual narrative temporality for the spectator in a way that intensifies its experience in other prose and poetic fiction where the dual temporality is necessary but must be activated by the beholder in the act of reading. Because the figures who inhabit plays must operate in fiction's world of dual temporality, a dramatic character's self, like Macbeth at moments of crisis, is always both future and present at once. The combination in drama of character's paradox in general and fiction's paradox of time results in a paradox that is paramount for understanding *Macbeth*, the paradox of agency. In drama, characters appear to act with freedom, but the audience experiences them with the knowledge that even their most apparently free actions are controlled by the actor and determined in advance and for eternity by the script.

*

Even in the most rudimentary forms of drama, the paradoxes of character, time, and agency that originate in the dual nature of the dramatic medium are experiences that belong to the audience. They are the necessary disposition into which the drama places audiences. Although these paradoxes exist for any actual theatrical event, they have no necessary bearing on experiences that characters have in the play.[6] Yet, in a way that is more characteristic than exceptional for a Shakespearean play, *Macbeth* exploits these paradoxes, doubling and redoubling drama's already redoubled paradoxes of fiction, torturing them in such a way that they become the sources of horror for Macbeth. When Macbeth learns prematurely of his fate, his resulting sense of divided selfhood and struggles with his own agency with respect to fulfilling his fate recreates on-stage the paradoxes the audience is already experiencing with him simply because he is a character in a play. Macbeth becomes an experiential version of what he already is in the viewer's perception. He is hopelessly divided, being both a self and no self, both his present and his future selves, both predetermined and free to fall.

It is not just through Macbeth's aporia that the audience re-experiences the paradoxes of drama; these experiences permeate the construction of the entire environment of the play, which itself presents a world shot through with the properties of the dramatic medium. In general, the theatricality of Macbeth's world appears in the system of figuration. Even in the eighteenth century, Walter Whiter took notice of the prevalence of images that are "borrowed from the *Stage*," connecting obscure and troublesome images like the "keen knife" that can see wounds and the Heavens that "peep through the blanket of the dark" to staged representations of tragedy itself (63–65). When the play speaks of the problems of identity, it employs the idiom of the theater to articulate them. The two truths the Weird Sisters have told of Macbeth's identity are "happy prologues to the swelling act." We are probably all familiar with how the play repeatedly tropes Macbeth's acquisition of new identity (and its eventual divestment) in sartorial metaphors that would literally hold true for the relationship between a change in identity and clothing that would be required for the stage: "Why do you dress me/ In borrow'd robes?" (1.3.108–109); "Now does he feel his title/ Hang loose upon him, like a giant's robe/ Upon a dwarfish thief" (5.2.20–22). So thoroughly are issues of identity bound up with metaphors of clothing that it is difficult to discern the direction and kind of metaphoricity in Macbeth's appeal to his fellow thanes after the discovery of Duncan's murder: "Let's briefly put on manly readiness/ And meet together in the hall." (2.4.131–32). Is assuming a manly identity being spoken of metaphorically as putting on clothes, or is Macbeth referring to changing into clothes of battle metonymically in terms assuming the abstract qualities of fortitude and preparedness that are normally associated with it ("manly readiness")? Where identity is a dressing, death is the ultimate, violent undressing, a prelude, perhaps, to Macbeth's description of Murther as "Tarquin's ravishing strides" (2.1.55). Macdonwald is killed when he is "unseam'd from the nave to th'chops" (1.2.22). The growth of horror out of familiar theatrical images is most pronounced when Macbeth speaks euphemistically of Duncan's prospective murder as the "deep damnation of his *taking off*" (1.7.20), as if the killing of a king in all its horror amounted to nothing more than removal from the stage.[7] Of course, at his most critical moment in the play, Macbeth will further invest the metaphor of death as a theatrical departure with the appropriate horror by relating existence in its most nihilistic sense to "a poor player/ That struts and frets his hour on the stage/ And then is heard no more" (5.5.24–26).

But while the system of theatrical figuration in which the play couches identity offers a partial depiction of how the play recreates for characters the programmatic experiences the audience has of them, the fullness of this recreation is located more in the systematic ambiguity and atmosphere of equivocation in which Macbeth and all other characters must operate. Lucy Gent has observed how the play's equivocation extends far beyond the witches' prophecies to form the structure of the play itself: "Equivocation is not so much a major theme in the play, as a number of critics have observed, but the very condition of the play" (422).[8] More than any other Shakespeare play, *Macbeth* presents an atmosphere where the equivocality and uncertainty normally confined to the audience's experience also plague the characters. Duncan's opening question, "What bloody man is that?" and the difficulties that he has getting the story of the battle from the Captain echo the process of differentiation the audience is experiencing along with him. The atmospheric ambiguity receives its most pronounced expression in the Weird Sisters' equivocations and foul/fair paradoxes, but it is not limited to their vatic riddles. The equivocal environs create problems of intelligence throughout and prefigure the problems of differentiation and discernment that Macbeth must endure in his own struggle for identity.

The equivocal environment of the play matches up to the theater so well because the theatrical medium continuously presents itself as an experience of two opposing interpretations at once. Others critics have made similar connection between the equivocal environment and theater. Stephen Booth's extensive study of the multifarious ways equivocation saturates the play cleverly ties the inconclusiveness on stage by analogy to the nature of tragedy itself, which he claims is an attempt to define, and therefore limit, events that are so horrifying that they resist definition according to the normal schemata of human intelligibility (86). Although Booth's observations about the nature of tragedy may be true, I rather think that the tragedy of Macbeth arises from taking the general paradoxes of drama and turning them against the characters in the play. William Scott comes closer than Booth to recognizing the connection between equivocation and the experiences of the theater audience in general: "When, confronted at once thereafter with the deceptive truth of the prophecies, Macbeth denounces 'th' equivocation of the fiend/ That lies like truth . . .' (5.5.43–44), we should recall that it is the function of the player to lie like truth and of the audience to believe what it knows to be equivocation" (174). Accordingly, Macbeth's entire journey from credulity to discovery reenacts the process of theatrical discovery that the audience undergoes. Macbeth's sublime experiences of an equivocal reality correspond directly to those experienced by the audience which itself faces and embraces the reality of a spectacle that is equivocal by definition.

The systematic indefinition of the environment in the play (and, therefore, the environment of all plays) is concentrated into the figures of the witches. Banquo's bewilderment on first encountering the Weird Sisters recreates the problems of intelligibility with which the mind of the spectator must grapple endlessly in any encounter with dramatic character:

> What are these
> So wither'd and so wild in their attire,
> That look not like th'inhabitants o'th'earth
> And yet are on't? live you? or are you aught
> That man may question? You seem to understand me,
> By each at once her choppy finger laying
> Upon her skinny lips: you should be women,
> And yet your beards forbid me to interpret
> That you are so.
>
> (1.3.39–47)

Their essential questionability forbids their easy classification under the conventional categories of human identity and, thus, embodies the intellectual problem dramatic identity presents spectators who experience all characters as an endlessly irresolvable question of human being. Banquo's own surprise at their sexual ambiguity echoes the historically specific theatrical experience created by the underlying maleness of all female appearance in the transvestite theater in early modern England. Banquo's question following their first predictions merely compounds the problems of identity it seeks to resolve: "I' th' name of truth,/ Are ye fantastical, or that indeed/ Which outwardly you show?" (1.3.52–54). His question, like Horatio's "What art thou?" addressed to the Ghost in *Hamlet*, would appear at first to hinge on a question of appearance and reality: Are you just imaginary, or are you really these things you appear to be on the outside? But the way he formulates his question does not provide a means of resolving the problem of identity the witches so insistently introduce. Even if they were "that indeed" which they outwardly show, Banquo would be no closer to solving an identity which his previous line of questioning has shown to have no recourse to appearance and reality. If the witches are not fantastical, then they are what they appear. But what they appear to be is nothing, or at least nothing identifiable with respect to common rubrics of identity. The witches are ciphers, veritable non-entities, who seem "corporal" but whose corporeality is unreliable so as to be capable of melting "as breath into the wind" (1.3.81–82). Their material indistinctness makes the witches like dramatic characters who similarly present a contradiction that cannot be resolved by resorting to the mere problem of appearance and reality. Dramatic characters provide an experience in which the audience must apprehend them as being and not-being what they appear to be, as physical but able to appear, reappear, and disappear as if they were not. Not that the witches should be seen as symbolic stand-ins or allegorically metadramatic representations of the theater, although either term might be used to describe them. We are not dealing in the encoded world of symbols or encrypted substitutes. Rather, their inscrutability, the immeasurable problems of intelligibility they present for Banquo and later for Macbeth, creates and intensifies problems and paradoxes identical to the ones drama creates for its audiences.

While the witches' mere being is sufficient to recreate the problems of dramatic identity, their doings (that in "deed" which outwardly they show) only add force to the paradoxical experiences that are lodged in their being. The combination of existence and actions in the witches brings together the full complement of the paradoxical experiences intrinsic to dramatic fiction. The witches puzzling, equivocal, and "imperfect" speech (1.2.70) only deepens the bewilderment their appearance sets up. But as problematic as the witches' equivocal speech proves for Macbeth's identity, their revelation of preternatural knowledge itself, which his letter tellingly reports is "more . . . than mortal," (1.5.2–3) provides the source for the divided temporality that persistently disintegrates his identity. Their disclosure of his future requires him to live the paradoxes of drama that they themselves embody. His ensuing struggle with life as governed by fate or free will is a dramatization of the paradoxical apprehension the audience already has with him. Macbeth selectively acts throughout as if his actions are subject to fate and chance, depending usually upon which one will work to his advantage at the moment. The full force of Macbeth's ambivalence toward fate that results from his divided experience emerges in his invocation of fate after he recalls the witches' promise to make "the seed of Banquo kings": "Rather than so, come, fate, into the list,/ And champion me to th'utterance" (3.1.69–71). The semantic ambiguity of the idiom "champion me," which editors contend means both "fight on my side" and "fight against," alternately supports Macbeth's own divided sense of his life as internally or externally controlled.

Macbeth's anxiety over disintegration is indicative of the larger way the paradoxes embodied by the witches proliferate, spreading outward to create other versions of themselves in the world and characters that surround them. In Macbeth's experience, the defining event of his existence hinges both on misgivings about intermingling of future and present and on matters of identity. Macbeth's initial doubts over committing regicide turn on a kind of temporal incontinence that results from the interpenetration of future and present that will not allow the assassination to be "done, when 'tis done" (1.7.1). In accordance with the precedence set by the witches, future and present exist simultaneously. The present is always reemerging as the future in the "poison'd chalice" where the two are perversely intermixed. In this same speech, Macbeth's doubts shift from temporal indistinctness to identity. Macbeth hesitates because his roles as Duncan's "kinsman and his subject," as well as that of "host," make him one who "should against his murtherer shut the door" (1.7.15). To commit the deed would unsettle these inveterate premises of selfhood.

In the quarrel which follows, Lady Macbeth, who herself seems supernaturally attuned to the workings of Macbeth's psyche, appeals to this anxiety over integrity. While analysis of Lady Macbeth's strategy here has rightly focused first on the cheap shots she takes at his roles as man and husband ("From this time/ Such I account thy love"), we should not overlook the importance of identity in the specific form it has taken so far in the arguments she puts forth. Her appeal to Macbeth's anxiety takes two forms. First, her appeal aggravates his anxiety over the loss of integrity. Where, for Macbeth, the prospect of murdering the king creates problems of identity, Lady Macbeth insists that his reluctance to do the deed creates an equivalent form of the disintegrated self: "Art thou afeard/ to be the same in thine own act and valour,/ As thou art in desire?" (1.7. 39–41). Macbeth responds to this new challenge to integrity by appealing to the effect that the murder would have on identity at an even more fundamental level of identity, the level of humanity itself: "Pr'ythee, peace, I dare do all that may become a man" (1.7.45–46). Lady Macbeth's response shifts the terms of the argument from humanity to manliness: "What beast was't then,/ That made you break this enterprise to me?/ When you durst do it, then you were a man" (1.7.46–48). But in the very moment of attacking his masculinity, Lady Macbeth moves from aggravating his fears of disintegration to assuaging them, assuring him, "To be more than what you were, you would/ Be so much more the man" (1.7.50–51). Lady Macbeth's calculus of identity seems designed to address the very fears that Macbeth has had all along. For Macbeth, to add to identity through murder is to be more than one self at once and annihilate the self in monstrosity. For his wife, to raise one's stature, to become a greater version of the self, even by the means of apparent self-dislocation, is simply to be more of what one already is. Lady Macbeth has been applying this paradoxical equation since our initial encounter with her. Dramatic character's condition of self-dispossession is one Lady Macbeth willingly embraces when she invokes the

"Spirits/ That tend on mortal thoughts" to "un-sex" her and exchange her "woman's milk for gall" (1.5.40–41, 48).

The troubling hypothetical image of herself as an infanticide, which she offers as proof of her own fealty to her word, also serves ironically to comfort Macbeth:

> I have given suck, and know
> How tender 'tis to love the babe that milks me:
> I would, while it was smiling in my face,
> Have pluck'd my nipple from his boneless gums,
> And dash'd the brains out, had I so sworn,
> As you have done to this.
>
> (1.7.54–59)

Lady Macbeth's ability to subordinate her most basic human and womanly instinct to the larger imperative of consistency, to another version of the future, and survive intact offers Macbeth a model for thinking of his own self in relation to his prospective crime. And that his argument turns from philosophical scruples to logistics ("If we should fail?") shows that this model of reasoning is ultimately effective in convincing him.

However, although Lady Macbeth's argument and example might persuade her husband to go through with the murder, the act fails to provide or restore a sense of unity in any permanent way. In fact, the opposite occurs. The very actions that Macbeth takes to establish the identity the witches promise him works against the very identity that is promised to him.[9] On a practical level of identity, the more Macbeth takes measures to preserve his kingship, by dispatching his enemies (and their families when the enemy is not to be found), the more he erects the foundations of his own demise. Late in the play, when the rebel forces are gathering near Dunsinane, Angus will speak of the "minutely revolts" that are the result of Macbeth's own "faith-breach" (5.2.18). Yet, the most pronounced version of his ironic self-annihilation can be seen when Macbeth tries to engineer his own fate and change Banquo's destiny. The more he tries to usurp the prerogative of the witches as ministers of fate, the more his language and actions bring him into alignment with them.[10] The apostrophe to Night that he delivers before his marveling wife borrows the incantatory cadence of conjuration that is the province of the witches:

> Come seeling night,
> Scarf up the tender eye of pitiful Day,
> And, with thy bloody and invisible hand,
> Cancel and tear to pieces, that great bond
> Which keeps me pale.
>
> (3.2.45–49)

It is worth noting that his conjuration of Night is itself indicative of the paradox of agency into which the play casts him. Although the encroaching darkness the First Murderer speaks of at the beginning of the next scene makes it look as if Macbeth has some influence, we know that Night comes willy-nilly. Macbeth's second encounter with the Weird Sisters is marked by his attempts to control the situation and the outcome: "I conjure you by that which you profess" (4.1.50). Macbeth persistently ignores the witches' instructions on how to interact with the visions before him, and the scene ends with Macbeth himself casting a curse on "the pernicious hour" (4.1.133). This alignment is significant because, as noted above, the witches are veritable non-entities. To usurp their role is to risk abrogating identity.

*

Given the play's focus on Macbeth's problems of identity, the audience should not be surprised that Macbeth's paradox of identity fails to individuate him from other characters. In fact, those moments that seem designed to crystallize the moral disparity between Macbeth and those who oppose him only make such distinctions murkier. Such is the experience of both Macduff and Malcolm when they meet in 4.3. in an effort to galvanize their resistance against Macbeth. Malcolm might be the rightfully anointed heir of Scotland, but the audience does not get to experience the "king-becoming graces" (4.3.91) that in theory should attend his kingship until after hearing him accuse himself of a viciousness that surpasses Macbeth's. As it is with any dramatic character, the process of realizing Malcolm's identity involves the experience of him as not being the self that he is. Furthermore, Malcolm himself acknowledges that the device of self-denigration he is using to test Macduff's priorities, and so differentiate him from Macbeth, is similar to stratagems Macbeth has used in an effort to seduce Malcolm into a settlement: "Devilish Macbeth/ By many of these trains hath sought to win me/ Into his power" (4.3.117–19). Although Malcolm claims that Macduff's impassioned reaction to his ploy reveals him as a "child of integrity," the actual effect that this device has on his interlocutor is a cognitive disintegration identical to the rapt state in which the witches' prophecies left Macbeth. At the end of his confession of his own virtue, Malcolm is forced to ask Macduff, "Why are you silent?" Macduff responds, "Such welcome and unwelcome things at once/ 'Tis hard to reconcile" (4.3.137–38). And, as it was for Macbeth, Macduff's cognitive disintegration is followed by the question of what it means to handle his predicament, in this case the murder of a wife and child, "as a man" (4.3.221).

Lady Macbeth, likewise, shares her husband's temporal self-dislocation. The last time the audience sees her is in the sleepwalking scene, where her existence is one of bodily dispossession, "eyes . . . open," but "senses . . . shut" (5.1.23–24). Where for Macbeth the self is dislocated by the coincidence of present and future selves, for his wife the dislocating force is a past version of herself which rehearses over and over again in the present the particulars of her crime: "[W]ho would have thought the old man to have so much blood in him?"; "To bed, to bed: there's knocking at the gate" (5.1.36–37, 62).[11] The present for Lady Macbeth is a perpetual reiteration of the past, and she is clearly "rapt," insensible alike to both temporal states of selfhood. For the audience, however, that Lady Macbeth is dispossessed by a version of her self intensifies the paradoxical experience of self-dispossession that her condition as sleepwalking instills in the first place. After all, we, like the doctor and the gentlewoman, observe her altered state in the prurient hope that her real self will emerge. By nullifying Lady Macbeth's self through a doubling of it, the play doubly redoubles the audience's experience of dramatic character's paradox of self-dispossession. But the play adds a further irony to this intensification. As with Macbeth in 3.1., the change we observe in Lady Macbeth is really no change at all. From her first "Come ye spirits which tend on mortal thoughts," Lady Macbeth's existence has been predicated on her willingness to let her self be displaced by forces outside herself. Instead of nullifying her, the sleepwalking scene realizes the self Lady Macbeth has been asking to be all along.

Unlike his wife, Macbeth continues to resist the temporal dislocations that are the defining experiences of dramatic character. After Lenox reports Macduff's flight to England, Macbeth seems set on resolving the temporal disjunction that has troubled him throughout: "From this moment,/ The very firstlings of my heart shall be/ The firstlings of my hand" (4.2.146–48). By collapsing thought and action, Macbeth is attempting to evacuate the future self that initially shook his "single state of man." Yet, despite his resistance, we are not surprised when Macbeth's deterioration is another version of the dislocated self. When Angus reports of the revolts of Macbeth's men, Menteth speaks of the King as a body in revolt against itself: "Who shall blame/ His pester'd sense to recoil and start,/ When all that is within him does condemn/ Itself for being there" (5.2.22–25). Macbeth in crisis is a continuous figure of the self as a process of evacuation. Macbeth's condition at the end of the play is a permanent realization of this divided condition of selfhood. Macbeth is reduced to a severed head, an experience for the audience in which the self is emptied of "all that is within him."

That the end is the same whether a character invites or resists self-dislocation only further points up the game *Macbeth* is playing with the duality of dramatic experiences. This game resides in the way the play presents a series of reinforcing instances in which experiences that are normally the source of pleasure for the audience are turned against the characters in the play. In *Shakespearean Tragedy and its Double*, Kent Cartwright describes how plays achieve "spectatorial distance" when "audience members . . . for a moment shift their attention from character to performer" and specifically how "Shakespearean tragedy can systematically appropriate this detachment from the fictional persona and engagement with the actor so as to heighten emotional power and complicate the meaning of the play" (1). Cartwright then analyzes Desdemona's death-scene by showing how, through a series of interruptions and surprising resuscitations, the play deliberately and repeatedly turns our attention to the body of the actor. Cartwright's illuminating analysis of *Othello*, which builds significantly on Maynard Mack's earlier theoretical work on engagement and detachment in Shakespeare's plays, certainly resembles the ideas that I am putting forth here. But I am not arguing that Macbeth's moments of self-dislocation result in anything as anticlimactic as the detachment of having our attention turned to the body of the actor.[12] Instead of detachment, I am suggesting that in Macbeth's temporal self-dislocation we re-experience as horrible an experience that we are already having, one that we normally encounter as pleasure.[13] The paradoxes of drama that Macbeth redoubles are the necessary and relentless experiences of drama. We cannot experience drama without placing the mind into what the phenomenological theorist Stanton Garner has called the theater's perpetual "oscillation between the perceptual levels" of "is" and "as if" (47). Although the mind may not be actively attending to the paradoxes of drama, the perception remains as part of the structural experience of the theater. And to have this pleasurable experience stoked in the way that *Macbeth* does is not to have the artificiality of the theater raised to the level of conscious awareness but merely to experience the pleasures of dramatic imitation in a more intense form.

For spectators, the result of this intensification is not an increased distancing from the spectacle, but a greater enfolding into it. By exaggerating the paradoxes of theater, the play casts the audience into the same aporia and sense of wonderment into which it has cast its principal figures. But, as we have already seen, the shape into which characters are thrown is already one and the same with the audience's experience of them as characters. The circular totalization of the empathy between characters and audience on which the entire play is structured is both the mark of Shakespeare's pre-eminence and the captivating force that draws us to the play and holds our imaginations so firmly when we see it.

Notes

1 All Quotations from *Macbeth* are from Kenneth Muir's New Arden Edition of that play.
2 Italics mine. Although "rapt" is an editorial emendation dating back to Pope of the folio's "wrapt," the context here suggests that the two terms are synonymous. The *OED* defines wrapt so that it is essentially synonymous with enraptured (Wrapped: 5).
3 This work differs from Hopkins in that where she suggests that the uncanny environment in Macbeth emerges from the perversion of terms denoting bourgeois domesticity, I am suggesting that this feeling in Macbeth comes from a recreation of the experiences that are already part of the theatrical experience. In this way, my reading offers a reason why the play would borrow from the quotidian materials of life. The theater takes normal, everyday properties of life and defamiliarizes them, infusing the real with the qualities of what is not.

4 Lynne M. Robertson also notes that Macbeth's decapitation at the end of the play is "the culmination of a process of disembodiment that has been steadily emerging from the second act of the play onwards" (34).

5 The clarifying brackets in Arivam's thoughts of this quotation are mine. Those in the quotation from Aristotle are Aviram's. The translation of Aristotle is also his.

6 I use the phrase "actual theatrical event" to distinguish between those events that are literally theatrical fictions and those that are metaphorically theatrical. Distinguishing seems necessary given the tendency in modern critical schools, especially New Historicism and Cultural Materialism, to dissolve the distinction between what is literally theatrical and what is merely theatrical-like. Bert States provides a splendid critique of the modern habit of invoking performance in its metaphorical sense (a defining feature of a number of disciplines) and then "forgetting" that it is a metaphor (2). The point here is not to contest any of these theories, but to limit the range of applicability of my theory of dramatic fiction.

7 The *OED* lists Shakespeare as the first author to have used "taking off," as a metaphor for murder (83: f). In effect, Shakespeare is inventing a metaphor for murder that is consistent with the sartorial imagery of the play.

8 A number of excellent studies of the uncertain environments exist. See Booth (King Lear); Knight; and McElroy.

9 James Calderwood has noted a pattern of "uncreation" in the play through which Macbeth's "[s]eeking to be more than he was . . . ultimately renders himself . . . nothing" (*If It Were Done* 57).

10 George Walton Williams offers a more detailed account on the verbal echoing in the play that links Macbeth to the witches.

11 The effect that her condition has on the doctor is the same as the aporia we have seen before in Macbeth and Macduff when faced with spectacles of uncertainty: "My mind she has mated, and amaz'd my sight./ I think, but dare not speak" (5.1.75–76).

12 This feeling of anticlimax is so often the case in readings that present themselves as metadramatic because they end in the statement that the audience is reminded that it is watching a play—an idea that is implicit in the term metadrama. This assumption supports even the nuanced and sophisticated metadramatic readings of James Calderwood in which the author argues that Hamlet exists as a divided self of character and actor; "Plays, however, give rise to a reinforcing division of identity because in them we can also distinguish between character and actor. . . . If we are absorbed in the play as fictional life, the actor . . . is artfully erased, consumed by the character Hamlet. If we become conscious of the actor for some reason (forgotten lines, extraordinary performance, a fit of coughing), then it is Hamlet who is erased, along with the fiction of life in Elsinore" (*To Be* 31). My point is that the experience of the theater is always a paradoxical combination of character and actor. In the experience of the audience, the actor is not erased by absorption in theatrical event, any more than the fiction is erased by the consciousness of the actor. The two exist simultaneously in the experience of the audience whether it attends to them or not.

13 The distinction between experience and awareness to which Stephen Booth's work often resorts is useful for understanding the distinction I am putting forth here. See particularly Booth's description of how *Macbeth* allows viewers to experience the potential of living outside the morality dictated by their own judgment: "By 'experience of such potential,' however, I do not mean—as I might seem to mean—'experience of recognizing such potential' " (King Lear 115). See also his description of how the eventfulness of Shakespeare's language consists of "substantively negligible, substantively irrelevant relationships among elements in a syntax to which those relationships do not pertain and by which those relationships are filtered from consciousness" ("Shakespeare's" 3).

Works cited

Aviram, Amittai. "Lyric Poetry and Subjectivity." *Intertexts* 5.1 (2001): 61–86.

Booth, Stephen. King Lear, Macbeth, *Indefinition, and Tragedy.* New Haven: Yale UP, 1983.

—— "Shakespeare's Language and the Language of Shakespeare's Time." *Shakespeare Survey* 50 (1997): 1–17.

Calderwood, James L. *If It Were Done:* Macbeth *and Tragic Action.* Amherst: U of Massachusetts P, 1986.

—— *To Be and Not To Be: Negation and Metadrama in* Hamlet. New York: Columbia UP, 1983.

Cartwright, Kent. *Shakespearean Tragedy and its Double: The Rhythms of Audience Response.* University Park: Penn State UP, 1991.

Dollimore, Jonathan. *Radical Tragedy: Religion, Ideology and Power in the Drama of Shakespeare and his Contemporaries.* 2nd ed. Durham: Duke UP, 1983.

Garner, Stanton. *Bodied Spaces: Phenomenology in Contemporary Performance.* Ithaca: Cornell UP, 1994.

Gent, Lucy. "The Self-Cozening Eye." *Review of English Studies* 34 (1986): 419–28.

Hopkins, Lisa. "Household Words: *Macbeth* and the Failure of Spectacle." *Shakespeare Survey* 50 (1997): 101–10.

Horwich, Richard. "Integrity in *Macbeth*: The Search for the 'Single State of Man.' " *Shakespeare Quarterly* 29.3 (1978): 365–73.

Knight, G. Wilson. "Macbeth and the Metaphysic of Evil." *The Wheel of Fire.* 1930. London: Methuen, 1965: 140–59.

Knights, L.C. "How Many Children Had Lady Macbeth: An Essay on the Theory and Practice of Shakespeare Criticism." *Explorations: Essays in Criticism Mainly on the Literature of the Seventeenth Century.* New York: Stewart, 1947. 15–54.

McElroy, Bernard. "*Macbeth*: The Torture of the Mind." *Shakespeare's Mature Tragedies.* Princeton: Princeton UP, 1973. 206–37.

Mack, Maynard. "Engagement and Detachment in Shakespeare's Plays." *Essays on Shakespeare and Elizabethan Drama: In Honor of Hardin Craig.* Ed. Richard Hosley. Columbia: University of Missouri Press, 1962. 275–96.

Muir, Kenneth, ed. *Macbeth.* New Arden Shakespeare, 1962. London: Methuen, 1984.

Robertson, Lynne M. "Getting a Head in a Warrior Culture: Shakespeare's *Macbeth* and the Problem of Identity." *Connotations* 7.1 (1997): 33–43.

Scott, William O. "Macbeth's—And Our—Self-Equivocations." *Shakespeare Quarterly* 37.2 (1986): 160–74.

States, Bert, "Performance as Metaphor." *Theatre Journal* 48 (1996): 1–26.

Whiter, Walter. "Specimen of a Commentary on Shakespeare." (1794) *Shakespeare*: Macbeth: *A Casebook.* 1968. Ed. John Wain. London: Macmillan, 1982.

Williams, George Walton. " 'Time for such a word': Verbal Echoing in *Macbeth*." *Shakespeare Survey* 47 (1994): 153–59.

13 The personating of Queens

Lady Macbeth, Sarah Siddons, and the creation of female celebrity in the late eighteenth century

Laura Engel

Her Majesty had express'd herself surprised to find me so collected in so new a position, and that I had conducted myself as if I had been used to a court. At any rate, I had frequently personated Queens.

(Siddons 22)

It is difficult for the frequent playgoer to disembarrass the idea of Hamlet from the person and voice of Mr. K. We speak of Lady Macbeth, while we are in reality thinking of Mrs. S.

(Charles Lamb, quoted in Bate 112)

In 1957, at the thirty-fifth annual Pageant of the Masters in Irvine, California, the actress Bette Davis posed as Sarah Siddons in a recreation of Sir Joshua Reynolds's portrait of Siddons as *The Tragic Muse*. In a photograph of the event, Davis appears in full eighteenth-century garb, seated on a mock throne, glaring down at a woman who reaches up to her in a gesture of devotion.[1] That an organizer of the event chose Davis to portray the eighteenth-century diva Sarah Siddons is a testament to the lasting quality of a category of identity that Siddons invented: the modern female superstar. The idea of the actress as a Queen, as an untouchable ideal, an exemplar of femininity, and a sublime being, originated with Siddons. Her celebrity status was the result of carefully crafted visual strategies on stage, on canvas, and in print that worked to convince audiences that she was, as William Hazlitt remarked, "tragedy personified. She was the stateliest ornament of the public mind" (5: 312).

Out of all of Siddons's roles she was perhaps best known for her legendary portrayal of the doomed Queen Lady Macbeth.[2] Siddons's performance of Shakespeare's devious heroine was lauded by critics, adored by audiences, and the subject of numerous portraits, engravings, and her own notes on how to perform the part.[3] According to Siddons's "Remarks on the Character of Lady Macbeth," written sometime after 1815 and published in Thomas Campbell's *Life of Mrs. Siddons* (London, 1834), Lady Macbeth's duplicitous and ambitious persona is ultimately softened and counteracted by her madness and breakdown.[4] The sleepwalking scene, Siddons claimed, should be seen not as the confession of a guilty murderess, but rather as the triumph of Lady Macbeth's femininity and compassionate nature. Her success at transforming Lady Macbeth from an ambitious usurper into a noble heroine is the theatrical equivalent of what she managed to achieve in her own career. Siddons's attempt to ally her portrayal of Lady Macbeth with an authentic, feminine persona mirrored her own desire to blur the boundaries between her roles on and off stage. In doing so, she provided a model for female celebrity that masked her role as an "ambitious candidate for fame" and instead posited her celebrity as an un-staged legitimate phenomenon.

In her study *Sexual Suspects*, Kristina Straub argues that the public's fascination with the private lives of eighteenth-century players extended to surveillance over their bodies. Straub writes: "The public's gaze is seen in theatrical discourse as a powerful and often problematic act of control—even oppression—exercised over a body of individuals professionally vulnerable to surveillance and public scrutiny" (13). Siddons herself endured this kind of relentless public attention; however, unlike other female performers whose private lives and public antics created scandal, Siddons's unique position engendered another model of public fascination, a model similar to the worship of the British Monarchy. As Shearer West has argued, Siddons's public and private roles represented "interlocking components;" her career was "anomalous" in a time when actresses were considered "dispensable or interchangeable" ("Public and Private" 3). Critics saw Siddons's ability to portray royalty as a perfect analogy for the level of her achievement and for her personal qualities. A reviewer of her last performance as Lady Macbeth notes: "Mrs. Siddons's conception of the propriety and demeanor of the character of Lady Macbeth marks the superior and unrivalled qualities of her genius. Mrs. Siddons's performance of this part becomes, therefore, a fine moral lesson: and the guilty strings of conscience are shown to be severer accusers than human laws" ("Mrs. Siddons's Departure"). According to her first biographer James Boaden, Siddons was so natural while performing that it was difficult to see her as "acting," a talent that expressed her exemplary Britishness. He writes: "So natural are her gradations and transitions, so classical and direct her speech and deportment. She is sparing in her action because English nature does not act much; but is always proper, picturesque, graceful and dignified" (172). So imprinted was the idea of Siddons as the embodiment of the British nation that when George III ordered a royal service at St. Paul's Cathedral to celebrate his miraculous recovery from madness, Siddons played the figure of Britannia.[5] Siddons's regal celebrity status reinforced "Britannia's" role as a benevolent ruler of a continuously expanding empire.[6]

During her reign as the Queen of the British theatre, portraits of Siddons that aided in promoting her celebrity emphasized many qualities portrayed in visual representations of the actual Queen, King George III's wife Queen

Charlotte. In the latter part of the eighteenth century, King George III and Queen Charlotte were visible and popular public figures. Historian Linda Colley credits George III with revitalizing and revising the ways in which British subjects saw the monarchy. Largely through portraiture and public appearances, George III created an image of the royals as paradoxically ordinary and extraordinary, both remote and accessible (206). Colley explains: "George III was on a different level from his subjects, the inhabitant of splendid palaces and the fulcrum of unprecedented ceremony; but he was also a husband, a father, a mortal man subject to illness, age and every kind of mundane vulnerability, and therefore, essentially the same as his subjects" (232).[7] Like the King, Queen Charlotte used visual images to present herself as both royal and ordinary. Well-known artists Thomas Gainsborough, Sir Joshua Reynolds, Benjamin West, and William Beechey depicted the Queen as a fashionable, attractive woman whose duties involved both her regal obligations and her position as a wife and mother.[8] The same artists were also involved in painting portraits of Sarah Siddons. Similar to depictions of Queen Charlotte, Siddons's portraits promoted the vision of her as both a public celebrity and a private individual.

In the present chapter, while comparing portraits of Siddons with paintings of Queen Charlotte, I will consider how Siddons invokes similar images of royalty and maternity to envision and redefine the character of Lady Macbeth in her "Remarks on the Character of Lady Macbeth." In examining Siddons's "Remarks" in relation to her affiliation with a variety of "Queens"—real Queens (Queen Charlotte) staged Queens (Lady Macbeth), and projected Queens (her own status as a celebrity diva)—I find evidence of Siddons's particular strategies for fashioning her celebrity. By positing Lady Macbeth's character, and by extension her own celebrity, as authentic and natural performances, Siddons effectively casts herself as a legitimate female star rather than an ambitious, power-seeking diva.

Siddons and Lady Macbeth

Siddons's portrayal of Lady Macbeth went beyond the expectations of her early audiences. She established traditions associated with the role that would survive on stage in actresses' performances for generations to follow.[9] As Bernice W. Kliman notes, "Her performances are worthy of close study, because she may be the best actor who has ever played the role of Lady Macbeth and because actors have emulated her in many individual choices—if not the entire characterization" (28). Much of our information about the innovation and impact of Siddons's performance of Lady Macbeth comes from a wealth of contemporary commentary about her actions and presence on stage as well as her own detailed analysis of the role. Significantly, Siddons's "Remarks on the Character of Lady Macbeth" have garnered less scholarly attention than the extensive comments about her performances of the role, and the portraits of her as Lady Macbeth painted by a variety of well-known artists. Kliman writes, "She herself wrote about her intentions and about the character of Lady Macbeth, though many critics think she surpassed her own analysis" (28), and Russ McDonald suggests that Siddons's "Remarks" "are to some degree a hindrance in that they are retrospective, summarizing a characterization shaped and tweaked for some thirty years. In other words, what they describe may not have been what spectators at Drury Lane saw in February of 1785" (38). Although the "Remarks" clearly cannot recapture exactly what Siddons did on stage, the document is an important record of how Siddons imagined and designed the role over many years, in the same way that she invented and promoted a carefully crafted image of herself as a performer.

The "Remarks" as a document pose some compelling questions because the text is embedded within a biography written and edited by someone else. The "Remarks" are set off by quotation marks in Campbell's biography, where they make up almost a whole chapter. The "Remarks" can be seen then as both a private and a public document. At the same time that it is authenticated by the quotation marks it is still part of the fabricated thread of Campbell's narrative. The fact that it is not a separate document allows Siddons to put forth an analysis and an opinion while still remaining within the authorized confines of another person's text. Her "Remarks" appear to be spontaneous and non-scripted, rather than a deliberate image-making strategy.

Catherine Burroughs, one of the few critics who considers the "Remarks" to be an important text in its own right, reads the document as evidence of Siddons's model for a method of acting that "had implications for living a more enlightened life off stage" (*Closet Stages* 56). Using a passage from Siddons quoted by Thomas Campbell in the biography, Burroughs emphasizes Siddons's anxieties about the difficulties in portraying such an unlikable heroine. Burroughs explains Siddons's process:

> Schooling herself to tolerate negative characters in order to make herself more capable of empathizing with the strange, the threatening, and the despicable, she confessed that she had for several years, 'perceived the difficulty of assuming a personage [Lady Macbeth] with whom no one feeling of common general nature was congenial or assistant. One's own heart could prompt one to express, with some degree of truth, the sentiments of a mother, a daughter, a wife, a lover, a sister &c, but to adopt this character must be an effort of the judgment alone.'
>
> (Burroughs, *Closet Stages* 56)

Burroughs argues that Siddons "persisted in trying to suspend her judgment about Lady Macbeth in order to inhabit the character in a way that would make more humanely explicable her variety of behaviors" (*Closet Stages* 57). This displays her "sympathetic curiosity," a quality that allies her with other Romantic women writers.

Although Burroughs's reading allows for the complexities of Siddons's take on the role of Lady Macbeth, she does not consider the possibility that Siddons's humanizing of the character had more than "sympathetic" motivations. Siddons's project of portraying Lady Macbeth as a recognizable mother, daughter, and wife, a character whose nature at one time was "congenial," was directly tied to promoting her own public image for audiences who had difficulty making the distinction between her identities on and off stage. As Judith Pascoe suggests, "Siddons as a wife and mother was just as public a persona as Siddons as Lady Macbeth, but the former role contained the latter one, rendering it less threatening to a society unused to demonstrable female desire" (24).

Throughout her analysis of Lady Macbeth, Siddons returns to Lady Macbeth's initial role as a would-be Queen, which of course involves acting as a gracious hostess to the soon to be murdered King Duncan while doing everything she can to support her ambitious husband. Highlighting Lady Macbeth's beauty, strength, and devotion to Macbeth, Siddons is able to revise the more diabolical aspects of this Lady Macbeth's character. From the outset, Siddons urges her readers to rethink their previous concept of a monstrously aspiring heroine:

> In this astonishing creature one sees a woman in whose bosom the passion of ambition has almost obliterated all the characteristics of human nature; in whose composition are associated all the subjugating powers of intellect and all the charms and graces of personal beauty. You will probably not agree with me as to the character of that beauty; yet, perhaps, this difference of opinion will be entirely attributable to the difficulty of your imagination disengaging itself from that idea of the person of her representative which you have been so long accustomed to contemplate.
>
> (Siddons, "Remarks," in Campbell 2: 10–11)

In this enticing introduction Siddons admits that she has a new, original, and perhaps unwelcome interpretation of Lady Macbeth.[10] Siddons contends that despite Lady Macbeth's "dreadful language" and "remorseless ambition," she is essentially "feminine, nay perhaps even fragile." She has suffered in the past and she uses those memories to fuel her motivation of her weaker husband. Separating Lady Macbeth's "ambition" from her true "nature," Siddons suggests that she is under some kind of unnatural spell that compels her to behave like a "perfectly savage creature" (2: 18).

Siddons uses images of Lady Macbeth's "personal beauty" to soften the deviousness of her motives and sentiments in the first act of the play. She writes, "Lady Macbeth, thus adorned with every fascination of mind and person, enters for the first time, reading a part of one of those portentous letters from her husband. . . . Now vaulting ambition and intrepid daring rekindle in a moment all the splendors of her dark blue eyes" (2: 13–14).

Directing attention to Lady Macbeth's "dark blue eyes" gives readers a moment to visualize the "fascination" of Lady Macbeth's person. In a similar fashion, promoting "personal beauty" was an integral part of designing images of Siddons and Queen Charlotte. In portraits of Siddons as "herself," her elegant figure and classical features created the illusion of a "larger than life" grandeur. It was this grandeur that convinced critics that she was of a higher class. Thomas Davies writes: "The person of Mrs. Siddons is greatly in her favor just rising above the middle stature, she looks, walks, and moves like a woman of superior rank" (quoted in Highfill et al. 14: 10). *The Morning Post* for Saturday, December 30, 1775, comments: "Her figure is a very fine one; her features are beautifully expressive; her action is graceful and easy, and her whole deportment that of a gentlewoman" (quoted in Matthews and Hutton 35).

Thomas Gainsborough's portrait of Siddons (1783–1785) is a testament to her grandeur as a Lady (Figure 13.1). In this painting, Siddons is "out of costume" playing herself, yet still in costume as a grand woman of society. She wears a white-and-blue-striped silk "wrapping gown" with lace sleeves (Ribeiro, *Art of Dress* 73).[11] She holds a fur muff in her hand and a hat with feathers and bows sits gracefully angled on her head. Her hair is partially powdered with natural color showing through. She stares confidently and seriously into the distance, the soft folds of her dress contrasted with her angular features and the line of the black necklace across her pale skin. Although this portrait was clearly recognizable as Siddons by viewers, Gainsborough softened Siddons's features, particularly her characteristic nose. In a legendary story about the creation of this painting, Gainsborough became frustrated with Siddons's image exclaiming, "Damn the nose—there's no end to it!" (Whitley 370).[12]

Gainsborough also manipulated aspects of Queen Charlotte's presence in his famous portrait of her, completed in 1781 (Figure 13.2). In this painting, Charlotte stands against a backdrop similar to the portrait by Benjamin West (discussed below). She is dressed in an elaborate "robe a la francaise"—a costume worn regularly at the Royal court. She holds a delicate fan between her fingers as she gazes contentedly at the viewer. Aileen Ribeiro comments that although the elaborate mix of fabrics and lace in this costume could "easily look ridiculous," Gainsborough's skill in blending the "cobwebby" material of the dress with the Queen's powdered hair and flowered headdress against the landscape in the background makes this portrait a remarkable success (*Art of Dress* 62).[13] Eighteenth-century observers were impressed with the attractive representation of an otherwise ordinary-looking Queen. Sir Henry Bate-Dudley remarked in the *Morning Herald*: "The Queen's is the only happy likeness we ever saw portrayed of her Majesty: the head is not only very highly finished but expresses all that amiableness of character which so justly distinguishes her." James Northcote explained that the "drapery was done in one night by Gainsborough and his nephew; they sat up all night, and painted by candlelight. This in my opinion, constitutes the essence

Figure 13.1 Thomas Gainsborough, *Mrs Siddons* (1785). By permission of The National Gallery, London.

of genius, the making of beautiful things from unlikely subjects" (quoted in *Gainsborough and Reynolds* 50).

Just as Gainsborough created the idea of status, wealth, and noble bearing with his portrait of Siddons, Queen Charlotte appears magically beautiful in his representation of her. Through visual imagery, both women were endowed with qualities that they did not innately possess. These qualities contributed to promoting their public images. Eighteenth-century observers'

Figure 13.2 Thomas Gainsborough, *Queen Charlotte* (1781). By permission of The Royal Collection.

reactions to these portraits suggest that this is what the public wanted to see—a beautiful Queen and a noble actress. Interestingly, these very different women participated in similar self-fashioning strategies. The goal of each was clearly to create an accessible image that sold her most attractive features. Queen Charlotte and Sarah Siddons had much in common; despite their disparate backgrounds they were celebrities and public figures, subject to the same standards of judgment with respect to femininity and style.

Curiously, in her "Remarks" Siddons describes Lady Macbeth as having "dark blue" eyes. Siddons, herself, had dark brown eyes. Similar to the idealized visual makeovers performed in portraits of Siddons and of Queen Charlotte, Siddons's vision of Lady Macbeth is that of a woman more conventionally beautiful than Siddons herself. In her "Remarks" Siddons faced a similar task of eighteenth-century portraitists. In painting a likeable version of Lady Macbeth, she had to succeed at making "beautiful things from unlikely subjects."

One of the most difficult tasks Siddons faced in portraying Lady Macbeth's "personal beauty" occurs at the beginning of the play, when Lady Macbeth refers to the vexed possibility that she was once a mother. In the eighteenth century emphasizing the virtues of domesticity and motherhood was a way of desexualizing the female figure, a process that was particularly important to the creation of a woman's public image. Popular portraits of Queen Charlotte and Siddons linked their personas to their role as mothers, presenting them as powerful figures because of their benevolent role as domestic guardians. Benjamin West's portrait of Queen Charlotte (not pictured) depicts her standing poised against a grand column with her children in the background. The painting conveys the idea that the Queen's glory comes from her position as a wife and mother to the King's children who will eventually rule the country.[14] West's image of Queen Charlotte suggests that eighteenth-century women could not be onstage or directly in the foreground without indirectly representing something else. In the painting, Charlotte's body, while beautifully clothed and positioned, is not a body of titillation or desire. She modestly gathers the folds of her costume in front of her lower torso and her bosom is disguised by a large decorative bow. The small, tamed lap dog at her feet signifies the idea of domesticity and fidelity inherent in the Queen's personality. The production of children is thus not seen as the result of multiple sexual acts, but as a duty and function of an eighteenth-century wife.

In William Hamilton's portrait of Siddons as Isabella, from Thomas Southerne's *Isabella* (one of her most celebrated parts), Siddons's gestures and position signify her role as a devoted mother.[15] The painting depicts the moment in the play when Isabella's reversal of fortune compels her to beg for food and money in order to support her family. Dressed all in black, Siddons looms above her son, her arms gracefully outstretched. She stares off in the distance with a look of pathos as she clutches the boy's hand.[16] Siddons's gestures recreate her presence on stage as a serious accomplished performer while lending credence to her "real life" image as a good mother and a devoted wife. This interplay of gesture, costume, and staging worked to promote the idea of Siddons as representative of the best qualities of her sex while de-emphasizing the sexual nuances of her presence and her performances.[17]

While the role of Isabella was a perfect vehicle for Siddons's project of representing herself as a self-sacrificing mother, portraying Lady Macbeth as tenderly maternal would prove to be more of a challenge. In her "Remarks" Siddons attempts to reveal Lady Macbeth's hidden maternal instincts by translating her cruelest speech—in which she describes dashing out the brains of her mysterious child—into a more palatable psychological reading of the incident. According to Siddons, this is a moment of pure persuasion for Lady Macbeth, "Her language to Macbeth is the most potently eloquent that guilt could use. It is only in soliloquy that she invokes the powers of hell to unsex her. To her husband she avows, and the naturalness of her language makes us believe her, that she had felt the instinct of filial as well as maternal love" (2: 18). Siddons imagines Lady Macbeth to be thinking "I, too have felt with a tenderness which your sex cannot know; but I am resolute in my ambition to trample on all that obstructs my way to a crown. Look to me and be ashamed of your weakness" (2: 19). Revised in this way, the line does not suggest that Lady Macbeth has harmed her child or even realistically would harm her child, but that this is the most powerful image that she can conjure that would make Macbeth understand her deadly resolve. Siddons explains: "The very use of such a tender allusion in the midst of her dreadful language, persuades one unequivocally that she has really felt the maternal yearnings of a mother towards her babe, and that she considered this action the most enormous that ever required the strength of human nerves for its perpetration" (2: 18).

Siddons's emphasis on Lady Macbeth's mothering instincts is significantly tied to her own performances and pregnancies. In April 1794, Siddons played Lady Macbeth at the lavish reopening of the new Drury Lane Theatre while she was five months pregnant with her sixth child. This was not the first time she had performed while pregnant. In 1775, she gave birth to her second child Sally halfway through a performance at Gloucester; in 1782, eight months pregnant with her fifth child, Siddons played both Hermione in the *Distressed Mother* and Nell in *The Devil to Pay at Bath*.[18] She was not shy about acknowledging that providing for her children was the main reason for her theatrical career. Siddons could be an adored celebrity because she was to all appearances also a devoted mother and wife. She remained in a passionless marriage with her husband, the unsuccessful actor William Siddons, wisely avoiding scandals associated with affairs and liaisons with powerful men, a practice that proved to be the downfall of many of her theatrical contemporaries.[19] Although Siddons seemed to have the power to transcend the limitations of her own body during her performances, it is significant that audiences saw her appear as Lady Macbeth while she was pregnant. The double nature of her persona as the character and the pregnant actress must have collided in these moments and helped to underscore Siddons's characterizations of Lady Macbeth as a potentially sympathetic figure.[20]

Once the murder of Duncan is accomplished and Lady Macbeth becomes the "legitimate" Queen, her persona undergoes a significant transformation. Siddons writes "The golden round of royalty now crowns her brow, and royal robes enfold her form; but the peace that passeth all understanding is lost to her forever" (2: 21–22). Siddons explains how she portrayed Lady Macbeth's "loss of peace" on stage: "Under the impression of her wretchedness, I, from this moment, have always assumed the dejection of countenance and manners which I thought accordant to such a state of mind" (2: 22). Suddenly Lady Macbeth displays "striking indications of sensibility, nay tenderness and sympathy" (2: 22–23) towards her husband. She becomes meek and repentant: "The sad and new experience of affliction has subdued the insolence of her pride and the violence of her will" (2: 23), and she loses her sharp ability to be duplicitous.

In the famous banquet scene, where Macbeth encounters Banquo's bloody ghost, Siddons describes the difficulty of conveying Lady Macbeth's vulnerable position:

> Dying with fear, yet assuming the utmost composure, she returns to her stately canopy; and, with trembling nerves, having tottered up the steps to her throne, that bad eminence, she entertains her wondering guests with frightful smiles, with over-acted attention, and with fitful graciousness; painfully, yet incessantly, laboring to divert their attention from her husband.
>
> (Siddons, "Remarks," in Campbell 2: 27)

Here Siddons emphasizes Lady Macbeth's discomfort with her new-found royal status; she "totters up the steps to her throne," which Siddons labels a "bad eminence," and she is unable to naturally control her actions. She is overly solicitous and fitful. Siddons goes on to explain how difficult it is to perform this scene well: "What imitation, in such circumstances as these, would ever satisfy the demands of expectation? The terror, the remorse, the hypocrisy of this astonishing being . . . present, perhaps, one of the greatest difficulties of the scenic art, and cause her representative no less to tremble for the suffrage of her private study, than for its public effect" (2: 28).

In her analysis Siddons shifts the focus of this scene from Lady Macbeth's machinations to her own anxieties about performing the part. Siddons effectively invites the reader to equate their sympathy with Lady Macbeth's inner monologue with an appreciation of Siddons's (the actress's) own private struggle to understand and perfect her portrayal of the role. Siddons suggests that Lady Macbeth should be pitied because she is suffering so much from the dreadful knowledge of the crime she has participated in committing. She then proposes that she should be admired for her skill in performing this complex train of emotions. Thus both of these "illegitimate" Queens, the usurping

Lady Macbeth and the ambitious actress Sarah Siddons, are asking to be exempt from harsh judgments about their presumptuous behavior—Lady Macbeth for her wrongdoings and Siddons for daring to inhabit a powerful and threatening female persona.

Interestingly, according to Siddons, Lady Macbeth's ultimate demise is the result of the sacrifices that she made for her husband. Her own pain leads her to redirect all of her attentions towards Macbeth. Siddons writes, "Yes; smothering her sufferings in the deepest recesses of her own wretched bosom, we cannot but perceive that she devotes herself entirely to the effort of supporting him" (2: 24). This is not only a transformation from her formerly narcissistic monstrousness, but also a radical departure from the persona of her youth. Siddons suggests to her readers that as a child Lady Macbeth had no boundaries set for her and no limits on her power:

> Let it be here recollected, as some palliation of her former very different deportment, that she had, probably, from childhood commanded all around her with a high hand; had uninterruptedly, perhaps, in that splendid station enjoyed all that wealth, all that nature had to bestow; that she had, possibly, no directors, no controllers, and that in womanhood her fascinated lord had never once opposed her inclinations.
>
> (Siddons, "Remarks," in Campbell 2: 24–25)

In this passage, Siddons sounds very much like a contemporary actress employing a Stanislavski-inspired approach to understanding the inner workings of her character.[21] She creates a past and set of memories for Lady Macbeth which provide her with a psychological narrative and rationale for Lady Macbeth's actions. The description of Lady Macbeth's happiest days, her life in the "splendid station" where she had enjoyed "all that wealth, all that nature had to bestow" and ruled all around her with "no directors" and "no controllers" (not even her "fascinated husband"), are a far cry from what she descends to at the end of the play. As in the beginning of her analysis, Siddons returns to the details of Lady Macbeth's appearance: "Behold her now, with wasted form, with wan and haggard countenance, her starry eyes glazed with the ever-burning fever of remorse, and on their lids the shadow of death" (2: 31).

Both of these tactics, giving Lady Macbeth a past and inviting readers to visualize Lady Macbeth's "wasted form," are similar to strategies used in the portraits of Siddons and Queen Charlotte. In images of the actress and the Queen viewers are asked to equate their visual personas with recognizable models of female identity. Charlotte becomes a dutiful mother and a lovely woman, Siddons becomes an aristocratic fashion plate and a woman who performs for the good of her children. Siddons similarly transforms the ruthless Lady Macbeth into a noble heroine for her audiences with a strategic vision of the role. At the end of the play Lady Macbeth is no longer an unnatural, cruel demon, but a passionate, grief-stricken woman who gave up a life of comfort and glory in order to promote her thankless husband.

In Siddons's analysis, Lady Macbeth self-destructs because, unlike Macbeth, she has had no outlet for her true feelings. Siddons explains, "His heart has therefore been eased, from time to time, by unloading its weight of woe; while she, on the contrary, has perseveringly endured in silence the utter most anguish of a wounded spirit" (2: 32–33). This repression results in her collapse, "her frailer frame, and keener feelings, have now sunk under the struggle—his robust and less sensitive constitution has not only resisted it, but bears him on to deeper wickedness" (2: 33). For Siddons's performance of Lady Macbeth to be effective she must convince audiences that underneath Lady Macbeth's mask of ambition and cruelty lies a fragile feminine body that will ultimately be destroyed, an idea that is implicitly tied to Siddons's own exhausting career as an actress. Given that the "Remarks" were written at the end of Siddons's career after many years of performing Lady Macbeth the document might also be seen as conveying Siddons's subtle musings on the physical and emotional price she paid for her extraordinary fame.[22] The revised version of a domestic and oppressed Lady Macbeth in Siddons's "Remarks" is directly related to her attempts to dissociate her theatrical image from scandal and to mitigate the stigma of her public role as a manipulative and powerful celebrity.

Siddons as "the murder-loving Melpomene"

While several portraits of Siddons as Lady Macbeth worked to convey her noble portrayal of the character to audiences—for example, George Henry Harlow's *Siddons as Lady Macbeth* and Thomas Beach's *John Philip Kemble as Macbeth and Sarah Siddons as Lady Macbeth* (1786)—a less successful painting was William Beechey's *Sarah Siddons with the Emblems of Tragedy* (1793).[23] The portrait displays Siddons turning mischievously towards the viewer, holding a dagger in one hand and the mask of tragedy in the other (Figure 13.3). Fashion historian Aileen Ribeiro remarks that although Siddons wears "the traditional black dress of tragedy," the "pelisse gown with a white frilled collar" and "the white turban, exotic in inspiration" ("Costuming the Part" 116) are unmistakably *au courant* for the 1790s. Siddons is thus dressed "as herself" in a contemporary costume even while holding a theatrical mask and a prop from *Macbeth*.

The critic Anthony Piscine found the image vulgar and inappropriate. Rather than depicting "the murder-loving Melpomene" Beechey had instead created "a gypsey in sattin disporting at a masquerade" (quoted in Ribeiro, "Costuming the Part" 116). What seemed startling and disturbing about this image for eighteenth-century viewers was Siddons's dual role in the portrait: as an actress, and as herself. In other portraits of Siddons as Lady Macbeth, she is clearly in costume, immersed in the character and a specific scene. Similarly, portraits of Siddons "out of character," such as Thomas

Figure 13.3 William Beechey, *Sarah Siddons with the Emblems of Tragedy* (1793). By permission of The National Portrait Gallery.

Gainsborough's painting of Siddons as a grand society lady, do not display visual references to her career as an actress.[24] The natural, effortless, unconscious quality of theatricality that Siddons so carefully strategized and perfected is destroyed in Beechey's painting by her obvious unmasking; a gesture that marks her awareness of her own performances.

The failure of Beechey's portrait (it was never sold and found in his studio after he died) underscores that the key to a positive formulation of celebrity for an actress was to always keep the act of performance hidden.[25] Returning then to the image we began with, it is not surprising that the most enduring portrait of Sarah Siddons, Reynolds's *The Tragic Muse*, portrays the actress as an allegorical Queen—a mythic representation of tragedy floating in the clouds. There she is separated from her "real" self, from the daily negotiations involved in being an actress, from the realities of her body, and from the manipulative tactics of fashioning her celebrity.

For Siddons, "personated Queens"—real and imagined—made it feasible for her to embody an unprecedented form of female celebrity, and to transform one of the most ruthless stage heroines into an exemplar of femininity. Using images of royalty and maternity as models for legitimate forms of theatrical display, both in her characterization of Lady Macbeth and in the building of her own career, made it possible for Siddons not to appear to be too ambitious, too theatrical, or too independent. Ironically, Lady Macbeth's rise and fall remains a perfect paradigm for the paradoxes inherent in society's view of famous women. Contemporary female celebrities, from Hillary Clinton to Madonna, still consistently face the challenge of conquering a public uneasy about women in power. For successful women to be seen as sympathetic they must be simultaneously passive and powerful, domestic and professional, compassionate and driven, divine and ordinary. In the end Lady Macbeth's sleepwalking becomes oddly analogous to the task of every famous woman: to project a natural, passive, and unconscious mode of feminine power that softens the dangerous paradoxes of female ambition, desire, and success.

Notes

1   For more on this event see West (*The Image* 114). West explains that in the first performance of Garrick's Shakespeare Jubilee in 1785, Sarah Siddons was wheeled in as a part of the opening act seated in the pose of *The Tragic Muse*. Similar to her famous role as Shakespeare's Hermione, Siddons poses as she appears in Reynolds's portrait of her, magically coming to life as the painting is enacted on the stage.

2   For more on Siddons's biography and performance history see Manvell; Asleson (*A Passion*).

3   For an analysis of portraits of Siddons as Lady Macbeth see McPherson ("Masculinity").

4   This is the date that Siddons's biographer Roger Manvell provides (120).

5   See McPherson ("Picturing Tragedy"). McPherson sees Siddons's portrayal of Britannia as an example of her status as ideal model for heroic portraiture (419).

6 Felicity Nussbaum demonstrates that issues of maternity and sexuality became an essential factor in the formulation of the British Empire. Eighteenth-century English women were increasingly defined in relation to their maternity and domesticity, which was the opposite of what was believed to have been the unrestrained sexuality of colonized women. Nussbaum explains: "England's national imperative to control women's sexuality and fertility in the eighteenth century is connected to the formation of a national identity coincident with the emergence of its second empire" (96).

7 See also Hibbert (particularly 78, 79; 304–306; 390–92, discussing the King's popularity).

8 Colley notes that although Charlotte was not seen as particularly glamorous, she was "just as important as a totem of morality as her husband was" (268).

9 For more about the legacy of Siddons's portrayal of a variety of Shakespearean heroines see McDonald (1–50).

10 Siddons's reference to "the person of her representative which you have been so long accustomed to contemplate" may refer to the actress Mrs. Pritchard who was known for her portrayal of Lady Macbeth on the London stage between 1744 and 1768. One of Siddons's new additions to the performance of Lady Macbeth was to break with Mrs. Pritchard's tradition of holding the candle in the sleepwalking scene.

11 According to Ribeiro, this type of gown was also known as a "Levite," a name that came from a costume worn by actresses playing the Jewish priestess character in Racine's *Athalie*.

12 In a small miniature of Siddons in the National Portrait Gallery her nose is twice the size, almost to the point of a caricature; most likely Siddons's real nose was somewhere in between these representations.

13 Ribeiro also notes that it would have taken nearly twenty yards of fabric to make this dress.

14 Colley notes that Queen Charlotte "delighted in having her smiling and abundant maternity commemorated in art, often posing with books on child care in her hands or on her dressing table" (268).

15 Asleson argues that Siddons's role as Isabella in Thomas Southerne's play *Isabella* is connected to the late eighteenth-century cult of sensibility. Asleson adds: "Of the numerous representations of Siddons as Isabella that appeared between 1782 and 1785, several focused on a private interview between the mourning mother and son—one of the most emotionally wrenching scenes in the play" ("Crafting" 53; for a reproduction of Hamilton's portrait of Siddons as Isabella, see 54).

16 Apparently Siddons's moving performance as Isabella affected her own young son, who played opposite her in several performances. The *Morning Post* of October 10, 1782 reports: "Mrs. Siddons of Drury Lane Theatre, has a lovely little boy about eight years old. Yesterday in the rehearsal of the 'Fatal Marriage' the boy, observing his mother in the agonies of the dying scene, took the fiction for reality, and burst into a flood of tears, a circumstance which struck the feelings of the company in a singular manner" (quoted in Matthews and Hutton 37). Just as Siddons's child was unable to distinguish between his real mother and the part his mother was playing, the boundaries between art and life are similarly complicated by the image in Hamilton's painting.

17 Siddons was not shy about bringing her children on stage with her, a marketing technique that reminded audiences that she was earning a living on stage for her family. Although she was famous for this role, she also became sick of it. In a letter to Viscountess Percival on November 24, 1795, Siddons writes: "I am now acting in a grand Pantomime calld Alexander the Great in which I have a very bad part and a very fine dress. Will go it several nights I suppose: well, anything is better than saying Isabella over and over again until one is so tired" (Siddons's

Correspondence, Harvard Theater Collection). Traces of Siddons's frustration and exhaustion are not evident in her portraits, which instead suggest that her life on stage mirrors her activities off stage.

18 For an excellent chronology of Siddons's performances and events in her life and career see Asleson (*A Passion* xiv–xv).

19 Although Siddons's career was not entirely free from criticism—she was accused of being greedy, masculine, and overly ambitious—she always seemed to recover her lofty reputation. Five thousand mourners lined the streets of London for her funeral procession. Other actresses, such as Mary Robinson, Mary Wells, and Dorothy Jordan, were less fortunate. Despite liaisons with wealthy and powerful men (the Prince of Wales, the journalist and officer Edward Topham, and the Duke of Clarence), these actresses died penniless and alone. Robinson's and Wells's association with extra-marital affairs and scandal certainly contributed to their demise in the public sphere. For more on the details of the lives and careers of Robinson, Wells, and Jordan, see Highfill et al.; and also for Dorothy Jordan, see Tomalin.

20 For more on Siddons acting while pregnant see Laura Rosenthal's excellent essay.

21 For more on the connections among contemporary theories of acting and performance practices in the eighteenth century see Roach.

22 In her letters Siddons often complained of fatigue and depression. In a letter to Miss Wynn on Monday, October 8, 1787, Siddons writes: "I am almost dead of Belvidera, as done in every limb as if I had been severely beaten." And on Sunday, July 26, 1789, "I am to play Rosalind for them next Wednesday—I hope to be in better spirits then I am this day which has been spent in weeping" (Siddons's Correspondence, Harvard Theater Collection).

23 For reproductions of these portraits see Asleson (*A Passion* 11, 12).

24 For more on images of Siddons as "herself" see West ("The Public and Private Roles").

25 For a history of the Beechey portrait see Roberts (45).

Works cited

Asleson, Robyn. *A Passion for Performance: Sarah Siddons and her Portraitists*. Los Angeles: The Paul J. Getty Museum, 1999.

——— " 'She was Tragedy Personified': Crafting the Siddons Legend in Art and Life." *A Passion for Performance: Sarah Siddons and her portraitists*. Ed. Robyn Asleson. Los Angeles: The Paul J. Getty Museum, 1999. 41–56.

Bate, Jonathan, ed. *The Romantics on Shakespeare*. London: Penguin, 1992.

Boaden, James. *Memoirs of Mrs. Siddons Interspersed with Anecdotes of Authors and Actors*. London: Henry Colburn, 1827.

Burroughs, Catherine R. *Closet Stages: Joanna Baillie and the Theater Theory of British Romantic Women Writers*. Philadelphia: U of Pennsylvania P, 1997.

Campbell, Thomas. *Life of Mrs. Siddons*. 2 vols. London: Effingham Wilson, 1834.

Colley, Linda. *Britons: Forging the Nation 1707–1837*. New Haven: Yale UP, 1992.

Gainsborough and Reynolds: Contrasts in Royal Patronage. London: The Queen's Gallery, Buckingham Palace, 1994.

Hazlitt, William. *The Complete Works of William Hazlitt*. Ed. P.P. Howe. 21 vols. London: J.M. Dent and Sons, 1930.

Hibbert, Christopher. *George III*. New York: Basic Books, 1998.

Highfill, Phillip Jr., Kalman Burnim, and Edward Langhans. *A Biographical Dictionary of Actors, Actresses, Musicians, Dancers, Managers and other Stage Personnel in London 1660–1800*. Carbondale: Southern Illinois UP, 1991.

Kliman, Bernice W. *Shakespeare in Performance:* Macbeth. 2nd ed. Manchester and New York: Manchester UP, 2004.

Manvell, Roger. *Sarah Siddons: Portrait of an Actress*. London: Heinemann, 1970.

Matthews, Brander and Laurence Hutton, eds. *The Kembles and their Contemporaries*. Boston: L.C. Page, 1886.

McDonald, Russ. *Look to the Lady: Sarah Siddons, Ellen Terry, and Judy Dench on the Shakespearean Stage*. Athens: U of Georgia P, 2005.

McPherson, Heather. "Masculinity, Femininity and The Tragic Sublime: Reinventing Lady Macbeth." *Studies in Eighteenth-Century Culture* 29. Ed. Timothy Irwin and Ouinda Mostefai. Baltimore: Johns Hopkins UP, 2000.

—— "Picturing Tragedy: Mrs. Siddons as the Tragic Muse Revisited." *Eighteenth-Century Studies* 33.3 (2000): 401–30.

Mrs. Siddons' Departure from the Stage. The Portfolio 3rd Series, vol. 1 (January 1813). Siddons's Papers. Harvard Theater Collection, Cambridge, Massachusetts.

Nussbaum, Felicity A. *Torrid Zones: Maternity, Sexuality, and Empire in Eighteenth-Century Narratives*. Baltimore: Johns Hopkins UP, 1995.

Pascoe, Judith. *Romantic Theatricality: Gender, Poetry, and Spectatorship*. Ithaca: Cornell UP, 1997.

Ribeiro, Aileen. *The Art of Dress: Fashion in England and France 1750–1820*. New Haven: Yale UP, 1995.

—— "Costuming the Part: A Discourse on Fashion and Fiction in the Images of Actresses in England, 1776–1812." *Notorious Muse: The Actress in British Art and Culture 1776–1812*. Ed. Robyn Asleson. New Haven: The Paul Mellon Centre for British Art with Yale UP, 2003.

Roach, Joseph R. *The Player's Passion: Studies in the Science of Acting*. Ann Arbor: U of Michigan P, 1993.

Roberts, William. *Sir William Beechey, R.A.* London: Duckworth, 1907.

Rosenthal, Laura. "The Sublime, the Beautiful, the Siddons." *The Clothes that Wear Us*. Ed. Jessica Munns and Penny Richards. Newark: U of Delaware P, 2003. 56–79.

Shakespeare, William. *Macbeth*. Ed. G. Blakemore Evans and J.J. Tobin. *The Riverside Shakespeare*. 2nd ed. Boston: Houghton Mifflin, 1997.

Siddons, Sarah. *The Reminiscences of Sarah Kemble Siddons 1773–1785*. Ed. William Van Lennep. Cambridge: Widener Library, 1942.

Straub, Kristina. *Sexual Suspects: Eighteenth-Century Players and Sexual Ideology*. Princeton: Princeton UP, 1992.

Tomalin, Claire. *Mrs. Jordan's Profession: The Actress and the Prince*. New York: Knopf, 1991.

West, Shearer. "The Public and Private Roles of Sarah Siddons." *A Passion For Performance: Sarah Siddons and her Portraitists*. Ed. Robyn Asleson. Los Angeles: The Paul J. Getty Museum, 1999. 1–39.

—— *The Image of the Actor: Verbal and Visual Representation in the Age of Garrick and Kemble*. New York: St. Martin's, 1991.

Whitley, William T. *Thomas Gainsborough*. London: Smith, Elder, 1915.

14 Politicizing *Macbeth* on U.S. stages

Garson's *MacBird!* and Greenland's *Jungle Rot*

Stephen M. Buhler

There may be no one play that can be characterized as the definitive Shakespearean text for the American experience, but a select few have made their presence felt throughout the history of the United States. Early on, *Richard III* and *Othello* were most frequently presented (Sturgess 16–17, 56–57); the relatively unproblematic depiction—at least in stage versions—of a tyrant's rise and fall and the profoundly problematic consideration of blackness in the midst of white culture understandably connected with the issues at work in the nation's political and economic founding. In time, however, *Hamlet* and *Julius Caesar* figured prominently on stage and through references in public discourse. Charles H. Shattuck has commented on the enduring popularity of both plays, captured vividly in the partnership of Edwin Booth and Lawrence Barrett in the late nineteenth century (2: 31–48); the acclaim, of course, was mingled with notoriety, since Edwin's brother John Wilkes Booth had been President Abraham Lincoln's assassin in 1865, casting himself in the role of a tyrannicide such as Shakespeare's Brutus (Furtwangler 97–100). Late twentieth-century political references regularly return to Hamlet. George Shultz, Secretary of State for President Ronald Reagan, has repeatedly insisted that the United States should not become "the Hamlet of nations," keeping itself from decisive action by undue concern for consequences (Shultz A25; see also Cartelli 99). Not long after the time that Shultz first drew this analogy, filmmaker Oliver Stone proclaimed the United States a nation of Hamlets in his film *J.F.K.*, as his cinematic rendering of conspiracy theorist Jim Garrison equates America with the Prince of Denmark seeking to solve the mystery of Old Hamlet's death: "We have all become Hamlets in our own country, children of a slain father-leader whose killers still possess the throne" (quoted in Steel 32).

Both *Julius Caesar* and *Hamlet* center on political assassination; so does a third, perennially troubling and inspiring candidate for the "American Shakespeare," *Macbeth*, which has itself figured in the processes of self-fashioning an identity for the United States. *Macbeth* was specially adapted by two late twentieth-century playwrights to address specific political crises. What attracted the writers was not only the topical pertinence of the subject matter, although their plays do react to recent assassinations, but the writers were also drawn to the play's and Shakespeare's more general resonances in American political culture. This chapter will consider in detail the impact of Shakespearean adaptation in the ideas advanced and explored by Barbara Garson in her 1966–1967 play *MacBird!* and by Seth Greenland in his 1995–1997 play *Jungle Rot.* These plays each consider the significance of an actual assassination—that of John F. Kennedy in 1963 and that of Patrice Lumumba in 1960—in shaping national policy and expressing national values.

Shakespeare's *Macbeth* was itself produced in the highly charged political context of James's first years as the English king. As Jonathan Bate has documented (61–104), the political significances of Shakespeare's plays were regularly transformed and increased throughout their performance histories in England; Kim C. Sturgess makes it clear that this continued in the nascent United States (57–70). Rival performances of *Macbeth* in nineteenth-century New York City would lead to bloodshed and death in the context of establishing a separate national identity. When the famed English actor-manager William Charles Macready dared to stage a production of the play in competition with the equally famed American actor-manager Edwin Forrest, Nativist fervor erupted into violent protest, which was violently suppressed by the military. At least thirty-one people died and over one hundred were injured in the Astor Place riot on the night of May 10, 1849 (Shattuck 1: 82–85). Macready was seen as the embodiment of aristocratic elitism and foreign dominance; Forrest as the champion of American "independence" and the rights of "Workingmen! [and] Freemen!!" (Shattuck 1: 80, 83; Sturgess 41–42).[1] In this context, it may seem uncanny that *Macbeth* may well have been Abraham Lincoln's favorite among Shakespeare's plays.[2]

After the assassination of President John F. Kennedy, much was made of alleged parallels between his death and that of Lincoln. Political activist and writer Barbara Garson, however, was struck instead by the possible significance of inexact parallels between the assassinations of Kennedy and of King Duncan in *Macbeth.* Garson claims the play began as a "slip of the tongue": during an antiwar speech given at Berkeley in August 1965, she "quite accidentally referred to the First Lady of the United States as Lady MacBird Johnson" (Garson ix). From there, Garson planned simply on writing a skit based on Shakespeare's *Macbeth,* but the project quickly grew to a full-length play, *MacBird!,* which was published throughout its various stages of revision and which had its first professional theater production, off-Broadway, in early 1967. The actors at the Village Gate theater in New York City included Stacy Keach in the title role, along with Cleavon Little, William Devane (who would later specialize in portraying Kennedys or Kennedyesque figures), and Rue McClanahan as Lady MacBird. On the page and on the stage, *MacBird!* was an unqualified, if outrageously controversial, success: Robert Brustein optimistically declared that the play "helps to destroy anxieties merely by making our nightmares tangible and manifest" (30); Dwight

Macdonald praised Garson's "adaptation of the Shakespearean material, the joke always depending on deftly using the familiar old lines to comment on the actual current situation" (12).

Garson's skill in adaptation and her additional interest in situating Macbeth within the Shakespearean canon as well as the contemporary context are evident from the beginning of *MacBird!*, as the Prologue borrows from *Henry V* in its general outline and from *Hamlet* in significant details:

> Oh, don't employ your own imaginations
> To piece out imperfections in our plot.
> For things that seem, I beg you, know no seeming;
> Your very lack of thoughts must cloak our kings.
>   (Garson 2; cf. *Henry V* Prologue, 23, 28)[3]

Garson strategically acknowledges that the parallel between recent events in American history and the story presented by Shakespeare in Macbeth is less than exact. She does not take seriously—although not a few Americans did—the theory that Lyndon Johnson was complicit or directly involved in the assassination of President John F. Kennedy; there are therefore "imperfections" in the plot of her drama and in the plotting that the drama depicts. Having made the point through her middle-class Everyman chorus, "dressed in standard business attire" (1), Garson invokes conspiratorial thinking immediately by echoing *Hamlet*. When Gertrude asks Hamlet why his father's death "seems so particular" with him, the Prince explodes: "I know not 'seems'" (1.2.76). To introduce a paraphrase of one of Hamlet's earliest expressions of doubt about the demise of the previous ruler—his suspicion that there was something particular about how Old Hamlet left his throne, his marriage, and this world—simply invites similar questions about the American Presidency in the middle 1960s. So, too, does the larger political comment that a lack of public inquiry provides necessary cover for the current regime: "lack of thoughts must cloak our kings."

Macbeth, as the source play proper, comes into sharper focus with the appearance of the Three Witches, who playfully embody American anxieties over "the specter of Communism" (in Marx and Engel's famous phrase) as they represent three aspects of the American Left in the middle of the twentieth century: a "student demonstrator, beatnik stereotype," a Black Muslim, and an old-school labor organizer, "wearing a worker's cap and overalls." Their identities and allegiances are confirmed by their speech, as the Black Muslim calls out "I come, soul brothers!" in a parody of the Second Witch's address to her familiar, Graymalkin, while the Wobbly announces that "Comrades call!," rather than "Paddock calls" (1; cf. *Macbeth* 1.1.1–9). In the next scene, Garson's First Witch will recount what occurred at an unsuccessful antiwar demonstration, the Second Witch will exult over inner-city riots and looting: "A joyful throng comes pouring out of doors/ A brick in either hand—they're going shoppin' " (7). The Third Witch offers both praise and admonition in lines indebted, yet again, to *Hamlet*. This time, however, the speaker imitated is Polonius:

> Young witch, it's time you learned these lasting lessons.
> Be thou militant but by no means adventurist.
> The working class and their objective interests
> Grapple to our cause with hoops of steel . . .
> Neither a burrower from within nor a leader be,
> But stone by stone construct a conscious cadre.
> And this above all—to thine own class be true
> And it must follow, as the very next depression,
> Thou canst not then be false to revolution.
> (8; cf. *Hamlet* 1.3.61–80)

Divisions among dissenting groups are important satiric targets for Garson, even as her sharpest wit and criticism are aimed at the policies that inspired dissent. An unintentionally haunting aspect of the first scene is its setting, which is a "Hotel corridor at [the] Democratic convention" (3) that took place in Los Angeles, California, in 1960; the real-life events that would ultimately overshadow Garson's text are themselves foreshadowed by this suggestion of the site of Robert Kennedy's assassination in 1968, in a hotel corridor after a political rally, also in Los Angeles.

When we first meet Robert in the play, he is enough of a politician to be deeply distrustful of MacBird, the character based on Lyndon Johnson. In a scene parodying the machinations that led to Johnson being nominated as John Kennedy's running mate, Robert borrows from Caesar's assessment of the spare, ambitious Cassius: "He has a fat, yet hungry look. Such men are dangerous" (5; cf. *Julius Caesar* 1.2.194–95). John, however, is convinced that MacBird presents no threat to a Ken O'Dunc—the name blends together Kennedy and Duncan—dynasty, shifting the Shakespearean intertext to *Richard II* and John of Gaunt's paean to England, now remade in the image of the United States as superpower.

> His [MacBird's] name will just stand second on the ticket.
> You, Bob, are still the second in succession.
> And Ted is next . . . and princes yet unborn . . .
> And for this land, this crownéd continent,
> This earth of majesty, this seat of Mars,
> This forceful breed of men, this mighty world,
> I see a . . . *New Frontier* beyond her seas.
> She shall o'erflow her shores and burst her banks,
> Eastward extend till East does meet with West,
> And West until the West does touch the East
> And o'er this hot and plaguéd earth descend

> The Pox Americana, a sweet haze,
> Shelt'ring all the world in its deep shade.
>   (5–6; cf. *Richard II* 2.1.40–66)

Garson's facility with blank verse and with adroit quotation from Shake-speare (note her glance at the "[states] unborn and accents yet unknown" in which the assassination of Julius Caesar will be enacted [3.1.111–13]) only serve to strengthen her topical commentary, especially the anxiety over various "hot spots" and "hotbeds of unrest" abroad and at home exhibited by several American administrations. MacBird himself is less than thrilled by his encounter with "a nigra and a filthy beatnik" accompanied, as his Crony observes, by "a bum done up in worker's duds" (7). It is striking how little Johnson's often strenuous efforts on behalf of Civil Rights softened his critics' animus toward him. Here, though, MacBird listens to his critics, who offer him a glimpse of future power: Garson's Witches prophesy that MacBird will first be Vice-President of the United States and then President.

That promise seems a remote possibility in light of the Ken O'Dunc clan's dismissiveness toward their political ally. As soon as MacBird accepts the offer to run for Vice-President, John Ken O'Dunc verbally anoints his younger brother as heir:

> All you who are nearest to us, know
> We will establish our estate upon
> The eldest, Robert, whom we now do name
> The Lord of Laws, henceforth our closest counsel.
> In all affairs of state we are as one.
> To him entrust your thoughts as though to me.
>   (15; cf. *Macbeth* 1.4.37–42)

The intertextual play with Duncan's investiture of his son Malcolm is espe-cially rich. The combination of John's dynastic obsessions and Robert's personal arrogance, coupled with the vision of the future granted by the Witches, goads MacBird into inviting John Ken O'Dunc to Texas and his doom. Unlike Duncan, who promises "signs of nobleness" for "all deservers" (41–42), Ken O'Dunc reserves all authority for himself and his brother. Like Macbeth, MacBird is already deep in contemplation of whatever is needful to achieve the promised goal:

> This Lord of Laws be blasted, there's the rub
> For in my way it lies. Stars, hide thy fires.
> Let no light see my black and deep desires.
>   (18; cf. *Macbeth* 1.4.50–51)

Intriguingly, the echo of Hamlet's most famous soliloquy ("ay, there's the rub" [3.1.64]) here works against the play's conventional association—which will culminate in a scathing sendup of Adlai Stevenson—of the Prince with indecision. (This is the understanding of the character of Hamlet reflected in George Shultz's phrase, noted above.) The anger at John's imperial vision of a coronation, not an inauguration, and at Robert's current power as Attorney General (the "Lord of Laws") as well as his future power as heir apparent seems to allow for no uncertainty.

But uncertainty returns, thanks to Garson's Shakespearean source. Garson presents Lady MacBird as a Lady Macbeth figure—making it clear that the play's title derives from the nickname of 'Lady Bird' Johnson. When her husband balks at considering any further the death of John Ken O'Dunc, Lady MacBird responds to his direct quotation from Macbeth with a simple, chilling yet hilarious assertion that flawlessly continues the blank verse.

MacBird:
    I dare do all that may become a man.
    Who dares do more is none.
Lady MacBird:
                        I'm not a man.
    I am a lady and a Southern hostess.
                (22; cf. 1.7.46–48)

Along the way, Garson comments on sexual politics in 1960s America, pitting the stereotypically domineering strength of a matriarch from the South against the calculated hypermasculinity of John Ken O'Dunc, whose Aide earlier refers to "A psychosexual index of the symbols/ We use in predetermining his image" (16).

The coronation scene subtly feeds conspiratorial thinking in two ways. It does so, first, by having the Earl of Warren—based, of course, on Chief Justice of the Supreme Court Earl Warren—comment on his crowning of "the realm's elect anointed head" (23). The real Warren had been asked to lead the commission that investigated the circumstances surrounding John Kennedy's assassination; Garson's play goes on to articulate profound doubt about that investigation. Second, the Earl of Warren sounds uncannily like one of the conspirators plotting against the life of another Shakespearean monarch, Henry V. Garson's Earl declares that "Never was monarch better feared or loved/ Than this majesty" (23) which closely follows the protestations of Richard, Earl of Cambridge, before his involvement in the plot against King Henry is revealed (*Henry V* 2.2.25–26). After John Ken O'Dunc delivers an abbreviated and versified version of John Kennedy's Inaugural Address ("Ask now how you can profit off your country/ But ask what you can give to serve the state," 25), MacBird assumes the identity of a later Richard in the Yorkist camp, the future Richard III:

This here is[4] the winter of our discontent,
Made odious by that son of . . .

> [the Crony completes the sentence with a simple "Yeah"]
> Now do our princelings pipe in tenor tones,
> Our bass-voiced elder statesmen cast aside,
> Our ancient counselors yield to college pups . . .
> But I am not cut out for merry meetings,
> For fancy foods and poetry and lutes.
> I am stamped out in stern and solid shape,
> And thank the lord I lack the frippery
> To sport and blithely laugh in foreign tongues
> While lightly touching on affairs of state
> At fox hunts, polo parties, garden teas.
>> (25–26; cf. *Richard III* 1.1.1–31 and also
>> 2.1.73, "I thank my God for my humility.")

While the intergenerational rivalry recalls that of Antony against Octavius in *Antony and Cleopatra*, Garson also suggests more than a hint of class-based resentment against the Kennedy family's successful appropriation of the trappings of New England privilege (despite the questionable sources of the fortune amassed by its paterfamilias Joseph Kennedy). This resentment, along with Lady MacBird's encouragement, strengthens MacBird's resolve to strike down the new president and to take his place.

The play's version of the assassination borrows heavily from news accounts and reenactments of Kennedy's actual assassination in Dallas, Texas, on November 22, 1963. Garson's stage directions call for a backdrop depicting "a six-story building toward the left, a grassy hill and a railroad overpass toward the right" and, just after a shot is heard, for a projector to show "an X in a sixth-floor window of the building" with "trajectory lines" extending from it. After MacBird himself, rather than a Jack Ruby figure, dispatches with the individual suspected of the crime, the surviving Ken O'Dunc brothers find the resolution far too convenient. Even the notably dim Ted can figure things out, almost quoting Marcellus in *Hamlet*: "There's something rotten in the State of—" (37; cf. 1.4.90). Before he can specify whether he means the state of Denmark or the State of Texas, Lady MacBird faints, calling attention away from the brothers. Act 1 of *MacBird!* ends with its title character calling for order and trust: "Good countrymen, this madness must abate./ Be calm, my friends, I speak as head of state" (37).

In contrast to such decisive words, the beginning of Act 2 offers the indecisive musings of the Egg of Head, Lord Stevenson. This devastating portrait of Adlai Stevenson draws heavily from *Hamlet*, as first the "Great Egg" conflates Ophelia's grief over the Prince's insanity with Macbeth's own description of the slain Duncan:

> Oh, what a noble mind was here brought down!
> The statesmen's, soldier's, scholar's eye, tongue, sword,
> The expectancy and rose of this fair state,

The glass of fashion and the mold of form . . .
And I, of statesmen most deject and wretched,
That sucked the honey of his many vows,
Now see that noble and most sovereign leader,
His silver skin laced with his own bright blood,
That unmatched form and feature of grown youth,
Blasted with a rifle! Woe is me!
To see what I have seen; see what I see!
     (40–41; cf. *Hamlet* 3.1.150–61 and *Macbeth* 2.3.112)

The Egg of Head is then invited by Robert to see the reality of John's demise and the nature of MacBird's regime. Playwright Garson continues to rely on the conventional reading of Hamlet's character as avoiding or deferring action to inform our response to Stevenson's reply:

To see, or not to see? That is the question.
Whether 'tis wiser as a statesman to ignore
The gross deception of outrageous liars,
Or to speak out against a reign of evil
And by so doing, end there for all time
The chance and hope to work within for change.
To work within the framework, there's the rub . . .
In speaking out one loses influence.
The chance for change by pleas and prayers is gone.
The chance to modify the devil's deeds
As critic from within is still my hope.
To quit the club! Be outside looking in!
This outsideness, this unfamiliar land
From which few travelers ever get back in—
It puzzles mind, it paralyzes will,
And makes us rather bear those ills we have
Than fly to others that we know not of.
Security makes cowards of us all.
     (41–43; cf. *Hamlet* 3.1.55–82)

Scholar Tom Blackburn, in a recent study of *MacBird!*, notes how Garson indicts several individuals "in the liberal Democratic ranks" for being either "equally corrupt" with Johnson and the Kennedys or else "easily manipulated" (141). What makes the Egg of Head susceptible to manipulation is his fear that being left outside the sphere of influence is "something worse than death" (42). As a result, he moderates or suppresses—self-censors—the critiques he might have delivered. Robert Brustein was surely correct, in his review of the 1967 stage production, to note that "Garson reserves her satiric spleen not so much for certain personalities in American political life as for a system of government within which it has become impossible to act with honor" (31); even so, there is sense of almost personal betrayal in her indict-ment of Stevenson. The rueful savagery of the satire here recalls Pope's assault on Joseph Addison as "Atticus" in his *Epistle to Dr. Arbuthnot*.

Robert Ken O'Dunc, in response, assumes another Shakespearean role, that of Cassius in *Hamlet*, urging Brutus to strike a blow against tyranny. Robert dismisses MacBird as

> *Your* President perhaps, but for myself
> I had as lief not be alive as be
> In awe of such a thing as that . . .
> I was born free as he and so were you.
> We both have come as close to being chief.
> MacBird! MacBird! *(In a crowlike call.)* What coarseness in
> that sound . . .
> The fault, dear Egg, is never in our stars
> But in ourselves that we are underlings.
> (43; cf. *Julius Caesar* 1.2.94–97, 140–41)

But by assigning Stevenson the role of Brutus, the Egg of Head can again take refuge in readings of Shakespeare that were standard during the mid-twentieth century. Brutus, like Hamlet, was seen as a well-meaning reformer, an ineffectual liberal, unable to confront political realities with the necessary forcefulness advised by Cassius and ultimately demonstrated by Mark Antony and Octavius after the death of Julius Caesar. The Egg of Head admits as much to Robert: "I know you think I'm acting like a toad/ But still I choose the middle of the road" (44).

Not every one in the body politic is as willing as the play's Stevenson to suppress his or her own suspicions. Enough rumblings arise to cause the new President concern. MacBird confides to the Earl of Warren that he would "like a full investigation,/ Conducted by a man a such repute/ That we may put an end to all these doubts" and that Warren is the only man to do it (48). The Earl responds with another approximate echo of Hamlet: "Oh, cursed spite/ That ever I was born to set things right" (see *Hamlet* 1.5.188–89). When MacBird assures Warren that he isn't being "asked to set things *right*" but rather to quell dissent, the Earl offers a variation on the Danish theme: "Oh, whine and pout,/ That ever I was born to bury doubt" (48). Garson again uses *Hamlet* to mark a satirical target as accommodative, as insufficiently principled. Just before acceding to the President's request, Warren strikes another pose that recalls the popular conception of the Prince of Denmark: "This tragic ambiguity makes me hesitant" (49).

Although the play's language frequently visits *Hamlet*, its structure is firmly grounded in the plot of *Macbeth*. Here the usurper employs federal initiatives, rather than favoritism, to sustain his hold on power: Johnson's wide-ranging package of programs dubbed the Great Society is here trans-formed into the Smooth Society, an attempt to buy compliance. Macbeth's reliance on fear to keep his followers in line survives, however: comparing the United States to a "garden carefully pruned" (with a nod to the Gardener's political allegory in Act 3, Scene 4 of *Richard II*), MacBird threatens to "lop off any branch that looks too tall,/ That seems to grow too lofty or too fast" (54). The language of the garden leads almost directly to Lady MacBird's entrance, uttering "Out, out damned odor, out!" (57; cf. Macbeth 5.1.35) and strewing flowers in the manner of the mad Ophelia. Lady Bird Johnson's Beautification and Conservation campaigns, which sought to minimize and ameliorate the aesthetic damage done by development and roads to the nation's countryside, becomes yet another cover-up:

> Flowers by the roadside . . . plant these flowers . . .
> Let all the land be lined with living blooms.
> Yet all the petals of the summer's roses
> Can never sweeten this accursed land.
> (58; cf. *Macbeth* 5.1.50–51)

Where Lady Macbeth remains concerned about the marks of guilt on her own "little hand," Lady MacBird recognizes the stains on the entire nation. Despite his wife's despair at hiding the guilt they share, MacBird decrees that the beautification program begin.

What leads MacBird to the world-weariness he ultimately shares with Macbeth is Vietnam. After Mac Namara—based on Secretary of Defense Robert McNamara, whom Johnson retained from the Kennedy administration, and a character whose name suits the source text almost too well— informs the President of problems with the "war in Viet Land," MacBird's resolve begins to weaken: "I git to be a-weary o' this show/ And wish my country didn't need me so" (59; cf. *Macbeth* 5.5.48–49). Perhaps sensing this weakness, Robert—now "Bobby"—convenes a group of conspirators in a manner that recalls the council at Brutus's house in *Julius Caesar* as well as the convocation of Scottish exiles in *Macbeth*. The discussion touches on such current events in 1966 as Senator Wayne Morse's brave questioning of the conflict in Vietnam and Adlai Stevenson's sudden death, which Garson's characters do not hesitate to suggest was suspicious. Before learning of the Egg of Head's death, the Wayne of Morse bitterly criticizes him in the same language with which Hamlet excoriates himself:

> Oh, what a rogue and peasant slave is he!
> Is it not monstrous how he bows and begs?
> He lives but in a fiction, in a dream,
> Wherein he plays the hero. But awake,
> A dull and muddy-mettled fellow he.
> (66–67; cf. *Hamlet* 2.2.550–52, 567–68)

Morse also describes Vietnam in terms borrowed from *Hamlet*: the conflict is a "carnal, bloody, and unnatural act" marked by "accidental bombing, casual slaughters" (69; cf. Horatio's account in 5.2.381–82). After Morse leaves—"I'm off to fight the war," he proclaims with delicious ambiguity—the play shows Robert deciding to make use of Morse and the antiwar sentiment he cultivates in order to bring MacBird down. Act 3 opens with MacBird's office beset by demonstrators; he attempts to dismiss them as treasonous, but Lady MacBird visits him with a vision, drawn from an actual incident, of a Buddhist monk setting himself ablaze in opposition to the war (Jones 268–69).

The Witches catalog these events in their next scene. The Beatnik recounts the confrontations at Berkeley, California, over free speech; the Black Muslim describes the violence visited on those calling for civil rights and racial equality; the Worker offers a vision of the horrors of war. Amid all this, MacBird enters, observed by Robert Ken O'Dunc. Once MacBird receives his false assurances of security and success, Robert asks the Witches what real news they have for him. The Third Witch, speaking in the tones of Old Hamlet, seeks to shock Robert with the truth of John's death: "List, list, oh, list!/ The serpent that did sting thy brother's life/ Now wears his crown!" (83; cf. *Hamlet* 1.5.22, 39–40). Robert is notably unimpressed and is insistent that he is "no prince Hamlet, nor was meant to be" (83). The line recalls the famous passage in T.S. Eliot's "The Love Song of J. Alfred Prufrock" (esp. 111), but the meaning is deliciously subverted. Prufrock, arguably, invokes Hamlet to suggest that he will never stop considering potential outcomes and act; Robert does so to announce that he has never hesitated, never second-guessed himself, never shrunk from action. But he then proceeds to act like Hamlet, enlisting the aid of the Witches as the Prince recruited the visiting Players to perform *The Mousetrap*. What results is a minstrel show version of the banquet haunted by Banquo in *Macbeth*, as the Witches contrast the nation's ongoing grief for the late John Ken O' Dunc with the alleged happiness of the one person who could gain by that death: "de Macky Bird am singing/ Happy as the day is long" (95). After the song, MacBird "sees the figure of Ken O' Dunc" in the person of Robert and reacts as Macbeth does at Banquo's ghost. Robert eventually reveals himself and, to the accompanying strains of music from the film *High Noon*, challenges the President to a showdown: "Mark me, MacBird. Tomorrow we shall meet./ And damned be he that first cries out 'retreat' " (96).

By having Robert visit the Witches and co-opt their vatic authority, Garson has already suggested that the regime which will replace that of her Macbeth figure is not substantially different from the tyrant's own. Robert's appropriation of Macbeth's famous last line—"And damned be he that first cries 'Hold, enough!' " (5.8.34)—makes the suggestion yet clearer. Such an interpretation of Shakespeare's text would be realized for the screen by Roman Polanski later in the decade: Polanski's film concludes with the image of Donalbain, the resentful younger brother to the rightful successor, entering the Witches' cave (Buhler 88). In his essay "*MacBird!* and *Macbeth*,"

Blackburn wonders whether "Garson's imagined cycle of endless corruption and disloyalty indeed mirror[s] a countertext in *Macbeth*?" (143); directors like Polanski would find evidence of such a cycle within their purposefully revisionist takes on the Shakespearean play text. Garson's play concludes with as bitter a critique of the entire Kennedy clan as it has offered of Lyndon Johnson. As Macbeth takes solace in the prophecy that no "one of woman born" (*Macbeth* 5.8.13) is a threat to him, MacBird continues to place credence in his Witches' assurance that "No man with beating heart or human blood/ Shall ever harm MacBird or touch his throne" (81). When he and Robert confront each other on the convention floor, MacBird is informed that any one of the Kennedys—the anti-Hamlets from shortly after birth—could bring him down. Robert informs him that

> At each male birth, my father in his wisdom
> Prepared his sons for their envisaged greatness . . .
> To free his sons from paralyzing scruples
> And temper us for roles of world authority
> Our pulpy human hearts were cut away.
> And in their place, precision apparatus
> Of steel and plastic tubing was inserted.
> The sticky, humid blood was drained and then
> A tepid antiseptic brine injected. . . .
> And so, MacBird, that very man you fear,
> Your heartless, bloodless foe now lifts his spear. (107)

The fatal blow is never delivered, however. MacBird instead dies of coronary failure, but not before he appropriates yet another line from *Hamlet*: "There cracks a noble heart!" (107; cf. Horatio in 5.2.359). With his adversary dead, Robert appropriates MacBird's tactics and policies. He promises the delegates that he will find out whoever is responsible for their fallen leader's death: "The plotters of his downfall, now obscure,/ I vow to bring to light, to bring to trial" (108). Further, he will "follow my great predecessor's path/ In hewing out the Smooth Society"; the play ends with the image of banners bearing the names of MacBird and Robert (or "Bobby" in Lisa Lyons's illustration, which appears in the Grove edition of the script) waving in the breeze "side by side" (109).

History would overtake Garson's satiric vision. Before the next Democratic convention in 1968, Lyndon Johnson would withdraw his name from consideration, and Robert Kennedy would campaign hard as an alternative both to Hubert Humphrey—Johnson's Vice-President and designated successor— and to Senator Eugene McCarthy, the more ardent antiwar candidate. Robert also ran effectively as a bearer of the Kennedy mystique, which would make his assassination (by a Jordanian immigrant distraught over the candidate's position on Israel and the Palestinians) all the more haunting. On the night of the shooting, June 4, 1968, Robert Kennedy had just won the California primary and was well on his way toward winning his party's nomination; he died two days later, from the results of the head wound caused by the gunman's bullets (Palermo 245–49). In the aftermath of the assassination, productions of *MacBird!* across the nation were cancelled.[5]

Seth Greenland would nevertheless follow Garson's lead by using *Macbeth* as a basis for critiquing American culture during the 1990s. In his play *Jungle Rot*, Greenland specifically addresses problematic aspects of American foreign policy. Although set in the Congo (known for some time as Zaire) in 1960, his play *Jungle Rot* also comments on persistent efforts by U.S. officials to shape the political destinies of other nations. In its first production, at the Cleveland Play House in 1995, *Jungle Rot* could draw upon fresh memories of Iran-Contra in the previous decade and upon the perennial outrage inspired by the knowledge that the Central Intelligence Agency of the U.S. had plotted the assassination of Patrice Lumumba, the newly independent nation's first prime minister.[6]

In exploring the realpolitik of assassination, Greenland enters into dialogue not only with Garson's engagement with Shakespeare, but also with Orson Welles's "Voodoo" *Macbeth* production of 1936. At the invitation of John Houseman, Welles directed a Federal Theatre Project staging of Shakespeare for the Works Progress Administration at a Harlem theater, with an all-black company (France 56–58). Welles chose to set his production of *Macbeth* in nineteenth-century Haiti, drawing parallels between and among early black independence movements, Eugene O'Neill's *The Emperor Jones*, and the events of Shakespeare's play. The results were controversial, as some defenders of the production nevertheless expressed uneasiness at the concept's implicit skepticism toward black self-rule and even toward black artistry (Anderegg 25; Fraden 175). Both Richard France (70) and Zanthe Taylor (49) cite Edward R. Murrow's comment that the show was permeated by a "blackface attitude." In *Jungle Rot*, Greenland further problematizes the racial skepticism evident in Welles's stage *Macbeth:* his play closely scrutinizes American insistence that people of certain races simply cannot be trusted to govern themselves properly. Greenland invokes the Wellesian precedent from the very first scene. Welles had conceived of Shakespeare's Witches as practitioners of Voodoo: drumming and chanting fiercely, they effectively suggested the presence of malign powers; it was reported that the performers cast in the roles were actual adepts. Greenland's play opens with the "sound of drumming" that becomes louder until "three young African men in native garb" speak the lines that begin *Macbeth*.

Man #1:
　　When shall we three meet again? In thunder, lightning, or in rain?
Man #2:
　　When the hurly-burly's done. When the battle's lost and won. (7)[7]

Here, though, there will be no open battle; the action is entirely covert. The object of these Witches' machinations is a feckless, middle-aged intelligence officer, operating under the cover of being a career (though minor) diplomat. As the stage directions indicate, John Stillman has "gone slightly to seed through a combination of gin, moral wavering and the equatorial sun" (7). Stillman will be offered the chance of promotion and reassignment to the United States if he succeeds in assassinating Lumumba. The third "Witch" explains that a sign will herald Stillman's hope for advancement and will also "present a quandary of the moral stripe" (8).

The doubling of roles in the case of Greenland's play further complicates any prior conviction as to whether the Congolese can or cannot handle power. Greenland's "Witches" are played by actors who also assume other roles in the political landscape of the nascent state, all in response to foreign interference. Thus, Burkino is a well-paid, utterly independent informer (the independence helps to drive up his price); M'Bekan and Ndolo are rebel soldiers, who are associated with rival factions in the Congo—especially in Katanga Province, where Lumumba met his death—and are also associated with attempts to keep the new nation free from all forms of colonialist influence. The problems intensify with competing external factions that insist upon fighting the Cold War in the Congo. Greenland's Lumumba, true to his real-life counterpart, expresses his conviction that Africans must chart their own paths. In statements made to the audience, which is placed in the role of a group of reporters at a press conference, Lumumba states that the African peoples, not just the Congolese, "want to be a force of peaceful progress. A force of conciliation. An independent and united Africa will make a large and positive contribution to world peace . . . The Congo is neutral!" (17). In steering clear of the West, Lumumba is ready to accept support from the Soviet Union, which makes him deeply suspect in American eyes. John Stillman sees Lumumba as "the only guy who can keep the lid on this place now that the Belgians are gone." One of his associates, however, declares Lumumba "an African Castro" (17–18); here Greenland deliberately recalls revelations that the CIA had been involved with attempts on the Cuban leader's life as well.

Less indebted to Shakespeare's language than Garson, Greenland comes closer to *Macbeth* in one crucial plot element: the direct involvement of Lady Macbeth in the assassination attempt. Patience Stillman has run out of patience by the time of the play's action. Her husband seems destined to remain posted at one "godforsaken backwater" (21) after another; they have arrived in Leopoldville after Bucharest in the chilliest days of the Cold War and Algeria during its own struggles toward independence (22). Longing to return to the United States and to reestablish herself socially, she is thrilled at the prospect of her husband's involvement in an important operation and in the potential rewards for its success. Mrs. Stillman exclaims

> John, this is wonderful news! It's a vote of confidence in you, darling! Someone in Washington has taken note of the work you've been doing

and when this job came up they decided John Stillman was their man. This is the most exciting thing that's happened to us in years! (39)

She is even more excited to learn that the plot involves her serving as hostess for a dinner party, during which the prime minister will be poisoned: "I finally get to entertain! My God, how much good news can I take at one time?" (40). Sensing Stillman's reluctance and moral repugnance, a special operative enlists Patience to do the actual killing. She must wear lipstick that will interact with wine: once Lumumba has had a drink, she "must contrive to kiss Lumumba on the lips" (48). In explaining the plan, Felix Bender,[8] sent from Washington, warns her "not to drink the wine you serve him or it will do to you what the asp did to Cleopatra" (48); in this offhand reference, playwright Greenland deftly connects his play with *Antony and Cleopatra*, Shakespeare's own examination of political intrigue on the African continent. Although Patience declares the assassination John's "patriotic duty" (39), she joins the conspiracy out of sheer self-interest: "This opportunity represents the antidote to years of obscurity, frustration and resentment. This is our chance to break the awful cycle of futility" (48). The faintest echo of Macbeth's "Tomorrow, and tomorrow, and tomorrow" (5.5.19) can be heard in Patience's desperate, darkly comic attempt to avoid despair.

Like Lady Macbeth, Patience Stillman is ultimately unable to commit the crime herself. Instead, playwright Greenland borrows—as Garson often does—from *Hamlet* as well as from *Macbeth*. Lumumba never does drink wine; Patience faints twice (outdoing Lady Macbeth's response to the discovery of Duncan's murder); a misguided American who has drunk wine attempts to revive her with mouth-to-mouth resuscitation, thereby poisoning himself with her lipstick; John Stillman reveals the full plan to Lumumba, who retreats, but only after concluding that the U.S. ambassador to the Congo will not, after all, be arriving at Patience's dinner party. Just in case the audience misses the connection with *Hamlet*, in which poison similarly dispatches an unintended target or two, the doomed American's wife watches as he "keels over and crashes to the floor" and then observes that she's "never seen one glass of wine affect him this way!" (68). Another connection with *Hamlet* is John's hesitation: as the circumspect Prince of Denmark is succeeded by the confident Fortinbras, John Stillman is replaced with a company man unbothered by scruples. After the plot fails and John prepares to return home in disgrace and relief, John tells his erstwhile aide Walter Clark:

> You're the perfect choice. You don't equivocate, you don't hesitate and you display a remarkable instinct for the jugular vein. You'll do well, Walter. Never mind what happens in the Congo. There are plenty of other places your services will be required. Places where our interests might not be aligned with those of the local population. And between you and me, I would say that probably describes much of the world. Your opportunities should be endless. (74)

That Walter's approach to world affairs and moral action would remain in the ascendant is made clear by the final scene, in which the "three natives" reappear. They remind us that Lumumba may have "triumphed over the CIA" this time, but his "victory, though sweet, was all too brief" (74). Soon Africa's "tropical air grew thick and cold" in the atmosphere of Cold War rivalry between superpowers and Patrice Lumumba "soon was murdered by other mad men" (75), after the leader was turned over to his political enemies.

If Garson's play was overtaken by real-life events, Greenland's was overtaken by popular perception. While the play enjoyed some success in the mid-1990s, later attempts to revive *Jungle Rot* have had to confront the resurgence of the conviction—advanced by new proponents of a Pax Americana both within the Bush II administration and throughout the news media—that American interests necessarily align with those of local populations, whether they know it or not. In Chicago, during the Spring of 2004, two theater productions attempted to respond to the implications of the U.S. invasion of Iraq. One was of a classic play, Bernard Shaw's *Heartbreak House*, by the Goodman Theater; the other was of *Jungle Rot* by the Noble Fool Company. Despite public announcements that revisiting Shaw's play was meant to connect with contemporary developments, the actual staging stressed the historical differences between the United States in the early twenty-first century and the time and place depicted by Shaw: each act, for example, was introduced with songs from Great Britain in the years before the Great War. The production was moderately successful at the box office. In contrast, the Noble Fool production of *Jungle Rot* coincided with the intensification of financial difficulties for the company, whose entire complex—just blocks away from the Goodman Theater—shut down early in the run. The problems were exacerbated by a then widespread popular sentiment averse to questioning the validity of any Pax Americana.

Looking at the stormy performance histories of *MacBird!* and *Jungle Rot*, the superstitious or the facetious might simply point to the dangers supposedly implicit in staging the Scottish Play in any form. More to the point, however, is the capacity of the source play and its imitators for examining not only the specifics of assassination but also the darkest impulses that might provoke any exercise of political power. *Macbeth* and its appropriations appear, like Banquo's ghost, as reminders of violent attempts to achieve, wield, and maintain power. As such, they are equally unwelcome but persistent contributors to the hybrid texts that are "American Shakespeare" and U.S. political identity.

Notes

1 See Sturgess on the processes of naturalizing Shakespeare as a harbinger of U.S. attitudes and on views of his plays as "democratic entertainment" (86). Richard Nelson's play *Two Shakespearean Actors* focuses on the night of the Astor Place riots.

2 Furtwangler (71) has discovered a personal account written by the Marquis de Chambrun, who was part of a group traveling with Lincoln just days before his assassination: at least in retrospect, the Marquis finds "a vague presentiment" in Lincoln's feeling prompted to read the passage depicting Macbeth's sense of guiltiness after the murder of Duncan, his pausing to comment upon it, and his choosing to read aloud once again the same scene. The historical moment combines the spirit of Nativism, a civil war over the nature and future of the American nation, and a leader himself destined for violent death meditating on a play that explores assassination, premonition, and armed struggles over the right to define a nation through its leader.

3 Page references from *MacBird!* will be noted in the text. Quotations from Shakespeare's plays are taken from *The Riverside Shakespeare* and will also be noted in the text.

4 "This here is" was likely meant by Garson to be pronounced "this here's"—but with a hint of two syllables, Texas-style.

5 My Shakespearean colleague Bob Hall, for example, had been slated to direct the show for the Nebraska Repertory Theatre later that summer.

6 See Heinz and Donnay's account of Lumumba's last days. Two earlier plays were also inspired by these and related events: Aimé Césaire's *A Season in the Congo* and Conor Cruise O'Brien's *Murderous Angels*.

7 Page references from *Jungle Rot* will be made in the text.

8 The name recalls that of CIA operative Felix Leiter in Ian Fleming's James Bond novels; the character is based on Dr. Sidney Gottlieb, CIA chief technical officer, who actually did prepare a tube of poisoned toothpaste, which was never used, for Lumumba.

Works cited

Anderegg, Michael. *Orson Welles, Shakespeare, and Popular Culture*. New York: Columbia UP, 1999.

Bate, Jonathan. *Shakespearean Constitutions: Politics, Theatre, Criticism 1730–1830*. Oxford: Clarendon, 1989.

Blackburn, Tom. "*MacBird!* and *Macbeth:* Topicality and Imitation in Barbara Garson's Satirical Pastiche." *Shakespeare Survey* 57 (2004): 137–44.

Brustein, Robert. "*MacBird!* on Stage." *New Republic* 11 Mar. 1967: 30–32.

Buhler, Stephen M. *Shakespeare in the Cinema: Ocular Proof*. Albany: State U of New York P, 2002.

Cartelli, Thomas. "Prospero in Africa: *The Tempest* as Colonialist Text and Pretext." *Shakespeare Reproduced*. Ed. Jean E. Howard and Marion F. O'Connor. New York: Methuen, 1987.

Césaire, Aimé. *A Season in the Congo*. Trans. Ralph Manheim. New York: Grove, 1968.

Eliot, T.S. *Collected Poems, 1909–1962*. New York: Harcourt, Brace, and World, 1963.

Fraden, Rena. *Blueprints for a Black Federal Theatre, 1935–1939*. Cambridge: Cambridge UP, 1994.

France, Richard. *The Theatre of Orson Welles*. Lewisburg: Bucknell UP, 1977.

Furtwangler, Albert. *Assassin on Stage: Brutus, Hamlet, and the Death of Lincoln*. Urbana: U of Illinois P, 1991.

Garson, Barbara. *MacBird!* New York: Grove, 1967.

Greenland, Seth. *Jungle Rot*. New York: Dramatists Play Service, 1997.

Heinz, G. and H. Donnay. *Lumumba: The Last Fifty Days*. Trans. Jane Clark Seitz. New York: Grove, 1969.

Jones, Howard. *Death of a Generation: How the Assassinations of Diem and JFK Prolonged the Vietnam War*. New York: Oxford UP, 2003.

Macdonald, Dwight. "Birds of America." Rev. of *MacBird! New York Review of Books* 7.9 (1 Dec. 1966): 12–14.

Nelson, Richard. *Two Shakespearean Actors*. London: Faber and Faber, 1990.

O'Brien, Conor Cruise. *Murderous Angels: A Political Tragedy and Comedy in Black and White*. Boston: Little, Brown, 1968.

Palermo, Joseph A. *In His Own Right: The Political Odyssey of Senator Robert F. Kennedy*. New York: Columbia UP, 2001.

Shakespeare, William. *The Riverside Shakespeare*. 2nd ed. Ed. G. Blakemore Evans. Boston: Houghton Mifflin, 1997.

Shattuck, Charles H. *Shakespeare on the American Stage*. 2 vols. Washington, DC: Folger Shakespeare Library, 1976–87.

Shultz, George P. "Act Now." *Washington Post* 6 Sept. 2002: A25.

Steel, Ronald. "Mr. Smith Goes to the Twilight Zone." Rev. of *J.F.K.*, dir. Oliver Stone. *New Republic* 3 Feb. 1992: 30–32.

Sturgess, Kim C. *Shakespeare and the American Nation*. Cambridge: Cambridge UP, 2004.

Taylor, Zanthe. "Singing for Their Supper: The Negro Units of the Federal Theater Project and Their Plays." *Theater* 27.2 and 3 (1997): 43–59.

15 *Macbeth* in Chinese opera

Bi-qi Beatrice Lei

For roughly three hundred years after his debut on the English stage, Shakespeare remained unknown to China. It was not until the turn of the twentieth century that, as part of wholesale Westernization and modernization, Western drama was made available.[1] Seen as a progressive humanist thinker, Shakespeare was among the first and most influential playwrights ever imported.[2] His early theatrical impact, however, was largely confined to Western-style drama; direct contact with traditional Chinese theatre remained rather sparse.[3] In the mid-1980s, artistically conscious Sinocization of Shakespeare as Chinese opera began to emerge in both China and Taiwan, and *Macbeth* has been a favorite.[4] Li Ruru, who has written extensively on China's Shakespeare, in a recent essay reviewed several *Macbeth* productions and analyzed how they reflect the adapters' individual personalities, artistic experiences, and theatrical and generic backgrounds (Li, "A Drum" 177). No less importantly, these adaptations also epitomize the distinct sociopolitical situations and cultural atmospheres of the two worlds separated by the Taiwan Strait. This chapter examines three adaptations—the Kunqu opera *The Story of Bloody Hands*, the Beijing opera *The Kingdom of Desire*, and the Sichuan opera *Lady Macbeth*—with a focus on their subtle transfiguration of thematic emphases, philosophical concerns, and ethical sentiments. As different degrees of assimilation, transfiguration, and registration of native values ensue, the fair–foul contention and confusion in Shakespeare's original become further complicated by intercultural and inter-generic conflicts.

*

Long before its clash with Western civilization, old China enjoyed its own musical and physical theatre or, more correctly, theatres.[5] Despite their enormous diversity, these indigenous genres together form a group identity—Chinese opera (*xiqu*).[6] Traditional Chinese opera approximates total theatre as it combines music, speech, pantomime, dance, acrobatics, martial art, and pageantry. In lieu of verbal signs—monologues and dialogues—it is arias, percussive beats, elaborate body movements, and colors that constitute the most eloquent vehicles of dramatic expression. Performance is highly codified and stylized in every aspect: minimal stage setting, symbolic props, anachronistic costume, anti-naturalist face painting, standardized character types, and stylized acting.[7] Self-consciously anti-illusory and stagy, the Chinese theatre is characterized by what Brecht has called "the alienation effect" (91–99).

Realism, the mainstream on the Western stage, was entirely foreign to the Chinese audience. Nevertheless, when the concept was first introduced to China in the early twentieth century, it was eagerly embraced as it corresponded to the particular needs of the time. Self-deemed the "Central Kingdom," China's ancient empire had enjoyed unsurpassed glory for millennia, but it suffered a drastic decline when confronted by the challenges of the modern age. From the nineteenth century onward, overpopulation and bureaucratic corruption created enormous social problems and local riots. The domestic commotion was further complicated by foreign affairs. While China persevered in closed-door policies since the early eighteenth century, the rapidly industrializing Western powers and Japan would not leave her alone. The Qing regime's resistance to foreign penetration led to repeated imperialist invasion, culminating in humiliating treaties starting around 1840. In 1911, the Qing dynasty was overthrown and the new Republic was founded, but civil wars continued to rage across the country and imperialist threats persisted. Politically, socio-economically, and culturally, China was experiencing unprecedented upheaval. Anxious for reform and modernization, in 1919 young intellectuals initiated a cultural renaissance, known as the May Fourth Movement. New literature written in colloquial vernacular and addressing contemporary problems was propagated to educate the masses and to liberate the mind. In particular, a new realist "spoken drama" (*huaju*) tackled pressing issues such as women's rights, the worker's movement, and anti-imperialist sentiment; masterpieces from the West were imported to serve as models of the new drama.[8]

Although the musical drama continued to entertain the general population and outstanding artists continued to flourish, reform-minded intellectuals saw it as an outdated theatre both in form and in content: its primitive aesthetics embodied feudal values.[9] The Communist Party of China (CPC), founded in 1921, held a very clear cultural policy—art should serve politics—and launched sustained dramatic reform beginning in the early 1930s.[10] While retaining most formalistic elements of traditional opera, communist playwrights and producers modified historical plots, characters, and themes to accommodate revolutionary ideology. The dual theme of anti-feudalism and anti-Japanism was especially popular during the Sino-Japanese War (1937–1945), and historical stories were recast to express this sentiment. After the People's Republic was established in 1949, dramatic reform was further institutionalized by the Mao regime.[11] Traditional opera endured a serious crisis during the Cultural Revolution (1966–1976), which aimed at smashing the "Four Olds"—old ideas, culture, customs, and habits. Religion, Confucian morals, classical literature and arts came under severe attack and were brought to the edge of extinction. Operatic theatre survived in the politically correct "model plays," but Mao's wife Jiang Qing banned all other plays. Many theatrical professionals were persecuted, and most costumes, props, and scripts were destroyed during the decade.

While Red China favored changes, in Taiwan, cultural traditions were carefully preserved. In 1949, Chiang Kai-shek and his Nationalist (KMT) government retreated to Taiwan, maintaining the original name of the Republic of China. Nevertheless, it was the People's Republic in the mainland that the world came to recognize as *the* China. Refusing to be thus marginalized, the Chiang regime—the father and son who together ruled Taiwan for sixty years after Taiwan's liberation from Japanese colonizers after World War II— promoted traditional arts as a link to the cultural China of several millennia. The bulk of the artifacts of imperial China, safely transported to Taiwan and put on display in Taipei's National Palace Museum, served as the symbols of the orthodoxy. Deliberately contradicting the practices of Red China, Taiwan's KMT government encouraged traditional culture. Calligraphy, for instance, was a mandatory exercise for every student from elementary through high school, and the models most often used were the masterpieces from the eighth-century Tang dynasty. Along the same line, Beijing (Peking) opera was elevated to the status of "national drama."[12] In the 1950s and 1960s, it was performed regularly, especially as the entertainment for troops, and specialized schools were established by the government to foster the tradition.[13]

Yet, despite all the government support, traditional opera gradually declined in the 1970s. Cut off from living sources and restricted by traditionalist ideology and political censorship, the opera troupes were confined to a small repertoire and to standardized acting styles. Young students were taught to copy the existing models, as faithfulness to tradition ensured authenticity and orthodoxy. Contrary to Red China's fervor for reformation and revolution, Taiwan's troupes often employed conventions for conventions' sake, without considering the changing tastes of the audience. As a result, traditional opera was losing its appeal to young audiences, who preferred TV and movies to this old-fashioned theatre. Furthermore, ineffective administration of the troupes, lack of discipline among the students/ apprentices, and low artistic standards in general all agonized aspiring artists.[14]

Even though traditional theatre suffered a serious decline, it never completely died out, as was the case with classical novels and with classical poetry (Liu and Liao 11). Indeed, the old theatre was only awaiting a renaissance, which finally came about in the late 1970s. In Taiwan, Chiang Senior died in 1975; the son who succeeded him was more willing to accommodate changes in both political and cultural spheres. Vibrant energy circulated in all cultural domains, with dynamic interaction between and reflection upon tradition and innovation, East and West, self and other. On the big stage, the Cloud Gate Dance Troupe invoked ancient myths and folklore in their modern dance; on the small stage, the Little Theatre Movement imported avant-garde ideas; in movie theatres, the so-called Taiwan New Wave filmmakers gave prominence to realist depictions of local life; in schools, students rejected Western pop music and composed their own "campus folksongs." Even the most conservative traditional theatre was infused by this vitality. In 1979, the Beijing opera actress Kuo Hsiao-chuang launched a revolution by incorporating concepts and practices from Western theatre. Her plays moved at a much faster pace and featured dramatic tension and character psychology. Most significantly, she reformed the technical aspects, adopting enriched lighting, scene, and costume design.[15] Kuo's hybrid novelty won immediate applause, especially from young audiences. Traditional opera was no longer seen as outdated and dull, but as an art form full of possibilities. Kuo's success encouraged further attempts to revitalize the stale tradition of operatic theatre, and various means were employed. It was under these circumstances that Shakespeare was summoned.

Back across the Taiwan Strait, Mao survived his rival Chiang only by one year; his death brought an end to the devastating Cultural Revolution. Chinese theatre in this decade was not only vertically isolated from its native tradition but also horizontally isolated from the rest of the world—foreign theatre was not performed at all (Mackerras, "The Masses" 167). The new regime under Deng Xiaoping tried to heal the damage of Cultural Revolution with socialist modernizations, and one of the therapies was the open-door policy—economic, scholarly, and cultural exchanges with the outside world were renewed. Ambivalence, however, followed these intercultural encounters, even to the extent of an identity crisis, and a strong reactionary nationalist spirit began to glare in the cultural atmosphere. On the one hand, amazement with and envy of other cultures often turned sour; on the other, disappointment and frustration with home environs often manifested themselves as pride and prejudice. Traditional theatre used foreign sources not to revive and improve itself, as in the case of Taiwan, but to outdo its alien rivals—to assert its own greatness. Shakespeare, a cultural icon of the West, became a convenient agent.[16]

*

In 1986, the first Chinese Shakespeare Festival was held in Shanghai and Beijing. Sixteen of Shakespeare's plays (twenty-eight productions) were staged in spoken drama and in traditional opera by troupes from various regions of the country.[17] In addition to performances, the festival also incorporated a scholarly conference. This new vogue of Shakespeare deviated from pre-Cultural Revolution practices. Then, Shakespeare was mostly honored as a humanist, whose stories illustrated progressive values; his plays were modernized and/or localized, made accessible, in order to propagate these values and to raise political and aesthetic consciousness. The adaptations of the 1980s, however, delivered a different political message. Shakespeare no longer served as a teacher, a model, but was mainly used as a touchstone to validate and propagate the worth of traditional theatre. Huang Zuolin opined:

> We can find a lot of common characteristics in Shakespeare's drama and traditional Chinese drama. We can also see some strong points in each which the two types of drama may learn from each other. There is no doubt that we shall make more contributions to the theatrical circles of the world if we perform Shakespeare's plays by using some stage techniques of traditional Chinese drama when we introduce the works of this great dramatic poet to Chinese audiences. And in the meantime we can make our brilliant theatrical and consummate stage techniques known to countries all over the world.[18]

Although Huang talked about a two-way traffic between East and West, his emphasis was plainly on the export, not the import. This was echoed by Zhang An Jian:

> As is known to us all, Shakespearean drama is a bright pearl of Western culture and traditional Chinese drama is a treasure of Eastern art. If we mix them together, it will not only make Shakespeare known to more Chinese audiences but also cause traditional Chinese theatre to exert a widespread influence upon the theatrical circles of the world. This is really a matter of great importance.[19]

Such was the kind of argument that surrounded the historic national event.

The Story of Bloody Hands (*Xie shou ji*), a Kunqu performance of *Macbeth* by Shanghai Kunju Opera Troupe, attracted the most attention of the nine adaptations (Figure 15.1). Kunqu (*Kunju, Kun* opera) is the oldest operatic form in China: it was fully developed by the end of the sixteenth century and its nationwide dominion extended for over two hundred years. It features strict and refined aesthetic codes, and approximates total theatre more than any of China's regional theatres. It was also the wet nurse of many younger genres, providing them with stories, role types, poetry, music, and acting styles. While some local genres are more open to new materials, Kunqu stands as the most conservative and aristocratic form, rehearsing plays written hundreds of years ago and resisting changes. This quality makes the Shakespeare adaptation particularly intriguing. Vaguely set in historical China, *Bloody Hands* compresses Shakespeare's original plot into eight scenes revolving around Macbeth and his wife.[20] Due to the nature of the genre—extensive arias and choreographic movement—Shakespeare's characters and lines were significantly trimmed. Such cutting, however, is common enough in modern productions of Shakespeare and almost inevitable for musical adaptations.

More remarkable than the condensation is the substantial enhancement of supernatural elements in the process of Sinocization. The play starts with a

Figure 15.1 Macbeth and Lady Macbeth in the Kunqu adaptation *The Story of Bloody Hands* (*Xie shou ji*). By permission of Shanghai Kunju Opera Troupe.

grotesque dance of the three weird sisters—one tall and two dwarfish, using special crouching steps (Figure 15.2). The fair–foul paradox manifests not only in their equivocal lines but also in the masks they wear behind their heads.[21] Surprised by them while returning from the battlefield, Macbeth asks: "Are you human or ghost?"[22] "Neither, but composed of cosmic essences over a thousand years." Contrary to Shakespeare's original, the weird sisters are visible and audible to Macbeth alone, who addresses them as "Madam Fairy." They greet Macbeth, prophesize his advancement and coronation, and explicitly warn him of Banquo, who could spoil his good fortune if Macbeth did not "root out the malady entirely." Their message is

Figure 15.2 Macbeth and the three weird sisters in the Kunqu adaptation *The Story of Bloody Hands* (*Xie shou ji*). Courtesy of Shanghai Kunju Opera Troupe.

understood to be nothing less than oracular. In scene six, when the troubled King Macbeth goes back to consult them, they call him "Heaven's Favorite" and explicitly tell him that the words are directly from the Jade Emperor (the supreme ruler over heaven and earth in popular religion). The supernatural force, then, is fully institutionalized. Played by cross-dressed male actors of remarkable acrobatic skill, these odd fairies have very powerful visual impact and carry much greater authority than their counterparts in Shakespeare.

Lady Macbeth is also approached by a higher power. Even before she learns of Macbeth's triumph and advancement, she has an alarming vision of tigers occupying the dragon bed—both animals being conventional symbols for royalty—and does not know how to interpret it. After Macbeth reveals the witches' prophecy, she immediately associates her dream with it. She understands that he has always had political aspirations: "Having been by your side for many years, I know your mind well. You are unwilling to submit to anyone, yet hesitant and irresolute, and have therefore missed many good opportunities." Now the oracles sanction their shared desire and prompt them to take action. She incants a rhyme:

> Regal status pronounced,
> Tigers and dragons descried—
> Oracles from heavens,
> Cataclysm if defied.

Significantly, the oracles also deliver an implied threat—disobedience against divine will can be disastrous. When he is left alone, Macbeth hallucinates, seeing a sword in the air, and wavers. Then the chant is again heard offstage and eventually reassures him.

> Auspicious signs, one after another, have foretold triumph.
> The dragon-spring sword, bestowed by heavens, points to the direction.
> The crown is nearly in hand—no more hesitation!
> God help my dear wife!
> Together we shall accomplish this undertaking,
> And become queen and king!

He then proceeds to murder Duncan. Seeing the task accomplished, Lady Macbeth again invokes providence: "Thanks to help from heavens, my lord is truly blessed!" Emphasizing divine intervention, the play provides a powerful rationale for the couple's regicide.

Bloody Hands is a world inhabited not only by fairies but also by ghosts. In Shakespeare, Banquo's ghost is pale and silent and, depending on the director, could even be wholly imaginary; here, his presence at the banquet scene is much more substantial, engaging Macbeth in stylized fighting. Ji Zhenhua, the actor who plays Macbeth, employs many physical techniques in this dramatic episode—head shaking, hair spinning, knee-bending jumps, whirling and turning, sword play, etc.—to show Macbeth's frenzy and panic, suggesting the formidable power of Banquo's ghost. In addition to the banquet scene, Lady Macbeth's sleepwalking scene—a brief scene in the original—is markedly elaborated and transformed into a spectacular and most memorable ghost scene. The frightful ghosts of Duncan, Banquo, Lady Macduff (who is also Lady Macbeth's sister in the adaptation), and a parrot (whose neck was wrung for revealing the crime) each emerge from a darkened background, assaulting Lady Macbeth not only verbally but also physically. She scoffs at some and begs others for pardon, but all to no avail, as the avenging ghosts together chase her around the stage, waving their sword or "water sleeves" (*shuixiu*, long white silk extensions of regular sleeves, conventional costume in traditional opera) and breathing fire, demanding that she surrender her life.[23] After a prolonged struggle—performed with superb physical movement and marvelous manipulation of four-foot-long water sleeves set to clamorous percussive beats—Lady Macbeth collapses in the end, literally beaten to death by the ghosts. Three supernatural scenes—"Banquet Disturbed," "Consulting the Witches," and "Bedchamber Insanity"—each more intense and sensational than the one before, immediately precede the eighth and final scene "Bloody Retribution," to overwhelming cumulative effect.

Supernatural elements do not merely furnish the play with thrilling sensations and astonishing spectacles but in fact downplay the couple's moral responsibility. As Lady Macbeth makes explicit, not to kill Duncan is a transgression of divine will, and that can have disastrous consequences. Exertion of political ambition is therefore intriguingly transfigured into a submissive act. Indeed, that the play portrays Macbeth in the "mature man" (*laosheng*) character type indicates that he is not a complete villain. In traditional Chinese theatre, all dramatis personae fall into distinct role types, and the moral quality of a given character can be easily recognized.[24] A villain typically appears as a "great painted face" (*dahualian*), while a "mature man" is usually the protagonist that serves the moral center or at least deserves sympathy.[25] Though ambitious, proud, suspicious, and murderous, the Kunqu Macbeth is no less a victim steered by external forces. As for Shakespeare's positive characters—Duncan, Banquo, Malcolm, Macduff, and Lady Macduff—they all deserve some pity, but none of them has a strong enough personality in the adaptation to hold the moral center; their main significance lies in their being victimized. Reshaping the characters, *Bloody Hands* betrays a strong distrust of the individual and evinces a willing submission to structure and authority. Highlighting the melodramatic avenging ghosts as a means of justice and thematizing karmic causality, the play is not essentially Buddhist, Taoist, or Confucian; rather, its sentiment is an offspring of popular religion. It is noteworthy that fairies, ghosts, oracles, and providential retribution—supernatural or even superstitious materials from popular religion—were considered part of the "Four Olds" and were actively opposed during the Cultural Revolution; indeed, it was why many old plays were banned.[26] Recapitulating these motifs, *Bloody Hands* signifies an avowedly nostalgic return to old China.

Huang Zuolin, the artistic director of *Bloody Hands*, was a student in England in 1935, when Brecht wrote his essay on Chinese operatic theatre. The German playwright's admiration of Beijing opera master Mei Lanfang, Huang recalled, "inspired me with great national pride" (96). Huang later built a successful career in Western-style spoken drama and cinema, but his faith in traditional theatre as cultural redemption for his confused, weakened, and impoverished country never wavered.[27] He was anxious, however, that cultural hybridization could be more destructive than constructive: "Our conventional theater has already lost more and more audiences. If we use our drama to perform Shakespeare's plays, the production might be 'neither fish nor fowl,' which would make the situation of our conventional theater even worse and damage the intact theatrical tradition."[28] As a result, *Bloody Hands* turned out to be an "out-and-out sinicized Shakespeare production" (Zhang Xiao Yang 157).[29] The transformation is not merely linguistic, generic, or stylistic, but it also manifests the political, social, and cultural atmosphere of China in its post-Cultural Revolutionary era. Intercultural exchange or rehabilitation of a centuries-old genre was not the main reason that Chinese critics universally lauded the Kunqu *Macbeth*—the play and its acceptance bespoke more complex sentiments of a people that were traumatized, nostalgic, and fervently nationalistic.

*

The Kingdom of Desire (*Yuwang chengguo*), a Beijing opera *Macbeth* by the Taipei-based Contemporary Legend Theatre (CLT), is of a different tone than the Kunqu adaptation. Premiering also in 1986, the play is in many ways more modern than *Bloody Hands*. The director-actor Wu Hsing-kuo broke away from established conventions and created an entirely novel theatre, and this bold endeavor may be attributed to the youth of the people involved. While Shanghai Kunju Opera Troupe was an established troupe with an 80-year-old artistic director and an acting staff in full bloom, the artists of the CLT were almost all in their twenties when Wu founded it. Indeed, this performance was the professional debut in traditional theatre for the adapter, the director, the producer, the set designer, and the costume designer.[30] These young people were free from the restraints of tradition, a heavy burden for long-term practitioners. The costumes of Macbeth and his wife, for example, follow no theatrical conventions.[31] Macbeth's ornate fish-scaled armor recalls the terracotta warriors of the First Qin Emperor's mausoleum newly unearthed near Xian (Figure 15.3). The wide sleeves and the long train in the back of each of Lady Macbeth's gowns also deviate significantly from conventions of traditional opera.[32] Another example is the solo dance performed at the banquet scene. Lin Hsui-wei, a modern dancer and choreographer, puts on three masks in turn—representing three forces within the protagonist (Shih 254)—and her dancing style is utterly alien to the traditional theatre (Figure 15.4). These and still more innovations shocked audiences and critics alike and stimulated enormous controversy.

In spirit, *Kingdom of Desire* is much more secular than *Bloody Hands*. There are no fantastic scenes of fairies or ghosts, no mention of strange dreams or a hallucinatory sword. Instead, the play takes pains to furnish psychological bases for the characters' actions.[33] When Macbeth reveals the prophecy to his wife, she immediately suspects that Banquo may betray Macbeth by informing Duncan, which might potentially cause Macbeth's ruin. Duncan's unexpected visit at night, his unreasonable suspicion about an apparently loyal subject, and his doubtful military strategy further confirm her apprehensions. Fear for his life, as well as political ambition, prompt Macbeth to take immediate action. His attempt to murder Banquo and Fleance is in turn psychologically justified by Lady's Macbeth's pregnancy, by the prospect of siring his own male heir. Her subsequent miscarriage, in addition to her guilty conscience, then provide a rationale for her feeble physical and mental state as shown in the sleepwalking scene.

Kingdom of Desire concocts an amoral universe distinct from Shakespeare's.

Figure 15.3 Macbeth in his war dress in the Beijing opera adaptation *The Kingdom of Desire* (*Yuwang chengguo*). By permission of the Contemporary Legend Theatre.

Contrary to Shakespeare's reverent king, the Beijing opera Duncan is cowardly, incompetent, indiscreet, suspicious, and even tyrannical, thus attenuating the horror of regicide. This Duncan is a sovereign unworthy of loyal service and unwavering devotion, and his court is as degenerate: except for the brave Macbeth and Banquo, the nameless court officials are all hopelessly useless and even clownish. Banquo, though valiant, is no less ambitious than Macbeth, anxious to make his son Macbeth's heir. Further down the hierarchy, the faithless soldiers and guards are disposed to abandon or betray their masters out of self-interest. As Shih Wen-shan has argued, *Kingdom of Desire* "reveals a morally sickened world: it opens with rebellion and ends with a mirrored image of killing" (251). The Macbeth couple's ambition, calculation, and criminality are perfectly at home in this moral chaos and

Figure 15.4 The mask dance at the banquet scene in the Beijing opera adaptation *The Kingdom of Desire* (*Yuwang chengguo*). Courtesy of the Contemporary Legend Theatre.

political turmoil. After hearing the Mountain Spirit's prophecy, Banquo asks rhetorically: "Who does not crave for high position and thick state pension?" This common ambition is reinforced by Lady Macbeth:

> Lo! The sun sets and the moon rises—
> The wheel of fortune is spinning constantly.
> It's time for all men of courage to compete,
> But only the strongest procures sovereignty.

In a world dominated by the law of the jungle, the Macbeth couple's usurpation is naturalized. No supernatural agent, it seems, is needed to tempt them into sin.

Not only more secular than *Bloody Hands, Kingdom of Desire* is also earthier than Shakespeare's original.[34] Consider Shakespeare's three weird sisters. They are said to be women with beards (1.3.45–46), a physical appearance that defies our common experience of gender.[35] They certainly act strangely, sailing in sieves, preparing soup with peculiar ingredients, and conjuring spirits. They do not "tread upon the ground" but "dance and vanish" (4.1). Interestingly, they are endowed with a unique mode of expression. Throughout the whole play, they and Hecate alone get to sing. They employ paradoxes and riddles, using a "highly stylized or ritualized" speech (Regan 92). Audibly different from natural speech, their speech pattern distinguishes them from the other characters and reinforces an uncanny image "not like th'inhabitants o' th' earth" (1.3.41). This eeriness is not to be found in the Mountain Spirit, their counterpart in the Beijing opera adaptation. At first look, the Mountain Spirit strikes the audience as peculiar with her long scattered hair and a long white smock. Judged by her speech and action, however, she seems a perfectly ordinary and natural figure. No aria is assigned to her; instead, she talks in a comparatively realistic style—the only special vocal technique she employs is her witchlike laugh which echoes in the dark forest. Rather than dancing, tumbling, and flying, she only walks and makes turns. In the opening scene, she claims that she will "ride on clouds and smoke, drive thunder and lightening, penetrate darkness, and cross over to the light." Nothing of the kind, however, appears on stage. Indeed, nothing in her looks, speech, or movements betrays any otherworldliness. Rather, her white smock and black hair make her almost identical to Lady Macbeth in her bedchamber save for their different hairstyles.[36]

The same realism applies to the ghost of Banquo at the banquet scene. He wears no special costume or makeup in order to look ghostly—all he has is a black veil upon his face. While he is alive, Banquo declaims, sings, struts, and mimes with extraordinary skills not incomparable to the grand battement and the arabesque in ballet; now dead, he merely walks quietly on stage. It is noteworthy that his death "naturalizes" not only his own movements but also those of Macbeth. As a rule, fighting in the play is done as stylized martial art, for both generals and soldiers alike. Macbeth's final collapse is a most memorable scene: shot by one of his own men, he turns a breathtaking back somersault from a standing position, leaping eight feet off the stage. Having not only safely but also elegantly landed on his feet, he falls on his back without bending his spine or knees. These amazing acrobatics are the highlight of the performance, consistently winning resounding applause. Macbeth's encounter with Banquo's ghost in the banquet scene, however, is presented in a different style. Waving his sword in the air, he chases the ghost clumsily around the stage, despite desperate efforts by Lady Macbeth to stop him. He climbs up the dining table, trying to threaten the ghost from above, but ends up tumbling down—the renowned martial artist and skilled dancer Wu shows no sign of his art in these movements. This crudely natural movement is so out of character for Macbeth and the operatic tradition that it creates an almost comic effect.

A distinct natural style separates the Mountain Spirit and Banquo's ghost from the world inhabited by the other dramatis personae: stylistically speaking, they belong more to the spoken drama, which valorizes realism and naturalism. Acting style, indeed, was what Wu saw as the most serious problem with traditional Chinese theatre:

> Beijing opera combines arias, dance, drama, and acrobatics. A good actor needs to attend to all these aspects to thrive. However, most actors can only fulfill the technical requirements; few can actually melt into the character, creating profound and moving performance. In addition, the fixed role types of *sheng* [male roles], *dan* [female roles], *jing* [painted face], and *chou* [clowns] also restrict the actor's interpretation of a role. As Neo-Confucianism in traditional Chinese culture emphasizes the golden mean, abidance to rules, and order, human nature is overridden by ethical principles and deprived of the freedom of expression. As a result, the characters lose contact with true humanity, and hence the power to move.
>
> ("From Tradition" 51)

Such discontent had been voiced early in the twentieth century, and Western-style spoken drama was imported as a solution to the problem. Wu's case, however, was different. Despite the harsh constraints imposed upon performing artists, to completely renounce conventional acting styles would be unthinkable for him. He was enamored with traditional opera and had no desire to abolish it—he has emphasized over and over that his intention was to revitalize it ("From Tradition" 50). Chinese opera, however, is a world that lives by its distinct conventions; stripped of them, the theatre would lose its compass and point of reference. Any modification, therefore, had to be conducted with considerable care. Like Ji had done in *Bloody Hands*, Wu also fused existing role types in his portrayal of Macbeth, employing the acting styles of "mature man," "warrior," and "great painted face." Yet for Wu, this reform within the existing framework was not enough. His vision of the novel theatre was something more radical, as in the works of Ariane Mnouchkine and Ninagawa Yukio (Wu, "On the Wings"). How could he liberate acting from standardized styles, breathing new life into Beijing opera, without destroying it altogether? The supernatural elements already prominent in Shakespeare's original afforded him poetic license. While supernatural elements provide *Bloody Hands* with opportunities to exhibit superb physical techniques passed down from the Kunqu tradition, they allow CLT to experiment and negotiate, blending realist and naturalist acting styles into Beijing opera.

Kingdom of Desire fuses various theatrical models: Shakespeare, realist and naturalist acting, and avant-garde intercultural theatre; it is also indebted to other fields of art. As founding members of Cloud Gate, both Wu and Lin were well versed in modern dance and effortlessly incorporated movements from it. In addition, Wu had learned a great amount from musicals and from cinema. The soldiers' ensemble singing and acting in the last scene, for instance, bears the imprimatur of Broadway. The influence of cinema is especially striking. Unnerved by the news that revolts and attacks are erupting all over his kingdom, King Macbeth gallops off to the forest to seek the Mountain Spirit for advice. While the whip in his hand—the conventional symbol for a horse on stage—is conveniently lifted from the indigenous theatrical tradition, his body movement on horseback mimics slow motion in cinema, highlighting his internal commotion. In particular, the influence of Kurosawa Akira's *The Throne of Blood*, a film adaptation of *Macbeth*, seems decisive. Catherine Diamond remarked, "In fact, *Kingdom of Desire* is not a Beijing opera of *Macbeth* but an adaptation of *Throne of Blood*" (118). This may be overstated, as I have pointed up other important sources and inspiration for Wu's creation. Wu's open-minded eclecticism and adventurous exploration of various materials have received polarized responses from audiences and critics.[37] In a sense the heterogeneity of *Kingdom of Desire*, as well as the diversified reaction to it, epitomizes the vibrant energy circulating in Taiwan in the 1980s. Soon, martial law was to be replaced by market law.

*

The Kunqu and Beijing opera adaptations did not exhaust all the possibilities for Sinocizing *Macbeth* in the form of traditional opera. Since 1986, more attempts have been made in the Chinese-speaking communities, such as the Yue opera *General Malong* (*Malong jiangjun*) and the Cantonese opera *The Rebel Hero* (*Yingxiong panguo*).[38] The Sichuan opera *Lady Macbeth* (*Makebai furen*), premiered in 1999, is the most intriguing. Regional Sichuan opera, in contrast to the more classical and national forms of Kunqu and Beijing opera, is much closer to the common people. Its language is more colloquial, and it is more adaptable to changing political, social, and cultural mores. Indeed, it was the first recorded operatic genre to have adapted Shakespeare's play.[39] Not surprisingly, *Lady Macbeth* registers the impact of contemporary realities. Deng's open-door policy had been in place for twenty years, and Chinese society was becoming increasingly diverse and dynamic. Communism was being qualified by capitalism, collectivism by individualism, and ideological dogmatism by pragmatism or even opportunism. Feminism also emerged. All these currents surge through the play.

Written by Xu Fen, *Lady Macbeth* is virtually a solo performance by Tian Mansha, who plays the title character. The role of Macbeth, who dominates most of the action and delivers extensive soliloquies in Shakespeare, is completely suppressed: he is silent throughout the play and merely walks around the stage, pantomiming lightly with simple gestures. Much of the play is presumably dialogue between the couple, but what Macbeth says is available to us only through Lady Macbeth's fragmentary quotation. His facial expression is also minimal, as it is hard to detect on his face heavily painted in gold. This drastic reduction of Macbeth and expansion of Lady Macbeth is phenomenal, but not totally incomprehensible. In fact, Lady Macbeth's responsibility in the terrible crime of regicide has been emphasized and over-emphasized by critics and adapters alike. Often Macbeth seems a weak and innocent victim of his scheming and manipulative wife, a femme fatale who, like Eve, serves as an instrument for her man's downfall. Both *Bloody Hands* and *Kingdom of Desire*, indeed, apportion the blame to Lady Macbeth: it is her powerful rhetoric born of womanish superstition or suspicion, if not ambition, that compels him to proceed. This "fiend-like queen" (5.8.35), however, subsists primarily in relation to her king: her eloquence justifies Macbeth's criminal action and her insanity and death plague him and further dramatize his downfall. Conversely, the Sichuan opera adaptation is keenly gender-conscious in presenting Lady Macbeth as a three-dimensional character, who exposes her psychology in a first-person confession.

In Shakespeare, Macbeth's letter reaches home before he does, informing Lady Macbeth about the weird sisters' prophecy and its partial fulfillment. In the adaptation, Lady Macbeth waits in suspense. After congratulating Macbeth on his victory over the rebel forces, she immediately asks: "What did the King reward you with?" Learning of his new title, she ponders, "Then, you are above tens of thousands, and only below one person!" She sighs, "In fact, with your wisdom and courage, it would be a shame for you to be under anybody, even just one person!" The idea of usurping the throne seems perfectly reasonable. "Why not?" she repeats the rhetorical question, and narrates her initial encounter with Macbeth in the third person:

> The past springs up in this instant:
> A belle wandered in the garden.
> Looking out from an ornate tower,
> She spotted a handsome youthful gallant.
> Gracefully he moved, like a lush tree combed by the zephyr;
> Majestically he stood, like a lofty mountain pillaring the azure.
> His bow he bent; straight fell wild geese from the clouds.
> In the woods, he badgers captured with bare hands.
> With the gallant the belle did elope,
> Discerning he was not of ordinary mould.
> Extraordinary, exceptional,
> He surely deserves to sit in the golden throne.
> No longer to be commanded by anybody,
> Between heaven and earth the sole sovereign *you* will be.

The last line reveals that this seemingly legendary romance is her own story. After she finishes this aria, the last line is echoed by an offstage chorus:

"Between heaven and earth the sole sovereign *I* will be." This female voice speaks her true mind. Her aspiration for power is unambiguous and deeply rooted, and she married Macbeth precisely because he showed the potential to help her fulfill this desire. Unlike in the other two adaptations, here Macbeth is used as an instrument for her ambition, and this also explains his silence.

Lady Macbeth then instantly conceives a murder plan. While Macbeth is offstage entertaining the king, she grabs a shining, two-foot-long steel knife and starts to sharpen it. This is a nightmarish scene indeed, as she grinds the knife left and right and grins, making petrifying cackles (Figure 15.5). She argues with Duncan in her imagination: "Old Fool King, people all commend

Figure 15.5 Lady Macbeth sharpening her knife in the Sichuan opera adaptation *Lady Macbeth* (*Makebai furen*). By permission of the Youth Sichuan Opera Troupe of the Sichuan Opera School.

you for your great wisdom. If you were truly wise, you should abdicate in favor of a more competent person—you should yield your crown to my husband Macbeth!" Legend has it that emperors Yao (2357–2255 BCE) and Shun (2255–2205 BCE) abdicated in their old age. Rather than passing the crown to their sons, they assigned competent successors outside their families to guarantee a peaceful transition of power and good government, and their selfless love for the people has been celebrated by the Confucians as exemplifying the political virtue of the Golden Age. Lady Macbeth's allusion to this political legend is extremely ironic—she and Macbeth are the polar opposites of these saintly kings. Shamelessly, she justifies their regicide: "Your lack of bounty— not our lack of duty—is to blame for your death tonight!"

That Lady Macbeth is ambitious is not a new invention—what is striking is her blatant honesty about it. The way she articulates her desire also reinforces her ingenuity. Contrary to the arias in other operatic adaptations, those in *Lady Macbeth* are not delivered with stringed or winded instruments; instead, they are only accompanied by occasional percussive beats. The overall effect of using unaccompanied arias is that, rather than polished pieces of musical art—sophisticated, elaborate, and ornate—they sound like a genuine voice from her heart. Significantly, there is no mention of witches or fairies, of nocturnal dream or waking vision, of prophecy obscure or unequivocal. Lady Macbeth does not need to invoke the authority of supernatural beings —her ambition is fully conscious, her rationale sound, and her action premeditated. Nor is Duncan's suspicion or Banquo's betrayal—reasonable sources of anxiety and fear for the couple in *Bloody Hands* and in *Kingdom of Desire*—an issue here. For the Sichuan opera Lady Macbeth, desire for power suffices all; other excuses or disguises are utterly unnecessary. Such frankness is only conceivable in an overtly pragmatic society, where individuals are prioritized over structure, where self-interest overrides ethical principles, where economic opportunism extends to moral and political opportunism. Terry Eagleton has called Shakespeare's Lady Macbeth a "bourgeois individualist" (4), but not until the end of the millennium did such a woman find a home on the Chinese stage. She makes it plain that her ambition is not unique—she is only lucky to have fulfilled it. Happily queened on the golden throne in the golden palace hall, she relishes her good fortune:

> For this eye-dazzling radiance of gold,
> How many have marched and battled in agony?
> How many have made their journey to Hades?
> How many have destroyed their own family?
> How many friends have turned deadly enemies?

Four questions in a row concisely summarize all human history. Her desire is only typical, not exceptional, and her regicide is posited as a minor offence compared to the terrible crimes of many usurpers. This argument even extends to the audience across the fourth wall. When the chorus accuses her for lack of conscience, she bitterly refutes it. Directly speaking to the audience, she says, "I'm afraid *you* would only be more vicious and venomous if *you* were in my shoes!" This disruption of theatrical illusion is very powerful when delivered as a complete surprise.

The finale of *Lady Macbeth* is perhaps the most Shakespearean of all three operatic adaptations. It is her guilty conscience, manifested in the imagined blood stains on her hands, and her fear of being discovered—not the attack of avenging ghosts or the trauma of miscarriage—that eventually defeat her. Her panic is vividly portrayed in the hand-washing scene. Eight serving ladies stand in circles, forming three human wash basins, while Lady Macbeth rushes from one to another, rubbing her hands rigorously. The serving ladies' long white water sleeves, reflecting a bluish light, comprise the water for her wash; and in a dramatic lighting change, the "water" instantly turns red the moment her bloody hands touch them (Figure 15.6). The play's ingenious use of lighting, colors, human props, pantomime, and flashback creates a surreal and futuristic ambience. The play starts and ends with a knock on the door while Lady Macbeth turns her back to the audience in the center of the stage, a symmetrical structure which further enhances the dreamlike atmosphere. The actress Tian's superb techniques based on her training as a Sichuan opera actress, however, remind the audience that they are watching an ancient theatrical genre—electrifying are her expressive body movements and unbelievable maneuvering of the five-foot-long, two-foot-wide water sleeves.

Figure 15.6 Lady Macbeth washes her hands in the Sichuan opera adaptation *Lady Macbeth* (*Makebai furen*). By permission of the Youth Sichuan Opera Troupe of the Sichuan Opera School.

Formalistically, the play is a dialectic between futurity and pastness; its spirit, however, is essentially a product of present-day China.

*

Dennis Kennedy has remarked that "the universality we so often admire derives not from Shakespeare's transcendence but from his malleability, from our own willingness to read in the pastness of the texts and find ourselves there. What selves we find depends on who we are" (301). Underneath their iridescent theatricality, the three adaptations of *Macbeth* each inculcate values structured by their distinct sociopolitical and cultural environs. In the Kunqu *Bloody Hands*, Shakespeare was used to celebrate the ancient theatrical tradition and to reaffirm concerns and sentiment that had been deliberately destroyed in the previous decade. The Beijing opera *Kingdom of Desire*, conversely, resorted to Shakespeare's authority for artistic experiments in an attempt to revitalize a stale theatre and to create a new aesthetic. In *Lady Macbeth*, Shakespeare became a site for intellectual exploration of ethics, gender, and Zeitgeist. All three plays have toured in Europe as well as Asia, stirring international audiences with their arresting music and dazzling spectacles; *Bloody Hands* visited Macbeth's Scotland and *Kingdom of Desire* has made its way to Shakespeare's London.[40] As products and processes of transculturation and acculturation, the operatic *Macbeths* illustrate, illuminate, and inform both the Shakespearean text and the Chinese-speaking worlds.

Notes

1 For a concise account of the early importation of Western drama, see Mackerras, *Chinese Drama* (104–13).
2 See He (150–54), Li ("The Bard" 50–64, *Shashibiya* 11–51) and Levith (1–23) for accounts of Shakespeare in China before the Cultural Revolution.
3 Zhang Xiao Yang (143–44) and Li (*Shashibiya* 39–40) have listed and discussed some pre-Cultural Revolution operatic adaptations, but no detailed references are available; also see Mackerras, "Operatic Adaptations" 24–25.
4 Brockbank speaks of the phenomenon as "a Shakespeare renaissance in China" (195). For a survey of operatic adaptations in the 1980s and 1990s, see Wang Shu-hua (119–45).
5 As of this writing, over three hundred indigenous forms exist across the Chinese-speaking communities.
6 Wichmann has observed three distinct features shared by all national and local theatres: synthesis, convention, and stylization (185).
7 See Hsü's account of the conventions of traditional Chinese theatre 35–50.
8 See Mackerras, *Chinese Drama* (104–12).
9 Many important literary figures and intellectual leaders—Hu Shih, Qian Xuan-tong, Fu Sinian, and Liu Pan-nung among others—spoke of traditional theatre as backward, primitive, and childish; see Liao (440–42, 445–49).
10 Later, Mao Zedong pronounced the official position in his "Talks at the Yenan Forum on Literature and Art" (1942); see Mackerras ("The Masses" 156–60).

11 For CPC's dramatic reform before the Cultural Revolution, see Wang An-chi, *Contemporary Chinese Opera* (11–51); Mackerras (*Chinese Drama* 119–29).

12 Guy has written on how Beijing opera obtained the status of "national opera" and its political implications (90–95).

13 For the development of Beijing opera in Taiwan in the 1950s and 1960s, see Wang An-chi, *Fifty Years* (1: 43–101).

14 Wu, "On the Wings."

15 Wang An-chi has summarized the significance of Kuo's reform (*Fifty Years* 1:108–109).

16 Chen has discussed Shakespeare's role as a cultural Other in China's Occidentalist theatre after the Cultural Revolution (43–58).

17 See Brockbank (203–204) and Li ("The Bard" 69–70) for a list of the productions.

18 Huang Zuolin, "The Prospects of Shakespeare's Plays on the Chinese Stage: A Speech Given at the Seminar of China's Inaugural Shakespeare Festival," in *Shakespeare in China*, ed. Shakespeare Association of China (Shanghai: Shanghai Literature and Art Press, 1987) 14, quoted in Zhang Xiao Yang (134).

19 Zhang An Jian, "The Treasure Shakespeare Has Left Us: A Reflection on the Inaugural Chinese Shakespeare Festival," in *Shakespeare's Triple Play: Research, Performance, and Teaching*, ed. Zhang Si Yang et al. (Changchun: Northeast Normal University Press, 1988), 218, quoted in Zhang Xiao Yang (134).

20 For a parallel plot analysis between Shakespeare's *Macbeth* and *Bloody Hands*, see Li (*Shashibiya* 127).

21 Tatlow has discussed the weird sisters in terms of visual metaphor of doubleness (200–201); this topic is then elaborated by C.Y. Alexander Huang.

22 In my discussion of the Chinese adaptations, I refer to all the characters with their Shakespearean names, not their Sinocized names, for the sake of convenience and clarity. The lines quoted, as well as other citations of Chinese texts, are my translation unless otherwise noted.

23 For a concise account of water sleeves and their different movements, see Scott (96–107).

24 See Hsü (43–44) for a full list of role types.

25 Ji remarked that he incorporated acting styles of the "mature man," the "great painted face," and the "warrior" in portraying Macbeth. His costume and makeup, however, is distinctly that of the "mature man."

26 Cf. Mackerras ("The Masses" 167).

27 As early as in 1962, Huang suggested balancing the predominant influence of Constantine Stanislavski in spoken drama by integrating elements of Chinese traditional theatre, but his theory did not win much sympathy; see Mackerras (*Chinese Drama* 162–63).

28 Huang Zuolin (Huang, "The Prospects" 13), quoted in Zhang Xiao Yang (133).

29 Li also considers *Bloody Hands* to be fully Sinocized, "completely authentic *kunqu*" ("Theatre" 38–39).

30 The adapter Lee Hui Ming was a Chinese major fresh out of college; the director Wu Hsing-kuo was a Beijing opera actor and modern dancer; the producer Lin Hsiu-wei was a modern dancer and choreographer; the set designer Deng Kuen-yen was an architect; the costume designer Lin Ching-ru had never designed for traditional theatre (Hu 25).

31 As Hsü has pointed out, the standardized costume in traditional theatre is "a self-contained system," a "mixture of Chinese dress ranging from T'ang (CE 618–906) to Ch'ing dynasty (CE 1644–1911)" which "does not conform in details to any particular period" (45). The standardized costume conveys "the social status and temperament of the characters" at one glance (44–45).

32 Shih associated Lady Macbeth's "tail" with that of the serpent and scorpion, hence an externalization of her character (242).

33 Diamond attributed all the deviations from Shakespeare to the influence of Kurosawa's 1957 film *The Throne of Blood* (118, 120–22).

34 I have discussed the supernatural elements of *Kingdom of Desire* in "Painting Ghost and Spirit in Natural Colors: *The Kingdom of Desire*, a Chinese Opera Adaptation of Shakespeare's *Macbeth*," Eleventh Annual Conference of the Group of Early Modern Cultural Studies (Newport Beach, October 2003).

35 Citations of Shakespeare are from *The Riverside Shakespeare*.

36 Shih remarked, "One sees the mirror image of the Mountain Spirit in Lady Aoshu [Lady Macbeth]" (253). The connection between Lady Macbeth and the witches has been thoroughly explored by critics; see Rose (87–88), Stallybrass (196–200), and Braunmuller (33–35). Rosenberg has discussed the productions that emphasize the "dissonant, masculinized femininity" shared by Lady Macbeth and the witches (158–205, 165). Most discussions and practices, however, tend to present the Lady as a witchlike figure instead of naturalizing the weird sisters, as *Kingdom of Desire* does.

37 Shih has surveyed the controversy raised by the premiere of *Kingdom of Desire* (269–80).

38 Li has listed three more operatic adaptations in China since 1986 ("A Drum" 169).

39 In 1914, Ya An Sichuan Opera Troupe staged *Murdering His Elder Brother and Marrying His Sister-in-Law*, an adaptation of *Hamlet* (Zhang Xiao Yang 143).

40 *Bloody Hands* was performed in Scotland, England, and Northern Ireland (1987) and Singapore (1993); *Kingdom of Desire* has toured England (1990), Korea (1991), Japan (1993), Hong Kong (1994), Germany (1996), Holland (1996, 2001), France and Spain (1998), and the United States (2005); *Lady Macbeth* has toured Germany, Holland, and Macao (2001).

Works cited

Braunmuller, A.R. "Introduction." *Macbeth*. By William Shakespeare. The New Cambridge Shakespeare. Cambridge: Cambridge UP, 1997. 1–93.

Brecht, Bertolt. *Brecht on Theatre: The Development of an Aesthetic*. Ed. and trans. John Willett. London: Methuen, 1978.

Brockbank, J. Philip. "Shakespeare Renaissance in China." *Shakespeare Quarterly* 39.2 (1988): 195–204.

Chen Xiaomei. *Occidentalism: A Theory of Counter-Discourse in Post-Mao China*. 2nd ed. Lanham: Rowman and Littlefield, 2002.

Diamond, Catherine. "*Kingdom of Desire*: The Three Faces of *Macbeth*." *Asian Theatre Journal* 11.1 (1994): 114–33.

Eagleton, Terry. *William Shakespeare*. Reading Literature Series. Oxford: Basil Blackwell, 1986.

Guy, Nancy A. "Peking Opera as 'National Opera' in Taiwan: What's in a Name?" *Asian Theatre Journal* 12.1 (1995): 85–103.

He Qi-Xin. "China's Shakespeare." *Shakespeare Quarterly* 37.2 (1986): 149–59.

Hsü Tao-Ching. *The Chinese Conception of the Theatre*. Seattle: U of Washington P, 1985.

Hu Huizhen. "*Yuwang chengguo* shinian: Wu Hsing-kuo huishou 'fei-chuantong' de yishi" (Ten Years after *The Kingdom of Desire*: Wu Hsing-kuo Recalls the Beginning of "Non-Traditional"). *Performing Arts Review* 48 (1996): 24–25.

Huang, C.Y. Alexander. "Shakespeare and the Visualization of Metaphor in Two Chinese Versions of *Macbeth*." *Comparative Literature and Culture* 6.1 (2004). 3 June 2004 <http://clcwebjournal.lib.purdue.edu/clcweb04-1/huang04.html>.

Huang, Zuolin. "A Supplement to Brecht's 'Alienation Effects in Chinese Acting.' " *Brecht and East Asian Theatre: The Proceedings of a Conference on Brecht in East Asian Theatre.* Ed. Anthony Tatlow and Tak Wai Wong. Hong Kong: Hong Kong UP, 1982. 96–110.

Ji Zhenhua. "Wo yan Kunju *Xie shou ji*" (My Acting in Kunju *The Story of Bloody Hands*). *Kunqu: Minzhu yishu jingshen de jingkou* (Kunqu: The Well of National Art Spirit). 15 Dec. 2004 <http://balrog.sdsu.edu/~shu/kunqu.htm>.

Kennedy, Dennis. "Afterword: Shakespearean Orientalism." *Foreign Shakespeare: Contemporary Performance.* Ed. Dennis Kennedy. Cambridge: Cambridge UP, 1993. 290–303.

Lee Hui-ming. *Yuwang chengguo* (The Kingdom of Desire). Taipei: International Studio of Frankfurt, 2000.

Levith, Murray J. *Shakespeare in China.* London: Continuum, 2004.

Li Ruru. "Chinese Traditional Theatre and Shakespeare." *Asian Theatre Journal* 5.1 (1988): 38–48.

—— "The Bard in the Middle Kingdom." *Asian Theatre Journal* 12.1 (1995): 50–84.

—— *Shashibiya: Staging Shakespeare in China.* Hong Kong: Hong Kong UP, 2003.

—— " 'A Drum, A Drum—Macbeth Doth Come': When Birnam Wood Moved to China." *Shakespeare Survey* 57 (2004): 169–85.

Liao Ben. *Xiju: Zhongguo yu dongxifang* (Drama: China and East–West). Taipei: Xuehai, 1999.

Liu Yanjun and Liao Ben. *Zhongguo xiju de chantui* (The Evolution of Chinese Drama). Beijing: Wenhua Yishu, 1989.

Mackerras, Colin. *Chinese Drama: A Historical Survey.* Beijing: New World Press, 1990.

—— ed. *Chinese Theatre: From Its Origin to the Present Day.* Honolulu: U of Hawaii P, 1983.

—— "Theatre and the Masses." *Chinese Theatre.* Ed. Colin Mackerras. Honolulu: U of Hawaii P, 1983. 145–83.

—— "Zhongguo difang xiqu gaibian Shashibiya" (Chinese Regional Operatic Adaptations of Shakespeare). Trans. Song Weike. *Chung-Wai Literary Monthly* 28:1 (1999): 20–31.

Regan, Stephen. "Macbeth." *Shakespeare: Texts and Contexts.* Ed. Kiernan Ryan. New York: Macmillan, 2000. 81–123.

Rose, Mark. *Shakespearean Design.* Cambridge, MA: Belknap Press of Harvard UP, 1972.

Rosenberg, Marvin. *The Masks of Macbeth.* Newark: U of Delaware P, 1978.

Scott, A.C. *The Classical Theatre of China.* New York: Macmillan, 1957.

Shakespeare, William. *Macbeth. The Riverside Shakespeare.* Ed. G. Blakemore Evans. Boston: Houghton Mifflin, 1974. 1312–42.

Shih Wen-shan. "Intercultural Theatre: Two Beijing Opera Adaptations of Shakespeare." Dissertation, University of Toronto, 2000.

Stallybrass, Peter. "*Macbeth* and Witchcraft." *Focus on Macbeth.* Ed. John Russell Brown. London: Routledge and Kegan Paul, 1982. 189–209.

Tatlow, Antony. *Shakespeare, Brecht, and the Intercultural Sign.* Post-Contemporary Interventions Series. Durham: Duke UP, 2001.

Wang An-chi. *Dangdai xiqu, fu juben xuan* (Contemporary Chinese Opera, Including Selected Plays). Taipei: Sanmin, 2002.

—— *Taiwan Jingju wushi nian* (Fifty Years of Beijing Opera in Taiwan). 2 vols. Yilan: National Center for Traditional Arts, 2002.

Wang Shu-hua. "Zhongsheng xuanhua li de Shashibiya" (A Tale of Two Cities: Shakespeare Adaptations in Shanghai and Taipei). *Chung-Wai Literary Monthly* 29.10 (2001): 117–47.

Wichmann, Elizabeth. "Traditional Theatre in Contemporary China." *Chinese Theatre: From Its Origin to the Present Day*. Ed. Colin Mackerras. Honolulu: U of Hawaii P, 1983. 184–201.

Wu Hsing-kuo. "Cong chuantong zouru Shawong shijie" (From Tradition to Shakespeare's World). *Chung-Wai Literary Monthly* 15.11 (1987): 50–51.

—— "Cheng yuwang zhi yi" (On the Wings of Desire). *Chuanqi shinian* (Ten Years of Legend). Tenth Anniversary Performance Program of *The Kingdom of Desire*. Taipei, 1996. N. pag.

Xu Fen. *Makebai furen* (Lady Macbeth). *Xu Fen xiju zuopin xuan* (Selections of Xu Fen's Dramatic Works). Ed. Chengdu City Cultural Bureau. 2 vols. Chengdu: Sichuan People's, 2001. 987–95.

Zhang Xiao Yang. *Shakespeare in China: A Comparative Study of Two Traditions and Cultures*. Newark: U of Delaware P, 1996.

16 *Macbeth*

Recent migrations of the cinematic brand

Kim Fedderson and
J. Michael Richardson

Macbeth belongs to the people who are doing it at this particular time. Even though we are aware of past traditions, we don't want necessarily to repeat them, but to make it very much our own.

(Ian McKellen, *Macbeth*, DVD)

There it was, saved forever, perfect . . . I couldn't match McKellen so I had an artistic temper tantrum.

(Chris Philpott, *Scenes from Macbeth*)

Everyone wants him!—to BE him [Shakespeare].

(Billy Morrissette, *Scotland, PA*, press kit)

"I want to be king!"

(Al Pacino, *Looking For Richard*, VHS)

The history of what was once England's most valuable cultural commodity—Shakespeare—bears striking similarities to the histories of some of the other commodities which the former empire has, in the course of its rise and fall, produced and exported. Take for example the Jaguar: a car that was once an iconic expression of British national culture and is now an asset largely in the hands of a lost colonial possession—America. As recounted in the online "Brief chronological history of the marque," the story of the Jaguar is unwittingly overwritten by motifs from Arthurian romance. The tale begins demotically with the establishment of Swallow cars by a young British motorcyclist named Billy Lyons in 1922. Later, re-christened "Jaguar," the brand gains prominence in England, becoming a bearer of the character and heritage of the national identity. In 1954, a period the "chronological history" calls "The British Invasion," Billy Lyons, himself re-christened and now Sir William Lyons of Wappenbury Hall, begins exporting cars to a "former colony . . . in earnest." We are told that this postwar period is a buoyant time when "The Empire Strikes Back," though success proves short-lived. Following Lyon's death in 1985, Jaguar succumbs to "A Better Idea," and in 1989, Jaguar is acquired by the Ford motor company. Refurbishing the brand, but capitalizing on its prestige and using funding provided by its former proprietors, Ford develops a new model, the X200: "Jaguar's smaller, more affordable saloon car, would be built at the Castle Bromwich plant." The elegy ends with a former colony's having appropriated the brand and marketing it back to its former owners. Now it's the emancipated child of the empire who strikes back.

There is something of this in the history of an imperial brand that we call SHAKESPEARE (by this neologism we are not referring to the historical author, nor to the texts of his works, but to the cultural value that is contingently imputed to them both through the history of their reception). Emerging in cultural locations where national identities and the production and consumption of cultural commodities intersect, narratives like that of the Jaguar reflect the insecurities and ambitions of national identities moving through imperial, colonial, and post-colonial contexts. Such narratives often exhibit a common structure, typically passing through predictable phases: (1) the establishment of the imperial brand; (2) the exportation of the imperial brand to its colonies; (3) colonial production and consumption of the imperial brand and its replication and mutation into various hybridic forms in the colonies; and, finally, though certainly not inevitably, (4) the colonial appropriation and re-deployment of the brand. We can see all of these phases on display in the history of the imperial brand SHAKESPEARE, especially as it moves out of its traditional high cultural locations, on or near the center, into popular culture locations on the periphery. The contours of this narrative are particularly evident in various filmed versions of *Macbeth* which we will examine, beginning with the imperial restatement of the play, the Royal Shakespeare Company's 1979 film of *Macbeth*, and then turning to a variety of colonial responses to that production, most notably a Canadian production, Chris Philpott's (1989) *Scenes from Macbeth*, and a recent American production, Billy Morrissette's *Scotland, PA* (2004). We conclude by examining the strategy of appropriation Al Pacino uses throughout his career, both on stage and in film, to lay claim to SHAKESPEARE.

*

There is at any given time a prevailing consensus which informs what readers will consider to be a *Macbeth*. This consensus is not *The Tragedie of Macbeth*, the play-text, nor a particular production, a *Macbeth*; rather it is the product of a series of dispersed but interconnected cultural preferences regarding the way in which the play-text should be realized in performance at any given time. This normative *MACBETH* is, in effect, a brand, and like all brands finds itself subject to proprietary control. While conceptions of the brand's origin—variously, the author, the play-text, the original conditions of the play's production and/or reception, etc.—are inevitably present in considerations of who owns it and controls its circulation, questions concerning its propriety are always answered in the present, not in the past. At any given moment, access to the play-text is mediated by a culturally constructed and historically specific illusion of the proper. This is not Shakespeare, the long dead and inaccessible author of the text, but SHAKESPEARE an evolving brand consisting of "a network of discursive practices, legitimating strategies and institutional pressures ... demarcating a zone of cultural transmission that includes various sixteenth and seventeenth century texts, their textual and performative history, and our labor and conversation with them" (Worthen 12).

Performances of *Macbeth* are grounded not upon the play-text alone, but on SHAKESPEARE, a historically contingent notion that delimits preferred ways of actualizing *The Tragedie of Macbeth*, thus creating a normative *MACBETH*. Without entering into the prolonged debate about whether primacy and authority reside in text or in performance, we can, at least for the sake of argument, assume that in the realms of both text and performance there exist aesthetic objects which we would, with varying degrees of comfort and confidence, designate *Macbeth*s. Friedman reasonably moderates between these polarities of text and performance, defining a performance as "an enactment that expresses one version of the significance of a text that demonstrably falls within that text's range of meaning" (39). In this view, the play-text is conceived of as a delimited field of signification, which can be made to mean many things, but which is not ultimately indeterminate. There are any number of ways that a given performance can be a *Macbeth* without necessarily being a version of *The Tragedie of Macbeth*, but its existence as such is always relational and depends upon a complex interplay of the specific signs the performance uses; the manner in which it uses those signs and the expectations this use intends (e.g. decorous imitation, ironic inversion, parodic play, etc.); and the reader's place within specific reading formations and familiarity with various interpretive canons and conventions. These signs may be used or read in ways that intentionally or unintentionally transform the production of the play-text into something that may not be immediately recognizable to all as a *Macbeth*. There are numerous films, such as *Joe Macbeth*, *Throne of Blood*, *Men of Respect*, *In the Flesh*, *MacHomer*, etc., which would not necessarily be recognized by all as *Macbeth*s.

Such films, transposed into different time periods, genres, or idioms, will be seen by many to still be *Macbeth*s, due to their deployment of plot motifs and situation, character types, thematic concerns, imagery, etc. clearly derived from the play-text and constituting its horizon of intelligibility. These minimum conditions for recognizability are what are decisive in determining what different viewers at different times and places will acknowledge to be a *Macbeth*, or at least *Macbeth*-like. The length and completeness of the performance are not, however, especially decisive in this regard—as, for instance, can be seen in the 30-minute animated versions of Shakespeare's plays produced by the BBC. The animated Shakespeares, while compact, still flow smoothly and continuously as narratives, and although they necessarily omit much of the text, cannot be said to be fragmentary in the way that Philpott's

Scenes from Macbeth, for instance, is fragmentary. Philpott's film advertises itself as a series of fragments, both in its title (*Scenes from*, not the entirety of, *Macbeth*) and in the title cards that indicate which scene is being presented at which time. Another instance is Miroslaw Rogala's *Macbeth: The Witches Scenes* which is even more elliptical. This videotape is part of a "unique futuristic production of Shakespeare's *Macbeth* (conceived by Byrne Piven) featuring interactive live action and video sequences projected on a large video screen" (liner notes to 1994 VHS version). As with Philpott, the title contains the crucial word "scenes" telling us that the performance is fragmentary and, like Philpott, Rogala includes title cards to inform us of which scene is being performed. The presence of the other crucial term, "Macbeth," in the titles of both productions confirms the films' desire to be affiliated with *MACBETH*. *Macbeth: The Witches Scenes*, with a running time of 17:38 is considerably shorter than *Scenes from Macbeth* (45 minutes) and omits even more of the plot and characters, but enough remains, and it is handled with sufficiently sophisticated and evocative imagery that "demonstrably falls within" *The Tragedie of Macbeth*'s range of meaning, to be recognizable and intelligible as a *Macbeth*.[1] All performances of the play, whether they be full-scale productions, compacted ones, or fragmentary ones, insofar as they situate themselves within the delimited field of signification established by the play-text and activate its minimum conditions of intelligibility (which will vary from one historically situated audience to another), belong to *MACBETH*.

This *MACBETH* is just as subject to historicity as SHAKESPEARE, the larger brand of which it, like all the other plays and poems, is just one particular part. Theater historians have chronicled the succession of various fashions in the performance of *Macbeth*, showing how each performance situates itself within the line of succession extending from the play-text, makes its particular claim to being an authoritative version of it, and in so doing contributes to the evolution of the norm. Not unlike the struggle for recognition within *The Tragedie of Macbeth*, performances contend with each other as they aspire within their particular historical contexts to be recognized as *MACBETH*.

*

The British claim to *Macbeth* is all but unassailable. Anyone setting out to make a *Macbeth* today inevitably contends in some fashion with Trevor Nunn's Royal Shakespeare Company (RSC) *Macbeth* featuring Ian McKellen. In the DVD commentary, McKellen tells us that "when John [Bowen] said to me one day that he thought that our *Macbeth* would do for the current generation and maybe for others afterwards, I knew we were on to something good" ("The Scottish Play: An Explanation"). The film, based on an earlier stage production, was widely regarded as the successful culmination of a postwar British tradition of performance, which was itself the extension of a line of succession stretching all the way back to Richard Burbage.

In "*Macbeth*: 1946–80 at Stratford-upon-Avon," Gareth Lloyd Evans notes that the "acting surrounding the Principals—Ian McKellen and Judi Dench—was, by far, the strongest of the period under review" (107), a period that included such Macbeths as Ralph Richardson's (1952), Laurence Olivier's (1955), Eric Porter's (1962), Paul Scofield's (1967), and Nicol Williamson's (1974). Evans's survey points out various flaws in the earlier stage productions, essentially documenting their failure to become *MACBETH*. Ralph Richardson's performance as Macbeth, says Evans, "did nothing to rescue the history of recent productions from mediocrity" (91). Laurence Olivier's (1955) surpassed great hopes for many viewers, "though the pleasures in the memory must not be allowed to obscure the fact that it did not, by any means, receive total critical acclaim" (92–93). Of Eric Porter's (1962), Evans notes that "The production and the acting had a kind of worthy dullness about them and it almost seemed as if Olivier had left little for anyone to do except, as Porter did, to present an uncluttered 'reading' of the role" (100).

By the time Paul Scofield aspires to *Macbeth* in 1967, writes Evans, "Stratford was ready for *Macbeth*; the memory of Olivier was less sharp, and Porter had left no enervating challenge. Scofield, a classical actor with huge experience, seemed an obvious choice" (102). Unfortunately, the "production's pace was slow, the lighting was capricious, the grouping sometimes seemed *ad hoc*, and some effects (notably Banquo's ghost) were awkwardly achieved" (103). However, the truly insurmountable problem was that Scofield's conception of Macbeth himself conflicted with that of the director, Peter Hall: "Scofield acted as if in tortured regret for a virtuousness that was slipping away and must be recaptured: Hall directed as if goodness and virtue had long ago disappeared from the world" (103).

Trevor Nunn, who was Hall's successor as artistic director of the RSC, signaled a kind of fealty to the legacy of his predecessor by retaining Hall's essentially "Christian" reading of the play. However, as a relative newcomer who had yet to impose "a trade mark on this company that was different from Hall's" (Evans 105), made the surprising and not altogether successful choice of Nicol Williamson for his Macbeth. Williamson employed an acting style that "is introvertive to such a degree as sometimes to seem to ignore the presence of others on the stage. The actor 'recites' to his colleagues rather than engaging them in dialogue" (105). Evans further notes that despite the eccentricities of Williamson's acting, "it was Nunn's production which excited the longest-lasting comment" (106).

In his second staging of *Macbeth*, Nunn did not repeat the miscasting of the principals, instead using McKellen and Dench, and produced a stage version which, despite a few flaws, "achieved the kind of indelibility in the memory which, ironically, might well sentence Stratford theatre-goers and actors alike to another seven years' absence from this play's rich and frightening potency" (Evans 109). Evans's prediction has turned out to be spot on. Despite the challenges of Adrian Noble in his 1994 stage version at the Barbican (RSC) with Derek Jacobi in the lead, and of Gregory Doran in his

1999 Swan production with Antony Sher, there has been no stage version to unseat that of McKellen and Dench.

The "indelibility" of the RSC stage production was soon enhanced by the production's being filmed in a fashion that adheres closely to the stage production. Both are noteworthy for starkness and simplicity in sets and costumes, the intention being to ensure, in McKellen's words, that "nothing got in the way of Shakespeare's words and the impact they had on the audience" ("Introduction"). Nunn describes the film as being an effort to "photograph the text" (quoted in McKellen, "Introduction").

McKellen claims that this film version accomplishes, even more effectively than previous elaborately staged versions, what Shakespeare himself would have wished, given that his original theater was small enough that the actors could be easily seen, used simple scenery, had no artificial lighting effects, and employed workaday costumes, leaving only actors and language. An advantage of film over stage, says McKellen, lies in things like its ability to have soliloquies delivered in close-up to the camera, so that they become direct addresses to each and every member of the audience (McKellen, "The Scottish Play"). He is much more interested in the opportunities film affords for the control and manipulation of the audience perspective than he is with the presentation of a spectacle in the classic realist mode that we see in such *Macbeth*s as Roman Polanski's which provide a minute depiction of a seemingly "real" landscape. McKellen says Shakespeare can be "overdesigned," and that this is the kind of "betrayal" that happens when Shakespeare is put into a very large theater in which the audience is too far away to see the actors well and thus needs the spectacle of costume, set design, and lighting effects to look at ("The Scottish Play"). For him and for Nunn, an overly elaborate production that exploits spectacle, costumes, scenery, etc. can seriously distract the audience from what they see as the core of Shakespeare—language.[2]

The RSC production is "Shakespeare on the cheap" but, McKellen argues, thereby captures the essence of Shakespeare ("The Scottish Play"). He notes a few instances where spectacle can be simply distracting and not at all helpful, e.g. having Banquo's ghost "corporeally there on the stage," which he notes would be "daft" since like the "air-drawn dagger" he is "only there in Macbeth's imagination." He also argues that masterful acting aided by understanding camera work can accomplish what no amount of spectacle, voice-over, or fabricated narrative links can. McKellen points out that you do not stop acting just because you are not speaking, that Dench creates the breakdown of Lady Macbeth without speech and that the camera is able to capture her as she is thinking, but not speaking ("The Scottish Play"). Because the camera directs and focuses the gaze of the viewer in a way not so readily possible on the stage (except at the cost of "naturalness"), it can be enormously helpful in keeping the viewer's attention on the words and character. In terms of the valorizing of character and language, McKellen notes that Prime Minister Harold Wilson responded most to Ross, because he is most familiar with that character type, and argues that a production should not limit the characters by costumes, etc. to a particular historical period: "you can make an audience . . . see what is not just modern but eternal in these characters—there will always be Ross's around to take advantage of the political situation." For McKellen, the main strength of this production is what he calls its "emptiness"—its refusal to set itself in medieval Scotland, or indeed any readily recognizable time and place—because this means that "any audience, watching it anywhere in the world can relate it to their experience of politics" ("The Scottish Play").[3]

Interestingly, the same dramatic and critical values underlie the quite differently realized McKellen–Loncraine *Richard III*. In the introduction to the screenplay, McKellen stresses the importance of not allowing anything to disturb or distract from the "clarity of storytelling" ("Introduction" 12). For *Richard III*, however, the setting chosen was not the "empty" one of the RSC *Macbeth*, but rather a fully realized fascist Britain of the 1930s, a setting which is fully designed but not "overdesigned." McKellen explains that this specific era was chosen because the historical events of *Richard III* occurred just a couple of generations before Shakespeare's first audiences saw them dramatized, and the parallel period for today would be the 1930s, which were also, appropriately, a decade of tyranny throughout Europe, "the most recent time when a dictatorship like Richard III's might have overtaken the United Kingdom" (13). In other words, the fictionalized, but quite specific, historical setting is justified on the grounds of recognition: the audience recognizes the allusion to a relatively recent period of tyranny, and thus can make the connection with the events and political themes of Shakespeare's text. The general aim is the same as that in his *Macbeth*, but the means to accomplish that end are changed because the political theme is somewhat different; the concrete trappings of a militaristic dictatorship carry the point more effectively than would a minimalist *Richard III*.[4]

Writing somewhat more theoretically, McKellen notes that

> Mixing words and pictures, the screen has its own language. So, in adapting *Richard III* I was translating. Translation is an inexact art, carrying responsibilities to respect the author's ends, even as you wilfully tamper with the means. I hadn't asked for Shakespeare's permission to fashion a film from his play. The least I could do was, change by change, cut by cut, ask myself whether he would have approved. . . . Not having him present to consult, I think of his having just left the rehearsal room, soon to return with the gentle query I've sometimes heard from living playwrights: "What the hell do you think you're doing to my play?"
>
> ("Introduction" 15)

Even though the mode of translation for *Macbeth* is quite different from that for *Richard III*, the justification for it, as presented by McKellen, is quite similar in that it focuses on the ability of the audience to grasp what McKellen sees as the essence of the play and relate to it immediately.

As in his *Macbeth*, he is not interested in the production's being historically accurate because "Shakespeare is writing about people with particular
natures" which in certain important respects transcend the particularities
of nationality and era ("The Scottish Play"). Thus the McKellen *Macbeth*
and *Richard III* are animated by the same philosophy of performance, but
this philosophy mandates neither historical verisimilitude nor bare stage
simplicity. What it does mandate is sensitivity to the language and characters;
a knowledge of how to use the available means of production to empower and
support high-quality acting; and an awareness of the capabilities and needs
of the audience. Verisimilitude if necessary, but not necessarily verisimilitude.
The McKellen *Macbeth*'s exploitation of those features and strengths of
the cinematic mode of production that facilitate a fixation on the play's
language and characters goes a long way towards explaining why Evans
found it indelibly etched in his memory. In achieving this, the film became
for its time the ruling *MACBETH*, and thus a target: something to aim for
and at.

*

The value of SHAKESPEARE, the imperial brand, had been established long
before McKellen arrived on the scene. Once securely established at the center,
SHAKESPEARE could migrate outwards. The history of SHAKESPEARE's
dispersion into colonial spaces has only recently begun to be explored
(Brydon and Makaryk; Fischlin), but inevitably SHAKESPEARE's arrival
unleashes a complex dynamic of compliance and resistance as the margin
writes and rewrites the cultural commodity exported by and imported from
the center. In 1953, English actor and director Tyrone Guthrie fulfilled the
hopes of many culturally insecure Canadians when he was persuaded by Tom
Patterson and the town council of Stratford, Ontario, to establish the Shakespearean Stratford Festival on the banks of its own Avon River. It quickly
became the center of theatrical culture in Canada, and its ambivalent
embrace of imperial culture in a colonial, now post-colonial, space reveals
much about the insecurities of the Canadian identities now no longer tethered
to the British empire and wary of assimilation into American culture. While it
is much more, as a colonial outpost, the festival is one of the principal sites of
SHAKESPEARE in Canada. While it began with an English actor, Alec
Guinness, speaking the first lines of *Richard III*, it now produces Shakespearean and non-Shakespearean plays and serves as a training ground for locally
produced Shakespeareans. Some of these, for example, William Hutt and
Richard Monette, would establish their careers almost exclusively within
Canada while others, notably William Shatner and Christopher Plummer, hav-
ing gained recognition there would migrate elsewhere within popular culture.

The influence of imperial culture at Stratford was also contested. With
the help of the Canadian Broadcasting Corporation, Paul Almond, a
Montreal-born filmmaker, made an unorthodox *Macbeth* in 1961. This

Macbeth, filmed using a *film noir* black and white set on a foggy and indefinable soundstage festooned with geometric obelisks, challenges the colonial mimicry implicit in the doublet and hose traditionalism then in place at the Festival Theatre. And yet this film reveals its own colonial insecurities, not just in its need to keep doing Shakespeare, but also in the casting of a pre-Bond Sean Connery in the role of *Macbeth*—his highland brogue was expected to supply the requisite authenticating resonance. Almond would later become a significant figure in the development of a specifically nationalist cinema (more specifically, French Canadian) through such films as *Isabel* and *Act of the Heart*, which, in yet another colonial irony, would bring another Canadian actor, Genevieve Bujold, to international attention.

Chris Philpott's similarly conflicted compliance and resistance is manifest throughout his *Scenes from Macbeth*. His hope, typically perhaps stereotypically Canadian, is simply for some degree of brand affiliation. His modest ambitions are further inhibited by a colonial angst more paralyzing than the inevitable anxiety of influence. He feels like the outsider he is, and this feeling of estrangement magnifies the anxiety that afflicts even those well within the establishment. Philpott expresses his loyalty to the imperial brand by virtue of deciding to make a *Macbeth* and not something altogether non-Shakespearean. Indeed, the film desperately wants to be a contribution to *MACBETH*. Its 45 minutes puts a number of scenes from the play-text into a modern business setting in Toronto and mixes the original language with contemporary idioms; the scenes are carefully selected so as to present a viewer not familiar with Shakespeare's text the essence of the plot, the most significant characters, the most famous scenes, and the most quoted speeches. There is sufficient narrative, linguistic, and thematic material retained and appropriately ordered to allow us to see this film as a *Macbeth* as opposed to, say, a *Hamlet*, yet sufficient variation introduced to allow us to distinguish it from other performances of *Macbeth*. There are some notable omissions from the cast and hence the narrative: Macduff is mentioned but does not appear, Malcolm and Donalbain are omitted, a host of lords and minor characters are either omitted or remain nameless in the film, but this in itself, along with the transplanting of the story from medieval Scotland to the Toronto of the late 1980s, is not enough to disqualify *Scenes from Macbeth* from a place within *MACBETH*.

Nonetheless, Philpott, as both a Canadian and as a relative newcomer in film and in SHAKESPEARE, feels nearly overwhelmed by both McKellen and the McKellen *Macbeth*. Confronting McKellen, who comes to his *Macbeth* furnished with a largely uncontestable pedigree—educated at Cambridge, invited by Sir Laurence Olivier to join the National Theatre Company, later a member of the Royal Shakespeare Company, knighted (elevated just like Billy Lyons), and already recognized as the heir apparent of the line of twentieth-century British Shakespeareans (e.g. Olivier, Gielgud, Richardson, Scofield)—Philpott responds with a subaltern petulance arising from his own feeling of inadequacy. He recalls watching McKellen's *Macbeth* and just being stupefied at how brilliant it was and how if interpretation meant getting closer and closer to the author's intention then all interpretation of this speech ('tomorrow and tomorrow and tomorrow') was now dead, because there it was, saved forever, perfect. Attempts to 'freshen' the text with unusual interpretations like Nicol Williamson's horrific reading in the BBC Macbeth, were inadequate. All that was left was to smash the reading. That's what I tried to do. I couldn't match McKellen so I had an artistic temper tantrum.

(personal correspondence 1998)

Despite its desire to be recognizable as a *Macbeth*, the film is in open, if ultimately ineffectual, revolt against conventional *Macbeth*s not only by virtue of its setting, but also by other liberties it takes with the text and with traditions of production and interpretation. Given his strong reaction to McKellen's performance of the speech, it is no surprise that the most radical gesture in Philpott's minor insurrection is the film's presentation of the "tomorrow and tomorrow and tomorrow" speech three times in a row, using three completely different styles and generic conventions: (1) as an unvarnished and inexpressive recitation in which the actor playing Macbeth adheres strictly to the text, suppressing all dramatic inflection, attempting to neutralize his self so that the text passes through him intact, untouched, undefiled—the ultimate in paranoid loyalty to a text or a brand; (2) as a wildly parodic standup comedy routine retaining the correct words, but alluding, via voice and mannerisms, to Groucho Marx, Jerry Lewis, the Three Stooges, and Le Petomane,[5] in effect subjecting the text to Philpott's unruly desires; and (3) as a drunken rant in a noisy underpass while his potential audience, the people in the cars, hurtle by him, oblivious to his barely audible performance; here the actor playing Macbeth still adheres faithfully to his text, but fails to connect with his audience at all. These multiple and incompatible renderings of the speech enact both Philpott's fidelity to SHAKESPEARE and his desire to do something willfully distinctive within it. But these versions also disrupt both the narrative flow of the film and our sense of what conventions to mobilize when reading it, making the point of the revolt unclear and nullifying its chances of success.

While not all the signs of revolt against *MACBETH* disrupt the narrative in this way, they do, sometimes individually and certainly cumulatively, destabilize our sense of what conventions and reading practices to deploy when viewing the film, suggesting the very kind of not fully focused but incredibly vehement energy captured in Philpott's own designation: tantrum. Sometimes in the film, these signs of revolt against *MACBETH* are on a small verbal scale; for example, the first speech in the film is Macbeth's saying "So foul and fair a day I have not seen," followed immediately by Banquo's prosaic, anachronistic, and bathetic "Yeah"; later the divorced Banquo goes to pick up his son and his ex-wife delivers the incredibly banal line "Fleance, your dad's here." Sometimes revolt is signaled by a jarring and even comic incongruity, as in having Macbeth's letter of Act 1, scene 5 appear, word for word, on Lady Macbeth's answering machine; or having Macbeth kill Duncan with a pool cue after Macbeth has snorted cocaine to screw his courage to the sticking point; or having Macbeth arrange Banquo's murder by meeting the murderers in a toilet stall in a nightclub; or having Macbeth during the banquet scene try to swallow all the food on the table while the live crabs served to the guests try to scramble out of their bowls, and, in the background, Banquo's murdered body struggles against the straps that hold it down on a gurney; or having a profoundly disturbed Lady Macbeth perform the sleepwalking scene walking down Yonge St. in her bathrobe in broad daylight shouting the Shakespearean lines while walking right past the restaurant where the anti-Macbeth conspiracy is forming (and a sign reading "Fully Licensed" is foregrounded). Finally, Philpott's Macbeth is killed in a drive-by shooting, the gunman being in a pickup truck. This pickup truck is loaded with Christmas trees, which some viewers will realize are this film's version of Birnam wood's coming to Dunsinane. This way of killing Macbeth has troublesome relations with the play-text itself, since an ambush is not comparable to an invasion, for instance, and we do not know what the relationship of the gunman to Macduff is, or if indeed he is connected to Macduff at all—but the dying Macbeth recalls the prophecy about his vulnerability only to one of woman born and is told by the police officer attending him that Macduff was untimely ripped from his mother's womb, so some relevance is hinted at. More significantly, we do not know how to respond to this scene emotionally: the drive-by is a serious and tragic conclusion, even if not the most dignified way for Macbeth to be done in, but the recognition of the trees' relationship to the witches' prophecy is purely comic.

Philpott clearly wants to be recognized as belonging to SHAKESPEARE, but belonging means to submit, willingly, to certain constraints required to make one recognizable as an "affiliate." The anxiety of influence in his letter suggests that Philpott both wants to affiliate himself with his predecessors, but also to make his own voice heard, to belong but simultaneously to escape the restrictions of belonging. As Macbeth feels tied to the stake by his enemies at the end of the play, but will still die with harness on his back, so Philpott feels similarly tied down by the McKellen *Macbeth*, but still will kick against it. *Scenes from Macbeth* closes with a poignant image depicting this struggle against imprisonment in a tradition, an image which shows the deadening burden which the latterly coming individual inherits. As Philpott's Macbeth lies on the ground, two police officers draw a chalk outline around his "corpse" as though he were already dead, and indeed he appears so at first glance. But then the "corpse" rouses itself and protests that it is not dead, getting more and more frantic as the police explain to him that he must be dead since the witches' prophecies have all come to pass. We last see this Macbeth struggling to escape the chalk outline as one policeman brings it towards completion and the other policeman holds Macbeth down; the screen goes dark; and, finally, we hear both birds singing and Macbeth/ Philpott still crying out in protest.

In *Scenes from Macbeth*, Philpott, despite attempting some radical alterations to the play, has no desire to mount a serious challenge to the imperial claim. His film is the result of the colonial subject's conflicted position: in service to the masters, but living at a potentially liberating distance. His individual "Scenes," as he implies in his letter, constitute an interesting series of tantrums done to and with *Macbeth* in order to gain recognition both at home and abroad, in effect to be noticed. His *Macbeth* is a fine adaptation (really a quasi-production) of the play. It meets the minimum conditions of recognizability as a *Macbeth* and, like McKellen's version, picks up and develops aspects of the play that transcend both its original medieval setting and the early modern context of its composition, thus encouraging viewers to revisit their current biases and modes of reading *Macbeth*. The anxiety that Philpott feels when faced with McKellen and the McKellen production is that of the colonial subject in the face of an empire he cannot begin to dream of seriously challenging. *Scenes from Macbeth* is a hybrid and carnivalesque response that seeks to differentiate itself from the more pious productions we would see in a Stratford (Ontario) production. In its effort to be distinctive, *Scenes from Macbeth* fashions Philpott as someone in Canada doing something interesting with *MACBETH*; it shows him as, in effect, making a pitch in hopes to gain affiliation with the head office. It is reminiscent of the time Canadian Prime Minister Pierre Elliott Trudeau in a moment of naughtiness did a pirouette behind the Queen's back—but on national television. In this respect, Philpott's film, unlike Trudeau's dance number, can be said to be a failure—Trudeau could and did patriate the constitution for Canadians, but *MACBETH* stays stubbornly British. Philpott and his film are relatively unknown; both he and his film end up like his Macbeth riffing on the "tomorrow" speech to a potential audience—SHAKESPEARE and its luminaries like McKellen—who remain blissfully unaware of his existence.[6]

*

Philpott's *Scenes from Macbeth* shows us one response to the colonial predicament of establishing an identity on the margin. In a typical Canadian manner, Philpott seeks recognition by submitting to tradition. He acknowledges and respects the cultural authority of the materials he chooses to work with and seeks recognition within SHAKESPEARE, adapting himself to it via a fraught though not abject strategy of homage, compromise, and improvisation.

Billy Morrissette's *Scotland, PA*, an American reworking of *Macbeth* set in a Pennsylvania fast food restaurant in the 1970s, reveals an alternate response to the colonial predicament. Morrissette seeks recognition by revolting against SHAKESPEARE, though in this instance this is a very simplistic and limited conception of SHAKESPEARE. For Morrissette, SHAKESPEARE is little more than an oppressive "Britishness"—i.e. elitism, classism, classicism, and presumption of cultural authority—suffocating the American spirit. In his enthusiasm for doing something new and revolutionary, Morrissette fecklessly tilts against this straw man. In the end, however, neither he nor his film is capable of offering any coherent substitute for the tradition it sets out to displace.[7]

Scotland, PA clearly affiliates itself with *Macbeth* through the names of its characters and the structure of its plot. The online press kit accompanying the film explicitly refers to it as a "black comedy retelling of Shakespeare's *Macbeth*," casting a "skewed glance" at the play and "sending it up for reappraisal." Morrissette's film, he claims, has enough "cultural and national self-confidence . . . to throw off any trace of earlier English theatrical traditions and practices" (*Scotland, PA*, press kit).

Of course, there's nothing revolutionary in the practice of adapting Shakespearean narratives and themes to the cultural imperatives of one's own historical time and place. Indeed, Michael Bogdanov, in his *Shakespeare on the Estate* (BBC, 1994) and later his *Macbeth* (Channel 4, 1997), feels the need to challenge the orthodoxies of SHAKESPEARE, and does so by actively working with a diverse group of common people: "Asian youths, various representatives of the large black community, drunks, homeless, unemployed" (quoted in Abele). Unlike Morrissette, who belittles all of his characters, Bogdanov treats his similarly plebeian characters in a serious and dignified fashion, and there seeks the means by which a seemingly irrelevant SHAKESPEARE could be revivified.

There's nothing inherently wrong in the satiric strategy of resisting, interrogating, or even rejecting longstanding standards of value. But to succeed satire requires an identifiable object, a discernible standard against which characters and institutions can be judged, and at least some characters treated with sufficient dignity to enlist our interest and sympathy. All of the characters in *Scotland, PA* are the objects of a derisive gaze, and it is far from clear whether the target of the bathetic incongruity between the characters and their tragic emplotment is American working-class culture in the 1970s or Jacobean tragedy. The film leaves us wondering whether the point is to suggest that the overarching concerns of tragedy (ambition, guilt, justice) are too inflated to square with contemporary experience, or whether the lives of these fast food workers and their associates are simply too puny for us to recognize their tragic implications. Morrissette's inability to clearly identify the targets of his satire and the norms against which their various failings can be measured undermines the satire. All that's left is unfocused farce full of the sounds of the 1970s and furious incident but ultimately signifying nothing.

Morrissette's response to his colonial predicament is fraught with contradictions. On the one hand, he clearly wants recognition within SHAKESPEARE and to see himself, like Loncraine, Almereyda, and Luhrmann, as one of the new adapters of the Bard. On the other hand, he derisively claims that the seriousness of members of SHAKESPEARE, from Olivier to Trevor

Nunn, amounts to little more than efforts to "morally or culturally shape and uplift the public, that is, to act as a kind of social bra" (*Scotland, PA*, press kit). He seems to think that the most authentic response to Shakespeare's work is not serious engagement but "smart-ass wryness," as is evident in what first attracted him to *Macbeth*: "it was not the plot, not the theme, not the meaning, not the 'Tomorrow and tomorrow and tomorrow' speech that touched him, but the fact that almost everyone had 'Mac' in their name" (*Scotland, PA*, press kit). Unlike McKellen and Philpott who seek recognition within SHAKESPEARE, Morrissette largely wishes to capitalize on *Macbeth*, but, finding that the burden that tradition imposes on him is too onerous, he grows resentful, and attempts to jettison that baggage and remake tradition in his own image. That image, however, rarely becomes anything more than a puerile sketch comedy designed to outrage the grownups. Morrissette, like Twain's Duke and the Dauphin in *Huckleberry Finn*, who also bring Shakespeare to the New World, does not so much make a *Macbeth* as exploit *MACBETH* to make a name for himself in American popular culture. In this endeavor he may very well be quite successful, but as a contribution to SHAKESPEARE, *Scotland, PA* is an incoherent adolescent rant, not the ludic and subversive, intentionally fractured postmodern refiguration of a canonical text that it claims to be.

*

As Macbeth's reign is coming apart at the seams, Angus says of the usurper: "now does he feel his title/ Hang loose about him like a giant's robe/ Upon a dwarfish thief" (5.2.21–22). Philpott feels acutely his dwarfishness in relation to SHAKESPEARE, but, like Disney's sorcerer's apprentice, gamely tries to wear its robes with a semblance of poise. Morrissette denies that the robes belong to a giant at all, and he dons them with a cockiness that fails to conceal their ill fit. In laying claim to SHAKESPEARE, there is a third and final contender whose strategy for being "king and safely thus" warrants consideration. Al Pacino, the most serious challenger to the imperial claim on SHAKESPEARE has not even made a *Macbeth*; he is, however, fully prepared to assume the giant's robes, and claim them as his and America's right. He doesn't so much make a *Macbeth*, as do a Macbeth. In *Looking for Richard*, his documentary about producing *Richard III*, Pacino attempts Macbeth's unrealized ambition to displace the King—in this instance, the British claim on SHAKESPEARE—and install himself as the first in a new line of succession. McKellen's and Pacino's careers are an interesting study in contrasts. Given his recognition within, and gentrification through, SHAKESPEARE, McKellen, like Shatner and Plummer, is able to migrate out from the imperial Shakespearean center into popular culture. He lands roles in such projects as *Lord of the Rings*, *Gods and Monsters*, and *Apt Pupil* precisely because of his success in the center. Through these sorts of roles, McKellen becomes enough of a household name that he moves even further from the center and finds himself in *X Men* (cast as the nemesis of a similarly transplanted Shakesbrit, Patrick Stewart).

Pacino's path is the inverse of McKellen's—a move out of the formerly colonial space into the heart of the empire. *Looking for Richard* closes with Pacino in street clothes intoning the opening of *Richard III* on the stage of the simulated Globe that the American actor and film and TV director Sam Wanamaker has built on the shores of the Thames where the original Globe once stood. Pacino goes looking for SHAKESPEARE, and his film effects the familiar chiasmus of colonial and imperial exchange evident in such new world narratives as *A Connecticut Yankee in King Arthur's Court*. Here origin and effect switch places and a youthful colonial offspring saves or restores its flagging imperial progenitor. *Looking for Richard* contends that the vitality of *Richard III* and SHAKESPEARE has been sapped by traditions of British theatrical orthodoxy. Exiled to the new world, SHAKESPEARE finds sanctuary among the commoners, and there purified and restored to its original health, it returns and reclaims its place in the center.

Unlike McKellen, Pacino acquires his notoriety and establishes his prestige through popular culture, in such essentially American films as *Panic in Needle Park*, *Dog Day Afternoon*, *The Godfather*, and *Serpico*. Nonetheless, he has always felt the pull of English national culture. He appeared in stage versions of *Richard III* (1972–1973, 1979), *Hamlet* (1979), and *Othello* (1979). He also participated in a number of plays in Joseph Papp's Public Theater. Pacino shares the values and the anxieties that inform the Public Theater. The Public "is an American theater in which all the country's voices, rhythms, and cultures converge" (The Public Theater, "History"), specifying its values as populist, nationalist, and hybrid. In implied contrast to elitist English classical traditions, The Public dedicates itself "to achieving artistic excellence while developing an American theater that is accessible and relevant to all people" (The Public Theater, "Mission"). But paradoxically, this populist and nationalist melting pot of a theater is in perpetual collision with the classical and elite: The Public began as the "Shakespeare Workshop," still produces "new plays, musicals, productions of Shakespeare, and other classics," remains the "permanent summertime home of free Shakespeare in Central Park," and shoulders responsibility for training "the next generation of classical performers through the Shakespeare Lab" (The Public Theater, "History"). The Public is a nationalist theater that nonetheless remains obsessively concerned with imperial culture, allaying its anxieties about its own cultural prestige by affiliating itself with what it implicitly rebels against. The Public tries to fuse two different senses of value—the traditional, aristocratic, values of the empire, however vestigial, and the democratic, populist values of America, however conflicted. These are the very anxieties that rise to the surface in Pacino's *Looking for Richard*.

In the documentary, Pacino alleges that a SHAKESPEARE mired in imperial traditions of performance and scholarship becomes an inaccessible and antiquarian pleasure reserved for the elite, and thus can no longer find its proper, popular, audience. His quest, depicted in the documentary, is to restore Shakespearean art to its rightful place in world culture by returning it to its populist, democratic roots, which are immediately recognizable to him as a modern American hero.[8] It is in this respect that Pacino most resembles Shakespeare's Macbeth. Just as Macbeth sought to usurp the throne and install himself as the first in a new line of succession, so Pacino contests the cultural authority of imperial SHAKESPEAREs with a view to establishing a relocated American line of succession. Ignoring McKellen's definitive accomplishments within SHAKESPEARE, rejecting out of hand Philpott's deferential contribution, and with much grander ambition than Morrissette's adolescent strivings, Pacino claims SHAKESPEARE as his own. Just as the Jaguar was lost to the empire and found a new home within America, Pacino appropriates SHAKESPEARE and markets it within a global marketplace.

Notes

1 Originally, Rogala's *Macbeth: The Witches Scenes* was part of a larger stage production of *Macbeth* which premiered on November 10, 1988 at the Noyes Cultural Arts Center, Evanston, Ill. Subsequently released as a separate video, *The Witches Scenes* now stands alone acting as a metonymic proxy for that production and a synecdochal iteration of *Macbeth*.

2 The overly melodramatic film of the staged version of *Macbeth* featuring Jeremy Brett and Piper Laurie presents a much more decorated set, offering a spectacle to compensate for its inability to engage the audience with the play's language.

3 For discussions about the problematic representation of place in *Macbeth* see Holland; Lehmann.

4 This is not to say that there is not also some loss, especially in the area of historicity— gone from this *Richard III* are arguments about the divine nature of kingship, for instance, but in their stead are other signs that Richard has disrupted what some characters in the play, and many members of the audience perhaps, would regard as the natural order of things.

5 Le Petomane: late nineteenth, early twentieth-century French performer who perfected flatulence as a performance art. See Nohain and Caradec.

6 Chris Philpott's career has since moved in non-Shakespearean directions. He has written, produced, and/or directed a number of feature-length films, some of which have received awards at venues such as the Palm Beach International Film Festival and the Phoenix Film Festival. These films include *Fairytales and Pornography* (2003), *The Happy Couple* (2002), and a film of the Dostoevsky novella *The Eternal Husband* (1998).

7 For a more sympathetic account of *Scotland, PA*, see Lehmann; Shohet. Shohet claims that *Scotland, PA* is an "intelligent if far from pious . . . take on *Macbeth*" which derives its critical edge from its "thoroughgoing engagement with details of the Shakespearian text and with textures of the 1970s" (187). While the setting certainly calls attention to the pervasive commodification of experience, declining political, social, and economic agency, and reconfiguration of gender roles characteristic of the era, whether it critically examines these issues or merely puts them on display for our amusement is debatable.

8 For a more detailed development of this argument, see Fedderson and Richardson.

Works cited

Abele, Elizabeth. "*Macbeth*." Rev. of *Macbeth*, dir. Michael Bogdanov. 26 January 2007 <http://www.imagesjournal.com/rarchive.htm>.

"Brief chronological history of the marque." 18 March 2005 <http://www.fordmotorcompany.co.za/corporate/history/jaguar.asp>.

Brydon, Diana and Irena R. Makaryk, eds. *Shakespeare in Canada: A World Elsewhere?* Toronto: U of Toronto P, 2002.

Evans, Gareth Lloyd. "*Macbeth*: 1946–80 at Stratford-upon-Avon." *Focus on Macbeth*. Ed. John Russell Brown. London: Routledge and Kegan Paul, 1982. 87–110.

Fedderson, K. and Richardson, M. "Looking for Richard in *Looking for Richard*." *Postmodern Culture* 8.2 (1998). 26 Jan. 2007 <http://www3.iath.virginia.edu/pmc/text-only/>.

Fischlin, Daniel. *Canadian Adaptations of Shakespeare Project*. 2004. 18 March 2005 <http://www.canadianshakespeares.ca/>.

Friedman, Michael D. "In Defense of Authenticity." *Studies in Philology* 99.1 (2002): 33–56.

Holland, Peter. " 'Stands Scotland Where It Did?': The Location of *Macbeth* on Film." *Macbeth*. Ed. Robert S. Miola. New York: W.W. Norton, 2004. 357–80.

In the Flesh. Dir. Stuart Canterbury and Antonio Passolini. VCA Interactive. 1998. VHS and DVD.

Joe Macbeth. Dir. Ken Hughes. Perf. Paul Douglas and Ruth Roman. Film Locations, 1955.

Lehmann, Courtney. "Out Damned Scot: Dislocating *Macbeth* in Transnational Film and Media Culture." *Shakespeare, The Movie II: Popularizing the Plays on Film, TV, Video, and DVD*. Ed. Richard Burt and Lynda E. Boose. New York: Routledge, 2003. 231–51.

Looking for Richard. Dir. Al Pacino. Fox Searchlight Pictures, 1996.

Macbeth. Dir. Orson Welles. Perf. Orson Welles and Jeanette Nolan. Mercury Productions/Republic, 1948.

Macbeth. Dir. Paul Almond. CBC Television, Canada. 1961.

Macbeth. Dir. Roman Polanski. Perf. Jon Finch, Francesca Annis, and Martin Shaw. Columbia Pictures, 1971. DVD. Tristar Home Entertainment, 2002.

Macbeth. Dir. Trevor Nunn. Perf. Ian McKellen and Judi Dench. Thames Television, 1978. DVD. Fremantle Home Entertainment, 2004.

Macbeth. Perf. The Independent Eye. Theatre 2000. 5 February 1994. VHS. 1995.

Macbeth on the Estate. Dir. Penny Woolcock. BBC2, U.K. 1997.

"*Macbeth on the Estate*." *British Theatre Guide*. 12 Aug. 2005 <http://www.britishtheatreguide.info/articles/140497.htm>.

Macbeth. Dir. Michael Bogdanov. Channel 4, U.K. 1997.

Macbeth. Dir. Arthur Allan Seidelman. Bard Productions. DVD. Century Home Video, 1981.

Macbeth: The Comedy. Dir. Alision L. LiCalsi. Tristan Films, 2001.

Macbeth: Shakespeare: The Animated Tale. Dir. Nikolai Serebirakov. Christmas Films and Soyuzmultifim. 1992.

Macbeth: The Witches Scenes. Dir. Miroslaw Rogala. VHS. 1994.

MacHomer: The Simpsons Do Macbeth. Written and perf. Rick Miller. 1995. 26 Jan. 2007 <http://www.canadianshakespeares.ca/a_machomer.cfm>.

McKellen, Ian. "Introduction." *William Shakespeare's "Richard III": A Screenplay Written by Ian McKellen and Richard Loncraine, Annotated and Introduced by Ian McKellen.* Woodstock: Overlook, 1996. 7–37.

—— "Introduction to *Macbeth*." *Macbeth*. Dir. Trevor Nunn. Perf. Ian McKellen and Judi Dench. Thames Television, 1978. DVD. Fremantle Home Entertainment, 2004.

—— *Ian McKellen.* 26 Jan. 2007 <http://www.mckellen.com/>.

—— "The Scottish Play: An Explanation." *Macbeth*. Dir. Trevor Nunn. Perf. Ian McKellen and Judi Dench. Thames Television, 1978. DVD. Fremantle Home Entertainment, 2004.

Men of Respect. Dir. William Reilly. Columbia Pictures, 1991. DVD. Sony Pictures, 2003.

Nohain, J. and F. Caradec. *Le Petomane, or, Gone with the Wind.* Trans. Warren Tute. London: Sphere, 1967.

Philpott, Chris. Personal Correspondence to J.M. Richardson. 13 March 1998.

The Public Theater. "History." 26 Jan. 2007 <http://www.publictheater.org/about/history.php>.

—— "Mission." 26 Jan. 2007 <http://www.publictheater.org/about/mission.php>.

Richard III. Dir. Richard Loncraine. United Artists, 1995. VHS.

Scenes from Macbeth. Written and dir. Chris Philpott. Philpott Productions, 1989. VHS.

Scotland, PA. Dir. Billy Morrissette. Perf. James LeGros, Maura Tierney, and Christopher Walken. Lot 47, 2001. DVD. Sundance Channel Home Entertainment, 2005.

Scotland, PA, press kit. 18 March 2005 <http://lot47.com/scotlandpa/press.html>.

Shakespeare on the Estate. Dir. Michael Bogdanov. BBC, U.K. 1994.

Shohet, Lauren. "The Banquet of Scotland (PA)." *Shakespeare Survey* 57 (2004): 186–95.

Throne of Blood. (*Kumonosu-Jo.*) Dir. Akira Kurosawa. Perf. Toshiro Mifune and Isuzu Yamada. Toho, 1957.

Worthen, W.B. "Staging 'Shakespeare': Acting, Authority, and the Rhetoric of Performance." *Shakespeare, Theory, and Performance.* Ed. James C. Bulman. London and New York: Routledge, 1996. 12–28.

17 Hypermedia *Macbeth*

Cognition and performance

Bruno Lessard

Minds are media, and vice versa.
  (W.J.T. Mitchell, "Addressing Media")

It will come as no surprise to anyone who has been watching the cultural recuperation of Shakespeare since the coming of film and television to witness the apparition of "digital Shakespeares."[1] This "post-cinema Shakespeare"[2] has appeared on the Internet and on CD-ROM, but those digital productions are often perceived as derivative commodities or simply unelaborated efforts characteristic of the cultural moment in which we live. However, as this chapter would like to show, digital adaptations of *Macbeth* are fascinating productions that actualize visually the very cognitive mechanisms readers of *Macbeth* perform when they read the play. Digital adaptations would stage the very processes our modular minds go through when we read *Macbeth*, and the study of such processes prompted by digital artworks allows us to gain insight into the analogous mechanisms that take place in our embodied minds. Combining touch, sight, and hearing, digital transformations of *Macbeth* refashion the way in which we understand information processing and the manner in which we assimilate Shakespeare. Even though some may argue that we have always read "hypertextually," one of digital technologies' major contributions would be to make apparent the cognitive mechanisms and performances that were neglected in the last decades, returning us to hearing, reading, and viewing positions that relate to oral poetry, stage performance, codex, and film.

Envisioning digital performance as an elaboration on previous types of performance, we may be tempted to look at *how Macbeth* signifies rather than at *what* it means. Such an inquiry would try to trace the migration from playscript, to printed text, to hypermedia. In the following pages an online adaptation of *Macbeth* entitled *HyperMacbeth*, by Italian digital artist dlsan (b. 1968), and Voyager's CD-ROM *Macbeth*, edited by A.R. Braunmuller, will serve as illustrations of the principal challenges facing future hypermedia adapters in the age of digital Shakespeares.

It should be pointed out at the outset that these two works in no way represent the future of Shakespeare in digital environments. Rather, they are useful examples of the creative strategies that have been used to transfer *Macbeth* from its traditional textual basis to computer screen in a way that reflects the desire to reshape performance in the digital era. As I argue, our understanding of "digital Shakespeare" would gain from the latter's inclusion within the history of performance. In fact, it can only be comprehended if seen within such a framework that not only refers to performance theory but also to performance across media.[3]

Performance and media migration

Elaborating on the work of Marshall McLuhan and Walter Ong, medievalist Paul Zumthor and historian Roger Chartier have written extensively on performance and media migration.[4] More concretely, they have paid attention to the manner in which orality and performance somewhat keep returning in newer media environments. Departing from critical positions that see fractures and schisms between historical periods and transitions, they have positioned performance as the recurring background against which to evaluate change in mediatic practices. It is the constant recycling and reappearance of performance, rather than its supposed disappearance, that is crucial to Zumthor and Chartier and that shall be investigated in the two digital *Macbeth*s examined here.

Zumthor's early work on oral poetry has shown that the categories (e.g. text, author) with which we study "literature" cannot account for the performative moments in medieval poetics. The later Zumthor was interested in the resurgence of orality in the twentieth century and examined what Walter Ong calls "secondary orality," that is, the presence of aural stimuli in various technological inventions that do not resemble the ones in past oral cultures. Interestingly, this concern for the transformation and recycling of orality was accompanied by a reconsideration of reading in terms of performance. In one of his late works, Zumthor remarks: "I am particularly convinced that the idea of performance must be largely extended; it should include all those actions that today concern the word *reception*" (emphasis in original, 19).[5] Zumthor goes on to argue that, in words that call to mind cognitive theory, it is reception as corporeal and sensorial perception that should attract our critical attention, reminding us that it is the human body that actually *receives* the literary work. In short, the medievalist's preoccupation was the possibility of developing concepts derived from performance theory to analyze embodied readers at work.

Chartier's work also addresses orality and performance, but his deals more directly with the representation and the reception of the written word in the digital age. Comparing various modes of reading, Chartier asks the following question: "How do we situate within the long history of the book, of reading, and of relations to the written word, the revolution that has been predicted, has in fact already begun, which transforms the book (or the written object) as we know it—with its quires, its leaves, its pages—into an electronic text to be read on a screen?" (*Forms* 14) The French historian's contribution would lie in the identification of the digital representation of texts as a critical moment in the history of reading. Commenting on the current "revolution," he notes: "The revolution of the electronic text will also be a revolution in reading. To read on a screen is not to read in a codex ... in place of the immediate apprehension of the whole work, made visible by the object that embodies it, it introduces a lengthy navigation in textual archipelagos that have neither shores nor borders" (*Forms* 18). Even though Chartier's rhetoric may seem to border on excessiveness as to the radical nature of the "revolution" hypertext has brought, he nevertheless hits the mark when he underlines the way in which new modes of writing and representation of the written word call for a reconsideration of what we do as readers.

Both Zumthor and Chartier demand that we approach a text (printed or virtual) in terms of performance, and that we inscribe this performance within the long history of oral and silent reading. The changing nature of performance is to be understood in terms of media migration, and the virtual representation of Shakespeare's plays in both scholarly editions and digital adaptations will have to begin with the reassessment of Zumthor's and Chartier's theses. Combined with Zumthor's and Chartier's insights, cognitive theory and recent research on digital performance will guide the forthcoming analysis of digital *Macbeth*s.

Cognition, Shakespeare, and performance

One of the most controversial analogies in cognitive science has concerned the comparison of the human brain with the computer: "When we put together the incoming sensory pathways with the outgoing motor ones, we have a reliable picture of what the brain does: it functions not unlike a computer in sifting and analyzing data and arriving at appropriate responses" (Kinney, *Lies* 32). The manner in which neurones and synapses interconnect to generate cerebral activity that leads to perception and to what is known as "cognition" is a nodal process that would recall hyperlinking. Of course, the point is not to claim that the brain *is* a computer, *pace* certain digital enthusiasts; it far exceeds what any future computer will be able to perform. The comparison is interesting because, as Nycole Paquin has argued, when the brain juggles with percepts and concepts, "perception becomes a performance, a cognitive event" (181).[6] Moreover, this performance as "cognitive event" would influence the manner in which we perceive literature in general. According to Mark Turner: "We would focus on how the embodied human mind uses its ordinary conceptual capacities to perform those acts of language and literature" (6).[7]

In Shakespeare studies, Mary Thomas Crane and Arthur F. Kinney have used cognitive theory to rejuvenate critical perspectives on the Bard's plays.[8] Whereas Crane posits a theory of human subjectivity within which "The body and the embodied brain structure meaning through complex linkages and networks that have a subterranean multiplicity from which simpler ideological structures emerge" (33), Kinney's cognitive and hypertextual framework to analyze Shakespeare's work and culture seems most helpful in the proposed approach to digital productions. In his writings Kinney revises the new historicist agenda by combining it with what he has called "hypertextual criticism." This combination would reorient current new historicist approaches and offer a critical reading that would be, to use Kinney's adjective, "hypertextual": "The center of interest now . . . is not [*Macbeth*'s] relationship to the margins, or to the beginning and the ending, but to a web of meaningful interrelations that are mutually enhancing at any nodal point in the play" (*Lies* 41). Kinney's cognitive and hypertextual outlook pictures Shakespeare's plays as an enormous database from which scholars make meaningful connections.

Having to work with a multitude of texts and versions, contemporary editors of Shakespeare's plays can use various digital and multimedia techniques to enhance their work in a way that actually demonstrates how unstable and uncertain textual editions of Shakespeare have always been. Moreover, the various versions of a given play entail a form of navigational performance that digital technologies make tangible. W.B. Worthen notes: "Rather than rendering the *text* less stable and coherent, hypertext in this sense perhaps approaches the performative by more openly situating the text on the permeable horizon of performance, where meanings arise from what we do to texts in order to make something from them" (emphasis in original, 213). Adding the notion of performance to the reconceptualization of reading in digital media, Worthen underscores the manner in which recent technologies seem to displace performance from actor to interactor.

My contention is that the interactor's embodied mind, when facing a digital rendition of *Macbeth*, reproduces the very associative mechanisms that the hypermedia technology performs itself. On the one hand, there is a cause-and-effect relationship between the hypermedia linkages and the interactor's cognitive linkages, but it should be made clear that there is no question as to what or who comes first; a digital work is an artistic invitation to perform within the algorithmic confines the creator has programmed. This creative agency must be allowed to the artist prior to assessing what the interactor will make of the work. On the other hand, the interactor's cognitive task cannot be bypassed in the process; she has to explore the digital work creatively, using her mnemonic skills, her knowledge of the play, her memories of film adaptations of the play, and then she will notice the analogous nature between what is taking place on the computer screen and what goes on in her mind as she reads the play in its textual environment.

Even though the interactor is bound to a program, her choices will be her own. The performance of the interactor does not lie in the clicking on links; rather, her cognitive and bodily performance analyzes the textual, visual, and sound effects attributed to each of the words, figures out why certain words are hyperlinked to others, and projects in her mind an unseen version of the play. This is where performative agency enters the stage. Thus envisaged, digital adaptations and editions would act as mirrors that return potential images in the disguised form of performative moments.

Digital Macbeths: dlsan's *HyperMacbeth* (2001) and the Voyager Shakespeare's *Macbeth* (1994)

Digital artist dlsan's *HyperMacbeth*[9] has been described as "an experimental representation of a dramatic text" ("the HyperMacbeth"). In a critical assessment from *Wired* magazine, Chloe Veltman has remarked that this "new treatment of *Macbeth* on the Internet probably won't impress Shakespeare purists." Indeed, the hypertextual activities and multimedia setting *Hyper-Macbeth* proposes appear to date back to the days of early Internet art experimentation. However, such critical stances on the work, as positive or negative as they may be, often disguise hasty judgments that could blind one to the role dlsan's piece actually plays in digital media's reconfiguration of performance.

Contrary to the account of the digital piece in *Wired*, I would question any enthusiastic description of *HyperMacbeth* as to its unpredictability, open-endedness, and non-linearity. The radical nature of digital media does not reside in the most obvious moments of bewilderment. As in numerous digital adaptations of literary works, it is not the work per se but its hypermedia configuration that should interest us, and the way in which it relates to various modes of cultural and technological appropriation that recycle and reshape performance.

Combining extracts from three of the play's soliloquies with industrial music and flashy colored strips, dlsan's *HyperMacbeth*'s originality and innovative treatment rest in the artist's unmentioned concept of performance. The hypermedia treatment *Macbeth* receives points to various modes of textual and visual reception that recall several episodes in the history of reading. To borrow Veltman's words, it is its "screen cluttered with undulating shards of text, colors, and music" that we must analyze to locate the website's innovative features.

The interactor has one initial task to perform: at the bottom of the screen appear officer Seyton's well-known words to Macbeth: "The queen, my lord, is dead" (5.5.16),[10] while the top of the screen features the Italian translation of the quotation which reads "La regina, mio signore, è morta" (Figure 17.1). Apparently, the first step in order to explore this website is to choose either the words in English or the ones in the Italian translation. This choice reminds the interactor that *Macbeth* is a play that is experienced and performed not only in English but also in translation into several languages. Moreover, dlsan's use of translation acts as a *mise en abyme* of the process of digitally translating *Macbeth* into hypermedia.

The interactor who decides to work with the quotation in English can click

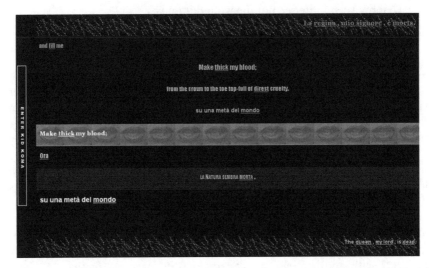

Figure 17.1 Web page from *HyperMacbeth*. <http://www.dlsan.org/macbeth/ the_mac.htm>. By permission of Matteo Santoni, a.k.a dlsan.

on the following hyperlinked words: "queen," "my lord," and "dead." The selection of the word "queen," for example, provokes the word "come" to appear on screen in two different places; the color, font, and type of the word are dissimilar to the color, font, and type used for "The queen, my lord, is dead." Moreover, the word "come" is also hyperlinked. The invitation to select the word "come" forces the interactor to imagine what will come next: another isolated word, a string of words, or a complete quotation? As the interactor keeps clicking on hyperlinked words, the screen space does not erase previous words or sentences. One assumes that it is purposely done to make it more difficult for the interactor to find the latest quotation. The interactor thus rereads previous quotations before finding the latest hyperlinked quotation.

Dlsan's choice of hyperlinking "queen" with "come" may seem odd or at least arbitrary. After all, the artist could have chosen several other soliloquies in the play. However, the decision makes sense if considered in light of Lady Macbeth's own (be)coming. Having read of Duncan's arrival, Lady Macbeth summons the "Spirits that tend on mortal thoughts" to "unsex" her and fill her body with "direst cruelty." The interactor soon realizes that dlsan's emendations reflect the visual atmosphere he has created to portray Lady Macbeth's macabre and "unnatural" request:

> make thick my blood, [. . .]
> Come to my woman's breasts,
> And take my milk for gall [. . .]
> Come, thick Night [. . .]

That my keen knife see not the wound it makes,
Nor Heaven peep through the blanket of the dark,
To cry, "Hold, Hold!"

(1.5.43–54)

Even though the interactor does not decide what words are to follow after clicking on a specific word or set of words, she nevertheless has to perform the cognitive task of suturing these links with her own knowledge of the play. Indeed, in order to make sense of dlsan's "textual jump-cuts" in Lady Macbeth's soliloquy, the interactor must recall the actual phrasing of the passage and judge if the digital artist's strategies and choices shed new light on the soliloquy. In this case, the procedural quality of the hyperlinks parallels Lady Macbeth's evolution or becoming in that they force a type of "reading" that is performative in its evolutionary processes.

Should the interactor decide to select "my lord," dlsan will challenge her knowledge of the play with the combination of a passage at the beginning of Act 2 with another in Act 1, Scene 7. Both passages feature Macbeth soliloquizing: "Now o'er the one half world / Nature seems dead, and wicked dreams abuse / The curtain'd sleep [. . .]" (2.1.49–51) and "this even-handed Justice / Commends th'ingredience of our poison'd chalice / To our own lips." (1.7.10–12) This probably is the most difficult hyperlink with which to come to terms, because it combines a first speech in Act 2 that is followed by another that precedes it in Act 1. The temporal flow of the play being questioned and redesigned by dlsan, the interactor must realign the speeches in her mind prior to revealing what this editorial maneuver entails.

Macbeth's first soliloquy characterizes the manner in which his potential murderous deed affects the supposedly peaceful order of sleep. Suffering from bad dreams, Macbeth points out that nightmares now haunt his sleeping hours, depriving him of peace of mind. The second soliloquy, even though it returns us to Act 1, Scene 7, which precedes the beginning of Act 2, adds complementary information to the portrayal of Macbeth's perturbed spirit. Having noted the bad dreams that trouble his sleep, Macbeth comments in Act 1, Scene 7 that he is to be given a taste of death if the murderous plan is executed. Dlsan's joining together of these two seemingly unrelated passages hints at the tragic ending of the play before the actual denouement. The interactor's internal linking of these passages constitutes an important task if the hyperlinks are to be effective.

In the case of the third word, "dead" (in "The queen, my lord, is *dead*" (5.5.16)), the interactor does not have to look for the passage to which it refers because it directly precedes Macbeth's celebrated "She-should-have-died-hereafter" soliloquy, and it is the only one dlsan has included in its entirety (5.5.17–28). If performed in the chronological order I have adopted to explain it more clearly in these pages, the journey ends with the meaning of life "signifying nothing" (5.5.28). The interactor bearing in mind that the word that triggers the soliloquy is "dead," the choice of the soliloquy is apt to represent Macbeth's sense of life's meaninglessness after so many unjustified deaths.

As the interactor soon realizes, performing dlsan's website is different from reading *Macbeth* in a book. Actually, when *Wired* reporter Veltman mentions that "The 'sound and fury' is the artist's [dlsan's] way of capturing something of the experience of going to the theater," she may be closer to the truth than might be expected. Indeed, it is precisely in the performative process dlsan's piece evokes that its novelty lies. The interactor may find all the clicking repetitive, but what about the reading and aural performances that take place without being noticed? Dlsan has commented that "In theater, every performance is different. People may know the text and the story, and maybe the actors and director, but they don't know how the performers will act" (quoted in Veltman). The website would transfer performance from the reception of actors' performances to the reception of virtual words in unforeseen contexts. Interactors must make decisions in order for this virtual "play" to unfold.

Interestingly, Veltman mentions that *"HyperMacbeth* works as a kind of pastiche on the conventions of annotating Shakespeare on the Web." As in most Internet versions of *Macbeth*, the interested reader who clicks on a hyperlinked word will be given either a definition of the word or other instances of the word in Shakespeare's plays. Dlsan's adaptation, on the other hand, offers hyperlinked words that trigger other words and music. This cyberspace *Macbeth* resists scholarly explanations characteristic of textual editions and revels in its own colorful obscurity.[11]

The second visual transformation of *Macbeth* to which we turn is the digital edition of the play edited by A.R. Braunmuller. The Voyager CD-ROM features ten sections from which the interactor can choose, and Shakespeare scholar David S. Rodes guides the interactor in her digital navigation. It is the nature of the interactor's task that I want to examine here via the interaction with both the CD-ROM and Rodes's own audio performance.

The CD-ROM welcomes the interactor with an audio quote from *Macbeth*. Willingly or not, this audio segment configures the entry in the CD-ROM environment. The reading activities characteristic of the textual *Macbeth* will not be the only ones that the interactor's body and mind will perform. On the contrary, reading faculties will have to give way to aural and visual decoding. Moreover, the visual and oral functions will be combined with various physical movements that trigger the images or the sound clips. Listening to the opening passage, the interactor quickly tries to identify to whom the voice-over may belong and to what film version of the play it is referring. These cognitive moments provoke a series of questions that will remain unanswered until the interactor unfamiliar with *Macbeth* explores the CD-ROM.

The introduction to the CD-ROM unwillingly points to the various human senses that will be summoned throughout the digital journey. While some preliminary remarks are spoken, the interactor views various paintings, drawings, and maps that she will be able to see later in other sections on the CD-ROM. Sight and hearing, two senses that come together in the filmic experience, combine to evoke images and webs of meanings in the informed interactor's mind. The challenge for the interactor is to process the visual, textual, and audio information this virtual *Macbeth* proposes.

The combinatorial skills that the CD-ROM promotes emphasize mental activities that Rodes addresses in his introduction, saying that there are "many ways to realize *Macbeth*; script is not fixed or static." In fact, he demands that we "make our own." In other words, the Shakespearean text is not a monolithic entity waiting to be resuscitated in the same ways over and over again, that is, either textually or cinematically. Arthur Kinney (*Lies*) has shown that the 1606 *Macbeth* is, among other things, a collection of various political and theological discourses that activate a plethora of reception strategies. The manner in which *Macbeth* has successfully made it into painting, film, television, and digital media must attract our attention to the fluid boundaries and flexible content that incorporate these various discourses. As Laurie Osborne has argued: "the multiple media that are beginning to converge in reproductions of Shakespeare relate directly to colliding materials within the plays" (141). The creative performances in which we engage to receive these materials echo Rodes's plea for an open-ended *Macbeth* to which we can actually collaborate, so to speak. The personalized reception of political, historical, and theological material the CD-ROM proposes is a first step in this participatory direction.

The interactor's performance is necessarily related to the database that contains the play in its digital form. In the section entitled "Characters in the Play," the interactor chooses a character, say, Lady Macbeth, and gains access to all of her speeches. Upon selecting a particular hyperlinked speech, the interactor returns to the digital edition of the play where she will be able to read notes and commentaries on the very same speech. Moreover, some speeches are associated with audio speeches. For example, if one were to select Macbeth's "She-should-have-died-hereafter" soliloquy (5.5.17–28), one could hear an English actor's rendering of the same lines.

Similarly, the section on the CD-ROM that is entitled "Clips Gallery" allows the interactor to view particular cinematic sequences that relate to certain dramatic scenes. For example, clicking on "Act 1, scene 3" makes the screen split so that in the right-hand portion of the screen a textual representation appears whereas the left-hand side presents Welles's version of the scene. The only drawback is that Welles's and Kurosawa's film versions cannot be seen at the same moment, depriving the interactor of a comparative scene analysis. Finally, in the same section, the text and the filmic sequence are associated so that one can click on a particular line of the text, and the visual and aural accompaniment will start from there.

The manner in which the CD-ROM actualizes the imaginary journey in digital space is accentuated in the section "Picture Gallery." This section offers a map of Scotland on which the interactor can click to view the various geographical areas mentioned in the play (e.g. Birnam wood). This section takes the interactor on a spatial reconsideration of Shakespeare's surroundings via virtual traveling. It points to and fills in the gaps in understanding that might arise, for, as Courtney Lehmann points out, recent adaptations of *Macbeth* tend to "dislocat[e] Scotland from its moorings in *any place at all*, as 'Scotland' becomes synonymous, for better or for worse, with a state of *mind*" (emphases in original, 235). The virtual zone and atmosphere Lehmann describes may also be present in the case of an Internet piece such as dlsan's. The CD-ROM, on the other hand, presents more general geographical spaces characteristic of Shakespeare's plays and life and offers supplementary information. For example, a digital tour takes us to Shakespeare's London, and we can click on a particular location of our choice (e.g. Bear Garden). Finally, the picture gallery contains more than eighty pictures, photographs, and production stills where the interactor can see, among others, famous Shakespearean actors such as Richard Burbage, various portraits of the Bard, and paintings.

Surprisingly, the most unexpected feature on the CD-ROM is the one that concerns popular entertainment via performance and personification. Entitled "*Macbeth* Karaoke," this rehearsal space proposes to enter a character's mind, for example Macbeth, in order to recite his part. Following the black dot that jumps from line to line, the interactor mouths Macbeth's words as they could be performed by a professional actor. The physical experience of pronouncing Shakespeare's words implies a corporeal mode of reception different from that of the individual reading of the play. Moreover, the inclusion of a virtual karaoke machine possesses underlying motivations that must be emphasized.

The importance of this section lies in the reasons Rodes mentions to justify its presence on the CD-ROM. The critic seems to position aurality as a primary function on the CD-ROM. Reminding us of the opening audio quotation, the karaoke section recalls the introduction to the digital environment in which vision is somewhat downplayed. Indeed, it is the speaking of words aloud that the digital karaoke machine suggests. Rodes elaborates on the importance of aurality: "Plays are meant to be spoken, not merely read, and only in sounding out the words can an actor or critic begin to hear the clues as to meaning and emotion that are conveyed in the repetition and variation of sound and in the modulation of rhythm." The critical position Rodes seems to be holding clearly privileges the oral work of the (inter)actor rather than her textual understanding of the play.

Actually, it is to the notion of performance that Rodes turns to explain his comment. He notes: "In a silent reading, one can stop to muse or drift—or go to the laundry; but in performance, the text becomes a script that moves compellingly onward." However, Rodes does not seem to take into consideration the hybrid spaces that performance entails, for acting relates to both silent and oral reading practices. More importantly, the interactor facing a computer screen is not in the same position as the actor standing up on stage.

Ultimately, Rodes elaborates on his notion of performance and comments on the function of memory in acting. He remarks: "Memory is, after all, like a muscle and benefits from challenging exercise. . . . All Renaissance education, including Shakespeare's, was based on memorization and repetition—and his great dramatic art grows from this very practical act." The reading and acting practices Rodes privileges place cognition and memory as aural activities. The inscription of textual matters does not seem to be primordial anymore in such a digital environment; it is the individualized performance of the interactor that is encouraged. "*Macbeth* Karaoke" proposes an unprecedented occasion to digitally perform in a way that combines text, screen, and orality.

Digital performances and archiving

The interpretation of two digital adaptations of *Macbeth* may serve several purposes. First, it allows the reader to understand what it is exactly that digital media can add to existing intertextual, visual, and cinematic transformations. Second, combined to a historical consideration of reading and viewing practices, such a critical endeavor permits a complete picture of the various transitions that have occurred in the performance of the Shakespearean text, from Elizabethan theatergoers to CD-ROM and web interactors. An ensuing conclusion is that it is in the refashioning of performance in various media contexts that we must envisage future adaptations of Shakespeare's plays.[12] The two digital adaptations with which we are concerned teach interesting lessons in terms of media migration and performance that more traditional adaptations on film do not, and future digital adapters of *Macbeth* (or other of Shakespeare's plays for that matter) may want to elaborate on their most successful and appealing features.

The first criterion that should be examined by digital creators concerns the medium itself. The adaptation that is found on the Internet implies a virtual community of interactors who can access the work from anywhere in the world as long as they have access to an Internet connection. Different from the collective reception of a play in performance and from the individual reading of *Macbeth*, the digital Shakespearean performance joins together several roles that were once dissociated. Moreover, the interactor perusing dlsan's work will be able to complement her navigational activity with other Shakespeare-related websites on which she will be able to find missing information (e.g. to what act and scene do the words "The queen, my lord, is dead" refer?). In this sense, dlsan's piece is an artistic take on *Macbeth*, but it is deprived of the reference material found in Internet editions of the plays.

The CD-ROM edition of *Macbeth*, on the other hand, functions according to other spatial and material economies. The interactor can only access the play using the CD-ROM; it will not be found online. One must purchase or at least have access to a university library that owns the CD-ROM. Whereas an online piece can be updated, the artist being able to add other quotations and hyperlinks, the CD-ROM is a "Read-Only-Memory" medium; it cannot be modified. This implies that recent cinematic adaptations of *Macbeth* will have to wait for future CD-ROMs (or, more likely, DVD-ROMs) to migrate to a more comprehensive digital environment that will be able to integrate the increasing list of cinematic *Macbeth*s.

These material considerations, while part of the history of digital media, point to the obsolescence of current media supports. Will we be able to visit dlsan's website or to run Braunmuller's edition of the play in ten years? What will become of other digital Shakespeare projects? Have Shakespeare scholars begun to archive and to protect those products that may disappear in a few years due to collective neglect? Apropos of impending archiving, Ron Burnett has commented:

> When the computer becomes a personal archive for all of the images of a generation (moving and still), the questions of storage, retrieval, and cataloguing will become even more pressing. What will have to change is the way in which users relate to the information they are collecting. This means that new concepts of memory and retrieval will be needed as well as new kinds of imagescapes. (70)[13]

Similarly, the ephemeral nature of critical writings that discuss digital art-works will have to be considered.[14] This aspect of scholarly work may give us pause, but it should not refrain us from investigating the way in which performance migrates from one older media environment to a more recent one. Refusing to pay attention to these issues will result in unbridgeable gaps in the reception of "post-cinema" Shakespeare.

It is precisely the possible disappearance of a certain type of Shakespeare adaptations that is at stake. For, as digital media seem to incorporate preceding ones rapidly, dlsan's *HyperMacbeth* and the Voyager CD-ROM embody two instances of performance across media that present us with a reverberated history of hearing, reading, and viewing strategies in a navigational practice that is quite unprecedented. It is the manner in which the interactor is allowed to combine various cognitive and performative faculties that makes digital adaptations worthwhile. *Macbeth* takes shape in and through the interactor's embodied mind; it is no longer confined to either the page or the cinema screen. Digital *Macbeth*s propose an enhanced Shakespearean experience that returns us to the very bodily and cognitive mechanisms that performance once implied. The death of the author and of the book having been pronounced, one awaits the (re)birth of the performer in its intermedial dimensions.

Dlsan's and Braunmuller's projects are not unprecedented visual achievements; they must be envisaged as transitory moments in the history of performance and media that goes from the representation of Shakespeare on stage, page, cinema screen, television screen, and computer screen. They conform to what David Saltz has described as "interactive performance environments."[15] As Shakespeare did not write for publication but for performance, digital artists do not create for posterity but for the revival of performance in an age given to visual spectacle. To understand these recent digital performances, it is the very categories themselves with which we have analyzed Shakespeare's plays that have to be reformulated: "What is 'character' on a CD-ROM? What is 'performance' on the Internet? . . . future reconsiderations of acting will increasingly need to accommodate trans-media projects in order to adequately account for the future post-cinema responses to Shakespeare" (Hopkins et al. 163).

The return of literary works in digital format, J. Hillis Miller has argued, would offer an uncanny site of performative reiteration: "The new existence for literary works in databases and on the Internet turns those works into innumerable, murmurous swarm of ghosts that return and can return again at our command" (101–103). One might add that *Macbeth*'s eerie and ghostlike effects on the reader are given a new existence in the performative moments Miller describes in the spectral atmosphere of digitized texts. The peculiar force of a play such as *Macbeth* may reside in its belated revival in digital environments that themselves give voice and "body" to the already expressed themes of return and haunting.[16] The activation of these moments of uncertainty and deferral, however, relies on the interactor to be triggered, making the person sitting at the computer the principal agent in Macbeth's posthumous digital performance.

Notes

1 Moreover, the principal task is not only to note the recycling of Shakespeare in the digital era but also to develop models and concepts to analyze "digital Shakespeares." Osborne (2003) points to such a task in an essay on animation and Shakespeare: "By the early twenty-first century, the many media in which Shakespeare can be produced are being drawn together to entertain and to teach; the flourishing CD-ROMs, websites, and DVDs raise the pressing question of how we should approach new productions of Shakespeare, where mixed media become multimedia" (153).

2 I borrow the expression "post-cinema Shakespeare" from Hopkins et al. (2003) in which the authors argue that " 'post-cinema' implies an explosion of forms that includes video, animation, CD-ROM, the Internet, and the resuscitation and revitalization of live performance/theater as a valid and vital art that in its 'liveness' provides a radical response to a mediatized society" (140). In this chapter I would like not only to describe the material conditions under which post-cinema Shakespeare takes place but also the manner in which the notion of performance is transformed in "digital Shakespeares."

3 Analyses of digital works often take the shape of surveys or catalog entries. For example, several critics have paid attention to "digital Shakespeares," but their writings do not seem willing to engage in detailed interpretations of digital editions or adaptations. For previous accounts of Shakespeare in the digital world, see Saeger; Feldmann; Werstine; Donaldson ("Digital," "Electronic"); Friedlander ("Playing," "Shakespeare"); Mullin ("Digital," "Shakespeare"). This chapter

furthers the ideas I have been developing in digital adaptation and performance theory. See Lessard ("Interface," "The Environment").

4 See the following writings: McLuhan; Ong; Zumthor; Chartier (*Forms, Culture*). The last reference contains three additional chapters that were not part of Chartier's 1995 book.

5 Translation mine.

6 Translation mine.

7 Literary theorists, on the other hand, have been somewhat reluctant to draw on the results of cognitive theory. Turner's ground-breaking *Reading Minds* and Spolsky's *Gaps in Nature: Literary Interpretation and the Modular Mind* and *Satisfying Skepticism: Embodied Knowledge in the Early Modern World* are examples of treatments of the human mind that processes literary information. More recently, certain literary scholars have turned to the *representation* of cognitive activities in literary works, and others have examined modern literary works' representation of technology and cognition. See Tabbi and Wutz; Johnston; Hayles; Tabbi.

8 See Crane; Kinney (*Lies, Shakespeare's*).

9 The reader will be able to find information on the artist at <http://ol;www.dlsan.org>.

10 References to *Macbeth* are from Kenneth Muir's Arden edition of the play.

11 Veltman cites Christiane Paul, author of *Digital Art* (2003), who has mentioned that "*HyperMacbeth* looks at Shakespeare's text as a form of remixable poetry" (cited in Veltman). The interactor's performance, even though it is less demanding and stressful than the DJ's, takes place in the mind where she has to combine incoming bits and pieces of texts.

12 The analysis of performance in digital environments is a relatively recent field of inquiry. Ground-breaking writings are Laurel; McKenzie; and Case. More recently, Saltz has questioned the use of performance art in the case of digital artworks; Causey has inquired into the area of liveness, immediacy, and presence in a performative realm deprived of the "fleshy other"; and Ryan ("Introduction," *Narrative*) has discussed the future of interactive drama and narrative as a multimedia construct.

13 French new media critic Couchot touches on this issue in the context of the future of the CD-ROM (44–45).

14 One way to give a chapter like this one a perennial existence would be to digitize it and to make it accessible (either online or on CD-ROM) to the person interested in dlsan's website or the Voyager CD-ROM. In other words, interactors should not have to search for such critical pieces; these writings should be adjacent to the digital works themselves if they can be run.

15 Contrary to conventional performative settings such as the theater and the music hall, Saltz argues that digital artists create other spatial venues to perform: "interactive performance environments provide contexts within which actions are performed" (123).

16 For an insightful analysis of the performative and the uncanny in *Macbeth*, see Garber (87–123).

Works cited

Burnett, Ron. *How Images Think*. Cambridge: MIT P, 2004.

Case, Sue-Ellen. *The Domain-Matrix: Performing Lesbian at the End of Print Culture*. Bloomington and Indianapolis: Indiana UP, 1996.

Causey, Matthew. "Postorganic Performance: The Appearance of Theater in Virtual Spaces." *Cyberspace Textuality: Computer Technology and Literary Theory*. Ed. Marie-Laure Ryan. Bloomington: Indiana UP, 1999. 182–201.

Chartier, Roger. *Culture écrite et société. L'ordre des livres (XIVe–XVIIIe siècle)*. Paris: Albin Michel, 1996.

—— *Forms and Meanings: Texts, Performances, and Audiences from Codex to Computer*. Philadelphia: University of Pennsylvania Press, 1995.

Couchot, Edmond. "Le cédérom de demain." *Navigations technologiques: poésie et technologie au XXIe siècle*. Ed. Ollivier Dyens. Montreal: VLB Editeur, 2004. 35–45.

Crane, Mary Thomas. *Shakespeare's Brain: Reading with Cognitive Theory*. Princeton: Princeton UP, 2001.

dlsan. *HyperMacbeth*. 2001. 26 Jan. 2007 <http://www.dlsan.org/macbeth/the_mac.htm>.

Donaldson, Peter S. "Digital Archive as Expanded Text: Shakespeare and Electronic Textuality." *Electronic Text: Investigations in Method and Theory*. Ed. Kathryn Sutherland. New York: Clarendon Press, 1997. 173–97.

—— "The Electronic Archive in the Classroom: Multimedia Shakespeare at MIT." *Teaching Shakespeare through Performance*. Ed. Milla Cozart Riggio. New York: Modern Language Association of America, 1999. 390–412.

Feldmann, Doris. "Multimedia Shakespeares." *Anglistik im Internet*. Ed. Doris Feldmann and Thomas Rommel. Heidelberg: Carl Winter Universitätsverlag, 1997. 129–43.

Friedlander, Larry. "Playing in Cyberspace: Experiments in Computer-Mediated Shakespeare." *Teaching Shakespeare through Performance*. Ed. Milla Cozart Riggio. New York: Modern Language Association of America, 1999. 413–32.

—— "The Shakespeare Project: Experiments in Multimedia." *Hypermedia and Literary Studies*. Ed. Paul Delany and George P. Landow. Cambridge: MIT P, 1991. 257–71.

Garber, Marjorie. *Shakespeare's Ghost Writers: Literature as Uncanny Causality*. New York: Routledge, 1987.

Hayles, N. Katherine. *How We Became Posthuman. Virtual Bodies in Cybernetics, Literature, and Informatics*. Chicago: U of Chicago P, 1999.

Hopkins, D.J., Catherine Ingman, and Bryan Reynolds. "Nudge, Nudge, Wink, Wink, Know What I Mean, Know What I Mean? A Theoretical Approach to Performance for a Post-Cinema Shakespeare." *Performing Transversally: Reimagining Shakespeare and the Critical Future*. Ed. Bryan Reynolds. New York: Palgrave Macmillan, 2003. 137–70.

Johnston, John. *Information Multiplicity: American Fiction in the Age of Media Saturation*. Baltimore: Johns Hopkins UP, 1998.

Kinney, Arthur F. *Lies Like Truth: Shakespeare*, Macbeth, *and the Cultural Moment*. Detroit: Wayne State UP, 2001.

—— *Shakespeare's Webs: Networks of Meaning in Renaissance Drama*. New York: Routledge, 2004.

Laurel, Brenda. *Computers as Theatre*. Reading, MA: Addison-Wesley, 1993.

Lehmann, Courtney. "Out Damned Scot: Dislocating *Macbeth* in Transnational Film and Media Culture." *Shakespeare, the Movie, II: Popularizing the Plays on Film, TV, Video, and DVD*. Ed. Richard Burt and Lynda E. Boose. New York: Routledge, 2003. 231–51.

Lessard, Bruno. "The Environment, the Body, and the Digital Fallen Angel in Simon Biggs's *Pandaemonium*." *Milton in Popular Culture*. Ed. Greg Colon Semenza and Laura Knoppers. New York: Palgrave Macmillan, 2006. 213–23.

—— "Interface, corporéité et intermédialité. *Sonata* de Grahame Weinbren." *Parachute* 113 (2004): 60–69.

McKenzie, Jon. "Virtual Reality: Performance, Immersion, and the Thaw." *Drama Review* 38.4 (1994): 83–106.

McLuhan, Marshall. *The Gutenberg Galaxy: The Making of Typographic Man.* Toronto: University of Toronto Press, 1962.

Miller, J. Hillis. *Black Holes.* Stanford, CA: Stanford UP, 1999.

Mitchell, W.J.T. "Addressing Media." *What Do Pictures Want? The Lives and Loves of Images.* Chicago: U of Chicago P, 2005. 201–21.

Mullin, Michael. "Digital Shakespeare: A Retrospective and Update." *Teaching Shakespeare through Performance.* Ed. Milla Cozart Riggio. New York: Modern Language Association of America, 1999. 373–89.

—— "Shakespeare on the Web." *Shakespeare Matters: History, Teaching, Performance.* Ed. Lloyd Davis. Newark: U of Delaware P, 2003. 119–37.

Ong, Walter. *Orality and Literacy: The Technologizing of the Word.* New York: Routledge, 1982.

Osborne, Laurie. "Mixing Media and Animating Shakespeare Tales." *Shakespeare, the Movie, II: Popularizing the Plays on Film, TV, Video, and DVD.* Ed. Richard Burt and Lynda E. Boose. New York: Routledge, 2003. 140–53.

Paquin, Nycole. *Le corps juge: sciences de la cognition et esthétique des arts visuels.* Montreal: XYZ, 1997.

Paul, Christiane. *Digital Art.* New York: Thames & Hudson, 2003.

Ryan, Marie-Laure. "Introduction." *Narrative across Media. The Languages of Storytelling.* Ed. Marie-Laure Ryan. Lincoln: U of Nebraska P, 2004. 1–39.

—— *Narrative as Virtual Reality: Immersion and Interactivity in Literature and Electronic Media.* Baltimore: Johns Hopkins UP, 2001.

Saeger, James P. "The High-Tech Classroom: Shakespeare in the Age of Multimedia, Computer Networks, and Virtual Space." *Teaching Shakespeare into the Twenty-First Century.* Ed. Ronald E. Salomone and James E. Davis. Athens, OH: Ohio UP, 1997. 271–83.

Saltz, David Z. "The Art of Interaction: Interactivity, Performativity, and Computers." *Journal of Aesthetics and Art Criticism* 55.2 (1997): 117–27.

Shakespeare, William. *Macbeth.* Ed. A.R. Braunmuller. New York: Voyager Co. 1994.

Shakespeare, William. *Macbeth.* Ed. Kenneth Muir. The Arden Shakespeare. New York: Routledge, 1995.

Spolsky, Ellen. *Gaps in Nature: Literary Interpretation and the Modular Mind.* Albany, NY: State U of New York P, 1993.

—— *Satisfying Skepticism: Embodied Knowledge in the Early Modern World.* Burlington, VT: Ashgate, 2001.

Tabbi, Joseph. *Cognitive Fictions.* Minneapolis, MN: U of Minnesota P, 2002.

Tabbi, Joseph and Michael Wutz, eds. *Reading Matters: Narrative in the New Media Ecology.* Ithaca: Cornell UP, 1997.

Turner, Mark. *Reading Minds: The Study of English in the Age of Cognitive Science.* Princeton, NJ: Princeton UP, 1991.

Veltman, Chloe. "Sound and Fury of HyperMacbeth." *Wired* May 29, 2002. 26 Jan. 2007 <http://www.wired.com/news/culture/0,52761-0.html>.

Werstine, Paul. "Hypertext as Editorial Horizon." *Shakespeare and the Twentieth Century: The Selected Proceedings of the International Shakespeare Association*

World Congress, Los Angeles, 1996. Ed. Jonathan Bate, Jill L. Levenson, and Dieter Mehl. Newark: U of Delaware P, 1998. 248–57.

Worthen, W.B. *Shakespeare and the Force of Modern Performance*. Cambridge: Cambridge UP, 2003.

Zumthor, Paul. *Performance, réception, lecture*. Longueil, Québec: Le Préambule, 1990.

18 Sunshine in *Macbeth*

Pamela Mason

Received opinion would have it that darkness pervades *Macbeth* and theatrical productions nowadays are often boringly predictable in their staging. Technical resources can reproduce "Thunder and lightning" very effectively, forcing audiences to peer through the "fog and filthy air."

But it was not always so. In Shakespeare's theatre the Witches did not have such influence. They would express their desire that they might meet again in "thunder, lightning, or in rain," but they could not ensure that would be the case. Even in England it is possible that the sun could shine on the day of performance. In an open-air performance, sunlight can combat the forces of darkness and present the natural world's resistance to any attempt to control the weather. The Witches' mantra "Fair is foul, and foul is fair" is not one that Jacobean audiences would therefore automatically endorse and, consequently, performances of this play could set up a dynamic of debate and challenge. The world of the play was never simply the world of the audience. A "willing suspension of disbelief" may be possible but not the denial of faith necessary to sustain the Witches' power. Productions today ensure that we lose sight of the fact that the action of the play happens in contested space. Members of an audience who are on their feet and engaged with the play are prepared to collaborate in the creative process. They fulfill the role defined for them by the Chorus in *Henry V* and go to the theatre prepared to work. Today we are denied that vigorous engagement.

Perhaps the problem of *Macbeth* being shrouded in darkness owes something to the academic closet. A.C. Bradley's view of the play has prescribed its presentation:

> Darkness, we may even say blackness, broods over this tragedy. It is remarkable that almost all the scenes which at once recur to memory take place either at night or in some dark spot. . . . The Witches dance in the thick air of a storm, or, "black and midnight hags," receive Macbeth in a cavern. The blackness of night is to the hero a thing of fear, even of horror; and that which he feels becomes the spirit of the play. (333)

Macbeth has become "cabin'd, cribb'd and confin'd" by assumptions that have denied it the range of interpretative openness granted the other tragedies. Whilst four centuries of performances have illuminated so many diverse elements of Shakespeare's plays, *Macbeth* seems curiously untouched by the process. Its merit is generally unquestioned, but it is too often assumed that it lacks the subtlety, challenge, and rich layering of *Hamlet*, *Othello* and *King Lear*. It is the only one in the group deemed suitable to be studied by those as young as 11 and the only one of the four set as an examination text for adolescents. How a play which so effectively exploits fear, apprehension, superstition and anxiety can be regarded as a safe curriculum choice is perhaps explained by the assumption that we know where we are with it. It simply deals with dark forces, doesn't it?

The manufactured darkness provided in the modern theatre for the first five scenes in the play makes the King's description of the Macbeths' castle heavily ironic.[1] The implication is usually that his perception is dulled by age or shaped by a hopelessly naive and optimistic spirit:

> The castle hath a pleasant seat; the air
> Nimbly and sweetly recommends itself
> Unto our gentle senses.
>
> (1.6.1–3)

But in a theatre open to the elements, the King's words would be more likely to ring true. The invocation 23 lines earlier, "Come, thick night/ And pall thee in the dunnest smoke of Hell" has not worked. The King's description makes it absolutely clear that the natural world resists such attempts at manipulation. Dark deeds are not the product of the environment and we ought to remember that "It's not the place's fault" (Larkin). For the King and for us, there is the prospect of comfort and ease from the "air" which "sweetly recommends itself/ Unto our gentle senses." Banquo's sense of reverence grants the place the name of "temple," which is confirmed by the presence of the diminutive "martlet." He is confident that "heaven's breath/ Smells wooingly here." The imagery of "pendent bed" anticipates the gentle rocking of the "procreant cradle," confirming the insistent fertility made explicit in "breed." And just as the King's opening line had remarked upon the quality of the "air," so Banquo concludes that "The air is delicate."

It is not the perceived sunlight that is ironic, for the description of natural light would have been confirmed by the wider expanse of the theatrical space. What is discordant and potentially poignant is the appearance in this place of the isolated figure of the Lady. Ideas about the fecundity of life-affirming light, nurturing, and domestic harmony find little reflection in the single figure of a childless wife. The sunlight in this scene makes it absolutely clear that metaphorical darkness has to be evoked and created by those who are choosing to challenge the pattern and temperament of the natural world. Darkness is only inevitable and inexorable as part of a natural cycle which will take us back to sunlight. Banquo had shared the encounter with the

Witches and had heard their prophecy, but he is able to respond sensitively, as the King does, to the prevailing atmosphere. Their perception will illuminate the actions and choices made by Macbeth and his Lady.

Productions ought, indeed, to emphasize that it is not the place's fault. It can seem that Macbeth is surrounded by the spiritual darkness of an unholy alliance between the Witches and his Lady, but at this point in the play Macbeth has decided not to come to greet his King. He has chosen to avoid the sweet and nimble air. His wife has to speak for herself and her husband as she offers "our service." She has to use words ("every point twice done, and then done double") to create a duality to fill the void of her husband's absence. She covers for her absent husband as she speaks of "our house" and "we rest," but her words fail to convince and the King demands:

> Where's the Thane of Cawdor?
> (1.6.20)

It is a question which goes unanswered. All his wife can do is to reiterate assurances of hospitality, but the King's words emphasize Macbeth's absence. The King speaks of "his [i.e. Macbeth's] home" and he instructs the Lady to "Conduct me to mine host" because:

> We love him highly,
> And shall continue our graces towards him.
> (1.6.29–30)

The play will map a journey into darkness, but the darkness is not all-pervasive. It is a darkness that will benefit from constant light to enable an audience to observe action and character clearly. That kind of illumination would have been taken for granted in Shakespeare's theatre.

Our modern stage's enthusiasm for darkness is paralleled by another kind of obfuscation, one which ironically has been carried out in the name of enlightenment. To read the play in its only authoritative text (that of the 1623 Folio) is to see it quite differently from the way it is presented to the modern reader. Its editorial history has involved a process of reshaping (and supposedly clarifying) the text, preventing readers and actors from engaging directly with the original play. The roughness of the verse, which editors have thought it appropriate to regularize, may in fact contain rich material for consideration. There are particular issues in terms of lineation. It is accepted that as the Folio was set in formes the process of casting off the text presented problems in terms of layout. Many pages of the Folio provide examples of how the compositors struggled to accommodate either too little or too much text.[2] But this "white space" argument has been used to justify a great deal of editorial intervention which has gone far beyond what can be defended simply on those grounds. The style of *Macbeth* is frequently unconventional. Prose accommodates both the naturalism of a Porter who has been drinking and the domestic exchange of mother and son. At times the blank verse is regular and the fluency of dove-tailed lines affirms the clarity of the Old Man's choric commentary or establishes that, despite the apparent contradictions, Malcolm and Macduff do indeed speak the same language and share the same values. Towards the end of the England scene the taut regularity of the verse provides a secure framework to contain and offer reassurance to Macduff as he struggles to come to terms with the news of the murder of his family. We also have the shorter, more emphatically rhythmic pulse of the Witches.

Elsewhere there is much that is fragmentary and unusual. It has been customary to present Compositors A and B as scapegoats for the irregularity. In his New Cambridge edition of the play A.R. Braunmuller states that "the main difficulty partly created by A and B is the play's lineation, its setting out of verse and prose and the regularity of its verse" (251). Others go further in defining the precise shortcomings of the compositors, concluding that A "had a regrettable tendency to rearrange normal blank verse into a succession of irregular lines" and B "had a tendency to set up prose as if it were verse" (Wells and Taylor 637, quoted in Braunmuller 251). However, there needs to be some caution in seeking scientific precision. It is dangerous to argue that, because sections of text can be rearranged to offer more regular lines than appear in the Folio, an editor should re-lineate. The belief that "the text is disfigured by mislineation" (Muir xiv) may deny the possibility that the play offers at times jagged and irregular verse as a means of communicating the tidal pressures, tensions, and complexities of emotions which the characters are experiencing. Editorial tidying may be erasing characteristics of the original text which could offer clues and guidance to reader and actor. It is disconcerting to realize that much excellent, stimulating criticism founded upon close reading which attends to scansion, enjambement, use of short lines, and metrical irregularity has in fact been working on an adapted text. In the absence of any other textual evidence than that which appears in the Folio, it seems necessary to adopt a more cautious approach before tampering with the layout of a text which is in so many ways unusual and unconventional.

This is a complex and controversial issue but it seems appropriate to raise questions about the way in which extensive conjecture about the characteristics of Compositors A and B has paved the way for extensive re-lineation of this text. Having decided that there are "eccentricities" or what is also termed "villainy," it has been asserted that: "it follows inescapably that, wherever possible, eccentricities in . . . setting of lines should be corrected" (Brooke 214). In *Shakespeare's Producing Hand* (1948) Richard Flatter argues a theatrical case for an attention to pauses and stage action. He challenges the insistence of setting out as many lines as possible in iambic pentameter. Although Nicholas Brooke in editing his Oxford edition of the play is not insensitive to such notions he dismisses Flatter's case for having "no understanding of the compositor's eccentricities" (Brooke 215). Where Flatter argues that the Captain's speech (1.2.7–23) represents "the broken utterance of a seriously wounded man" Brooke counters with: "In fact, *simple rearrangement* [my italics] shows it to be regular and rhetorically impressive in the manner of a Senecan messenger" (215). The question must be not whether Shakespeare wanted his Captain to be a seriously wounded man or a Senecan messenger, but whether an editor or the reader/actor should be making that decision. Modern editions have sanitized the play.

In the scene discussed earlier (1.6), "simple rearrangement" allows Macbeth's Lady to sustain the regularity of the verse established by the King and Banquo. In the Folio text she begins securely enough, but four lines into her speech her rhythm falters. She then has three lines of awkward sounding verse as her clockwork runs down before the King's slightly odd, abrupt question gives new impetus to the scene:

> *Lady*   All our service
>   In every point twice done, and then done double,
>   Were poor and single business to contend
>   Against those honours deep and broad
>   Wherewith your Majesty loads our house.
>   For those of old, and the late dignities,
>   Heaped up to them we rest your hermits.
> *King*   Where's the Thane of Cawdor?
>
>   (1.6.21–28)

Although she had urged her husband to dissemble only 20 lines earlier ("look like the innocent flower/ But be the serpent under it"), perhaps she does not find it that easy. And where is he, anyway? All major editions reorder her lines to smooth out the awkwardness and thereby allow her to finish with a half-line which the King's question completes. However, this "simple rearrangement" does not produce totally regular verse. One set of irregular lines has been replaced with another set of less irregular lines, which look tidier on the page but make a different kind of theatrical sense:

> *Lady*   All our service
>   In every point twice done, and then done double,
>   Were poor and single business to contend
>   Against those honours deep and broad wherewith
>   Your Majesty loads our house. For those of old,
>   And the late dignities heap'd up to them,
>   We rest your hermits.
> *King*   Where's the Thane of Cawdor?
>
>   (1.6.14–20)

The revision gives her greater fluency and assurance.

Other editorial additions have also contributed to shaping our perceptions of the play, perhaps unhelpfully. No one would argue that it would make sense to follow the punctuation of the Folio text slavishly. Fashions change and to standardize the punctuation in order to help a modern reader is both a sensible and uncontested policy. However, there is an issue, possibly peculiar to this play, concerning the use of exclamation marks. In the Folio text of *Macbeth* only two exclamation marks are used, but modern editions have been littered with them. If the view is taken that greetings, warnings, cries, shouts, prophecies, announcements, and exclamations need to be signaled by the addition of the exclamation mark then all dramatic texts face the risk of being infested. The text of *Macbeth* has been particularly distorted for its readers and by extension for its audiences by such an approach. One particular characteristic of the Witches is their repeated phrases of greeting ('Hail, hail, hail') or prophecy. Adding exclamation marks to the text encourages an eyebrow-raising, melodramatic delivery which may well have contributed to the perceived banality of much of the Witches' dialogue. It is no part of an editor's job to indicate that lines should be whispered or declaimed, be it enigmatically or winsomely. Liberal scattering of exclamation marks needs to be curtailed. *Fowler's Modern English Usage* urges restraint in the use of the exclamation mark. It acknowledges that the conventions for poetry are different but Burchfield's remark that "excessive use of exclamation marks . . . add a spurious dash of sensation to something unsensational" is apposite (273). In recent years there has been a shift in editorial policy and A.R. Braunmuller's New Cambridge edition (1997) is significantly more restrained than earlier editions. But some issues and inconsistencies remain. After the discovery of Duncan's murder Macduff's utterance "O horror, horror, horror" looks and reads very differently if printed plainly. With editorial intervention it is fragmented and the markings imply an equality between the phrases and urge a regularity of delivery, "O horror! horror! horror!" The following 23 lines have a further eighteen exclamation marks in Muir's edition (2.3.64–88) and it is customary for this section to be heavily accented.

However, perhaps the most striking example of editorial and theatrical collusion which has distorted the play centers upon the character who has come to be known as Lady Macbeth. Who is she and what is she? Quite simply she is not to be found in Shakespeare's play. The Folio stage direction for the fifth scene in the play reads *"Enter Macbeths Wife alone with a letter"* and for Act 3, Scene 2 the stage direction reads *"Enter Macbeths Lady, and a servant."* She is consistently described simply as *"Lady"* in the speech headings. The designation distinguishes her from her counterpart who is described as *"Macduffes Wife"* in the stage direction to Act 4, Scene 2 and is *"Wife"* throughout her speech headings. Shakespeare's text emphasizes the marital relationship for both women and makes a simple but clear distinction between them in the speech headings: Lady as against Wife. Nowhere in Shakespeare's play (and there is no list of characters in the Folio) is there any reference to the characters as they have become known, from Rowe onwards, both critically and theatrically.[3] Lady Macbeth and Lady Macduff are evidence of how the play has been reinvented in ways which distort Shakespeare's text.

Simon Forman's account of seeing the play (in April 1611) emerges from his experience of the play in performance, before the intervention of any editorial process. He did not see her as Lady Macbeth; to him she is "his [Mackbeth's] wife," a phrase which is used twice, and later in his account she becomes "mackbet's quen" (Salgado 31–32). Stage directions and speech headings do not register verbally in the theatre and Forman's account is a useful reminder of the need to engage with the identity a character is granted within the text and through the words that are spoken.

"Lady" is used just three times in the play. All three references occur in 2.3 within 44 lines. It is Macduff who addresses Macbeth's wife as "gentle lady" (83) and he again uses the term when he voices concern for her, "Look to the lady" (119), in a phrase that is repeated by Banquo seven lines later (126). "Queen" is used three times in the play: there is one reference to Edward's wife in the England scene but the other two both refer to Macbeth's queen. The announcement of her death grants her the title for the first time, "The Queen, my lord, is dead" (5.5.16), and the play's final reference to the Macbeths defines them, in Malcolm's words, as "this dead butcher, and his fiend-like Queen" (5.9.35). "Wife" is used thirteen times in the play: there is one reference to "a sailor's wife" (1.3.4), but the other twelve are divided eight to four in favor of Macduff's wife. The spoken text of the play makes it clear that the titles Lady Macbeth and Lady Macduff have developed from outside, not inside, the play.

In many ways, of course, a character's name is not particularly important. Elsewhere in Shakespeare's plays there are examples of characters whose impressive names, like Claudius in *Hamlet* and Archidamus in *The Winter's Tale*, remain unknown to audiences. But in the case of this particular Lady there is perhaps some cause for concern about the way in which she has become labeled. Initially, appending "Macbeth" to her "Lady" was a fairly straightforward way of attaching her to her husband. However, over the passage of time the name "Lady Macbeth" has encouraged a notion of the character as someone with social aspirations and political ambition. Her husband is the straightforward "Macbeth" with no titular indication of ambition. Coining "Lady Macbeth" contributes to the sense that a scheming woman appropriates a title, facilitating the assumption that she represents the stereotype of the self-seeking, manipulative and cold-hearted wife. However innocent or sensible the original editorial decision may have been, there is no doubt that now "Lady Macbeth" has achieved a cultural identity which constrains attempts to look afresh at the role.

Apart from the invention of her name, editors have arguably encouraged Macbeth's Lady to be stereotyped through the addition of what has become one of the most famous moments of dramatic action not just in this play but in the canon. Lady Macbeth's faint, like the exchange of foils in *Hamlet* or the disappearance of the banquet in *The Tempest*, is a sequence which always excites interest in the *way* it is done on stage. Yet there is no textual requirement for the lady's faint. She calls for assistance, "Help me hence, hoa," but the Folio text lacks any stage direction to indicate what action

might accompany her words. Rowe inserted "*Seeming to faint*" and his add-
ition was accepted by Pope, Theobald, Hanmer, Warburton, and Capell.
Collier, however, removed the indication of "seeming" and preferred "*Lady
Macbeth swoons*," which he inserted at Banquo's line "Look to the lady."
Hunter (New Penguin) emends that to "*swooning*." Although Muir, Wells and
Taylor, Brooke, and Braunmuller all resist adding any stage direction, their
editions acknowledge and accept the tradition of the faint. In the lines that
follow, Macduff and Banquo direct attention to Macbeth's wife through a
repeated command ("Look to the lady"), but there is no stage direction in
response. Rowe instructed "*Lady Macbeth is carried out*" and subsequent
editors have modified the wording but not the sense of his suggestion: "*Lady
Macbeth is taken out*," "*Exit Lady Macbeth, attended*," "*Exit Lady Macbeth,
helped*." Generally the exit is marked following Banquo's instruction, but
Braunmuller inserts it after Macduff's comment.

Lady Macbeth's appeal for help has been traditionally interpreted as
preceding a swoon. Critical attention has focused upon whether it is real or
feigned and upon whether it is possible (or advisable) to seek to make such a
decision evident theatrically. However, it is not necessary for her to faint. The
text indicates that she appeals for assistance to leave the stage and more significant than her action is the fact that, although Macduff alerts the assembly
to take note of her, six lines later his command is precisely echoed by Banquo.
The absence of stage directions in the Folio text leave this section interestingly open to interpretative choices about stage grouping, about Macbeth's
inability (or unwillingness?) to respond to his wife and about the positioning
and the manner of the exit.

The textual additions and emendations reveal that interpretative assumptions about Lady Macbeth have been smuggled in here under the cloak of
editorial impartiality. Rowe's "seeming" established the moment as illustrative
of the lady's ability to dissemble. The combination of "seeming" and "faint-
ing" is powerful in its indictment not only of her but more generally of female
duplicity. She has been accused of exploiting an assumed feminine weakness
for more sinister motives. It lies at the heart of the cultural anxiety about the
character.

When it is suggested that the faint might be genuine, it serves to reveal her
weakness in contrast to her husband's resilience under pressure and as such
she is judged to fail him. Braunmuller is brisk in his judgment that "Whatever
her action, she fails to perform the part she promised" and he cites her earlier
words, "we shall make our griefs and clamour roar/ Upon his death"
(Braunmuller 156 n.). The only major editorial inquiry that this sequence has
prompted is Braunmuller's response to Banquo's repetition of Macduff's
line: "Look to the lady." His edition includes extensive speculation about
the kind of errors that this "repetition bracket" might indicate by reference
to the characterization of Macduff and Banquo (259–61). If we strip away all
the accumulation of editorial interference, the text is opened up for a range of
interpretative possibilities to be explored.[4]

What could Macbeth's wife do to prompt the comments of Macduff and Banquo? Of course she might faint but there are other possibilities. A lady who swoons confirms conventional attitudes about female weakness which this particular lady may be faking. However, her words ("Help me hence, hoa") could be delivered as an ineffectual, imperious summons for an attended exit with the aim of signaling an end to the gathering. She could be asking for assistance after she has vomited. More inventively, her sense of anger at her husband's spinelessness could prompt frustration which causes her to crush the glass of water she may be holding. She looks down and sees blood on her hands. Crucially, she must do something which draws attention to herself. It may or may not be a deliberate ploy to distract attention from her husband. It may or may not be related to illness, real or imagined. Most important is the recognition that her behavior at this moment is undefined and whatever choice is made here will have consequences for the way in which her character is viewed. It may remain most likely that she will faint but there is a need for transparency in the editorial and critical decisions that are made in order to liberate readers and actors to recognize that this is a moment of *choice* not a moment which simply confirms conventional assumptions about female behavior.

Although most modern editors have abstained from inserting a stage direction prescribing the faint,[5] annotation accepts the tradition. And editors accept without question that the Lady leaves the stage at this point by inserting a stage direction to remove her from the stage on or just before Banquo's line: "Look to the lady." Not only is the exit inserted, but the manner of it is indicated through additions such as *"taken out," "attended," "helped."* But why is it always thought necessary to remove her before the *Exeunt*?

Banquo's command "Look to the lady" is the beginning of a speech which might resonate more powerfully if allowed to be heard while she is still on stage. His words prompt a communal awareness of the need to recognize how "our naked frailties" which "suffer in exposure" need to be "hid." This action needs to take place before those he addresses meet again. When he states that "Fears and scruples shake us," he is again drawing attention to a shared experience which might well register more strongly if the Lady remains on stage. Having been silent for 15 lines, Macbeth urges the assembly to "put on manly readiness." That would certainly be capable of richer resonance if the Lady had remained and she could then leave the stage at the *"Exeunt"* with all but Malcolm and Donalbain. Of crucial importance is the need to preserve the openness of the text and ensure that readers know where editorial intervention has taken place. The issue in this particular instance is not simply that an early exit has been inserted by editors but that the manner of that exit has been prescribed.

It certainly would seem that the relationship between editorial work and theatrical practice is cause for concern. Studying Shakespearean performance both historically and on the contemporary stage rightly informs academic approaches today and yet, while editors often flex their directorial muscles in conjectural stage directions, directors and actors seem to be either ignoring their efforts or resisting such academic intrusion. The matter of Macbeth's death has suffered particularly in this respect.

The sequence from Macbeth's entrance, "they have tied me to a stake," to the end of the play is presented as *Scena Septima* in the Folio. It is a scene of action and reflection showing first of all Macbeth's vigorous dispatch of Young Siward. We see Macbeth's confidence in his invincibility from all except "he/ That was not borne of Woman." Macduff's invocation to Fortune, "Let me find him," engages with the central prophecy of the play. The short pieces of dialogue and the repeated instructions in the stage directions for *Alarums* create the tension, excitement, and unpredictability of battle. Malcolm is guided to the safety of the castle by Siward who, not knowing of his son's death, gives reassurance that the "Noble Thanes do brauely." His assertion that "little is to do" is followed by Macbeth's entrance denouncing heroic suicide. Macduff's command, "Turne Hell-hound, turne," splendidly crafts the confrontation between the two who have been juxtaposed but kept apart so far on stage. After an exchange, Macduff declares "My voice is in my Sword" and as described there follows *Fight: Alarum*. Macbeth's confidence in his "charmed Life" is restated to be defeated by Macduff's revelation of the manner of his birth, "Dispaire thy charme." From confidence through withdrawal ("Ile not fight with thee") to defiance ("I will not yield") the action is graphically described: "Before my body,/ I throw my warlike Shield." The stage direction then requires them to "*Exeunt fighting. Alarums.*" In the Folio this comes at the bottom of the left-hand column of print and the next column is headed by "*Enter Fighting, and Macbeth slaine.*" The repeated "*Alarums*" are followed by "*Retreat, and Flourish.*" The stage picture is crafted with "*Enter with Drumme and Colours*" for Malcolm's entrance. Twenty-seven lines later the Folio SD reads "*Enter Macduffe; with Macbeth's head*" and he announces:

> Haile King, for so thou art.
> Behold where stands
> Th'Usurpers cursed head.

With a directed "*Flourish*" Malcolm is acclaimed king. Simon Forman's account of a performance in 1611 gives some description of stage business but Macbeth's death is dealt with in seven words: "after in the battle Macduff slew Macbeth" (Salgado 32).

Editors have judged this section to need work. There has been some reluctance to follow the Folio and new scenes have frequently been marked after Macbeth's death and Malcolm and Siward's exit (e.g. Barnet). Dover Wilson's New Cambridge edition (1947) divides Act 5 into eight scenes. The Arden edition (1951) and New Cambridge edition (1997) give it nine scenes while the Oxford Complete Works manages eleven! In following Pope's inserted break after Macbeth's death Stanley Wells argues that it "seems right, less for considerations of place (Muir) than because a time interval may be presumed" (Wells and Taylor 544). Of modern editions only the Oxford single edition follows the Folio division and Nicholas Brooke argues lucidly for that decision:

> The fact is that scenes 2–6 represent the preparations for battle when the two armies must be understood to be in separate locations . . . Scene 7 is the battle itself which is continuous, where a number of incidents happen before our eyes and the rest is off-stage. The Folio arrangement is therefore, entirely rational, and any other forgets the reality of the theatre for an improbable series of mini-scenes designated "Another part of the field." (206)

Even more problematic is the matter of the stage directions relating to Macbeth's death. The lineation in the Folio is seen by some to support the case for emendation. Dyce had argued that "The stage-directions given by the Ff in this scene are exquisitely absurd" (Furness, ed. *Macbeth* 345) and all editions after Pope to the end of the nineteenth century chose to keep the first and remove the second. They had Macbeth pursue Macduff off-stage and cut the Folio direction, *"Enter Fighting, and Macbeth slaine."* Dover Wilson indulged in a characteristic flight of fancy and suggested: "they fight to and fro beneath the castle wall, until at length 'Macbeth' is 'slain' " (84). In Braunmuller's 1997 New Cambridge edition, the layout works hard to preserve the sense of the original though additions are still felt to be necessary:

> *Exeunt*[,] *fighting. Alarums*
> *Enter* [*Macbeth and Macduff,*] *fighting*[,] *and Macbeth slain*
> [*Exit Macduff, with Macbeth's body*]

He offers two notes. The first (on ll. 1–2) refutes some earlier judgments:

> Many editors have doubted F's SDs here, suggesting that they are con- fused, or imprecise, or represent two different stagings (one for the out- door, one for the indoor theatre?). However inadequate, the SDs convey a shifting duel, moving from place to place on stage.

His second note justifies his addition by reference to Malcolm's line:

> I would the friends we miss were safe arrived.

Braunmuller suggests that this "seems to stipulate a stage empty of dead bodies, and Macduff needs to remove Macbeth's body in order to 'behead' it" (Braunmuller 236 n.). Recent editors have worried about the practical arrangements for removing Macbeth's body and have felt the need to indicate textually that Macduff should remove it. There has not been any engagement with R.G. White's reasonable point that the stage direction which follows: *Retreat, and Flourish* might provide a solution. In 1883 he wrote:

> It is possible that Shakespeare, or the stage-manager of his company did not deny the audience the satisfaction of seeing the usurper meet his doom, and that in the subsequent "retreat" his body was dragged off the stage for its supposed decapitation.
>
> (quoted in Furness, ed. *Macbeth* 345)

Rather than explore theatrical possibilities in this way, editors often seem to prefer the Shavian approach to preparing the text for a reader. They like to promote the sense of moment-by-moment revelation and give a sense of actuality for the reader. It can, of course, amount to authorial intervention.

Twenty-seven lines after Macbeth is killed on stage the Folio text instructs:

> *Enter Macduffe, with Macbeths head.*

The Jacobean audience would read the iconography as the public display of the consequence of Macbeth being a traitor. It defies naturalism in the most fundamental of ways and the notion that readers need to be told that Macbeth's body must be removed from the stage in order that his head should be cut off seems unnecessary. Malone added the detail "on a pole" from Holinshed and Dover Wilson followed him. Recent editors leave the stage direction unamended, but once again in their notes they sometimes feel the need to be prescriptive. Hunter states that "presumably the head is on a pole" and similarly Brooke suggests "Presumably the head is on the end of his lance." Both cite Macduff's phrase, "Behold where stands . . .," in support.

Perhaps academics need to concentrate upon how our only authoritative text is crafted. The language, characterization, and interpretative possibilities of what is printed in the Folio all merit analysis. Indeed, we might make a convincing case for simply retaining Shakespeare's words and worry less about how stage business might have been achieved on Shakespeare's stage or might be achieved today. We might leave invention to the actors and directors! Narrow-minded attempts to recreate a first performance on the Elizabethan stage by speculating about curtains, use of the discovery space or from which door a character might enter can seem to lock the play in the museum case of history. Editorial edicts about who removes the body or whether Macbeth's severed head should be displayed on a pole or a lance have had little influence upon stage practitioners and must be of doubtful use to readers. The assumption that it is necessary to add descriptions about removing bodies or to indicate to whom a character is speaking implies a degree of prescription which would seem to be alien to all our convictions about the interpretative richness of a Shakespearean text. Dover Wilson's imaginative, descriptive additions are often mocked, but is it not worryingly patronizing to think that the speech heading ALL which prefaces the penultimate speech in *Macbeth* should require emendation? The Folio reads:

ALL   Hail, King of Scotland!

but in the Oxford Complete Works it reads:

ALL BUT MALCOLM   Hail, King of Scotland!

We might do well to remember Furness's warning. He takes as his starting point concern about editorial intrusion in the matter of stage directions, but he moves on to offer some cautionary words about an editor's role:

> Where stage directions occur in the Qq or Ff they are to be reverently accepted, and they are also respectable in Rowe, as indications of stage tradition, but in other cases, where they are devised by editors, they are apt to be intrusive and are mostly superfluous. They belong more to the province of the actor than to that of the editor. We editors readily lose sight of the fact that we are, for the most part, mere drudges, humble diggers and delvers in forgotten fields, and from close poring over the words of a dramatic character we are apt to forget ourselves, and bound in imagination for one wild moment on the stage to dictate action to the player-folk themselves.
>
> (Furness, ed., *Othello* 193)

For all the editorial attention *Macbeth* has received, a case still needs to be made for the Folio text. Although it is a very short play, it is almost always cut in performance and it has become customary to play it without an interval. Two highly acclaimed productions in recent years in Stratford-upon-Avon have not only delivered the play as a continuous piece of action but were also first staged within the smaller theatres. Both the 1976 (The Other Place) and 1999 (Swan Theatre) productions were filmed to be shown on television, where an insistent use of close-up sustains the tight focus. In both productions darkness prevails.

The intense, one-room experience at The Other Place gave the audience the sense of being trapped in the world of the play and there could be no escape until the release provided by the protagonist's death. In a similar way Greg Doran swathed the audience at the Swan in darkness. His "fog and filthy air" obscured the Weird sisters from the audience's view. While undoubtedly for some this was chillingly effective, it might be felt that the director here was being educated by Willy Russell's Rita. Her solution to the staging problems of *Peer Gynt* is to "Do it on the radio" (Russell 27).

To deny a Shakespearean audience the opportunity to see what is happening seems oddly perverse. It may be an acknowledgment that audiences today have lost the capacity to engage simultaneously with words and images which do not correlate in any simple, straightforward way. Shakespeare urged his audiences to "work" and "Think, when we talk of horses, that you see them" (*Henry V*, Chorus 3.25; Chorus 1.26). There is a real danger of theatre today striving so vigorously to replicate the more naturalistic experiences of film and television that it will render itself redundant. The Witches are actors who have the capacity to prompt the illusion of fear, apprehension, and curiosity in the soldiers who encounter them. They are representations. They are not real. Putting out the lights so that we cannot see them is treating members of the audience as if they are children who can be easily frightened by the dark. As Theseus says:

> . . . in the night, imagining some fear,
> How easy is a bush supposed a bear?
> (5.1.21–22)

But as Hippolyta points out, Theseus is missing the point. His account denies the essence of the theatrical experience. She counters his tentative assertion, persuasively arguing for the totality of the experience:

> But all the story of the night told over,
> And all their minds transfigured so together,
> More witnesseth than fancy's images,
> And grows to something of great constancy;
> But howsoever, strange and admirable.
> (5.1.23–27)

It is the "howsoever" of the theatrical experience that we are in danger of losing. With *Macbeth* we may already have lost it.

Notes

1 Bradley asserts this is "an ironical passage" (333).
2 See Hinman (xvi–xvii).
3 G.K. Hunter in his New Penguin edition (1967) is unusual in resisting the renaming of Macduff's wife and he lists her as such in "The Characters in the Play." Although he describes Macbeth's wife as Lady Macbeth in the same list he does follow the Folio speech prefixes in describing her as "Lady" and her counterpart as "Wife."
4 Julia's "faint" at the end of *The Two Gentlemen of Verona* is similarly open to interpretation. The text will support her action as deliberate distraction not female weakness.
5 Hunter, however inserts "*Swooning.*"

Works cited

Barnet, Sylvan, ed. *Macbeth*. New York: Signet, 1963.
Bradley, A.C. *Shakespearean Tragedy: Lectures on* Hamlet, Othello, King Lear, *and* Macbeth. London: Macmillan, 1904.

Braunmuller, A.R., ed. *Macbeth*. New Cambridge Shakespeare. Cambridge: Cambridge UP, 1997.

Brooke, Nicholas, ed. *Macbeth*. Oxford Shakespeare. Oxford: Oxford UP, 1988.

Burchfield, R.W. *The New Fowler's Modern English Usage*. Oxford: Clarendon, 1996.

Flatter, Richard. *Shakespeare's Producing Hand: A Study of His Marks of Expression to be Found in the First Folio*. London: William Heinemann, 1948.

Furness, H.H., ed. *Macbeth*. New Variorum Edition of Shakespeare. Philadelphia: J.B. Lippincott, 1873.

——— , ed. *Othello*. New Variorum Shakespeare. Philadelphia: J.B. Lippincott, 1873.

Hinman, Charlton. *The Norton Facsimile: The First Folio of Shakespeare*. New York: Norton, 1968.

Hunter, G.K., ed. *Macbeth*. New Penguin Shakespeare. New York: Penguin, 1967.

Larkin, Philip. "I remember, I remember." *The Less Deceived: Poems*. London: Marvell Press, 1955.

Muir, Kenneth, ed. *Macbeth*. Arden Shakespeare. London: Methuen, 1951.

Russell, Willy. *Educating Rita*. London: Methuen Drama, 1986.

Salgado, Gamini. *Eyewitnesses of Shakespeare: Firsthand Accounts of Performances 1590–1890*. London: Sussex UP, 1975.

Wells, Stanley and Gary Taylor, with John Jowett and William Montgomery. *William Shakespeare: A Textual Companion*. Oxford: Clarendon, 1987.

Wilson, John Dover, ed. *Macbeth*. New Cambridge Shakespeare. Cambridge: Cambridge UP, 1947.

Notes on contributors

Rebecca Lemon is Associate Professor of English at the University of Southern California.

Jonathan Baldo is Associate Professor of English at the Eastman School of Music, University of Rochester, New York.

Rebecca Ann Bach is Associate Professor of English at The University of Alabama at Birmingham.

Julie Barmazel is Lecturer at California State University Channel Islands.

Abraham Stoll is Associate Professor of Renaissance Literature at the University of San Diego.

Lois Feuer is Professor of English at California State University, Dominguez Hills.

Stephen Deng is Assistant Professor in the Department of English at Michigan State University.

Lisa A. Tomaszewski has taught English and film at Drew University and Fairleigh Dickinson University.

Lynne Dickson Bruckner is Associate Professor of English at Chatham University, Pittsburgh.

Michael David Fox is the Artistic Director of The New American Theater and dramaturg for the Diavolo dance theater, both in California.

James Wells is Associate Professor of English at Belmont University, Nashville.

Laura Engel is Assistant Professor of English at Duquesne University, Pittsburgh, where she specializes in Eighteenth-Century British Literature and Drama.

Stephen Buhler is Professor of English at the University of Nebraska-Lincoln.

Bi-qi Beatrice Lei is Assistant Professor at the Department of Foreign Languages and Literature, the National Tsing Hua University, Taiwan.

Kim Fedderson is the Dean of Social Sciences and Humanities at Lakehead University, Ontario.

J. Michael Richardson is Professor of English, specialising in Renaissance Literature, at Lakehead University, Ontario.

Bruno Lessard is a Social Sciences and Humanities Research Council of Canada Postdoctoral Fellow in the Department of Film (Future Cinema Lab) and in the Communication and Culture Programme at York University in Toronto.

Pamela Mason is a former Fellow of the Shakespeare Institute and Lecturer in English, The University of Birmingham. She is co-editor, with Sandra Clark, of the Arden Shakespeare's forthcoming Arden Third Series *Macbeth*.

Nick Moschovakis has taught at institutions including The University of the South, George Washington University, and Reed College.

Index

Related titles from Routledge*

Routledge Guides to Literature Series:
Shakespeare and Renaissance Studies

Editorial Advisory Board: Richard Bradford (University of Ulster at Coleraine), Jan Jedrzejewski (University of Ulster at Coleraine), Duncan Wu (St. Catherine's College, University of Oxford).

Routledge Guides to Literature offer clear introductions to the most widely studied authors and literary texts. Each book engages with texts, contexts and criticism, highlighting the range of critical views and contextual factors that need to be taken into consideration in advanced studies of literary works. The series encourages informed but independent readings of texts by ranging as widely as possible across the contextual and critical issues relevant to the works examined and highlighting areas of debate as well as those of critical consensus. Alongside general guides to texts and authors, the series includes 'sourcebooks', which allow access to reprinted contextual and critical materials as well as annotated extracts of primary text.

- *Ben Jonson*
  By James Loxley
- *William Shakespeare's The Merchant of Venice: A Sourcebook*
  Edited by S. P. Cerasano
- *William Shakespeare's King Lear: A Sourcebook*
  Edited by Grace Ioppolo
- *William Shakespeare's Othello: A Sourcebook*
  Edited by Andrew Hadfield
- *William Shakespeare's Macbeth: A Sourcebook*
  Edited by Alexander Leggatt
- *William Shakespeare's Hamlet: A Sourcebook*
  Edited by Sean McEvoy
- *William Shakespeare's Twelfth Night: A Sourcebook*
  Edited by Sonia Massai

*Some books in this series were originally published in the Routledge Literary Sourcebooks series, edited by Duncan Wu, or the Complete Critical Guide to English Literature series, edited by Richard Bradford and Jan Jedrzejewski.

Available at all good bookshops
For a full series listing, ordering details and further information please visit:
www.routledgeliterature.com

Related titles from Routledge

Accents on Shakespeare Series
General Editor: Terence Hawkes

Books in the *Accents on Shakespeare* series provide short, powerful, 'cutting-edge' accounts of and comments on new developments in the field of Shakespeare studies. In addition to titles aimed at modular undergraduate courses, it also features a number of spirited and committed research-based books.

The *Accents on Shakespeare* series features contributions from leading figures and the books include:

- *Shakespeare and Appropriation*
  Edited by Christy Desmet and Robert Sawyer
- *Shakespeare Without Women*
  Dympna Callaghan
- *Philosophical Shakespeares*
  Edited by John J. Joughin
- *Shakespeare and Modernity: Early Modern to Millennium*
  Edited by Hugh Grady
- *Marxist Shakespeares*
  Edited by Jean E. Howard and Scott Cutler Shershow
- *Shakespeare in Psychoanalysis*
  Philip Armstrong
- *Shakespeare and Modern Theatre: The Performance of Modernity*
  Edited by Michael Bristol and Kathleen McLuskie
- *Shakespeare and Feminist Performance: Ideology on Stage*
  Sarah Werner
- *Shame in Shakespeare*
  Ewan Fernie
- *The Sound of Shakespeare*
  Wes Folkerth
- *Shakespeare in the Present*
  Terence Hawkes
- *Making Shakespeare*
  Tiffany Stern
- *Spiritual Shakespeares*
  Edited by Ewan Fernie
- *Presentist Shakespeares*
  Edited by Terence Hawkes and Hugh Grady
- *Shakespeare, Authority, Sexuality*
  Alan Sinfield

Available at all good bookshops
For a full series listing, ordering details and further information please visit:
www.routledgeliterature.com

Related titles from Routledge

Alternative Shakespeares 3
Edited by Diana E. Henderson

This volume takes up the challenge embodied in its predecessors, *Alternative Shakespeares* and *Alternative Shakespeares 2*: to identify and explore the new, the changing, the radically 'other' possibilities for Shakespeare Studies at our particular historical moment.

Alternative Shakespeares 3 introduces the strongest and most innovative of the new directions emerging in Shakespearean scholarship – ranging across performance studies, multimedia and textual criticism, concerns of economics, science, religion, and ethics – as well as the "next step" work in areas such as postcolonial and queer studies that continue to push the boundaries of the field. The contributors approach each topic with clarity and accessibility in mind, enabling student readers to engage with serious 'alternatives' to established ways of interpreting Shakespeare's plays and their role in contemporary culture.

The expertise, commitment and daring of this volume's contributors shine through each essay, maintaining the progressive edge and real-world urgency that are the hallmark of *Alternative Shakespeares*. This volume is essential reading for students and scholars of Shakespeare who seek an understanding of current and future directions in this ever-changing field.

Contributors include: Kate Chedgzoy, Mary Thomas Crane, Lukas Erne, Diana E. Henderson, Rui Carvalho Homem, Julia Reinhard Lupton, Willy Maley, Patricia Parker, Shankar Raman, Katherine Rowe, Robert Shaughnessy and W. B. Worthen.

Diana E. Henderson is Professor of Literature at MIT.

ISBN 13: 978–0–415–42332–8 (hbk)
ISBN 13: 978–0–415–42333–5 (pbk)
ISBN 13: 978–0–203–93409–8 (ebk)

Available at all good bookshops
For ordering and further information please visit:
www.routledgeliterature.com

New in Paperback from Routledge

Dramatists and their Manuscripts in the Age of Shakespeare, Jonson, Middleton and Heywood: Authorship, Authority and the Playhouse
Grace Ioppolo

'Ioppolo's book, often iconoclastic, can also be bracingly funny ... it brings the opportunity to think again in new and fresh ways about the manuscripts at the book's centre and their place in the culture and practices of the early modern theatre.' – *The Library*

This book presents new evidence about the ways in which English Renaissance dramatists such as William Shakespeare, Ben Jonson, Thomas Heywood, John Fletcher and Thomas Middleton composed their plays and the degree to which they participated in the dissemination of their texts to theatrical audiences. Grace Ioppolo argues that the path of the transmission of the text was not linear, from author to censor to playhouse to audience – as has been universally argued by scholars – but circular. Authors returned to their texts, or texts were returned to their authors, at any or all stages after composition. The reunion of authors and their texts demonstrate that early modern dramatists collaborated in various ways and degrees in the theatrical production and performance of their plays, and that for early modern dramatists and their theatrical colleagues authorship was a continual process.

Extant dramatic manuscripts, theatre records and accounts, as well as authorial contracts, memoirs, receipts and other archival evidence, are used to prove that the text returned to the author at various stages, including during rehearsal and after performance. This monograph provides much new information and case studies, and will be a fascinating contribution to the fields of Shakespeare studies, English Renaissance drama studies, manuscript studies, textual study and bibliography and theatre history.

Grace Ioppolo is reader in English and American Literature at Reading University, UK.

ISBN 13: 978–0–415–33965–0 (hbk)
ISBN 13: 978–0–415–47031–5 (pbk)
ISBN 13: 978–0–203–44942–4 (ebk)

Available at all good bookshops
For ordering and further information please visit:
www.routledgeliterature.com

Related titles from Routledge

Engines of the Imagination
Jonathan Sawday

'This is a magisterial work of myth-busting, and a marvellous demonstration of how art and literature may be used to reanimate the material imagination of an historical period. The old idea of the Renaissance as a pretechnological pause, or paradise, is gone for good.' – *Steven Connor, Birkbeck College, University of London, UK*

How did men and women in earlier ages respond to their technologies? In his characteristically lucid style, Jonathan Sawday explores poetry, philosophy, art, and engineering to reveal the lost world of the machine in the pre-industrial culture of the European Renaissance.

In the Renaissance, machines and mechanisms appealed to familiar figures such as Shakespeare, Francis Bacon, Montaigne, and Leonardo da Vinci, as well as to a host of lesser-known writers and artists in the sixteenth and seventeenth centuries. This intellectual and aesthetic engagement with devices of all kinds would give rise to new attitudes towards gender as well as towards work and labour, and even fostered the beginnings of the new sciences of artificial life and reason which would be pursued by Descartes, Hobbes, and Leibniz in the later seventeenth century.

But, writers, philosophers, and artists often had conflicting reactions to the technology that was beginning to surround them. For at the heart of the creation of a machine-driven world were stories of loss and catastrophe. Was technology a token of human progress or was it, rather, a sign of the fall of humanity from its original state of innocence? These contradictory attitudes are part of the legacy of the European Renaissance. This historical legacy helps to explain many of our own attitudes towards the technology that surrounds us, sustains us, and sometimes troubles us today.

Jonathan Sawday is Professor of English Studies at the University of Strathclyde, Glasgow. He has taught at universities in Britain, Ireland, and the United States. As well as writing many articles and essays on Renaissance literature and culture, he is the author of the *The Body Emblazoned* (Routledge, 1995) and co-editor (with Tom Healy) of *Literature and the English Civil War* (1990), and (with Neil Rhodes) *The Renaissance Computer* (Routledge, 2000).

ISBN 13: 978–0–415–35061–7 (hbk)
ISBN 13: 978–0–415–35062–4 (pbk)
ISBN 13: 978–0–203–69615–6 (ebk)

Available at all good bookshops
For ordering and further information please visit:
www.routledgeliterature.com

Related titles from Routledge

King Lear: New Critical Essays
Edited by Jeffrey Kahan

Is *King Lear* an autonomous text, or a rewrite of the earlier and anonymous play *King Leir?* Should we refer to Shakespeare's original quarto when discussing the play, the revised folio text, or the popular composite version, stitched together by Alexander Pope in 1725? What of its stage variations? When turning from page to stage, the critical view on *King Lear* is skewed by the fact that for almost half of the four hundred years the play has been performed, audiences preferred Naham Tate's optimistic adaptation, in which Lear and Cordelia live happily ever after. When discussing *King Lear*, the question of what comprises 'the play' is both complex and fragmentary.

These issues of identity and authenticity across time and across mediums are outlined, debated, and considered critically by the contributors to this volume. Using a variety of approaches, from postcolonialism and New Historicism to psychoanalysis and gender studies, the leading international contributors to *King Lear: New Critical Essays* offer major new interpretations on the conception and writing, editing, and cultural productions of *King Lear*. This book is an up-to-date and comprehensive anthology of textual scholarship, performance research, and critical writing on one of Shakespeare's most important and perplexing tragedies.

Contributors include: Jeffrey Kahan, R.A. Foakes, Richard Knowles, Tom Clayton, Cynthia Clegg, Edward L. Rocklin, Christy Desmet, Paul Cantor, Robert V. Young, Stanley Stewart and Jean R. Brink.

Jeffrey Kahan is Associate Professor of English at the University of La Verne in California, and completed his Ph.D at the Shakespeare Institute, University of Birmingham. He is the author of *Reforging Shakespeare* (Lehigh, 1998) and *The Cult of Kean* (Ashgate, 2006) and editor of *Shakespeare Imitations, Parodies and Forgeries, 1710–1820* (3 vols. Routledge, 2004).

ISBN 13: 978–0–415–77526–7 (hbk)
ISBN 13: 978–0–203–09008–4 (ebk)

Available at all good bookshops
For ordering and further information please visit:
www.routledgeliterature.com